FleaMarket Trader

THOUSANDS OF ITEMS
WITH
CURRENT VALUES

Eleventh
edition

Edited by
Sharon & Bob Huxford

COLLECTOR BOOKS
A Division of Schroeder Publishing Co., Inc.

The current values in this book should be used only as a guide. They are not intended to set prices, which vary from one section of the country to another. Auction prices as well as dealer prices vary greatly and are affected by condition as well as demand. Neither the Editors nor the Publisher assumes responsibility for any losses that might be incurred as a result of consulting this guide.

Searching For A Publisher?

We are always looking for knowledgeable people considered to be experts within their fields. If you feel that there is a real need for a book on your collectible subject and have a large comprehensive collection, contact Collector Books.

Editorial assistants: Mike Drollinger, Nancy Drollinger, Linda Holycross, Donna Newnum, Loretta Woodrow.

Cover design by: Beth Summers
Book design by: Mary Ann Dorris

Introduction

The *Flea Market Trader* is a unique price guide, geared specifically for the convenience of the flea market shopper. Several categories have been included that are not often found in general price guides, while others on antiques not usually seen at flea markets have been omitted. The new categories will serve to introduce you to collectibles that are currently coming on, the best and often the only source for which is the marketplace. As all of us who religiously pursue the circuits are aware, flea markets are well informed on current values, those 'really great' buys remain on the table. Like most pursuits in life, preparation has its own rewards; and it is our intention to provide you with the basic tool of education and awareness toward that end. But please bear in mind that the prices in this guide are meant to indicate only general values. Many factors determine actual selling prices; values vary from one region to another; dealers pay various wholesale prices for their wares, and your bargaining skill is important too.

We have organized our listings into general categories for easy use; if you have trouble locating an item, refer to the index. Unless another condition code is present in the description line, the values we have suggested reflect prices of items in mint condition. NM stands for minimal damage, VG indicates that the item will bring 40% to 60% of its mint price, and EX should be somewhere between the two. Glassware is assumed clear unless a color is noted. Only generally accepted abbreviations have been used.

We would like to take this opportunity to thank each author, dealer, and auction house who allowed us to use their photographs.

The Editors

Advertising Collectibles

As far back as the turn of the century, manufacturers used characters to identify with their products. They were always personable, endearing, amusing, and usually succeeded in achieving just the effect the producer had in mind, making their product line more visual, more familiar, and therefore one the customer would more often than not choose over the competition. Magazine ads, display signs, product cartons, and TV provided just the right exposure for these ad characters. Elsie the Cow became so well known, that at one point, during a random survey, more people recognized her photo than one of the president!

There are scores of advertising characters and many have been promoted on a grand scale. Today's collectors search for the dolls, banks, cookie jars, mugs, plates, and scores of other items modeled after or bearing the likenesses of their favorites, several of which are featured below.

Condition plays a vital role in evaluating vintage advertising pieces. Our estimates are for items in at least near-mint condition, unless another condition code is present in the description. Try to be very objective when you assess wear and damage.

For more information we recommend *Zany Characters of the Ad World* by Mary Jane Lamphier; *Advertising Character Collectibles* by Warren Dots; and *Huxford's Collectible Advertising*. All are published by Collector Books.

See also Black Americana; Breweriana; Character and Promotional Drinking Glasses; Fast Food Collectibles; Novelty Radios; Novelty Telephones; Pin-Back Buttons.

Ad Characters

Admiral Appliances Admiral bank, vinyl, M **20.00**

Atlas Annie doll, prestuffed cloth, 1977, 15½" **15.00**

Aunt Jemima cookie jar, figural, plastic, F&F Mold, NM **400.00**

Baby Ruth beanbag doll, Hasbro, 1970s, EX **35.00**

Barlow & Eaton Kitty, black, 1983, 8", M **15.00**

Baskin-Robbins Honey Hill Bunch ice cream store w/2 kids, 1977, MIB **55.00**

Bell Telephone operator or white lineman, 15", MIB, ea ...**60.00**

Betty Crocker doll, Kenner, 1974, 13", G **30.00**

Big Boy ashtray, figural on rim, ceramic, NM **375.00**

Big Boy bank, vinyl, slender, small checks, 1970s, M in package **35.00**

Big Boy bank, 1973, 9", EX ...**18.00**

Big Boy die-cut menu, ca 1956, M **150.00**

Big Boy salt & pepper shakers, ceramic, Elias Brothers, 1991, pr **35.00**

Big Buster Popcorn tin container, full, M **85.00**

Bonnie Breck doll, w/accessories & booklet, Hasbro, 1972, 9", MIB **35.00**

Bumble Bee Tuna bank, bee on green base, vinyl, 1960s, 7", EX **45.00**

Buster Brown camping kit, aluminum pan & bucket w/lid, 1930s, EX ..**120.00**

Buster Brown doll, stuffed cloth, 1974, 14", NM **35.00**

Buster Brown hand puppet, cardboard, 1950s, EX **10.00**

Buster Brown magic slate, 1950s-60s store give-away, M **20.00**

Buster Brown shaving mug .**175.00**

Buster Brown whistle, pictured w/Tige, rectangular, EX+ ..**32.00**

Campbell Kids cheerleader doll, vinyl, 1967, 8", EX **75.00**

Campbell Kids Christmas ornament, glass, 1991, MIB (sealed) **8.00**

Campbell Kids cup, girl's face, F&F mold, MIB **25.00**

Campbell Kids doll calendar, 1989, M **8.00**

Campbell Kids dolls, special edition, 1988, MIB, pr **65.00**

Campbell Kids hotpad holder, painted plastic, recent, 6", M ..**12.00**

Cap'n Crunch doll, cloth, General Mills, 1982, lg, EX **15.00**

Cap'n Crunch nodder, sm **75.00**

Ceresota Flour boy, printed cloth, name on shirt, early, 17", EX **100.00**

Charlie Chocks doll, printed cloth, 1970-71, 20", EX **25.00**

Charlie Tuna telephone, plastic, mk Star-Kist Foods Inc, 1987, 10", MIB **60.00**

Chester Cheeto doll, stuffed, Cheetos label on tennis shoes, 22", EX **15.00**

Chicken of the Sea mermaid, cloth w/yarn hair, painted face, 13", MIP **12.00**

Chiquita Banana doll, printed material, uncut, 1950s, 11x17", NM .**45.00**

Christian Brothers Brandy St Bernard, Dakin, 1982, 12", EX **30.00**

Columbia Ice Cream tray, girl w/dog & horse, 16x13", VG **200.00**

Comfort Inn Choice-a-saurus dinosaur, PVC, M **8.00**

Count Chocula flicker ring ...**100.00**

Count Chocula vinyl figure, 1975, 8", EX **80.00**

Blue Bonnet Sue salt and pepper shakers, Nabisco, by Benjamin & Medwin, discontinued, $15.00 for the pair.

Caribbean Coconut Rum Witch sipper cup, plastic, Made in China, 7½", from $4.00 to $5.00.

Cracker Jack sailor, vinyl head, Vogue, 1980, 13", M in worn package **40.00**

Crocker Spaniel girl, Crocker National Bank, 8", VG .**12.00**

Curad Taped Crusader bank, plastic, 1977, 8" **60.00**

Dow Scrubbing bubble figure, vinyl, 1989, 3½", EX, from $10 to **15.00**

Elsie the Cow, stuffed body w/vinyl head & hooves, 12" **75.00**

Elsie the Cow coffee mug, from $55 to **65.00**

Elsie the Cow container, Borden's Instant Starlac, 5-qt **55.00**

Elsie the Cow cookbook, Borden's Eagle Brand 70 Magic Recipes **12.00**

Elsie the Cow cut-out face w/name at bottom **6.00**

Elsie the Cow ice cream dish, face logo, paneled glass sides, footed .**38.00**

Elsie the Cow place mat, Elsie w/family, M **8.00**

Elsie the Cow playing cards, NMIB **20.00**

Elsie the Cow soap, Beauregard, M in original holder **145.00**

Elsie the Cow soap, Elsie in the Looking Glass, M in original holder **145.00**

Elsie the Cow star, Elsie's face & signature on tin, 18" dia **375.00**

Elsie the Cow tumbler, tall **45.00**

Energizer Bunny, plush, w/sunglasses, mail-in premium, 24", M ..**50.00**

Energizer Bunny flashlight, squeezable vinyl, 1991, MIP (sealed) **12.00**

Ernie the Keebler Elf, stuffed plush, 1981, 24", VG **40.00**

Ernie the Keebler Elf, vinyl, 1970s, 7", M **25.00**

Eveready Cat bank, plastic, 1981, 6" **12.00**

Farmer Jack bank, vinyl, 1986, 7", EX **55.00**

Franken Berry, vinyl, General Mills, 1975, 8", NM **95.00**

Franklin Life Ben Franklin doll, stuffed cloth, G **8.00**

Fruit Stripe Gum figure, Yipe zebra, bendable, M **30.00**

Funny Face frisbee, set of 4 ....**35.00**

Funny Face Goofy Grape pitcher, red **100.00**

Funny Face walker, set of 4 w/coins **350.00**

Hamburger Helper Helping Hand clock, MIB **45.00**

Harley Hog, leather jacket w/Harley logo, w/tags, 9", M **30.00**

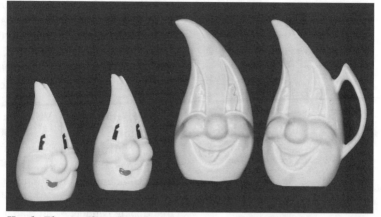

Handy Flame salt and pepper shakers, gas utility company, ca 1950s, 4", $25.00 for the pair; sugar bowl and creamer, 6", $45.00. (Photo courtesy Lee Garmon)

Harry Hood, vinyl, Hood Dairies, NM **95.00**

Heinz Ketchup Ant, figure, bendable PVC, 4½", EX **10.00**

Hershey bear, vinyl face, Ideal, 1982, 12", EX **30.00**

Hershey ornament, bear on milk carton, wood, 1985, 4½", MIB **8.00**

Hush Puppy bank, vinyl, mk Hush Puppy Brand Casuals, 1970, 8" **30.00**

Hush Puppy whistle, molded plastic dog figural, M **5.00**

IGA Stores Tablerite Kid, litho cloth, 12" **20.00**

Jack Frost rag doll, 1960s, 18", VG **10.00**

Jeans Man, doll, Jordache/Mego, 12", MIB **30.00**

Jersey-Creme tray, girl in bonnet holds glass, 12" dia, G ..**50.00**

Jolly Green Giant, stuffed cloth, 16", M **45.00**

Jordache Cheerleader, pom-pon action, Mego, 11½", MIB (sealed) **12.00**

Jordache Jeans lady, Mego, all original, 1981, 11½", MIB (sealed) **18.00**

Jumbo Popcorn tin container, 10-lb, M **145.00**

Kool-Aid Kid, pigtails & freckles, 1989, 14", MIB **39.00**

Kraft Macaroni & Cheese Cheesasarus bank, mail-in premium, M **35.00**

Libby girl, talking, Mattel, 1974, 15", VG **25.00**

Little Caesar's Pizza-Pizza man, plush, 1990, EX **5.00**

Lucky Lymon doll, vinyl, talker, 1990, 7½", MIB **35.00**

Mad Money court jester keychain, Lady Luck Casino, 3", MIP **10.00**

Magic Chef figure, vinyl, 7½", EX+ **20.00**

Marky Maypo, vinyl, blue pants & shire, red hat & neckerchief, 10", M **55.00**

McGruff Crime Stopper dog, Dakin, all original, 1987, 16", M **40.00**

Mr. Peanut ashtray, metal with standing figure, 6x6", EX, $25.00.

MD Toilet Tissue Daisy, stuffed cloth, 1977, 16", EX ...**15.00**

Miss Clairol Glamour Misty, original bathrobe, Ideal, 1965, 12", EX **35.00**

Miss Tastee, plastic, w/cloth dress & banner, G **20.00**

Missy, Wrangler Action Figure, Ertl, w/accessories, 1982, 4", MOC **6.00**

Missy, Wrangler girl, in western attire, 1982, 11½", MIB ..**45.00**

Mr Peanut bank, tan plastic, hat unlocks bank, USA, 1960s, 8½", NM **35.00**

Mr Peanut figure, bendable PVC, 1991, 6", EX **10.00**

Mr Peanut wind-up toy, plastic, 8½", EX **300.00**

Mr Salty, stuffed cloth, VG+, from $12 to **20.00**

Nestle P'Nutty or Semi-Sweetie, all original, 1984, 10", ea **15.00**

Nestle Quik bunny, plush, mail-in, M **20.00**

Oreo Cookie bendee, 4", M **8.00**

Pfizer Doctor, all original, 1960s, 18", EX on original stand **65.00**

Pillsbury Doughboy, stuffed cloth, 1970s, 14", EX **15.00**

Pillsbury Poppin' Fresh, stuffed, 1972, 11", EX **15.00**

Pillsbury Poppin' Fresh, vinyl, 1972, 7", NM **15.00**

Postal bear, dressed as letter carrier, all tags, 20", M **95.00**

Pillsbury Poppin' Fresh hand puppets, Bun-Bun or Poppie, EX, $25.00 each; Biscuit the cat, rare, EX, $35.00.

Reddy Kilowatt coin, Light for Freedom, Diamond Jubilee 1879-1954 ....**8.00**

Reddy Kilowatt earrings, Your Favorite Pin-Up, 1", pr, MOC **12.00**

Reddy Kilowatt hot mat, face w/atoms in orbit, cardboard, 5½" **15.00**

Reddy Kilowatt lighter, Florida Power & Light Co, gold-tone **18.00**

Reddy Kilowatt lighter, Zippo, full-body portrait **75.00**

Reddy Kilowatt Magic Gripper, yellow rubber w/logo, 4½", MIP **20.00**

Reddy Kilowatt oven mitt, white w/yellow trim & Reddy's face **20.00**

Reddy Kilowatt patch, Safety Club, Reddy's face in hard hat, 3" dia **8.00**

Reddy Kilowatt soda bottle cap, Your Electric Servant, plastic **5.00**

Reddy Kilowatt tie clip, For Better Living, 1953, MOC **15.00**

Reddy Kilowatt tie tack, Reddy's face on pewter **16.00**

Ronald McDonald, litho cloth, 1971 ....**10.00**

Sergio Valente brunette lady, Toy Time, 1982, 4", MOC **6.00**

Sergio Valente man, 1982, 12", MIB **25.00**

Shakey Chef, litho cloth, 18" **20.00**

Shaklee rabbit, 1970, 7", EX ...**12.00**

Smokey Bear, stuffed, gray badge & belt buckle, 1960s, EX **50.00**

Snoboy, California Stuffed Toys, 15", EX **10.00**

United Airlines Menehune of Hawaii, 9", $75.00. (Photo courtesy June Moon)

Sweet Heart of the Corn, vinyl w/cloth clothes, 1981, 9", NM **20.00**

Texaco Cheerleader, red & white clothes, raincoat, 11½", M **70.00**

Tony the Tiger, cloth, terry cloth shirt, EX+ **85.00**

Toucan Sam, vinyl, 1984, 5", MIB **45.00**

Travel Lodge Sleepy Bear, vinyl, M **45.00**

Trix Rabbit, vinyl, 1977, 8½", EX **30.00**

Tyson Chicken Quick, stuffed, seated, 13", EX **15.00**

Vigorine Pig, litho cloth, premium, 17" **20.00**

Airline Memorabilia

Collectors now seek nearly every item used by or made for commercial (i.e., non-military) airlines. The primary focus of interest are items actually used on the planes such as dishes, glassware, silver serving pieces and flatware, wings and badges worn by the crew, playing cards, and junior wings given to passengers. Timetables and large travel agency plane models are examples of advertising items which are also widely collected. Pre-war items are the most desirable, and items from before 1930 are quite rare. For further information we recommend contacting Mr. Dick Wallin, who is listed in the Directory under Illinois.

Demitasse cup and saucer, Alitalia, gray and silver logo, $40.00. (Photo courtesy Dick Wallin)

Butter pat, American Airlines, blue & silver **25.00**
Butter pat, BOAC, gold net .**25.00**
Cup & saucer, China Airlines, Blue Leaf **20.00**
Cup & saucer, Delta, Signature pattern **15.00**

Cup & saucer, demitasse; Alitalia, gray & silver logo **40.00**
Cup & saucer, demitasse; Eastern, Rosenthal **40.00**
Cup & saucer, demitasse; Pan American, President (eagle & stars) **35.00**
Cup & saucer, Pan American, Bauscher, gold rim **15.00**
Cup & saucer, TWA, china, marked on side & bottom **25.00**
Cup & saucer, TWA, red stripe & gold starburst **15.00**
Flight computer, American Airlines pilot's, in leather pouch, 1933 ....**245.00**
Lapel pin, North American employee's, 10k gold-filled w/emerald, 1940s **33.00**
Lapel pin, Northrop employee's, gold triangle form,w/hallmark, 1950s **23.00**
Napkin, Air Atlanta, shows logo, 21x16", M **5.00**
Patch, Eastern, blue & yellow embroidered block letters, 10x2" **5.00**
Plate, United Airlines, blue pinstripes & name **600.00**
Plate, USAAF, china, 6¾" .**10.00**
Playing cards, Northwest Orient **12.50**
Playing cards, Ozark Arlines, 1984 World's Fair **10.00**
Postcard, Eastern, Golden Falcon, DC-7B **5.00**
Print, United's DC-6 Mainliner 300, prop plane, 12x15½" matted **35.00**
Route map & schedule, United Airlines, 1943, 4-page **9.00**
Salt & pepper shakers, Eastern, glass w/metal top, pr .**8.00**

Salt & pepper shakers, Singapore Airlines, china, pr **35.00**

Silverware, American Airlines Flagship, each pc: from $25 to **35.00**

Souvenir packet, Jal-Wings of New Japan, booklet form, 1950s, 6x10" **22.00**

Swizzle stick, TWA **2.00**

Teapot, United Airlines, silver logo & name **45.00**

Teaspoon, Iberia **25.00**

Wings, Delta, plastic w/pin-back closure, junior size **2.50**

Wings, Delta, w/logo **12.50**

Akro Agate

This company operated in Clarksburg, West Virginia, from 1914 to 1951, manufacturing marbles, novelties, and children's dishes, for which they are best known.

Though some were made in clear solid colors, their most popular, easy-to-identify lines were produced in a swirling opaque type of glass similar to that which was used in the production of their marbles. Their trademark was a flying eagle clutching marbles in his claws. Refer to *The Collector's Encyclopedia of Children's Dishes* by Margaret and Kenn Whitmyer (Collector Books) for more information.

Chiquita, creamer, cobalt, 1½" .**14.00**

Chiquita, saucer, baked-on colors, 3⅛" **3.00**

Chiquita, teapot, green opaque, w/lid, 3" **14.00**

Chiquita, 22-pc set, green opaque, MIB **78.00**

Concentric Rib, plate, opaque colors not green or white, 3¼" **7.00**

Stacked Disc and Interior Panel, solid opaque colors, 21-piece boxed set, from $325.00 to $375.00. (Photo courtesy Margaret and Kenn Whitmeyer)

Octagonal, 21-pc, mixed colors, sm, $195.00.

Concentric Rib, sugar bowl, green or white opaque, 1¼" **10.00**

Concentric Rib, teapot, white opaque, w/lid, 3⅜" **12.00**

Concentric Rib, 8-pc set, green or white opaque, MIB **33.00**

Concentric Ring, bowl, cereal; any opaque color, lg, 3⅜" **22.00**

Concentric Ring, creamer, blue marbleized, lg, 1⅜" **45.00**

Concentric Ring, cup, cobalt transparent, sm, 1¼" .**30.00**

Concentric Ring, sugar bowl, cobalt transparent, lg, 1⅜" **45.00**

Interior Panel, bowl, cereal; azure blue, lg, 3⅜" **30.00**

Interior Panel, creamer, azure blue, sm, 1¼" **32.00**

Interior Panel, creamer, blue & white, lg, 1⅜" **32.00**

Interior Panel, cup, green & white, sm, 1¼" **15.00**

Interior Panel, pitcher, topaz transparent, sm, 2⅞" **15.00**

Interior Panel, plate, green transparent, sm, 3¼" **6.00**

Interior Panel, plate, red & white, lg, 4¼" **16.00**

Interior Panel, set, 21-pc, yellow opaque, lg, MIB **450.00**

Interior Panel, sugar bowl, green transparent, w/lid, lg, 1⅜" .**27.00**

Interior Panel, sugar bowl, pink lustre, sm, 1¼" **27.00**

Interior Panel, teapot, green & white, sm, 3⅜" **35.00**

Interior Panel, teapot, lemonade & oxblood, w/lid, lg, 3¾" ...**65.00**

Interior Panel, teapot, red & white, w/lid, lg, 3¾" **65.00**

Miss America, creamer, white w/decal **55.00**

Miss America, cup, white **40.00**

Miss America, sugar bowl, forest green, w/lid **65.00**

Miss America, teapot, orange & white, w/lid **125.00**

Octagonal, bowl, cereal; lt blue, lg, 3⅜" **20.00**

Octagonal, creamer, blue or white, sm, 1¼", ea **14.00**

Octagonal, cup, pumpkin, closed handle, lg, 1½" **15.00**

Octagonal, tumbler, white, sm, 2" **10.00**

Raised Daisy, creamer, yellow, sm, 1¼" **45.00**

Raised Daisy, plate, blue, sm, 3" **14.00**

Raised Daisy, teapot, green, no lid, sm, 2⅜" **30.00**

Raised Daisy, tumbler, blue, sm, 2" **55.00**

Stacked Disc, creamer, any opaque color not green or white, sm, 1¼" **14.00**

Stacked Disc, cup, white, sm, 1¼" **6.00**

Stacked Disc, plate, green or white, sm, 3¼", ea **3.00**

Stacked Disc, sugar bowl, gr opaque, sm, 1¼" **10.00**

Stacked Disc, tumbler, pumpkin, sm, 2" **21.00**

Aluminum

From the late 1930s until early in the 1950s, kitchenwares and household items were often crafted of aluminum, usually with relief-molded fruit or flowers on a hammered background. Today many find that these diversified items make an interesting collection. Especially desirable are those examples marked with the manufacturer's backstamp or the designer's signature.

You've probably also seen the anodized (colored) aluminum pitchers, tumblers, sherbet holders, etc., that were popular in the late '50s, early '60s. Lately, they're everywhere, and with a wide range in asking prices. Tumblers in good condition with very little wear seem to be about $2.00 to $3.00 each. The pitchers are fairly common and shouldn't be worth much more than about $12.00.

Our advisor for this category is Dannie Woodard, author of *Hammered Aluminum, Hand Wrought Collectibles*; *Hammered Aluminum, Hand Wrought Aluminum Book II*; and publisher of *The Aluminist*, a newsletter printed six times a year. Her address is in the Directory under Texas. See also Clubs and Newsletters.

Ashtray, Bittersweet, hammered, Wendell August #60, 5½" dia **38.00**
Basket, bread; hammered, duck on pond, oval w/twisted handle, Cromwell **12.00**

Beverage server, on stand with holder for candle or sterno, Buenilum, $195.00. (Photo courtesy Dannie Woodard)

Basket, hammered, china plate insert, floral frame, Farberware, 12" **38.00**
Basket, hammered, sq knot handle, fern & flowers, Canterbury Arts, 9" **18.00**
Basket, hammered frame w/flowers, Paden City insert, Cromwell, 14" **35.00**
Basket, polished w/stamped flowers, unmarked, 7" **7.00**
Bowl, hammered, Big-Horn sheep, Hand Forged #2, 8¾" dia .**25.00**
Bowl, hammered, blackbird & fleglings, DePonceau, 5¾" dia **25.00**
Bowl, hammered, footed, berries along scallops, Cellini Craft, 11½" **85.00**

Bowl, hammered, hunter, LA Handwrought (bell symbol), 15" dia **95.00**

Bowl, hammered, intaglio floral band, Everlast, 9" dia ...**10.00**

Bowl, hammered, looped handles, Buenilum, 6" dia **8.00**

Bowl, hammered, petal design, grapes in center, Wendell August #807 ....**85.00**

Bowl, machine-embossed pattern, Wrought Aluminum, 7" **7.00**

Bowl, polished, repousse flowers, butterfly handles, Hand Forged **12.00**

Bowl, simulated hammer marks, mum, Federal Silver Co, 7½" dia **8.00**

Butter dish, Crisscross glass lid, tulip finial, aluminum tray, R Kent **20.00**

Butter dish, polished, glass insert for ¼-lb stick, loop finial, Buenilum **25.00**

Butter dish, polished, stamped Bali Bamboo, patterned insert, Everlast **22.00**

Candlestick, anodized/polished, crystal ball, Kensington .**45.00**

Candlestick, hammered, flower sprigs, Findley, 3½x5" .**28.00**

Candlesticks, hammered, double platform, lotus leaves, W August, pr **175.00**

Candlesticks, hammered, saucer base, twisted stem, W August, 8x6", pr **195.00**

Candy dish, divided glass, hammered holder & lid, R Kent, 6" dia **35.00**

Candy dish, hammered, curled handle, flowers, Kraftware, 4½" sq **6.00**

Drippings jar with matching salt and pepper shakers, anodized chartreuse, $15.00 for the set.

Candy dish, hammered lid w/fruits, thick glass dish, unmarked Everlast **45.00**

Casserole, hammered, Bali Bamboo, bamboo finial, Everlast, 7" dia **25.00**

Casserole, hammered, Bittersweet, bar on lid, W August #735, 9x13½" **125.00**

Casserole, hammered, footed ring style, fan handles, Crown, 8½" dia **35.00**

Casserole, hammered, intaglio flowers, side handles, Everlast, 9¼" **15.00**

Casserole, hammered, pea pod finial, Everlast #1038, 7" dia **18.00**

Chafing dish, hammered, grape clusters on lid, Everlast, 10" dia **35.00**

Chafing dish, hammered, tulip, ribbon/flower handles, Rodney Kent **27.00**

Coaster, hammered, tropical fish, Wendell August **15.00**

Coasters, embossed chrysanthemums, 8 in caddy w/leaves, Continental **35.00**

Coasters, embossed tulips, ribbon & flowers on caddy handle, R Kent **35.00**

Coasters, hammered, rose, 6 in caddy w/curled handle, Everlast **25.00**

Coasters, hammered, spiral design, Everlast, set of 6 ....**18.00**

Coasters, polished, beaded rim, 8 in caddy w/looped handle, Buenilum **30.00**

Cocktail shaker, Chrysanthemum, pouring spout, Continental #550, 12" **55.00**

Condiment server, hammered, Apple Blossom, glass jar, W August #592 ....**35.00**

Condiment server, hammered, Ferris-wheel style, 3 dishes, Everlast **65.00**

Creamer & sugar bowl, hammered, Chrysanthemum, Continental #515 ....**45.00**

Creamer & sugar bowl w/tray, hammered, Bali Bamboo, Everlast #B21 ....**45.00**

Creamer & sugar bowl w/tray, plain, World **20.00**

Crumber, hammered, tray & brush, grapes, scalloped, Everlast **35.00**

Crumber, hammered, tray & brush, looped handles, Buenilum **35.00**

Crumber, hammered, tray w/hanging brush, rose, Everlast .**35.00**

Drink mixer, hammered, 1-pc, lg hole for spoon, Everlast, 7" **60.00**

Gravy boat, hammered, Chrysanthemum, w/tray, Continental #610 ....**35.00**

Gravy boat, hammered, loop handles, attached tray, w/ladle, Buenilum **35.00**

Ice bucket, hammered, applied leaves on lid, Everlast Ice Cooler #5008 ....**25.00**

Ice bucket, hammered, roses, side handles, Everlast, 9½" **45.00**

Ice bucket, hammered, tulip finial, flower handles, Rodney Kent **35.00**

Ice bucket, polished, footed, loop finial, Knight Kraft **28.00**

Jewelry, hammered bracelet, zinnia, links, Wendel August **55.00**

Smoking set, turquoise ceramic cigarette box with four ashtrays and tray, Wendell August Forge, from $95.00 to $135.00. (Photo courtesy Dannie Woodard)

Jewelry, hammered cuff bracelet, flowers & leaves, unmarked ...**25.00**

Jewelry, stamped bracelet, western motif ea section, unmarked **55.00**

Ladle, gravy; polished, double-loop handle, unmarked Buenilum **15.00**

Ladle, punch; polished, twisted double-loop handle, unmarked Buenilum **55.00**

Lamp, hammered aluminum & walnut w/aluminum shade, Wendell August **650.00**

Match box cover, hammered, Wendell August, penny box sz **35.00**

Match box cover, polished, stylized fish, Palmer-Smith, kitchen size **55.00**

Match folder cover, polished, ducks, unmarked **5.00**

Meat server, hammered, well & tree, Continental #544, 15½x11" **65.00**

Napkin holder, hammered, ribbon-&-flower-band feet, Rodney Kent **27.00**

Napkin holder, polished, cactus, Farber & Shlevin **12.00**

Napkin holder, polished, machine-embossed roses, World .**15.00**

Patio cart, hammered, intaglio leaves, w/serving pcs, Everlast **650.00**

Pitcher, hammered, applied floret & leaves, World **45.00**

Pitcher, hammered, flared at top, Everlast **25.00**

Pitcher, hammered, ice guard, Bali Bamboo, Everlast **55.00**

Pitcher, hammered, intaglio flowers, twisted handle, Everlast, 6" **35.00**

Pitcher, hammered, looped & twisted handle, Buenilum **35.00**

Pitcher, hammered, mum, leaf handle, Continental **45.00**

Pitcher, hammered, Pine, ice guard, Wendell August #760 ....**85.00**

Pitcher, hammered, thin, grooved band at center, Italy **10.00**

Pitcher, hammered, Wild Rose, Continental **35.00**

Pitcher, polished, straight sides, twisted handle, Buenilum **15.00**

Punch bowl, spun, R Wright, 5½x11½", +cups & tray & bottle opener **1,250.00**

Punch bowl & ladle, hammered, grapes, Wendell August **350.00**

Punch bowl & ladle, hammered, ped base, +hooks & glass cups, Everlast **225.00**

Salad fork & spoon, bamboo design on wooden finials, unmarked, pr **35.00**

Silent butler, hammered, apple blossoms, Wendell August #95, 7" dia **45.00**

Silent butler, hammered, bird on twig, NS Co, 6" **18.00**

Silent butler, hammered, cattails, unmarked, 5x6" **15.00**

Silent butler, hammered, Corduroy, wood handle, Continental #1505, 8" **18.00**

Silent butler, hammered, flower cluster, Henry & Miller, 4½x6" **15.00**

Silent butler, hammered, fruits, oval, Everlast, 7x9" **25.00**

Silent butler, hammered, rose, Everlast, 6" dia **18.00**

Silent butler, hammered, roses bouquet, Canterbury Arts, 6" dia **25.00**

Silent butler, hammered, tulip, Rodney Kent, 7½" dia ...**22.00**

Silent butler, polished, intaglio roses, World, 6¼" **12.00**

Smoking set, hammered tray, ashtrays & box, +pottery box, W Ausust #75 ....**150.00**

Smoking stand, hammered, ducks on tray, Wendell August #926, 22¼" **275.00**

Tidbit tray, hammered, grapes, 3-tiered, ring handle, Everlast, 14" **22.00**

Tidbit tray, machine embossed, tiered, unmarked **10.00**

Tidbit tray, polished, floral, side handle, Hammercraft **7.00**

Tray, bread; hammered, grapes, handles w/leaves, World **15.00**

Tray, bread; hammered, tulip, scalloped edge, Rodney Kent **15.00**

Tray, bread; hammered, Wild Rose, Continental **15.00**

Tray, bread; machine embossed, pansy, National Silver Co .**8.00**

Tray, bread; polished, stamped wild rose, unmarked **7.00**

Tray, hammered, Bali Bamboo, handles, Everlast, 14½x20½".**45.00**

Tray, hammered, Bittersweet, tab handles, Wendell August, 9½x14" **55.00**

Tray, hammered, Chrysanthemum, handles, Continental #524, 11x22" **45.00**

Tray, hammered, giant cactus, tab handles, Wendell August, 13¼x21" **195.00**

Tray, hammered, horseback riders & lakes, bar handles, A Armour, 9x13" **95.00**

Tray, hammered, intaglio flowers, ribbed tab handles, Everlast, 9x11" **18.00**

Tray, hammered, lake scene, loop handles & fluted rim, Cromwell, 15½" **25.00**

Tray, hammered, Oak Leaf & Acorn, handles, Continental #520, 17¼" **35.00**

Tray, hammered, polo players, winners' names, 4-23-39, W August, 8x23" **95.00**

Tray, hammered, rose bouquet, Everlast, 12" sq **20.00**

Tray, spun, raffia-wrapped hand grips, Russel Wright, 14½" dia **65.00**

Animal Dishes With Covers

Popular novelties for part of this century as well as the last, figural animal dishes were made by many well-known glasshouses in milk glass, slag, colored opaque, or clear glass. Many on the market today are reproductions, and though they're well worth your attention, don't overpay, thinking they're the originals. Beware! Refer to *Covered Animal Dishes* by Everett Grist (Collector Books) for more information.

Atterbury Duck, any color, unmarked LG Wright, 11" **70.00**

Bird on jar, milk glass, marked Avon on base **10.00**

Bull's head, mustard jar, purple slag, LG Wright, no ladle **35.00**

Cat on ribbed base, milk glass, Westmoreland, #18, 5" ..**35.00**

Chick, salt dish, milk glass w/yellow paint, Westmoreland, #3, 1" **24.00**

Dog on wide-rib base, amber, Westmoreland, 5½" **65.00**

Dolphin w/fish on lid, milk glass, Kemple **115.00**

Duck, soap dish, clear, painted bill **15.00**

Duck on cattail base, milk glass, unknown maker, 5½" **120.00**

Duck on wavy base, blue opaque, Westmoreland, #10 ....**75.00**

Eagle mother on lacy base, milk glass, Westmoreland ..**125.00**

Fish, Flat; green transparent **75.00**

Fish on collared base, clear frosted, Central Glass **150.00**

Fox on lacy base, milk glass, Westmoreland, #1 ....**150.00**

Hen, amberina, LE Smith, 5½" .**75.00**

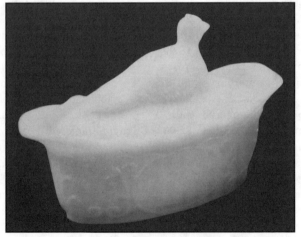

Quail on base with embossed scrolls, milk glass, unknown maker, 5½" , $65.00.

Swan, Raised Wings; milk glass with socket-molded eyes, Westmoreland, $85.00 to $95.00.

Hen, colors other than milk glass, Westmoreland Specialty, 5½" **85.00**

Hen, milk glass w/blue opaque head, Westmoreland Specialty, 5½" **65.00**

Hen, Straight Headed; clear, attributed to Indiana Glass, 5½" **35.00**

Hen on nest, red slag, LG Wright, 5½" **95.00**

Hen on sleigh, milk glass, Westmoreland, 5½" **85.00**

Hen w/chicks, milk glass, red comb, split-rib base, unmarked, 5½" **75.00**

Lamb on basketweave base, amber, LG Wright, 5½" **35.00**

Lamb on split-rib base, amber, Kemple, 5½" **45.00**

Lovebirds on nest, almond, Westmoreland, #20 ....**65.00**

Lovebirds on nest, crystal satin, Westmoreland, #20 .....**45.00**

Owl, med blue, footed, LG Wright, 4x6½" **65.00**

Owl on basketweave base, amber, LG Wright, 5½" **65.00**

Owl on basketweave base, blue slag, LG Wright, 5½" **75.00**

Pintail duck, milk glass, Kemple, 5½" **65.00**

Quail on scroll base, milk glass, 5½" **65.00**

Rabbit, Mule-Eared; blue opaque, 5½" **55.00**

Robin on twig nest, antique blue, Westmoreland, #7 ....**65.00**

Rooster, blue opaque w/white head, Westmoreland Specialty, 5½" .**85.00**

Rooster, white carnival, LE Smith, tall **45.00**

Rooster on nest, red slag, LG Wright, 5½" **95.00**

Rooster on ribbed base, milk glass, Westmoreland, #2, 5" ...**25.00**

Santa on Sleigh, milk glass w/painted details, Westmoreland, 5½" .**95.00**

Squirrel, milk glass, split-rib base, unmarked McKee, 5½" .**185.00**

Swan, Closed-Neck; milk glass, Westmoreland Specialty .**75.00**

Swan, crystal, unknown maker, recent, sm **10.00**

Swan on knobby basketweave base, amber, Patent Appl'd For, 7" **165.00**

Turkey, amethyst, LE Smith, med **35.00**

Turkey, crystal, LE Smith, med .**35.00**

Turkey, green carnival, LE Smith, lg **50.00**

Turkey, milk glass, split-rib base, unmarked McKee, 5½" .**110.00**

Turkey on woven base, lilac mist, LG Wright, 5½" **40.00**

Turtle, knobby back, dark green, LG Wright, lg **125.00**

Turtle on basketweave base, amber, LG Wright **20.00**

Appliances

Old electric appliances are collected for nostalgic reasons as well as for their unique appearance and engineering. Especially interesting are early irons, fans, vacuum cleaners, and toasters. Examples with Art Deco styling often bring high prices at today's auctions and flea markets. But remember, condition is important. Be sure they're reasonably clean and in excellent working condition before paying listed prices.

Blender, Oster, chrome base .**40.00**

Blender, Waring, chrome base, heavy glass, EX **35.00**

Chafing dish, Chase #17087 .**125.00**

Coffee urn set, Royal Rochester Floral **95.00**

Corn popper, Dominion **75.00**

Fan, Emerson, brass cage, 6-blade, 1908 ....**150.00**

Fan, Emerson, oscillating, 12" **130.00**

Fan, Knapp #145, battery .**150.00**

Fan, Mesco DC Fan, #3695 .**85.00**

Fudge sauce warmer, Johnston's, 1930s **45.00**

Heater, General Electric, bulb type **45.00**

Ice cream mixer, Smoothie, bullet shape, MIB **95.00**

Mixer, General Electric, green stripe **55.00**

Percolator, Coffee Maid, Deco style, chrome, 1950s **45.00**

Percolator, Porcelier #120 ...**85.00**

Percolator, Westinghouse #283881, EX **65.00**

Toaster, Bersted #87 ....**40.00**

Toaster, Dominion, single slice **150.00**

Toaster, General Electric #129T75 ....**45.00**

Toaster, Handy Hot **35.00**

Toaster, Majestic, 2-slice, tip-out style **75.00**

Toaster, Royal Rochester #1340 ....**55.00**

Toaster, Torrid No T-70, NM, $65.00.

Toaster, Sun Chief #680 ......**25.00**

Toaster, Sunbeam #T-1-C ...**75.00**
Toaster, Torrid Swing Around, EX **85.00**
Toaster, Universal #E947 ...**75.00**
Toaster, Westinghouse #5422, white **65.00**
Vacuum cleaner, Airway, 1922, w/original bag **145.00**
Vacuum cleaner, Gurell Guild Electrolux, EX **175.00**
Vacuum cleaner, Universal Supreme No E440, ca 1942 ....**125.00**
Waffle iron, Manning Bowman Twin O'Matic **85.00**
Waffle iron, Universal #E2024 .**35.00**

Ashtrays

Even though the general public seems to be down on smoking, ashtrays themselves are beginning to be noticed favorably by collectors, who perhaps view them as an 'endangered species'! Some of the more desirable examples are those with embossed or intaglio designs, applied decorations, added figures of animals or people, Art Deco styling, an interesting advertising message, and an easily recognizable manufacturer's mark.

Bald man singing w/mouth open wide, Sweet Adeline at base, Japan **25.00**
Calico donkey w/cigarette panniers & tray on back, Japan, 3¼" **30.00**
Car w/rumble seat tray, blue lustre, Japan, 2", from $15 to **25.00**
Card suit shape w/cat head & feet extended from ends, Japan, 3¾" **18.00**

Card suit shape w/clown seated at side, tan & blue lustre, Japan, ea **20.00**
Card suit shape w/mouse musician at side, Japan, 1½" **15.00**
Ceresota Flour, boy in center, gold trim, 4 rests, 7" dia **5.00**
Clown at side of canoe ashtray, lustre, Japan **15.00**
Clown w/indented tummy, card suit button on costume, lustre, Japan **15.00**

Clown, snuffers on each shoulder and in base, marked Japan, 5¼", $50.00. (Photo courtesy Carole Bess White)

Coon Chicken Inn, 4" dia **35.00**
Cowboy hat, green w/red band, Japan, 3" L **10.00**
Deco-style falcon beside 6-sided tray, maroon & green, Japan, 3¼" **30.00**
Devil's head relief in center of metal tray, 3 rests, Occupied Japan **15.00**
Duck pr, yellow ducks by tan lustre tray, Japan, 2", from $10 to **15.00**

Electrolux, blue & chrome sweeper applied on base, 5½x6½" **120.00**

Floral decor embossed on metal, Occupied Japan **3.00**

Flower on orange lustre w/green rim, Noritake mark, 3" dia **30.00**

Frog w/white lustre tummy, green w/open mouth, Japan, 3" **20.00**

Little Orphan Annie & Sandy beside tan & white lustre tray, Japan, 3" **100.00**

Monkey w/hat beside tray, blue & tan lustre, Japan, 2½" ..**20.00**

Otard Cognac, white w/blue lettering, made in France, triangular, 6" **15.00**

Peacock figural, tail is tray, white lustre, striker base, Japan, 3" **18.00**

Rabbit beside tray, white lustre w/red & blue, Japan, from $20 to **45.00**

Ralston Purina, dog's feeding bowl style, graphic on white, 6" .**35.00**

Revolutionary War musicians, multicolor shiny glazes, Japan, 3" **12.50**

Souvenir of Colorado, metal w/embossed scenes, 3 rests .**4.00**

Souvenir of Long Beach, embossed scenes on metal, Occupied Japan **4.00**

Souvenir of NY City, metal, embossed Statue of Liberty, Occupied Japan **15.00**

Souvenir of Washington DC, embossed metal, Occupied Japan **12.50**

Westfella Cream Separators, plastic & tin cream separator, 5" **35.00**

Tire Ashtrays

Tire ashtrays were introduced in the teens as advertising items. The very early all-glass or glass and metal types were replaced in the early 1920s by the more familiar rubber-tired varieties. Hundereds of different ones have been produced over the years. They are still distributed by the larger tire companies only, but no longer contain the detail or color of the pre-World War II tire ashtrays. Although the common ones bring modest prices, rare examples demand retail prices of up to several hundred dollars. Our tire ashtray advisor is Jeff McVey; he is listed in the Directory under Idaho. You'll also find information on how to order his book, *Tire Ashtray Collector's Guide,* which we recommend for further study.

Pennsylvania Vacuum Cup Oilproof 34x4, 1-pc, all glass, $200.00. (Photo courtesy Jeff McVey)

Allstate SR Balloon, amber insert shaped like disc wheel ..**80.00**

Atlas 5.50-17 4 Ply, clear insert embossed Atlas **75.00**

BF Goodrich Comp T/A, clear insert w/manufacturer's mark .**30.00**

Continental R (3 times), clear insert w/3 rests, embossed horse logo **50.00**

Dunlop (Ireland), pink Carrigaline Pottery insert imprinted D **100.00**

Englebert (Belgium), metal insert resembles wheel cover ..**75.00**

Firestone Heavy Duty High Speed..., amber insert, Texas Expo, 1936 ....**125.00**

Firestone Radial 23 (tractor tire), clear insert w/manufacture's mark **25.00**

General Ld250 Haf-Trac, clear insert w/manufacturer's mark **30.00**

Gillette Super Traction, clear insert embossed Gillette w/polar bear **125.00**

Goodrich Silvertown Heavy Duty Cord 36x6, embossed green insert **45.00**

Goodyear Balloon All Weather 33x6.00, green disk-wheel insert **85.00**

Goodyear 6.70-15 4 Ply, clear insert w/dealer's imprint **40.00**

Hood Arrow Heavy Duty 6 ply 6.00-20, clear insert w/dealer's sticker **100.00**

Kelly-Springfield Steelmark Radial, clear insert w/manufacturer's mark **25.00**

Kleber Colombes 6.40-15 Grand Raid, aluminum Kleber Colombes insert **60.00**

Lee of Conshohocken Truck-Bus, clear insert w/dealer's sticker **100.00**

Miller Deluxe Long Safe Milage, clear insert embossed Miller Tires **80.00**

Pennsylvania Vacuum Cup Oilproof 34x4, 1-pc, all glass **200.00**

Phillips 66 Deep Cleat...(tractor), clear insert w/manufacturer's mark **45.00**

Remington Cushion-Aire 79 Dual..., clear insert w/manufacturer's mark **35.00**

Seiberling All-Tread, clear insert w/dealer's sticker **40.00**

Toyo Radial Z-2 (Japan), clear insert w/manufacturer's imprint **40.00**

US Royal Heavy Duty Six, amber insert, matchbox holder marked US Tires **85.00**

Zenith, clear insert w/manufacturer's imprint **45.00**

Autographs

Autographs of famous people from every walk of life are of interest to students of philography, as it is referred to by those who enjoy this hobby. Values hinge on many things — rarity of the signature and content of the signed material are major considerations. Autographs of contemporary sports figures or entertainers often sell at $10.00 to $15.00 for small signed photos. Beware of forgeries. If you are unsure, ask established dealers to help you.

Acuff, Roy; inscribed & signed 8x10" black & white glossy **10.00**

Aiello, Danny; signed 8x10" black & white glossy .**14.00**

La Rue, Lash; signed lobby card, $40.00.

Allyson, June; signed 8x10" black & white glossy **10.00**

Anka, Paul; signed 8x10" black & white glossy **50.00**

Autry, Gene; inscribed & signed copy of his fan club magazine .**25.00**

Bardot, Bridgette; signed 8x10" color glossy **32.00**

Mansfield, Jayne; inscribed card, matted and framed with vintage photograph, $345.00.

Belafonte, Harry; inscribed & signed 8x10" black & white glossy **12.00**

Bellamy, Ralph; inscribed & signed 8x10" black & white glossy **8.00**

Bishop, Joey; inscribed & signed 8x10" black & white glossy **4.00**

Bronson, Charles; signed 8x10" black & white glossy **10.00**

Brooks, Mel; inscribed & signed 8x10" black & white glossy **9.00**

Brynner, Yul; signed 8x10" black & white glossy **75.00**

Burns, George; inscribed & signed 8x10" black & white glossy **8.00**

Buttons, Red; inscribed & signed 8x10" black & white glossy **6.00**

Cagney, Jim (James); signed 8x10" black & white glossy **95.00**

Campell, Glen; inscribed & signed 8x10" black & white glossy **20.00**

Clark, Roy; inscribed & signed 8x10" black & white glossy **5.00**

Clooney, Rosemary; inscribed & signed 8x10" black & white glossy **5.00**

Conway, Tim; inscribed & signed 8x10" black & white glossy **5.00**

DeHaviland, Gloria; signed 8x10 black & white glossy **35.00**

Domino, Fats; signed 8x10" black & white glossy **18.00**

Fontaine, Joan; signed 8x10" black & white glossy **10.00**

Foreman, George; signed 5x6" newspaper photo knocking Moore out **16.00**

Graf, Steffi; signed Adidas brochure **12.00**

Harrison, Rex; signed 8x10" black & white glossy **35.00**

Heston, Charlton; signed 8x10" black & white glossy **15.00**

Holden, Williams; signed 8x10" black & white glossy **70.00**

Jones, James Earl; signed 3x5" white card & a signed xeroxed article **35.00**

Jones, Quincy; signed 8x10" black & white glossy **15.00**

Joyner, Florence Griffith; signed Classic Games Card in color **20.00**

Keyes, Evelyn; signed 8x10" black & white glossy **30.00**

Leigh, Janet; signed 8x10" black & white glossy **10.00**

Lewis, Carl; signed 4x6" color action photo on card w/stats on back **20.00**

Loren, Sophia; signed 8x10" color glossy **20.00**

Louganis, Greg; signed Hall of Fame Trade Card, color, ready to dive **10.00**

Stuart, Jimmy; signed 8x10" color photo, $45.00.

Marino, Dan; signed (w/#13) 6x8" black & white glossy of him in play **16.00**

Marvin, Lee; signed 8x10" black & white glossy **100.00**

Michener, James A; signed magazine cover **40.00**

Minnelli, Liza; signed 8x10" black & white glossy **12.00**

Moore, Clayton; 8x10" black & white glossy also signed Lone Ranger **25.00**

Newton, Wayne; inscribed & signed 8x10" black & white glossy **12.00**

O'Conner, Sandra Day; signed Supreme Court card **25.00**

Page, Patti; inscribed & signed 8x10" black & white glossy **4.00**

Peck, Gregory; inscribed & signed 8x10" black & white glossy **15.00**

Powell, Jane; signed 8x10" black & white glossy **15.00**

Presley, Priscilla; inscribed & signed 8x10" black & white glossy **12.00**

Prosky, Robert; inscribed & signed 8x10" black & white glossy .**5.00**

Randolph, Joyce; inscribed & signed 8x10" black & white glossy **5.00**

Redford, Robert; signed 8x10" black & white glossy **50.00**

Rehnquist, William H; signed Supreme Court card **40.00**

Reynolds, Burt, inscribed & signed 8x10" color glossy **9.00**

Reynolds, Burt; inscribed & signed 8x10" black & white glossy **7.00**

Reynolds, Debbie; signed 8x10" color glossy **15.00**

Rivers, Joan; signed 8x10" black & white glossy **6.00**

Robards, Jason; signed 8x10" black & white glossy **8.00**

Robinson, Sugar Ray; signed 4x5" black & white magazine photo in ring **40.00**

Simon, Carly; inscribed & signed 8x10" black & white glossy **16.00**

Storm, Gale; signed 8x10" black & white glossy **12.00**

Trump, Donald; inscribed signed 8x10" black & white glossy **28.00**

Turner, Ted; signed black & white 8x10" glossy photo **15.00**

Ullman, Liv; signed 8x10" black & white glossy **12.00**

Walker, Hershel; inscribed & signed magazine cover in uniform **10.00**

West, Mae; signed 8x10" black & white glossy **85.00**

Williams, Esther; signed 8x10" black & white glossy **10.00**

Williams, Robin; signed 8x10" black & white glossy **18.00**

Williams, Vanessa; signed photo on 5x7" paper stock **25.00**

Automobilia

Many are fascinated with vintage automobiles, but to own one of those 'classy chassis' is a luxury not all can afford! So instead they enjoy collecting related memorabilia such as advertising, owners' manuals, horns, emblems, and hood ornaments. The decade of the 1930s produced the items that are most in demand today, but the '50s models have their own band of devoted fans as well. Usually made of porcelain on cast iron, first-year license plates in hard-to-find excellent condition may bring as much as $200.00 for the pair. See also License Plates.

Clock, Ford, neon (not working), 3-color metal face, 18x18", EX, $800.00.

Bank, Ford dog w/washcloth, marked Florence Ceramics **45.00**

Book, Automobile Quarterly's World of Cars, w/dust jacket, 1971, NM **15.00**

Book, Ford at Fifty, w/dust jacket, 107-page, 9x12", EX **20.00**

Book, Mercedes for the Road, 1946-74, Rasmussen, w/dust jacket **15.00**

Hood ornament, GMC, chrome with green and black paint, now desk accessory, 3x6½", EX+, $60.00.

Book, The Porsche Book, Boschen & Barth, w/dust jacket, EX **15.00**

Book, Thunderbird!, Ray Miller, Glenn Embree, 4th edition, EX **20.00**

Brochure, Chevrolet Trucks for 1942, EX **50.00**

Brochure, DeSoto, partial color, 4-page, 1951, opens to 11x15½" **40.00**

Catalog, DeSoto, Twentieth Century Travelog, part color, M ...**45.00**

Catalog, sales; LaSalle 1939, spiral bound, 28-page, 12x9¼" .**85.00**

Catalog, sales; Oldsmobile, 1952, 16-page, 11x8½", M **30.00**

Chauffeur's badge, Colorado, 1953 ....**20.00**

Coin, Pontiac, chief's portrait, Chief of the Sixes, General Motors **10.00**

Door guards, Reed's Protective, 1960s, MIP **5.00**

Gauge, compression; Hastings, ca 1930s **20.00**

Headband, Pontiac, w/feather, 1951 Silver Anniversary give-away, M **22.00**

Lighter, chrome w/cloth-covered wire, 6-volt plug-in **15.00**

Magazine, Car Life, February, 1954, Volume 1, #1 ....**10.00**

Magazine, Motor Life, Indy '55 feature, June 1955 ....**5.00**

Magazine, Sports Cars Illustrated, January, 1958 ....**5.00**

Magnatray, plastic, attaches to dash, 3x9" **10.00**

Manual, Chilton's Repair Guide & Tune-Up, 1970-83 ....**6.00**

Manual, Dodge Body Service, 1973, M **12.00**

Medal, St Christopher, gold-tone badge shape, 1950s **15.00**

Mug, Chevrolet 1961 Truck Sales Award, ceramic w/gold, bow-tie logo **20.00**

Owner's manual, Chevrolet, 1949, EX **10.00**

Owner's manual, Ford, cover wear, 1951, EX **1200**

Owner's manual, Hudson 8, 1935, EX **30.00**

Paperweight, GM Golden Milestones...1908-58, 2" brass oval in Lucite **45.00**

Pencil, mechanical, Armstrong Tires, rhino logo, EX **15.00**

Pencil, Oldsmobile 1950s logo, Jack Frost Motors, wooden, M **2.00**

Pin-back button, Chevrolet, Watch the Leader, tin, ¾" dia, EX **10.00**

Playing cards, AAA, lighthouse scenes, double deck, early 1960s, M **10.00**

Playing cards, Ford oval logo, double deck (blue & white decks), M **10.00**

Postcard, Chevrolet Monte Carlo, 1970, M **5.00**

Postcard, Corvette, orange, 1974 .**4.00**

Postcard, Olds Toronado, turquoise w/vinyl roof, 1967, M **5.00**

Poster, Buick, Vacation Check-Up, family in sedan, 1950s, 36x23", NM **180.00**

Promotional vehicle, 1955 T-bird convertible, black, AMT, EX **135.00**

Promotional vehicle, 1966 Ford Mustang Fastback, working radio, NM **150.00**

Promotional vehicle, 1967 Chevrolet Fleetside pick-up, orange, NM **125.00**

Promotional vehicle, 1971 Plymouth Roadrunner, copper w/stripes, EX **125.00**

Ring, Pontiac Service Craftsman, sterling, signed Balfour .**125.00**

Sign, Chrysler Plymouth Sales..., porcelain, 2-sided, 18x35", EX **295.00**

Sign, Pontiac, neon, Chief in circle, red & blue, new, 18x26" **185.00**

Suicide knob, black plastic w/silver stripes, ca 1950 ....**30.00**

Thermometer, Buick Motor Cars, porcelain, white on black, 27", VG **200.00**

Tie, National Corvette Restorers Society, multicolor on navy .**5.00**

Tie bar, GMC trucks, red & blue V-6 emblem **10.00**

Tie pin, Firestone Service, 14k solid gold top, older shield logo, NM **25.00**

Tire pressure gauge, Dodge, yellow w/orange & black lettering, 2x3" **65.00**

Watch fob, Awarded for Loyalty in the Cause of Good Roads, US flag **35.00**

Autumn Leaf

Autumn Leaf dinnerware was a product of the Hall China Company, who produced this extensive line from 1933 until 1978 for exclusive distribution by the Jewel Tea Company. The Libbey Glass Company made co-ordinating pitchers, tumblers, and stemware. Metal, cloth, plastic, and paper items were also available. Today, though very rare pieces are expen-

Clock, ca 1956, electric, from $400.00 to $550.00.

Creamer and sugar bowl, Rayed, from $60.00 to $80.00.

sive and a challenge to acquire, new collectors may easily reassemble an attractive, usable set at a reasonable price. Hall has produced special club pieces (for the NALCC) as well as some limited editions for an Ohio company, but these are well marked and easily identified as such. Refer to *The Collector's Encyclopedia of Hall China* by Margaret and Kenn Whitmyer (Collector Books) for more information. Our advisor for this category is Gwynne Harrison; she is listed in the Directory under California.

Baker, French; 2-pint, from $125 to **150.00**
Bowl, cereal; 6½", from $8 to .**12.00**
Bowl, cream soup; from $25 to **35.00**
Bowl, salad; 9", from $15 to .**25.00**
Bowl, vegetable; divided oval, 10½", from $80 to **125.00**
Bowl, vegetable; oval, from $15 to **25.00**
Bowl, vegetable; oval, w/lid, from $50 to **75.00**
Candle holders, 1989 club pc, from $225 to **250.00**

Candlesticks, metal, 4", pr, from $70 to **100.00**
Candy dish, metal base, from $450 to **550.00**
Clock, electric, from $400 to ..**550.00**
Coffeepot, all china, 4-pc, from $275 to **350.00**
Coffeepot, Rayed, 8-cup, from $30 to **45.00**
Cookbook, 1984 club pc **45.00**
Cookie jar, Tootsie, Rayed, from $250 to **300.00**
Creamer & sugar bowl, Rayed, 1930s style, from $60 to **80.00**
Drip jar, from $15 to **20.00**
Gravy boat w/underplate, from $40 to **55.00**
Jug, ball from, #3, from $35 to ..**40.00**
Jug, utility; Rayed, from $20 to **25.00**
Mug, chocolate; 4-pc set, 1992 club pc, from $80 to **100.00**
Plate, 10", from $10 to **15.00**
Plate, 6", from $5 to **8.00**
Plate, 9", from $8 to **12.00**
Platter, oval, 13½", from $20 to .**28.00**
Salt & pepper shakers, Casper, ruffled, regular, pr, from $20 to **30.00**

Salt & pepper shakers, range size, pr, from $20 to **30.00**

Souffle baker, 4½", from $40 to **50.00**

Stack set, 4-pc, from $70 to .**100.00**

Teacup, regular, ruffled-D, from $7 to **10.00**

Teapot, Aladdin, from $40 to **50.00**

Teapot, Donut, 1993 club pc, from $100 to **125.00**

Teapot, long spout, Rayed, 1935, from $45 to **60.00**

Teapot, Newport, 1978, from $175 to **200.00**

Tray, metal, oval, from $75 to.**100.00**

Tray, tidbit; 2-tier, from $80 to......................................**100.00**

Tumbler, gold & frost on clear glass, Libbey, 15-oz, from $50 to **65.00**

Tumbler, iced tea; frosted glass, Libbey, 5½", from $15 to **20.00**

Vase, bud; sm or regular decal, from $175 to **225.00**

Warmer, round, from $125 to **165.00**

Avon

Originally founded in 1886 under the title California Perfume Company, the firm became officially known as Avon Products Inc. in 1939. Among collectors they are best known not for their cosmetics and colognes but for their imaginative packaging and figural bottles. Avon offers something for almost everyone with cross-collectibles including Fostoria, Wedgwood, commerative plates, Ceramarte steins, and hundreds of other quality items. Also sought are product samples, awards, magazine ads, jewelry, and catalogs. Their Cape Cod glassware has been sold in vast quantities since the '70s and is becoming a common sight at flea markets and malls. Our advisor Tammy Rodrick is listed in the Directory under Illinois. See also Cape Cod.

Avon Assortment Gift Set, 8-pc, 1931-33 ....**100.00**

Beauty Kit for Fingers, 4-pc, 1938-39 ....**75.00**

Pheasant decanter, 1972-74, $10.00; Quail decanter, 1973-75, $9.00.

Colonial Set, perfume & face powder, 1943 ....**65.00**

Derringer Cologne Pistol, 1977 .**10.00**

Dutch Pipe, 1973 ....**10.00**

Esquire Men's Set, 3-pc, 1940 .**75.00**

Extra Special Male After Shave, 1977 ....**5.00**

Faithful Laddie Collie, 1977 ..**5.00**

Gift Set #21, 3-pc, 1933-35 ..**75.00**

Gold Box Gift Set, 3 perfumes, 1944 ....**75.00**

Kodiak Bear, 1977 ....**5.00**

Little Folks Xmas Gift Box Set, 4 perfumes, 1933 ....**200.00**

Minuet Set, boxed, 4-pc, 1944 ....**100.00**

Opposing Chess Set, 7 different pcs, 1975, MIB **10.00**

Orchid Set, 3-pc, 1939 ....**50.00**

Peek A Boo Set, 3-pc, 1944 ..**75.00**

Pepper Box Pistol Replica, 1977 .**10.00**

Smart Move Chess Piece, 11-pc, 1971-76, MIB **10.00**

Spectator Set, 3-pc, 1939 ...**100.00**

Threesome Set (renamed Mayfair Set in 1939), 1936-38, 3-pc **50.00**

Twenty Paces Set, gun replicas, 1967, MIB **50.00**

Vanity Book, double compact & lipstick, 1934 ....**50.00**

Vanity Book, double fan compact & lipstick, 1931-32 ....**75.00**

Young Hearts Set, cologne, talc, bubble bath, 1953 ....**100.00**

Banks

After the Depression, everyone was aware that saving 'for a rainy day' would help during bad times. Children of the '40s, '50s, and '60s were given piggy banks in forms of favorite characters to reinforce the idea of saving. They were made to realize that by saving money they could buy that expensive bicycle or a toy they were particularly longing for.

The most popular (and expensive) type of older bank with today's collectors are the mechanicals, so called because of the antics they perform when a coin is deposited. Over three hundred models were produced between the Civil War period and the first World War. On some, arms wave, legs kick, or mouths open to swallow up the coin — amusing nonsense intended by the inventor to encourage and reward thriftiness.

Most of the original banks have become very expensive, and some have been known to sell for as much as $20,000.00. Because of this, many collectors can't afford the old banks and are opting for some of the modern mechanicals that are emerging on the collectible market, including Book of Knowledge and James D. Capron, which are reproductions with full inscriptions stating that they are replicas of the originals. Beware of unmarked modern reproductions. See also Advertising; Character Collectibles; Disney.

Book of Knowledge Banks

Always Did 'Spise a Mule (Jockey), EX **175.00**

Boy on Trapeze, rare, NM .**650.00**

Bull Dog Bank, EX+, from $225
to **300.00**
Butting Buffalo, NM **350.00**
Cabin, w/original box & documents, M **415.00**
Cat & Mouse, M **425.00**
Creedmoor, NM **400.00**
Dentist, Special Medallion Series, M **350.00**
Eagle & Eaglets, eaglets chirp for food, NM **450.00**
Hometown Battery Bank, M .**395.00**
Humpty Dumpty, Special Medallion Series, w/original box & documents, M ...**375.00**
Indian Shooting Bear, NM .**425.00**
Jonah & the Whale, NM, from $295 to **325.00**
Leap Frog, Special Medallion series, NM+ **395.00**

Boy on Trapeze, Book of Knowledge, rare, NM, $650.00. (Photo courtesy Dan Iannoti)

Magician Bank, NM+ **365.00**
Milking Cow, NM **365.00**
Organ Bank (Girl & Boy), NM .**335.00**
Owl (Turns Head), EX **275.00**
Punch & Judy, NM **355.00**
Tammany, Special Medallion Certified, M **295.00**
Teddy & the Bear, NM **310.00**
Trick Pony, EX+ **250.00**
Uncle Sam, NM+ **375.00**
US & Spain, w/original cannon ball, NM **340.00**
William Tell, coin rings bell in castle, NM+ **340.00**
World's Fair, bronze version, M **395.00**

Other Modern Mechanicals

Auto Bank, John Wright, 1974, coin on hood flips into car, NM **745.00**
Elephant, James Capron, EX+ **280.00**
Elephant, John Wright, w/original box & documents, M ...**245.00**
Galloping Cowboy, Y/Japan, 1950s, battery-op, man on white horse, MIB **440.00**
Ice Cream Freezer (semimechanical), John Wright, scarce, M **110.00**
Magic Bank, James Capron, NM **950.00**
Mason, Black Face, John Wright, M **925.00**
Mercury Rocket, Duro, D15, silver metal, no paint or trap, 1960s, EX **55.00**
Merry-Go-Round (semimechanical), John Wright, scarce, M .**110.00**
Mule Entering Barn, James Capron, mule jumps in, dog runs out, NM **700.00**

Organ Grinder, NYC/Japan, 4 actions, rare, 8", NMIB .**660.00**

Penny Pineapple, Wilton, commemorating statehood, 1st edition, NM **675.00**

Penny Pineapple, Wilton, 2nd edition, rpr, EX **295.00**

Santa Claus, John Wright, w/original box & documents, M **290.00**

Satelite Bank, Duro, D25, gold w/nose cone marble, 1960s, w/key, NM **225.00**

Strato XU 232, Duro, D24, green, w/key, NM+ **135.00**

Trick Dog, James Capron, NM **625.00**

Uncle Sam, John Wright, imported, w/original box, M **235.00**

Uncle Sam & Arab, John Wright, commemorating 1975 oil embargo, NM **1,300.00**

Washington at Rappahannock, John Wright, original, 1977, M **675.00**

Wild West Bank, Vacument/Kansas State Bank, 1960s, VG **85.00**

Barware

Gleaming with sophistication and style, vintage cocktail shakers are skyrocketing in value as the hot new collectible of the '90s. Young trend-setters are using this swank and practical objet d'art to serve their pre-dinner drinks. Form and function never had a better mix. The latest acquisition from America's classic Art Deco past is occasion enough for a party and a round of martinis.

In the 1920s it was prohibition that brought the cocktail hour and cocktail parties into the home. Today the high cost of dining out along with a more informed social awareness about alcohol consumption brings at-home cocktail parties back into fashion. Released across the country from after a half century of imprisonment in attics and china closets, these glass and chrome shaker sets have been recalled to life — recalled to hear the clank of ice cubes and to again become the symbol of elegance.

For further information we recommend *Vintage Bar Ware* by Stephen Visakay. Our advisors for this category are Arlene Lederman (listed in the Directory under New York) and Stephen Visakay (listed in the Directory under New Jersey).

Glass, cobalt w/applied sterling rooster design **100.00**

Glass, cobalt w/white silkscreened recipes, 1930 ....**75.00**

Glass, ruby red, chrome top, w/applied sterling design, 1930s **95.00**

Glass, ruby red, chrome top, 1930s-40s **65.00**

Mixer, chrome w/painted cast-iron base, Stevens Electric Co, 1934, 13" **150.00**

Napkins, cloth, various deisgns, 1930s-40s, 4x6" **2.00**

Serving set, all chrome, unmarked, 1940s, teapot, shaker, tray & 6 cups **65.00**

Shaker, aluminum cylinder, unmarked, 1930s-40s ...**35.00**

Shaker, aluminum cylinder w/red or black plastic lid, West Bend, 1933 ....**45.00**

Shaker, Blue Moon, chrome w/blue top, Chase, #90066 .....**100.00**

Shaker, chrome, recipes, colored plastic handle, Forman Bros, 1930s **75.00**

Shaker, chrome cylinder, red-painted top cap, Revere, ca 1938 ....**125.00**

Shaker, chrome dumbbell shape, not stamped w/maker's name, 1930s **150.00**

Shaker, chrome penguin, screw-off knob on beak, no mark, 1930s **200.00**

Shaker, chrome skyscraper, cylindrical, Revere (Norman Bel Geddes) **350.00**

Shaker, chrome skyscraper w/Bakelite lid, Manning-Bowman, 12" **85.00**

Shaker, chrome teapot style, Catalin trim, Revere, ca 1938 ....**200.00**

Shaker, chrome teapot w/black handle, Krome-Kraft, 1930s-1950s **35.00**

Shaker, clown w/3 chrome balls, 4 attached bells, wooden handle **200.00**

Shaker, frosted lady's leg, chrome top, removable slipper, unmarked **175.00**

Shaker, Gaiety, chrome w/black rings, Chase, #90034 ....**45.00**

Shaker, generic type, chrome or stainless, color plastic handle, 1930s **28.00**

Shaker, glass dumbbell, various colors, chrome top, 1930, from $125 to **175.00**

Shaker, green glass w/chrome top, flashed & cut decoration **75.00**

Shaker, lady's leg, cobalt glass w/chrome top, removable shoe, unmarked **450.00**

Shaker, cobalt with fired-on white sailboats, 11",
$37.50; matching ice bowl, $35.00; tumbler, $12.50.

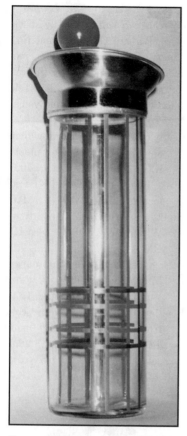

Tam-o-Shaker, glass cylinder with red & blue stripes, chrome top, 1930s, 12", $95.00. (Photo courtesy Stephen Visakay)

Shaker, lady's leg, red glass w/ chrome top, removable slipper, unmarked **250.00**

Shaker, silver-plated penguin, stamped Napier Pat-D-101559, 1930s **750.00**

Tray, chrome, 1930s **20.00**

Tray, glass on black wood w/painted recipes, handles, 1940s ..**35.00**

Tray, glass on wood w/rooster decor, 1930s, 12x18" **35.00**

Tray, metal w/painted rooster & weather vane, 1950s, 12x16" **15.00**

Bauer

The Bauer Company moved from Kentucky to California in 1909, producing crocks, gardenware, and vases until after the Depression when they introduced their first line of dinnerware. From 1932 until the early 1960s, they successfully marketed several lines of solid-color wares that are today very collectible. Some of their most popular lines are Ring, Plain Ware, and Monterey Modern. Refer to *The Collector's Encyclopedia of California Pottery* by Jack Chipman for more information.

Baking dish, Ring, black only, w/lid, M **100.00**

Bean pot, Plain, black, handles, 4-qt **200.00**

Bowl, berry; white **25.00**

Bowl, cereal; white **55.00**

Bowl, flower; Hi-Fire, orange-red, deep, 5" **55.00**

Bowl, lug soup; w/lid, 5½" .**160.00**

Casserole, in rack, w/lid, 7½" .**150.00**

Casserole, Ring, w/lid, 4" ..**150.00**

Cigarette jar, blue, w/lid ...**275.00**

Coffeepot, Plain, individual .**85.00**

Cookie jar, Ring, w/lid **275.00**

Cup & saucer, Monterey, white .**40.00**

Custard cup, Ring, Hi-Fire style, white **25.00**

Custard cup, Ring, standard, black only **55.00**

Ewer, Cal Art, blue **150.00**

Gravy boat, Al Fresco, coffee brown or Dubonnet **18.00**

Jug, ball; Ring, blue **275.00**

Marmalade, Plain, black ...**200.00**

Mustard jar, orange-red, w/lid .**275.00**

Pitcher, beater; Ring, w/lid .**300.00**

Coffee server, Ring, jade green, 6-cup, $50.00; with black lid, $30.00.

Plate, chop; all colors but white, 13" **50.00**
Plate, Contempo, all colors, 10" .**10.00**
Plate, soup; burgundy, 7½" .**80.00**
Platter, La Linda, light brown, pink or gray, 12" **22.00**
Refrigerator stack set, in rack, complete **275.00**
Spice jar, orange-red, #3, w/lid .**200.00**
Stein, Ring, black, cylindrical, 5" **200.00**
Teapot, Aladdin, 4-cup **125.00**
Teapot, Ring, wooden handle, 6-cup **100.00**

The Beatles

Beatles memorabilia is becoming increasingly popular with those who grew up in the '60s. Almost any item that could be produced with their pictures or logos were manufactured and sold by the thousands in department stores. Some have such a high collector value that they have been reproduced,

beware! Refer to *The Beatles: A Reference and Value Guide* by Michael Stern, Barbara Crawford, and Hollis Lamon (Collector Books) for more information. Our advisor for this category is Bojo (Bob Gottuso), who is listed in the Directory under Pennsylvania.

Belt buckle, gold-color metal w/black & white photo under plastic, EX **40.00**
Book, Beatles Forever, 1970s collectors edition, VG+ **9.00**
Book, Beatles on Broadway, Whitman, 1964, 8½x12", EX **17.00**
Book, paperback; Yellow Submarine, Max Wilk, Signet, pocket size, VG **18.00**
Booklet, '65 concert souvenir, color front, black & white inside, 12" **28.00**
Booklet, Official Fan Club, green cover, 1971, 20-page, 8½x11" ...**18.00**

Doll, George Harrison, Applause, 1988, 24", NM, $85.00. (Photo courtesy June Moon)

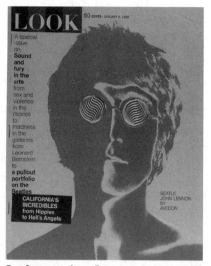

Look magazine, January 9, 1968, with psychedelic photos of Beatles inside, NM, $40.00. (Photo courtesy June Moon)

Cake decorations, miniature replicas of Revell dolls, 3", EX **60.00**

Coin, sterling silver, John Lennon portrait, 1940-80, limited edition **20.00**

Decorations, Yellow Submarine, 20 cardboard popouts on 9½x15" sheet **45.00**

Diary, vinyl w/black & white photos, 1965, 3x4", EX **30.00**

Flasher button, I Like Beatles, 1st names & faces, Vari-Vue, 2½" **25.00**

Gumball record charm, black plastic, face on 1 side, label on back **7.00**

Hairbrush, Genco, 1964, MIP .**40.00**

Headband, Love the Beatles, blue, Betterwear, MIP **55.00**

Key chain, Come Together, new, M **15.00**

Mobile, 4 punch-out portraits w/stage, Whitman, EX **150.00**

Mug, plastic w/color paper insert, head shots of ea, 4" **18.00**

Paperweight, Official Beatles Fan in thick acrylic, '70s, 3½x4¼" **90.00**

Picture sleeve, Nobody Told Me, Lennon, unused, NM **10.00**

Pin, Yellow Submarine figural, cloisonne on brass, 1½" ..**8.00**

Pin-back button, I Believe in Yesterday w/photo, brown on cream, 1¾" **4.00**

Poster, Dell #2, black & white photos on red, Dell #2, 19x54", EX **32.00**

Press book, Yellow Submarine, United Artists, w/ad slicks, etc, 13x18" **85.00**

Ring, gold-tone metal w/group photo, EX **45.00**

Scarf, triangular, black on red w/leatherette cord, 1960s, M **70.00**

Scrapbook, stickers in corner, Whitman, G **35.00**

Spoon, bright silver-tone w/color portrait, 4½", 4 for **24.00**

Stick pin, Yellow Submarine hand-painted tin diecut, 1968, ⅞" **35.00**

Sunglasses, John Lennon style, various color lenses, ea pr **6.00**

Switchplate, Yellow Submarine Snapping Turk, MIP (sealed) **25.00**

Thimble, black & white portrait on plastic (ea different color), 4 for **16.00**

Wallet, bifold, pictures under plastic, brown vinyl, 3½x4½" **200.00**

Wallpaper, single panel, 1964, 21x21", VG+ **30.00**

Wig, Lowell Toys, M on VG card .**110.00**

Beatnik Collectibles

The 'Beats,' later called 'Beatniks,' consisted of artists, writers, and others disillusioned with Establishment mores and values. The Beatniks were nonconformist, Bohemian free-thinkers who expressed their distain for society from 1950 to 1962. From a collector's point of view, the most highly regarded Beat authors are Allen Ginsberg, Lawrence Ferlinghetti, and Jack Kerouac. Books, records, posters, pamphlets, leaflets, and other items associated with them are very desirable. Although in their day they were characterized by the media as a 'Maynard G. Krebs' (of Dobie Gillis TV fame), today the contributions they made to American literature and the continuation of Bohemianism are recognized for their importance and significance in American culture.

Our advisor for this category is Richard Synchef; he is listed in the directory under California. Values are for examples in excellent to near-mint conditions.

Magazines

City Lights, #3, Spring 1953, San Francisco: City Lights, early Ferlinghetti publication...**50.00**

Evergreen Review #2, San Francisco Scene, NY: Grove Press, 1959 ....**65.00**

Fruitcup, Beach Books Texts & Documents, San Francisco, 1969 (only issue)............**75.00**

Life, Squaresville Vs Beatsville, September 21, 1959 ....**25.00**

Playboy, Beat Issue, July 1959, Ginsberg, Corso, Kerouac, etc **40.00**

Paperback Books

Brown, William; Beat, Beat, Beat; NY: Signet, 1959, cartoons of Beatniks **25.00**

Feldman, Gene; Beat Generation & Angry Young Men, NY: Dell, 1959, anthology.....**35.00**

Ginsberg, Allen; Planet News 1961-1967, City Lights/Pocket Poets #23, 1st printing...**40.00**

Kerouac, Jack; Oharma Bums, Signet, 1959, 1st printing.**50.00**

Kerouac, Jack; Tritessa, NY: Avon, 1960, 1st printing **75.00**

Krim, Seymour (editor); Beats, Greenwich, CT: Fawcett, 1960, anthology..............**45.00**

Mandel, George; Beatville USA,
NY: Avon, 1961 ....**30.00**

Records

Bruce, Lenny; I Am Not a Nut,
Elect Me, LP, Fantasy #7007,
red vinyl, 1969 ....**50.00**
Bruce, Lenny; Lenny Bruce -
American, LP, Fantasy #7011,
red vinyl, 1961 ....**50.00**
Poetry reading, Greenwich Village
Cafe Bizarre, LP, Musitron
Audiotron Fidelity, NY ..**75.00**
San Francisco Poets, LP, NY: Hanover,
1959, Rexroth, Whallen, Ginsberg,
Ferlinghetti, McClure (impor-
tant)..............................**125.00**

Miscellaneous

Booklet, Burroughs, Wm; Prospectus
for Naked Lunch, NY: Grove
Press, 1962, 16-page. **150.00**
Cigarette holder, black plastic, on
display cardboard, 1950s,
12".................................**20.00**
Folder, promo; Beat Generation,
MGM, w/VanDoren, Cochoran,
Danton, rare, 8½x11"...**225.00**
Handbill, McClure, Michael; The
Beard, controversial play,
later banned, pink w/black let-
ters, 7½x11"................**300.00**
Poster, poetry reading, Ginsberg,
Ferlinghetti, McClure, etc, August
7, 1971, UC Berkeley, Pavley
Ballroom, 9x14" **100.00**

Beer Cans

If you can remember flat-top
beer cans that had to be opened with
those punch-type openers, chances
are you were a high school or college-
age student during the early 1930s.
The cone-top with the bottle-cap lid
was patented about 1935. It wasn't
until the 1960s that the aluminum
can with a pull-tab opener became
commonplace. Even some of the latter are being collected today, and
there are hundreds of brands and
variations available. Many are
worthless, and most are worth very
little, but some have considerable
value, and we've listed a few examples of each. Just be sure to grade
condition very carefully. No. 1:
'new,' rust-free; No. 2: only tiny
dents or scratches, still rust-free;
No. 3: only minor fading, scratching,
and rust; No. 4: all of the above,
and more pronounced.

In the following listings, all

**ABC Beer, Extra Dry, orange,
silver, and white, 12-oz, Grade
2, $5.00.**

cans are the 11- to 12-oz. size unless stated otherwise, and unless otherwise described, values are for cans in Grade 1 condition. Our advisor for this category is Steven Gordon; he is listed in the Directory under Maryland.

Fisher's Old German Style, Auburndale, FL, Grade 2, $3.00.

Ballantine Beer, flat top, few sm brown spots, 16-oz **70.00**

Ballantine Bicentennial 1976, from 50¢ to **1.00**

Big Cat Malt Liquor, pull tab, sm spots, 16-oz **3.00**

Brew 102 Beer, ziptop, bottom opened, clean **5.00**

Brown Derby Beer, punch top, bottom opened, few sm scratches **10.00**

Buckhorn Hamms, pull tab, from 50¢ to **1.00**

Budweiser, flat top, air sealed, 16-oz **15.00**

Chippewa Pride, pull tab, multi-color w/scenic view **1.00**

Club Special Beer, pull top, bottom open, clean **50.00**

Colt 45 Stout Malt Liquor, pull tab, few minor spots **12.00**

Crossroads Pilsner, pull tab, red can w/2 labels, 12-oz **1.00**

Fitger's, pull tab, yellow w/red star, 12-oz **1.00**

Gambrinus Ohio State, stainless steel **2.50**

Gamecock Cream Ale, ring tab, bottom opened, clean **26.00**

Harley Daytona 1993, aluminum **50**

Hudepohl 1975 Cincinnati Reds, pull tab, from 50¢ to **1.00**

Jamaica Sun Beer, pull tab, very minor spots **15.00**

Miller Genuine Draft, St Patrick's Day Sweepstakes on back, air sealed **13.00**

Milwaukee Brand Cream Ale..**1.00**

National Bohemian, Triple Crown Winners **1.00**

National Bohemian Beer, pull tab, very fine scratches **15.00**

Olbrau Beer, flat top, bottom opened, clean **26.00**

Old Grimes, pull tab, white w/2 labels, 12-oz **1.00**

Olde English Malt Liquor, pull tab, full, light surface spots, 16-oz **10.00**

Orbit Beer, pull tab, bottom opened, clean **16.00**

Ortliebs, coal mining scene, aluminum **1.00**

Polish Countess, pull tab, bronze w/2 labels, 12-oz **1.00**

Regal Select Beer, pull tab, 16-oz **5.00**

Robin Hood Cream Ale, pull tab....**50**

Schlitz, white w/brown label, aluminum **50**
Schlitz Tall Boy, flat top, bottom opened, sm marks, 1969, 24-oz **6.00**
Schmidt Betsy Ross 1976, from 50¢ to **1.00**
Spur Spout Malt Liquor, pull tab, air sealed, 16-oz **30.00**
State Line, white w/2 labels, pull tab, 12-oz **50**
Tennents Beer, flat top, clean .**33.00**
Walters Light Ale 1976, stainless steel **1.00**

Bronze, temple rattle from Japan, God of Thunder handle, 6" **40.00**
Bronze, Town Crier w/wooden handle, heavy, 9" **90.00**
Glass, amberina, pressed diamond daisy pattern, 6" **175.00**
Glass, carnival, pressed diamond daisy pattern, 6" **350.00**
Glass, clear, pressed diamond daisy pattern, 6" **45.00**
Silver, marked 925 for Taxco Mexico, flower handle w/stem back, 4½" **35.00**

Bells

The first large bell to be placed atop a church was in Italy, 400 A.D. Since then such bells have announced morning services, vespers, deaths, christenings, fires, and community news. Countries have used them en masse to peal out the good news of Christmas, New Year's, and the ending of World Wars I and II. They were also rung in times of great sorrow such as the death of President Abraham Lincoln. For further information we recommend our advisor (author of several books) Dorothy Malone Anthony, who is listed in the Directory under Kansas. See also Clubs and Newsletters.

Brass, 2 cranes hold gongs for happiness, 6" **35.00**
Bronze, Buddha's temple, 4 panels of 9 snails each, monkey handle **40.00**
Bronze, peacock handle, bumps on bottom of openwork rattle, 4" .**50.00**

Bronze, Robin Hood as handle, by Ballantyne, 6½", $225.00. (Photo courtesy Dorothy Malone Anthony)

Silver, ship handle w/embossed Dutch scenes around bell, 2¾" **75.00**

Black Americana

This is a wide and varied field of collector interest. Advertising, toys, banks, sheet music, kitchenware items, movie items, and even the fine arts are areas that offer Black Americana buffs many opportunities to add to their collections. Caution! Because some pieces have become so valuable, reproductions abound. Watch for a lot of new ceramic items, less detailed in both the modeling and the painting. Our advisor for this category is Judy Posner, who is listed in the Directory under Pennsylvania. Refer to these books for more information: *Black Collectibles Sold in America* by P.J. Gibbs, and *Black Dolls, An Identification and Value Guide, 1820-1991*, by Myla Perkins. (Both are published by Collector Books.)

Perfume, Karoff, Picanette, Stuart Products, 1938, 4¼", $85.00.

Album cover, Little Black Jungle Band Storybook, for 78 rpm record **50.00**

Autograph, Butterfly McQueen, w/framed photo as Prissy, 11x14" **225.00**

Bill hook, Duluth Imperial Flour, Chef litho on cardboard, 7¼x3" **145.00**

Birthday card, sympathetic child, full color, 1930s, EX **30.00**

Book, Amelia Jane Again, Enid Blyton, hardcover, Dean & Son Ltd, 1946 ....**70.00**

Book, Men About Town Minstrels, cardboard cover, 1938, 157 pages, EX **60.00**

Book, Pickaninny Twins, LF Perkins, hardcover, 1931, 1st edition, EX **165.00**

Box, cardboard, Fun To Wash Washing Powder, Mammy color litho, 7¼" **65.00**

Box, sample; Cream of Wheat, Rastus w/bowl, 1940s, 3¼x2x1¼", EX **95.00**

Coaster, Sambo's Restaurant Bicentennial, paper, multicolor, 3½", M **16.00**

Coffee mug, Sambo's Restaurant, trademark w/gold on ivory, 1950s, M **40.00**

Cookie jar, Aunt Jemima, F&F Mold & Die **400.00**

Creamer, Mammy face, ceramic, multicolor paint, 2x2⅞" .**60.00**

Creamer, Uncle Mose, F&F Mold & Die, EX **70.00**

Dinner bell, girl praying in white gown, ceramic, gold trim, 1940s **55.00**

Doll, Topsy, handmade topsy-turvy, modern materials, 1930s pattern, M **50.00**

Dolls, Mammy & Topsy, compo on wood, handmade, 1930s, 8" & 4", pr **295.00**

Figurine, Porter, painted cast metal, railroad accessory, 1930s, 2" **45.00**

Frying pan, cast iron w/embossed & painted Mammy, 4½" L ..**45.00**

Glass slide, Uncle Mose in rocker, full color, 1900s, 4x3¼" .**28.00**

Greeting card, Valentine, Mammy color litho, Tuck, easel back, EX **48.00**

Humidor, man's bust, multicolor high glaze, 8½", EX **425.00**

Lapel pin, man's tintype on gold-tone metal, ca 1900, 1½" dia, EX **75.00**

Magazine ad, Aunt Jemima pancakes, black & white, 1958, 10½x14", EX **28.00**

Matchbook, Sambo's Restaurant, Sambo w/pancakes & tiger, 1960s, M **32.00**

Menu, souvenir; Club Plantation, naughty lady cover, 1940s, 5x6½" **70.00**

Salt and pepper shakers, Japan, $50.00 for the pair; matching cruet, $45.00.

Paint book, Golly's Magic, 8-page booklet w/coupon, 1970s, 4½x6" **38.00**

Pancake shaker, Aunt Jemima, blue plastic w/embossed figure, 8½" **85.00**

Pancake shaker, Aunt Jemima, yellow plastic, F&F Mold & Die, NM **100.00**

Pencil holder, celluloid, man in alligator's mouth, 1930s, 8" .**65.00**

Plate, Bit of the Old South, slaves at work, Vernon Kilns, 1940 .**65.00**

Plate, souvenir; Uncle Tom's Cabin, gold border, Dresden Ontario **125.00**

Playing cards, Tamko Roof, waiter w/tray backs, double deck, EX **150.00**

Postcard, Busy Line, couple on telephones w/Black Cupid on wire, 1920s **28.00**

Postcard, 4 of a Kind, 4 men in fancy clothes, Germany, 1908 ....**55.00**

Poster, Aunt Jemima Ready Mix..., family at breakfast, color, 13x20" **165.00**

Puzzle, Coon Chicken Inn souvenir, optical illusion, 1940s **125.00**

String holder, chalkware Mammy, 6¼", $200.00.

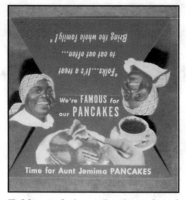

Table card, Aunt Jemima, dated 1953, M, $45.00. (Photo courtesy Judy Posner)

Recipe book, Fine Old Dixie Recipes, Mammy cover, w/songs & poems, 1939 ....**65.00**

Recipe book, Kentucky Fare, Mammy at kettle on cover, 1953, 28 pages **40.00**

Recipe cards, Aunt Jemima premium, set of 16 ....**255.00**

Sack, paper, Aunt Jemima Corn Meal, colorful, 1950s, 5-lb **55.00**

Salt & pepper shakers, Mammy, Luzianne, F&F, pr ...**150.00**

Salt & pepper shakers, Aunt Jemima & Uncle Mose, F&F, 3½", pr **45.00**

Salt & pepper shakers, Aunt Jemima & Uncle Mose, F&F, 5", pr **75.00**

Salt & pepper shakers, boy & watermelon slice, ceramic, 1940s, EX, pr **75.00**

Salt & pepper shakers, butler & maid, ceramic, brown skin, 4¾", pr **135.00**

Salt & pepper shakers, children sit on carrots, ceramic, old, pr ...**85.00**

Salt & pepper shakers, girl sits on watermelon slice, ceramic, 5", pr **175.00**

Salt & pepper shakers, Mammy & maid, ceramic, Japan, 4½", pr **55.00**

Salt & pepper shakers, nude body forms holder, head & melon shakers **300.00**

Salt & pepper shakers, praying hands, ceramic, w/gold, Japan, '50s, pr **65.00**

Scorecard, Hit the Jack w/Robertson's, golliwog, '70s, 5x4½", M **22.00**

Shopping bag, Golly It's Good, golliwog w/Robertson's Marmalade, 1970s **165.00**

Syrup, Aunt Jemima figural, plastic, F&F Mold & Die **60.00**

Teapot, Gone w/the Wind commemorative of Mammy, rare matt glaze, 1988 ....**175.00**

Thermos, Sambo's Restaurant, plastic, Aladdin, 1970s, 10¼", EX **95.00**

Tumbler, mint julep; Aunt Fanny's Cabin ad on frosted glass, 7" **28.00**

Wall pocket/vase, Chef, ceramic, brown skin, hangs or sits, 1940s, 5" **150.00**

Watch fob, Green River Whiskey, copper/silver-tone, man on horse **125.00**

Black Cats

This line of fancy felines was marketed during the 1950s mainly by the Shafford (importing) Company, although black cat lovers accept similarly modeled, shiny glazed kitties of other importing firms into their collections as well. Some of the more plentiful items maybe purchased for $15.00 to $35.00, while the

Cruets, Shafford, 7½", $50.00 to $60.00 for the pair.

Shafford six-piece spice set in a wooden rack usually sells for as much as $145.00. These values and the ones that follow are for items in mint paint, a very important consideration in determining a fair market price. Shafford items are often minus their white whiskers and eyebrows, and this type of loss should be reflected in your evaluation. An item in poor paint may be worth even less than half of given estimates. Note: Unless 'Shafford' is included in the descriptions, values are for cats that were imported by another company.

Ashtray, flat face, Shafford, 4¾" **18.00**
Ashtray, head shape w/open mouth, Shafford, 3" **18.00**
Cigarette lighter, sm cat stands on book beside table lamp ..**65.00**
Condiment set, upright cats, yellow eyes, 2 bottles + pr of shakers in wire stand ...**85.00**

Cookie jar, lg cat head, Shafford **85.00**
Creamer & sugar bowl, Shafford **45.00**
Cruet, slender form, gold collar & tie, tail handle **12.00**
Cruets, cojoined cats, Royal Sealy, 1-pc, 7¼" **40.00**
Decanter, long cat w/red fish in his mouth as stopper **50.00**
Desk caddy, pen forms tail, spring body holds letters, 6½" ...**8.00**
Mug, Shafford, 3½" **50.00**
Pitcher, squatting, mouth spout, Shafford, 5", 14½" circumference **75.00**
Planter, cat & kitten in a hat, Shafford-like paint **25.00**
Planter, upright cat, Shafford-like paint, Napco label, 6" ...**20.00**
Salt & pepper shaker, cat on back, yellow eyes, shaker ea end, 10½" **60.00**
Salt & pepper shakers, round 'teapot' cat, Shafford, pr, from $40 to **50.00**

Spice set, 6 sq shakers in wooden frame, yellow eyes **125.00**

Teapot, bulbous body, head lid, green eyes, Shafford, 4½" **30.00**

Teapot, panther-like appearance, gold eyes, sm **20.00**

Teapot, yellow eyes, 1-cup ...**30.00**

Tray, flat face, wicker handle, Shafford, lg **125.00**

Blade Banks

In 1903 the safety razor was invented, making it easier for men to shave at home. But the old, used razor blades were troublesome, because for the next twenty-two years, nobody knew what to do with them. In 1925 the first patent was filed for a razor blade bank, a container designed to hold old blades until it became full, in which event it was to be thrown away. Most razor blade banks are 3" or 4" tall, similar to a coin bank with a slot in the top but no outlet in the bottom to remove the old blades. These banks were produced from 1925 to 1950. Some were issued by men's toiletry companies and were often filled with shaving soap or cream. Many were made of tin and printed with an advertising message. An assortment of blade banks made from a variety of materials — ceramic, wood, plastic, or metal — could also be purchased at five-and-dime stores. Our advisor, David C. Giese, is listed in the Directory under Virginia.

Advertising, Ever-Ready, The Razor You Treasure, metal top removes **65.00**

Advertising, Ever-Ready for Old Blades, metal **65.00**

Advertising, Gem Record Shaves, book form **60.00**

Advertising, JB Williams Co for New & Old Blades, metal **70.00**

Advertising, JB Williams Co Safe for Razor Blades, metal. .**65.00**

Advertising, Lamglois Shaving Cream, metal **60.00**

Advertising, Listerine, glass jar, originally held soap **25.00**

Advertising, Mennen, w/shaving stick **65.00**

Tony the Barber, Ceramic Arts Studio, 5", from $65.00 to $75.00.

Advertising, Mennen Lather Shave, metal **60.00**

Advertising, Palmolive, for used razor blades **60.00**

Advertising, Red Devil Lye, paper label **70.00**

Advertising, Red Seal Lye, paper label **70.00**

Advertising, St National Bank of Kansas City, For Your Used..., paper **30.00**

Advertising, US Deck Paint, metal can w/sailing ship **80.00**

Advertising, Wardonia, for used blades, plastic **25.00**

Advertising, Williams Shaving Cream, metal **60.00**

Barber, ceramic, hand to his chin, 6" **65.00**

Barber, ceramic, w/comb & scissors in his pocket, 5¼" ..**65.00**

Barber, ceramic, 4" **65.00**

Barber chair, ceramic, 5" ...**150.00**

Barber chair, ceramic, 5¾" .**160.00**

Barber pole, ceramic, Blades .**40.00**

Barber pole, ceramic, face & beret hat **80.00**

Barber pole, ceramic, half form, fits flat to wall, New Place for..., ...**75.00**

Barber pole, ceramic, man's face, parting hair, Gay Blades .**70.00**

Barber pole man, ceramic, doubles as shaving mug w/bank in head, 7" **180.00**

Barber pole man, wood w/metal arms & key lock, 9" **180.00**

Barbersol, glass container w/slot in lid **45.00**

Craftsman Thin Blades, plastic .**35.00**

Dandy Dan, plastic barber figure w/metal arms **40.00**

Discarder Blades, metal **60.00**

Donkey, ceramic, Listerine...**35.00**

Elephant, ceramic, Listerine ..**40.00**

For Used Razor Blades, metal .**60.00**

Frog, ceramic, yellow or green, used blades in bottom ..**80.00**

Looie the barber, ceramic, w/razor in right or left hand, ea **160.00**

Man's face, ceramic, smiling w/eyes closed **67.00**

Man w/vest on, wood, unscrew to empty blades **70.00**

Mushroom, ceramic, embossed man shaving **30.00**

Ocean Spray Cranberry Sauce, metal **60.00**

Owl, ceramic, 6" **75.00**

Razor Brush, ceramic, Blades, 5½", variations, ea **65.00**

Soap dish, metal, doubles as bank, Old Blades **200.00**

Wall plate, brass, For Used Razor Blades **25.00**

Yellow ware, ceramic pig w/Razor Bank embossed on back .**175.00**

Barber pole, ceramic, face with derby hat, arms hold razor and brush, $90.00; Barber pole, ceramic, face, derby hat, no arms, $80.00. (Photo courtesy David Giese)

Blue Ridge

Some of the most attractive American dinnerware made in the 20th century is Blue Ridge, produced by Southern Potteries of Erwin, Tennessee, from the late 1930s until 1956. More than four hundred patterns were hand painted on eight basic shapes. The Quimper-like peasant-decorated line is one of the most treasured and is valued at double the prices listed below. For the very simple lines, subtract about 20%, and add 20% for more elaborate patterns. Refer to *Blue Ridge Dinnerware, Revised Third Edition,* by Betty and Bill Newbound (Collector Books) for more information.

Pitcher, Virginia, #2, $75.00.

Basket, aluminum edge, 7" .**14.00**
Bonbon, flat shell, Pixie, china .**90.00**
Bowl, hot cereal **10.00**
Bowl, mixing; med **20.00**
Bowl, vegetable; w/lid **70.00**
Butter dish **45.00**
Cake lifter **25.00**
Casserole, w/lid **45.00**
Chocolate pot **175.00**
Creamer, '50s shape **12.00**

Creamer, regular shape **8.00**
Cup & saucer, regular shape .**12.00**
Custard cup **12.00**
Gravy boat **22.00**
Leftover, w/lid, sm **15.00**
Mug, child's **25.00**
Pitcher, Abby, earthenware .**75.00**
Pitcher, Chick, china **95.00**
Pitcher, Spiral, 7" **65.00**
Plate, Christmas Tree **65.00**
Plate, dinner; Premium; 10½" .**45.00**
Plate, party; w/cup well & cup .**30.00**
Plate, 7" **10.00**
Relish, crescent shape, individual **15.00**
Relish, deep shell, china **55.00**
Salt & pepper shakers, Bud Top, pr **35.00**
Salt & pepper shakers, tall & footed, china, pr **50.00**
Sugar shaker, regular shape, w/lid **15.00**
Teapot, Ball shape **100.00**
Teapot, rope handle **75.00**
Tidbit tray, 3-tier **30.00**
Vase, boot form, 8" **85.00**

Blue Willow

Inspired by the lovely blue and white Chinese exports, the Willow pattern has been made by many English, American, and Japanese firms from 1950 until the present. Many variations of the pattern have been noted — mauve, black, green, and multicolor Willow ware can be found in limited amounts. The design has been applied to tinware, linens, glassware, and paper goods, all of which are treasured by today's collectors. Refer to *Blue Willow* by

Mary Frank Gaston (Collector Books) for more information. See also Children's Dishes; Royal China.

Bank, kitten figure, unmarked Japan, 9¼" **250.00**
Bowl, covered vegetable; marked Adderly, 6x10" **150.00**
Bowl, covered vegetable; marked Japan, 9" **75.00**
Bowl, pedestal base (no decoration), Holland mark, 4x7½" ...**125.00**
Bowl, soup; Homer Laughlin .**12.00**
Bowl, soup; marked Barker Bros Ltd, 7½" **20.00**
Bowl, vegetable; Homer Laughlin, oval **30.00**
Bowl, vegetable; Variant center pattern, Pictorial rim, unmarked, 10" **20.00**
Butter dish, rectangular, holds ¼-lb stick, marked Japan .**60.00**
Butter pat, marked England, 3½" **25.00**
Cake plate, Traditional pattern, handles, English mark .**75.00**
Coffeepot, graniteware, unmarked, 6" **90.00**
Compote, footed, marked Shenango China, 3x6" **50.00**
Creamer, hotel ware, Shenango China, individual size ..**25.00**
Creamer, squat, unmarked American, 2½" **10.00**
Cup, farmer's; Japan, lg **35.00**
Cup & saucer, demitasse; marked Japan **15.00**
Egg cup, double; unmarked Japan, 3¼" **30.00**
Gravy boat, marked Shenango China, 6" L **45.00**
Ladle, Traditional center pattern, unmarked, 8" **140.00**

Napkin ring, unmarked, 1½" .**75.00**
Pie server, marked Made in Japan, 10" **30.00**
Pitcher, Chicago Jug-style, Buffalo Pottery, 3-pt **400.00**
Pitcher, triangular shape, marked Doulton, 6" **200.00**

Candlesticks, 6", $50.00 for the pair.
(Photo courtesy Mary Frank Gaston)

Plate, Canton pattern, marked Shenango China, ca 1960, 10½" **45.00**
Plate, Homer Laughlin, 7" **6.00**
Plate, Variant center pattern w/Pictorial border, unmarked, 6" **8.00**
Platter, Homer Laughlin **30.00**
Relish, rectangular w/scalloped edge, marked John Maddock, 11" **55.00**
Salt & pepper shakers, ceramic & wood, unmarked, 5", pr .**20.00**
Sugar bowl, w/lid, marked Japan, 3½" **25.00**
Teapot, Mandarin pattern w/Variant border, CT Maling **150.00**
Teapot, unmarked Homer Laughlin, 6-cup **50.00**
Tumbler, willow border on clear glass, 5" **17.50**

Bobbin' Head Dolls

Bobbin' head dolls made of papier-mache were produced in Japan during the 1960s until about 1972. They are about 7" tall, hand painted in bright colors, then varnished. Some represent sports teams and their mascots, and these are the most collectible. They've been made in countless variations. Base color indicates when the doll was made. During 1961 and '62, white bases were used; today these are vey scarce. Green bases are from 1962 to '66, and gold bases were used from 1967 until 1972. If you want to learn more about them, we recommend *The Bobbing Head Collector and Price Guide* by our advisor Tim Hunter, listed in the Directory under Nevada. Another scource that deals primarily with nodders but includes bobbin' heads as well is *Figural Nodders* by Hilma R. Irtz. See also Clubs and Newsletters.

Baseball

Atlanta, gold base **145.00**
Boston, blue hat, green base .**200.00**
Chicago Cubs, miniature ...**450.00**
Cincinnati, green base **225.00**
Detroit, gold base **160.00**
Houston Colts, white base .**250.00**
KC A's, green base **275.00**
KC A's, miniature **300.00**
Maris, white base **475.00**
Minnesota, green base **110.00**
Philadelphia, white base ...**190.00**
San Diego, gold base **100.00**
Texas, gold base **125.00**
Washington, green base **300.00**

Basketball

Baltimore, Little Dribbler, Black or White player, ea **145.00**
Chicago, Little Dribbler, Black or White player, ea **90.00**
Globetrotters **275.00**
Knicks, 1962, sq base **300.00**
Lakers, 1968, round gold base .**60.00**
Sonics, Black player **450.00**

Football

Airzona State Sun Devil head .**345.00**
Atlanta, realistic face **110.00**
Atlanta, toes up **175.00**
Big Eight, boy head, from $100 to **250.00**
Chicago, 1962, sq **105.00**
Cleveland, realistic face **250.00**

Green Bay Packers, 1967, $110.00. (Photo courtesy Tim Hunter)

Dallas, 1962, Black **500.00**
Dallas, 1968 merger, gold
  base **200.00**
Dallas Texans, 1961, toes up, red
  base **550.00**
Detroit, toes up **145.00**
Miami, 1965, ear pads **425.00**
Mid-American, boy head, from $50
  to **90.00**
Minnesota, toes up, Black .**450.00**
Montreal, various sizes & decals, sim-
  ilar to 1962 NFL Dolls ...**240.00**
NY Giants, 1968 merger, gold
  base **85.00**
Pittsburgh, toes up **155.00**
San Diego, 1968 merger **100.00**
St Louis, 1968 merger, gold
  base **30.00**
Stanford Indian head **375.00**
Washington, 1962, sq **200.00**
Winnipeg, various sizes & decals, sim-
  ilar to 1962 NFL dolls **200.00**

Hockey

Baltimore Clippers **200.00**
Boston, 1962, sq **450.00**
Boston, 1967, gold **475.00**
Boston Braves **475.00**
Chicago, 1962, mini **65.00**
Detroit, Canada, high skate .**425.00**
Los Angeles, 1967, gold **425.00**
New York, 1962, sq **175.00**
Portland Buckaroos **400.00**
San Diego Gulls **375.00**
St Louis, 1967, gold (gold uniform
  add 20%) **450.00**
Toronto, 1962, mini **35.00**

Nonsports

Canadian Mountie, Canada souvenir, Made in Japan, 5" .**35.00**
Colonel Sanders, ca 1950s, 7" .**75.00**

Shriners, Japan, from $50.00 to $70.00 each. (Photo courtesy Hilma R. Irtz)

Director **125.00**
Li'l Abner character, ea, from $90
  to **110.00**
Pig Pen **225.00**
Poll Parrot **700.00**
Reddy Kilowatt **600.00**
Roy Rogers **200.00**
Schroeder **160.00**
Sgt Snorkel **125.00**
Shriner, in tuxedo, bow tie & fez,
  Japan, 6¾" **70.00**
Six Flags **300.00**
Topo Gigo **75.00**
Yosemite Sam **500.00**
Zero **125.00**

Bookmarks

Bookmarks have been around
as long as books themselves, yet
only recently has bookmark collecting been growing in popularity.
Most collectors like modern ones as
well as the antique; there is so
much available that a person could
establish a collection in a short
time and on a limited budget.
Many of the modern bookmarks

from publishers and advertisers are free. Bookmarks are found in almost any material, brass, plastic, and paper to antique silk, silver, and celluloid (the latter three the hardest to come by and therefore the most highly prized). The old paper ones are still plentiful and modestly priced. Dated commemorative bookmarks, old or new, are the most popular with collectors. Our advisor for bookmarks is Joan L. Huegel, who is listed in the Directory under Pennsylvania. See also Clubs and Newsletters.

Aluminum,embossed heart shape w/Teddy Roosevelt picture in center **8.00**
Brass, souvenir of Drakes Well, Titusville PA, ca 1950, 2" .**2.50**
Celluloid, advertising w/page flap, rose-shaped top **4.00**
Chamois, hand-painted Easter greetings, flowers, pale yellow, ca 1900 ....**5.00**
Felt, souvenir from 1982 World's Fair in Knoxville, MIP ...**3.00**
Leather, Queen's Silver Jubilee/ coat of arms on white, 1977 ....**4.00**
Metal, dog figure on top, 2" ...**1.50**
Paper, America's Hope Is Dingman's Soap, colorful ad **3.00**
Paper, Dr Schilling's health preserving elastic corset ad .**3.00**
Paper, NY City skyline, plain on reverse, ca 1930 ....**2.00**
Paper, Price & Temple Pianos ad, blue embossed flowers **2.50**
Paper, Wright's Coal Tar Soap, page flap **2.00**
Plastic, Smokey the Bear on yellow heart shape, modern **1.50**
Silk, Memorial Day, patriotic colors, 1910, 7" **5.00**

Bottle Openers

Figural bottle openers are models of animals, people, and various inamimate objects designed for the sole purpose of removing a bottle cap. To qualify as an example, the cap lifter must be part of the figure itself. Among the major producers of openers of this type were Wilton Products; John Wright, Inc.; L & L Favors; and Gadzik Sales. These and advertising openers are very collectible. Our advisor for this category is Charlie Reynolds; he is listed in the Directory under Virginia. The FBOC (Figural Bottle Opener Collectors) are listed under Clubs and Newsletters.

Elephant, painted cast iron, mouth open, trunk up, VG+, $45.00.

Alligator, F-136, painted cast iron, head down, NM **90.00**

Black Face, F-402C, painted brass, wall mount, NM **95.00**

Cinderella Slipper, F-210, gold-painted cast-iron shoe form, M **35.00**

Clown, F-417, painted cast iron, wall mount, M **95.00**

Cowboy w/Guitar, F-27, painted cast iron, M **185.00**

Deco Dog, F-82, painted cast iron, long stylized shape, NM .**65.00**

Elephant, F-48, painted cast iron, mouth open, trunk up, NM **60.00**

English Pointer, F-79, painted cast iron, NM **90.00**

Flamingo, F-120, painted cast iron, EX/NM **175.00**

Foundry Man, F-29, painted cast iron, man pouring metal, NM **175.00**

Hanging Drunk, F-415, painted cast iron, wall mount, M **110.00**

Lamppost Drunk, F-1, painted cast iron, leg out, NM ...**20.00**

Mallard Duck, F-106, painted cast iron, realistic, bright colors, NM **90.00**

Miss Four Eyes, F-408, painted cast iron, w/ringlets, wall mount, NM **115.00**

Parrot, F-111, painted cast iron, head up, mouth open, NM **90.00**

Pelican, F-130a, hollow base metal, NM original paint **175.00**

Pretzel, F-232d, brass, NM ...**5.00**

Rooster, F-97, painted cast iron, opener in tail, NM **80.00**

Sea Gull, F-123, painted cast iron, perched on stump, NM **70.00**

Skunk, F-92c, painted cast iron, NM **125.00**

Squirrel, F-91, painted cast iron, down on all fours, NM .**150.00**

Straw Hat Arrow Signpost, F-13, painted cast iron, EX+ .**24.00**

Bottles

Bottles have been used as containers for commercial products since the late 1800s. Specimens from as early as 1845 may still be occasionally found today (watch for a rough pontil to indicate this early production date). Some of the most collectible are bitters bottles, used for 'medicine' that was mostly alcohol, a ploy to avoid paying the stiff tax levied on liquor sales. Spirit flasks from the 1800s were blown in the mold and were often designed to convey a historic, political, or symbolic message. Even bottles from the 1900s are collectible, especially beer or pop bottles and commercial containers from defunct bottlers. Refer to *Bottle Pricing Guide, Third Revised Edition,* by Hugh Cleveland (Collector Books) for more information.

Dairy Bottles

The storage and distribution of fluid milk in glass bottles became commonplace around the turn of the century. They were replaced by paper and plastic containers in the mid-1950s. Perhaps 5% of all US dairies are still using some glass, and glass bottles are still widely used in Mexico and some Canadian provinces.

Milk-packaging and distribution plants hauled trailer loads of glass bottles to dumping grounds during the conversion to the throwaway cartons now in general use. Because of this practice, milk bottles and jars are scarce today. Most collectors search for bottles from hometown dairies; some have completed a fifty-state collection in the three popular sizes.

Bottles from 1900 to 1920 had the name of the dairy, town, and state embossed in the glass. Nearly all of the bottles produced after this period had the copy painted and then pyro-glazed onto the surface of the bottle. This enabled the dairyman to use colors and pictures of his dairy farm or cows on the bottles. Collectors have been fortunate that there have been no serious attempts at this point to reproduce a particularly rare bottle!

Amador Goat Dairy, Glendale AZ, maroon pyro, sq, 1-qt, EX .**45.00**
Baker Farm Exeter NH, black pyro, cream top, sq, 1-qt **28.00**
Borden's, Phoenix Store Jug, yellow-brown label, round, ½-gal **18.00**
Borden's, red pyro, wide mouth, sq ½-pt **6.50**
Brookville Dairy...PA, Rich Whole Milk..., orange pyro, round, 1-qt **32.00**
Central's New Space Saver... Willmar MN, red pyro, cream top, 1-qt **22.50**
Clover Farm Dairy..., cloverleaf, red & green pyro, round, 1-qt **18.00**

Connelly Brothers Patented July 8th 1930, embossed cream top, 1-qt, EX **85.00**
Dairy Dale...Meyersdale PA...You Can Whip Our..., blue pyro, 1-qt **20.00**
Danville Producers...US Is a Sound Investment..., orange pyro, 1-qt **88.00**
Deary Bros Dairy Specialists, red pyro, round, 1-qt **12.50**
Detrick Bros, Snydersville PA, yellow pyro, round, 1-qt **18.00**
Dublin Coop..., You Owe It to Your Country..., red pyro, squat, 1-pt **30.00**
ER Warner Dairy/Store Bottle, brown pyro, round, 1-qt .**12.50**
Faircroft Dairy...Ridgway PA... Best for Baby..., orange pyro, 1-qt **17.50**
Fargo's Dairy, Batavia NY, boy & girl, red pyro, round, 1-qt, EX **35.00**
Fox Dairy, Fostoria O..., black pyro, sq, baby top, 1-qt **85.00**
Foxden Farm Quality...Controlled, cow's head, orange pyro, round, 1-qt **16.00**
Freemans Dairy, Best by Test, red pyro, creamer size, ½-oz, NM **18.00**
Frye's Dairy...Leominster Mass, orange pyro, double baby top, 1-qt **90.00**
Fulton Dairy, EK Rowlee, brown pyro, round, 1-qt **15.00**
Getz's Dairy, Manchester NH, windmill scene, orange pyro, round, 1-qt **20.00**
Gillet & Sons..., America First Last Always, eagle, orange pyro, 1-pt **35.00**

Goshen Dairy...New Phila O, embossed, round, slight stain, 1-qt **22.50**

Hess & Sons Dairy, orange pyro, tall & round, 1-qt **12.50**

Hoppy's Favorite..., Hoppy on horse, red & black pyro, sq, 1-qt **75.00**

Horne's Dairy...Skowhegan ME, barn scene, yellow pyro, round, 1-qt **16.00**

HR Noyes Dairy, red pyro, sq, baby top, 1-qt, EX **65.00**

Indian Hill Farm...Greenville ME, Indian head, orange pyro, 1-qt **20.00**

Kent Dairy, red pyro, creamer size, ¾-oz **15.00**

Meadow Gold Milk in shield, red pyro, round, 1-qt **20.00**

Merrifield Creamery, Athol MA & banner, red pyro, round, 1-qt **16.00**

Midwest Dairy..., Buy War Bonds..., minuteman, orange pyro, 1-qt, EX **80.00**

Model Dairy, Bowling Green O, embossed cream top, round, 1-qt, EX **90.00**

Morning Star Dairy, Chattanooga TN, embossed, round, 1-qt, EX **14.00**

Netherland, Dutch girl & boy, red pyro, sq, 1-qt, EX **25.00**

Palmerton Sanitary Dairy...PA, embossed, round, ½-pt, VG .**25.00**

Pellissier, Riverside & 3-leaf symbol, orange pyro, round, 1-qt **15.00**

Pine State...Bangor ME, green pyro, baby top, sq, 1-qt, NM ...**75.00**

Property of Liberty Milk Co, Statue of Liberty, embossed, round, 1-qt **10.00**

Quinnequack Farm, Guernsey Milk, orange pyro, round, 1-qt .**20.00**

Raw Goat Meat...Sandy Hook CT, orange pyro, sq, 1-qt **45.00**

Realicious Cooperative...Prepared & Ready..., green pyro, round, 1-pt **35.00**

Rider Dairy Co, red pyro, sq, 1-qt **20.00**

Cloverleaf Farms, red pyro, cream top, $35.00.

San a Pure Dairy...Findlay OH, embossed cream top, 1-qt, EX **90.00**

Shamokin Sanitary..., They Guard Your..., red pyro, round, 1-pt, VG **55.00**

Simmons Dairy, Vernon Center NY, cow & tree, orange pyro, round, 1-qt **20.00**

Steere Dairy, Meadville PA, green pyro, ribbed neck, 1-qt ..**16.00**

Sundale Diary, Electropured, green pyro, round, 1-qt .**12.50**

Sunshine Dairy, orange pyro, baby top, sq, 1-qt, VG **45.00**

Sunshine Milk, Bridgeport CT, farm scene, orange pyro, round, 1-qt **12.50**

Vermont Country Egg Nog, maroon pyro on green glass **9.00**

Walens Dairy, Lincoln ME, Milk Is..., black & orange pyro, round, 1-qt **22.50**

Walnut Crest Farm...Westbrook ME, maroon pyro, round, 1-qt .**15.00**

Wason-MacDonald Co, Haverhill MA, orange pyro, maroon banner, 1-qt **15.00**

Waterville Dairy...Waterville ME..., 4-leaf clover, maroon pyro, 1-qt **15.00**

White Springs...NY/Drink Milk... Buy War Bonds, orange pyro, 1-qt **75.00**

Wiley's Health Drinks...Winfield KS, green pyro, round, 1-qt ...**20.00**

Worcester Farm, Keene NH, Pure Milk, red pyro, round, 1-qt .**15.00**

Soda Bottles With Applied Color Labels

This is an area of bottle collecting that has recently shown strong and sustained growth. Market prices have been climbing steadily. Refer to *The Official Guide to Collecting Applied Color Label Soda Bottles*, Volumes I and II, by Thomas Marsh for more information. Mr. Marsh is listed in the Directory under Ohio.

Arrow Up, green, 1-qt **15.00**

Big Dot, clear, 10-oz **10.00**

Canfield's, clear, 9-oz **10.00**

Chester Club, clear, 8-oz **25.00**

Delaware Punch, clear, 7½-oz .**15.00**

Fresca, green, 1-qt **15.00**

Freshy, green, 12-oz **15.00**

Gill's, clear, 10-oz **20.00**

Hazel Club, clear, 1-qt **35.00**

Dillon Beverages, orange pyro, 16-oz, $10.00.

Indian Mound Spring, green, 17-oz **15.00**

Knight Club, clear, 7-oz **15.00**

London Dry Ginger Ale, green, 1-qt **25.00**

Maple Spring, clear, 7-oz **15.00**

Milton Spring, green, 8-oz ...**15.00**

Moxie, aqua, 7-oz **20.00**

Old Faithful, clear, 12-oz **25.00**

Pop Stop Beverages, clear, 12-oz **10.00**

Purity's Ginger Ale, green, 1-qt .**15.00**

Raleigh's, clear, 12-oz **15.00**

Sahara Dry, clear, 7-oz **20.00**

Seal Rock Spring (Pale Dry), green, 7-oz **15.00**

Shirley, clear, 12-oz **10.00**

Split Rock Ginger Beer, green, 7-oz **15.00**

Tab, clear, 20-oz **10.00**

Tom Thumb, clear, 6½" **20.00**

Valley Beverages, green, 1-qt .**15.00**

Wheaton's, green, 8-oz **20.00**

Wise-Up, green, 7-oz **15.00**

Miscellaneous

Ackers English Remedy Throat & Lungs, blue.....................**22.00**

Allens World Hair Restorer, bright root beer-amber **15.00**

Atwood's Vegetable Jaundice Bitters, aqua, EX label, 12-sided .**80.00**

Buena Yerba Bitters, amber, lg .**50.00**

Capitol City Bottling Works Baton Rouge LA, Hutchinson soda **25.00**

Chevalier C Old Castle Whiskey..., castle, yellow-golden amber, 1-qt **45.00**

Dickey Chemist SF, cobalt, applied top **40.00**

Dr Bull's Superior Stomach Bitters..., amber, applied top, NM **180.00**

Dr HA Ingram's Nervine Pain Extract, aqua, rolled lip, pontiled **30.00**

Dr Kilmer's Swamp Root Cure, aqua, London variant, 7½" **15.00**

Eagle/Eagle, GII-113, aquamarine blue, Pittsburgh, 1-pt ...**115.00**

EG Booze (Clevinger), amber, cabin form, cured applied top **200.00**

EN Lightner Sarsaparilla & Co, Detroit, MI, aqua **100.00**

Dr. Mann's Celebrated Aqua Balsam, Galion, Ohio, deep aqua, rare, $210.00; Dr. J. Blackman's Genuine Healing, clear, 5½", $35.00; Graffenerg Co. Dysentery Syrup, aqua, 5½", $45.00.

Fletcher's Tomato Sauce, yellow-lime green, ground top, crude **12.00**

Foleys' Kidney & Bladder, amber, 9¼" **18.00**

Gargling Oil Lockport NY, teal green, scarce 7½" size .**145.00**

Geelemann Brewing Co, Milwaukee, amber, blob top, 1-pt **20.00**

Glass & Co, crossed anchors, med blue-green, cleaned, light haze **75.00**

Greens Lung Restorer, Santa Abie... CA, aqua, very crude **65.00**

Halls Sarsaparilla, JR Gates, aqua, applied mouth, crude **75.00**

Harrison's Columbian Ink, aqua, 8-sided, open pontil **110.00**

Hawthorn Spring Saratoga, olive green, 1-pt **60.00**

Home Brewing Co, Indianapolis IN, amber, blob top, 1-qt **20.00**

Jr Spaldings Rosemary & Castor Oil, dark aqua, rolled lip, pontiled **75.00**

Keeley Treatment Inebriety, clear, 5¾" **55.00**

King Solomons Bitters Seattle WA, amber, bold embossing **110.00**

Knowlton Saratoga NY, dark forest green, high shoulder, whittled, 1-qt **250.00**

MB Shaw Bottling Works, Pen Yan NY, aqua, 1-pt **10.00**

McCarthy & Moore Waterbury CN, Hutchinson soda ...**30.00**

McLanes American Worm Specific, aqua, open pontil **35.00**

Monticello Club Pure Rye, clear, 1-qt **20.00**

Mrs Allen's World Hair Restorer, dark amethyst, applied top **150.00**

Nafis Automatic Acidity Test USA, amber, tooled neck, 11½", EX **20.00**

National Kidney & Liver Cure, amber **70.00**

Old Homestead's Wild Cherry Bitters, orange-amber, cabin form **290.00**

Rickleys' Sarsaparilla Apothecary Dover NH, aqua, smooth base **110.00**

Roses Lime Juice, flattened bladder, dark olive green, 9" **120.00**

Sandwich cologne, light pink-amethyst, 12-sided, pontiled, 8¼" **270.00**

Sarasota Star Spring, amber, dug, 1-qt **50.00**

St Clairs Hair Lotion, cobalt, tooled lip, bruise, 7⅜" ...**75.00**

Star (poison), cobalt, wide mouth, 6" **190.00**

Sun Drug Poison, green, irregular hexagon, NM **155.00**

Terre Haute Brewing, Terre Haute IN, amber, blob top, 1-pt **15.00**

Tree, Summer/Summer, GX-17, aquamarine, flat collar, open pontil, 1-pt **285.00**

Violin, bright yellow-green, pontil, 9¾" **25.00**

Wagner & Weber Wagner SD, Hutchinson soda **35.00**

Wallace's Tonic Bitters, Chicago, amber, sq **60.00**

Warner's Safe Cure London, emerald-olive, 1-pt **90.00**

Warner's Safe Diabetes Cure, rich chocolate-amber w/olive tint **95.00**

Warner's Safe Tonic, deep amber, pt-sz slug plate variant, NM **175.00**

Boyd Crystal Art Glass

Since it was established in 1978, this small glasshouse located in Cambridge, Ohio, has bought molds from other companies as they went out of business, and they have designed many of their own as well. They may produce several limited runs of a particular shape in a number of the lovely colors of glass they themselves formulate, none of which are ever reissued. Of course, all of the glass is handmade, and each piece is marked with their 'B-in-diamond' logo. Most of the pieces we've listed are those you're more apt to find at flea markets, but some of the rarer items may be worth a great deal more. Our advisor for this category is Joyce Pringle who is listed in the Directory under Texas.

Angel, Vaseline **24.00**
Artie the Penguin, Crystal Carnival **9.25**
Artie the Penguin, Waterloo .**8.50**
Boyd Airplane, Waterloo **18.50**
Bunny Salt, Mint Green **20.00**
Bunny Salt, Vanilla Corral ...**6.75**
Candy the Carousel Horse, Banana Cream **7.00**
Chick Salt, Nile Green **7.25**
Chick Salt, Oxford Gray **18.00**
Duck Salt, Cobalt **15.00**
Duck Salt, Spinnaker Blue ...**9.50**
Eli & Sara (Amish couple), Chocolate **16.00**
Elizabeth, Chocolate Carnival .**8.50**
Elizabeth, Lime Carnival **45.00**
Jennifer, Capri Blue **9.00**

Jennifer, Crystal Carnival (test color) **20.00**
Louise, Firefly **42.50**
Louise, Zak Boyd Slag **12.00**
Mini Vase, Dogwood Slag **12.00**
Owl, Capri Blue **9.00**
Owl, Peanut Butter **25.00**
Sammy Squirrel, Windsor Blue, retired **8.50**
Skippy the Dog, Mint Green .**8.00**
Skippy the Dog, Sunburst **5.00**
Train, Alexandrite Carnival, 6 pcs **82.50**
Tucker Car, Cashmere Pink .**13.50**
Tucker Car, Cobalt **20.00**
Willie the Mouse, Classic Black .**7.50**
Willie the Mouse, hand painted, Christmas 1993 ....**18.00**
Zak Elephant, Olympic White Carnival **45.00**

Breweriana

Beer can collectors and antique advertising buffs as well enjoy looking for beer-related memorabilia such as tap knobs, beer trays, coasters, signs, and the like. While the smaller items of a more recent vintage are quite affordable, signs and trays from defunct breweries often bring three-digit prices. Condition is important in evaluating early advertising items of any type.

Ashtray, Anheuser-Busch, brass w/embossed & painted eagle, EX **60.00**
Bank, Budweiser Barley Malt Syrup, tin can form, VG .**35.00**
Clock, Bud Man on face of 9" dia watch, w/band, wall hanging, EX **75.00**

Display figure, Anteek Beer, composition, 22½", EX, $300.00.

Clock, Mitchell's Premium, glass face, 15" dia, EX **220.00**

Coaster, Empire Beer Chicago..., blue w/orange & red reverse, 4½" **85.00**

Corkscrew, Anheuser-Busch, engraved brass plate, embossed eagle logo **35.00**

Door push, Hanley's Ale, glass, red background, 11" L, VG .**60.00**

Flashlight, Schlitz, bottle shape, 1969, MIB **12.00**

Globe, Anheuser-Busch, milk glass, etched logo, 8" dia **230.00**

Match holder, Anheuser-Busch, eagle logo on front & back **185.00**

Mug, Anheuser-Busch, heavy metal, logo on bronze color, mini .**45.00**

Mug, Jim Beam Budweiser, Clydesdale, ceramic, 1983 convention **85.00**

Napkin holder, Budweiser, 1983 Jim Beam convention, Clydesdales, EX **40.00**

Paperweight, Anheuser-Busch, 70 Million Barrels, Lucite, 1986 ....**75.00**

Paperweight, Schlitz, brewery scene encased in glass, EX **100.00**

Plate, Anheuser-Busch, Cheers, N Rockwell, metal, Benedictine, 10", EX **70.00**

Salt shakers, Bud Man, ceramic, Ceramarte labels on base, pr, EX **200.00**

Sign, Bud Dry, red & blue neon, 23" wide, EX **40.00**

Sign, Dick's Quincy Beer, plastic over tin button, 9", EX+ **150.00**

Sign, Schiltz, lighted metal bottle, 20", EX **175.00**

Sign, Schlitz, lighted rotating globe w/wooden base, 9x12", EX .**30.00**

Sign, Schlitz, metal under glass, gold foil on brown, 8x12", VG+ **80.00**

Sign, Loewer's Gambrinus Brewery Co, embossed tin, 20x26", G, $300.00.

Sign, Stroh's Bohemian Beer, cardboard, easel back, 1950s, 14x18", EX **100.00**

Stein, Budweiser, 50th Anniversary Collector Series, 6½", from $110.00 to $140.00.

Stein, Anheuser-Busch, Santa's Helper, MIB 65.00

Stein, Budweiser, Our Kind of Town, Chicago, ceramic, EX 65.00

Stem, Anheuser-Busch, gold etched logo, 6", NM 30.00

Stem, Pilsner; Gansett Pilsner, engraved words, 9", EX+ .50.00

Tablecloth, Anheuser-Busch, red, white & brown, 48" sq, EX .20.00

Tap figure, Bud Man, colorful, 1970s, EX 95.00

Tap knob, Mitchell's Premium, black Bakelite w/metal insert, G .80.00

Tip tray, Bevo in gold letters on wood-grain ground, 6½", EX+ 300.00

Tip tray, Frank Jones Ale, name in shield, tin litho, 5" dia, EX+ 45.00

Tip tray, Goldschmidt Brothers, triangle logo, tin litho, 4", EX 40.00

Tray, Fidelio, fox hunters, ca 1935, 12" dia, VG+ 30.00

Tray, Hornung's Beer, bottle & awards, 1930s, EX 40.00

Tray, Ranier, Evelyn Nesbitt, 13" dia, G 50.00

Tumbler, Fox DeLuxe, red-painted logo on clear, 6" 30.00

Tumbler, Iroquois Brewing, Indian logo painted on clear, 3½" 50.00

Tumbler, Schlitz etched in clear, World logo, gold rim, 3½" .45.00

Breyer Horses

Breyer collecting has grown in popularity throughout the past several years. Though horses dominate the market, cattle and other farms animals, dogs, cats, and wildlife have also been produced, all with exacting details and lifelike coloration. They've been made since the early 1950s in both glossy and matte finishes. (Earlier models were glossy, but from 1968 until the 1990s when both glossy and semigloss colors were revived for special runs, matte colors were preferred.) Breyer also manufactures dolls, tack, and accessories such as barns for their animals. For more information and listings, see *Schroeder's Collectible Toys, Antique to Modern* (Collector Books).

Arabian Stallion, matt sorrel, 1973-91 ....15.00

Belgian, matt chestnut, 1965-80 ....45.00

Black Beauty, matt black, 1980-93 ....15.00

Bucking Bronco, matt gray, 1961-67 ....200.00

Buckshot, matt grulla, 1971-73 ....45.00

Stud Spider, 1978-83, with booklet by James Brolin and original box (both add value to model), $60.00. (Photo courtesy Carol Karbowiak Gilbert)

Clydesdale Mare, matt chestnut, 1969-89 ....**25.00**

Friesian, matt black, 1992-95 .**25.00**

Gem Twist, matt alabaster, 1993-95 ....**25.00**

Ginger, matt chestnut, 1980-93 ....**15.00**

Halla, matt bay, 1977-85 .....**50.00**

John Henry, matt dark bay, 1988-90 ....**35.00**

Keen, matt chestnut, 1980-93 ....**15.00**

Kipper, matt chocolate brown, 1986 ....**80.00**

Merrylegs, matt dapple gray, 1980-93 ....**10.00**

Mesteno the Foal, matt light dun, 1993-present **7.00**

Mighty Tango, matt dapple gray, 1980-91 ....**20.00**

Moose, #79, 1966-95 ....**25.00**

Morgan, matt black w/diamond star, 1965-87 ....**40.00**

Mustang Stallion, matt chestnut, 1976-90 ....**20.00**

Rearing Stallion, matt palomino, 1965-85 ....**30.00**

Rojo, matt red dun, 1995 to present **15.00**

Sagr, matt sorrel, 1983-93 ..**20.00**

St Bernard, #328, 1972-80 ..**35.00**

Swaps, matt chestnut, 1975-90 .**30.00**

Bubble Bath Containers

Figural bubble bath containers were popular in the 1960s and have become highly collectible today. The Colgate-Palmolive Company produced the widest variety called Soakies. Purex's Bubble Club characters were also popular. Most Soaky bottles came with detachable heads made of brittle plastic which cracked easily. Purex bottles were made of a softer plastic but lost their paint easier. Condition affects price considerably.

The interest collectors displayed in the old bottles prompted many to notice foreign-made products. Some of the same characters have been licensed by companies in Canada, Italy, the UK, Germany, and Japan, and the bottles they've designed have excellent detail. They're usually a little larger than domestic bottles and though fairly recent are often reminiscent of those made in the US during the 1960s. The following prices are for containers in excellent to near-mint condition, unless noted otherwise.

Baloo Bear (Jungle Book), Colgate-Palmolive, 1960s, slipover only, NM **25.00**
Bamm-Bamm, Purex, 1960s, black & white, NM **30.00**
Barney Rubble, Soaky, MIB .**20.00**
Batman, Avon, MIB **25.00**
Bozo the Clown, EX **25.00**
Broom Hilda, VG **35.00**
Casper the Friendly Ghost, EX **30.00**
Cecil Sea Serpent, Purex, green, 1960s, NMIB **75.00**
Cinderella, Colgate-Palmolive, movable arms, 1960s, NM **35.00**
Creature From the Black Lagoon, NM **95.00**
Dick Tracy, Soaky, 1965, 10", EX+ **45.00**
Donald Duck, Colgate-Palmolive, white & blue, 1960s, NM .**30.00**
Dum Dum, VG **25.00**
El Kabong, Knickerbocker, 1960s, black, yellow & white, rare, NM **75.00**
Felix the Cat, red, VG **35.00**
Fred Flintstone, Colgate-Palmolive, EX **20.00**
Fred Flintstone, Purex, black & red, 1960s, NM **30.00**
Gumby, Perma Toy, No More Tears, 1987, 9½", M (sealed) **20.00**

Brutus and Popeye, Colgate, 1960, NM, $40.00 each.

Jiminy Cricket, Colgate-Palmolive, green, black & red, 1960s, NM **30.00**
Lippy the Lion, Purex, 1960s, EX **55.00**
Mickey Mouse, band leader, Colgate-Palmolive, 1960s, red, NM **30.00**
Mickey Mouse, red shirt, VG .**20.00**
Mr Jinx w/Pixie & Dixie, Purex, orange w/gray mice, 1960s, NM **30.00**
Muskie, Soaky, NM, from $25 to **35.00**
Peter Potomus, Soaky, w/original tag, M **12.00**
Pinocchio, Soaky, 1960s, NM..**20.00**
Pluto, Colgate-Palmolive, 1960s, orange w/cap head, NM .**25.00**
Porky Pig, EX **15.00**
Quick Draw McGraw, Purex, orange & blue or orange only, 1960s, NM, ea **40.00**

Yogi, Cindy, and Boo Boo, Damascar/Italy, 1994-95, NM, $35.00 each. (Photo courtesy Matt and Lisa Adams)

Sailor, Avon, VG 10.00

Secret Squirrel, Purex, yellow & purple, 1960s, NM **60.00**

Snaggle Puss, Purex, 1960s, pink w/green hat, NM **50.00**

Speedy Gonzalez, Colgate Palmolive, blue & red, 1960s, NM **30.00**

Spouty the Whale, Soaky, w/original tag, M **12.00**

Tennesse Tuxedo, 1960s, NM .**30.00**

Three Little Pigs, Tubby Time, 1960s, NM, ea **35.00**

Thumper (Bambi), Colgate-Palmolive, 1960s, light blue & white, NM **30.00**

Touche Turtle, Purex, EX ...**35.00**

Wally Gator, Purex, powder, on tummy, green, 1960s, NM **50.00**

Winsome Witch, Purex, blue & black, 1960s, NM **30.00**

Woodsy Owl, Lander Company, early 70s, brown, green & yellow, NM **30.00**

Cake Toppers

The first cake toppers appeared on wedding cakes in the 1880s and were made almost entirely of sugar. The early 1900s saw toppers carved from wood and affixed to ornate plaster pedestal bases and backgrounds. A few single-mold toppers were even made from poured lead. From the 1920s to the 1950s bisque, porcelain, and chalkware figures reigned supreme. The faces and features on many of these were very realistic and lifelike. The beautiful Art Deco era was also in evidence.

Celluloid kewpie types made a brief appearance from the late 1930s to the 1940s. These were quite fragile because the celluloid could be easily dented and cracked. The true Rose O'Neill kewpie look-alike also appeared for awhile during this same period.

During and after World War II and into the Korean Conflict of the 1950s, groom figures in military dress appeared. Only a limited amount were ever produced; they are quite rare. From the 1950s into the 1970s, plastics were used almost exclusively. Toppers took on a vacant, assembly-line appearance with no specific attention to detail or fashion.

In the 1970s, bisque returned and plastic disappeared. Toppers were again more life-like. For the most part, they continue that way today. Wedding cakes now show off elegant and elaborate cake toppers — especially those from Royal Doulton and Lladro.

Toppers should not be confused with the bride and groom doll sets of those same earlier periods. While some smaller dolls could and did serve as toppers, they were usually too unbalanced to stay upright on a cake. The true topper consisted of a small bride and groom anchored to (or a part of) a round flat disk which made it extremely stable for resting on a soft, frosted cake surface. Cake toppers never did double-duty as play items. Our advisor is Jeannie Greenfield, who is listed in the Directory under Pennsylvania.

Bisque couple, early 1900s, reflect fashion of the day, 4½" .**40.00**
Bisque Kewpies, 1920s crepe-paper clothes, molded plaster base, 3" **45.00**
Celluloid Kewpies, crepe-paper outfits, bride wears headband, 3" **25.00**

Military, WWII era (48-star flag), all plaster, 6", $45.00. (Photo courtesy Jeannie Greenfield)

Marine dress uniform on groom, all bisque, 4½" **35.00**
Sailor uniform on groom, all plaster, 4½" **35.00**
1920s couple, all bisque, bride in dropped-waist gown, 4" .**30.00**

California Potteries

In recent years, pottery designed by many of the artists who worked in their own small studios in California during the 1940s through the 1960s has become highly sought after, and prices on the secondary market have soared. As more research is completed and collectors are introduced to the work of previously unknown artists, the field continues to expand. Items made by Kay Finch, Brayton, Howard Pierce, and Sascha Brastoff often bring high prices (especially the Finch

Adams, Matthew; Lighters, $115.00 each. (Photo courtesy Pat and Chris Secor)

pieces) and have been considered very collectible for several years. Now such names as Matthew Adams, Marc Bellair, and deLee are attracting their share of attention. It's a fascinating field, one covered very well in Jack Chipman's *Collector's Encyclopedia of California Pottery* (Collector Books).

Adams, Matthew

Bowl, Alaska in gold, bear scene, bright yellow, w/lid, signed, 5" deep **185.00**

Lighter, light blue w/walrus, rounded top, signed, #183, 5½" **115.00**

Planter, polar bear, green & white, 4½" **95.00**

Salt & pepper shakers, Eskimo design, blue w/gold, bulbous, 4", pr **65.00**

Vase, polar bear design, blue & white, bulbous top, #1262, 8½" ..**265.00**

Bellaire, Marc

Ashtray, Clown, multicolor on cream, 7" **45.00**

Ashtray, Mardi Gras, triangular shape, 8½" **165.00**

Compote, Cave Painting, 4-footed, 6x12" **125.00**

Figurine, birds, tan, green leaf design, gold trim, pr ...**195.00**

Figurine, bowl, bird w/long neck form, multicolor w/gold trim, 17" **315.00**

Vase, Balinese Women, hourglass shape, 8" **125.00**

Brastoff, Sascha

Ashtray, enamel ware, hooded, 5½" **40.00**

Ashtray, lg pipe shape w/cigarette holder, green w/gold trim **135.00**

Ashtray, Rooftops , 13x5" ...**50.00**

Bowl, Alaska, walrus, gray footed, 3½" **45.00**

Bowl, Star Steed, 5½" sq **55.00**

Candle holder, resin, green, round **45.00**

Compote, Alaska, w/native, footed, 8" **65.00**

Dish, Pagoda design, #C-2 ...**50.00**

Figurine, horse head, satin-matt crackle, 7½" **250.00**

Brastoff, Sascha; Compote, ivory with gold and silver dove, 9½", $65.00.

Nut dish, Vanity Fair design, #01, 3" **50.00**

Pitcher, Fruit design, dark brown, 6" **110.00**

Plate, dinner; Winrock, porcelain, stamped marks, 11" **45.00**

Plate, Surf Ballet design, blue w/platinum trim **22.00**

Tray, white w/platinum & gold, #F-3, 9¾" **40.00**

Vase, Alaska, #082, 8" **75.00**

Vase, enamel & copper, 5" ...**70.00**

Vase, Surf Ballet design, 5" **68.00**

Brayton Laguna

Creamer & sugar bowl, eggplant glaze, 2½" **65.00**

Figurine, Ann, seated child, Childhood series, 4" **135.00**

Figurine, baby leaning against pillow, 6x6" **75.00**

Figurine, bear, seated, 3½", from $18 to **22.00**

Figurine, Chinese girl w/child on her back **95.00**

Figurine, Fifi & Mimi, fancy cats, 9", pr **200.00**

Figurine, monkey & organ grinder **85.00**

Figurine, owl, woodtone w/white crackle, 6" **45.00**

Figurine, Pluto, sniffing, Walt Disney line, 3¼x6" **175.00**

Figurine, toucan, multicolor, glossy, in-mold marks, 1950s-60s, 9" **125.00**

Flower holder, Swedish Maid .**75.00**

Planter, Provincial wheelbarrow .**20.00**

Plate, solid pink or maroon, early, 10½" **40.00**

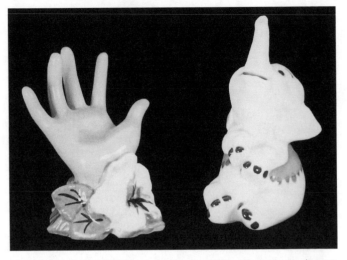

Cleminson, Ring holders: elephant and hand figurals, $45.00 each.

Teapot, brown stain w/white crackle decor, XC-35 ....**50.00**

Teapot, Webton Ware, white w/blue peasants **40.00**

Vase, bud; Provincial design ..**30.00**

Wall plaque, Blackamoor ..**175.00**

Cleminson Pottery

Bowl, cereal; clown in center, from $60 to **80.00**

Canister, marked Flour, white w/blue flowers **65.00**

Cup, My Best Gal, lg **20.00**

Egg cup, double, painted as lady w/spoon & apron, early .**25.00**

Match holder, butler **55.00**

Mug, Special Achievement ..**32.00**

Pitcher, Gala Gray, 7" **30.00**

Planter, blue bathtub w/pink flowers, 7" L **50.00**

Plaque, heart form w/pansies .**18.00**

Ring holder, bulldog **25.00**

Salt & pepper shakers, Distlefink, brown, pr, from $20 to ..**30.00**

Sprinkler, Chinese boy **35.00**

Toothbrush holder, baby's face .**55.00**

Wall pocket, frying pan **26.00**

Wall pocket, pink diaper, from $15 to **20.00**

De Forest of California

Condiment jar, American **50.00**

Condiment jar, Italian Jam .**45.00**

Pitcher, water; pig face, rare .**265.00**

deLee

Bank, bunny w/purse, 9", from $65 to **100.00**

Figurine, Annie, w/basket & platner, 10", from $75 to ...**100.00**

Figurine, girl in long skirt w/fan, 7½", from $25 to **35.00**

Wall pocket, skunk, DeStinker, 6", from $25 to **35.00**

Finch, Kay

Bowl, swan, green interior, #4956, 6" **150.00**

Finch, Kay; Figurine, Afghan dog with wings, #4964, $350.00.

Figurine, angel, white w/sm blue flowers & wings, #114 ....**60.00**
Figurine, choir boy, kneeling, #211 ....**85.00**
Figurine, donkey w/baskets, #4769, sm **95.00**
Figurine, elephant, #4804, 5", from $160 to **175.00**
Figurine, kittens, Muff & Puff, #182/#183, pr **150.00**
Figurine, owl, Toot, #188, 5¾", from $100 to **125.00**
Figurine, pig, Smiley, #164, 7x8", from $250 to **300.00**
Figurine, squirrel, 1¾" **45.00**
Mug, Santa, white **100.00**
Vase, flared oval, white w/green ivy, 10½x10x6" **125.00**

Florence Ceramics

Angel, 7", from $80 to **100.00**
Boy, modern, bust form, 9¾", from $250 to **275.00**
Charmaine, white, 9", from $275 to **300.00**

Emily, flower holder, 8", from $40 to **50.00**
Josephine, blue, 9", from $150 to **200.00**
June, planter **50.00**
Marilyn, w/hat box, pink, 8½", from $175 to **300.00**
Nancy, bud vase **50.00**
Roberta, moss, 8½", from $200 to .**275.00**
Wendy, planter, 6" **50.00**

Keeler, Brad

Keeler, Brad; Figurine, cat, silver tag, 5x7", $20.00.

Bowl, shell form, 9" **18.00**
Figurine, cat, Siamese, 4x6" .**50.00**
Figurine, colt, original label, 7" **20.00**
Figurine, Li'l Red Riding Hood, original label **60.00**
Lobster dish, divided **65.00**
Plate, chicken form, 7-color, 7" .**35.00**
Tray, tomato form **38.00**

Schoop, Hedi

Dish, leaf form w/angel figurine, maroon w/gold trim **75.00**
Figurine, ballet dancer, pink w/platinum mottling, 10", from $135 to **150.00**
Figurine, brunette in yellow w/ flower basket, sticker, 9½" .**70.00**

Figurine, girl in blue, skirt to side, basket on head, 12" **98.00**

Figurine, lady in long pink & black dress, w/umbrella, tall ..**90.00**

Figurine, Oriental boy w/basket, yellow & black w/dragon **45.00**

Figurine/planter, Oriental boy w/oboe & girl, black & white, 10½", pr **200.00**

Lamps, Oriental man & lady, gold trim, pr **400.00**

Lamps, slender ladies (matching), green w/gold trim, pr ..**495.00**

Twin Winton

Ashtray, Hillbilly Line (Men of the Mountains), Clem on his back **50.00**

Ashtray, poodle, kitten, elf or Bambi, ea **40.00**

Bank, Dobbin **50.00**

Bank, foo dog **50.00**

Bank, nut w/squirrel **50.00**

Bank, sailor elephant **40.00**

Bank, Teddy bear **40.00**

Candy jar, Candy House **45.00**

Candy jar, old shoe **45.00**

Canister set, House, Cookies, Flour, Sugar, Coffee & Tea, 5-pcs **450.00**

Ice bucket, bathing in barrel .**250.00**

Ice bucket, Hillbilly Line (Men of the Mountains), Clem bathing in barrell......................**250.00**

Napkin holder, Ranger bear .**85.00**

Pitcher, bronco on side, cowboy handle **85.00**

Planter, squirrel & stump ...**45.00**

Pretzel bowl, Hillbilly Line (Men of the Mountains), bathtub form **40.00**

Salt & pepper shakers, barrel, pr **50.00**

Salt & pepper shakers, Dutch girl, pr **35.00**

Salt & pepper shakers, hen on nest, pr **50.00**

Salt & pepper shakers, Hillbilly Line (Ladies of the Mountains), pr **35.00**

Salt & pepper shakers, rooster, pr .**30.00**

Sugar bowl & creamer, hen & rooster **100.00**

Weil Ware

Butter dish, Rose **13.50**

Coffeepot, Bamboo, w/lid **75.00**

Figurine, girl, lifted chin, sgraffito floral skirt, lg **50.00**

Figurine, sailor boy w/flowers before white vase, 10¾" .**40.00**

Platter, Blossom, 13" **22.00**

Vase, Ming Tree, w/coralene, 8½" **40.00**

Wall pocket, Oriental girl **40.00**

Weil, Figurine, girl in green with flowers, $60.00.

Yona

Candy jar, clown, from $60 to ..**65.00**
Figurine, angel, Be Kind to Animals, 5" **28.00**
Figurine, Chinaman w/basket, 12" **20.00**
Figurine, Europeans in blue, man w/cape, lady w/bucket, 8¾", pr **75.00**
Figurine, girl w/bouquet, applied flowers, brown & white dress **55.00**
Nut/mint dish, red & white stripes, striped handle ..**32.00**
Pill jar, from $30 to **35.00**

Cameras

Whether buying a camera for personal use, adding to a collection, or for resale, use caution. Complex useable late model cameras are difficult to check-out at sales and you should be familiar with the camera model or have confidence in the seller's claims before purchasing one for your personal use. If you are just beginning a camera collection, there are a multitude of different types and models and special features to select from in building your collection; you should have on hand some of the available guide books listing various models and types. Camera collecting can be a very enjoyable hobby and can be done within your particular funding ability.

If you are buying for resale, it can be a very profitable experience if you are careful in your selection and have made arrangements with buyers who have identified their requirements to you. Generally, buying the low-cost, mass-produced cameras is not advisable; you may have a difficult time finding a buyer for such cameras. Of these low-cost types, only those that are mint, or new in the original box, have any appreciable appeal to collectors. Very old cameras are not necessarily valuable — it all depends on availabilty and and number made. The major criterion is quality; prices offered for mint-condition cameras may be double or triple those of average wear items. You can expect to find that foreign-made cameras are preferred by most buyers because of the general perception that their lenses and shutters are superior. The German- and Japanese-made cameras dominate the 'classic' camera market. Polaroid cameras and movie cameras have yet to gain a significant collector's market.

The cameras listed here represent only a very small cross section of thousands of cameras available. A (+) at the end of the line indicates cameras that are generally considered as the most popular user-type cameras and does not include later model Auto-Focus cameras or Point and Shoot cameras. The values given are for cameras with average wear and in good working order; they represent average retail prices with limited guarantees. It is very important to mention that purchase prices at flea markets, garage sales, or estate sales would have to be far less for them to be

Exakta V Varex, ca 1950, from $75.00 to $100.00.
(Photo courtesy Gene's Cameras)

profitable to a resaler who has the significant expense of servicing the camera, testing it, and guaranteeing it to a user or collector. Our advisor, Gene Cataldo (of Gene's Cameras), is listed in the Directory under Alabama.

Agfa Billy, early 1930s **25.00**
Agfa Isolette **30.00**
Agfa Karat 3.5, 1940 ....**40.00**
Alpa 7, 1952-1959 ....**350.00**
Ansco Memar, 1956-1959 ....**35.00**
Argus A2F, 1931-1941 ....**20.00**
Argus C3, black brick type, 1940-
    1950 ....**10.00**
Baldi, by Balda-Werk, Germany,
    1930s **40.00**
Bosley B2 ....**30.00**
Canon A-1 (+) **180.00**
Canon AE-1 (+) **110.00**
Canon AE-1P (+) **150.00**
Canon F-1 (+) **250.00**
Canon IIB, 1949-1952 ....**275.00**
Canon III, 1951-1953 ....**225.00**
Canon J, Seiki Kogaku, 1939-
    1940 ....**7,000.00**
Canon J-II, Seiki Kogaku, 1945-
    1946 ....**6,500.00**

Canon S-11, Seiki Kogaku, 1946-
    1947 ....**600.00**
Canon 7, chrome, 1961-1964 ..**300.00**
Ciroflex, 1940s **35.00**
Conley, folding plate type, 1900-
    1910 ....**100.00**
Contax II, 1936-1942 ....**375.00**
Contax III, 1936-1942 ....**325.00**
Contessa 35, 1950-1955 .....**175.00**
Deica II D, 1932-1938 ....**270.00**
Detrola Model D, Detroit Corp,
    1938-1940 ....**30.00**
Eastman Folding Brownie Six-20 .**15.00**
Eastman Premo Camera, many
    models, ea **50.00**
Edinex, by Wirgin **70.00**
Exakta II, 1949-1950 ....**150.00**
Graflex Pacemaker Crown Graphic,
    various sizes, ea **200.00**
Graflex Speed Graphic, 1938-
    1947, miniature **150.00**
Hit Camera, novelty type, Japanese,
    sm **15.00**
Kodak, vest pocket folding, vari-
    ous models, ea **30.00**
Kodak Bantam, Art Deco design,
    1935-1938 ....**30.00**
Kodak Box Brownie 2A **7.00**

Kodak Box Hawk-Eye No 2A ..**5.00**
Kodak Medalist I, 1941-1948 .**150.00**
Kodak Retina Model I, Germany **50.00**
Kodak Retina Model II, Germany **75.00**
Kodak Retina Model IIa, Germany **100.00**
Kodak Retina Model IIc **125.00**
Kodak Retina Model IIIc ...**130.00**
Kodak Retina Model IIIC ..**500.00**
Kodak Retina Reflex, various models, ea **90.00**
Kodak Retinette, various models, Germany **45.00**
Kodak View Camera, early 1900s, various sizes, ea **175.00**
Kodak 35, w/rangefinder, 1940-1951 ....**30.00**
Konica Autoreflex (+) **80.00**
Konica Autoreflex TC **70.00**
Konica FS-1 (+) **100.00**
Konica III, 1956-1959 ....**85.00**
Leica IIIc, 1940-1946 ....**225.00**
Leica IIIF, 1933-1939 ....**275.00**

Leica IIIg, 1956-1960 ....**600.00**
Leica M3, 1954-1966 ....**650.00**
Mamiya-Sekor 500TL, 1966 ..**50.00**
Mercury, Model II, CX, 1945 .**40.00**
Minolta HiMatic, various models, ea **20.00**
Minolta SR-7 ....**50.00**
Minolta SRT 101 (+) **75.00**
Minolta SRT 202 (+) **100.00**
Minolta XD, XD-7, or XD-11, 1977, ea **175.00**
Minolta X700 (+) **135.00**
Minolta-17, miniature, various models, ea **25.00**
Minox B (Spy Camera) **130.00**
Miranda Automex II, 1963 ..**90.00**
Nikon EM **80.00**
Nikon F, w/various finders, meters **175.00**
Nikon FA (+) **225.00**
Nikon FG (+) **125.00**
Nikon FM (+) **175.00**
Nikon S, 1951-1954 ....**425.00**
Nikon S2, 1954-1958 ....**400.00**
Nikon S3, 1958-1960 ....**900.00**

Wizard Folding Plate Camera, ca 1898, from $125.00 to $175.00. (Photo courtesy Gene's Cameras)

Olympus OM-1 (+) **125.00**
Olympus OM-10 (+) **85.00**
Olympus OM-2 (+) **160.00**
Olympus Pen EE **30.00**
Olympus Pen F, 1963-1966 .**150.00**
Olympus 35 IV, 1949-1953 ..**50.00**
Pentax K-1000 (+) **110.00**
Pentax ME (+) **90.00**
Pentax Spotmatic F (+) **135.00**
Pentax Spotmatic SP1000 (+) ..**100.00**
Pentax Super Program (+) ..**160.00**
Plaubel-Makina II, Germany,
    1933-1939 ....**200.00**
Praktica FX, 1952-1957 ....**50.00**
Realist Stereo, 3.5 lens **120.00**
Regula, King, various models,
    fixed lens, ea **40.00**
Regula, King, w/interchangeable
    lens **90.00**
Ricoh KR-30 (+) **115.00**
Rolleicord II, 1936-1950 ....**90.00**
Rolleiflex Automat, 1937 ...**150.00**
Samoca 35, 1950s **40.00**
Seroco, folding plate type, Sears,
    1901, 4x5" **125.00**
Supersport Dolly, w/rangefinder,
    1935-1941 ....**150.00**
Topcon Uni **60.00**
Univex, Universal Camera Co,
    1935-1939 ....**25.00**
Voightlander Vito II, 1950 ...**50.00**
Voigtlander Bessa, folding type,
    1931-1949 ....**40.00**
Voigtlander Bessa Rf, w/
    rangefinder, 1936 ....**140.00**
Voigtlander Vitessa L, 1954 .**175.00**
Wizard, Manhatten Optical Co,
    1896-1910 ....**150.00**
Yashica A, Twin Lens reflex .**50.00**
Yashica 124, Twin Lens reflex ..**130.00**
Zeiss-Ikon Box Tengor 43/2, 1934-
    1938 ....**35.00**
Zeiss-Ikon Juwell (275/11), Ger-
    many, 1927-1939 ....**500.00**

Zeiss-Ikon Nettar, folding roll
    film, various sizes **35.00**
Zeiss-Ikon Super Ikonta B
    (532/16), 1937-1956 .....**160.00**
Zorki 4, Russian **70.00**

Candlewick

Candlewick was one of the
all-time bestselling lines of The
Imperial Glass Company of Bellaire, Ohio. It was produced from
1936 until the company closed in
1982. More than 741 items were
made over the years; and, though
many are still easy to find today,
some (such as the desk calendar,
the chip and dip set, and the
dresser set) are a challenge to collect. Candlewick is easily identified by its beaded stems, handles,
and rims characteristic of the tuft-
ed needlework of our pioneer
women for which it was named.

Ashtray, #400/172, heart form,
    4½" **9.00**
Bowl, #400/51H, heart w/hand,
    6" **25.00**
Bowl, fruit; #400/1F, 5" **12.00**
Candle holder, #400/100, 2-
    light **20.00**
Candle holder, #400/86, mush-
    room shape **22.00**
Coaster, #400/78, 4" **6.00**
Creamer, #400/31, plain foot .**9.00**
Fork & spoon set, #400/75 ...**35.00**
Ladle, marmalade; #400/130, 3-
    bead stem **10.00**
Mayonnaise set, #400/52/3, tray,
    bowl & ladle **45.00**
Mustard jar, #400/156, w/spoon .**30.00**
Pitcher, #400/424, plain, 80-oz .**55.00**

Salt and pepper shakers, #400/96, beaded feet, chrome lids, $25.00 for the pair.

Plate, #400/62D, handles, 8½" .**12.00**

Plate, canape; #400/35, off-center indent, 6" **11.00**

Relish bowl, #400/217, oval, handles, 10" **40.00**

Salt & pepper shakers, #400/109, individual, pr **10.00**

Stem, champagne/sherbet; #3800, 6-oz **25.00**

Stem, cocktail; #400/190, 4-oz .**18.00**

Stem, water; #400/190, 10-oz ..**18.00**

Teacup, #400/35 ....**7.50**

Tumbler, #400/19, 12-oz **22.00**

Tumbler, water; #400/18, 9-oz .**40.00**

Vase, #400/87 R, rolled rim, beaded handles, 7" **35.00**

Cape Cod by Avon

Now that Avon has discontinued their Cape Cod line, don't be surprised to see prices on the upward swing. They've been making this dark ruby red glassware since the '70s. In addition to the place settings (there are plates in three sizes, soup and dessert bowls, a cup and saucer, tumblers in two sizes, three different goblets, a mug, and a wine glass), there are many lovely accessory items as well. Among them you'll find a cake plate, a pitcher, a platter, a hurricane-type candle lamp, a butter dish, napkin rings, and a pie plate server. Note: mint-in-box items are worth about 20% more than the same piece with no box.

Bell, marked Christmas 1979 on bottom, 6½", from $20 to .**25.00**

Bowl, dessert; 1978-80, 5" ...**12.00**

Bowl, serving; 1986, 8¾" **25.00**

Bowl, soup/cereal; 1991, 7½" **13.00**

Butter dish, holds ¼-lb stick, 1983-84, 7" L, from $20 to **25.00**

Candle holder, hurricane type w/clear chimney, 1985 ..**25.00**

Candle holders, squat form, 1983-84, 2½x3¾" dia, pr, from $15 to **18.00**

Candlestick, 1975-80, 5-oz, from $7 to **9.00**

Goblets, 6", $9.00 each.

Candlesticks, 8½", pr, from $25 to **30.00**

Candy dish, footed, 1987, 3½x6" dia, from $12 to **15.00**

Condiment dish, divided, rectangular, 1985, from $12 to **15.00**

Creamer, footed, 1981-84, 4" .**12.50**

Cruet, 1975-80, 4", from $10 to .**13.00**

Cup & saucer, 1990, 3½", from $9 to **12.00**

Decanter, w/stopper, 1977-80, 16-oz, from $18 to **22.00**

Dessert server, wedge-shape stainless, plastic handle, 1981-84, 8" L **15.00**

Goblet, champagne; 1991, 5¼" .**12.50**

Goblet, water; 1976-90, 6" **9.00**

Goblet, wine; 1992, 5¼", from $4 to **6.00**

Heart box, 1989, 4" wide, from $20 to **25.00**

Mug, pedestal foot, 1982-84, 5" .**10.00**

Napkin rings, set of 4, 1989 ..**20.00**

Pie plate, server, 1991, 11" dia, from 35 to **40.00**

Pitcher, water; footed, 1984, 8¼", from $35 to **40.00**

Plate, bread & butter; 1992, 5¾" dia **8.50**

Plate, cake; footed, 1991, 3½x10¾" dia **50.00**

Plate, dessert; 1980, 7¼" **6.50**

Plate, dinner; 1982-83, 11", from $14 to **16.00**

Platter, 1986, 10¾x13½" **24.00**

Relish, 9¼", 5½" **20.00**

Salt & pepper shakers, marked May 1978 on bottom, pr, from $18 to **22.00**

Sauce boat, footed, 1988, 8" L ..**25.00**

Sugar bowl, footed, 1980-83, 3½" **12.50**

Tidbit tray, 2-tier, brass handle, 1987, 9¾", from $30 to **35.00**

Tumbler, footed, 1988, 3¾" **7.50**

Tumbler, straight sided, 1990, 5½", from $8 to **10.00**

Vase, footed, 1985, 8", from $20 to **25.00**

Wine glass, footed, 5" **7.50**

Carnival Chalkware

Chalkware statues of Kewpies, glamour girls, assorted dogs, horses, etc., were given to winners of carnival games from about 1910 until the 1950s. Today's collectors especially value those representing well-known personalities such as Disney characters and comic book heroes. Refer to *The Carnival Chalk Prize* by Tom Morris for more information. Mr. Morris is in the Directory under Oregon.

American eagle, marked God Bless America, ca 1935-45, 12" .**65.00**

Betty Boop, short skirt, hands on hips, ca 1930-40, 14½" **265.00**

Bulldog by ashtray, w/2 wells for cigarette pack & matches, 8x7½" **35.00**

Cat & goldfish bowl, ca 1930-45, 9½" **65.00**

Cat sitting in overstuffed chair, ca 1930-40, 5½" **35.00**

Charlie McCarthy, top hat & bow tie, ca 1930-40, 13" **75.00**

Circus elephant, bank, ca 1940-50, 12" **45.00**

Dog, lg expressive eyes, flat back, 1940-50, 6½" **8.00**

Donald Duck, ca 1940, 7" **30.00**

Donkey, head & ears up, teeth showing, ca 1940-50, 12" **25.00**

Ferdinand the Bull, ca 1940-50, 9½" **50.00**

Girl sitting & winking, hand painted, Winkie 1919, 6" **60.00**

Hen w/chick, bank, ca 1935-45, 7¼x9" **50.00**

Little Sheba, hand painted, original feathers, ca 1920s, 13" **155.00**

Mickey Mouse, ca 1930-40, 12" **95.00**

Pekinese dog, ca 1935-40, 7¼x10½" **40.00**

Beach Bather, no mark, 1940-50, 7½x9", $55.00. (Photo courtesy Tom Morris)

Penguin, resembles Kool Cigarette penguin, glass eyes, 1935-45, 7¼" **35.00**

Popeye, hand to ear, ca 1930-40, 11½" **115.00**

Skunk, resembles Disney's Flower, ca 1945-50, 4½" **35.00**

Wimpy, Popeye's friend, ca 1930-40, 8" **45.00**

Carnival Glass

From about 1905 until the late 1920s, carnival glass was manufactured by several major American glasshouses in hundreds of designs and patterns. Its characteristic iridescent lustre was the result of coating the pressed glassware with a sodium solution before the final firing. Marigold, blue, green, and purple are the most common colors, though pastels were also used. Because it was mass produced at reasonable prices, much of it was given away at carnivals. As a result, it came to be known as carnival glass. Refer to *The Standard Encyclopedia of Carnival Glass* by Bill Edwards (Collector Books) for more information.

Acorn Burrs, creamer, amethyst **260.00**

Acorn Burrs, punch cup, marigold, Northwood **45.00**

April Showers, vase, green, Fenton **150.00**

Arcs, bowl, white, Imperial 8".**175.00**

Aztec, creamer, clambroth .**250.00**

Balloons, compote, smoke, Imperial **90.00**

Band of Roses, tray, marigold .**75.00**

Banded Diamonds, bowl, amethyst, Crystal, 5" **75.00**

Banded Grape, creamer, marigold, Fenton, mini **75.00**

Banded Panels, compote, amethyst, Westmoreland **55.00**

Beaded Cable, candy dish, white, Northwood **200.00**

Beaded Shell, tumbler, blue, Dugan **180.00**

Beaded Swirl, compote, blue, English **60.00**

Bells & Beads, nappy, peach opal, Dugan **100.00**

Birds & Cherries, bonbon, amethyst, Fenton **65.00**

Blackberry Block, tumbler, blue, Fenton **75.00**

Blackberry Spray, hat, blue, Fenton **40.00**

Blackberry Wreath, bowl, ice cream; marigold, Millersburg, 10" .**100.00**

Booker, mug, marigold **160.00**

Bouquet, tumbler, blue, Fenton .**40.00**

Broken Arches, bowl, green, Imperial, 8½" **75.00**

Bubbles, lamp chimney, pastel **50.00**

Butterflies, bonbon, amethyst, Fenton **70.00**

Butterfly, bonbon, green, regular, Northwood **100.00**

Butterfly & Berry, butter dish, marigold, w/lid, Fenton .**150.00**

Butterfly and Tulip, bowl, marigold, footed, Dugan, 10½", $320.00. (Photo courtesy Bill Edwards)

Button & Fan, hatpin, amethyst .**60.00**

Cambridge Hobstar, napkin ring, marigold, Cambridge **50.00**

Cane, wine, pastel, Imperial ..**75.00**

Cannonball Variant, pitcher, marigold **240.00**

Carnival Honeycomb, bonbon, amethyst, Imperial **55.00**

Checkerboard, punch cup, marigold, Westmoreland **90.00**

Cherry, bowl, amethyst, Millersburg, rare, 7" **95.00**

Chrysanthemum, bowl, blue, flat, Fenton, 9" **80.00**

Coin Dot, bowl, green, Fenton, 6" .**40.00**

Concave Diamond, tumbler, vaseline **190.00**

Cornucopia, vase, marigold, Fenton, 5" **70.00**

Cosmos & Cane, tumbler, advertising; white, rare **250.00**

Cut Arcs, compote, blue, Fenton **55.00**

Daisy & Cane, spittoon, blue, rare, English **250.00**

Dandelion, mug, green, Northwood **600.00**

Diamond & Sunburst, wine, amethyst, Imperial **60.00**

Diamond Point Columns, spooner, marigold, Imperial **40.00**

Double Dolphins, candlesticks, pastel, Fenton, pr **90.00**

Duncan, cruet, marigold, National Glass **600.00**

Enameled Grape, tumbler, blue, Northwood **45.00**

Engraved Daisy & Spears, goblet, marigold, 4½" **75.00**

Fans, cracker jar, marigold, metal lid, English **150.00**

Fenton's Arched Flute, toothpick holder, blue, Fenton **100.00**

Fern Panels, hat, blue, Fenton ..**50.00**

Fine Cut Rings, celery tray, marigold, English **160.00**

Fishscales & Beads, bride's basket, peach opal, complete, Dugan **140.00**

Florentine, candlesticks, Celeste blue, Fenton & Northwood, pr .**150.00**

Flute, sherbet, green, Northwood **45.00**

Flute & Cane, milk pitcher, marigold, Imperial **115.00**

Frosted Block, butter dish, marigold, w/lid, Imperial **70.00**

Garden Path, bowl, fruit; amethyst, Dugan, 10" .**115.00**

Gothic Arches, vase, green, Northwood, 8" **85.00**

Grape, Heavy; nappy, amethyst, Imperial **55.00**

Grape, water bottle, amethyst, rare, Imperial **250.00**

Grape & Cherry, bowl, blue, English, rare, 8½" **180.00**

Halloween, tumbler, marigold, 2 sizes **175.00**

Hawaiian Moon, tumbler, cranberry flash **90.00**

Heavy Prisms, celery vase, marigold, English, 6" **85.00**

Hex Base, candlesticks, marigold, pr **75.00**

Hobstar & Cut Triangles, rose bowl, green, English **70.00**

Hobstar & Fruit, bowl, peach opalescent, Westmoreland, rare, 6" **100.00**

Holly, Panelled, creamer, marigold, Northwood **90.00**

Intaglio Daisy, bowl, marigold, English, 4½" **30.00**

Inverted Coin Dot, bowl, green, Northwood-Fenton **70.00**

Inverted Prisms, creamer, marigold, English **70.00**

Inverted Strawberry, spooner, blue **150.00**

Iris, goblet, buttermilk; green, Fenton, scarce **65.00**

Jackman, bottle, whiskey; marigold **50.00**

Lattice, bowl, pastel colors, Dugan, various sizes **85.00**

Laurel Leaves, plate, smoke, Imperial **60.00**

Leaf Rays, nappy, peach opalescent, Dugan, either exterior **50.00**

Leaf Tiers, creamer, marigold, footed, Fenton **85.00**

Lustre & Clear, sugar bowl, pastel colors, Imperial **60.00**

Lustre & Flute, bonbon, green, Northwood **60.00**

Lustre Rose, fernery, green, Imperial **65.00**

Maize, syrup (cruet), clear, Libbey, rare **235.00**

Many Prisms, perfume, marigold, w/stopper **75.00**

Moderne, saucer, marigold ..**30.00**

Moonprint, jar, blue, w/lid, English **85.00**

Morning Glory, funeral vase, amethyst, Imperial **300.00**

Multi-Fruit & Flowers, cup, green, Millersburg, rare **90.00**

Mystic, vase, marigold, footed, Millersburg, rare **165.00**

Oklahoma, decanter, marigold, Mexican **850.00**

Optic & Buttons, salt cup, marigold, Imperial **850.00**

Orange Peel, cup, teal, Westmoreland **35.00**

Orange Tree, powder jar, blue, w/lid, Fenton **95.00**

Orange Tree Orchid, tumbler, green, Fenton **55.00**

Parlor, ashtray, blue **95.00**

Peach, pitcher, white, Northwood **775.00**

Peacock, bowl, ice cream; amethyst, Millersburg, 5" **190.00**

Peacock & Dahlia, bowl, blue, Fenton, 7½" **100.00**

Peacock & Urn, compote, amethyst, Fenton **90.00**

Peacock & Urn & Variants, bowl, green, Millersburg, 6" ...**210.00**

Pickle, paperweight, amethyst, 4½" **65.00**

Pine Cone, plate, green, Fenton, 6½" **275.00**

Pineapple, compote, blue, English **58.00**

Plain Jane, basket, smoke, Imperial **75.00**

Propeller, compote, green, Imperial **70.00**

Puzzle, bonbon, peach opalescent, stemmed, Dugan **100.00**

Question Marks, plate, cake; stemmed, amethyst, Dugan, rare **450.00**

Raindrops, bowl, marigold, Dugan, 9" **65.00**

Raspberry, pitcher, milk; green, Northwood **375.00**

Rolled Ribs, bowl, marigold opalescent, New Martinsville .**150.00**

Rose Bouquet, creamer, marigold **60.00**

Rose Garden, vase, letter; blue, Sweden **190.00**

Rose Spray, compote, Celeste blue, Fenton **190.00**

Round-Up, bowl, amethyst, Dugan, 8¾" **180.00**

S-Repeat, cup, amethyst, Dugan, rare **120.00**

Seaweed, bowl, green, Millersburg, rare, 5" **470.00**

Shell, plate, green, Imperial, 8 .**375.00**

Silver Queen, tumbler, marigold, Fenton **70.00**

Single Flower, bowl, banana; peach opalescent, Dugan, rare, 9½" **350.00**

Sowerby Wide Panel, bowl, black amethyst, Sowerby **75.00**

Spiderweb, candy dish, smoke, w/lid, Northwood **40.00**

Split Diamond, bowl, sauce; amethyst, flat, English .**70.00**

Star, bowl, marigold, English, 8" .**50.00**

Strawberry, bonbon, green, Fenton **65.00**

Stretched Diamond, tumbler, marigold, Northwood, rare **175.00**

Ten Mums, tumbler, blue, Fenton, rare **80.00**

Thin & Wide Rib, vase, green, ruffled, Northwood **150.00**

Seaweed, bowl, green, 9", $375.00.
(Photo courtesy Bill Edwards)

Thistle, vase, marigold, English, 6" **45.00**

Thistle & Lotus, bowl, blue, Fenton, 7" **70.00**

Three Flowers, tray, smoke, center handle, Imperial, 12" **70.00**

Thumbprint & Spears, creamer, green **60.00**

Tulip & Cane, compote, marigold, Imperial **45.00**

Twins, bowl, fruit; pastel colors, w/base, Imperial **35.00**

US Diamond Block, shakers, marigold, US Glass, pr .**80.00**

Vintage, powder jar, amethyst, w/lid, Dugan **120.00**

Water Lily & Cattails, tumbler, marigold, Northwood .**200.00**

Western Thistle, pitcher, cider; blue **350.00**

Whirling Star, cup, marigold, Imperial **20.00**

Wide Panel, bowl, teal, Westmoreland, 7½" **70.00**

Wide Panel, goblet, marigold, Northwood-Fenton-Imperial **40.00**

Woodpecker, vase, wall; green, Dugan **90.00**

Wreath of Rose, bowl, nut; marigold, Dugan/Diamond **70.00**

Wreathed Cherry, toothpick, amethyst, old only, Dugan..**175.00**

Zig Zag, tumbler, blue, decorated, Fenton **50.00**

Zip Zip, flower frog holder, marigold, English **60.00**

474 Variant, compote, green, Sweden, 7" **90.00**

Cat Collectibles

Cat lovers are often quite fervent in their attachment to their pets, and for many their passion extends into the collecting field. There is no shortage of items to entice them to buy, be they figural pieces, advertising signs, postcards, textiles, books, candy containers, or what have you. Marbena Fyke has written two amusing and informative books called *Collectible Cats, Identification and Value Guide*, Volume I and Volume II. If you're a cat lover yourself, you're sure to enjoy them. See also Black Cats.

Apron, Kliban, cat playing guitar pictured, M **15.00**

Boot scraper repro, walking cat form, cast iron, 10½x18", EX **75.00**

Box, cat form, overall Oriental florals, Made in China, 4½x7½" **65.00**

Cookie jar, Kliban playing guitar, Sigma, from $150 to **175.00**

Figurine, chocolate-point Siamese, Bing & Grondahl #2308, 5½" **240.00**

Figurine, cloisonne, lavender & wine w/blue & gold, China, 3" .**20.00**

Figurine, red tabby Persian, Shafford, 1967, 10" L **45.00**

Cookie jar, Kitty Cucumber, $50.00. (Photo courtesy Marilyn Dipboye)

Figurine, Siamese, Beswick #2139 (discontinued), 13¾" ...**140.00**

Figurine, sleeping kitten, porcelain, painted details, Japan, 4" L **65.00**

Music box, Kitty Cucumber, plays White Christmas, 1988-89 .**48.00**

Pillow, Kliban figural, 22" L, M .**22.00**

Pin, brushed gold figure w/rhinestones, green winking eye **18.00**

Pin, gold-tone lion w/black stripes, rhinestone mouth & beard .**24.00**

Planter, ceramic figural, white w/colored flowers, Portugal, 10" **27.00**

Salt & pepper shakers, Cat's Pajamas, F&F Mold & Die Co, pr, from $35 to **45.00**

Salt & pepper shakers, Owl & the Pussy Cat in boat, F&F Mold & Die Co, from $65 to ...**75.00**

Teapot, ceramic figure, Victorian dress, bouquet spout, tail handle **30.00**

Teapot, Miss Kitty, Kittens of Knightsbridge, ceramic, F&F, from $65 to **75.00**

Teapot, Reigning Marie Cattoinette, ceramic, F&F ..**85.00**

Cattail Dinnerware

Cattail was a dinnerware pattern popular during the late 1920s until sometime in the 1940s. So popular, in fact, that ovenware, glassware, tinware, and even a kitchen table was made to coordinate with it. The dinnerware was made primarily by Universal potteries of Cambridge, Ohio, though a catalog from Hall China Co., circa 1927, shows a three-piece coffee service, and there may have been other pieces. It was sold for years by Sears Roebuck and Company, and some items bear a mark with their name.

The pattern is unmistakable — a cluster of red cattails (usually six, sometimes one or two) with black stems on creamy white. Shapes certainly vary; Universal used a minimum of three of their standard mold designs. Shapes used by Universal were Camwood, Old Holland, Laurella, and possibly others. Some Cattails say 'Wheelock' on the bottom. Wheelock was a department store in Peoria, Illinois.

Batter jug with metal lid, $80.00; bowl, $15.00. (Photo courtesy Ken and Barbara Brooks)

If you are trying to decorate a '40s vintage kitchen, no other design could afford you more to work with. To see many of the pieces that are available and to learn more about the line, read *The Collector's Encyclopedia of American Dinnerware* by Jo Cunningham. Our advisors for Cattail Dinnerware are Ken and Barbara Brooks, who are listed in the Directory under North Carolina.

Bowl, Old Holland shape, marked Wheelock, 6" **6.00**
Butter dish, w/lid, 1-lb **45.00**
Cake cover & tray, tinware .**30.00**
Can, step-on, tinware **30.00**
Canisters, tinware, 4-pc set .**45.00**
Casserole w/cover, several different styles, ea **30.00**
Cookie jar **85.00**
Cracker jar, barrel shape **75.00**
Creamer, Laurella shape **16.00**
Custard cup **7.00**
Gravy boat w/liner **35.00**
Jug, refrigerator; w/handle ..**30.00**
Jug, side handle, cork stopper **32.00**
Kitchen scales, tinware **37.00**
Match holder, tinware **35.00**

Pie plate **25.00**
Pie server, hole in handle for hanging, marked Universal Potteries **25.00**
Pitcher, ice lip; glass **100.00**
Pitcher, utility or milk **25.00**
Plate, dinner; Laurella shape, from $12 to **15.00**
Plate, dinner; 3-compartment .**25.00**
Plate, salad or dessert; round .**5.00**
Plate, serving; early, marked Universal...Oven Proof..., from $30 to **35.00**

Coffeepot, 3-piece, $65.00. (Photo courtesy of Ken and Barbara Brooks)

Platter, oval **25.00**
Salad set: fork, spoon & bowl .**50.00**
Salt & pepper shakers, different
    styles, pr **15.00**
Saucer, Old Holland shape,
    marked Wheelock **6.00**
Shakers, glass, salt, pepper, flour
    & sugar shakers, w/red metal
    tray **40.00**
Stack set, 3-pc w/lids **40.00**
Sugar bowl, 2 handles, w/lid ..**16.00**
Tablecloth **85.00**
Teapot, w/lid, from $30 to **35.00**
Tumbler, iced tea; glass **35.00**
Tumbler, marked Universal Potteries,
    scarce **65.00**
Tumbler, water; glass **30.00**
Waste can, oval, tinware **30.00**

Ceramic Arts Studio

Whether you're a collector of American pottery or not, chances are you'll like the distinctive styling of the figurines, salt and pepper shakers, and other novelty items made by the Ceramic Arts Studio of Madison, Wisconsin, from about 1938 until approximately 1952. They're not especially hard to find — a trip to any good flea market will usually produce one or several good buys of their shelf sitters or wall-hanging pairs. They're easily spotted, once you've seen a few examples; but if you're not sure, check for the trademark: the name of the company and its location.

Ashtray, Peek-a-boo pixie, 5"
    wide **60.00**
Bank, paisley pig, 3" **70.00**
Canoe **110.00**

Figurine, Al, hunter w/gun .**75.00**
Figurine, Alice's Mad Hatter .**195.00**
Figurine, Collie puppy playing,
    2¼" **22.00**
Figurine, Dachshund, 3½" L ..**40.00**
Figurine, FiFi, 3" **50.00**
Figurine, guitar boy, 5" **65.00**
Figurine, Gypsy tambourine girl,
    7" **75.00**
Figurine, Hiawatha **125.00**
Figurine, kitten playing w/ball of
    yarn, 2" **30.00**
Figurine, mermaid baby,
    seated **50.00**
Figurine, Minnehaha **195.00**
Figurine, Pioneer Susie, w/broom,
    5" **50.00**
Figurine, square dance boy,
    6½" **55.00**
Figurine, squirrel w/jacket,
    2¼" **45.00**
Figurine, Wee Scotch boy & girl,
    3¼", pr **45.00**
Flowerpot, sq **30.00**
Jug, horse head **60.00**
Salt & pepper shakers, Hindu
    boys, pr **110.00**
Salt & pepper shakers, snuggle
    type: cow & calf, 5½", 2½",
    pr **85.00**
Salt & pepper shakers, snuggle
    type: rabbit mother & baby,
    running, pr **95.00**
Salt & pepper shakers, Suzette
    on Pillow, white poodle, 4",
    pr **85.00**
Salt & pepper shakers, snug-
    gle type: dog & doghouse,
    pr **75.00**
Salt & pepper shakers, snuggle
    type: mouse & cheese wedge,
    3", pr **30.00**
Salt & pepper shakers, fish,
    upright tails, 4", pr **65.00**

Shelf sitter, boy w/puppy,
4¼" **65.00**
Shelf sitter, cowgirl, 4¾" .**65.00**
Shelf sitter, Pete & Polly parrots,
7½", pr **125.00**

Salt and pepper shakers, snuggle bear mother and baby, $75.00 for the pair.

Shelf sitter, Young Love boy &
girl, 4½", pr **95.00**

Cereal Boxes and Premiums

When buying real estate, they say 'location, location, location.' When cereal box collecting its 'character, character, character.' Look for Batman, Quisp, Superman, or Ninja Turtles — the so-called 'Grain Gods' emblazoned across the box. Dull adult and health cereals such as Special K or Shredded Wheat, unless they have an exciting offer, aren't worth picking up (too boring). Stick to the cavity-blasting presweets aimed at kids, like The Jetsons, Froot Loops, or Trix. You can hunt down the moldy FrostyOs and Quake from childhood in old stores and pantries or collect the new stuff at your supermarket. Your local cereal aisle — the grain ghetto — is chock full of future bluechips, so squeeze the moment! The big question is: once you've gotten your flaky treasures home, how do you save the box? If you live where pests (bugs or mice) aren't a problem, display or store the box unopened. Otherwise, eat its contents, then pull out the bottom flaps and flatten the package along the fold lines. If you don't want to flatten the box, empty it by gently pulling out the bottom flaps and removing the bag. Be sure to save the prize inside, called an inpack, if it has one; they're potentially valuable too. Prices are for cereal boxes that are full or folded flat, in mint condition. For further information we recommend *Cerealizing America, The Unsweetened Story of American Breakfast Cereal,* by Scott Bruce and Bill Crawford, and *Cereal Box Bonanza* by Scott Bruce. Scott (Mr. Cereal Box) is our advisor for this category; he is listed in the Directory under Massachusetts. See also Clubs and Newsletters.

Boxes

Alpha Bits, Fun & Games (Lovable Truly), 1966 ....**190.00**
Bozo's Little O's, 1986 ....**35.00**
Corn Flakes, Vanessa Williams,
1984 ....**70.00**

Count Chocula, Star of David (Lugosi),1988 ....**30.00**

ET's, Michael Jackson album, 1984 ....**85.00**

Fruity Freakies, Freakie iron-on, 1975 ....**225.00**

Huck Hound All Stars, 1965 .**625.00**

King Vitaman, light trucks, 1971 ....**215.00**

Mickey Mouse Puppets, canister, 1965 ....**45.00**

Mr T, Mr T stickers, 1984 ....**70.00**

Puffa Puffa Rice, Hawaiian Outrigger, 1967 ....**70.00**

Quake, Quake playmate, 1966 ....**675.00**

Quangaroos, fury-wheel, 1972 .**550.00**

Quisp, ray gun offer, 1968 .**875.00**

Rice Krispies, Monkeemobile, 1967 ....**300.00**

Super Sugar Crisp, Archies record, 1970 ....**175.00**

Toasted Corn Flakes, Holleb's Brownie, 1930 ....**30.00**

Toasties, Hoppy Wild West cards, 1950 ....**1,250.00**

Wheaties, Redskins NFL Champs, 1988 ....**25.00**

Premiums

Apple Jack mug & bowl, 1967, from $75 to **100.00**

Donkey Kong Junior Pez dispenser, from $75 to **100.00**

Dr Dolittle medical bag, 1967, from $50 to **75.00**

ET/Michael Jackson album & poster, 1984 ....**90.00**

Frankenberry squeeze toys, 1980, ea, from $50 to **75.00**

Freakie figures, plastic, 1973, from $10 to **20.00**

Freakies plastic mug & bowl, 1975 ....**90.00**

Freakies wall clock, 1975, from $100 to **150.00**

Gabby Hayes cannon ring, 1950 .**240.00**

Gary Lewis's Doin' the Flake record, 1964, from $35 to **50.00**

Jean LaFoote plastic bank, 1973 ....**90.00**

Cornelius C. Sugarcoat walking toy, 1958, $275.00. (Photo courtesy Scott Bruce)

Jungle Book swingers, 1977 .**10.00**

Lovable Truly inflatable figure, 1964, from $100 to **150.00**

Marky Maypo vinyl figure, 1960s, from $50 to **75.00**

Moonstones Moon buggies, 1976 ....**25.00**

Pink Panther (Flakes) 5-in-1 spy kit, 1970, from $50 to .**100.00**

Quisp ceramic bank, 1971 ..**1,150.00**

Quisp friendship figural ring, 1966 ....**1,250.00**

Quisp or Quake playmate (stuffed toy), 1966, from $125 to ..**150.00**

Quisp propeller beanie, 1966 .**525.00**

Quisp ray gun, 1968 ....**275.00**

Sgt Preston Klondike land deed, 1955 ....**13.00**

Spoonmen spoonriders, 1958, from $20 to **30.00**

Tobor the robot, 1958 ....**75.00**

Tony the Tiger, inflatable, 1953, 30", from $150 to **250.00**

Tony the Tiger (head), cookie jar, 1965 ....**115.00**

Toolie Birds, plastic, 1971, from $15 to **25.00**

Trix rabbit mug, place mat & bowl, 1964 ....**90.00**

US Navy frogmen, 1955, 3", from $25 to **35.00**

USS Nautilus submarine, 5" L, 1960 ....**65.00**

Winnie-the-Pooh spoonriders, 1965, from $10 to **20.00**

Yellow Submarine rub-on sheets, 1969 ....**40.00**

Chalkware

Just beginning to show up in co-ops and at flea markets, funky chalkware plaques (lots of fruit and birds, some of ships or courting couples) appeal to collectors who are getting into the '60s and '70s retro look. Most of it you'll find is marked Miller Studio, though other companies made and marked it as well, and some is unmarked. Miller dated their items, and in addition to the wall plaques (some with thermometers), you might also find bookends and other items. It's very inexpensive right now — our values are mall prices, so naturally they're going to be a high retail. (Dealers who do the leg work in order to offer their customers a good selection must ask more for their merchandise, especially when paying high booth rent.)

Plaque, pink poodle on black, Miller Studios, 1969, from $10.00 to $12.00.

Bookends, frog w/banjo, Stern, pr **15.00**

Note pad holder, Don't You Forget It, w/fruit, Miller, 1968 ...**9.00**

Plaque, bluebird on blossoming cherry branch, 6" **9.50**

Plaque, cherry cluster, CAP, 1969, 12" **12.00**

Plaque, Dutch boy & girl, full figure, 5", pr **12.00**

Plaque, elephant, white w/blue trim, 8" **10.00**

Plaque, fish people, 6", pr, from $12 to **15.00**

Plaque, flower in full bloom w/bee, 6" **9.00**

Plaque, fruit (various), 3", set of 3 ....**12.00**

Plaque, fruit arrangement w/banana, apple, grapes & pear, 11" **12.00**

Plaque, galleon, black & gold, Miller Studio, 1964, lg **8.00**

Plaque, grape cluster, purple w/green leaves, 12" **12.00**

Plaque, Have a Nice Day, sunflower & bird, Miller Studio, 1974, 6½" **10.00**

Plaque, lovers in garden, 12" ..**15.00**

Plaque, parrot, exotic colors, Miller Studio, 1967, 14" **15.00**

Plaque, swan pr on oval, Miller Studio, 1986, sm **9.50**

Plaque, Victorian couple, sq w/bow at top, 13" **16.00**

Pot holder/plaque, apple face & pear face, Miller, 1970, 5", pr **22.00**

Pot holder/plaque, face of Amish boy & girl, Miller, 1970, pr **22.00**

Pot holder/plaque, Mexican boy & girl, full figure, 6", pr **20.00**

Thermometer/plaque, bluebird on branch, Miller Studio, 1972 ....**15.00**

Thermometer/plaque, lady poodle in bubbly tub, Miller Studios, 1973 ....**15.00**

Character and Promotional Glassware

Once routinely given away by fast-food restaurants and soft-drink companies, these glasses have become very collectible; and though they're being snapped up by avid collectors everywhere, you'll still find there are bargains to be had. The more expensive are those with Disney or Walter Lantz cartoon characters, super-heroes, sports greats, or personalities from Star Trek or the old movies. For more information refer to *Collectible Drinking Glasses* by Mark E. Chase and Michael J. Kelley (Collector Books) and *The Collector's Guide to Cartoon and Promotional Drinking Glasses* by John Hervey (L-W Book Sales).

Ranger Joe, Hazel Atlas, red on milk glass, 3", $10.00.

Al Capp, Li'l Abner, Sneaky Pete's
Hot Dogs, 1975, indent base,
$40 to **80.00**

Al Capp, Unwashable Jones/
Schmoos, 1949, Federal,
4¾" **22.00**

Archies, Betty & Veronica Give a
Party, Welch's, 1971, 4¼", $3
to **5.00**

Batgirl, Pepsi, Super Moon Series,
1976, 6½", NM **12.00**

BC Ice Age, Arby's, 1981, 6 different, ea: $3 to **5.00**

Beatles/Mopheads, Yea! Yea! Yea!,
Canadian, 6½" **30.00**

Big Baby Huey, Action Series,
Harvey/Pepsi, late 1970s, 5",
$8 to **12.00**

Big Boy, 50th Anniversary, 1986,
$5 to **7.00**

Blue Fairy (Pinocchio), blue
image w/verse on back, 1940,
4⅜" **20.00**

Broom Hilda, Sunday Funnies,
1976, rare, $100 to **150.00**

Bullwinkle, Static Pose Series,
PAT Ward/Pepsi, late 1970s,
5", $25 to **30.00**

Burger Chef & Jeff, Burger
Chef, Now We're Classified,
$15 to **25.00**

Burger Chef & Jeff, Burger Chef,
1975, $8 to **10.00**

Care Bears, Pizza Hut, 1983,
Friend Bear or Good Luck
Bear, $7 to **10.00**

Clara Peller, Where's the Beef?,
Wendy's, 1985, 6", $5 to ..**8.00**

Currier & Ives, Collector Series,
Arby's, 1978, 4½", $3 to ..**5.00**

Davy Crockett, Holiday Freeze, 7",
from $10 to **15.00**

Dick Tracy, Domino's Pizza, mid-
1970s, Brockway, $100 to .**125.00**

**Underdog, Action Series,
Leonardo TTV/Pepsi, 5",
from $15.00 to $20.00.**

Empire Strikes Back, Burger
King/Coca-Cola, 1980, $3
to **7.00**

ET, Collector Series, Pizza
Hut/Pepsi, 1982, $2 to **3.00**

Flintstone Kids, Pizza Hut, 1986,
$2 to **3.00**

Gasoline Alley, Sunday Funnies,
1976, $8 to **15.00**

Go-Go Gophers, Leonardo
TTV/Pepsi, 6", $15 to **20.00**

Green Lantern, Super Moon Series,
Pepsi, c DC, 1976, $40 to .**60.00**

Henery Hawk, Static Pose
Series, Pepsi, 1973, side
logo, $25 to **40.00**

Heritage Bicentennial Collector
Series, Coca-Cola, 1976, set
of 4 ....**28.00**

Horace Horsecollar, Musical
Notes, Disney, 1937, red &
blue, 4¼" **85.00**

Huckleberry Hound & Yogi Bear, Hanna-Barbera/Pepsi, 1977, $15 to **25.00**

James Bond 007, from R Moore movies, 1985, 4 different, ea: $10 to **15.00**

Josie & the Pussycats, Hanna-Barbera/Pepsi, 1977, $15 to **25.00**

King Kong, Coca-Cola, 1976, 4 different, ea: $5 to **8.00**

Little Orphan Annie, Sunday Funnies, 1976, $8 to **15.00**

Mummy, Universal Studios, 1960s, tall, from $35.00 to $45.00. (Photo courtesy June Moon)

McDonaldland, Action Series, McDonalds, 1977, 6 different, ea: $3 to **5.00**

Mickey Mouse, Bosco, black on clear, 1930s, 3" **45.00**

Mickey Mouse, vertical name, 1930s, 4¼", NM **45.00**

Mickey Mouse Through the Years, Sunoco, 1988, 6 different, ea: $5 to **7.00**

Minnie Mouse, Disney/Hook's Drugs, 1984, $12 to **15.00**

Nursery Rhymes, Big Top Peanut Butter, 1950s, $3 to **5.00**

Pac-man, Arby's, 1980, 4½", $2 to **4.00**

Pierre the Bear, LK's, 1977, 4 different, ea: $3 to **5.00**

Pinocchio, red image w/verse on back, 1940, 4¾" **20.00**

Pittsburgh Penguins, Elby's Big Boy, 1989, 4 different, ea: $6 to **8.00**

Pluto at Disneyland, Coca-Cola **10.00**

Rescuers, Bianca or Penny, WDP/Pepsi, 1977, ea: $10 to **12.00**

Rescuers, Madame Medusa, WDP/Pepsi, 1977, $25 to ..**30.00**

Riddler, Super Moon Series, Pepsi, DC Comics, 1976, $40 to ..**60.00**

Robin, Super Moon Series, Pepsi, 1976, $10 to **15.00**

Shazam!, DC Comics Super Heroes/Pepsi, round base, '78, 5⅝", $15 to **25.00**

Snoopy, Sports Series, Dolly Madison, 4 different, ea ..**5.00**

Snow White & 7 Dwarfs, Disney/Bosco, 1938 ....**37.00**

Spider-Man, Super Heroes, 7-Eleven/Marvel Comics, 1977, $25 to **30.00**

Star Trek, Dr Pepper, 1976, 4 different, ea: $15 to **20.00**

Star Wars, Burger King/Coca-Cola, 1977, 4 different, ea: $5 to ..**7.00**

Superman the Movie, DC Comics, 1978, 6 different, ea: $5 to .**10.00**

Tom & Jerry, Action Series, MGM/Pepsi, '75, 2 different, 5", ea: $6 to **10.00**

Urchins, American Greetings/ Coca-Cola, 1976-78, 6 different, ea: $3 to **5.00**

Winnie the Pooh for President, WDP/Sears, 1970s, $7 to .**10.00**

Wizard of Oz, Swift & Co, Tinman, plain bottom, green, $12 to .**18.00**

Wolfman, Universal Studios Monsters, early 1980s, short, $65 to **85.00**

Woody Woodpecker, Walter Lantz/Pepsi, Brockway, 1970s, $10 to **20.00**

Wyatt Earp, OK Coral, black, gold & green, 4⅞" **25.00**

Character Collectibles

One of the most active areas of collecting today is the field of character collectibles. Flea markets usually yield some of the more common items — toys, books, lunch boxes, children's dishes, and sheet music are for the most part quite readily found.

Trade papers are also an excellent source. Often you will find even the rare and hard-to-find listed for sale. Disney characters, television personalities, and comic book heroes are among the most sought after.

For more information, refer to *Schroeder's Collectible Toys, Antique to Modern* (Collector Books), and *Cartoon Friends of the Baby Boom Era* by Bill Bruegman (see the Directory under Ohio).

See also Advertising; Books; Bubble Bath Containers; Cereal Boxes; Character and Promotional Drinking Glasses; Character Watches and Clocks; Cookie Jars; Fast Foods; Games; Lunch Boxes; MAD Collectibles; Movie Memorabilia; Pencil Sharpeners; Puzzles; Star Trek; Star Wars; Novelty Telephones; Western Heroes; View-Master Reels and Packets.

Batman

Batman was created in 1939 by Bob Kane. He's been imortalized in comic books, TV and movie cartoons, and finally on the silver

Batman belt, Lee, with tag, elastic, child-size, 1982, M on card, $25.00.

screen. A plethora of related merchandise has been marketed over the years. Items from the late '60s are often marked National Periodical Publications.

Batman, bank, Batman bust, Mego, plastic, 1974, 8", M **60.00**
Batman, belt, Lee, w/tag, elastic, child-size, 1982, M **15.00**
Batman, bicycle siren, Empire, 1970s, M (VG box) **10.00**
Batman, charm bracelet, 1966, 8", MOC **50.00**
Batman, Colorforms, 1966, NMIB **40.00**
Batman, figure, Joker, Presents, w/stand, 15", M **35.00**
Batman, night light, 1966, M ..**15.00**
Batman, pencil, w/Penguin topper, NM **2.00**
Batman, pogo stick, lg plastic bust, 1970s, VG **150.00**
Batman, snow-cone cup, 1960s, 5½", M **4.00**
Batman, String Art Kit, Smith, 1976, MIB (sealed) **65.00**
Batman, sunglasses, licensed 1966, w/paper label, scarce, M .**90.00**

Betty Boop

Betty Boop was developed by the Fleischer Studios in 1930. All in all, there were about one hundred black and white cartoons produced during the decade of the '30s. Very few of these early cels remain today. Many of the cartoons were copied and colored in the '60s, and many of these cels are still available. Hoards of related items were marketed in the '30s, and many others were produced over the next forty years. During the '80s, still others were marketed. One of the leading companies in this resurgence of popularity was Vandor; they came out with dozens of different ceramic items. Another innovative company is Bright Ideas of San Francisco; they feature items ranging from playing cards to Christmas tree light sets. King Features still owns the copyright, and all items should carry the appropriate labeling. Our advisor for Betty Boop is Leo A. Mallette, who is listed in the Directory under California.

Ashtray, reclining on piano, Vandor, 1981 ....**55.00**
Bookends, jukebox form, Vandor, 1981, pr **165.00**

Betty Boop doll, cloth with removable clothes, King Features, Colorforms, 1977, 18", M, $60.00.

Box, T-Bird, Vandor, 1986 ...**85.00**
Clock, bed of roses, Vandor ..**65.00**

Clock, covered wagon, Vandor, KS, 1985, rare, from $350 to ..**400.00**
Clock, full figure, Vandor, from $48 to **50.00**
Doll, Cameo Doll/Fleischer Studios, wood body, compo head, 13½", EX **800.00**
Egg cup, Vandor **30.00**
Fan, prewar Japan, paper & wood, moving eyes, 5", M **175.00**
Hand mirror, Vandor, 1983 .**150.00**
Mug, bust of Betty, Vandor, 1981 ....**35.00**
Picture frame, Vandor **45.00**
Salt & pepper shakers, Betty as car hop, Vandor, 1985, pr **45.00**
Tea set, Fleischer Studios, lusterware, 1930s, EX, from $500 to **600.00**
Utensil holder, Vandor, from $15 to **35.00**
Wall hook, figural, Vandor, 1984, rare **125.00**

California Raisins

In the fall of 1986, the California Raisins made their first commercials for television. In 1987 the PVC figurines were introduced. Initially there were four: a singer, two conga dancers, and a saxophone player. At this time Hardee's, the fast food restaurant, issued similar but smaller figures. Later that same year, Blue Surfboard (Horizontal), and three Bendees (which are about 5½" tall with flat pancake-style bodies) were issued for retail sale.

In 1988 twenty-one Raisins were made for sale in retail stores and in some cases used for promotional efforts in grocery stores:

Blue Surfboard (vertical), Red Guitar, Lady Dancer, Blue/Green Sunglasses, Guy Winking, Candy Cane, Santa Raisin, Bass Player, Drummer, Tambourine Lady (there were two styles), Lady Valentine, Male Valentine, Boy Singer, Girl Singer, Hip Guitar Player, Sax Player with Beret, and four Graduates. The Graduates are identical in design to the original four characters released in 1987 but stand on yellow pedestals and are attired in blue graduation caps and yellow tassels. Bass Player and the Drummer were initially distributed in grocery stores along with an application to join the California Raisin Fan Club located in Fresno, California. That same year, Hardee's issued six more: Blue Guitar, Trumpet Player, Roller Skater, Skateboard, Boom Box, and Yellow Surfboard. As was true with the 1987 line, the Hardee's characters were generally smaller than those produced for retail sales.

Eight more made their debut in 1989: Male in Beach Chair, Green Trunks with Surfboard, Hula Skirt, Girl Sitting on Sand, Piano Player, 'AC,' Mom, and Michael Raisin. That year the Raisins starred in two movies: *Meet the Raisins* and *The California Raisins — Sold Out*, and were joined in figurine production by five movie characters (their fruit and vegetable friends): Rudy Bagaman, Lick Broccoli, Banana White, Leonard Limabean, and Cecil Thyme.

First Commercial Issue, Guitar Player, red guitar, 1988, $8.00. (Photo courtesy Larry DeAngelo)

The latest release of Raisins came in 1991 when Hardee's issued four more Raisins: Anita Break, Alotta Style, Buster, and Benny. All Raisins issued for retail sales and promotions in 1987 and 1988, including Hardee's issues for those years, are dated with the year of production (usually on the bottom of one foot). Of those Raisins released for retail sale in 1989, only the Beach Scene characters are dated, and they are actually dated 1988. Hardee's Raisins, issued in 1991, are also undated.

In the last two years, California Raisins have become extremely popular collectible items and are quickly sold at flea markets and toy shows. On Friday, November 22, 1991, the California Raisins were enshrined in the Smithsonian Institution to the tune of *I Heard It Through the Grapevine*. We recommend *Schroeder's Collectible Toys*,

Antique to Modern, for further information about the many miscellaneous items relating to California Raisins that are available. Listings are for loose items in mint condition, and all are marked CALRAB. Our advisor, Larry De Angelo, is listed in the Directory under Virginia.

Beach Theme Issue, girl sitting in sand w/boom box, green shoes, 1988 ....**10.00**
Beach Theme Issue, girl w/grass hula skirt, white gloves, 1988 ....**10.00**
Beach Theme Issue, male in beach chair, orange sandals & glasses, 1988 ....**10.00**
Beach Theme Issue, male w/green trunks & surfboard, white gloves, 1988 ....**10.00**
Christmas Issue, Candy Cane Raisin, green glasses, red sneakers, 1988 ....**9.00**

Christmas Issue, Santa Hat, red cap & green sneakers, 1988 ...**9.00**

Commercial Issue, First; Singer, w/microphone, 1988 ....**8.00**

Commercial Issue, First; Sunglasses 1, eyes visible, 1988 ...**16.00**

Commercial Issue, First; Sunglasses 2, can't see eyes, 1988, M **8.00**

Commercial Issue, First; Winky, hitchhiker pose, 1988 ......**8.00**

Commercial Issue, Second; Bass Player, gray slippers, 1988 ....**8.00**

Commercial Issue, Second; Drummer, black hat, yellow feather, 1988 ....**8.00**

Commercial Issue, Second; Ms Delicious, girl w/tambourine, 1988 ....**12.00**

Commercial Issue, Third; Hip Band Guitarist (Hendrix), 1988 ....**22.00**

Commercial Issue, Third; Hip Band Microphone-Female, Applause, 1988 ....**9.00**

Commercial Issue, Third; Hip Band Microphone-Male, Applause, 1988 ....**9.00**

Commercial Issue, Third; Hip Band Saxophone, black beret, 1988 ....**15.00**

Graduates Post Raisin Bran Issue, Hands, yellow plastic base, 1988 ....**40.00**

Graduates Post Raisin Bran Issue, Saxophone, yellow plastic base, 1988 ....**40.00**

Graduates Post Raisin Bran Issue, Singer, yellow plastic base, 1988 ....**40.00**

Graduates Post Raisin Bran Issue, Sunglasses, yellow plastic base, 1988..........**40.00**

Hardee's 1st Promotion, Hands, thumbs touch head, 1987, sm **3.00**

Hardee's 1st Promotion, Microphone, right hand points up, 1987, sm **3.00**

Hardee's 1st Promotion, Saxophone, gold sax, no hat, 1987, sm ..**3.00**

Hardee's 1st Promotion, Sunglasses, orange glasses, 1987, sm ...**3.00**

Hardee's 2nd Promotion, Captain Toonz, blue boom box, Applause, 1988 .**3.00**

Hardee's 2nd Promotion, FF Strings, blue guitar, Applause, 1988 .**3.00**

Hardee's 2nd Promotion, Rollin' Rollo, w/hat marked H, Applause, 1988 ....**3.00**

Hardee's 2nd Promotion, SB Stuntz, yellow skateboard, Applause, 1988 ....**3.00**

Hardee's 2nd Promotion, Trumpy Trunote, w/trumpet, Applause, 1988 ....**3.00**

Hardee's 2nd Promotion, Waves Weaver, yellow surfboard, Applause, 1988 ....**4.00**

Hardee's 4th Promotion, Alotta Style, w/bags, Applause, 1991, MIP **12.00**

Hardee's 4th Promotion, Anita Break, w/boom box, Applause, 1991, MIP **12.00**

Hardee's 4th Promotion, Benny, bowling ball & bag, Applause, 1991, MIP **12.00**

Hardee's 4th Promotion, Buster, w/skateboard, Applause, 1991, MIP .**12.00**

Key Chains, First; Hands, hands up, thumbs at head, 1987 .**7.00**

Key Chains, First; Microphone, right hand points up, 1987 ....**7.00**

Key Chains, First; Saxophone, gold sax, no hat, 1987 .....**7.00**

Key Chains, First; Sunglasses, orange glasses, fingers at face, 1987 ....**7.00**

Key Chains, Graduate; Hands, thumbs touch head, Applause, 1988 .**35.00**

Key Chains, Graduate; Microphone, right hand points, Applause, 1988 ....**35.00**

Key Chains, Graduate; Saxophone, gold sax, Applause, 1988 ....**35.00**

Key Chains, Graduate; Sunglasses, fingers touch face, Applause, 1988 ....**35.00**

Key Chains, Second; Hip Band Guitarist (Hendrix), w/headband, 1988 ....**35.00**

Key Chains, Second; Hip Band Microphone-Female, yellow shoes, 1988 ....**25.00**

Key Chains, Second; Hip Band Microphone-Male, hand w/open palm, 1988 ....**25.00**

Key Chains, Second; Hip Band Saxophone, black beret, blue eyelids, 1988 ....**25.00**

Meet the Raisins 1st Edition, Banana White, yellow dress, 1989 ....**12.00**

Meet the Raisins 1st Edition, Lick Broccoli, red & orange guitar, 1989 ....**12.00**

Meet the Raisins 1st Edition, Piano, red hair, blue piano, 1989 ....**20.00**

Meet the Raisins 1st Edition, Rudy Bagaman, vegetable cigar, 1989 ....**12.00**

Meet the Raisins 2nd Edition, AC, hand in 'low five' position, 1989 ....**85.00**

Meet the Raisins 2nd Edition, Cecil Thyme, orange carrotlike, 1989 ....**85.00**

Meet the Raisins 2nd Edition, Leonard Limabean, purple coat, 1989 ....**85.00**

Meet the Raisins 2nd Edition, Mom, yellow hair, pink apron, 1989 ..**95.00**

Meet the Raisins, Second Edition, Cecil Thyme, 1989, $85.00. (Photo courtesy Larry De Angelo)

Post Raisin Bran Issue, Hands, hands point opposite ways, 1987 ...**4.00**

Post Raisin Bran Issue, Microphone, right hand makes fist, 1987 ....**6.00**

Post Raisin Bran Issue, Saxophone, inside sax painted black, 1987 ....**4.00**

Post Raisin Bran Issue, Sunglasses, orange glasses, 1987 ...**4.00**

Special Edition, Michael Raisin, silver microphone, stud belt, Applause **20.00**

Special Lovers Issue, Female, holding Be Mine heart, Applause, 1988 ....**8.00**

Special Lovers Issue, Male, holding I'm Yours heart, Applause, 1988 ....**8.00**

Special Raisin Club Issue, Tambourine Female, Applause, 1988 ....**12.00**
Unknown Issue, Blue Surfboard (horizontal), not connected to foot, 1988 ....**50.00**
Unknown Issue, Blue Surfboard (vertical), connected to right foot, 1988 ....**35.00**

Dick Tracy

The most famous master detective of them all, Dick Tracy stood for law and order. Whether up against Boris Arson or the Spider Gang, he somehow always came out on top, teaching his young followers in no uncertain terms that 'Crime Does Not Pay.' Many companies parlayed his persona through hundreds of items for retail sales; and radio premiums such as badges, buttons, secret code books, and rings were free just for 'sending in.' In 1990 with the release of the movie, a new round of potential collectibles appeared. Our advisor is Larry Doucet, who is listed in the Directory under New York. He offers free appraisals to anyone who will send a long SASE and detailed descriptions or photographs.

Book, coloring; Saalfield #399, uncolored, 1946, EX+ **40.00**
Book, Dick Tracy Meets the Night Crawler, Whitman, hardcover, 1945, EX **15.00**
Book, Dick Tracy Tempo, William Johnston, paperback, 1970, NM+ **15.00**
Calendar, Copy Express, color, limited quantities, 1988, NM **45.00**
Candy wrapper, Dick Tracy Candy Bar, Schutter, color, '50s, NM **40.00**
Charm, Dick Tracy, plastic head, gumball machine, EX ...**25.00**
Christmas-tree light bulb, multicolor glass, 1940s, 3¼", EX+.**65.00**
Colorforms Adventure Kit, 1962, NMIB...............................**65.00**

Game, Sunday Funnies, Ideal, 1970s, M, $75.00. (Photo courtesy Dunbar Gallery)

Figurine, painted lead, '30s . **30.00**

Flashlight, Secret Service, pocket size, VG **20.00**

Game, Dick Tracy Detective Game, full color, 14x20", EX+ **60.00**

Note pad, Tracy profile, Rick Fletcher signature, 1970s, 3½x7", M **15.00**

Pin-back, Dick Tracy Detective, Tracy in profile w/gun, '30s, EX **30.00**

Premium, Decoder Card, Post Cereal, red, early '50s, NM **40.00**

Premium, DT Flagship Plane, Quaker, balsa wood, 1930-39, EX+ (in box) **250.00**

Premium, Secret Code Book, Quaker, 1938, 12-page, 3x6", G **15.00**

Premium, Secret Service Patrol Badge, Quacker, blue & gold, 1930-39, EX+ **30.00**

Rubb'r Niks, flexible, includes: gun, wrist radio, holster, 6x9", NM **45.00**

Soaky, Colgate-Palmolive, 1965, 10", EX+ **45.00**

Tie clip, 1933 Chicago World's Fair, metal, 1¾x¾", EX+ **400.00**

Toy, Bullet gun, lugar w/6 bullets & colorful passport **20.00**

Watch, TV; plastic wrist watch viewer, 2 boxes of film strips, NM+ **20.00**

Disney

The movies of Walt Disney have been a part of every child's growing-up years, and the characters they feature as familiar as family. Though it's the items from the '30s and '40s that generally bring such high prices, even memorabilia from more recent movies are collectible. There are many books available for further study: *Character Toys and Collectibles, First and Second Series* and *Antique & Collectible Toys, 1870-1950* by David Longest; *Stern's Guide to Disney Collectibles* by Michael Stern (there are three in the series); and *The Collector's Encyclopedia of Disneyana* by Michael Stern and David Longest. Our advisor for this category is Judy Posner, see the Directory under Pennsylvania.

Area rug, Aristocrats, 46x60", old, EX **375.00**

Ashtray, 3 Little Pigs, lusterware, 1930s, EX **95.00**

Bank, Mickey Mouse, head form, 1971, 12", EX **25.00**

Bank, Mickey Mouse Club House, compo, MIB **25.00**

Bank/gum-ball machine, Scrooge McDuck, Superior/WD, 1989, 9½", MIB **20.00**

Bell, souvenir; Tinker Bell, gold-tone metal, 1950s, 3", EX **59.00**

Book, Lady, Whitman Tell-a-Tale, EX **24.00**

Book, Mickey Mouse & the Boy Thursday, Whitman, 1948, 96-page, EX **35.00**

Bubble pipe, Donald Duck, w/soap powder & spoon, 1950s, 8", MIB **45.00**

Candy container, Rocketeer, Topps, plastic helmet, 2½", M **3.00**

Cane, wood w/compo Mickey at top, Borgfeldt, 1930s, 29", EX **300.00**

Card game, Mickey Mouse Shuffled Symphonies, 1930s, NM, $95.00.
(Photo courtesy Dunbar Gallery)

Card, Christmas; Studio, 1978, unused **75.00**

Ceiling light cover, Winnie the Pooh, EX **40.00**

Change purse, Tinkerbell, vinyl, EX+ **25.00**

Charm, long-billed Donald Duck, costume jewelry, enamel, 1930s, EX **65.00**

Clock, alarm; Mickey Mouse figural, Bradley, 1970s, MIB .**79.00**

Colored pencil set, 1950s, MIB **40.00**

Colorform Sew-ons, Mickey & Minnie, 1960s, MIB **45.00**

Colorforms, Sleeping Beauty, dress designer, 1959, MIB **65.00**

Cup, Mickey Mouse, Safteyware, Mickey, yellow plastic, 1930s, 3", EX **40.00**

Doll, Cinderella, Effanbee, 1985, MIB **50.00**

Figure, Bambi, Character Novelty Company, velvet, 1940s, 12½", EX **85.00**

Figure, Kaa (Jungle Book), cloth, 1967, M **39.00**

Figure, Tramp pup, plush, hang tag remains, 1960s, 12", EX .**29.00**

Figure, Vulture (Jungle Book), cloth, 1967, M **39.00**

Figurine, Baby Flower (the skunk), Shaw Pottery, 3¼", M ...**79.00**

Figurine, Big Bad Wolf, bisque, 1930s, 3½", EX **85.00**

Figurine, Donald's nephew/baseball catcher, Shaw Pottery, 2⅞", EX **95.00**

Figurine, Eeyore, ceramic, older, colorful, 1960s, EX **55.00**

Figurine, Flora (Sleeping Beauty fairy), Hagen-Renaker, 1959, EX **250.00**

Figurine, Mickey Mouse, Leeds, airbrushed pastels, signed, 1940s, M **95.00**

Figurine, Peter Pan, Magic Memories, limited edition, M .**125.00**

Figurine, Pinocchio, Evan K Shaw, minor rub on hat, 1940s, EX **295.00**

Jack-in-the-box, Winnie the Pooh, working, EX **85.00**

Jump rope, Pluto, 1970s, MOC **12.00**

Kaleidoscope, Mickey Mouse, VG **50.00**

Lamp, figural; Donald Duck, Universal Lamp Company, 1969-71, 9½", EX **75.00**

Lamp, figural; Pooh & Eeyore, plastic, works, EX **55.00**

Hot water dish, Donald Duck, Walt Disney
Enterprises, 1930s-40s, $130.00.

Light shade, ceiling; Mickey,
Donald, Minnie & Pluto,
1950s, 14", M 79.00

Mirror, figural Bambi, Thumper,
Flower & Friend Owl, 1960s,
20x24", NM 250.00

Music box, Donald Duck/engineer,
Mickey Mouse Club song,
1960s, EX 75.00

Music box, Mickey & Minnie, Love
Story, 1970s, EX 75.00

Music box, Mickey Mouse, Yankee
Doodle, Bicentennial, Schmid,
EX 75.00

Music box, Mickey Mouse dressed
as cowboy, Schmid, M ..75.00

Night light, Mickey & Donald,
Haunted House, Enesco,
1988, MIB 50.00

Night light, Snow White figural,
plastic, color, 1950s, EX ..125.00

Night light, TV shape, Mickey Mouse
Club, plastic, 1950s, EX ...89.00

Nodder, Donald Duck, plastic,
Walt Disney Productions, 2",
EX 38.00

Party bags, Who Framed Roger
Rabbit, for party favors, plastic, MIP 20.00

Pencil toppers, figural, Nightmare
Before Christmas, ea 6.00

Perfume bottle, Donald Duck, med
bill, figural, colorful, 1940s,
EX 59.00

Pillowcase, Minnie Mouse,
embroidered, framed, 23x20",
EX 150.00

Pin, costume jewelry, Peter Pan,
color, 1950s, EX 35.00

Pin, Mickey & Pluto, multicolored
enamel, 1930s, EX 125.00

Pistol, Mickey Mouse Bubble
Buster, Kilgore, 1930s, 7",
NM 275.00

Planter, Donald Duck, Leeds, airbrushed, signed, 1940s, 7",
EX 75.00

Plate, bicentennial; Mickey Mouse,
Schmid, MIB 55.00

Plate, dinner; Mary Poppins, plastic, Sun Valley Melmac, 9½",
M 29.00

Print, glow-in-the-dark; Snow
White & Dopey, 1940s, original frame, M 48.00

Print, glow-in-the-dark; 3 Little
Pigs Silly Symphony, color,
EX 49.00

Puzzle, Black Hole, Whitman, 1979, 500-pc, unopened ..**32.00**

Record player, Peter Pan, G ...**40.00**

Salt & pepper shakers, figural, Donald Duck & Ludwig Von Drake, '50s, pr **165.00**

Salt & pepper shakers, Kanga & Roo, Enesco, 1964, pr ..**195.00**

Salt & pepper shakers, Snow White & Dopey, Enesco, 1960s, pr .**275.00**

Sheet music, Honest John, 1939, EX **45.00**

Shooting Gallery, Mickey Mouse, 1970s, MOC **12.00**

Spoon, Mickey Mouse, Post Toasties, silverplated, 1930s, EX+ ..**25.00**

Stove, Snow White & the Seven Dwarfs, MIB **75.00**

Switch plate, Winnie the Pooh, WDP, EX+ **6.00**

Switch plate, 3 Little Pigs, plastic, color, 1950s, MIB **32.00**

Tea set, Mary Poppins, plastic, 1964, MIB **95.00**

Tractor, Donald Duck driving, Sunruco/Canada, rubber, 5", EX+ **115.00**

Tray, Disneyland, multicolored litho tin w/very primitive map, EX **75.00**

Tray, lap type, Donald Duck, Casey Jr, 1961, VG+ **24.00**

Wall pocket/planter, Dumbo in the Tree, shelf-sitter, 1940s .**50.00**

Flintstones

Anyone alive today knows that Fred, Wilma, Barney, Betty, Pebbles, and Bamm-Bamm lived in Bedrock, had a dinosaur for a pet, and preferred bowling over any other sport. The invention of Hanna-Barbera who introduced them all in 1959, they met with immediate, sustaining success. To date literally thousands of items featuring the Flintstone crew have been sold such as games, playing cards, pin-back buttons, cookie jars, puzzles, toys, dolls, T-shirts, etc., so today's collectors can build a large and varied collection of Flintstones memorabilia with ease.

Bank, Bamm-Bamm & Dino, from $85 to **90.00**

Bank, Barney, w/bowling ball, Homecraft, 1973, NM ...**30.00**

Bank, Pebbles on Dino, Vandor, 1989, from $45 to **60.00**

Bowl, plastic, 1978, EX **15.00**

Clothes hanger, Bamm-Bamm, 1975, EX **20.00**

Earring tree, Fred, EX+ **35.00**

Erasers, figural, rubber, 6 different characters, 2", EX ...**50.00**

Felt picture kit, 1976, MIB (sealed) **20.00**

Mug, Barney Rubble, Vandor ..**20.00**

Mug, Fred Flintstone, Vandor, 1989, from $15 to **20.00**

Pebble's Fortune Teller, MIP ..**5.00**

Salt & pepper shakers, Pebbles & Bamm-Bamm, Vandor, 1989, pr **40.00**

Super Putty, 1980, MOC **15.00**

Vehicle, Flintmobile, Mattel, 1993, MIB **10.00**

Wall plaque, Bedrock City, 1976, EX **20.00**

Wonder Slate, 1973, MIP (sealed) **15.00**

Garfield

America's favorite grumpy cat, Garfield has his own band of

Bank, football player, Enesco, $45.00.

devotees who are able to find a good variety of merchandise modeled after his likeness. Garfield was created in 1976 by Jim Davis. He underwent many changes by the time he debuted in newspapers in 1978. By 1980 his first book was released, followed quickly in 1981 by a line of collectibles by Dakin and Enesco. The stuffed plush animals and ceramic figures were a huge success. There have been thousands of items made since, with many hard-to-find items being produced in Germany, the Netherlands, England, and other European countries. Banks, displays, PVCs, and figurines are the most desirable from these countries. Our advisor for this category is Adrienne Warren, see the Directory under New Jersey.

Bank, Denver Broncos, vinyl, Enesco, MIB **16.00**
Christmas ornament, Fun in Santa's Sleigh, 1984 .....**45.00**

Clock, Time To Eat, red case, checkerboard background, Sunbeam, EX **12.00**
Cup, A Garfield Float, Pizza Hut, 1992, EX **3.00**
Diecast, Ertl, Garfield in Space Shuttle, M **5.00**
Doll, plush, Uncle Sam, w/tag, M **20.00**
Doll, PVC, in duck innertube, EX .**3.50**
Door chime, wood, Garfield face, Enesco, MIB **25.00**
Figurine, ceramic, Zodiac Virgo, Enesco **15.00**
Hopper, Kat's Meow, wind-up, fuzzy **4.00**
Mug, Santa Garfield standing next to toy sack **5.00**
Musical birthday candle, plays Happy Birthday when lit, Hallmark, MIB **15.00**
Musical Birthday-action, Enesco, MIB **16.00**
Night light, Off the Wall, Prestigeline #PT-5658 ....**15.00**
Nutcracker, wood, Enesco, 8", MIB **35.00**

Phone, lift receiver & eyes open, 1980s, from $15 to..........**35.00**

Pin, Garfield sitting, cloisonne, Kats Meow, MOC **5.00**

Switch plate, Garfield & Odie in tree, Prestigeline #PT-5659, MIP **12.00**

Tin, Christmas cookies, 8" **5.00**

Wacky wind-ups, Cake Walkin', Back to Bed, Tubin', MIP, ea **6.00**

Water dome, Ready, Aim, Romance!, Enesco, MIB .**12.00**

Howdy Doody

The Howdy Doody show was introduced in 1951, and the puppet host and his cast of friends, Buffalo Bob, Flub-a-Dub, Clarabelle, Mr. Bluster, and the Princess became pals to their rapt TV audiences. Merchants filled their shelves with an enormous variety of licensed merchandise. Even into the '70s and '80s, Howdy Doody continued to be marketed, though on a much smaller scale. For further reading see *Howdy Doody, Collector's Reference and Trivia Guide* by Jack Koch (Collector Books).

Bandana, Howdy on horse w/lasso, 1988, 19x19", EX, from $5 to **15.00**

Bank, Howdy's head, Vandor, ceramic, from $75 to ...**125.00**

Bank, musical, Leadworks, Howdy coming out of piano, 1988 ..**65.00**

Bath towel, Howdy on horse, 38x21", M **125.00**

Beanie, red felt w/white felt panel, 1950s, EX **50.00**

Belt buckle, metal, 1976, 2½" ..**35.00**

Bowl, cereal; white w/decals, Taylor-Smith Company, 5½", EX .**15.00**

Camera, Sun Tray, ca 1950-54, M (illustrated card) **90.00**

Can, juice; Welch's Grape Juice Concentrate, Kagran Corp, 1955 .**30.00**

Clock, alarm; Howdy as cowboy, brass, twin bells, Leadworks, 1976, EX **45.00**

Cushion, inflatable, Best Seal Corp, 13" sq **10.00**

Decals, Clarabelle & Mr Bluster, for NBC Inc, 1971 ....**5.00**

Ear muffs, furry, Vacu-U-Form Howdy on ea side, 1950s ..**100.00**

Football, Howdy pictured, 8" .**60.00**

Howdy Doody Figurine Painting Kit, VG in box, $85.00; Howdy Doody's Electric Carnival Game, Harett Gilman Inc., VG in box, $40.00.

Game, Dominos, Ed-U-Card, 1950-54, EX, from $80 to **350.00**

Game, 3 Ring Electric Circus, Harriet-Gilman, 1950, EX, from $35 to **225.00**

Hand puppet, Howdy in TV style box, Kaysam, latex, 1950s, EX **95.00**

Handbag, red, child's size, Howdy's face, 1950s, EX **95.00**

Handkerchief, Howdy on bronco, multicolored, Bob Smith, 8x8" **32.00**

Key chain, flasher, 1950s **18.00**

Mask, rubber w/movable mouth, EX **50.00**

Mug, ceramic, shows 6 characters, 1971 ....**30.00**

Pencil, Howdy's head on top, 1950-54, from $12 to **40.00**

Pinball, Ja-Ru #2312, NBC Inc/King Features Syndicate, 1987, MIP **15.00**

Placemat, Howdy & Friends, color, 9½x12" **25.00**

Planter, seated on barrel, Lefton, 5x5x6½" **100.00**

Record, Story of Howdy Doody, 1976, 12" **10.00**

Ring, silver, raised face of Howdy & Doody, 1950s **95.00**

Salt & pepper shakers, Howdy's head, by Peter Puppet, 1950-54, 3", MIB **175.00**

Slippers, cloth w/plastic head on ea, by Carousel by Guy, 1988, M **15.00**

Spoon holder, ceramic, Vandor, from $35 to **50.00**

Squeeze toy, rubber, Howdy in airplane, Spunky **95.00**

Washcloth, Howdy/Clarabelle, terry-cloth mitt, Ulmann, 1950s, EX **35.00**

Wrist band, plastic **75.00**

Peanuts

First introduced in 1950, the *Peanuts* comic strip has become the world's most widely read cartoon. It appears daily in about 2,200 newspapers. From that funny cartoon about kids (that readers of every age could easily relate to) has sprung an entertainment arsenal featuring movies, books, Broadway shows, toys, theme parks, etc. And surely as the day follow the night, there comes a bountiful harvest of *Peanuts* collectibles. If you want to collect, you should know that authenticity is important. To be authentic, the United Features Syndicate logo and copyright date must appear somewhere on the item. In most cases the copyright date simply indicates the date that the character and his pose as depicted on the item first appeared in the comic strip.

Bank, Snoopy on watermelon, papier-mache **35.00**

Christmas ornament, Snoopy holding stocking, ceramic **30.00**

Cookie cutter, Snoopy on doghouse, Hallmark, MIP ..**15.00**

Cup, snack; Lucy, Thermos .**10.00**

Doll, pocket; Linus, Boucher Assoc, EX **15.00**

Glass, Lucy's Lemonade Stand ..**5.00**

Mug, Girls & Root Beer..., Snoopy, Determined, 1970s, 5" ..**20.00**

Radio, Snoopy on Doghouse, Determined **20.00**

Toy, Woodstock chirper, Determined **20.00**

Nodder, Woodstock, United Feature Syndicate, ca 1965 and 1972, $85.00. (Photo courtesy Hilma R. Irtz)

Wind-up, Snoopy football, Aviva, MIB **10.00**

Raggedy Ann and Andy

Designed by Johnny Gruelle in 1915, Raggedy Ann was named by combining two James Whitcomb Riley poem titles, *The Raggedy Man* and *Orphan Annie*. These early cloth dolls were dated and had painted-on features. You probably won't find those, but Applause made a line in the 1980s that range from $25.00 for a 12" doll, $40.00 for the 17" size, $60.00 for the 25" doll, and $100.00 and up for the large 36" size. Other dolls have been made by Knickerbocker and Hasbro. The Knickerbocker dolls from the 1960s run from $145.00 up to $500.00 depending on size; those from the '70s, about half as much.

Even their dolls from the 1980s run from about $25.00 to $100.00. Hasbro's bear a Playskool label and are still available.

Besides the dolls, scores of other Raggedy Ann and Andy items have been marketed, including books, radios, games, clocks, bedspreads, and clothing. In the last couple of years, collector interest has really taken off, and just about any antique mall you visit today will have an eye-catching display.

Compact, Ann, w/mirror & comb **3.50**
Cup, juice; Ann & Andy, Oneida Ware, 1969 ....**5.00**
Doll, Andy, Hallmark Cards, made in Korea, 5½", G **6.00**
Doll, Andy, Knickerbocker, jointed arms, legs, head, vinyl, 1970s, 6" **8.00**
Doll, Andy, Knickerbocker, 1979, 12", MIB **40.00**
Doll, Ann, blue flowered dress, Hasbro, 12" **11.00**
Doll, Ann, vinyl, jointed, blue dress w/red polka dots, vinyl, 6" .**10.00**
Doll, Ann, wind-up musical, head moves, Applause, 1986, 12" **45.00**
Doll, bean bag; Ann, Toy Works, 1991, 8½", M **12.00**
Finger puppet, Ann, Knickerbocker, 1972, MIP **10.00**
Hand puppet, Ann, Knickerbocker, 1973, MIP **25.00**
Paint-by-numbers set, w/paint & brush, 2-8x10" panels **4.50**
Pillow, stuffed; Ann or Andy, Bobbs-Merrill, 1973, G .**10.00**
Radio, AM, portable, Bobbs-Merrill, 1973, NM **25.00**

Raggedy Ann and Andy talking Bank, Janex Corp., copyright 1977, NM, $45.00.

Squeeze toy, Ann, made in Taiwan, 5" **1.50**

Stapler, Ann, Janex Corp, 1975 ....**15.00**

Talking alarm clock, battery cover missing, works, rare, 1974, G **25.00**

Wall plaque, Ann, plastic, Syroco Inc, 1977, 14" **10.00**

Smurfs

A creation of Pierro 'Peyo' Culliford, the little blue Smurfs that we have all come to love have found their way to the collectibles market of today. There is a large number of items currently available at reasonable prices, though some, such as metal lunch boxes, cereal premiums and boxes, and promotional items and displays, are beginning to attract special interest. Because the Smurfs' 'birthplace' was in Belgium, many items are European in nature. The values listed here are for items in mint condition. Our advisor for this category is Adrienne Warren, see the Directory under New Jersey. Those seeking further information may contact the Smurf Collectors' Club, listed in our Clubs and Newsletters section.

Alarm clock, Bradley, 2-bell windup, MIB **25.00**

Bank, Smurf in airplane, Wallace Berrie **20.00**

Box, Hardee's Fun Meal, 1988/1990, ea **6.00**

Car, Burago, Italy, MIB, $50 to ..**75.00**

Cottage, lg mushroom, MIB ..**50.00**

Doll, Smurfette, 1981, stuffed, 8", EX **10.00**

Doll Smurfs & Smurfette, plush, Wallace Berrie, M w/tag, ea, from $5 to **25.00**

Doll stroller, VG **25.00**

Figurine, advertising, PVC, several, M, from $35 to **100.00**

Figurine, pewter, M, from $15 to **35.00**

Figurine, porcelain, Wallace-Berrie, ea, from $15 to ..**20.00**

Figurine, PVC, several different, NM, ea, from $2 to **4.00**

Figurine, PVC, USA issue, M, from $3 to **4.50**

Fire truck, Ertl, diecast, loose .**5.00**

Fun House, wind-up, Galoob, MIB **15.00**

Jack-in-the-box, plastic, 1982, VG **45.00**

Jewelry, cloisonne, MOC, ea, from $5 to **10.00**

Music box, walking figure, light paint wear, 1982 ....**10.00**

Musical top, Ohio Art, tin litho, 1982, MIB **20.00**

Pencil case, w/Smurfette, M ..**3.00**

Playset, Windmill, MIB **45.00**

Playsets, Super Super, MIB, different editions, from $25 to **200.00**

Puzzle, Smurfette ice skating, Playschool, EX **8.00**

Radio & headset, AM, Power-Tronic, MIB **10.00**

Record player, 1982, EX **20.00**

Scooter, plastic, G **25.00**

Toothbrush & cup set, MIB .**25.00**

Tote bag, w/Smurfette, MIP ..**5.00**

Toy, Space Traveler, 1978, MOC **25.00**

Truck, lift; Hong Kong, MIB ..**10.00**

Vehicle, diecast, Ertl, MOC, ea ..**10.00**

Zipper pull, Brainy or Smurfette, hard plastic w/clip, 2½", ea ..**5.00**

Warner Brothers

Bugs Bunny and Porky Pig were some of the original Warner Brothers characters, first appearing in cartoon form in 1938. The studio closed in 1963, but they and several other characters (some of which we've featured below) remained popular with kids and collectors alike since the cartoons have been in syndication for TV ever since.

Bugs Bunny, bank, Homecraft, multicolored vinyl, 13", EX **25.00**

Bugs Bunny, bookends, 1970, EX, pr **20.00**

Bugs Bunny, Cartoon-O-Graph, NM (VG box) **15.00**

Bugs Bunny, cookie mold, 1978, EX **5.00**

Bugs Bunny, cup dispenser, 1989, MIP **8.00**

Bugs Bunny, diecast figure in train, Ertl, MOC **5.00**

Bugs Bunny, doll, Mighty Star, stuffed, 18", NM **15.00**

Bugs Bunny, game, Race in Space, Whitman, 1980, complete, EX **12.00**

Bugs Bunny, gumball dispenser, Bugs w/carrot on tree trunk, mini, MOC **10.00**

Bugs Bunny pencil holder, 1940s, 5x6x4", NM, from $50.00 to $125.00. (Photo courtesy Dunbar Gallery)

Bugs Bunny, jack-in-the-box, Mattel, 1970s, VG **15.00**

Bugs Bunny, lamp, Bugs in chair, 1970, EX **30.00**

Bugs Bunny, napkin, Happy Birthday, 1972, 24-count, MIP **5.00**

Bugs Bunny, planter, ceramic, 1950s, M **35.00**

Bugs Bunny, soap, 1930s, MIB **45.00**

Bugs Bunny, tablecloth, paper, 1972, 52x96", MIP **5.00**

Bugs Bunny, tray, litho metal, 1982, 17x12", EX **10.00**

Cool Cat, poster, 1968, M **10.00**

Daffy Duck, candle holder, painted bisque, 1980, M **35.00**

Daffy Duck/Pepe Le Pew, place mat, Pepsi, plastic w/graphics, 1976, NM **6.50**

Elmer Fudd, figure, American Pottery, 1940s, 6½", NM **75.00**

Elmer Fudd, Fire Chief pull toy, wood, 1950s, EX **60.00**

Elmer Fudd, pencil holder, diecast figure, 1940s, NM **125.00**

Elmer Fudd, pistol/flashlight, EX **15.00**

Elmer Fudd, wristwatch, Sheraton, 1972, M (orig package) ...**85.00**

Porky Pig, bank, 1972, 16", EX .**26.00**

Porky Pig, cookie mold, 1978, EX **5.00**

Road Runner, figure, PVC, Shell Gas premium, MIP **3.00**

Speedy Gonzales, doll, Mighty Star, cloth, 1971, EX+ ...**20.00**

Sylvester, blow-up figure, 1970, 8", EX **8.00**

Sylvester, doll, velour, 5", VG .**8.00**

Sylvester, hand puppet, cloth, 1990, EX **12.00**

Sylvester, rattle, 1975, EX **6.00**

Tasmanian Devil, doll, stuffed, Mighty Star, 12", NM **30.00**

Tasmanian Devil, figure, Taz on motorcycle, diecast, Ertl, 1989, MOC **25.00**

Tweety Bird, doll, Dakin, 1969, 7½", NM- **32.00**

Tweety Bird & Sylvester, bowl, plastic, EX **4.00**

Wile E Coyote, doll, Dakin, w/tag, 1968, 12", MIB **30.00**

Yosemite Sam, air freshener, Medeo, 1990, MIP **15.00**

Yosemite Sam, hand puppet, toothpaste premium, M .**12.00**

Yosemite Sam, transfer, Vogart, 1971, MIP **20.00**

Miscellaneous Cartoon and Kids' Show Characters

Alvin & the Chipmunks, doll, Alvin, stuffed, 1987, 7", EX **6.00**

Andy Panda (Woody Woodpecker), ring w/embossed figure, NM **20.00**

Aristocats, Colorforms, 1960s, NM (EX box) **38.00**

Babba Louie, figural fun bath, w/tag, 1976, M **15.00**

Banana Splits, tambourine, MIP **35.00**

Bozo the Clown, figure, Super Flex, MOC **20.00**

Bozo the Clown, gumball dispenser, figural, 1987, 2¾", MOC **10.00**

Bullwinkle, figure, Whamo, bendable, 1972, EX **20.00**

Buzz Sawyer, Christmas card, 1950s, unused, NM+ **14.00**

Capt Caveman, figure, plastic, 1970s, 3", EX+ **25.00**

Casper the Friendly Ghost, candy bucket, plastic, EX+ **30.00**

Dennis the Menace, night light, w/Ruff **55.00**

Deputy Dawg, bagatelle game, Imperial Toy, 1978, NM .**8.00**

Dr Dolittle, medical kit, Hasbro #1345, NMIB **75.00**

Dr Dolittle, stick horse, Toggle, AJ Renzi Plastic Corp, 1972, NMIB **40.00**

Dr Suess, doll, Lorax, Coleco, M .**30.00**

Family Affair, hat box, Buffy, 1969, EX **50.00**

Felix the Cat, flasher ring, Vari-Vue, 1960s-70s, M **25.00**

Ghostbusters, Ecto 500 Race Car, MIB **35.00**

Ghostbusters, tray, 1986, M .**30.00**

Gremlins, night light, Gizmo figure, MOC **25.00**

Gumby, cowboy outfit, MOC ..**18.00**

Gumby, jeep, Lakeside, no windshield, 1965, G (VG box) ..**18.00**

Heckle & Jeckle, magic slate, Lowe, 1952, EX+ **18.00**

Hong Kong Phooey, iron-on transfer, 1976, M **20.00**

Huckleberry Hound, rug, multicolored, 1950s, VG **35.00**

Inspector Gadget, Shrinky Dinks, Colorforms, 1983, MIB .**27.00**

Inspector Gadget, wastebasket, 1980s, NM **55.00**

Jetsons, cap, EX **8.00**

Land of the Lost, figure, Christa, Krofft, bendable, 1991, MOC **8.00**

Laurel & Hardy, bank, Hardy, Play Pal, 1974, 7", VG ..**22.00**

Little Lulu, jewelry box, Larami, 1973, NMIP (sealed) **12.00**

Mighty Mouse, bagatelle game, Imperial Toy, 1978, NM .**8.00**

Mister Magoo, tattoo wrapper, Fleer, 1967, 1½x3½", M .**15.00**

Mother Goose, jack-in-the-box, Mattel, 1971, working, EX+ .**25.00**

Muppet Babies, Shrinky Dinks, 1985, MIB **15.00**

Olive Oyl, mirror, King Features, 1980, 6¾x5½", G **5.00**

Olive Oyl, ponytail holder, King Features, 1958, MOC **30.00**

Pink Panther, jewelry set, 1989, MOC **12.00**

Bozo Circus Train, Multiple Toymakers #875, ca 1970, MIB, $70.00.

Pink Panther waste can, 1982, 11¾", M, $25.00.

Popeye, mug, Vandor, 1980 .**38.00**

Popeye, paper party cup, Happy Birthday, 3", M **8.00**

Popeye, pipe bubble blower & bubbles, MOC **20.00**

Popeye & Olive Oyl, salt & pepper shakers, Vandor, 1980, pr **125.00**

Princess of Power, talking toothbrush, NM **40.00**

Quick Draw McGraw, TV tray, metal, 1960s, unused, M **45.00**

Ricochet Rabbit, plate, Melmac, 1960s, 8", EX **25.00**

Road Runner, w/launcher & chute, Rayline, 1970s, MOC **40.00**

Rocky & Bullwinkle, sewing card, 1961, EX **25.00**

Scooby Doo, bank, vinyl w/felt vest, NM **25.00**

Scooby Doo, rubber stamp, 1982, MOC **10.00**

Sesame Street, tray, tin litho, 1971, 17x12", EX **12.00**

Simpsons, paper plates, Chesapeake, 9", 8 per package, MIP **4.50**

Spider-Man, book bag, canvas, EX **12.00**

Spider-Man, wall climber, PVC, w/suction cup, 3", M ...**25.00**

Superman, bread bag, 1966, NM **15.00**

Superman, kite, 1971, MIP .**22.00**

Superman, scissors, 1973, MOC **16.00**

Underdog, pillow, white inflatable vinyl, EX **23.00**

Woody Woodpecker, banjo, MIB **25.00**

Yogi Bear, bean pinball game, 1970s, MOC **10.00**

Character Watches and Clocks

Since the 1930s kids have enjoyed watches whose dials depicted their favorite cartoon character, western hero, or movie and TV personality. They're relatively scarce today (since they often met with abuse at the hands of their young owners) and as a result can be rather expensive to collect. The boxes they came in are even harder to find and are often tagged with prices about equal to that of the watch they contained. Condition is of the utmost importance when evaluating a watch or clock such as these — watch for rust, fading, scratches, or other signs of wear that will sharply decrease their values. Refer to *Comic Character Clocks and Watches* by Howard S. Brenner (Books Americana) for more information.

Clocks

Bambi Animated Alarm, blue case, Bayard, WDP, 1964, VG ..**225.00**

Batman & Robin, action pose on face, wind-up alarm, 1980s, 4½", M **15.00**

Batman Talking Alarm, Janex, w/Robin in Batmobile, 1974, 7x7x3", EX **90.00**

Betty Boop Alarm, China, w/Koko & Bimbo on round dial, 6", EX in box **55.00**

Bugs Bunny alarm clock, Ingraham, 1950s, 5" square, M, $375.00. (Photo courtesy Dunbar Gallery)

Bugs Bunny Talking Alarm, Eh Wake Up Doc, 1974, EX **30.00**

Donald Duck, Glen Clock of Scotland, in garden w/bird, 5½" sq, EX **250.00**

Donald Duck, pendulum weight w/moving eyes, 1960s, NM in EX box **100.00**

Dr Seuss Alarm, Cat in Hat, swinging arms for hands, 2-bell, 1978, 6" **70.00**

Green Sprout, talking alarm, M **36.00**

Mickey Mouse Alarm, Bayard, running on round face, 1960s, M in EX box **200.00**

Mickey Mouse Alarm, Germany, lg face, tin ears, red case, 1960, 5", EX **35.00**

Roy Rogers & Trigger Alarm, Ingraham, desert scene, 1950s, 4x4", EX **175.00**

Scrooge McDuck Alarm, Bayard, Scrooge & gold coins, 1950, 5", EX **155.00**

Smokey the Bear Alarm, Germany, Prevent..., 2-bell, 1960s, 7", EX .**100.00**

Snoopy Alarm, United Features Syndicate, playing tennis, 1958, 4", EX- **35.00**

Snoopy Doghouse Alarm, Salton, LED, 6", M **40.00**

Tom Mix Alarm, Germany, name & bust, gold case, 1950s, 3½", EX **75.00**

Watches

Alien, w/wraparound tail band, 1980s, MOC **20.00**

Bart Simpson, Nelsonics, LCD, 5-function, multicolor plastic, MOC **12.00**

Batman Action Watch, Gilbert, 1965, MIB **390.00**

Batman Binky Flasher, face flashes from Batman to Robin, 1960s-70s, NM **15.00**

Beauty & the Beast, Disney, quartz, limited edition, 1994, M .**150.00**

Bozo the Clown, 1971, MOC .**20.00**

Bugs Bunny, Timex/Warner Bros, carrots as hands, 1955 .**325.00**

Campbell's Soup Kid (boy), 50th Anniversary, working, 1982, EX **48.00**

Capt Marvel, w/original band, unused, M **350.00**

Batman wristwatch, man's, gold color, expansion band, black bat on face, May 1984, no other printing, from $55.00 to $60.00. (Photo courtesy Lee Garmon)

Dick Tracy, New Haven, working, original band, 1947, VG+ **125.00**

Dukes of Hazzard, Unisonic, LCD quartz, w/stainless band, 1982, MIB **40.00**

Goofy, Lorus, Walt Disney, Japan movement, runs backwards, 1991, M **30.00**

Hopalong Cassidy, 100th Anniversary, w/neckerchief & slide, MIB **100.00**

Jughead, Cheval, Archie Comic Pub, Hong Kong, plastic case, 1989, MIB **30.00**

Little Orphan Annie & Sandy, illustrated dial, gold-tone band, 1970, M **28.00**

Madonna, MOC **35.00**

Mickey Mouse, Ingersoll, measles face, 1947, MIB **350.00**

Minnie Mouse, Brio, Walt Disney World Showcase of Dolls, 1990, MIB **150.00**

New Kids on the Block, metal w/leather band, working, EX **12.00**

Six Million Dollar Man, Berger, Universal, Swiss movement, 1976, VG **75.00**

Snoopy, Armitron, quartz, gold face, leather band, 1989, M **80.00**

Snoopy Tennis Player, Times, UFS, Swiss movement, 1970s, VG **75.00**

Superman, New Haven, lg size, EX+ **475.00**

007 Sercret Service Wristwatch, Imperial, dial lights, 1984, MOC **56.00**

Children's Books

Books were popular gifts for children in the latter 1800s; many were beautifully illustrated, some by notable artists such as Frances Brundage and Maxfield Parrish. From this century tales of Tarzan by Burroughs are very collectible as are those familiar childhood series books, for example, The Bobbsey Twins and Nancy Drew.

Big Little Books

Probably everyone who is now forty to sixty years of age owned a few Big Little Books as a child. Today these thick hand-sized adventures bring prices from $10.00 to $75.00 and upwards. The first was published in 1933 by Whitman Publishing Company. Dick Tracy was the featured character. Kids of the early '50s preferred the format of the comic book, and the Big Little Books were gradually phased out. Stories about super heroes and Disney characters bring the highest prices, especially those with an early copyright. For more information see *Big Little Books* by Larry Jacobs (Collector Books).

Captain Midnight and the Moon Woman, #1452, EX, $75.00.

Andy Panda & the Pirate Ghosts, Whitman, #1459, 1949, NM **40.00**
Buck Jones, The Rough Riders, Whitman, #1486, 1943, NM **45.00**
Buck Rogers & the Depth Men of Jupiter, #1169, VG/EX **60.00**
Bugs Bunny & His Pals, Whitman, #1496, 1945, EX ...**40.00**
Chandu the Magician, #1093, EX **60.00**
Dick Tracy & the Crooks in Disguise, #1479, NM **90.00**
Donald Duck, Off the Beam, #1438, EX **45.00**
Felix the Cat, Whitman, #1439, 1945, EX+ **70.00**
Ghost Avenger, #1462, EX **38.00**
Green Hornet Cracks Down, Whitman, #1480, 1942, EX **75.00**
Man From UNCLE, Whitman, 1967, EX+ **15.00**
Mickey Mouse & the Magic Lamp, 1942, EX+ **75.00**
Polly & Her Pals on the Farm, #1060, VG+ **30.00**

Popeye & Castor Oyl the Detective, Whitman, #1497, EX **35.00**
Red Ryder & Hoofs of Thunder, #1400, NM **70.00**
Spike Kelly of the Commandos, Whitman, #1467, 1943, EX **20.00**
Tarzan Lord of the Jungle, Whitman, #1407, 1946, NM .**45.00**

Dick and Jane

Dick and Jane readers were very common first-grade textbooks from the 1930s until the mid-1970s. Not only were they used in public schools in the United States, they were also used on military bases worldwide and in Roman Catholic and Seventh Day Adventists' schools. Even today they're used in Mennonite and Amish schools. These books have been published in the US, Canada, the Philippine Islands, Australia, and New Zealand.

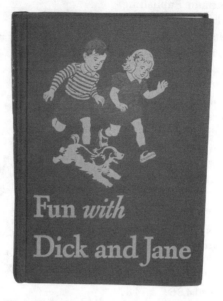

Fun With Dick and Jane, hardcover, 1946-47, VG, $125.00.

Before We Read, soft cover, school stamp, 1962, EX **75.00**

Dick & Jane, soft cover, 1936, VG+ **250.00**

Fun Wherever We Are, soft cover, 1962, VG **70.00**

Fun Wherever We Are, soft cover, 1965, G **40.00**

Fun With Our Family, soft cover, 1962, VG **70.00**

Fun With Our Family, teacher's edition, hardcover, 1962, G **75.00**

Fun With Our Friends, hardcover, 1962, VG **50.00**

Fun With Our Friends, teacher's edition, hardcover, 1962, EX **75.00**

Good Times With Our Friends, soft cover, 1953, VG **75.00**

Good Times With Our Friends, soft cover, 1954, G **50.00**

Guess How, hardcover, 1951, 6x8", VG **35.00**

Guess Who, soft cover, 1951, VG **70.00**

Guess Who, teacher's edition, soft cover w/school stamp, 1951, VG ..**75.00**

More Dick & Jane Stories, soft cover, 1934, VG+ **250.00**

New Friends & Neighbors, hardcover, 1956, VG **50.00**

New Fun With Dick & Jane, hardcover, 1951, VG **45.00**

New Guess Who, hardcover, school stamp, 1962, VG .**60.00**

New Guess Who, teacher's edition, hardcover, 1962, NM **75.00**

New Our New Friends, Cathedral edition, 1952, G **35.00**

New Our New Friends, hardcover, school stamp, 1956, G ...**50.00**

New Our New Friends, teacher's edition, hardcover, 1956, G .**50.00**

New Our New Friends, 2nd 1st-grade reader, 1945, VG+, from $55 to **65.00**

New We Come & Go, soft cover, 1956, VG **70.00**

New We Work & Play, 2nd of 3 pre-primers, soft cover, 1956, VG **65.00**

Our New Friends, 2nd 1st-grade reader, 1946, VG+ **60.00**

Sally, Dick & Jane, soft cover, 1962, VG **70.00**

Think-&-Do Book, workbook, soft cover, 1962, unused **20.00**

We Come & Go, 3rd/last primer, 1956, VG **30.00**

We Read More Pictures, soft cover, 1963, EX **75.00**

We Read More Pictures, teacher's edition, soft cover, 1951, VG **75.00**

We Talk, Spell & Write, soft cover, 1951, VG **75.00**

Little Golden Books

Little Golden Books (a registered trademark of Western Publishing Company Inc.), introduced in October of 1942, were an overnight success. First published with a blue paper spine, the later spines were of gold foil. Parents and grandparents born in the '40s, '50s, and '60s are now trying to find the titles they had as children. From 1942 to the early 1970s, the books were numbered from 1 to 600, while books published later had no numerical order. Depending on where you find the book, prices can vary from 25¢ to $30.00 plus. The most expensive are those with dust jackets from the early '40s or books with paper dolls and activities. The three primary series of books are the Regular (1-600), Disney (1-140), and Activity (1-52).

Television's influence became apparent in the '50s with stories like the Lone Ranger, Howdy Doody, Hopalong Cassidy, Gene Autry, and Rootie Kazootie. The '60s brought us Yogi Bear, Huckleberry Hound, Magilla Gorilla, and Quick Draw McGraw, to name a few. A TV Western title from the '50s is worth around $12.00 to $18.00. A Disney from 1942 to the early '60s will go for $8.00 to $15.00 (a few even higher; reprinted titles would be lower). Cartoon titles from the '60s would range from $6.00 to $12.00. Books with the blue spine or gold paper spine (not foil) can bring from $8.00 to $15.00. If you are lucky enough to own a book with a dust jacket, the jacket alone is worth $20.00 and up. Paper doll books are worth around $30.00 to $36.00. These prices are meant only to give an idea of value and are for 1st editions in mint condition. Condition is very important when purchasing a book. You normally don't want to purchase a book with large tears, crayon or ink marks, or missing pages.

As with any collectible book, a 1st edition is always going to bring the higher prices. To tell what edition you have on the 25¢ and 29¢ cover price books, look on the title page or the last page of the book. If it is not on the title page, there will be a code of 1/(a letter of the alphabet) on the bottom right corner of the last page. A is for 1st edition, Z would refer to the twenty-sixth printing.

There isn't an easy way of determining the condition of a book. What is 'good' to one might be 'fair' to another. A played-with book in average condition is generally worth only half as much as one in mint, like-new condition. To find out more about Little Golden Books, we recommend *Collecting Little Golden Books* (published by Books Americana).

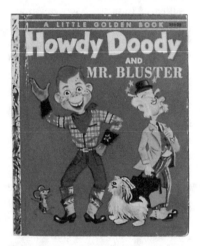

Howdy Doody and Mr. Bluster, $25.00.

Aladdin, Disney, #107-88, 1993, VG/EX **2.00**
Black Beauty, Saalfield, #1047, 1934, G **4.00**
Book of God's Gifts, #112, 4th edition, VG/EX **4.00**
Bugs Bunny & the Indians, #120, C edition, VG+ **12.00**

Christmas Carols, #26, 1946, 1st edition, EX **15.00**
Cowboy Millionaire, Saalfield #1106, VG **20.00**
Dennis the Menace, #386, B edition, VG/EX **7.00**
Elves & the Shoemaker, #307-56, B edition, VG/EX **4.00**
Golden Book of Birds, #13, 4th edition, EX **12.00**
Hansel & Gretel, #17, D edition, VG/EX **14.00**
Jetsons, 1962, EX **25.00**
Ken Maynard in Strawberry Roan, Saalfield, #1090, G **10.00**
Little Red Riding Hood, #300-65, 1992, illustrated by J Evers, EX **4.00**
Lone Ranger, #263, A edition, EX **22.00**
Mr Ed, #483, A edition, VG/EX **17.00**
Peter Pan, Disney, #104-68, 1992, VG/EX **2.00**
Robin Hood, #D126, 1st edition, VG/EX **12.00**
Sky, #270, A edition, 24 pages, VG/EX **10.00**
Story of Jesus, #27, D edition, VG/EX **12.00**
Uncle Wiggily, #148, A edition, VG/EX **14.00**
What Am I?, #58, B edition, VG/EX **10.00**

Series

Everyone remembers a special series of books they grew up with: The Hardy Boys, Nancy Drew Mysteries, Tarzan — there were countless others. And though these are becoming very collectible today, there were many editions of each, and most are very easy to find. As a result, common titles are sometimes worth very little. Generally the last few in any series will be the most difficult to locate, since fewer were printed than the earlier stories which were likely to have been reprinted many times. As is true of any type of book, first editions or the earliest printing will have more collector value. For further reading see *Collector's Guide to Chidren's Books, 1850 to 1950*, by Diane McClure Jones and Rosemary Jones (Collector Books).

Beverly Gray's Scoop, Clair Blank, McLoughlin, 1954, VG ..**15.00**
Bobbsey Twins at School, Laura Lee Hope, Grosset Dunlap, 1941, NM **15.00**
Bobbsey Twins on Ranch, LL Hope, Grosset Dunlap, 1935, w/jacket, VG **15.00**
Cherry Ames Cruise Nurse, Helen Wells, Grosset Dunlap, VG **5.00**
Chip Hilton: Championship Ball, Grosset Dunlap, 1948, w/jacket, VG **16.00**
Dana Girls: Clue of Rusty Key, C Keene, Grosset Dunlap, 1942, w/jacket **22.00**
Hardy Boys' Detective Handbook, Dixon, Grosset Dunlap, 1959, VG **10.00**
Hardy Boys: Missing Chums, Dixon, Grosset Dunlap, 1942, w/jacket, VG **60.00**
Lone Ranger, Fran Striker, Grosset Dunlap, 1938, w/jacket, VG .**15.00**
Lone Ranger & Gold Robbery, Striker, Grosset Dunlap, 1939, VG **35.00**

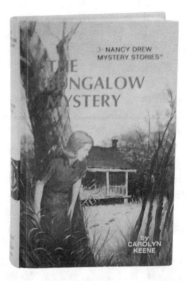

Nancy Drew, The Bungalow Mystery, third in series, Carolyn Keen, Grosset Dunlap #9503, 1960, EX, $6.00.

Oz: Princess of Oz, Baum, Reilly Lee, blue cloth cover, ca 1920, G .**95.00**
Oz: Woodman...Original Story, Baum, Reilly Lee, cloth cover, 1955, VG **20.00**
Tom Swift & His Jetmarine, Appleton, Grosset Dunlap, 1954, VG .**20.00**

Whitman Tell-A-Tale Books

Though the Whitman Company produced a wide variey of children's books, the ones most popular with today's collectors (besides the Big Little Books which are dealt with earlier in this category) are the 8" books known as 50¢ juveniles. They were published in a variety of series, many of which centered around radio, TV, and comic strips. For more information, photos, and current values, we recommend *Whitman Juvenile Books, Reference & Value Guide*, by David and Virginia Brown (Collector Books).

Bambi, #2548, 1972, VG/EX ..**4.00**
Cinderella, #2552, 1954, VG/EX .**7.00**
Donald Duck & the New Birdhouse, #2520, 1956, VG/EX **8.00**
Hooray for Lassie, 1964, EX ..**8.00**
Johnny Appleseed, #808, 1949, VG/EX **18.00**
Little Black Sambo, Helen Bannerman, 1950, VG **15.00**
Roy Rogers Sure 'Nough Cowpoke, VG **15.00**
Woody Woodpecker's Peck of Troubles, #2562, 1951, VG/EX **6.00**
Yogi Bear & the Super Scooper, 1961, EX+ **5.00**

Wonder Books

Though the first were a little larger, the Wonder Books printed since 1948 have all measured 6½" x 8". They've been distributed by Random House, Grosset Dunlap, and Wonder Books Inc. They're becoming very collectible, especially those based on favorite TV and cartoon characters. Steve Santi's book *Collecting Little Golden Books* includes a section on Wonder Books as well.

Baby Elephant, #541, 1950, VG/EX **6.00**
Copycat Colt, #545, 1951, illustrated by C Steiner, VG/EX **10.00**

Fred Flintstone's Surprising Corn, #918, 1976, VG/EX **6.00**

A Surprise for Felix, 1959, NM, $14.00.

How Peter Cottontail Got His Name, illustrated by Jackson, 1957, VG **15.00**
Huckleberry Hound, Handy Hound, Stand-Up Story Book, 1975, EX+ **5.00**
Little Peter Cottontail, pictorial boards, Mary & Carl Hauge, 1954, VG **30.00**
Little Schoolhouse, #310, 1958, VG/EX **5.00**
Peter Pan, #597, 1952 ....**5.00**
Peter Goes to School, #600, 1953, EX **5.00**
Roly-Poly Puppy, #549, 1950, VG/EX **7.00**
Sleeping Beauty, #635, 1956, VG/EX **5.00**
Three Little Pigs/Red Riding Hood, #609, 1975, 2-in-1 book....**14.00**
Tom Corbett's Trip to the Moon, 1950s, NM **35.00**
Traveling Twins, hardcover, 1953, 7x8", NM **8.00**

Teddy Bear Tales, Joan Walsh Anglund, Random House, first edition, 1985, NM, $18.00. (Photo courtesy Marvelous Books)

Miscellaneous

ABC & Busy Days, Samuel Lowe, soft cover, ca 1940, oblong, 8x11", VG **25.00**

Billy's Farm Friends, Volland, linen-like paper, 1923, VG **55.00**

Child's Garden of Verses, Stevenson, McLoughlin Color Classics, 1939, G **15.00**

Cinderella, Fern B Peat, Harper, stiff wrappers, 1931, 9x13", VG .**70.00**

Donald Duck in Bringing Up Father, Whitman, 1948, VG **22.00**

Ferdinand the Bull, Lawson, Viking, 1st edition, 1936, VG ...**145.00**

How 6 Found Christmas, Hyman, Little Brown, 1st edition, 5x8", VG **18.00**

Little Black Sambo, Whitman, pictorial boards, 1934, 6x7", VG **110.00**

Little House in Big Woods, Wilder, Harper & Bros, '53, 1st edition, VG **40.00**

Lullaby for Eggs, Jones, Bridgman, MacMillan, cloth cover, 1955, VG+ **25.00**

Morning Is a Little Child, Anglund, Harcourt, cloth, 1969, 8x10", EX **22.00**

Peter Pan & Wendy, Attwell, Barrie, Scribner, cloth cover, 1930, VG **65.00**

Raggedy Ann Stories, Gruelle, Bobbs-Merrill, hardcover, 1961, VG+ **25.00**

Santa Claus & Little Lost Kitten, Whitman, Fuzzy Wuzzy Book, 1952, VG **20.00**

Santa's Busy Day, pop-up, Polygraphic Co, 1953, 8x10", VG+ **85.00**

Teddie's Best Christmas Tree, Chapin, picture boards, 1929, VG **25.00**

Uncle Wiggily & the Barber, Garis, Platt & Munk, soft cover, 1939, EX **10.00**

Children's Dishes

In the late 1900s glass companies introduced sets of small-scaled pressed glass dinnerware, many in the same pattern as their regular lines, others designed specifically for the little folks. Many were of clear glass, but milk glass, opalescent glass, and colors were also used. Not to be outdone, English ceramic firms as well as American potteries made both tea sets and fully accessorized dinnerware sets decorated with decals of nursery rhymes, animals, or characters from children's stories. Though popularly collected for some time, your favorite flea market may still yield some very nice examples of both types. Refer to *The Collector's Encyclopedia of Children's Dishes* by Margaret and Kenn Whitmyer (Collector Books) for more information.

Ceramic

Bowl, Miniature Blue Willow, England, 2", from $30 to **35.00**
Casserole, Bluebird, Knowles-Taylor-Knowles, w/lid, 5½" **45.00**
Creamer, chauffeur w/lady, pink lustre trim, Germany, from $22 to **27.00**
Creamer, Daffodil, Southern Potteries, 3" **20.00**
Creamer, Orient, blue Oriental scene on white, from $20 to **25.00**

Cup, Violets, Buffalo **7.00**
Cup & saucer, Punch & Judy, blue on white, England, 1⅞", 4¼" **40.00**
Gravy boat, Kite Fliers, blue on white, England, 3¼" ...**100.00**
Mug, Blue Willow, Coalport, 1⅞" **22.00**
Plate, Athens, blue on white, Davenport, 3", from $5 to **8.00**
Plate, Holly, Germany, from $8 to **10.00**
Plate, Minuet, Salem China Co, 6¼" **5.00**
Platter, Gaudy Floral, multicolor on cream, 4", from $30 to **35.00**
Sugar bowl, Nursery Scene, Germany, w/lid, 3¼", from $18 to **20.00**
Sugar bowl, Roman Chariots, blue on white, England, 1½" **40.00**
Teapot, Greenaway child, Cleveron China USA, 3½" **70.00**
Teapot, Mini Floral, multicolor on cream, 6½", from $45 to ..**50.00**
Tray, Dimity, green on cream, rectangular, 4⅞", from $15 to **18.00**
Tureen, Calico, brown on cream, w/lid, 3¾", from $35 to **45.00**

Teapot, Mary Had a Little Lamb, 6¼", from $55.00 to $65.00.

Glass

Bowl, master berry; Fine Cut, crystal, 1¾" **75.00**

Bowl, Tulip & Honeycomb, crystal, Federal, 1¾" dia, from $60 to **70.00**

Bread baker, clear opalescent, Kidibake, Fry, #1928, 5" ..**65.00**

Butter dish, Beaded Swirl, crystal, Westmoreland, 2⅜" **50.00**

Butter dish, Sweetheart, crystal, Cambridge, 2" **20.00**

Cake stand, Baby Thumbprint, crystal, 3x4", from $90 to **110.00**

Casserole, pale blue, from Sunny Suzy set #260, w/lid, 10-oz **10.00**

Creamer, Cherry Blossom, Delphite Blue (beware of reproductions) **30.00**

Creamer, Moderntone, pastel, 1¾", from $6 to **7.00**

Creamer, Stippled Diamond, amber, 2¼", from $90 to **100.00**

Cup & saucer, Homespun, crystal, Jeannette, 1⅝", 3¼", from $16 to **19.00**

Grill plate, clear opalescent, Kidibake, Fry, 8" **27.50**

Mug, Liberty Bell, crystal, 2", from $100 to **125.00**

Pie plate, crystal, McKee, #97, 4½" dia **12.00**

Pitcher, Colonial Flute, crystal, 3¼" **22.00**

Plate, Doric Pansy, pink, Jeannette, 5⅞", from $7.50 to ..**8.50**

Plate, Laurel, Jade Green, McKee, 5⅞", from $7.50 to **8.50**

Punch cup, milk glass, US Glass, 1⅜" **25.00**

Ramekin, crystal w/red trim, from Betty Jane set, McKee, #294 ....**8.00**

Set, Doric Pansy, ultramarine, Jeannette, 14-pc, from $230 to **270.00**

Spooner, Hobnail w/Thumbprint Base, blue, 2⅞" **75.00**

Sugar bowl, Buzz Saw, crystal, Cambridge, w/lid, 2⅞" ..**32.00**

Sugar bowl, Laurel, French Ivory, McKee, 2⅜", from $20 to .**25.00**

Teapot, Moderntone, white, w/lid, 3½", from $95 to **110.00**

Tumbler, Nursery Rhyme, crystal, US Glass, 2" **22.00**

Mug, Stork and Peacock, forest green, $20.00.

Christmas

No other holiday season is celebrated to the extravagant extent as Christmas, and vintage decorations provide a warmth and charm that none from today can match. Ornaments from before 1870 were imported from Dresden, Germany — usually made of cardboard and sparkled with tinsel trim. Later, blown glass ornaments were made there in literally thousands of shapes such as fruits and vegetables, clowns, Santas, angels, and animals. Kugles, heavy glass balls (though you'll sometimes find fruit and vegetable forms as well) were made from about 1820 to late in the century in sizes from very small up to 14". Early Santa figures are treasured, especially those in robes other than red. Figural bulbs from the '20s and '30s are popular, those that are character related in particular. Refer to *Christmas Collectibles*, by Margaret and Kenn Whitmyer, and *Christmas Ornaments, Lights & Decorations*, by George Johnson (both by Collector Books) for more information.

Candy container, snowman, mica-covered cardboard with woolen carrot nose, Made in Germany, 9", from $45.00 to $55.00.

Bubble light, common-shaped base, 1940s, M **8.00**

Bubble light, rocket base, 1940s, M **18.00**

Bulb, ball w/stars, red **18.00**

Bulb, chick, multicolor paint on milk glass, NM **55.00**

Bulb, flower, peach shaded to gold, 1930s-50s, Japan, mini ..**30.00**

Bulb, golfing rooster, multicolor paint, NM **35.00**

Bulb, grapes, multicolor w/green leaves on milk glass, 3¼" ..**15.00**

Bulb, Humpty Dumpty (bust), milk glass, multicolor paint ...**45.00**

Bulb, Kewpie, painted details, 1930s-50s, Japan, mini .**35.00**

Bulb, rose, red paint, milk glass, lg **50.00**

Bulb, Santa, full figure w/pack, multicolor on milk glass, EX **45.00**

Bulb, 3 Men in a Tub, multicolor paint, EX **135.00**

Candle holder, Santa, red glass, Fenton **35.00**

Candy container, dwarf, cardboard w/glitter, painted face, 5" ..**45.00**

Candy container, house, cardboard litho, Japan, 1930s, 5x4x3" **45.00**

Candy container, Santa, papier-mache/cardboard/cotton clothes, 14", EX **300.00**

Candy container, Santa face, celluloid, on foil cornucopia container **40.00**

Candy container, Santa in sleigh, celluloid, 3¼", EX **50.00**

Candy container, snowball, celluloid, 2" **65.00**

Candy container, star medallion, Dresden, cardboard w/glitter, 3" **120.00**

Books, Santa's Tuney Toy, Polygraphic, 1956, from $10.00 to $15.00; Santa's Circus, White Plains Greeting Card Co., 1952, from $15.00 to $20.00. (Photo courtesy Margaret and Ken Whitmyer)

Cup & saucer, Father Chrismas w/toys, bisque, Germany ..**70.00**

Feather tree, green feathers, 5", EX **60.00**

Feather tree, red flower-tip branches, 6½" **55.00**

Fence, painted tin wire, 20" sq w/2-part 6" gate **110.00**

Fence, wooden, green paint, 12 sections, each section: 7x22", EX **90.00**

Garland, glass beads, 96" **25.00**

Light, Matchless Star, glass prisms, 1930s, 2", M **15.00**

Lights, Betty Boop, string of 10, NM **300.00**

Lights, Fantasia, Mazda, England, 1940, set of 12, MIB **235.00**

Ornament, angel's head diecut in spun-glass circle, 2½", VG ..**65.00**

Ornament, animal, cotton batting, pre-WWI, EX ea **30.00**

Ornament, bell, blown, gold w/white & green flower, 3" **22.00**

Ornament, bird, celluloid, on ring, Japan, 6" **50.00**

Ornament, butterfly, blown .**65.00**

Ornament, chenille candy cane, 12", M **12.00**

Ornament, clown's head, blown, pearly white, red, black & gold, 3" **50.00**

Ornament, dinner bell, blown, blue, 4½" **22.50**

Ornament, Father Christmas, scrap, heart shape w/tinsel, 6" ...**25.00**

Ornament, flower, blown, 3" ..**20.00**

Ornament, icicle, mold blown, pink, 1950s, 14" **35.00**

Ornament, lady's face in flower, mold blown, multicolor paint, 2½" **35.00**

Ornament, Santa in chimney, mold blown, multicolor paint, 1930s, 3" **45.00**

Ornament, scowling Indian, blown glass, multicolor paint, pre-1940, 3" **200.00**

Ornament, star, 6-pointed w/indents, blown, 3-color, 4½" **35.00**
Reindeer, lead, Germany, 2x1¾" ...**42.00**
Santa, papier-mache/cardboard, paper belt, Japan, 13", EX **85.00**
Santa, plastic, red & white, Irving, 4" **75.00**
Santa in sleigh w/2 reindeer, celluloid, Japan, 18", VG ...**45.00**
Santa w/green pack, bisque, Japan, 4½", EX **50.00**

Cigarette Lighters

Pocket lighters were invented sometime after 1908 and were at their peak from about 1925 to the 1930s. Dunhill, Zippo, Colibri, Ronson, Dupont, and Evans are some of the major manufacturers. An early Dunhill Unique model, if found in its original box, would be valued at hundreds of dollars. Quality metal and metal-plated lighters were made from the '50s to about 1960. About that time disposable lighters never needing a flint were introduced,

causing a decline in sales of figurals, novelties, and high-quality lighters.

What makes a good lighter? — novelty of design, type of mechanism (flint and fuel, flint and gas, battery, etc.), and manufacturer (and whether or not the company is still in business). Most of the lighters listed here are from the 1930s. Sizes listed are approximate. For further information, we recommend *Collector's Guide to Cigarette Lighters, Identification and Values*, by James Flanagan.

Miniature, Aladdin, chromium, lift-arm, mother-of-pearl, 1955,⅞x¾" **35.00**
Miniature, Occupied Japan, lift-arm, chromium, leather bands, 1948 ....**40.00**
Novelty, cigar shaped, Negbaur, plastic, 1955, 2½x⅝" **25.00**
Novelty, wooden shoe, hand painted, Holland, ca 1940, 2⅛x4½" **40.00**
Pocket, Aero-lite, chromium, lift-arm, mid-1930s, 2⅛x1" .**30.00**

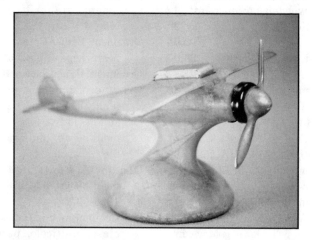

Table, airplane figural, metal with silver paint, 6" long, from $50.00 to $60.00.

Table, Scottie dog figural, painted cast metal, Strikalite, Made in USA, 3¼x3¾", $75.00.

Pocket, bottle shape, Johnny Walker, ca 1960s, 2⅜x⅝" **10.00**

Pocket, brass, lift-arm, ca 1985, 2¼x¾" **30.00**

Pocket, coin shape, 1965, 1¼" dia ..**10.00**

Pocket, Colbri, pouch style, ca 1954, 2⅛x2" **45.00**

Pocket, Colibri, lift-arm, silver, ca 1937, 2½x1⅜" **90.00**

Pocket, Dunhill, silverplated, butane, lift-arm, ca 1990, w/box ..**220.00**

Pocket, Evans, chromium, ca 1929, 2x1½" **60.00**

Pocket, General Electric logo, brushed finish, 1940 .....**65.00**

Pocket, Hilton, chromium, leather band, ca 1950s, 2x1⅝" ..**20.00**

Pocket, Parker, Flaminaire, chromium, butane, ca 1951, w/gift box .**40.00**

Pocket, Pereline, brass, w/key chain, mid-1950s, 1¼x1¼" **10.00**

Pocket, Prince, round, chromium, late 1950s, 1⅞" dia **20.00**

Pocket, shaped like a book, 1918, 2½x1¾", from $75 to ...**125.00**

Pocket, Strato Flame, chromium, butane, ca 1952, 1¾x2¼" ..**30.00**

Pocket, Tee-Vee, lift-arm, chromium, ca 1935, 1½x⅞" **25.00**

Pocket, Triangle, chromium & leather, lift-arm, 1920s, 1⅞x 1½" **70.00**

Pocket, tube-style, ca late 1950s, 2⅜x⅜" **15.00**

Pocket, Zenith, chromium, ca 1938, 2½x1½" **30.00**

Pocket, Zippo, Bearing Sales Co logo, brushed finish, 1940s **56.00**

Pocket, Zippo, Medalist logo, brushed finish, 1965 .....**27.00**

Pocket, Zippo, Slim, Shriner's Lodge design, 1970, orig box **34.00**

Table, cognac glass shape, stainless steel, ca 1960s, 5x2¾" **25.00**

Table, German, ceramic, 1958, 3¾x12⅝" **40.00**

Table, ice cream cone shape, plastic, 1960s, 3⅝x2½" **15.00**

Table, motorcycle, shape, chromium, butane fuel, 1985, 3½x6" ..**40.00**

Table, Occupied Japan, mother-of-pearl, lift-arm, ca 1948, 1¼x1⅜" **40.00**

Table, PGL, chromium, butane, 1960, 4¼x2½" **30.00**

Table, Shields, chromium, ca 1950s, 4½x6⅝" **30.00**

Table, Swank, television shape, ca 1960s, 2¾x4" **40.00**

Table, tankard shape, chromium, butane, early 1980s, 4¼x3" ..**25.00**

Table, Willie the Kool Penguin, painted metal, 4" **100.00**

Table, 8-ball form, plastic, 1965, 3x2½" **20.00**

Clothes Sprinkler Bottles

From the time we first had irons, clothes were sprinkled with water before ironing for the best results. During the 1930s until the 1950s when the steam iron became a home staple, some of us merely took sprinkler tops and stuck them into bottles to accomplish this task, while the more imaginative enjoyed the bottles made in figural shapes and bought the ones they particularly liked. The most popular were the Chinese men marked 'Sprinkle Plenty.' Some bottles were made by American Bisque, Cleminson of California, and other famous figural pottery makers. Many were made in Japan for the export market. Note that all of the Chinese men listed here are inscribed 'Sprinkle Plenty.'

Cat, Siamese; tan, ceramic, from $100 to **125.00**

Chinaman, Sprinkle Plenty, white, green & brown, holds iron, ceramic **135.00**

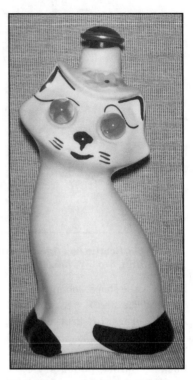

Cat with marble eyes, American Bisque, from $150.00 to $195.00. (Photo courtesy Ellen Bercovici)

Chinaman, variety of colors & designs, homemade ceramic, from $30 to **60.00**

Clothespin, red, yellow & green, plastic, from $15 to **25.00**

Dutch Boy, green & white, ceramic, from $125 to **145.00**

Elephant, pink & gray, ceramic, from $45 to **55.00**

Myrtle, Pfaltzgraph, ceramic, from $195 to **225.00**

Rooster, red & green, ceramic, from $100 to **125.00**

Sadiron, girl ironing **45.00**

Victorian lady w/purse **120.00**

Coin Glass

Coin Glass was originally produced in crystal, ruby, blue, emerald green, olive green, and amber. Lancaster Colony bought the Fostoria Company in the mid-1980s and is currently producing this line in crystal, green, blue, and red, but without frosted coins. (Beware — some people are sand blasting or satinizing the non-frosted coins!) The green and blue are 'off' enough to be pretty obvious, but the red is close. Here are some (probably not all) of the items currently in production: bowl, 8" diameter; bowl, 9" oval; candlesticks, 4½"; candy jar with lid, 6¼"; creamer and sugar bowl; footed comport; wedding bowl, 8¼". Know your dealer!

Emerald green is the most desired by collectors. You may also find some crystal pieces with gold-decorated coins. These will be valued at about double the price of plain crystal if the gold is not worn. Worn or faded gold seems to have little value. Our prices are for pieces with frosted coins. Numbers included in our descriptions were company-assigned stock numbers that collectors use as a means to distinguish variations in stems and shapes. For further information we recommend *Collectible Glassware from the '40s, '50s, & '60s* by Gene Florence (Collector Books).

Ashtray, #1372/114, amber, 7½" **.35.00**
Ashtray, #1372/115, amber, oblong **10.00**
Bowl, #1372/179, amber, 8" **75.00**

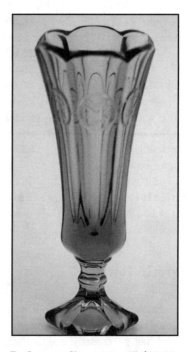

Bud vase, olive green, 8", $28.00.

Bowl, #1372/179, green, 8" .**125.00**
Bowl, nappy; #1372/499, clear, handled, 5⅜" **15.00**
Bowl, nappy; #1372/499, ruby or blue, 5⅜" **35.00**
Bowl, wedding; #1372/162, ruby, w/lid **100.00**
Candle holder, #1372/316, amber, 4½" **45.00**
Candle holder, #1372/316, green, 4½" **80.00**
Candy jar, #1372/347, blue or ruby, 6¼" **65.00**
Candy jar, #1372/347, clear, w/lid, 6¼" **30.00**
Candy jar, #1372/347, olive or amber, w/lid, 6¼" **35.00**
Cigarette box, #1372/320, clear, w/lid **40.00**
Cigarette box, #1372/374, w/lid, ruby or blue **85.00**

Creamer, #1372/680, olive ...**15.00**

Decanter, #1372/400, green, w/stopper, 1-pt, 10¼" ..**325.00**

Jelly, #1371/448, green **35.00**

Jelly, #1372/448, blue or ruby ...**30.00**

Pitcher, #1372/453, green, 32-oz, 6¼" **125.00**

Sugar bowl, #1372/673, olive, w/lid, 5⅜" **35.00**

Sugar bowl, #1372/673, ruby or blue, w/lid **45.00**

Tumbler, iced tea/high ball; #1372/64, crystal, 12-oz, 5⅛" **40.00**

Comic Books

Factors that make a comic book valuable are condition, content, and rarity, not necessarily age. In fact, comics printed between 1950 and the late 1970s are most in demand by collectors who prefer those they had as children to the earlier comics. Issues where the hero is first introduced are treasured. While some may go for hundreds, even thousands of dollars, many are worth very little; so if you plan to collect, you'll need a good comic book price guide such as Overstreets to assess your holdings. Condition is extremely important. Compared to a book in excellent condition, a mint issue might be worth six to eight times as much, while one in only good condition should be priced a less than half the price of the excellent example.

Adventures Into the Unknown, #102, American Comics Group, VG+ **8.00**

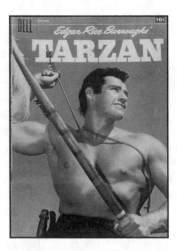

Tarzan and the Men of the Deep, Dell #108, c 1958, NM, $25.00.

Adventures of Bob Hope, #24, DC Comics, VG+ **28.00**

Adventures of the Fly, #9, Archie Publications/Radio Comics, VG **15.00**

All-American Western, #115, Kubert art, DC Comics, VG+ **50.00**

Amazing Adventures, #18, Marvel, NM **6.00**

Archie As Pure Heart the Powerful, #1, Archie Publications, NM **24.00**

Arizona Kid, #6, Marvel, Canada, VG **9.00**

Atom, The; #9, DC Comics, EX+ **65.00**

Batman, #129, DC Comics, VG ...**59.00**

Batman, #163, DC Comics, NM ..**90.00**

Beany & Cecil, #4, Clampett, 1963, EX+ **23.00**

Ben Bowie & Mountain Men, #11, Dell, VG **6.00**

Big Land, The; #812, Alan Ladd Cover, NM **70.00**

Black Diamond Western, #44, Golden Age, VG **7.00**

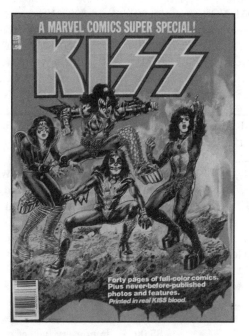

KISS Marvel Comic #1, printed with real KISS blood in red ink, $65.00. (Photo courtesy June Moon)

Bonanza, #207, 1962, EX **40.00**

Buffalo Bill, #6, 1951, VG **10.00**

Captain Midnight, #54, Golden Age, EX+ **60.00**

Challengers of the Unknown, #23, DC Comics, VG+ **20.00**

Cisco Kid, #3, Golden Age, EX ..**27.00**

Combat, #32, Dell, VG **2.00**

Crime Does Not Pay, #123, Golden Age, glossy, NM **25.00**

Dale Evans Queen of the West, #3, EX **60.00**

Dell Junior Treasury, #10, Tom Sawyer, NM **22.50**

Deputy, The; #1225, TV version, Henry Fonda cover, EX ..**30.00**

Don Winslow of the Navy, #2, Charlton Comics, VG+ ..**85.00**

Donald Duck in Disneyland, #1, NM **165.00**

Famous Funnies, #134, Eastern Color Printing Co, EX+ .**25.00**

Fantasy Masterpieces, #9, Marvel, EX **14.00**

Felix the Cat, #61, Toby Press, VG **30.00**

Fight the Enemy, #2, Tower Comics, NM **12.00**

Francis the Talking Mule, #465, EX **17.50**

Frontier Western, #4, Marvel, G..**6.00**

Ghostly Tales, #55, NM **6.00**

Girl From Uncle, #5, TV version, photo cover, EX **25.00**

Ha Ha Comics, #17, American Comics Group, 1945, VG .**11.00**

Holiday Comics, #4, LB Cole cover, 1951, VG **28.00**

Incredible Hulk, #108, Marvel, EX **20.00**

Krazy Kat Comics, #454, Dell, EX+ **15.00**

Laugh-In, #128, EX **5.00**

Light in the Forest, #891, photo cover, NM **60.00**

Lone Rider, #12, Superior Comics, EX **10.00**

Marge's Tubby, #5, VG- **11.00**

Marvel Super-Heroes, #14, Marvel, EX+ **45.00**

Movie Classics, McHale's Navy, VG+ **9.00**

Munsters, #4, Gold Key, VG+ ..**16.00**

Our Gang, #20, Dell, G **20.00**

Perfect Love, #4, St John Publishing, VG **11.00**

Pogo Possom, #2, Kelly cover art, VG **85.00**

Restless Gun, #1045, EX+ ...**40.00**

Sergeant Preston of the Yukon, #29, photo cover, VG+ ...**27.00**

Space Ghost, #1, TV version, Spiegle art, NM **230.00**

Space Man, #10, Dell, NM **5.00**

Superboy, #96, DC Comics, EX+ .**27.00**

Superman, #152, DC Comics, EX **20.00**

Superman's Girlfriend Lois Lane, #13, DC Comics, NM **95.00**

Tales From the Crypt, #28, Golden Age, VG+ **95.00**

Tales of the Unexpected, #31, DC Comics, EX **40.00**

Twilight Zone, #24, Dell, VG .**3.00**

Uncle Remus & Brer Rabbit, #129, VG **35.00**

Western Hero, #109, Golden Age, VG+ **20.00**

Western Roundup, #4, Dell, NM **40.00**

When Knighthood Was in Flower, #682, VG+ **14.00**

Wings of Eagles, The; #790, John Wayne cover, EX+ **90.00**

Wonder Woman, #119, DC Comics, EX **20.00**

Young Rebels, #1, NM **9.00**

Compacts

Prior to World War I, the use of compacts was frowned upon. It was not until after the war when women became liberated and entered the work force that the use of cosmetics became acceptable. A compact became a necessity as a portable container for cosmetics and usually contained a puff and mirror. Compacts were made in many different styles, shapes, and motifs and from every type of natural and man-made material. The fine jewelry houses made compacts in all of the precious metals — some studded with precious stones. The most sought-after compacts today are those in Art Deco style or made of plastic, figurals, and any that incorporate gadgets. Compacts that are combined with other accessories are also very desirable. Refer to *Ladies' Compacts of the 19th and 20th Centuries* (Wallace-Homestead Book Co.) and *Vintage Vanity Bags & Purses* and *Vintage Ladies' Compacts, An Identification Guide*, (both published by Collector Books). All three are written by our advisor, Roselyn Gerson; she is listed in the Directory under New York. Another good reference is *The Collector's Encyclopedia of Compacts I & II, Carryalls, and Face Powder Boxes* by Laura M. Mueller. See also Clubs and Newsletters.

Dark blue with gold grid design, pearl trim, Rex Fifth Avenue, 3½" dia, from $25.00 to $35.00.

Bracelet combination, plastic w/metal slide, Marlow Parisienne **250.00**

Brushed gold-tone metal, shows heart, arrow & I Love You, Dorset, 2½" dia **70.00**

Charm, hammered silver, mirror & powder well,⅝" dia, from $25 to **50.00**

Cloisonne, gilded metal w/painted flowers, sliding lipstick, La Mode **125.00**

Eastern Star on blue enamel, Stratton, 2¾" dia, from $60 to .**80.00**

Enamel, hand-painted Japanese couple in garden, 2½x2", from $50 to **75.00**

Gold-tone w/blue & gold enameling, mirror & compartments, 2¾" L **90.00**

Ivory celluloid, resembles hand mirror, 5x2½" dia, from $100 to ...**125.00**

Leather vanity, resembles book, Raquel, 2x3", from $80 to ..**125.00**

Lighter combination, black enamel w/Deco decor, Evans, 3¼x6¾" **200.00**

Mercedes Benz logo on brushed silver w/matching comb&case, 2¾" dia **125.00**

Mini, gold-tone metal w/enamel, resembles fan, 2½x1½" ..**50.00**

Mini/key chain combination, snakeskin, chain at rim, Italy, 1½" **90.00**

Mother engraved on brushed gold-tone metal, Elgin, 3x2¼" ..**80.00**

Plastic, blue & ivory, screw top lid, cord w/lipstick in tassel ..**300.00**

Plastic, multicolor striped glitter, 1930s, from $50 to **75.00**

Plastic dog w/bobbin' head applied to pearlized plastic lid, 3" ...**115.00**

Powder-grinder vanity, silver-tone, Dorothy Gray, 1¾x2" **55.00**

Powder-sifter type, engraved silver-tone metal, Elizabeth Arden, 2½" dia **80.00**

Red leather, attached lipstick sleeve, pull-out mirror, 3x3½" **140.00**

Repousse doves on polished gold-tone metal, 2⅞" dia, from $80 to **120.00**

Rhinestones cover gold-tone lid, Pilcher, 3½" dia, from $75 to **150.00**

Silver-tone w/orange black & silver Deco decor, 2" dia, from $50 to **75.00**

Silvered-metal, resembles coin, Elgin, from $150 to **200.00**

Snakeskin, crystal gray, back lid brushed gold-tone, 3x3", from $40 to **60.00**

Souvenir, Washington DC, heart-shaped silver-tone metal, from $40 to **60.00**

Suitcase style, gold-tone, Kigu logo, push-back handle, 3¼" L **165.00**

Vanity, enamel w/silver-tone mesh bottom, 4" dia, from $60 to **80.00**

Vanity, gold-tone & green enamel resembles package, Coty, 3x1⅞" **100.00**

Vanity, International Sterling, octagon w/handle, 2x3", from $80 to .**100.00**

Vanity, mother-of-pearl, rouge compartment on lid, Elgin, 2¾" sq **80.00**

Vanity, petit-point half-moon shape on gold-tone metal, 1930s **125.00**

Vanity, US Marine insignia on lid, compartments, mirror, 2¼" **50.00**

Vanity/lighter combo, orchids on white enamel, R Hudnut 3x4½" **175.00**

World glove, gold-tone ball shape, plastic interior, Kigu, 1⅛" **175.00**

Cookbooks

Advertising cookbooks, those by well-known personalities, and figural diecuts are among the more readily available examples on today's market. Cookbooks written prior to 1874 are the most valuable; they often sell for $200.00 and up. Refer to *A Guide to Cookbook Collecting* by Colonel Bob Allen and *The Price Guide to Cookbook and Recipe Leaflets* by Linda Dickinson for more information. (Both books are published by Collector Books.)

Bordon Co, Borden's Eagle Brand Magic Recipes, 1946, 28-page, VG **12.50**

The Hershey Recipe Book, 1930, $15.00.

Campbell Soup Co, Easy Ways to Delicious Meals, spiral, 1970, 204-page **8.00**

Campbell Soup Co, Prego Please!, 1985, 21-page, VG **4.00**

Carnation, Cooking w/a Surprising Difference, 1966, 48-page, VG **7.00**

Carnation, Fun To Cook Book, 1978, 48-page, EX **7.00**

Chelsea Milling Co, Hospitality in a 'Jiffy,' 1960s, 21-page, EX **2.50**

Eagle Brand, Dessert Lover's Hand-Book, 1969, 21-page, EX **8.00**

General Foods, All About Home Baking, 1963, 117-page, VG **4.00**

General Foods, Cookies Galore, 1956, 39-page, EX **12.00**

General Mills, Betty Crocker's Party Book, spiral, 1960 1st edition **12.00**

General Mills, Betty Crocker's Bisquick Cook Book, 1956, 26-page, VG **8.00**

Griswold, Aunt Ellen Booklet on Waterless Cooking, 1928, EX **20.00**

Hershey Foods, Hershey's 1934 Cookbook, spiral, 1971, 96-page, EX **6.00**

HJ Heinz Co, For Variety Cook w/Soup, 1970s, 31-page, EX **3.00**

Kellogg's, Housewife's Almanac, 1938, 35-page, VG **5.00**

Kellogg's, New Way of Living, 1932, 32-page, G **7.50**

Lever Bros, Aunt Jenny's 12 Pies Husbands Like Best, 1952, 21-page **6.00**

Lever Bros, Good Cooking Made Easy, 1942, 48-page, EX .**8.00**

Lipton, Souped Up Recipes From Lipton, spiral, 1978, 128-page, EX **8.00**

Minute Tapioca, Cook's Tour w/Minute Tapioca, 1931, 46-page, G **12.00**

National Biscuit Co, 50 Delicious Desserts, 1937, 16-page, EX .**14.00**

National Livestock & Meat Board, Meat...You'll Talk About, 1952, G **4.00**

Planters, They Taste So-o-o Good!, 1955, 48-page, EX **10.00**

Prince Macaroni, Prince Golden Macaroni Recipes, 1951, 31-page, VG **7.50**

Ralston Purina, Easy Guide to Good Eating..., 1950, 30-page, VG **3.50**

Rumford, Rumford New Use Cook Book, 1935, 22-page, G .**10.00**

Standard Brands, Royal Cook Book, 1932, 45-page, EX **15.00**

Standard Brands, Time-Tested Royal Recipes, 1950s, 31-page, VG **6.00**

Twin Pines Farm Dairy, Twin Pines Yogurt Recipes, no date, 16-page, VG **7.50**

United Fruit Co, Chiquita Banana Cookbook, 1962, 24-page, EX **5.00**

Waterless Ware, New Science of Waterless Cooking, soft cover, 1928 ....**15.00**

Wessen Oil, Quicker Ways to Better Eating, 1955, 100-page, EX .**6.00**

Appliances

American Cooker Recipe Book, soft cover, 1926, EX **20.00**

Frigidaire Corp, Frigidaire Recipe Book, 1931, EX **15.00**

Frigidaire Corp, Frigidaire-Frozen Delights, 1929, EX **17.50**

Gas Range, Cooking Is Fun, soft cover, 1955, EX **10.00**

General Electric, Refrigerator Menus & Recipes, 1927, 5th edition **10.00**

Home Comfort Cook Book, hardcover, 1924, 213-page, EX **35.00**

Knapp-Monarch Co, Chefster 7 in 1 Deep Frying, soft cover, 1950s **10.00**

Magic Chef Cooking, Dorothy E Shank, hardcover, 1935, 204-page, EX **15.00**

Mary Meade's Magic Recipes for the Osterizer, hardcover, 1966, EX **10.00**

Mirro Doughmaker & Bread Baking Kit Cook Book, soft cover, 1955 ....**8.00**

Mirro-Matic Pressure Pan Recipes, hardcover, 1952, EX **10.00**

SOME RECIPES FOR COOKING

The Gas Range and How to Use It, 1906, $25.00. (Photo courtesy Col. Bob Allen)

Mirro-Matic Pressure Pan Recipes, soft cover, 1946 ....**10.00**

Pressure Cooking, Ida Bailey Allen, hardcover, 1947, 403-page, EX **25.00**

Sears, Coldspot Operating Suggestions & Recipes, 1930s, 32-page, EX **15.00**

Servel Electrolux Refrigerator, Making the Most of Your..., 1941 ....**10.00**

Standard Electric Stove Co, Cook Book & Instructions, 1930, 32-page **20.00**

Jell-O

The Jell-O® Story: Peter Cooper dabbled with and patented a product which was 'set' with gelatin, a product that had been known in France since 1682. Peter Cooper's patent for an orange-flavored gelatin was granted in 1845 and was marketed from the 1890s through the early 1900s. Suffice it to say, it never did 'Jell' with the American public.

In 1897 Pearl B. Wait, a carpenter in Le Roy, New York, was formulating a cough remedy and laxative tea in his home. He experimented with gelatin and came up with a fruit-flavored dessert. His wife coined the name Jell-O®, and production began with four flavors: lemon, orange, raspberry, and strawberry.

Jell-O® is 'America's Most Famous Dessert.' In the infancy of advertising campaigns, this was the campaign slogan of a simple gelatin dessert that would one day become known around the world. The success story is the result of advertising and merchandising methods, new and different, having never before been employed. Well-groomed, well-trained, and well-versed salesmen went out in 'spanking' rigs drawn by beautiful horses into the roads, byroads, fairs, country gatherings, church socials, and parties to advertise their product. Pictures, posters, and billboards over the American landscape as well as full-page ads in magazines carried Jell-O® with her delicious flavored product into American homes. For further information we recommend our advisor, Col. Bob Allen, listed in the Directory under Missouri.

Calendar of Desserts-354 New Ideas & Recipes, 1940, 48-page **10.00**

Jack & Mary's Jello Recipe Book, 1937, $35.00. (Photo courtesy Col. Bob Allen)

Dessert Magic, 1944, 6th printing, 26-page **8.00**

Hostess Guide From..., boxed set of 38 cards, 1967 1st edition .**10.00**

It's Dessert Time, You Can Do Wonders..., 1953, 33-page **8.00**

New...Book of Surprises-Salads-Desserts, 1930, 23-page .**14.00**

New...Recipes Made w/the New Flavor, Lime, 1930, 11-page **14.00**

Recipes for Delicious Ice Cream-Jell-O Ice Cream Powder, 1936 ....**14.00**

Sweet Moments Desserts, 1966, 44-page **6.00**

Pillsbury

Bake Off Cookie Favorites, 1969, 64-page **4.50**

Baking Is Fun, Ann Pillsbury, 1948, 3rd edition, 1948, EX **8.00**

Busy Lady Bake-Off Recipes, 1966, 96-page, EX **6.00**

Butter Cookie Cook Book, Pillsbury's Best, 1957 ....**6.00**

Fabulous Pies From Pillsbury, Ann Pillsbury, 1961, 24-page **6.00**

Grand National Prize-Winning Recipes, 2nd Grand National, 1952, insert **3.50**

Money Saving Meals, 1970, 79-page, VG **4.00**

Nice 'n Easy Cook Book, 1968, 171 recipes **3.00**

Plain & Fancy, Hot Roll Mix, package insert, 1950 ....**3.50**

Short-Cut Breads, Pillsbury's Best, 1960 ....**6.00**

100 Prize Winning Recipes, 1953, 96-page **20.00**

12th Grand National Bake Off-100 Recipes, 1961, 96-page **25.00**

18th Annual Bake Off Recipes, 1967, 96-page **5.00**

3rd Grand National Bake-Off... Recipes, 1953, 96-page...**25.00**

7th Grand National Cookbook, 1956, 1st edition, 96-page, VG **12.00**

Kate Smith Chooses Her 55 Favorite Ann Pillsbury Cake Recipes, 1952, $8.00. (Photo courtesy Col. Bob Allen)

Miscellaneous

The Fun to Cook book,
1967, 48-page, EX, $6.00.
(Photo courtesy Colonel
Bob Allen)

Art of Good Cooking, Paula Peck, hard
cover, 1966, 368-page, EX .**12.50**
Better Homes & Gardens, spiral,
1949, EX **20.00**
Better Homes & Gardens Meals in
Minutes, hardcover, 1963, 62-
page **12.50**
Better Homes & Gardens Salad
Book, hardcover, 1959, 156-
page, EX **5.00**
Better Homes & Gardens...for
Two, Meredith Press, 1968,
96-page, G **8.00**
Book of Unusual Soups, Mary D Cham-
bers, 1930, 162-page, EX **30.00**
Fanny Farmer Cookbook, 1959 11th
edition, 1965 12th printing .**15.00**
Fireside Cook Book, JA Beard, 1949,
5th printing, 322-page **25.00**
French Chef Cookbook, Julia
Child, 1968, EX **30.00**
Good Things To Eat, Church &
Dwight, 1943, 15-page, VG ..**5.00**
Hawaiian Parties Indoor & Out, Castle &
Cooke, 1973, 33-page, VG **5.00**

Meals for Two Cookbook, Culinary Arts
Institute, 1949, 48-page, VG .**6.00**
Once in a While Cook, Birk & Co,
1952, 27-page, VG **3.00**
Pennsylvania Dutch Cook Book,
Culinary Arts Press, 1936, 48-
page, VG **10.00**
Southern Cook Book, Culinary
Arts Institute, 1972, 64-page,
EX **6.00**
Woman's Day Cook Book of
Favorite Recipes, 1958, 96-
page, EX **8.00**
50 Tasty Sandwich Recipes, Culinary Arts
Institute, 1949, 48-page, EX ..**6.00**

Cookie Cutters and Molds

Cookie cutters have come into
their own in recent years as wor-
thy kitchen collectibles. Prices on
many have risen astronomically,
but a practiced eye can still sort
out a good bargain. Advertising
cutters and product premiums,
especially in plastic, can still be
found without too much effort. Aluminum cutters with painted wood-
en handles are usually worth
several dollars each if in good condition. Red and green are the usual
handle colors, but other colors are
more highly prized by many. Hallmark plastic cookie cutters, esp-
cially those with painted backs, are
always worth considering if in good
condition.

Be wary of modern tin cutters being sold for antique. Many
present-day tinsmiths chemically
antique their cutters, especially if
done in a primitive style. These
are often sold by others as 'very

old.' Look closely, because most tinsmiths today sign and date these cutters.

To learn more, check *The Cookie Shaper's Bible* by Phillis Wetherill and Rosemary Henry. Ms. Henry also publishes *Cookies*, a newsletter for collectors. She is listed in the Directory under Virginia. See also Clubs and Newsletters.

Animals, metal outline, Davis Baking Powder, set of 4 ....**25.00**
Christmas tree, plastic w/impression lines, Dial Soap, 1981 ....**3.00**
Easter basket, pink plastic w/impression lines, Dan Dee Imports, 1968 ....**2.00**
Easter egg, blue plastic, Kellogg's Rice Krispies, 1982 ....**1.50**
Easter rabbit, pastel pink plastic, Kellogg's Rice Krispies, 1982 ....**1.50**
Female symbol, dark green plastic outline **4.00**
Flag, red plastic w/impression lines, back & handle, Tupperware, 1963 ....**5.00**
Fozzie Bear, brown hard plastic w/painted back, Hallmark, 1979 ....**10.00**
Gingerbread man, plastic w/impression lines, Dial Soap, 1981 ....**3.00**
Gingerbread Soap Twins, turquoise, Avon, 1965, set of 2 ....**10.00**
Halloween cat, aluminum w/self handle, Wrigley Gum, 1962 ....**5.00**
Peanut, tan plastic w/back & handle, Kroger Peanut Butter, 1985 ....**3.00**

Wear-Ever cookie cutter with five shapes on red plastic handle, $8.50.

Round, green plastic, marked For Bisquicks on handle, Bisquick, 2⅜" **6.00**
Round, metal, marked Marvel Flour on handle **7.00**
Round, metal w/egg-shaped handle, Egg Baking Powder, ca 1901 ....**40.00**
San Diego Zoo Elephant, white plastic w/painted back, Monogram, MOC **8.00**
Tom & Jerry, red plastic w/impression lines, Loew, 1956, ea ...**2.00**

Cookie Jars

The Nelson McCoy Pottery Co., Robinson Ransbottom Pottery Co., and the American Bisque Pottery Co., are three of the largest producers of cookie jars in the country. Many firms made them to a lesser extent. Today cookie jars are one of the most popular of modern collectibles. Figural jars are the most common (and the most valuable), made in an endless variety of subjects. Early jars from the 1920s and '30s were often decorated in 'cold paint' over the glaze. This type of color is easily removed — take care that you use very gentle cleaning methods. A damp cloth and a light touch is the safest approach.

For further information we recommend *The Collector's Encyclopedia of McCoy Pottery* by Sharon and Bob Huxford, *The Collector's Encyclopedia of Cookie Jars* by Joyce and Fred Roerig, *An Illustrated Value Guide to Cookie Jars* by Ermagene Westfall (all published by Collector Books), and *McCoy Cookie Jars From the First to the Last* by Harold Nichols (self-published). Values are for jars in mint condition unless otherwise noted.

American Bisque, Sailor Elephant, marked USA, $65.00.

American Bisque, Boy Lamb, sitting, marked USA, 13" ..**165.00**
American Bisque, Collegiate Owl, from $75 to **85.00**

American Bisque, Peasant Girl, unmarked, 10½" **375.00**
American Bisque, Schoolhouse, from $65 to **75.00**
Applause, '57 Chevy **80.00**
Brush, Cookie House, #W31 ..**85.00**
Brush, Dog & Basket **250.00**
Brush, Hen on Basket, unmarked **125.00**
Brush, Humpty Dumpty w/Peaked Hat **175.00**
Brush, Panda, #W21 ....**250.00**
Brush, White Hen on Basket ..**65.00**
Brush, 3 Bears **100.00**
California Originals, Cookie Monster, 1980 Muppets Inc **125.00**
California Originals, Eeyore, minimum value **450.00**
California Originals, Ernie, Muppets Inc #973, from $40 to **50.00**
California Originals, Ferdinand ..**75.00**
California Originals, Humpty Dumpty **125.00**
California Originals, Shoe House, mouse in door **40.00**
Cardinal China, Garage, Free Parking for Cookies **135.00**
Cardinal China, Sack of Cookies, from $45 to **55.00**
Cardinal China, Soldier **200.00**
Clay Art, Cow in Corn **50.00**
Clay Art, Primrose Cat **55.00**
Cleminson, Cookie Book **95.00**
Cleminson, Yellow Heart ...**300.00**
Cumberland Ware, Elephant ..**60.00**
De Forest of California, Chipmunk, black & white stripes, holds spoon **155.00**
De Forest of California, Fortune Cookie **25.00**
De Forest of California, Monkey, yellow hat **195.00**
Doranne of California, Jeep ..**95.00**

Doranne of California, Monkey in Barrel **70.00**

Enesco, Betsy Ross **225.00**

Enesco, Coke Machine **58.00**

Enesco, Ice Cream Shop **48.00**

Fitz & Floyd, Bunny Bonnet .**110.00**

Fitz & Floyd, Dot Kangaroo ..**175.00**

Fitz & Floyd, Holiday Leaves Deer **160.00**

Fitz & Floyd, Mother Rabbit, from $70 to **90.00**

Fitz & Floyd, Nutcracker Soldier **125.00**

Fitz & Floyd, Prunella Pig ..**125.00**

Fitz & Floyd, Santa in a Christmas Car **175.00**

Fitz & Floyd, Santa on Cookie Cycle, minimum value .**300.00**

Fitz & Floyd, Dot Kangaroo.**175.00**

Fitz & Floyd, Wonderland Teapot **75.00**

Happy Memories, Hopalong Cassidy **300.00**

Holiday Designs, Panda **50.00**

Holiday Designs, Pumpkin ..**35.00**

Holt Howard, Tiger **75.00**

Inarco, Raggedy Andy **75.00**

Japan, Cookies Can w/Raccoon ..**20.00**

Japan, Raggedy Ann Seated, Cookies lettered on hat **45.00**

Japan, Smiling Pear **20.00**

Maddux, Koala **75.00**

Maddux, Raggedy Andy, #2108 ..**300.00**

Maddux, Walrus **65.00**

Maurice of California, Gigantic Frog **195.00**

McCoy, Caboose, 1961, from $140 to **165.00**

McCoy, Clyde Dog, 1974, from $150 to **200.00**

McCoy, Cookie Barrel, 1958-67, from $40 to **45.00**

McCoy, Forbidden Fruit, 1967, from $65 to **75.00**

McCoy, Clown in Yellow Barrel, $130.00.

McCoy, Honey Bear, 1953-55, from $100 to **120.00**

McCoy, Liberty Bell, 1975, from $75 to **100.00**

McCoy, Mammy, Cookies on base, from $250 to **300.00**

McCoy, Modern Pineapple, no mark, from $75 to **100.00**

McCoy, Sad Clown, 1970-71, from $75 to **100.00**

McCoy, Wren House, 1959-60, from $150 to **175.00**

Metlox, Apple, Golden Delicious, 9½" **150.00**

Metlox, Calico Cat, cream w/blue ribbon **150.00**

Metlox, Duck, Francine **225.00**

Metlox, Koala **125.00**

Metlox, Lighthouse, minimum value **500.00**

Metlox, Pretzel Barrel, 11" ..**125.00**

Metlox, Squirrel Nut Barrel ..**175.00**

Metlox, Wheat Shock, 4-qt .**125.00**

Napco, Little Bo Peep **295.00**

Napco, Man w/Ice Bag, MIB ..**160.00**
National Silver, Mammy ...**200.00**
Norcrest, Emmet Kelly **90.00**
Omnibus, Safari Truck **45.00**
Pan American Art, Bartender .**225.00**
Pantry Pride, Yellow Tomato, gold
    handle **72.00**
Pottery Guild, Elsie in Barrel ..**495.00**
Red Wing, Bob White, un-
    marked **125.00**
Red Wing, Crock, white **60.00**
Red Wing, Grapes **225.00**
Red Wing, King of Tarts, white,
    unmarked **675.00**
Red Wing, Pineapple, yellow ..**200.00**
Regal China, Hobby Horse .**250.00**
Regal China, Tulip **300.00**
Robinson Ransbottom, Chef, gold
    trim, #411 ....**275.00**
Robinson Ransbottom, Dutch Boy,
    gold trim **425.00**
Robinson Ransbottom, Dutch
    Boy, unmarked **250.00**

Robinson Ransbottom, Hey Diddle
    Diddle, no gold **225.00**
Roman Ceramics, C-3PO **50.00**
Schmid, Gingerbread House Bak-
    ery **65.00**
Shawnee, Basketweave, hexago-
    nal, marked USA, minimum
    value **50.00**
Shawnee, Dutch boy (Jack), dou-
    ble-striped pants, marked
    USA **250.00**
Shawnee, Elephant, marked Shawnee
    60, minimum value **150.00**
Shawnee, Fruit Basket, yellow
    bowl, Shawnee 84, minimum
    value **160.00**
Shawnee, owl, brown w/gold trim,
    marked USA, minimum
    value **225.00**
Sierra Vista, Squirrel, Starnes
    label **165.00**
Sierra Vista, Train, smiling
    face **105.00**

Fitz & Floyd, Santa Cycle, $500.00 minimum value.

Cleminson, Potbellied Stove, $90.00.

Sigma, Circus Man w/Top Hat ..**175.00**
Sigma, Darth Vador **150.00**
Sigma, Hortense **175.00**
Sigma, Kliban Mama Cat ..**250.00**
Sigma, Peter Max **385.00**
Starnes, Pirate **300.00**
Treasure Craft, Conductor Bear .**50.00**
Treasure Craft, Cookie Barn .**45.00**
Treasure Craft, Dog on Sled ..**80.00**
Treasure Craft, Lion King ...**55.00**
Treasure Craft, Mrs Potts, from
    $60 to **70.00**
Treasure Craft, Snowman ...**60.00**
Twin Winton, Bambi **225.00**
Twin Winton, Chinese man wear-
    ing coolie hat **150.00**
Twin Winton, Cookie Barn, #41 ...**50.00**
Twin Winton, Log Cabin **50.00**
Twin Winton, Teddy Bear .**125.00**
Vandor, Betty Boop, standing .**500.00**
Vandor, Betty Boop Holiday
    1994 ....**125.00**
Vandor, Howdy Doody head ..**350.00**
Vandor, Mona Lisa **65.00**

Corkscrews

Webster's dictionary defines a corkscrew as an instrument consisting of a metal screw or helix with a sharp point and a traverse handle whose use is to draw corks from bottles. From early times this task was done by using the worm end of a flintlock gun rod. The history of corkscrews dates back to the mid-1600s, when wine makers concluded that the best-aged wine was that stored in smaller containers, either stoneware or glass. Since plugs left unsealed were often damaged by rodents, corks were cut off flush with the bottle top and sealed with wax or a metal cover. Numerous models with handles of wood, ivory, bone, porcelain, silver, etc., have been patented through the years. Our advisor for this category is Paul P. Luchsinger; he is listed in the Directory under Pennsylvania.

Armstrong-type concertina, all
    steel, bladed worm, 1880s, 5"
    closed **95.00**
Buffalo handle, straight pull, heli-
    cal worm/turned shaft, 1850s,
    5½ **45.00**
Cellerman's type, steel, straight-pull
    type, bladed worm, 1890s,
    5½" **15.00**
Challenge, steel, revolving han-
    dle, bladed worm, 1880s,
    6½" **100.00**
Continental, steel, continuous
    action, long bladed worm,
    1900s, 5¼" **22.50**
Edwin Walker, brass collar, bell cap
    w/lifter, wood handle, 5" .**27.50**

Folding bow type, steel, helical worm, 1890s, 2½" closed .**18.00**

Happy Face, ca 1935, 10', $85.00.

Hollwig, advertising Pabst Milwaukee, US Patent 1891 ....**75.00**

Hong Kong, bell shape, double lever, wing handle w/crown opener, 7" **25.00**

J Perille Depose Paris, steel, attached collar, driving handle, 1890s **50.00**

Monkey figural, chrome plated, helical worm is tail, 1930s, 2½" **60.00**

Negbaur USA pat'd, parrot figural, open mouth is cap lifter, 5" **50.00**

Nifty, Made in Pat in USA Vaughan Chicago, pocket style w/crown lifter **5.00**

Peerage England, brass pig figural handle, bladed worm, 1920s, 3½" **48.00**

Phoenix, Monopol type, steel, continuous action, bladed worm, 4¾" **48.00**

Rapid, Swiss made, brass plated, mid-1900s **135.00**

Shakerspeare portrait brass handle, bladed worm, 1930s, 7½" **30.00**

Solon, DRGM No 152004, steel w/open frame, long bladed worm, 4¼" **60.00**

Staghorn handle, 9 tools, early 1900s **65.00**

T-bar, steel, straight pull, helical worm, 1890s, 4½" **22.00**

West Germany, 2-prong cork extracter, steel w/black plastic casing, 5¾ **10.00**

Williamson's, bullet style, Pat 1900 ....**40.00**

Cracker Jack

The name Cracker Jack was first used in 1896. The trademark as well as the slogan 'The more you eat, the more you want' were registered at that time. Prizes first appeared in Cracker Jack boxes in 1912. Prior to then, prizes or gifts could be sent for through catalogs. In 1910 coupons that could be redeemed for many gifts were inserted in the boxes.

The Cracker Jack boy and his dog, Bingo, came on the scene in 1916, and have remained one of the world's most well-known trademarks. Prizes themselves came in a variety of materials, from paper and tin to pot metal and plastic. All items listed are marked Cracker Jack. For further information we recommend our advisor, Phil Helley, listed in the Directory under Wisconsin. Larry

White has written *Cracker Jack, the Complete Unofficial Guide for Collectors*.

Truck, tin litho, red, white, and black, CJ/Angelus, 1931, $65.00.

Baseball bat	**65.00**
Compass	**125.00**
Game, bead; German	**100.00**
Headdress	**125.00**
Jungle Book, animated	**100.00**
Movies, ea	**125.00**
Paper dolls, Bobby & Betty	**150.00**
Puzzle, jigsaw; 1931	**100.00**
Riddle cards, ea	**22.00**
Song book, Uncle Sam	**95.00**
Tray, mini, 2 sizes, ea	**130.00**
Visor, paper	**90.00**

Crackle Glass

At the height of productivity from the 1930s through the 1970s, nearly five hundred companies created crackle glass. As pieces stayed in production for several years, dating items may be difficult. Some colors such as ruby red, amberina, cobalt, and cranberry were more expensive to produce. Smoke gray was made for a short time, and because quantities are scarce, prices on these pieces tend to be higher than on some of the other colors, amythest, green, and amber included. Crackle glass is still in production today by the Blenko Glass Company, and it is being imported from Taiwan and China as well. For further information on other glass companies and values we recommend *Crackle Glass, Identification and Value Guide*, by our advisors, Stan and Arlene Weitman (Collector Books). You will find them in the Directory under New York.

Apple, emerald green, very fine crackle, Hamon, 1940s-1970s, 3¼" **50.00**
Ashtray, dark blue, bowl form w/3 rests, unknown, 7¼" **30.00**
Bottle, topaz amber fish w/green eyes, sits on fins, unknown, 15" **75.00**
Candle holder, sea green, bulbous w/narrow neck, Blenko, 1960s, 5¼" **50.00**
Cruet, blue, double-ball stopper, Rainbow, 1940s-1960s, 6½" **55.00**
Cruet, sea green, ball stopper, Pilgrim, 1949-1969, 6", from $40 to **70.00**
Decanter, crystal ovoid base, pinched sides, olive stopper, Blenko, 11" **60.00**
Decanter, ruby, double-ball form base w/ball stopper, Rainbow, 7¾" **75.00**
Decanter, tangerine, bulbous w/narrow neck, crackled top, Blenko, 13" **75.00**
Decanter, topaz, cylinder base, narrow neck, Rainbow, 1960s, 8½" **75.00**
Glass, cream, drop-over handle, unknown, 5½", from $35 to ...**50.00**

Cruet, amberina, Rainbow, late 1940s-1960s, 7", from $45.00 to $75.00. (Photo courtesy Stan and Arlene Weitman)

Glass, sea green, pinched sides, Blenko, late 1940s-1950s, 5¾" **50.00**

Hat, amberina, smooth bottom, Kanawha, 1957-1987, 2", from $35 to **40.00**

Jug, blue, clear drop-over handle, Pilgrim, 1949-1969, 4" ..**30.00**

Jug, teal, drop-over handle, Pilgrim, 1949-1969, 4", from $30 to **35.00**

Perfume bottle, olive green ball base, metal top, Rice, 3".**25.00**

Pitcher, dark amber, drop-over handle, Pilgrim, 1949-1969, 4" **25.00**

Pitcher, emerald green, pulled-back handle, unknown, 5½"....**45.00**

Pitcher, green, clear drop-over handle, Pilgrim, 1949-1969, 3½"....................................**35.00**

Pitcher, green, pulled-back handle, Williamsburg Glass, 1960, 4¾"........................**60.00**

Pitcher, lemon lime, clear pulled-back handle, Pilgrim, 1969, 4¼"....................................**25.00**

Pitcher, olive green, frilled top, attributed to Blenko 8¼"....................................**85.00**

Pitcher, tangerine, clear drop-over handle, Pilgrim, 1969, 3¾" **30.00**

Pitcher, topaz, clear drop-over handle, Pilgrim, 1949-1969, 3¾"....................................**25.00**

Vase, amberina, bulbous base, slender neck w/rolled rim, Hamon, 8"........................**75.00**

Vase, amberina, bulbous w/pinched rim, Pilgrim, 1949-1969, 4"..........................**65.00**

Vase, amberina, slender body w/flared top, Kanawha, 1957-1987, 7¾"........................**60.00**

Vase, amberina w/yellow ruffled top, applied trim, unknown, 5¼"....................................**80.00**

Vase, amethyst, bulbous w/pinched rim, Pilgrim, 1949-1969, 4"..........................**70.00**

Vase, crystal urn form w/blue rosettes, Blenko, 1940s-1950s, 8¾"....................................**90.00**

Vase, crystal w/applied sea green leaves, Blenko, 1940s-1950s, 7"....................................**75.00**

Vase, crystal w/ribbed sides, unknown, 10" **75.00**

Vase, emerald green, double neck, Blenko, 1940s-1950s, 4"....................................**60.00**

Vase, jonquil, crimped top, footed, Blenko, 1950s,7¼" **100.00**

Vase, sea green, clear drop-over handles, Blenko, 1940s-1950s, 7½"..................................**75.00**

Credit Cards

Credit items predate the 20th century and have been made from various types of materials. Celluloid tokens and paper cards were among the earliest, followed by paper and metal plates with holders, metal tokens, and, finally, plastic cards. They have been issued by merchants, oil companies, the travel and entertainment industries, and banks to name the most common. Credit card collecting is one of the fastest growing hobbies today. By their very nature, credit cards and charge tokens were usually deliberately destroyed, making older credit items fiercely sought after. Our advisor, Walt Thompson, is listed in the Directory under Washington.

American Express, violet color, 1969 ....**43.00**

Carte Blanche/Hilton hotels, 1960 ....**18.00**

Diners' Club National directory booklet, 1962 ....**10.00**

Diners' Club 1974, credit card **10.00**

Drexler Technology Corp Lasercard, optical memory card **18.00**

Esso Standard Oil Co, paper, 1959, as issued in holder, envelope **95.00**

Esso Standard Oil Co, papercard, 1960 ....**15.00**

Hess Bros, charge sample coin, no numbers **29.00**

Hilton Hotels, paper, credit card, late 1940s **33.00**

Hilton/Statler Hotels, paper, credit card, 1956 ....**9.00**

Kaufman, charge coin **20.00**

Lady Luck Casino, hotel card, joker emblem **8.00**

Marathon Oil Co, sample credit card, 1975 ....**4.00**

May & Malone, charge coin, scarce **31.00**

Sunoco, Sun Oil Company credit card, 1972, $8.00.

McLenna, McFeely, Prior, copper, charge coin **21.00**

Michigan Bankcard, charge card, 1969 ....**20.00**

National Express, credit card, 1974 ....**25.00**

Netherland Plaza/Terrace Plaza hotel, paper, 1956 ....**15.00**

Sak's 5th Ave, plastic, 1970s **8.00**

SEARS, aluminum, 1940s, sm, rare **90.00**

Shell Oil Co, nationwide, paper, 1956 ....**18.00**

Skydel's, paper department store charge card, 1954 ....**12.00**

Strawbridge Clothiers, Pilgrim & Indian, arrowhead shape **21.00**

Texas Oil Co, paper, national credit card, 1945 ....**20.00**

The PEP Boys, credit card, 1977 ....**42.00**

Vacuum Oil Co, paper, 1931, damage **25.00**

VISA, Diver's Card, Marine Midland Bank, fish scene, 1996 ....**28.00**

VISA, Humane Society, colorful, 1995 ....**10.00**

WT Grants, paper charge card, 1950s **11.00**

Cuff Links

What is this new attraction to cuff links as a collectible? To the surprise of many, cuff links are not really new to the hobby scene; they have been collectible for years. In fact, one of the main reasons for the formation of the National Cuff Link Society in 1991 was to provide a networking mechanism for collectors. The Society's quarterly publication, *The Link*, unites collectors throughout the world and provides ideas and research. Veteran collectors describe the hobby as the ideal collectible. They point out that cuff links are very available, affordable, easy to display, and do not require a lot of room to store. They also boast that it is the only collectible that can be worn on one's shirt sleeve.

Collectors also enjoy the virtually infinite number of cuff link designs available and the opportunities to specialize. Some of the most popular subjects for specialization are sports, fraternal emblems, advertising logos, animals, cars, and ships. Other enthusiasts limit their collections to the types of materials used in the manufacturing process. Examples of this category include wood, leather, plastic, fur, silver, and gold. Some collectors concentrate on the back of the cuff link — they specialize in various fastening devices that have evolved over the years.

Cuff link collecting is educational. They have always mirrored the economy, lifestyle, and history of their time. For example, the Victorian period's accent on color, glitter, and enamel was clearly reflected in the design of its cuff links. Likewise, the post-World War

II era's preference for ostenatious fashion gave birth to the bright and over-sized cuff links of that day. Cuff links also reveal a lot about the state-of-the art of design and workmanship at the time of their manufacture. For further information cuff links and *The Link*, contact Gene Klompus, society president, who is listed in the Directory under Illinois. See also Clubs and Newsletters.

Bon Ami Cleanser, barbell-type closure, enameled sterling, ca 1895, VG **160.00**
Compass, sterling, swivel toggle closure, w/matching tie bar, 1940s **125.00**
Enamel on sterling, blue & yellow pastel abstract design, ca 1955, EX **135.00**
Fleur-de-lis, silver & blue sq shape, Swank, 1960, ¾", G **8.00**

Knots, gold-tone, Hickok brand, 1955, w/matching tie bar, G **15.00**
Martin & Lewis, silver-tone, toggle closure, ca 1965 ....**85.00**
Mickey Mouse logo, black, yellow & red, ca 1940, VG in VG box **45.00**
Presidential Seal, Reagan presidency, base metal, G in original box **200.00**
Soccer balls, sterling, barbell-shape, S&S brand, 1902, ¾", M **150.00**
Square faced, brilliant red stone, wraparound closure, 1970, VG **25.00**
Watch cuff links (only 1 w/watch), Sheffield, G (watch slow) in box **110.00**

Related Items and Accessories

Collar button, gold-tone base metal, G, bag of 100 ......**10.00**

Cuff links, steer heads, sterling, manufactured by Fenwick and Sailors, $70.00. (Photo courtesy Gene Klompus)

Collar pin, silver color, Swank, ca 1965, 2", G w/original box .**4.00**

Set: key chain, ballpoint, cuff links & money clip, 1950s, fair w/box **22.00**

Shirt studs, gray mother-of-pearl faces, Krementz, ca 1935, 4-pc set **30.00**

Sleeve attacher for ca 1920 shirts, silver color, Patent 1898, 3", VG **15.00**

Tie bar, initial G in gold, ca 1948, 4" **3.00**

Tie tac, Beatle's face in silver, 1964, 4-pc set **150.00**

Tie tac, Kansas City Chiefs logo, ca 1970 ....**25.00**

Tie tac, NASA logo & ¾" space capsule, silver base metal, ca 1965 ....**50.00**

Czechoslovakian Glass

Items marked Czechoslovakia are popular modern collectibles. Pottery, glassware, jewelry, etc., were produced there in abundance. Refer to *Czechoslovakian Glass and Collectibles* by Dale and Diane Barta and Helen M. Rose (Collector Books) for more information.

Atomizer, frosted satin w/painted flowers, amber stem & foot, 5½" **95.00**

Basket, red, cased, applied black rim & handle, 6½" **80.00**

Bottle, cologne; amber cut base, amber intaglio drop stopper, 5¾" **135.00**

Bowl, cream w/multicolor wavy design, cased, inverted rim, 4½" **85.00**

Candlestick, black w/orange interior, wide flared rim, 3", pr **190.00**

Candlestick, mottled colors, cased, wide base, flared rim, 3" **55.00**

Decanter, clear w/painted floral design, w/stopper, 10½" .**70.00**

Honey pot, dark blue iridescent w/enameled decor, w/lid, 5" **95.00**

Lamp globe, multicolored mottle, cased, globular, 5½" **95.00**

Paperweight, clear w/multicolor base, 3 pink & white flowers, 3" **45.00**

Pitcher, clear w/painted scene, bulbous, clear handle, 6¾" .**175.00**

Pitcher, cobalt & red mottle, cased, cobalt handle, flared rim, 9" **125.00**

Pitcher, orange, cased, applied cobalt rim & handle, tricorner top, 5" **85.00**

Salt & pepper shakers, crystal duck forms, porcelain head tops, 2", pr **45.00**

Shot glass, clear w/enameled design, 1¾" **25.00**

Vase, autumn-colored mottle, cased, slim form w/4 clear feet, 11¾" **80.00**

Vase, black w/enameled exotic bird, cased, silver rim, 7¼" **145.00**

Vase, bud; dark blue w/enamel floral decor, 8¼" ..**75.00**

Vase, clear frosted, embossed running horses, ball form, 7" **90.00**

Vase, cobalt w/mottled colors, cased, applied cobalt handles, 8" **90.00**

Vase, crystal, floral intaglio, ball form, 5" **90.00**

Vase, dark amethyst w/gold design, footed, flared rim, 8½" **85.00**

Vase, frosted satin w/coralene crescent design, 4½" **65.00**

Vase, green w/red & brown overlay streaks, lamp chimney shape, 7" **150.00**

Vase, light blue, cased, pleated rim, clear handles, 7⅞" **110.00**

Vase, light green w/cobalt threads, fan form, 7¾" **200.00**

Vase, orange w/black serpentine decor, cased, slim, 8" **90.00**

Vase, orange w/blue mottled base, cased, ruffled rim, slim, 8½" **85.00**

Vase, pink w/white swirling stripe overlay design, ruffled rim, 8½" **125.00**

Vase, red, cased, applied black rim & 3 black angular handles, 4" **130.00**

Vase, red & orange mottle, cased, w/metal flower arranger, 4" **75.00**

Vase, red w/blue & yellow mottling, cased, flared rim, slim, 6½" **60.00**

Vase, red w/white mottling, cased, black edge on flared rim, 7" **80.00**

Vase, white w/green aventurine, cased, applied black rim, 8⅞" **110.00**

Vase, yellow, cased, applied black rim, classic form, 6¼" **70.00**

Vase, yellow w/silver bird & flower design, cased, slim form, 10" **100.00**

Vase, yellow-orange w/brown overlay at base, cased, bulbous, 4½" **60.00**

Vases: Yellow cased with red and brown mottle, 8", from $70.00 to $75.00; Yellow cased with black ruffled rim, 7", from $60.00 to $65.00.

Dakin

From about 1968 through the late 1970s, the R. Dakin Company produced a line of hollow vinyl advertising and comic characters licensed by Warner Brothers, Hanna-Barbera, and Disney as well as others. Some figures had molded-on clothing; some had felt clothes and accessory items. Inspiration for characters came from TV cartoon shows, comic strips, or special advertising promotions. Dakins were offered in different types of packaging. Those in colorful 'Cartoon Theatre' boxes command higher prices than those that came in clear plastic bags. Plush figures were also produced but the vinyl examples such as we've listed below are the most collectible. All are complete with clothes and accessories, and original tags are present unless otherwise noted. For further information and more listings we recommend *Schroeder's Collectible Toys, Antique to Modern* (Collector Books).

Foghorn Leghorn, vinyl, 1970, 8½", **EX+, $75.00.**

Baby Puss, Hanna-Barbera, 1971, EX+ **100.00**
Bambi, Disney, 1960s, MIP .**35.00**
Bozo the Clown, Larry Harmon, 1974, EX **35.00**
Bugs Bunny, Warner Bros, 1971, MIP **30.00**
Bull Dog, Dream Pet, EX **15.00**
Daffy Duck, Warner Bros, 1968, EX **30.00**
Deputy Dawg, Terrytoons, 1977, EX **40.00**
Donald Duck, orig tags, NMIP .**30.00**

Dumbo, Disney, EX+ **20.00**
Elmer Fudd, Warner Bros, in tuxedo, 1968, EX............**30.00**
Goofy, Disney, 1960s, EX **20.00**
Goofy Gram, Dog, You're Top Dog, EX **20.00**
Goofy Gram, Fox, Wanna See My Etchings?, EX **20.00**
Goofy Gram, Lion, Sorry You're Feeling Beastly!, EX **20.00**
Huckleberry Hound, Hanna-Barbera, 1970, EX+ **75.00**
Jack-in-the-Box, bank, 1971, EX **25.00**
Mickey Mouse, Disney, 1960s, cloth clothes, EX **20.00**
Mighty Mouse, Terrytoons, 1978, EX **100.00**
Monkey on a Barrel, bank, 1971, EX **25.00**
Oliver Hardy, Larry Harmon, 1974, EX+ **30.00**
Pebbles Flintstones, Hanna-Barbera, 1970, EX **35.00**

Pink Panther, Mirisch-Freleng, 1971, EX+ **50.00**

Porky Pig, Warner Bros, 1968, EX+ **30.00**

Scooby Doo, Hanna-Barbera, 1980, EX **75.00**

Scrappy Doo, Hanna-Barbera, 1982, EX+ **75.00**

Seal on a Box, bank, 1971, EX .**25.00**

Sylvester, Warner Bros, 1978, MIP (fun farm bag) **20.00**

Tiger in a Cage, bank, 1971, EX **25.00**

Tweety Bird, Warner Bros, 1966, EX+ **20.00**

Uncle Bugs Bunny, Warner Bros, 1975, EX+ **50.00**

Underdog, Jay Ward, 1976, MIB (cartoon theater box) ..**150.00**

Wile E Coyote, Warner Bros, 1968, MIB **30.00**

Yogi Bear, Hanna-Barbera, 1970, EX **60.00**

Decanters

The James Beam Distilling Company produced its first ceramic whiskey decanter in 1953 and remained the only major producer of these decanters throughout the decade. By the late 1960s, other companies such as Ezra Brooks, Lionstone, and Cyrus Noble were also becoming involved in their production. Today these fancy liquor containers are attracting many collectors. Our advisors for decanters are Judy and Art Turner of Homestead Collectibles, who are listed in the Directory under Pennsylvania.

Beam, Automotive Series, Bass Boat **29.00**

Beam, Automotive Series, Duesenberg Convertble, lt bl **110.00**

Beam, Automotive Series, Golf Cart **35.00**

Beam, Automotive Series, Space Shuttle **49.00**

Beam, Automotive Series, State Trooper, gray **65.00**

Beam, Automotive Series, Train, flat car **79.00**

Beam, Automotive Series, 1903 Ford Model A, black **49.00**

Beam, Automotive Series, 1929 Ford Police Car, blue **89.00**

Beam, Automotive Series, 1955 Chevy Corvette, copper .**85.00**

Beam, Automotive Series, 1957 Chevy Corvette, black ..**59.00**

Jim Beam, Siamese Cat, 1975, 11½", $18.00.

Beam, Automotive Series, 1969
Chevy Camaro, blue **49.00**
Beam, Automotive Series, 1978
Chevy Corvette, red **65.00**
Beam, Casino Series, Golden Gate,
1970 ....**10.00**
Beam, Casino Series, HC
Pinwheel **40.00**
Beam, Casino Series, Reno-Prima
Donna **9.00**
Beam, Centennial Series, Chicago
Fire **25.00**
Beam, Centennial Series, Key
West **9.00**
Beam, Centennial Series, San
Diego **9.00**
Beam, Club Series, Fox, blue .**50.00**
Beam, Club Series, Rocky
Mountain **10.00**
Beam, Convention Series, #8
Chicago, 1978 ....**10.00**
Beam, Convention Series, Pilgrim
Lady **40.00**
Beam, Customer Series,
Broadmoor Hotel **9.00**
Beam, Customer Series, Marina
City **10.00**
Beam, Executive Series, 1959
Tavern Scene **35.00**
Beam, Executive Series, 1972
Regency **15.00**
Beam, Foreign Series, Australia,
Koala **15.00**
Beam, Foreign Series, New
Zealand, Kiwi **5.00**
Beam, Oraganization Series, #2
Ducks Unlimited, Wood Duck,
1975 ....**45.00**
Beam, Organization Series, #10
Ducks Unlimited, Mallard,
1984 ....**95.00**
Beam, Organization Series, #15
Ducks Unlimited, Black Duck,
1989 ....**95.00**

Beam, Organization Series,
Bartenders Guild **9.00**
Beam, Organization Series, Elks .**9.00**
Beam, Organization Series,
Legion Music **10.00**
Beam, Organization Series, Shriner-
Moila w/Camel **15.00**
Beam, Organization Series,
Turtle **10.00**
Beam, People Series, Buffalo
Bill **15.00**
Beam, People Series, Hatfield .**19.00**
Beam, People Series, McCoy ..**19.00**
Beam, People Series, Viking ..**10.00**
Beam, Political Series, Boxer
Elephant, 1964 ....**190.00**
Beam, Political Series, Drum
Donkey, 1976 ....**19.00**
Beam, Political Series, Election
Democrat, 1988 ....**29.00**
Beam, Regal China Series,
Antique Trader **9.00**
Beam, Regal China Series,
Canteen **19.00**
Beam, Regal China Series,
Franklin Mint **9.00**
Beam, Regal China Series,
Jukebox **59.00**
Beam, Regal China Series, Mt St
Helens **20.00**
Beam, Regal China Series, Pony
Express **10.00**
Beam, Regal China Series, Seattle
World's Fair **10.00**
Beam, Regal China Series, Stone
Mountain **19.00**
Beam, Regal China Series,
Tombstone **9.00**
Beam, Regal China Series,
Yosemite **9.00**
Beam, Sports Series, Bing Crosby
33rd, 1974 ....**35.00**
Beam, Sports Series, Bowling
Pin **10.00**

Beam, Sports Series, Clint Eastwood **24.00**

Beam, Sports Series, Hula Bowl **14.00**

Beam, Sports Series, Louisville Downs **14.00**

Beam, Sports Series, US Open .**24.00**

Beam, State Series, Kansas .**39.00**

Beam, State Series, Ohio **9.00**

Beam, Trophy Series, Bird, Blue Jay **10.00**

Beam, Trophy Series, Dog, Setter **21.00**

Beam, Trophy Series, Fish, Rainbow Trout **15.00**

Beam, Trophy Series, Horse, Appaloosa **15.00**

Beam, Trophy Series, Panda Bear **20.00**

Brooks, Indy Racer Penske #2 .**75.00**

Famous First, Automotive Series, Airplane, Spirit of St Louis .**75.00**

Famous First, Automotive Series, Duesenberg **95.00**

Hoffman, Lucky Lindy **95.00**

Kingston Classics, Fire Truck .**95.00**

Lionstone, Boxers **65.00**

Lionstone, Rainmaker **25.00**

McCormick, Muhammad Ali .**175.00**

Mike Wayne, John Wayne bust .**65.00**

Mount Hope, Fireman & Soldiers **24.00**

Old Commonwealth, Fireman #3 On Call Red, 1983 ....**85.00**

Pacesetter, 1978 Corvette, yellow **35.00**

Wade, JB Barrel, blue or black, ea **95.00**

Depression Glass

Depression glass, named for the era when it was sold through dimestores or was given away as premiums, can be found in such varied colors as amber, green, pink, blue, red, yellow, white, and crystal. Mass produced by many different companies in hundreds of patterns, Depression glass is one of the most sought-after collectibles in the United States today. Refer to *The Pocket Guide to Depression Glass* by Gene Florence (Collector Books). See also Fire-King.

Aunt Polly, sugar bowl, blue, with lid, $30.00.

Adam, butter dish, pink, w/lid .**80.00**

Adam, coaster, green, 3¼" ...**20.00**

Adam, pitcher, pink, 32-oz, 8" .**40.00**

Adam, plate, grill; pink or green, 9" **20.00**

American Pioneer, bowl, crystal or pink, handled, 9" **25.00**

American Pioneer, goblet, wine; green, 3-oz, 4" **45.00**

American Pioneer, plate, crystal or pink, 6" **12.50**

American Pioneer, saucer, green **5.00**

American Pioneer, whiskey, crystal or pink, 2-oz, 2¼" **45.00**

American Sweetheart, creamer, pink, footed **13.00**

American Sweetheart, plate, salad; red, 8" **65.00**

American Sweetheart, sugar bowl, blue, footed, open **115.00**

Aunt Polly, bowl, green, 4¾x2" .**15.00**

Aunt Polly, creamer, blue **45.00**

Aunt Polly, tumbler, blue, 8-oz, 3⅝" **30.00**

Aunt Polly, vase, green, footed, 6½" **30.00**

Aurora, bowl, pink, deep, 4½" .**40.00**

Aurora, creamer, cobalt, 4½" ...**22.50**

Aurora, saucer **5.00**

Avocado, bowl, salad; crystal, 7½" **12.00**

Avocado, cup, green, footed, 2 styles **35.00**

Avocado, plate, luncheon; pink, 8¼" **17.00**

Beaded Block, bowl, celery; pink, 8¼" **13.00**

Beaded Block, bowl, 5½" sq ...**7.50**

Beaded Block, bowl, jelly; red, stemmed, 4½" **18.00**

Beaded Block, vase, bouquet; amber, 6" **12.00**

Block Optic, ice bucket, pink .**45.00**

Block Optic, mug, green **32.50**

Block Optic, plate, grill; green or pink, 9", ea **25.00**

Block Optic, sherbet, green, 5½-oz, 3¼" **6.00**

Block Optic, tumble-up night set, green **62.50**

Bowknot, bowl, berry; green, 4½" **16.00**

Bowknot, sherbet, green, low foot **16.00**

Cameo, bowl, sauce; crystal, 4¼" .**5.50**

Cameo, bowl, vegetable; green, oval, 10" **30.00**

Cameo, cup, yellow, 2 styles ..**7.50**

Cameo, plate, dinner; pink, 9½" **75.00**

Cameo, platter, yellow, closed handles, 12" **40.00**

Cameo, vase, green, 8" **35.00**

Cherry Blossom, bowl, soup; pink, flat, 7¾" **60.00**

Cherry Blossom, coaster, green **13.00**

Cherry Blossom, pitcher, pink, allover pattern, flat, 42-oz, 8" **52.50**

Cherry Blossom, plate, sherbet; pink or green, 6", ea **8.00**

Cherry Blossom, platter, Delphite, oval, 11" **40.00**

Cherry Blossom, tray, sandwich; pink or green, 10½", ea **25.00**

Cherryberry, butter dish, iridescent, w/lid **145.00**

Cherryberry, olive dish, green, w/handle, 5" **15.00**

Cherryberry, sugar bowl lid only, crystal **30.00**

Chinex Classic, bowl, cereal; browntone, 5¾" **5.50**

Chinex Classic, bowl, vegetable; castle decal, 9" **35.00**

Chinex Classic, cup, decal decorated **6.50**

Circle, bowl, green or pink, 5¼" .**10.00**

Circle, decanter, green or pink, w/handle **45.00**

Circle, pitcher, green or pink, 60-oz **35.00**

Circle, tumbler, water; green or pink, 8-oz, 4" **9.00**

Cloverleaf, bowl, dessert; yellow, 4" **25.00**

Cloverleaf, sherbet, yellow, footed, 3" **11.00**

Cloverleaf, tumbler, green, footed, 10-oz, 5¾" **22.50**

Colonial, bowl, berry; crystal, 4½" **9.00**

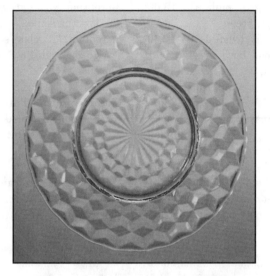

Cube, plate, luncheon; green, 8", $7.00.

Colonial, plate, grill; pink or green, 10" **25.00**

Colonial, spoon holder, pink .**125.00**

Colonial, whiskey, green, 1½-oz, 2½" **15.00**

Colonial Block, bowl, pink or green, 4" **6.50**

Colonial Block, butter tub, pink or green **40.00**

Colonial Block, creamer, white .**7.00**

Colonial Block, sugar bowl, white **5.50**

Colonial Fluted, bowl, cereal; green, 6" **9.00**

Colonial Fluted, cup, green ...**5.00**

Colonial Fluted, sherbet, green .**6.00**

Columbia, bowl, soup; crystal, low, 8" **20.00**

Columbia, plate, bread & butter; pink, 9½" **13.00**

Columbia, snack plate, crystal .**35.00**

Coronation, bowl, berry; red, 4¼" .**6.50**

Coronation, tumbler, pink, footed, 10-oz, 5" **20.00**

Cube, coaster, green, 3¼" **7.50**

Cube, sherbet, pink, footed ...**7.00**

Diamond Quilted, bowl, cereal; blue or black, 5" **15.00**

Diamond Quilted, goblet, cordial; pink or green, 1-oz **12.00**

Diamond Quilted, ice bucket, pink or green **50.00**

Diamond Quilted, plate, sandwich; pink or green, 14" **12.50**

Diamond Quilted, tumbler, water; pink or green, 9-oz **9.00**

Diamond Quilted, vase, blue & black, fan shape, dolphin foot **75.00**

Diana, ashtray, crystal, 3½" .**3.00**

Diana, plate, pink, 9½" **16.00**

Diana, platter, amber, oval, 12" .**13.00**

Dogwood, bowl, berry; pink, 8½" **60.00**

Dogwood, plate salver, pink, 12" .**30.00**

Dogwood, tumbler, pink, molded band **21.00**

Doric, bowl, berry; pink, 4½" ..**7.00**

Doric, cake plate, pink or green, 3-legs, 10", ea **21.00**

Doric, plate, grill; pink, 9" ...**15.00**

Doric, saucer, green **4.50**

Doric, tray, pink, handled, 10" .**12.50**

Doric & Pansy, bowl, green & teal, handled, 9" **35.00**

Doric & Pansy, plate, salad; green & teal, 7" **35.00**

Doric & Pansy, tumbler, green & teal, 9-oz, 4½" **90.00**

English Hobnail, ashtray, pink or green, 3" **20.00**

English Hobnail, bottle, toilet; ice blue, 5-oz **45.00**

English Hobnail, bowl, grapefruit; pink or green, 6½" **20.00**

English Hobnail, bowl, nappy; 6" sq **16.00**

English Hobnail, bowl pickle; pink or green, 8" **30.00**

English Hobnail, cup, ice blue .**25.00**

English Hobnail, tidbit, ice blue, 2-tier **75.00**

Floral, bowl, vegetable; green, oval, 9" **20.00**

Floral, candy jar, green, w/lid .**40.00**

Floral, plate, salad; pink, 8" .**10.00**

Floral, tumbler, juice; green, footed, 5-oz, 4" **21.00**

Floral & Diamond Band, bowl, berry; green, 4½" **9.00**

Floral & Diamond Band, compote, pink, tall, 5½" **15.00**

Florentine No 1, bowl, cereal; yellow, 6" **23.00**

Florentine No 1, plate, grill; pink, 10" **18.00**

Florentine No 1, plate, sherbet; crystal, green or pink, 6" .**6.00**

Florentine No 1, sugar bowl, yellow, w/lid **37.00**

Florentine No 2, bowl, yellow, 5½" **40.00**

Florentine No 2, candlesticks, crystal, 2¾", pr **100.00**

Florentine No 2, gravy boat, yellow **55.00**

Florentine No 2, plate, salad; crystal, green or pink, 8½", ea **9.00**

Florentine No 2, shakers, green, pr **42.50**

Flower Garden w/Butterflies, comport, black, footed, 7" ..**175.00**

Flower Garden w/Butterflies, cup, pink **65.00**

Flower Garden w/Butterflies, plate, blue or canary yellow, 7" **30.00**

Flower Garden w/Butterflies, tumbler, amber, 7½" **175.00**

Fortune, bowl, berry; pink or crystal, 4" **4.50**

Fortune, bowl, pink or crystal, roll edge, 5¼" **7.00**

Fortune, tumbler, juice; pink or crystal, 5-oz, 3½" **8.00**

Fruits, cup, green **8.00**

Fruits, sherbet, pink **7.00**

Georgian, bowl, vegetable; green, oval, 9" **60.00**

Georgian, hot plate, green, center design, 5" **47.50**

Georgian, plate, sherbet; green, 6" **6.00**

Hex Optic, bucket reamer, pink or green **55.00**

Hex Optic, ice bucket, pink or green, metal handle **18.00**

Hex Optic, sugar shaker, pink or green **165.00**

Hobnail, cup, pink or crystal, ea .**4.50**

Hobnail, goblet, iced tea; crystal, 13-oz **8.00**

Hobnail, whiskey, crystal, 1½-oz **6.00**

Homespun, creamer, pink or crystal, footed **10.00**

Homespun, platter, pink or crystal, closed handles, 13" ..**15.00**

Homespun, tumbler, pink or crystal, footed, 5-oz, 4" **7.00**

Indiana Custard, bowl, soup; French ivory, flat, 7½" ..**30.00**

Indiana Custard, plate, bread & butter; French ivory, 5¾" **6.50**

Indiana Custard, plate, salad; French ivory, 7½" **15.00**

Indiana Custard, saucer, French ivory **8.00**

Iris, bowl, sauce; iridescent, ruffled, 5" **25.00**

Iris, coaster, crystal **95.00**

Iris, goblet, iridescent, 4-oz, 5½" **125.00**

Iris, lamp shade, crystal, 11½" .**85.00**

Iris, vase, green or pink, 9" .**130.00**

Jubilee, candlesticks, pink or yellow, pr **185.00**

Jubilee, plate, sandwich; yellow, 13½" **50.00**

Jubilee, tumbler, water; yellow, 10-oz, 6" **35.00**

Lace Edge, bowl, pink, plain, 9½" **24.00**

Lace Edge, comport, pink, 7" ..**24.00**

Lace Edge, plate, pink, solid lace, 13" **32.00**

Laced Edge, bowl, opalescent, oval, 11" **140.00**

Laced Edge, bowl, opalescent, 5" **37.50**

Laced Edge, plate, dinner; opalescent, 10" **85.00**

Laced Edge, tumbler, opalescent, 9-oz **60.00**

Lake Como, creamer, white, footed **30.00**

Lake Como, platter, white, 11" .**65.00**

Laurel, bowl, soup; jade green, 7⅛" **32.00**

Laurel, cheese dish, white opalescent, w/lid **55.00**

Laurel, shakers, French ivory, pr **50.00**

Lincoln Inn, bowl, cereal; cobalt, 6" **14.00**

Lincoln Inn, goblet, water; black **17.50**

Lincoln Inn, saucer, blue **4.50**

Lincoln Inn, vase, pink, footed, 12" **95.00**

Lorain, creamer, crystal, footed **16.00**

Lorain, platter, yellow, 11½" .**42.50**

Lorain, relish, green, 4-part, 8" .**20.00**

Madrid, bowl, sauce; amber, 5" .**6.00**

Manhattan, tumbler, pink, footed, 5¼", $17.00.

Madrid, cookie jar, pink, w/lid .**30.00**

Madrid, Jello mold, amber, 2⅛" .**13.00**

Madrid, plate, relish; green, 10¼" **16.00**

Madrid, tumbler, blue, 5-oz, 3⅝" .**38.00**

Manhattan, bowl, sauce; crystal, handles, 4½"..................**9.00**

Manhattan, candy dish, pink, 3 legs..................................**11.00**

Manhattan, pitcher, pink, tilted, 80-oz. **60.00**

Manhattan, wine, crystal, 3½" .**5.50**

Mayfair (Federal), bowl, cereal; crystal, 6" **9.50**

Mayfair (Federal), bowl, sauce; green, 5" **12.00**

Mayfair (Federal), platter, amber, oval, 12" **27.50**

Mayfair (Federal), tumbler, amber, 9-oz, 4½" **27.50**

Mayfair/Open Rose, bowl, cereal; pink, 5½" **24.00**

Mayfair/Open Rose, bowl, vegetable; blue, 10" **65.00**

Mayfair/Open Rose, butter dish lid, pink **40.00**

Mayfair/Open Rose, cup, green or yellow, ea **145.00**

Mayfair/Open Rose, tumbler, water; green or yellow, 11-oz, 4¾", ea **200.00**

Miss America, cake plate, pink, footed, 12" **42.50**

Miss America, pitcher, crystal, 65-oz, 8" **46.00**

Miss America, plate, salad; crystal, 8½" **7.50**

Miss America, saucer, red ...**65.00**

Moderntone, bowl, cobalt, 5" .**25.00**

Moderntone, creamer, amethyst .**10.00**

Moderntone, plate, luncheon; cobalt, 7¾" **12.50**

Moderntone, tumbler, amethyst, 5-oz **30.00**

Moondrops, bowl, pickle; blue or red, 7½" **22.00**

Moondrops, candlesticks, green, ruffled, 2", pr **24.00**

Moondrops, comport, blue or red, 11½" **65.00**

Moondrops, gravy boat, crystal .**90.00**

Moondrops, powder jar, blue or red, 3-footed **175.00**

Moondrops, vase, green, rocket style, 9¼" **135.00**

New Century, ashtray/coaster, green, 5⅜" **28.00**

New Century, goblet, cocktail; green, 3¼-oz **22.50**

New Century, tumbler, pink, cobalt or amethyst, 10-oz, 5" **16.00**

No 610 Pyramid, bowl, master berry; pink, 8½" **30.00**

No 610 Pyramid, ice tub, crystal **55.00**

No 612 Horseshoe, bowl, vegetable; green or yellow, 8½", ea **30.00**

No 612 Horseshoe, sherbet, green **14.00**

No 616 Vernon, cup, crystal ..**8.00**

No 616 Vernon, tumbler, green or yellow, footed, 5" **35.00**

No 618 Pineapple & Floral, plate, dinner; crystal, 9⅜" **17.50**

No 618 Pineapple & Floral, plate, sandwich; amber or red, 11½" **16.00**

No 618 Pineapple & Floral, vase, crystal, cone-shaped, lg .**40.00**

Normandie, bowl, berry; amber, 5" **6.00**

Normandie, pitcher, pink, 80-oz, 8" **150.00**

Normandie, plate, dinner; iridescent, 11" **11.50**

Normandie, tumbler, juice; pink, 5-oz, 4" **85.00**

Old Cafe, bowl, crystal, 5" **5.00**

Old Cafe, candy dish, any color, low, 8", ea **11.00**

Old Cafe, vase, red, 7¼" **20.00**

Parrot, jam dish, amber, 7" .**35.00**

Parrot, platter, green, oblong, 11¼" **52.00**

Patrician, butter dish, amber or crystal, w/lid **90.00**

Patrician, plate, sherbet; pink or green, 6", ea 8.00

Patrician, tumbler, amber or crystal, footed, 8-oz, 5¼" 47.50

Patrician, cookie jar, amber, with lid, $85.00.

Petalware, creamer, crystal, footed 3.00

Petalware, platter, pink, oval, 13" 18.00

Petalware, saucer, monax, plain .2.00

Primo, cake plate, yellow or green, 3-footed, 10" 25.00

Primo, plate, dinner; yellow or green, 10" 20.00

Princess, ashtray, green, 4½" .70.00

Princess, relish, topaz or apricot, plain, 7½" 150.00

Princess, vase, pink, 8" 40.00

Radiance, bowl, bonbon; ice blue or red, 6" 30.00

Radiance, cup, punch; amber, flat 7.00

Radiance, decanter, ice blue or red, handled, w/stopper 165.00

Raindrops, bowl, fruit; green, 4½" 6.00

Raindrops, tumbler, green, 4-oz, 3" 5.00

Ribbon, bowl, berry; green, 4" .20.00

Ribbon, creamer, green, footed .15.00

Ribbon, shakers, black, pr ...45.00

Rose Cameo, bowl, cereal; green, 4½" 15.00

Rose Cameo, plate, salad; green, 7" 12.00

Rosemary, bowl, berry; amber, 5" 6.00

Roulette, cup, pink or green ..6.50

Roulette, tumbler, juice; pink, 5-oz, 3¼" 22.00

Round Robin, creamer, iridescent, footed 6.00

Round Robin, saucer, green ..2.00

Royal Ruby, bonbon, 6½" 8.50

Royal Ruby, cup, Old Cafe 8.00

Royal Ruby, plate, dinner; round, 9⅛" 11.00

Royal Ruby, sugar bowl, footed 8.00

Royal Ruby, tray, 6x4½" 12.50

Sandwich (Hocking), bowl, berry; crystal, 4⅞" 5.00

Sandwich (Hocking), creamer, green 27.50

Sandwich (Hocking), plate, dessert; crystal, 7" 10.00

Sandwich (Indiana), bowl, amber or crystal, 6" 4.00

Sandwich (Indiana), butter dish bottom, teal blue 42.50

Sandwich (Indiana), cup, red .27.50

Sandwich (Indiana), plate, sandwich; pink or green, 13" .25.00

Sandwich (Indiana), tumbler, amber, footed, 15-oz, 6½" 120.00

Sharon, bowl, cereal; amber, 6" 20.00

Sharon, candy jar, amber, w/lid .45.00

Sharon, plate, salad; pink, 7½" 23.00

Ships, cocktail shaker, blue & white **32.50**

Ships, tumbler, iced tea; blue & white, 12-oz **22.00**

Ships, tumbler, whiskey; blue & white, 3½" **27.50**

Sierra, bowl, cereal; pink, 5½" .**12.00**

Sierra, pitcher, green, 32-oz, 6½" **110.00**

Sierra, saucer, pink **6.00**

Sierra, sugar bowl lid only, pink or green, ea **16.00**

Spiral, bowl, berry; green, 4¾" ...**5.00**

Spiral, plate, sherbet; green, 6" .**2.00**

Spiral, preserve, green, w/lid .**30.00**

Strawberry, creamer, crystal, sm **12.00**

Strawberry, olive dish, pink, w/handle, 5" **13.00**

Strawberry, tumbler, iridescent, 8-oz, 3⅝" **20.00**

Sunflower, plate, dinner; pink, 9" **15.00**

Sunflower, saucer, green **10.00**

Swirl, butter dish bottom, pink **32.50**

Swirl, cup, ultramarine **15.00**

Swirl, plate, sherbet; delphite, 6½" **6.00**

Swirl, tumbler, pink, footed, 9-oz **18.00**

Tea Room, bowl, finger; green .**50.00**

Tea Room, ice bucket, pink .**50.00**

Tea Room, relish, green, divided .**25.00**

Tea Room, shakers, pink, pr .**50.00**

Twisted Optic, bowl, blue, 9" .**25.00**

Twisted Optic, candy jar, pink, footed, tall, w/lid **35.00**

Twisted Optic, mayonnaise, blue **35.00**

Twisted Optic, plate, luncheon; canary yellow, 8" **8.00**

US Swirl, bowl, berry; green, 4⅜" **6.00**

US Swirl, pitcher, pink or green, 48-oz, 8", ea **50.00**

Vitrock, bowl, fruit; white, 6" .**5.50**

Vitrock, plate, soup; white, 9" .**13.00**

Vitrock, sugar bowl, white **4.50**

Waterford, ashtray, crystal, 4" .**7.50**

Waterford, lamp, crystal, spherical base, 4" **26.00**

Waterford, plate, salad; pink, 7⅛" **8.00**

Waterford, plate, sherbet; pink, 6" **6.00**

Windsor, cake plate, crystal, footed, 10¾" **8.50**

Windsor, candlesticks, crystal, 3", pr **20.00**

Windsor, pitcher, green, 52-oz, 6¾" **55.00**

Windsor, plate, chop; pink, 13⅝" **45.00**

Dollhouse Furnishings

Collecting antique dollhouses and building new ones is a popular hobby with many today, and all who collect houses delight in furnishing them right down to the vase on the table and the scarf on the piano! Flea markets are a good source of dollhouse furnishings, especially those from the 1940s through the '60s made by Strombecker, Tootsietoy, Renwal, or the Petite Princess line by Ideal.

Bathtub, Tomy Smaller Homes .**8.00**

Bed, bright yellow, hard plastic, Marx, ¾" scale **5.00**

Bed, light pink, open headboard & footboard, Tootsietoy **18.00**

Bed, pink, Strombecker, ¾" scale **12.00**

Rocking chair, blue and pink, Renwal #65, $10.00; Stroller, blue and pink, Renwal #87, $35.00; Baby, Renwal #8, $10.00. (Photo courtesy Judy Mosholder)

Bed, turquoise bedspread, Ideal, 1969 ....**6.00**

Boudoir chaise lounge, blue, Ideal Petite Princess, #4408-1 .**18.00**

Buffet, brown or tan, Plasco ..**4.00**

Buffet, dark marbleized reddish brown, Ideal Young Decorator **15.00**

Chair, armless; pale blue, hard plastic, Marx, ½" scale ...**2.00**

Chair, barrel; ivory & brown, Renwal, #77 ....**8.00**

Chair, living room; yellow, no-base style, Plasco **3.00**

Corner cupboard, blue, Bestmade **4.00**

Cradle, Mattel Liddles **3.00**

Doll, baby w/diaper, Thomas, 2" .**4.00**

Doll, brother, tan suit, metal rivets, Renwal, #42 ....**28.00**

Doll, mother, rose dress, Renwal, #43, M **5.00**

Dresser, pink, low style, hard plastic, Marx, ½" scale **2.00**

Dresser, pink, tall style, Strombecker, ¾" scale ..**15.00**

Hamper, ivory, Ideal **4.00**

Hamper, pink, lid opens, Plasco **4.00**

Highboy, yellow, hard plastic, Marx, ¾" scale **5.00**

Hutch, metal, blue & white, doors & drawers open, Durham, ½" scale **8.00**

Ironing board, w/iron, pink & blue, Renwal, #32 ....**22.00**

Night stand, pink, Strombecker, ¾" scale **5.00**

Playpen, blue, hard plastic, Marx, ¾" scale **5.00**

Refrigerator, turquoise, F&F, ½" scale **2.00**

Refrigerator, 3 drawers, Tomy Smaller Homes **12.00**

Sink, bathroom; light green, Strombecker, ¾" scale **8.00**

Sink, blue, hard plastic, Marx, ¾" scale **5.00**

Sink, kitchen; pink, no-base style, Plasco **3.00**

Sofa, metallic gold w/metallic red base, Renwal, #78 ....**15.00**

Sofa, red w/brown trim, Jaydon **10.00**

Stool, pink, hard plastic, footed, Marx, ¾" scale **4.00**
Stove, ivory w/black trim, Ideal **15.00**
Table, dining; ivory, Tootsietoy .**15.00**
Table set, pedestal style, Ideal Petite Princess, #4427-1 ....**22.00**
Tub, pink w/blue trim, Renwal, #T95 ....**7.00**
Vanity, pink, round mirror style w/bench, Plasco **8.00**
Vanity, yellow, hard plastic, Marx, ½" scale **2.00**
Vanity w/bench, red, Allied ...**5.00**
Victrola, gold, Tootsietoy **35.00**

Dolls

Doll collecting is no doubt one of the most popular fields today. Antique as well as modern dolls are treasured, and limited edition or artists' dolls often bring prices in excess of several hundred dollars. Investment potential is considered excellent in all areas. Dolls have been made from many materials — early to middle 19th-century dolls were carved of wood, poured in wax, and molded in bisque or china. Primitive cloth dolls were sewn at home for the enjoyment of little girls when fancier dolls were unavailable. In this century from 1925 to about 1945, composition was used. Made of a mixture of sawdust, clay, fiber, and a binding agent, it was tough and durable. Modern dolls are usually made of vinyl or molded plastic.

Learn to check your intended purchases for damage which could jeopardize your investment. In the listings, values are for dolls in excellent condition unless another condition is noted in the line. They are priced 'mint in box' only when so indicated. Played-with, soiled dolls are worth from 50% to 75% less, depending on condition. Authority Pat Smith has written many wonderful books on the subject: *Patricia Smith's Doll Values, Antique to Modern; Modern Collector's Dolls* (eight in the series); *Vogue Ginny Dolls, Through the Years With Ginny;* and *Madame Alexander Collector's Dolls.* Patsy Moyer's books, *Modern Collector's Dolls, Volume 1,* and *Doll Values, Volume I,* are also highly recommended. (All are published by Collector Books.) See also Holly Hobbie; Strawberry Shortcake; Trolls.

American Character

In business by 1918, this company made both composition and plastic dolls, and many collectors count them among the most desirable American dolls ever made. Everything was of high quality, and the hard plastic dolls of the 1950s are much in demand. The company closed in 1968. All of their molds were sold to other companies.

Annie Oakley, hard plastic, original clothes, 1955, 17", EX ..**165.00**
Butterball, 1961, 18", M **145.00**
Cartwright: Ben, Hoss or Little Joe, 1968, 8", M, ea **135.00**
Cricket, 1964, 9", EX **15.00**
Freckles, face changes, 1966, 13", M **35.00**
Little Miss Echo, talker, 1964, 30", M **275.00**
Newborn Baby, vinyl, sleep eyes, rooted hair, 1958, 15", M **80.00**

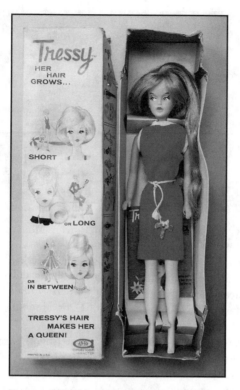

Tressy, 1963-64, 12½", MIB, $40.00. (Photo courtesy Cindy Sabulis)

Sally Says, talker, plastic & vinyl, 1965, 19", M **65.00**

Tressy, Miss America Character outfit, NM......................**50.00**

Annalee

Annalee Davis Thorndike made her first commercially sold dolls in the late 1950s. They're characterized by their painted felt faces and the meticulous workmanship involved in their manufacture. Most are made entirely of felt, though Santas and rabbits may have flannel bodies. All are constructed around a wire framework that allows them to be posi-

tioned in imaginative poses. Depending on rarity, appeal, and condition, some of the older dolls have increased in value more than ten times their original price. Dolls from the 1950s carried a long white red-embroidered tag with no date. The same tag was in use from 1959 until 1964, but there was a copyright date in the upper right-hand corner. From then until 1970, it was folded and sewn into the seam of the doll. After that they used a white satin tag with a copyright date. This was replaced in 1975 by a long white cotton strip which they folded over in 1982. The dates on these tags were not production

**Annalee, Gardener, Teacher, and Bowler Mouse, 1984, 7",
$75.00 each. (Photo courtesy Jane Holt)**

dates, merely copyright dates. Finally in 1986, the company initiated the practice of actually dating the dolls. Refer to *Teddy Bears, Annalee's, and Steiff Animals* by Margaret Fox Mandel (Collector Books). Our advisor for this category is Jane Holt; she is listed in the Directory under New Hampshire.

Angel on sled, 1990, 7" **40.00**
Angel w/star, 1984, 7" **50.00**
Bicentennial boy & girl mice, 1976, 7", pr **300.00**
Bride & groom frogs, 1980, 10", pr **300.00**
Choir girl, 1972, 18" **175.00**
Christmas goose, 1988, 10" .**40.00**
Clown, 1980, 18" **175.00**
Duck in raincoat, 1986, 5" ...**50.00**
Leprechaun, 1979, 10" **70.00**
Snowman, 1979, 10" **70.00**
Yum Yum bunny, various colors, 1966, 12" **550.00**

Arranbee

Made during the 1930s through the '50s, these composition or plastic dolls will be marked either 'Arranbee,' 'R&B' (until 1961), or 'Made in USA - 210.'

Littlest Angel, hard plastic, 1956, 10", M **50.00**
Miss Coty, vinyl, 1958, 10", M .**95.00**
My Angel, plastic & vinyl, re-dressed/played with, 1961, 17" **15.00**
My Dream Baby, vinyl & cloth, 1950, 15", EX **40.00**
Nancy Lee, hard plastic, 1950-59, 14", M **275.00**
Nancy Lee, vinyl, unusual eyebrows, re-dressed, 1954, 15", EX **80.00**
Nanette, walker w/jointed knees, 1957-59, 18", M, minimum value **325.00**
Storybook doll, composition w/molded hair, painted eyes, 10", M **185.00**

Barbie and Friends

Barbie has undergone some minor makeovers since 1959 — the

first one had just white irises but no eye color. Today those early Barbies are almost impossible to find, but if you can find one in mint condition, she's worth about $2,500.00 — add $1,000.00 more if the original box is with her. Refer to *The World of Barbie Dolls* and *The Wonder of Barbie, 1976 to 1986,* by Paris, Susan, and Carol Manos. Sibyl De Wein and Joan Ashabraner have written *The Collector's Encyclopedia of Barbie Dolls and Collectibles*; and *Barbie Fashion, Vol. I and Vol. II,* by Sarah Sink Eames are also excellent references. *Barbie Exclusives Book I and Book II* by Margo Rana, *The Story of Barbie* by Kitturah B. Westenhouser, *Barbie Doll Exclusives and More* by J. Michael Augustyniak, and *The Barbie Doll Years* by Patrick and Myrazona Olds are other titles of interest to collectors. All these books are published by Collector Books.

Values given for mint-in-the-box dolls will be from five to as much as seven times higher than the same doll in good, played-with condition.

Happy Holidays Barbie, 1994, gold gown with white fur trim, MIB, $165.00. (Photo courtesy Lee Garmon)

Allan, painted red hair, original clothes, straight legs, 1964, M **70.00**

Barbie, American Beauty Queen, 1991, MIB (sealed w/corner damage) **45.00**

Barbie, Ballroom Beauty, 1991 Wal-Mart special, MIB (sealed) .**40.00**

Barbie, Bubble Cut, 1961, blonde hair, original swimsuit, EX **175.00**

Barbie, Egyptian Queen, 1993, MIB (sealed) **65.00**

Barbie, Flight Time, 1989, MIB (sealed) **25.00**

Barbie, Holiday, 1991, MIB (sealed) **200.00**

Barbie, Parisienne, 1980, 1st in International series, MIB .**200.00**

Barbie, Truly Scrumptious, 1968, MIB **500.00**

Christie, Golden Dream, 1980 department store special, MIB (sealed) **40.00**

Francie, Malibu, original outfit, 1970, VG **45.00**

Ken, Busy, painted brown hair, all original, 1972, VG **65.00**

Ken, Totally Hair, 1991 department store special, MIB (sealed) **55.00**

Midge, titian hair, original swimsuit, straight legs, 1963, NM .**125.00**

PJ, Sweet Roses, 1983, MIB (sealed) **75.00**

Skipper, Jewel Secrets, 1986, MIB (sealed) **30.00**

Stacy, Talking, titian hair, original swimsuit, 1967, NM **165.00**

Betsy McCall

Tiny 8" Betsy McCall was manufactured by the American Character Doll Company from 1957 until 1963. She was made from fine quality hard plastic with a bisque-like finish and had hand-painted features. Betsy came with four hair colors — tosca, blond, red, and brown. She has blue sleep eyes, molded lashes, a winsome smile, and a fully jointed body with bendable knees. On her back is an identification circle which reads © McCall Corp. The basic doll could be purchased for $2.25 and wore a sheer chemise, white taffeta panties, nylon socks, and Maryjane-style shoes.

There were two different materials used for tiny Betsy's hair. The first was soft mohair sewn onto mesh. Later the rubber scullcap was rooted with saran which was more suitable for washing and combing.

Betsy McCall had an extensive wardrobe with nearly one hundred outfits, each of which could be purchased separately. They were made from wonderful fabrics such as velvet, felt, taffeta, and even real mink fur. Each ensemble came with the appropriate footware and was priced under $3.00. Since none of Betsy's clothing is tagged, it is often difficult to identify other than by its square snap closures (although these were used by other companies as well).

Betsy McCall is a highly collectible doll today but is still fairly easy to find at doll shows. The prices remain reasonable for this beautiful clotheshorse and her many accessories, some of which we've included below. For further information we recommend our advisor, Marci Van Ausdall, who is listed in the Directory under California. See also Clubs and Newsletters.

Child's dish, Homer Laughlin, w/fork & spoon, EX **50.00**
Coat & hat #3, for 8" doll, EX .**40.00**
Coloring book, Year Round Coloring, Saalfield, #9598, 1965 ....**10.00**
Doll, Ideal, w/wrist tag & curlers, 14", EX **175.00**
Doll, w/pink tissue & original pamphlet, MIB, minimum value **195.00**
Figurine, Heirloom Tradition/ Tomy, porcelain, October, 1984, M **10.00**
Outfit, Brunch Time, for 8" doll, MIB **45.00**
Paper dolls, Whitman #4744, 1971, cut, complete, w/original box **15.00**

Cabbage Patch

Special editions have been issued by Babyland General Hospital, Cleveland, Georgia, since 1978, and many of these are now valued at more than $500.00. But of the many varieties of retail-level Coleco dolls, few are worth more than they cost when new, simply because they were made in enormous quantities. We have listed a few exceptions below. Values are given for mint-in-box examples.

Coleco, 1983, freckled Black kid, from $225 to **400.00**

Coleco, 1983, black signature, minimum value **30.00**

Coleco, 1983, freckled boy or girl, minimum value **60.00**

Coleco, 1985, World Traveler, blue signature, from $40 to ..**70.00**

Coleco, 1986, Circus Kid, clown or ringmaster, from $50 to .**75.00**

Coleco, 1986, popcorn hair, from $30 to **125.00**

Hasbro, Teeny Tiny Premie Twins, Oriental or Hispanic set .**50.00**

Hasbro, 1989-94, minimum value **20.00**

Jesmar, Spain, 1983-85, from $30 to **150.00**

Tsukuda (Japan), 1983-85, minimum value **30.00**

Cameo

Best known for their Kewpie dolls, this company also made some wood-jointed character dolls with composition heads during the 1920s and '30s. Although most of the Kewpie molds had been sold to another company by then, the few that were retained by the company were used during the 1970s to produce a line of limited edition dolls. Kewpies marked 'S71' were actually made by Strombecker.

Miss Peep, ball-jointed shoulders & hips, 1970s-80s, 17", M ..**45.00**

Miss Peep, Black, vinyl, 1960s, 18", M **65.00**

Miss Peep, vinyl, 1960s, 15", M **40.00**

Miss Peep Newborn, vinyl & plastic, 1962, 18", M **40.00**

Pinkie, vinyl & plastic, 1950s, 10" or 11", M **135.00**

Kewpie Gal, by AMSCO, head marked Cameo, 11", MIB, $35.00. (Photo courtesy Glorya Woods)

Scootles, vinyl, 1964, 14", M, minimum value **185.00**

Celebrity Dolls

Dolls that represent movie or TV personalities, fictional characters, or famous sports figures are very popular collectibles and can usually be found for well under $100.00. Mego, Horsman, Ideal, and Mattel are among the largest producers. Condition is vital. If rather than mint in box, your dolls is mint without box, the value would drop about 65%. Dolls in only good or poorer condition drop at a very rapid pace. Our advisor for this category is Henri Yunes; he is listed in the Directory under New Jersey.

Cher, 1st issue, pink dress, Mego, 1976, 12", MIB (sealed) .**45.00**

Twiggy, Mattel, 1967, MIB, $350.00. (Photo courtesy Henri Yunes)

Christie Brinkley, Real Models, Matchbox #54611, 1989, 11½", MIB **35.00**

Dolly Parton, red gown, World Doll, 1987, 18", MIB (sealed) **90.00**

James Dean, Rebel Rouser outfit, DSI, 1994, MIB (sealed) **75.00**

Marie Osmond, Mattel, 1976, 11", MIB **50.00**

Marilyn Monroe, any of 4 outfits, Tri-Star, 1982, 15", MIB, ea **110.00**

Prince Charles, wedding attire, Peggy Nesbit/England, 1984, 8", MIB **100.00**

Roger Moore (as James Bond from Moonraker), Mego, 1979, 12", MIB **100.00**

Sally Field (Flying Nun), Hasbro, 1967, 5", MIB **80.00**

Soupy Sales, Knickerbocker, 1966, VG+ **80.00**

Chatty Cathy

Made by Mattel, this is one of the most successful lines of dolls ever made. She was introduced in the 1960s as either a blond or a brunette. By pulling a string on her back, Chatty Cathy could speak eleven phrases. During the next five years, Mattel added to the line with Chatty Baby, Tiny Chatty Baby, Tiny Chatty Brother, Charmin' Chatty, and Singing' Chatty. The dolls were taken off the market only to be brought out again in 1969. But the new dolls were smaller and had restyled faces, and they were not as well received. Our advisors for this category are Kathy and Don Lewis, authors of *Chatty Cathy Dolls, An Identification and Value Guide;* they are listed in the Directory under California.

Charmin' Chatty, auburn or blond hair, blue eyes, record, M **95.00**

Chatty Baby, brunette, red pinafore over white romper, MIB **200.00**

Chatty Baby, early, brunette hair, blue eyes, M **85.00**

Chatty Baby, open speaker, blond hair, blue eyes, M **75.00**

Chatty Baby, open speaker, brunette hair, brown eyes, M **125.00**

Chatty Cathy, brunette hair, brown eyes, M **150.00**

Chatty Cathy, later, open speaker grille, brunette w/brown eyes, M **150.00**

Chatty Cathy, mid-year/transitional, brunette w/blue eyes, M **125.00**

Chatty Cathy, Patent Pending, brunette w/blue eyes, M **130.00**

Singing Chatty, brunette hair, M **125.00**

Tiny Chatty Baby, blond w/blue eyes, M **75.00**

Tiny Chatty Baby, brunette w/brown eyes, M **125.00**

Deluxe, Deluxe Topper

Dolls by the Deluxe Reading Corporation may be marked either Deluxe Topper, Topper Corp., Topper Toys, Deluxe Toy Creations, or Deluxe Premium Corp. They're most famous for their teen fashion doll, Dawn. She was produced from the late 1960s to 1970, so her wardrobe is right in step with today's retro styles. Expect to pay from $10.00 to $15.00 for any of her outfits, mint in the box.

Baby Boo, battery-operated, 1965, 21", M **40.00**

Baby Magic, 1966, 18", M **45.00**

Betty Bride (Sweet Rosemary), 1-pc vinyl body, 1957, 30", minimum value **85.00**

Dawn, 6", MIB **30.00**

Li'l Miss Fussy, battery-operated, 18", M **30.00**

Penny Brite, child, 8", M **15.00**

Private Ida, of the Go Go's, 1965, 6", M **40.00**

Smarty Pants, battery-operated, 1971, 19", M **30.00**

Suzy Cute, move arm & face changes expressions, 7", M **25.00**

Tom Boy, of the Go Go's, 1965, 6", M **40.00**

Eegee

The Goldberger Company made these dolls, Eegee (E.G.) being the initials of the company's founder. Dolls marked 'Made in China' were made in 1986.

Annette, teen type, 11½", M **50.00**

Annette, walker, plastic & vinyl, 1966, 25", M **45.00**

Babette, Barbie look-alike, 1962, 11½", M, minimum value **60.00**

Baby, cloth & composition, 16", M, minimum value **95.00**

Baby Luv, cloth & vinyl, marked BT Eegee, 1974, 14", M **30.00**

Ballerina, foam body & limbs, vinyl head, 1967, 18", M **25.00**

Flowerkin, plastic & vinyl, marked F-2 on head, 1963, 16", MIB **55.00**

Gigi Perreaux, hard plastic & vinyl, open/closed mouth, 1951, 17", M **700.00**

Granny, rooted hair, painted eyes, from Beverly Hillbillies, 14", M **60.00**

Miss Sunbeam, plastic & vinyl, dimples, 1968, 17", M ...**25.00**

My Fair Lady, adult type, vinyl, jointed waist, 1956, 10½", M **50.00**

Posey Playmate, foam & vinyl, 1969, 18", M **15.00**

Tandy Talker, pull-string talker, plastic & vinyl, 1961, 20", M **45.00**

Effanbee

This company has been in business since 1910, continually producing high quality dolls, some of all composition, some composition and cloth, and a few in plastic and vinyl. In excellent condition, some of the older dolls often bring $300.00 and up.

Alice in Wonderland (Honey), hard plastic, redressed, 16" ..**145.00**

Alyssia, walker, hard plastic w/vinyl head, re-dressed, 20" **80.00**

American child, composition, closed-mouth boy, 15", M **950.00**

Babyette, cloth & composition, sleeping baby, 1946, 12", VG **100.00**

Barbara Joan, composition, open-mouth girl, 15", M **650.00**

Candy Kid, composition toddler, re-dressed, 1946, 12" ..**100.00**

Currier & Ives, plastic & vinyl, re-dressed, 12" **10.00**

Currier & Ives, plastic & vinyl, 12", M **35.00**

Fluffy, vinyl, 1954, 10", M ...**30.00**

Half Pint, plastic & vinyl, 1966 on, M **25.00**

Honey, hard plastic, EX face color, all original, 1949-55, 14" **225.00**

Li'l Sweetie, nurser w/no lashes or brows, 1967, 16", M **40.00**

Limited Edition Club, Princess Diana, 1982, M **95.00**

Mary Jane, walker, plastic & vinyl, w/freckles, 1960, 31", M **175.00**

Mickey, vinyl, molded-on hat, 1956, 11", VG **20.00**

Patsy Baby, cloth body, straight legs, 11", M **250.00**

Polka Dottie, re-dressed, 1953, 21", VG **50.00**

Suzie Sunshine, freckles, re-dressed, 1961 on, 18", EX **10.00**

Witch, designed by Faith Wick, all original, 18", M, minimum value **50.00**

Fisher-Price

Since the mid-1970s, this well-known American toy company has been making a variety of dolls. Many have vinyl heads, rooted hair, and cloth bodies. Most are marked and dated.

Baby Ann, #0204, vinyl & cloth, removable clothes, 1974-78, M **40.00**

Black Elizabeth, vinyl & cloth, removable skirt, 1974-78, M **40.00**

Jenny, #0201, vinyl & cloth, removable skirt, 1974-78, M **40.00**

Joey, #0206, vinyl & cloth, removable clothes, 1975, M **40.00**

Mary, #0200, vinyl face & hands w/cloth body, 1974-78, M .**40.00**

Natalie, #0202, vinyl & cloth, removable clothes, 1974-78, M **40.00**

Gerber Baby

The first Gerber Baby dolls were manufactured of cloth by an unknown

Doll, premium, Atlanta Novelty Company, 1979, blue-checked cloth body, removable eyelet-trimmed bib and skirt, 17', M, $90.00. (Photo courtesy Joan S. Grubaugh)

maker in 1936. Since that time six different companies have attempted to capture the charm of the charcoal drawing done by Dorothy Hop Smith of her friend's baby, Ann Turner (Cook).

Gerber began to issue premium items in the 1930s but discontinued them during World War II (1941-1945), and began again in 1946. In the '70s, Gerber began to expand their interest beyond food items into merchandising their related baby care line and insurance. Then in the '80s Gerber initiated a sales program of promotional items that were available to those somehow connected with the company. Later the '90s gave way to an emphasis on mass merchandising and entering into the area of toys that grow with your child. However, the sale of high quality food for infants and toddlers remains their first priority.

Besides premiums and sale items, Gerber made available many 'freebie' souvenirs through its company tours, the Tourist Center, and special events which they sponsored. An excellent new book, *Gerber Baby Dolls and Advertising Collectibles,* has written by our advisor, Jean Stryker Grubaugh (see the Directory under Ohio for ordering information).

Amsco, vinyl, pink & white rose bud sleeper, 1972-73, 10", MIB.**65.00**

Amsco, vinyl, plastic pants & bib-type shirt, 1972-73, 14", EX **35.00**

Amsco, vinyl, 2-pc dress w/shoes & socks, 1972-73, 14", EX **40.00**

Arrow Rubber & Plastic Corp, footed clown pajamas, 1956-67, 14", VG **45.00**

Arrow Rubber & Plastic Corp, jeans & shirt, 1956-67, 14" VG..................................**45.00**

Atlanta Novelty, 50th Anniversary, stuffed body w/vinyl head, arms & legs, eyelet skirt & bib, 1978, 17", MIB (sealed) .**90.00**

Atlanta Novelty, Drink & Wet, 1979, 17", w/accessories & trunk.............................**110.00**

Atlanta Novelty, flowered bed jacket w/matching pillow & coverlet, 1979, 17", MIB (sealed).........................**95.00**

Atlanta Novelty, w/ 'mama' voice, several different outfits, 1979-81, 17", MIB (sealed), ea **100.00**

Atlanta Novelty, zipper snowsuit w/matching hood, 1979, 17", MIB (sealed) **95.00**

Gerber Birthday Twins, white, 1989, 6", w/accessories & box **40.00**

Sun Rubber, 1955-1958, 12", nude or re-dressed, from $50 to......................................**75.00**

Toy Biz Inc, Food & Playtime Baby, 1994, 15", MIB.....**25.00**

Hasbro

Some of these dolls sold extremely well on the retail level during the 1980s — you probably remember the 'Real Baby' dolls. They came in two versions, one awake, the other asleep. They were so realistic that even grown-up girls had them on their Christmas lists! See also Jem and GI Joe.

Adam, World of Love Series, 1971, 9", M **15.00**

Dolly Darling, 1965, 4½", M ..**8.00**

Little Miss No Name, 1965, 15", M **90.00**

Real Baby, vinyl & cloth, open/closed mouth, 1984-86, 19", M **40.00**

Sleeping Beauty Storybook Doll, complete, 1967, 3", M ...**45.00**

That Kid, 1967, 21", M **90.00**

Horsman

During the 1930s, this company produced composition dolls of the highest quality. Today many of their dolls are vinyl. Hard plastic dolls marked '170,' are also Horsmans. They are best known for their 'Hee-Bee,' 'She-Bee,' and 'Patsy' dolls.

Angelove, plastic & vinyl, made for Hallmark, 1974, 12", M **20.00**

Baby Butterfly, Oriental, 12", M **250.00**

Baby Tweaks, cloth & vinyl, inset eyes, 1967, 20", M **25.00**

Ballerina, 1-pc vinyl body w/jointed elbows, 1947, 18", M **35.00**

Betty Jo, composition, re-dressed, 16", EX **100.00**

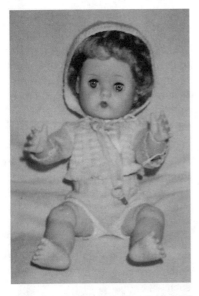

Baby Precious, with dynel rooted hair and sleep eyes, original clothes, 1954-56, $40.00. (Photo courtesy Linda Shelton)

Bye-Lo Baby, cloth & vinyl, Ward's 100th anniversary, 1972, 14", M **45.00**

Christopher Robin, 11", M ..**30.00**

Cinderella, plastic & vinyl, painted eyes, 1965, 11½", M .**25.00**

Crawling Baby, vinyl, 1967, 14", M **30.00**

Floppy, vinyl w/foam body & legs, 1965, 18", M **20.00**

Gold Medal doll, vinyl w/molded hair, re-dressed, 1953, 26", EX **90.00**

Life-size baby, plastic & vinyl, 26", M **200.00**

Mouseketeer boy or girl, 1971, 8", M **20.00**

Pippi Longstocking, vinyl & cloth, 1972, 18", M **25.00**

Ruthie, vinyl, 1958-66, 14", M .**25.00**

Snow White, Disney exclusive, 1981, 8", M **35.00**

Tuffie, vinyl, upper lip molded over lower, re-dressed, 1966, 16" **18.00**

Ideal

For more than eighty years, this company produced quality dolls that were easily affordable by the average American family. Their 'Shirley Temple' and 'Toni' dolls were highly successful. They're also the company who made 'Miss Revlon,' 'Betsy Wetsy,' and 'Tiny Tears.' For more information, see *Collector's Guide to Ideal Dolls* by Judith Izen. See also Shirley Temple; Tammy.

April Showers, battery-operated, hands & head move, 1968, 14", M **20.00**

Baby Crissy, pull string to make hair grow, 1973-75, 24", M **65.00**

Bamm-Bamm, plastic & vinyl, 1963, 12", M **15.00**

Betty Big Girl, plastic & vinyl, re-dressed, 1968, 32" **100.00**

Bizzie Lizzie, 1971, 18", M ..**35.00**

Black Kissy, 22", M **75.00**

Bonnie Braids, hard plastic & vinyl, re-dressed, 1951, 13½" **50.00**

Daddy's Girl, re-dressed, 1961-62, 29", EX **225.00**

Doctor Evil, jointed, w/face masks, 1965, 11", M, minimum value **75.00**

Electro-man, switch sets off alarm, light-activated, 1977, 16", M **265.00**

Giggles, plastic & vinyl, re-dressed, 16" **18.00**

Harmony, battery-operated, re-dressed, nonworking, 1971, 21" **20.00**

Harmony, battery-operated, 1971, 21", M **35.00**

Joey Stivic, 1-pc body, anatomically correct, 1976, 15", M **25.00**

Katie Kachoo, raise arm & she sneezes, 1968, 17", M ...**25.00**

King Little, composition & wood, 1940s, 9", M **265.00**

Kissy, 22", M **40.00**

Little Lost Baby, 3-faced, 1968, 22", M **50.00**

Mini Monster, 8½", M **10.00**

Miss Ideal, jointed, 1961, 25", M **365.00**

Penny Playpal, re-dressed, 1959, 32", EX **60.00**

Real Live Baby, head bobs, re-dressed, 1965, 20" **10.00**

Saralee, cloth & vinyl, 1950, 18", M **275.00**

Sparkle Plenty, Magic Skin (latex), 15", M **95.00**

Tabitha, cloth & vinyl, painted eyes, 1966, 15", M **35.00**

Tiffany Taylor, head swivels to change hair color, 1973, 19", M **28.00**

Tubsy, plastic & vinyl, battery-operated, 1966, 18", M .**20.00**

Wingy, hard plastic/vinyl, from Dick Tracy comics, 14", M **165.00**

Jem

The glamorous life of Jem mesmerized little girls who watched her Saturday morning cartoons, and she was a natural as a fashion doll. In 1985 Hasbro introduced the Jem line of 12" dolls representing her, the rock stars from Jem's musical group, the Holograms, and other members of the cast, including Rio, the only boy, who was Jem's road manager and Jerrica's boyfriend. Production was discontinued in 1987. Each doll was posable, joint-ed at the waist, heads, and wrists, so that they could be positioned at will with their musical instruments and other accessory items. Their clothing, their makeup, and their hairdos were wonderfully exotic, and their faces were beauti-fully molded. Our values are given for mint-in-box dolls. All loose dolls are valued at about $8.00 each.

Stormer, with blue curly hair and guitar, Hasbro, 1986, com-plete, MIB, $45.00. (Photo cour-tesy June Moon)

Aja, blue hair, complete w/accessories, MIB **45.00**
Ashley, curly blond hair, w/stand, 11", MIB **25.00**
Banee, straight black waist-length hair, w/stand, MIB **25.00**
Clash, straight purple hair, complete, MIB **45.00**
Danse, pink & blond hair, invents dance routines, MIB **45.00**
Jem, Roll 'N Curl, 12", MIB (sealed) **30.00**
Jem Roadster, AM/FM radio in trunk (working), scarce, EX, from $150 to **165.00**
Jem Soundstage, Starlight House #17, from $45 to **55.00**
Jem/Jerrica, Glitter & Gold, w/accessories, MIB **55.00**
Jetta, black hair w/silver streaks, complete, MIB **45.00**
Kimber, red hair, w/stand, cassette, instrument & poster, 12½", MIB **45.00**
Krissie, dark skin w/curly dark brown hair, w/stand, 11", MIB **25.00**
Pizzaz from Misfits, chartreuse hair, complete, MIB **45.00**
Raya, pink hair, complete, MIB .**45.00**
Rio, Glitter & Gold, complete, 12½", MIB **55.00**
Roxy, blond hair, complete, MIB .**45.00**
Shana of Holograms Band, purple hair, complete, EX, $30 to .**45.00**
Stormer, curly blue hair, complete, MIB **45.00**
Video, band member who makes video tapes, MIB **45.00**

Kenner

This company's dolls range from the 12" jointed teenage glam-our dolls to the tiny 3" 'Mini-Kins' with the snap-on changeable clothing and synthetic 'hair' ponytails. (Value for the latter: doll only, $8.00; doll with one outfit, $15.00; complete set, $70.00.)

Baby Bundles, nude, 16" **8.00**
Baby Won't Let Go, plastic & vinyl, rooted hair, 1977-93, 17", M **18.00**
Black Gabbigale, 1972, 18", M .**40.00**
Blythe, pull string to change eye color, 1972, 11½", M **35.00**
Cover Girl, bendable elbows & knees, 1979, 12½", M ...**85.00**
Crumpet, plastic & vinyl, 1970, 18", M **27.00**
Jenny Jones & Baby, vinyl, 1972, 9", 2½", M **20.00**
Sweet Cookie, 1972, 18", M .**28.00**

Liddle Kiddles

Produced by Mattel between 1966 and 1971, Liddle Kiddle dolls and accessories were designed to suggest the typical 'little kid' in the typical neighborhood. These dolls can be found in sizes ranging from ¾" to 4", all with posable bodies and rooted hair that can be restyled. Later, two more series were designed that represented storybook and nursery rhyme characters. The animal kingdom was represented by the Animiddles and Zoolery Jewelry Kiddles. There was even a set of extraterrestrials. And lastly, in 1979 Sweet Treets dolls were marketed.

Our values are for items that are mint on card or mint in box unless otherwise noted. Deduct

25% for dolls complete with accessories but with the box or card missing, and 75% if no accessories are included, but the doll itself is dressed. For further information we recommend *Schroeder's Collectible Toys, Antique to Modern* and *Liddle Kiddles* by Paris Langford (both by Collector Books). Our advisor, Cindy Sabulis, is listed in the Directory under Connecticut.

Kiddle Kologne #3705, Sweet Pea, with original cardboard base, Mattel, from $25.00 to 35.00. (Photo courtesy Cindy Sabulis)

Annabelle Autodiddle w/car & pusher, 1968-70, 4", from $35 to **45.00**
Apple Blossom Kologne, #3707, complete w/stand **25.00**
Babe Biddle & Her Car, #3503, EX **65.00**
Case, EX, any, from $20 to .**40.00**

Cinderiddle, ragged dress, complete, w/storybook, 1968, 3½", from $85 to **100.00**
Funny Bunny Kiddle, 2-pc bunny suit, 1968-69, 3¾", from $15 to **25.00**
Howard Biff Boodle, #3520, complete w/white shirt & yellow wagon **65.00**
Lois Locket, Black doll w/ponytails in jeweled locket, 1968-69, from $25 to **35.00**
Luscious Lime Kola Kiddle, 1968-69, 2", in 5" bottle, $35 to **45.00**
Mickey Mouse Skediddler, #3629, MIP **75.00**
Olivia Orange, #3730, complete **35.00**
Rapunzel & Prince, w/necklace & stand/book, 1969-70, 2", from $65 to **75.00**
Swingy Skediddle, blond in pink, orange skediddler/pusher, '69-70, 4" **55.00**
Trikey Triddle, w/balloon, trike, comb & brush, 1967, 2½", from $40 to **50.00**

Mattel

Though most famous, of course, for Barbie and her friends, the Mattel company also made celebrity dolls, lots of other action figures (the Major Matt Mason line and She-Ra, Princess of Power, for example), and in more recent years, 'Baby Tenderlove' and 'P.J. Sparkles.' The low side of our ranges indicate values for nonworking, played-with dolls, while the high side should be used to evaluate dolls still mint in the box. See also Barbie; Liddle Kiddles.

Baby First Step, talker, from $25 to **150.00**

Baby Small Talk, MIB **75.00**

Bozo the Clown, talker, from $10 to **150.00**

Bye-Bye Diapers, uses potty chair & claps hands, 1981, MIB (sealed) **25.00**

Cecil the Seasick Serpent, talker, from $45 to **300.00**

Downy Dilly, upsy-downsy, MIB (sealed) **135.00**

Goldilocks, Storybook Small-Talk, from $10 to **85.00**

Herman Munster hand puppet, talker, from $50 to **250.00**

Larry the Talking Plush Lion, from $20 to **175.00**

Li'l Drowsy Beans, blond hair, 11", MIB (sealed) **20.00**

Linus the Lionhearted, talker, from $10 to **100.00**

Mama Beans, cloth & vinyl, all original, 1974, 10", w/4" twins **20.00**

Miss Information, upsy-downsy, MIB (sealed) **150.00**

Pudgy Fudgy, upsy-downsy, MIB (sealed) **150.00**

Scooby-Doo, talker, from $35 to .**175.00**

Slugger, vinyl & cloth, rooted red hair, 1975, 5½" **15.00**

Tangie, cloth, vinyl & yarn, painted eyes, all original, 3½" **15.00**

Tender Love & Kisses, 1976, 14", MIB **25.00**

Tiny Baby Tender Love, molded hair, all original, 1971, M **20.00**

Tippee Toes, w/trike & horse, 1967, 16", MIB **100.00**

Mego

When you think of Mego, you think of action figures and celebrity dolls, but they also made lots of 'baby dolls' as well. For comprehensive coverage of Mego's action figures and celebrity dolls, see *Mego Toys, An Illustrated Value Guide*, by Wallace Chrouch (Collector Books).

Waltons, Mary Ellen and John Boy, cloth-dressed, 1975-76, 8", M, $18.00 each. (Photo courtesy Wallace Chrouch)

Batman, action figure, Super Heroes series, complete, 8", M **50.00**

Cochise, action figure, American West Series, complete, 8", M **45.00**

Davy Crockett, action figure, American West Series, complete, 8", M **50.00**

Lainie, jointed waist, battery operated, 1973, 19", M **35.00**

One Million BC, action figures, series of 5, 8", M, ea **20.00**

Super Woman, 4 figures in series, 1973, 8", M, ea **20.00**
Walton's, 6 figures in series, 1975, 8", M, ea **18.00**
Wizard of Oz, Wicked Witch, action figure, 1974, 8", M **30.00**
World's Greated Super Pirates, action figures, series of 4, 8", M, ea **60.00**

Nancy Ann Storybook

These dolls were first made in California during the 1940s. Some were made of bisque, while others were made of hard plastic. Both wigs and rooted hair were used, and they ranged in sizes from 5" up to 10" or 12". An extensive line of clothing was available, and there were wall cases and standing shelves to display them on. These dolls have been reintroduced in recent years.

Audrey Ann, toddler legs, marked Nancy Ann Storybook 12, 6", M **950.00**
Debbie, hard plastic & vinyl, re-dressed, 10", EX **40.00**
Debbie, hard plastic & vinyl, 10", M **100.00**
Margie Ann, bisque, in school dress, 6", M, minimum value .**165.00**
Muffie, walker, hard plastic, painted eyebrows, 8", M, minimum **75.00**
Nancy Ann Fairytale doll, vinyl, from 1960s, 5½", MIB ...**45.00**
Plastic, 1948-53, re-dressed, 3½" to 4½", ea **18.00**

Petal People

Uneeda Petal People are approximately 3" tall, Kiddle-like vinyl dolls with rooted hair and fabric clothing. Each doll has plastic shoes and comes inside a 12" flower attached to a flowerpot base. There are six different flowers and dolls — each a different color flower with a molded seat inside the petals. Each pot has a color-coordinated sticker with the accompanying doll's name, stock number, and a short poem. For further information we recommend *Liddle Kiddles, an Identification and Value Guide*, by our advisor, Paris Langford (listed in the Directory under Louisiana).

Dizzy Daisy, #30131, blond, yellow outfit, pink shoes, M, from $15 to ..**20.00**
Polly Poppy, #30128, brown hair, black & orange outfit, M, from $15 to **20.00**

Daffi Dill, #30130, brown hair, yellow and black outfit, white pearlized shoes in green daffodill, M, from $15.00 to 20.00. (Photo courtesy Pat Smith)

Rosy Rose, #30127, blond, red & black outfit, M, from $15 to.....................................**20.00**

Sunny Flower, #30129, brown hair w/yellow outfit, M, from $15 to..............................**20.00**

Tiny Tulip, #30126, blond w/pink & black outfit, M, from $15 to.**20.00**

Raggedy Ann and Andy

Raggedy Ann dolls have been made since the early part of the 20th century, and over the years many companies have produced their own versions. They were created originally by Johnny Gruelle, and though these dolls are practically nonexistent, they're easily identified by the mark, 'Patented Sept. 7, 1915.' P.F. Volland made them from 1920 to 1934; theirs were very similar in appearance to the originals. The Mollye Doll Outfitters were the first to print the now-familiar red heart on her chest, and they added a black outline around her nose. These dolls carry the handwritten inscription 'Raggedy Ann and Andy Doll/ Manufactured by Mollye Doll Outfiters.' Georgene Averill made them ca 1938 to 1950, sewing their label into the seam of the dolls. Knickerbocker dolls (1963 to 1982) also carry a company label. The Applause Toy Company made these dolls for two years in the early 1980s, and they were finally taken over by Hasbro, the current producer, in 1983. Refer to *The World of Raggedy Ann Collectibles* by Kim Avery (Collector Books).

Applause, tag in seam, 36", M, minimum value **150.00**

Applause doll, tag in seam, 1981, 12", M **28.00**

Averill, Georgene; red yarn hair, label in seam, 1960-63, 15", M **100.00**

Averill, Georgene; red yarn hair, tag in seam, 1950s, 18", M **185.00**

Hallmark, black yarn hair, brown legs, tagged, M, minimum value **600.00**

Knickerbocker, Beloved Belindy, Black doll, 1965, 15", VG .**400.00**

Knickerbocker, printed face, red yarn hair, tag in seam, 1960s, 8", M **65.00**

Knickerbocker, printed face, red yarn hair, tag in seam, 1980s, 16", M **20.00**

Nasco/Bobbs-Merrill, plastic & vinyl, rooted yarn hair, 1973, 24", M **145.00**

Remco

The plastic and vinyl dolls made by Remco during the 1960s and seventies are gaining popularity with collectors today. Many have mechanical features that were activated either by a button on their back or batteries. The Littlechap Family of dolls (1964), Dr. John, his wife Lisa, and their two children, Judy and Libby, came with clothing and fashion accessories of the highest quality. Children found the family less interesting than the more glamorous fashion dolls on the market at that time, and as a result, production was limited. These dolls in excellent condition are valued at about $20.00 each, while their outfits range from about $30.00 (loose and complete) to a minimum of $50.00 (MIB).

Baby Know It All, 1969, 17",
    M **18.00**
Baby Sad or Glad, 1966, 14",
    M **15.00**
Black Jumpsy, 1970, 14", M .**18.00**
Heidi, 1965, 5½", M **10.00**
Jan, Oriental, 5½", M **15.00**
Lindalee, cloth & vinyl, 1970, 10",
    M **20.00**
Littlechap Family, Dr John, 14½",
    M **95.00**
Littlechap Family, Libby, 10½",
    M **45.00**
Mimi, battery-operated singer,
    1972-73, 19", M **45.00**
Orphan Annie, plastic & vinyl,
    disk eyes, 1967, 15", M .**40.00**
Spunky, w/glasses, 5½", M ..**16.00**
Sweet April, vinyl baby, re-
    dressed, 1971, 5½", EX ...**2.00**
Tippy Tumbles, 1966, 16", M .**15.00**
Tumbling Tomboy, 1969, 16",
    M **15.00**
Winking Heidi, 1968, M **12.00**

Shirley Temple

The public's fascination with Shirley was more than enough reason for toy companies to literally deluge the market with merchandise of all types decorated with her likeness. Dolls were a big part of that market, and the earlier composition dolls in excellent condition are often priced at a minimum of $600.00 on today's market. Many were made by the

Ideal Company, who in the 1950s also issued a line made of vinyl.

Painted bisque, molded hair,
    Japan, 6", M **185.00**
Plastic & vinyl, 1982-83, Ideal,
    12", M **40.00**
Vinyl, 1950s, 12", M **225.00**
Vinyl, 1950s, 15", MIB **350.00**
Vinyl, 1972 Montgomery Ward
    reissue, 17", M in plain
    unmarked box **225.00**
Vinyl, 1973, red polka-dot dress,
    played with & dirty, 16" .**50.00**
Vinyl, 1984, marked Dolls,
    Dreams & Love, Henry
    Garfinkle Co, 36", M ...**275.00**

Tammy

In 1962 the Ideal Novelty & Toy Company introduced their teenage Tammy doll. Slightly pudgy and not quite as sophisticated looking as some of the teen fashion dolls on the market at the time, Tammy's innocent charm captivated consumers. Her extensive wardrobe and numerous accessories added to her popularity with children. Tammy had everything including a car, a house, and a catamaran. In addition, a large number of companies obtained licenses to issue products using the 'Tammy' name. Everything from paper dolls to nurse's kits were made with Tammy's image on them. Tammy's success was not confined to the United States. She was also successful in Canada and in several European countries. Doll values listed here are for mint-in-box

Tammy's Family by Ideal, Mother and Dad, Tammy and Ted, MIB, $50.00 each; Pepper, MIB, $40.00. (Photo courtesy Cindy Sabulis)

examples. (Loose dolls are generally about half mint-in-box value as they are relatively common.) Values for other items are for mint-condition items without their original packaging. (Items other than dolls with their original packaging or in less-than-mint condition would then vary up or down accordingly.) Our advisor, Cindy Sabulis, has co-authored a book with Susan Weglewski entitled *Collector's Guide to Tammy, the Ideal Teen* (Collector Books), which we highly recommend. Cindy is listed in the Directory under Connecticut.

Black Tammy, MIB **225.00**
Dodi, suntan, 1977, 9", MIB .**40.00**
Grown-Up Tammy, MIB **55.00**
Pepper, 1963, 9", MIB **40.00**
Pos'n Pepper, original clothes, 1964, 9", VG **20.00**
Pos'n Salty, MIB **80.00**
Tammy's car, minimum value .**75.00**
Tammy's Ideal House, minimum value **100.00**
Tammy's Mom or Dad, MIB, ea **50.00**
Ted, 1964, 12½", MIB **50.00**

Terri Lee

There were two sizes of this chubby charmer, the larger 16" to 18" and the Tiny Terri Lee, measuring 10". She was made during the 1950s and came from the factory with a daisy tied to her wrist and dressed in a variety of costumes. Some of these dolls were 'talkers' that came with an attachment at the base of the neck for a 'phone jack' to connect with a record player. Others were 'walkers,' and besides Terri Lee, they made a variety of babies and toddlers by other names.

Terry Lee, 16", M, $450.00; Tiny Terry Lee, 10", M, $200.00. (From the collection of Cyndie Matus)

Connie Lynn, 19", M, minimum value **365.00**

Jerri Lee, hard plastic, caracul wig, played with, re-dressed, 16" **195.00**

Majorette, hard plastic, M, minimum value **425.00**

Mary Jane (Terri Lee lookalike), walker, plastic, 16", M **300.00**

So Sleepy, re-dressed, played with, 9½" **80.00**

Tiny Terri Lee, re-dressed, played with, 10" **65.00**

Tiny Teens

Uneeda Tiny Teens are approximately 7" tall with rooted hair and eyelashes. Each doll came packaged in an oval-shaped card with a gold scalloped bubble that resembled a locket frame. These dolls were very well dressed and came with one or more accessories, a posing stand, and removable shoes. The dolls are marked UD, CO 1967 on the back of the shoulders. There are 12 dolls in the series. Our advisor, Paris Langford, is listed in the Directory under Louisiana.

Beau Time, blond, blue & white dress, MIP (sealed), from $10 .....**15.00**

Date Time, auburn hair, green & white gown, MIP (sealed), from $10 ....**15.00**

Fun Time, brunette, gingham trimmed outfit, MIP (sealed), from $10 ....**15.00**

Mini Time, brunette, jumpsuit w/overdress, MIP (sealed), from $10 to **15.00**

Party Time, auburn hair w/pink ribbon, MIP (sealed), from $10 to **15.00**

Prom Time, brunette w/crown & trophy, MIP (sealed), from $10 to **15.00**

Shower Time, blond, black slicker w/accessories, MIP, from $10 to **15.00**

Sport Time, blond, brown & gold pant outfit, MIP (sealed), from $10 to..............................**15.00**

Tea Time, blond in blue gingham dress, MIP (sealed), from $10 to **15.00**

Bride Time, blond hair, white lace dress with bouquet and white shoes, never removed from card, from $10.00 to $15.00. (Photo courtesy Pat Smith)

Vacation Time, yellow outfit, w/camera, MIP (sealed), from $10 to...............................**15.00**

Winter Time, blond, green & blue outfit, MIP (sealed), from $10 to....................................**15.00**

Uneeda

Uneeda dolls generally date from the 1950s through the '70s; they were made of vinyl and plastic, and some had cloth bodies. They made some mechanical talkers, nursing dolls, and a walker who turned her head with each step she took. Most are marked and dated.

Baby Dollikins, re-dressed, played with, 1958, 21".............**15.00**

Baby Dollikins, 1958, 21", M .**40.00**

Ballerina, vinyl, 14", M **20.00**

Bare Bottom Baby, 12", M ..**15.00**

Black Coquette, 1963, 16", M .**28.00**

Coquette, 1963, 16", M **25.00**

Grannykins, painted-on half glasses, 1974, 6", M **9.00**

Pollyanna, played with, 1960, 31" **45.00**

Pollyanna, 1960, 10½", M ...**25.00**

Serenade, battery-operated singer, 1962, 21", M **45.00**

Suzette, 1959-60, 1962, 10½", M **55.00**

Tiny Teen, 1957, 5", M **8.00**

Vogue

This is the company that made the 'Ginny' doll famous. She was first made in composition during the late 1940s, and if you could find her in mint condition, she'd bring about $450.00 on today's market. (Played with and in relatively sad condition, she's still worth about $90.00.) Ginnys from the 1950s were made of rigid vinyl. The last Ginny came out in 1969. Tonka bought the rights in 1973, but the dolls they produced sold poorly. After a series of other owners, Dakin purchased the rights in 1986 and began producing a vinyl doll that resembled the 1950-style Ginny very closely. For more information, we recommend *Collector's Guide to Vogue Dolls* by Judith Izen and Carol Stover (Collector Books).

Baby Dear, 1960-61, 17", M .**90.00**

Cowgirl Ginny, hard plastic with original outfit, 1957, M, $425.00. (From the collection of Kris Londquist)

Baby Dear Two, re-dressed, 27", EX **80.00**
Brickette, 1960, 22", M **60.00**
Ginny, hard plastic, sleep eyes, painted lashes, strung, 8", M **350.00**
Ginny, vinyl, round face, International, 1977, M, minimum value **50.00**
Ginny Cowgirl, strung, complete w/hat, M **425.00**
Ginny Hawaiian, brown doll, 8", M, minimum value **650.00**
Hug-A-Bye Baby, played with, 1975, 16" **8.00**
Jill, hard plastic, 1957-60, M .**185.00**
Love Me Linda, 15", M **20.00**
Welcome Home, 20", M **65.00**

Door Knockers

Though many of the door knockers you'll see on the market today are of the painted cast-iron variety (similar in design to doorstop figures), they're also found in brass and other metals. Most are modeled as people, animals, and birds; and baskets of flowers are common. All items listed are cast iron unless noted. Prices shown are for examples in excellent condition without damage and with original paint. For further information we recommend our advisor, Craig Dinner, listed in the Directory under New York.

Basket w/pink roses, green leaves on cream, blue trim, 3¼x2¼" **325.00**
Bathing beauty, blue eyes & suit, pink & green backplate, 5x2½" **575.00**

Cherub, blond hair with purple scarf and red roses on light blue background, 4x3", M, $500.00. (Photo courtesy Craig Dinner)

Castle, single flag, marked #630 & 631, lg **190.00**

Cherries, red w/green leaves, 3x3" **185.00**

Circus elephant's head, gray w/red trim, 6x5½" **525.00**

Colonial man, marked WS in triangle, Pat Apld For, 4¾x2½" **150.00**

Flower basket, multicolored w/blue bow, cream backplate, 4x3" **65.00**

Grapes, purple w/green leaves, 3x3" **185.00**

Pear, yellow w/multicolored flowers, 3¼x3" **175.00**

Poinsettia, red & green leaves w/yellow center, white backplate, 3" **265.00**

Rose, pink w/white highlights, green & yellow leaves on cream & green **215.00**

Woman in Bonnet, yellow & cream w/red roses, marked #615 .**375.00**

Doorstops

Doorstops, once called door porters, were popular from the Civil War period until after 1930. They were used to prop the doors open during the hot summer months so that the cooler air could circulate. Though some were made of brass, wood, and chalk, cast iron was by far the most preferred material, usually molded in amusing figurals — dogs, flower baskets, frogs, etc. Hubley was one of the largest producers. Refer to *Doorstops, Identification and Values* by Jeanne Bertoia (Collector Books) for more information. Beware of reproductions!

Rooster, flat casting, NM, 7x5½", $125.00 to $175.00.

Aunt Jemima, flat casting, 13¼x8", EX **325.00**

Basket of Tulips, Hubley, flat casting, 13x9", NM **325.00**

Boston Terrier, Hubley (others), full figure, 10x10", EX ..**65.00**

Cat, Sculptured Metal Studios, flat casting, 10¾x7½", EX **400.00**

Crocodile, wedge back, 5¾x11½", EX **75.00**

Daisy Bowl, Hubley, flat casting, #232, 7x6", EX **75.00**

Dolly Dimple, Hubley, full figure, 7¾x3¾", EX **275.00**

Donald Duck, Walt Disney Productions 1971, 8⅜x5¼", NM **225.00**

Duck by Bush, flat casting, 7½x10½", NM **375.00**

Duck w/Top Hat, flat casting, 7½x4¼", EX **250.00**

Dutch Boy, full figure, 8⅜x3⅜", EX **250.00**

Elk, flat casting, 11x10", EX .**125.00**

Flowered Doorway, flat casting, 7⅝x7½", EX **275.00**

Geisha, Hubley, full figure, 7x6", EX **200.00**

George Washington, flat casting, 12¼x6⅜", EX **425.00**

Gnome w/Shovel, flat casting, 9½x4½", EX **275.00**

Grapes & Leaves, Albany Foundry, flat casting, 7¾x6½", EX .**125.00**

Horse, full figure, Hubley, 7½x11", EX **100.00**

House w/Woman, Eastern Spec Mfg Co #50, 5¾x8½", EX **225.00**

Little Colonial Woman, full-figure hollow casting, 4¾x2⅝", EX ..**75.00**

Log Cabin, National Foundry, flat casting, 4⅝x10", EX ...**125.00**

Old Mill, flat casting, 6¼x8¼", EX **200.00**

Olive Picker, flat casting, #207, 7 ¾x8¾", EX **550.00**

Reading Girls, flat casting, 5x8⅝", EX **450.00**

Rooster, flat casting, 7x5½", EX **125.00**

Rose Basket, Hubley, flat casting, #121, 11x8", EX **125.00**

Scottish Highlander, flat casting, 15½x13", EX **275.00**

Shore Bird, flat casting, 10x6½", EX **275.00**

Spanish Girl, Hubley, flat casting, 9x5", NM **225.00**

St Bernard, Hubley, full figure, 3½x10½", EX **325.00**

Terrier (running), Spencer, Guilford Conn, wedge back, 4x7", EX **175.00**

Tiger Lilies, Hubley, flat casting, #472, 10½x6", EX **150.00**

Woman w/Muff, full-figure solid casting, 9¼x5", EX **200.00**

Woman w/Ruffled Dress, full-figure hollow casting, 6¼x 4¾", EX **150.00**

Egg Timers

The origin of the figural egg timer appears to be Germany, circa 1920s or 1930s, with Japan following their lead in the 1940s. Some American companies may have begun producing figural timers around this same era as well, but evidence is scarce in terms of pottery marks or company logos.

Figural timers can be found in a wide range of storybook characters (Oliver Twist), animals (pigs, ducks, rabbits), career and vocational uniformed people (chef, London Bobby, housemaid), or people in native costume.

All types of timers were a fairly uniform height of 3" to 4". If a figural timer no longer has its sand tube, it can be recognized by the hole which usually goes through the back of the figure or the stub of a hand. Most timers were made of ceramic (china or bisque), but a few are of cast iron and carved wood. They can be detailed or quite plain. Listings below are for timers with their sand tubes completely intact. Our advisor is Jeannie Greenfield; she is listed in the Directory under Pennsylvania.

Boy w/black cloak & cane, German, 3¾" **65.00**

Cat w/orange ribbon around neck, Occupied Japan, 2⅝" **25.00**

Chef stands by open barrel containing sand tube **40.00**

Dutch boy on telephone, in shades of blue, Germany **65.00**

Leprechaun, all brass, Ireland .**35.00**

Little girl sitting with phone, Germany, $50.00. (Photo courtesy Jeannie Greenfield)

Newspaper boy, Japan, 3¾"..**50.00**

Pig in chef's outfit, stands on hind legs **35.00**

Rooster, brown w/red, timer through mouth to back of head, Germany **30.00**

Scotsman w/bagpipes, plastic, England, 4½" **50.00**

Swiss/German boy in native costume plays flute **65.00**

Swiss/German girl in native costume plays guitar **65.00**

Telephone, black glaze on clay, Japan, 2" **20.00**

Veggie man, bisque, German, 4½" **60.00**

Elvis Presley

The King of Rock 'n Roll, the greatest entertainer of all time (and not many would disagree with that), Elvis remains just as popular today as he was in the height of his career. In just the past few months, values for Elvis collectibles have skyrocketed. The early items marked 'Elvis Presley Enterprises' bearing a 1956 or 1957 date are the most valuable. Paper goods such as magazines, menus from Las Vegas hotels, ticket stubs, etc., make up a large part of any Elvis collection and are much less expensive. His 45s were sold in abundance, so unless you find an original Sun label (one recently sold at auction for $2,800.00), a colored vinyl or a promotional cut, or EPs in wonderful condition, don't pay much! The picture sleeves are usually worth much more than the record itself! Albums are very collectible, and even though you see some stiff prices on them at antique malls, there's not many you can't buy for well under $25.00 at any Elvis convention.

Remember, the early mark is 'Elvis Presley Enterprises'; the 'Boxcar' mark was used from 1974 to 1977, and the 'Boxcar/Factors' mark from then until 1981. In 1982, the trademark reverted back to Graceland.

Our advisor is Rosalind Cranor, author of *Elvis Collectibles* and *Best of Elvis Collectibles* (Overmountain Press); see the Directory under Virginia for ordering information.

Beach hat, w/original photo hang tag, 1956 ....**125.00**

Belt buckle, pewter, 60th Anniversary, numbered, limited, in box **15.00**

Bottle of wine, Always Elvis, Collectors Series One, Boxcar Enterprises, Inc., licensed by Factors, 1978, poem by Col. Tom on back, sealed, M, $125.00. (Photo courtesy Lee Garmon)

Book, Solid Gold Memories, 1977, lg **25.00**

Bracelet, dog tags; on original card, 1956 ....**30.00**

Bracelet, EP Enterprises, color head shot, 1977 ....**14.00**

Button, You're Nothing But a Hound Dog, 1956, 1" **35.00**

Calender, pocket; RCA, 1977 .**7.50**

Card, Christmas; Western Union, 1959 ....**95.00**

Card, Easter; 1969 ....**15.00**

Christmas ornament, Hallmark, 1992, original box **25.00**

Coffee cup, plastic w/paper insert, 1977 ....**17.50**

Cologne, Be My Teddy Bear, in package with white teddy bear, 7½" **45.00**

Coloring contest form, Girls!, Girls!, Girls!, 1962 ....**30.00**

Concert ticket, unused, from Indiana, 1977 ....**35.00**

Cup, drinking; plastic, 1979 ..**7.50**

Decanter, McCormick, 1978, Elvis '77, plays Love Me Tender .**85.00**

Decanter, McCormick, 1979, Elvis '55, plays Loving You, 750 ml **75.00**

Decanter, McCormick, 1981, Aloha Elvis, plays Blue Hawaii, 750 ml **150.00**

Decanter, McCormick, 1984, Elvis Karate, plays Don't Be Curel, 50 ml **125.00**

Decanter, McCormick, 1987, Elvis Memories, plays several songs, 750 ml **695.00**

Doll, white jumpsuit, 1984, 12", in original box **75.00**

Flash button, color, 3" **17.00**

Flasher button, Love Me Tender, black & white, 3" **19.00**

Flasher keychain, full figure, yellow background, 2½x2" .**18.00**

Guitar, toy; Lapin, sealed on original card, 1984, lg **74.00**

License plate, TCB **6.00**

Lipstick, Hound Dog Orange, 1956, EX **325.00**

Lotion, Love Me Tender, 1984 .**25.00**

Lunch bag, paper **10.00**

Menu, Las Vegas souvenir, 10¾" dia, EX **40.00**

Movie still, Love Me Tender, original, 1956 ....**25.00**

Music box, 1968 Comeback, original box **68.00**

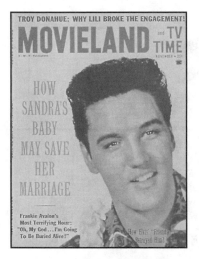

TROY DONAHUE: WHY LILI BROKE THE ENGAGEMENT!

MOVIELAND and TV TIME

HOW
SANDRA'S
BABY
MAY SAVE
HER
MARRIAGE

Frankie Avalon's
Most Terrifying Hour:
"Oh, My God...I'm Going
To Be Buried Alive!"

Magazine, Movieland and TV Time, November, 1961, EX, $20.00.

Necklace, gold plated, TCB, w/chain **20.00**

Pen, from Tickle Me promotion, w/original feathers, 1956 .**18.00**

Pencil, Sincerely Yours Elvis Presley, unused, 1956 ..**18.00**

Pin, Fan Club; original, blue & gold, 1956 ....**35.00**

Pin-back button, Always Yours, 1956 ....**35.00**

Pin-back button, Don't Be Cruel, 1956 ....**35.00**

Pitcher, glass w/multicolor decal of Elvis at the mike, +4 mugs **100.00**

Plate, Melmac, July, 1969, EX .**25.00**

Playing cards, Best of Elvis, MIB **5.00**

Postcard, Graceland, Highway 51, early '60s **22.00**

Postcard, Love Me Tender, color **7.50**

Shot glass, Rock 'N Roll **7.50**

Sideburns sticker, from vending machine, '50s **45.00**

Sweater clip, silver-tone w/image of Elvis, EX **18.00**

Tip tray, plastic, assorted photos, EX, ea **5.00**

Enesco Kitchen Accessories

Enesco is an importing company based in Elk Grove, Illinois. They're distributors of ceramic novelties made for them in Japan. During the 1960s, they sold a line of novelties originally called 'Mother-in-the-Kitchen.' Today's collectors refer to them as 'Kitchen Prayer Ladies.' Ranging from large items such as canisters and cookie jars to toothpick holders and small picture frames, the line was fairly extensive. Some of the pieces are very hard to find, and those with blue dresses are much more scarce than those in pink. Where we've given ranges, pink is represented by the lower end, blue by the high side. If you find a white piece with blue trim, add another 10% to 20% to the high end. For a complete listing and current values, contact our advisor, April Tvorak, who is listed in the Directory under Colorado.

Another Enesco line destined to become very collectible is called 'Kitchen Independence.' It features George Washington with the Declaration of Independence scroll held at his side, and Betsy Ross wearing a blue dress and holding a large flag.

Both lines are pictured in *The Collector's Encyclopedia of Cookie*

Kitchen Prayer Ladies tea set, from $175.00 to $275.00. (Photo courtesy April Tvorak)

Jars, Volume 1 and 2, by Joyce and Fred Roerig.

Dutch Boy and Girl

Cutting board, Kissin' Don't Last..., E-5821 ....**45.00**
Salt & pepper shakers, E-5816, very sm, pr **25.00**
Toothpick holder, E-6803 ....**30.00**

Kitchen Independence

Cookie jar, Betsy Ross **225.00**
Egg timer, George Washing-ton **50.00**
Napkin holder, George Washington, from $18 to **22.00**
Salt & pepper shakers, George Washington & Betsy Ross, pr **20.00**
Spoon holder, Betsy Ross, marked Spoon Storage on skirt, 5¾" **22.00**
Toothpick holder, George Washington (drummer), scarce **35.00**

Kitchen Prayer Ladies

Bank, from $145 to **175.00**
Candle holders, 4¼", pr, from $95 to **110.00**
Crumb sweeper, E-3350, from $150 to **175.00**
Egg timer, from $135 to **145.00**
Instant coffee jar, spoon-holder loop on side, from $85 to **95.00**
Photo holder, 6½", from $95 to **125.00**
Planter, 6½", from $65 to **75.00**
Plaque, cutting board on apron, 7⅜", from $45 to **55.00**
Salt & pepper shakers, pr, from $12 to **20.00**
Scouring pad holder, from $50 to **60.00**
Spoon holder, upright, from $45 to **50.00**
Sprinkler bottle, from $200 to **400.00**
Teapot, w/creamer & sugar bowl, from $175 to **275.00**

Snappy the Snail

Cookie jar **100.00**
Salt & pepper shakers, pr ...**16.00**
Spoon rest **12.00**
Tea bag holder **6.00**
Teapot, w/creamer & sugar
    bowl **125.00**

Miscellaneous

Figurine, cat or dog w/sad eyes, 6",
    ea, from $6 to **8.00**
Figurine, Kaa (snake), Disney,
    w/label **5.00**
Music box, Mary Poppins ..**200.00**
Spoon rest, Granny, 6¾" **18.00**

Farm Collectibles

As you drive through the country, you'll notice a trend toward more older decorations around homes and farmsteads. While making the outdoor scene nicer to view, the old pieces of horse-drawn machinery, wheels, fencing, and other items also depict bits of rural history.

Items collectors look for include actual scale models and toy tractors; tractor, seed, or other advertising items and giveaways; tools related to milking, blacksmithing, or other farming activities; windmills, weathervanes, and lightening rod balls; and many other miscellaneous antiques and collectibles. For further information we recommend our advisor, Gary Van Hoozer, listed in the Directory under Missouri. See also Clubs and Newsletters for information about *Farm Antiques News*.

Calf muzzle, wireware restrainer, $38.00.

Auger, earth; 5-ft, w/wooden handle **12.00**
Corn sheller, belt or crank driven, wooden frame, unmarked .**40.00**
Hook, hay grapple; resembles ice tongs **15.00**
Hook, hay grapple; 4 hooks .**25.00**
Horseshoe w/frog protector ...**3.00**
Log roller, w/hook **10.00**
Middlebuster, EX **50.00**
Mower wheel, cast iron w/lugs, horsedrawn **12.00**
Pig feeder, wooden, sm **20.00**
Plow, breaking; 6" shank, horsedrawn, w/single tree & hardware, restored **150.00**
Plow, horsedrawn **45.00**
Plow/cultivator, 5-shovel, horsedrawn **50.00**
Yard pump, Moniter, Baker Mfg Co, Evensville, Wis **60.00**

Fast Food Collectibles

Everyone is familiar with the kiddie meals offered by fast-food restaurants, but who knew that the toys tucked inside would become so collectible! Played-with items are plentiful at garage sales for nearly nothing, but it's best if they're still in the packages they originally came in. The ones to concentrate on are Barbies, the old familiar Disney characters, and those that tie in with the big blockbuster kids' movies. Collectors look for the boxes the meals came in, too, and even the display signs that the restaurants promote each series with are valuable. The toys don't have to be old to be collectible.

Our values are for toys that are still in the original packaging. A loose example is worth about 20% to 25% less than one still sealed. Our advisors for McDonald's® are Joyce and Terry Losonsky, authors of *Illustrated Collector's Guide to McDonald's® Happy Meal® Boxes, Premiums and Promotions*, *McDonald's® Happy Meal® Toys in the USA*, *McDonald's® Happy Meal® Toys Around the World*, and *Illustrated Collector's Guide to McDonald's® McCAPS®*. Terry and Joyce are listed in the directory under Maryland. Another recent reference is *McDonald's Collectibles* by Gary Henriques and Audre DuVall (Collector Books). Our advisors for restaurants other than McDonald's are Bill and Pat Poe (see Florida). See also Character and Promotional Drinking Glasses and Clubs and Newsletters.

Arby's, Babar's World Tour Finger Puppets, 1990, ea **2.00**
Arby's, Little Miss, 1981, 9 different, ea **4.00**
Arby's, Yogi Bear Fun Squirters, 1994, MIP, ea **4.00**
Burger King, Aladdin, 1992, MIP, ea **3.00**
Burger King, Archies, 1991, 4 different, MIP, ea **4.00**
Burger King, Beetlejuice, 1990, 6 different, ea **2.00**
Burger King, Bone Age, 1989, 4 different, ea **5.00**
Burger King, Dino Crawlers, 1994, 5 different, MIP, ea **2.00**
Burger King, Gargoyles 1995, MIP, ea, from $2 to **3.00**
Burger King, Lion King, 1994, 7 different, MIP, ea **4.00**
Burger King, Little Mermaid, 1993, 4 different, MIP, ea **3.00**
Burger King, Mini Record Breakers, 1989, 6 different, ea **2.00**
Burger King, Mini Sports Games, 1993, 4 different, MIP, ea .**3.00**
Burger King, Nerfuls, 1989, Officer Bob, Bitsy Ball or Scratch, ea **4.00**
Burger King, Pocahontas, 1995, 8 different, MIP, ea **3.00**
Burger King, Silverhawks, 1987, pencil topper **5.00**

Burger King, Archies, 1991, 4 different, MIP, ea, $4.00.

Burger King, Thundercats, 1986, Snarf 5.00

Burger King, Z-bots w/Pogs, 1994, 5 different, MIP, ea 2.00

Carl's Jr, Addams Family, MIP, ea 8.00

Carl's Jr, Amazing Mazes, MIP, ea 5.00

Carl's Jr, Reptile Inflatibles, MIP, ea 6.00

Carl's Jr, Rollerblade, 4 different, MIP, ea 5.00

Dairy Queen, Circus Train, set of 4, MIP 22.00

Dairy Queen, Space Shuttle, 6 different, MIP, ea 3.00

Dairy Queen, Tom & Jerry, 1993, 6 different, MIP, ea 6.00

Denny's, Dino-Makers, 1991, 6 different, MIP, ea 3.00

Denny's, Flintstone Dino-Racers, 1991, 6 different, MIP, ea .4.00

Denny's, Jetsons, Go Back to School, 1992, 4 different, MIP, ea 3.00

Denny's, Jetsons Space-Age Puzzle Ornaments, 1992, MIP, ea 3.00

Dominos Pizza, Noid, figure, bendable, 1988, 7", NM 10.00

Dominos Pizza, Noid Glider w/Power Prop, 1989, MIP 20.00

Frisch's Big Boy, Racers, 1992, ea 5.00

Frisch's Big Boy, Safari Fun, MIP, ea 4.00

Frisch's Big Boy, Sports Figures, 1990, ea 5.00

Hardee's, Apollo 13 Rocket, 1995, 3 different, MIP, ea 4.00

Hardee's, Dinosaur in My Pocket, 1993, 4 different, MIP, ea .3.00

Hardee's, Doodletop Jr's, 1996, 4 different, MIP, ea 3.00

Hardee's, Swan Princess, 1994, 5 different, MIP, ea 4.00

Hardee's, X-Men, 1995, 6 different, MIP, ea 3.00

Jack-in-the-Box, Bendable Buddies, 1991, 5 different, MIP, ea 8.00

Jack-in-the-Box, Garden Fun, 3 different seed packages, MIP, ea 5.00

Long John Silver's, Berenstain Bears Books, 1990, 8 different, ea 2.00

Long John Silver's, Free Willy 2, 5 different, ea 4.00

Long John Silver's, I Love Dinosaurs, 4 different, ea .4.00

Long John Silver's, Sea Watchers, 1991, miniature kaleidoscope, MIP 5.00

Long John Silver's, Treasure Trolls, 1992, pencil toppers, MIP, ea 3.00

McDonald's, Airport, 1986, MIP, ea 5.00

McDonald's, McDonaldland Fun Set, 1992, from K-Mart, Walmart, etc., EX, $4.00.

Wendy's, plush koala with original tag, 1989 World Wildlife Fund, 5¾", from $4.00 to $5.00.

McDonald's, Amazing Wildlife, 1995, 8 different, MIP, ea .**3.00**

McDonald's, American Tale Storybook, 1986, ea **2.00**

McDonald's, Astroniks, 1984, Regional, 6 different, ea .**14.00**

McDonald's, Barnyard (Old McDonald's Farm), 1986, 6 different, ea **8.00**

McDonald's, Bedtime, 1989, foam wash mitt, MIP **5.00**

McDonald's, Crazy Creatures w/Popoids, 1985, 4 different, ea **5.00**

McDonald's, Dink the Little Dinosaur, 1990, Regional, 6 different, ea **5.00**

McDonald's, Ducktail I, 1987, MIP, ea, from $5 to **6.00**

McDonald's, Flintstones, 1994, under age 3, Rocking Dino, MIP **5.00**

McDonald's, Fun w/Food, 1989, 4 different, MIP, ea **8.00**

McDonald's, Halloween Pals, 1990, ea **2.00**

McDonald's, Hook, 4 different, MIP, ea **3.00**

McDonald's, Lego Building Set, 1986, race car, 16-pc set, MIP **6.00**

McDonald's, Little Golden Book, 1982, 5 different, EX, ea **3.00**

McDonald's, Little Mermaid, 1989, 4 different, MIP, ea **5.00**

McDonald's, New Archies, 1988, 6 different, ea **8.00**

McDonald's, Piggsburg Piggs, 1991, Regional, 4 different, MIP, ea **5.00**

McDonald's, Runaway Robots, 1987, 6 different, ea **3.00**

McDonald's, Stomper Mini 4x4, 1986, MIP, ea **15.00**

McDonald's, Wild Friends, 1992, Regional, any except under age 3, MIP **4.00**

McDonald's, 101 Dalmatians, 1991, 4 different, MIP, ea **4.00**

Pizza Hut, Brain Thaws, 4 different, MIP, ea **4.00**

Pizza Hut, Marvel Comics, 4 different, MIP, ea **4.00**

Pizza Hut, Pagemaster, 4 different, MIP, ea **4.00**

Pizza Hut, Squirt Toons, 5 different, MIP, ea **5.00**

Roy Rogers, Animals II, 4 different, MIP, ea **3.00**

Roy Rogers, Space Meals, 4 different, MIP, ea **4.00**

Sonic, Flippin' Food, 1995, 3 different, MIP, ea **3.00**

Sonic, Squishers, 4 different, MIP, ea **5.00**

Subway, Cone Heads, 1993, 4 different, MIP, ea **4.00**

Subway, Inspector Gadget, 1994, 4 different, MIP, ea **4.00**

Taco Bell, Milk Caps, MIP, ea .**3.00**

Taco Bell, Sticker Sheets, Undersea Scene, MIP **3.00**

Target Markets, Muppet Twisters, 3 different, MIP, ea **4.00**

Target Markets, Targeteers, 1992, 4 different figures or vehicle, MIP **5.00**

Wendy's, Alf Tales, 1990, 6 different, MIP, ea **4.00**

Wendy's, Ballasaurus, 1992, 4 different, MIP, ea **4.00**

Wendy's, Potato Head II, 1988, 5 different, ea **4.00**

Wendy's, Rocket Writers, 1992, 5 different 4" vehicles, ea ..**2.00**

Wendy's, World Wild Life, 1988, 4 different books, ea **3.00**

White Castle, Bow Biters, 1989, Blue Meany, MIP **5.00**

White Castle, Castleburger Dudes, 1991, 4 different, MIP, ea .**4.00**

Fenton

The Fenton glass company, organized in 1906 in Martin's Ferry, Ohio, is noted for their fine art glass. Over one hundred thirty patterns of carnival glass were made in their earlier years (see Carnival Glass), but even their new glass is considered collectible. Only since 1970 have some of the pieces carried a molded-in logo; before then paper labels were used. See also Clubs and Newsletters.

Bells

Anticipation, limited edition.**32.00**

Aurora, Persian gold carnival, 7" **25.00**

Bicentennial, chocolate, Washington, Adams, Jefferson & Franklin, 7" **45.00**

Birds in Winter, bluebird in snow **33.00**

Cameo Satin, hand-painted flowers, Medallion #8267, 7" **25.00**

Custard, musical, Christmas deer scene, #7668 ....**40.00**

Daisy & Button, teal opalescent **25.00**

Faberge, Teal Marigold, #8466 .**40.00**

Prayer, Velva Rose **30.00**

Purple crystal w/etched roses .**35.00**

Sables Arch, red carnival, 6" ..**17.00**

Figurines

Alley cat, dark carnival, 10½" .**75.00**

Bear, black, sitting **16.00**

Bear, Primrose, reclining **24.00**

Bird, Rose Garden, short tail .**25.00**

Boy & girl, praying; Crystal Velvet, pr **32.00**

Happy Cat, made from Tiffin mold, signed FAGCA (the club owns the mold), Steigel Green Stretch, #9446, 1994, small, minimum value $50.00. (Photo courtesy Lee Garmon)

Bunny, tan custard w/hand-painted roses, artist signed **25.00**

Butterfly on stand, blue slag .**30.00**

Cat in slipper, blue opaque & milk glass **22.00**

Duck, custard w/hand-painted rose **34.00**

Fish paperweight, green carnival (rare color) **50.00**

Happiness Bird, red, 6½" **28.00**

Lion, Pink Pearl **27.00**

Rabbit, custard w/hand-painted daisies, artist signed **25.00**

Rabbit, iridescent blue, hollow, 1970s, 5½" **85.00**

Raccoon, hand-painted Hearts & Flowers **24.00**

Swan, Rosalene, open back .**38.00**

Wise Owl Decision Maker, black, #5180 ....**32.50**

Lamps

Courting, milk glass, #3893 .**130.00**

Fairy, Beaded, Colonial Pink .**35.00**

Fairy, Burmese w/decaled maple leaves, 2-pc **85.00**

Fairy, Heart, Rosalene, #8406RE **40.00**

Fairy, Heart, Rosalene, #846RE, 1976 ....**75.00**

Fairy, Hobnail, Spring Green .**30.00**

Fairy, Old Virginia, amber, 2-pc **24.00**

Fairy, owl, custard **25.00**

Fairy, Persian Medallion, custard, 3-pc **25.00**

Huricane, Black Rose, milk glass base, #7398BR **125.00**

Huricane, Dot Optic, blue w/milk glass base, #170, 11" **52.50**

Student, custard w/hand-painted scene, #7411, 21" **500.00**

Table, Emerald Green w/ivy decoration, #194, 24" **55.00**

Table, Moonstone, etched, ginger jar form, #893, 20" **200.00**

Miscellaneous

Banana boat, Silver Crest, low foot **48.00**

Basket, blue overlay, #218, 7¼x7¼" **60.00**

Basket, Burmese, plain, 7" ..**40.00**

Basket, Coin Dot, Mulberry, #1434MS **55.00**

Basket, Ming Crystal, #1616, 10x7" **65.00**

Basket, Threaded Diamond Optic, Rosalene, 3-toed, #8435RE **50.00**

Bonbon, Apple Blossom, 8" .27.50

Bonbon, Silver Crest, 5½" ...15.00

Bottle, scent; Hobnail, cranberry opal, #3865CR, no stopper 22.50

Bowl, Cherries & Orange Tree, purple carnival, lg 40.00

Bowl, Open Lace Basketweave, Ebony, 3" H 30.00

Bowl, Peach Crest, ruffled rim, 5¾" 15.00

Bowl, sauce; Fentonia, marigold carnival, ca 1913-15 ......35.00

Cake stand, Silver Crest, crimped rim, 5x13" 30.00

Candy box, Chessie, red carnival 50.00

Candy box, Chessie, Rosalene .250.00

Candy box, Chessie, teal carnival 60.00

Coasters, San Toy, #1490, 4", 4 for 55.00

Comport, Emerald Crest, double-crimped rim, #206, 6½" .35.00

Comport, Hobnail, milk glass, #3728, 6" 16.00

Comport, Silver Crest, ruffled, 6x8" 20.00

Comport, Silver Turquoise, 3½" 15.00

Goblet, Hobnail, milk glass, #A-106 ....18.00

Goblet, water; Lincoln Inn, crystal 35.00

Hat, Aqua Crest, 3½" 38.00

High shoe, Daisy & Button, amber carnival 22.00

Mug, butterfly, Favrene, made for FAGCA, 1985 ....60.00

Pitcher, juice; Hobnail, blue opalescent, w/4 glasses .60.00

Plate, Blacksmith, purple carnival, 1972 ....35.00

Plate, Persian Medallion, purple carnival 28.00

Rose bowl, Drapery, plum opalescent iridescent, 3-footed 47.50

Salt & pepper shakers, Hobnail, black & white, #3602, pr .12.50

Stein, Bicentennial, Patriot Red 38.00

Tobacco jar, Grape & Cable, red carnival 250.00

Tumbler, Hobnail, cranberry opalescent, barrel form, #3947CR 21.00

Van, vase, Ebony, #847 ....35.00

Vase, Burmese, pinched, #7359, 7" 32.50

Vase, Coin Dot, lime green opalescent, #1454, 9" 70.00

Vase, Empress, Blue Jade, #8252BJ 50.00

Vase, Hobnail, cranberry opalescent, #3855, 4" 25.00

Vase, Hobnail, Peachblow, crimped, #3856, 6" 30.00

Vase, Mulberry, old, 4½" 45.00

Vase, Silver Crest, top-hat shape, #1924, 4x4½" 42.00

Vase, Dancing Ladies, Mongolian Green, 1930, #901, 8½", $325.00.

Fiesta

Since it was discontinued by Homer Laughlin in 1973, Fiesta has become one of the most popular collectibles on the market. Values have continued to climb until some of the harder-to-find items now sell for several hundred dollars each. In 1986 HLC reintroduced a line of new Fiesta of which buyers should be aware. To date these colors have been used: cobalt (darker than the original), rose (a strong pink), black, white, apricot (very pale), yellow (a light creamy tone), turquoise, (country) blue, seamist (a light mint green), lilac, persimmon, periwinkle, and the newest color, sapphire blue (very close to the original cobalt). When old molds were used, the mark will be the same, if it is a molded-in mark such as on pitchers, sugar bowls, etc. The ink stamp differs from the old — now all the letters are upper case.

'Original colors' in the listings indicates values for three of the original six colors — light green, turquoise, and yellow. Refer to *The Collector's Encyclopedia of Fiesta* by Sharon and Bob Huxford (Collector Books) for more information. See also Clubs and Newsletters.

Bowl, cream soup; original colors **42.00**
Bowl, dessert; original colors, 6" **38.00**
Bowl, footed salad; original colors **270.00**
Bowl, fruit; medium green, 4¾" **450.00**
Bowl, fruit; original colors, 5½" **25.00**
Bowl, fruit; red, cobalt or ivory, 4¾" **32.00**
Bowl, nappy; '50s colors, 8½" .**62.00**
Bowl, nappy; original colors, 9½" **52.00**
Bowl, unlisted salad; yellow. **100.00**
Carafe, original colors **220.00**
Casserole, French; yellow ..**275.00**

Cup, demitasse; yellow, turquoise, or light green, $55.00;
Saucer, demitasse; yellow, turquoise, or light green, $15.00.

Individual sugar bowl, yellow, $95.00; Creamer, red, $200.00 (in standard yellow, $95.00); Figure-8 tray, turquoise $230.00 (in standard cobalt, $75.00).

Casserole, original colors ..**140.00**

Coffeepot, demitasse; original colors **335.00**

Coffeepot, red, cobalt or ivory **240.00**

Compote, sweets; original colors **72.00**

Creamer, individual; red ...**230.00**

Creamer, original colors **22.00**

Cup, demitasse; '50s colors .**340.00**

Egg cup, '50s colors **155.00**

Egg cup, red, cobalt or ivory .**70.00**

Marmalade, original colors .**225.00**

Mixing bowl, #2, original colors .**110.00**

Mixing bowl, #3, red, cobalt or ivory **130.00**

Mixing bowl, #5, original colors **150.00**

Mixing bowl, #7, original colors **275.00**

Mug, Tom & Jerry; original colors **55.00**

Pitcher, disk juice; yellow **45.00**

Pitcher, disk water; original colors **110.00**

Pitcher, ice; original colors ..**120.00**

Plate, '50s colors, 10" **50.00**

Plate, '50s colors, 9" **22.00**

Plate, chop; original colors, 13" **35.00**

Plate, compartment; '50s colors, 10½" **75.00**

Plate, compartment; original colors, 12" **50.00**

Plate, deep; medium green .**120.00**

Plate, medium green, 6" **18.00**

Plate, original colors, 7" **9.00**

Plate, original colors, 9" **12.00**

Plate, red, cobalt or ivory, 9" .**18.00**

Platter, original colors **35.00**

Salt & pepper shakers, original colors, pr **22.00**

Salt & pepper shakers, red, cobalt or ivory, pr **28.00**

Sauce boat, original colors ..**45.00**

Saucer, '50s colors **6.00**

Sugar bowl, w/lid, '50s colors, 3¼x3½" **70.00**

Sugar bowl, w/lid, original colors, 3¼x3½" **42.00**

Teacup, '50s colors **37.00**

Teacup, original colors **25.00**

Teapot, lg; original colors ..**175.00**

Teapot, med; original colors .**150.00**

Tray, figure-8; cobalt **80.00**

Tray, relish; mixed colors, minimum value **270.00**

Tumbler, juice; original colors .**38.00**

Tumbler, water; red, cobalt or ivory **72.00**

Vase, original colors, 8" **550.00**
Vase, red, cobalt or ivory, 12" .**1,100.00**

Fire-King Glass

From the 1930s to the '60s, Anchor Hocking produced a line called Fire-King; various patterns and colors were used in its manufacture. Collectors are just beginning to reassemble sets, so prices are relatively low, except for some of the Jade-ite pieces that are especially popular. Refer to *Collectible Glassware of the '40s, '50s, and '60s* by Gene Florence (Collector Books) and *Fire-King Fever '97* by our advisor, April Tvorak. She is listed in the Directory under Colorado.

Alice, cup & saucer, Jade-ite .**5.00**
Alice, cup & saucer, white or ivory **8.00**
Alice, plate, dinner; blue trim .**26.00**
American Artware, jewel box, fired-on color, ivory rose lid **20.00**

Apple Blossom, cake pan, round **14.00**
Bubble, bowl, vegetable; crystal or white **7.00**
Bubble, plate, dinner; Forest Green or ruby red **18.00**
Charm, bowl, serving; Azur-ite or Forest Green **16.00**
Charm/Square, bowl, soup; Jade-ite **22.00**
Charm/Square, dessert; Azur-ite or Forest Green, ea **16.00**
Charm/Square, plate, luncheon; Azur-ite or Forest Green .**5.00**
Charm/Square, plate, luncheon; Jade-ite, 8", minimum value **8.00**
Decal Dinnerware, bowl, serving **14.00**
Decal Dinnerware, cup & saucer **5.00**
Forest Green, batter bowl, 7⅝" .**14.00**
Forest Green, bowl, crimped rim, 8¼" **10.00**
Fruit, bowl, cereal; 5" **8.00**
Fruit, casserole, oval w/clear lid **16.00**
Gray Laurel, creamer & sugar bowl **12.00**

Multi-Fruit, batter bowl, $38.00. (Photo courtesy April Tvorak)

Sapphire Blue, mug, $28.00.

Gray Laurel, plate, dinner **8.00**

Jane Ray, bowl, flanged soup; Jade-ite **45.00**

Jane Ray, bowl, sauce; ivory .**12.00**

Jane Ray, cup & saucer, ivory, from $12 to **16.00**

Kitchenware, batter bowl, ivory, from $15 to **18.00**

Kitchenware, grease jar, decal .**28.00**

Laurel, bowl, cereal; Jade-ite .**12.00**

Laurel, salt & pepper shakers, Jade-ite, footed, pr, minimum value **45.00**

Laurel, sherbet, Jade-ite **6.50**

Lustre Shell, bowl, soup; 1965-76, 6⅜" **5.50**

Lustre Shell, cup, demitasse; 1965-76, 3½-oz **5.00**

Lustre Shell, platter, 1965-76, 13x9½" **6.50**

Lustre Shell, sugar bowl, w/lid, 1965-76 ....**6.50**

Peach Lustre, mug, household .**5.00**

Peach Lustre, platter, round ..**15.00**

Restaurant Ware, bowl, Jade-ite, rolled lip, 15-oz **12.00**

Restaurant Ware, coffee mug, Jade-ite, lightweight, 8-oz **8.00**

Restaurant Ware, cup & saucer **7.00**

Royal Lustre, bowl, vegetable; 1976, 8½" **12.00**

Royal Ruby, pitcher, tilted ball form, 42-oz **55.00**

Royal Ruby, tumbler, iced tea; 32-oz **12.50**

Royal Ruby, vase, crimped top, 7" **10.00**

Sapphire Blue, bowl, mixing; sm **16.00**

Sapphire Blue, measuring cup, 3-spout **25.00**

Sapphire Blue Ovenware, baker, 5⅝" dia **4.00**

Sapphire Blue Ovenware, coffee mug, thin, 8-oz **20.00**

Sapphire Blue Ovenware, custard cup, 4" **4.00**

Sapphire Blue Ovenware, pie plate, 9" **9.00**

Sheaf of Wheat, bowl, sauce; Jade-ite **15.00**

Sheaf of Wheat, plate, dinner; Jade-ite **35.00**

Soreno, butter dish, Avocado Green **12.00**

Swirl/Flat, bowl, sauce; ivory **3.00**

Swirl/Flat, cup & saucer, ivory .**4.00**

Swirl/Flat, plate, salad; Azur-ite .**8.00**

Swirl/Shell, plate, salad; Jade-ite **6.00**

Swirl/Shell, platter, Jade-ite, oval **30.00**

Turquoise Blue, bowl, cereal; 5" .**9.00**

Turquoise Blue, bowl, teardrop mixing; 3-qt **32.00**

Turquoise Blue, plate, dinner; 9" .**8.00**

Fishbowl Ornaments

Mermaids, divers, and all sorts of castles have been devised to add interest to fishbowls and aquariums, and today they're starting to attract the interest of collectors. Many were made in Japan and imported decades ago to be sold in 5-&-10¢ stores along with the millions of other figural novelties that flooded the market after the war. The condition of the glaze is very important; for more information we recommend *Collector's Guide to Made in Japan Ceramics* by Carole Bess White (Collector Books).

Bathing beauty atop lg sea turtle, multicolor & lustre glazes, 2½" **15.00**

Bathing beauty atop sea turtle, multicolor & lustre, 2½" **15.00**

Bathing beauty on coral & wave, multicolor, 4", from $20 to **30.00**

Bathing beauty on starfish, multicolor, glossy, 3½", from $30 to **40.00**

Boy on dolphin, multicolor matt glaze, 3¾", from $18 to .**28.00**

Castle, multicolor & tan lustre glazes, on white rocks, 5", from $15 to **20.00**

Castle, multicolor matt glaze, 2½", from $15 to **20.00**

Diver, orange matt glaze, 3¼", from $12 to **22.00**

Diver holding knife, white suit, brown boots & blue gloves, 4¾" **22.00**

Diver sitting in coral, black & red glossy glaze, 3½", from $12 to **18.00**

Fish, white w/orange stripes on seaweed base, 2½", from $12 to **22.00**

Castles, multicolored matt glazes, Japan, 2½" to 3", from $15.00 to $20.00 each. (Photo courtesy Carole Bess White)

Mermaid on conch shell, multicolor matt glaze, 3½", from $5 to **10.00**

Mermaid on snail, multicolor semigloss glaze, 4", from $30 to **45.00**

Mermaid riding sea horse, multicolor, glossy, 3¼" **15.00**

Pagoda, multicolor glossy glaze, 3½", from $15 to **20.00**

Torii gate, multicolor, glossy, 3¾", from $15 to **20.00**

Fisher-Price

Since about 1930 the Fisher-Price Company has produced distinctive wooden toys covered with brightly colored lithographed paper. Plastic parts were first added in 1949. The most valuable Fisher-Price toys are those modeled after well-known Disney characters and have the Disney logo. A little edge wear and some paint dulling are normal to these well-loved toys and to be expected; pricing information reflects items that are in excellent played-with condition. Mint-in-box examples are extremely scarce. For further information we recommend *Fisher-Price, A Historical Rarity Value Guide,* by John J. Murray and Bruce R. Fox (Books Americana); *Modern Toys, 1930-1980* by Linda Baker (Collector Books); and *Schroeder's Collectible Toys, Antique to Modern* (Collector Books). Our advisor for this category is Brad Cassidy; he is listed in the Directory under Ohio. See also Clubs and Newsletters.

Aero-Marine Search Team, #323, 1978-83 ....**15.00**

Chick Basket Cart, #302, 1957 ....**40.00**

Chubby Cub, #164, 1969-72 .**20.00**

Cookie Pig, #476, 1967 ....**50.00**

Cry Baby Bear, #711, 1967-69 .**40.00**

Dinette, #251, pedestal table w/4 chairs, ea set **2.00**

Rabbit Basket Cart, late 1950s, #301, 7x6", EX, $40.00.

Doggy Racer, #7, 1942 ....**200.00**
Fire Truck, #630, 1959 ....**50.00**
Honey Bee, #208, yellow & white, 1978 ....**10.00**
Humpty Dumpty, #736, plastic, 1972-79 ....**8.00**
Jolly Jallopy, #724, circus clown's roadster, 1965-78 ....**15.00**
Kitty Bell, #499, 1950 ....**100.00**
Mini Copter, #448, blue litho, 1971-83 ....**25.00**
Molly Moo Cow, #132, 1972-78 .**35.00**
Movie Viewer, #460, crank handle, 1973-90 ....**5.00**
Musical Duck, #795, 1952 .**100.00**
Oscar the Grouch, #177, 1977-84 ....**30.00**
Patch Pony, #616, 1963 ....**50.00**
Peek-A-Boo Block, #760, 1970-79 ....**20.00**
Perky Penguin, #786, 1973-75 .**30.00**
Pick-Up & Peek Puzzles, #500, 1972-86 ....**10.00**
Picture Disk Camera, #112, w/5 picture disks, 1968-71 ..**40.00**
Pocket Radio, #772, Jack & Jill, 1974-76 ....**15.00**
Pop-Up-Pal Chime Phone, #150, 1968-78 ....**40.00**
Pudgy Pig, #478, 1962 ....**50.00**
Sesame Street Characters, #940, 1977, ea **3.00**
Toot-toot Engine, #641, red litho, 1964-87 ....**3.00**
Tumble Tower Game, #118, w/10 marbles, 1972-75 ....**15.00**
Woodsey Bramble Beaver, #606, 32-pages, 1981 ....**20.00**

Fishing Collectibles

Very much in evidence at flea markets these days, old fishing gear is becoming popular with collectors. Because the hobby is newly established, there are some very good buys to be found. Early 20th-century plugs were almost entirely carved from wood, sprayed with several layers of enamel, and finished off with glass eyes. Molded plastics were of a later origin. Some of the more collectible manufacturers are James Heddon, Shakespeare, Rhodes, and Pflueger. Rods, reels, old advertising calendars, and company catalogs are also worth your attention, in fact, any type of vintage sporting goods is now collectible. For more information we recommend *Fishing Lure Collectibles* by Dudley Murphy and Rick Edmisten (Collector Books). Our advisor for this category is Dave Hoover; he is listed in the Directory under Indiana.

Lures

Bomber Water Dog, wooden, yellow w/black shadow wave, MIB **20.00**
Brooks Jointed Reefer, gray scale, red spot, cream belly, plastic, EX **10.00**
Creek Chub, Beetle, yellow w/green wings, EX **95.00**
Creek Chub, Husky Jointed Pikie #3018, glass eyes, silver flash, MIB **50.00**
Creek Chub, Pike, Baby #900, glass eyes, silver flash, EX+ **20.00**
Creek Chub, Pop & Dunk, glass eyes, golden shiner, EX+ **65.00**
Eger Frog Skin, Baby, white tack eyes, cup rig, EX **115.00**

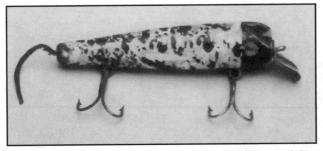

Vermillion Bait Co., Vermillion Meadow Mouse, metal diving lip, leather tail, red eyes, ca 1924, 3¾", $65.00. (Photo courtesy Dudley Murphy and Rick Edmisten)

Fly Rod, Christenson, perch, M in 2-pc wooden box **45.00**

Heddon, Baby Prowler, perch scale, 2¾", EX+ **20.00**

Heddon, Crazy Crawler Bullfrog #2120, EX **35.00**

Heddon, Mouse #210, bead eyes, w/whiskers, ears & tail intact, EX **40.00**

Heddon, Punkinseed Spook #380 Tiny, crappie, gold eye, EX+ **40.00**

Heddon, Stingaree, perch scale, MIB **25.00**

Heddon, Torpedo #130, painted eyes, shiner scale, MIB .**60.00**

Jinx, Frog Spot, sm, MIB **15.00**

Old Skipper Wobbler, lip stamped, red scale, EX **20.00**

Paul Bunyon Centipede, reddish-pink, 5", EX **125.00**

Pflueger, Fly Rod Grasshoper, green w/brown wings & legs, EX- **35.00**

Pflueger, Musky Mustang, painted eyes, red & white w/metal plate, EX+ **35.00**

Sambo, hook & spoon show light wear, EX- **40.00**

Shakespeare, Dopey, painted eyes, yellow perch, EX in box .**10.00**

Shakespeare, Frogskin, white tack eyes, flakes, EX **125.00**

Shakespeare, Palmer Gold Flutter Spoon, EX- **20.00**

Shakespeare, Swimming Mouse #6578, red & white, MIB .**25.00**

South Bend, Fish-O-Bite, perch, M in plastic-top box **20.00**

South Bend, Fly Rod Trout-Oreno, rainbow, screw hook holder, EX **10.00**

South Bend, Pal-O-Mine, jointed, glass eyes, pikie, 4½", VG+ .**20.00**

Reels

Airex, Bache Brown Mastereel, Model 3, half bail, VG ..**22.00**

Ambassadeur 5000, red grooved rims, 4-screw, light wear, EX **65.00**

Garcia Mitchell #300, full bail, EX **20.00**

Hirrocks-Ibbotson No 1870, MIB **20.00**

Langley Speedy, Model 510, black, MIB **20.00**

Hardy Viscount 150 Salmon Reel, extra spool and zippered case with leader compartment, 1x3⅞", EX, $70.00.

Pflueger Summit, jeweled, fancy
   plates, NM **25.00**
Pflueger Trump No 1943, jeweled,
   NM **20.00**
Shakespeare Marhoff, green rim,
   1964, NMIB **35.00**
South Bend 450-B, anti-backlash,
   VG **25.00**
Wooden, metal arrow back,
   click, double handle, 4",
   EX **70.00**

Miscellaneous

Bobber, Ideal, yellow, black &
   white stripes, yellow trailer
   ball end, 10" 115.00
Catalog, Abercrombie, 1951, Spring
   & Summer, outdoor equip-
   ment, EX- **35.00**
Catalog, Creek Chub, 1936, new
   lures, EX+ **250.00**
Catalog, Heddon, 1940, w/dealer
   supplement, EX+ **195.00**
Catalog, Heddon, 1951, 80 pages,
   full color, EX **85.00**
Catalog, South Bend, color charts,
   1941, EX **40.00**

Catalog, Winchester Firearms,
   component parts, 1962, 75
   pages, EX........................**20.00**
Decoy, Carl Christenson, Bluegill,
   glass eyes, 7", EX+ **75.00**
Decoy, Carl Christenson, Largemouth
   Bass, glass eyes, 9¾",
   EX+ **80.00**
Decoy, Dura Ducks, inflatable rubber, late 1940s, hen & drake
   pr, EX............................**30.00**
Decoy, Sunny Bashore, Crappie, glass
   eyes, full tail, 5½", EX+ .**195.00**
Plaque, Heddon, wooden, rainbow
   trout, 11x6", EX- **50.00**

Flashlights

The flashlight was invented in 1898 and has been produced by the Eveready Company for these past ninety-six years. Eveready dominated the flashlight market for most of this period, but more than one hundred twenty-five other US flashlight companies have come and gone to provide competition along the way. Add to that number over thirty-five known foreign flashlight manufacturers, and you end up with over one thousand different models of flashlights to collect. They come in a wide variety of styles, shapes, and sizes. The flashlight field includes tubular, lanterns, figural, novelty, litho, etc. At present, over forty-five different categories of flashlights have been identified as collectible. For further information we recommend consulting the *Flashlight Collectors of America*, see Clubs and Newsletters. Our advisor, Bill Utley, is listed in the Directory under California.

Aurora, all nickel **16.00**

BMG, USN, black, w/bull's-eye lens **22.00**

Bond, Bell Telephone, w/right-angle lens **15.00**

Burgess Sub, lithographed ..**42.00**

Chase Bomb Light, size & shape of donut w/o hole **52.00**

Chase Vest Pocket, brass **15.00**

Chestlite, green box lantern w/straps **18.00**

Delta, Red Buddy Lantern **9.00**

Embury Lantern, marked Pat .**24.00**

Eveready, Box Lantern, #4706, lg, w/slide switch **36.00**

Eveready, Canister Lantern, #4702 ....**32.00**

Eveready, Canister Lantern, #4708 ....**35.00**

Eveready, Captain, 3-cell **15.00**

Eveready, Cigarette-Case style, 2-C batteries, lg **26.00**

Eveready, Daylo Pistol **42.00**

Eveready, Daylo Vest Pocket, w/paper label, MIB **25.00**

Eveready, Wallite, black hammer-tone, oval **38.00**

Eveready, 1912 Cigarette Case, vest-pocket light **18.00**

Eveready, 1912 Vest Pocket, lg .**14.00**

Eveready, 1912 Vest Pocket, sil-verplated **32.00**

Eveready, 1914 Canister Lantern, #4708 ....**38.00**

Eveready, 1917 Liberty Daylo Box Lantern **32.00**

Eveready, 1930 Electric Candle, #1654 ....**52.00**

Eveready, 1931 Electric Candle, #1653 ....**54.00**

French Flasher **32.00**

Homart, Art Deco, 2- or 3-cell ...**18.00**

Homart, w/compass on end cap .**21.00**

Kwik-lite C, all nickel **18.00**

Lightmaster, Art Deco style .**16.00**

May, Baby Torch, 2-cell **24.00**

Motor Car, 2 'C' Electric Candle, Made in Hong Kong **24.00**

Niagara, Green Club Lantern .**14.00**

Purse light, rectangular, Patent 1934, 1¼x½x2¾" **18.00**

Rayovac, Art Deco style, cop-per **24.00**

Rayovac, bullet shape **10.00**

Rayovac, Handyman **15.00**

Rayovac, solid copper style ..**24.00**

Rudolph Red-Nosed Reindeer lapel lite **12.00**

Winchester, copper, Made in USA Olin, 6¾", $30.00.

Flower Frogs

Nearly every pottery company and glasshouse in America produced their share of figural flower 'frogs,' and many were imported from Japan as well. They were probably most popular from about 1910 through the 1940s, coinciding not only with the heyday of American glass and ceramics, but with the gracious, much less hectic style of living the times allowed. Way before a silk flower or styrofoam block was ever dreamed of, there were fresh cut flowers on many a dining room sideboard or table, arranged in shallow console bowls with matching frogs such as we've described in the following lines. Please note that these examples are all made in Japan. For further information see *Collector's Guide to Made in Japan Ceramics, Identification and Values,* by Carole Bess White (Collector Books). Our advisor, Nada Sue Krauss, is listed in the Directory under Ohio. See also specific pottery and glass companies.

Bird on knotty tree trunk, blue & multicolor lustre, 5" **23.00**
Birds among ivy covered vase, multicolor & tan lustre, 5¾" **22.50**
Dancing lady, attached 5" dia bowl, white w/yellow trim, 6½" **20.00**
Ducks on tan stump, lustre, Japan, 5", from $18 to ..**28.00**
Frog, blue lustre w/yellow belly, orange lustre base, Japan, 3x2¾" **15.00**

Penguins, blue lustre with pale yellow breasts on pearl lustre ice/snow base, marked Made in Japan, 4¾x3¾", $25.00.

Lotus bud flower, multicolor shiny glaze, 4½" wide **15.00**
Oriental lady, lime green on 3½" dia base, ca 1940s-50s, 13" ...**15.00**
Parrot on stepped base, multicolor, shiny & matt, 3¼", from $12 to **22.00**
Rosebud atop round tan lustre base, Japan, 2½", from $12 to **22.00**
Swan pair w/lily pads & flowers at bowl rim, multicolor lustre, 8" dia .**65.00**
Swans circle bowl w/2 swans at center, white, tan & black, 7" wide **100.00**
Swans circle low bowl, tan & blue lustre, Japan, 8" dia, from $75 to .**125.00**
Woodpeckers facing double flower, multicolor lustre, Japan, 10" wide **65.00**

Frankoma

Since 1933 the Frankoma Pottery Company has been producing dinnerware, novelty items, vases, etc. In 1965 they became the first American company to produce a line of collector plates. The body of the ware prior to 1954 was a honey tan that collectors refer to as 'Ada Clay.' A brick red clay (called 'Sapulpa') was used from then on, and this and the colors of the glazes help determine the period of production. Refer to *Frankoma and Other Oklahoma Potteries* by Phyllis and Tom Bess (Schiffer), and *Frankoma Pottery, Value Guide and More*, by Susan N. Cox, our advisor for this category. Susan is listed in the Directory under California.

Sculpture, Indian Chief, hand-painted headdress, ca 1950, 7½", $300.00.

Ashtray, Club Trade Winds, Sapulpa Clay, fish w/advertising, 7" **17.50**

Ashtray, dog form, Sapulpa Clay, #402 ....**15.00**

Ashtray, Dutch shoe, Sapulpa Clay, #466, 6" **21.00**

Ashtray, leaf form w/4 rests, Sapulpa Clay, #478, 15" .**15.00**

Ashtray, teardrop form, Woodland Moss, #F203, 13½" **12.00**

Baker, Lazybones, Prairie Green, #4v, 1½-qt **17.50**

Baker, Mayan Aztec, Desert Gold, #7u, 10-oz **10.00**

Bank, elephant form, Sapulpa Clay, #380, 4½" **8.00**

Bookend, boot form, Peach Glow, #433, pr **45.00**

Bookend, Ocelot on Rocks, Ada Clay, #422, pr **370.00**

Bookend, Pacing Ocelot, #112, Sapulpa Clay, pr **155.00**

Bowl, rice; Woodland Moss, #F34, 1960-79, 8" **8.00**

Bowl, Westwind, Country Blue, #6n, 1-qt **5.50**

Broach, Silla-Gem, 4-leaf clover, Woodland Moss **15.00**

Candle holder, Aladdin lamp form, White Sand, Sapulpa Clay, #309 ....**25.00**

Coaster, Sapulpa Clay, #LGC, lg .**3.00**

Cookie jar, Trojan horse on lid, Ada Clay, 3-qt **235.00**

Creamer, individual; Lazybones, Sapulpa Clay, #562 ....**7.00**

Figurine, Coyote, #102, White Sand, 12½" **45.00**

Figurine, Mare & Colt, White Sand, #103, 12" **45.00**

Figurine, Peter Pan, Sapulpa Clay, 6" **70.00**

Figurine, Terrier, Ada Clay, #161, 3" **80.00**

Flower arranger, wedding ring form, Ada Clay, #200, 12" **28.00**

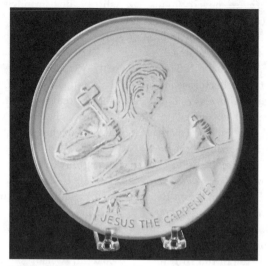

Plate, Teenagers of the Bible, Jesus the Carpenter, 1972, $45.00.

Flower holder, fish form, Ada Clay, #185, 3" **125.00**

Fondue pot w/cover, Peach Glow, #FD, 1969-73, 1½-qt **30.00**

Horseshoe, Ada Clay, #34 ..... **5.50**

Jug, Uncle Slug, Ada Clay, #10, 2¼" **18.00**

Lazy Susan, Wagon Wheel, Clay Blue, #94fc, 7 sections w/base, 15" **65.00**

Mug, boot form, Sapulpa Clay, #C33, 5" **9.50**

Mug, Mayan, Ada Clay, #83 **12.00**

Mug, Plainsman, Onyx Black, #5cl, 12-oz **5.50**

Mug, Political, elephant or donkey, Onyx Black, 1988, ea **20.00**

Mug, Political, 1978, elephant or donkey, Woodland Moss, ea .**34.00**

Mug, travel style **6.50**

Napkin ring, rabbit, Sapulpa Clay, #260 .... **3.00**

Pitcher, Plainsman, Brown Satin, #5d, 3-qt **18.00**

Planter, fluted sides, Peach Glow, #F33, 1974-1991, 3¾x7" .**7.00**

Planter, log form, Ada Clay, #9L, 11" long **14.00**

Planter, Mallard Duck, Woodland Moss, #208, 1960-79, 12" .**14.00**

Planter, Swan, w/open tail, Ada Clay, #228, 7½" **30.00**

Planter, turtle, Sapulpa Clay, #396, 7" **11.00**

Plate, Bicentennial, Symbols of Freedom 1976, White Sand, 8½" **50.00**

Plate, Cherokee Alphabet, Peach Glow, Sapulpa Clay, #7FS **22.00**

Plate, child's; elephant's head on long oval form, Sapulpa Clay, #257 .... **14.50**

Plate, Christmas 1979, The Star of Hope, White Sand, 8½" .**40.00**

Plate, Christmas 1984, Faith, Hope & Love, White Sand, 8½" **38.50**

Plate, Christmas 1991, Let There Be Peace, White Sand, 8½" **25.00**

Plate, Mayan Aztec, Woodland Moss, #7f, 9" **5.50**

Plate, Oral Roberts Easter 1972, White Sand, 8½" **10.00**

Plate, Teenagers of the Bible 1982, Mary the Mother, Desert Gold, 7" **20.00**

Ring holder/apple baker, Sapulpa Clay, #RH, 1988-1991 .....**5.00**

Salt & pepper shakers, barrel form w/tab handles, Ada Clay, 3", pr **18.50**

Salt & pepper shakers, Dutch shoe form, Woodland Moss, #915H, 4", pr **26.00**

Salt & pepper shakers, milk can form, Sapulpa Clay, 4½", pr **15.00**

Salt & pepper shakers, snail form, Ada Clay, #558H, 3", pr **12.00**

Sculpture, Circus Horse, Prairie Green, Ada Clay, #138, 6" .**125.00**

Sculpture, English Setter, #163, 2⅞" **65.00**

Sculpture, Gardener Girl, green dress **90.00**

Sugar bowl, Ada Clay, #92A .**17.00**

Teapot, Wagon Wheel, Red Bud, #94t, 6-cup **29.00**

Teapot, Westwind, Autumn Yellow, #6t, 6-cup **18.00**

Trivet, Liberty Bell, Woodland Moss, undated, 6" dia ...**11.00**

Trivet, White Buffalo Symbol of Indian Survival, Sapulpa Clay **7.50**

Tumbler, Club Trade Winds, Woodland Moss, #T1, 1-qt .**7.50**

Tumbler, Plainsman, Mauve, #5l, 12-oz **6.00**

Vase, bud; 2 handles at narrow neck, tapered body, Sapulpa Clay, 6" **6.00**

Vase, flared octagonal sides & foot, Sapulpa Clay, #38, 6" **6.00**

Vase, free-form w/foot, Ada Clay, 7" **15.00**

Vase, oil derrick form, Sapulpa Clay, #199 ....**9.00**

Vase, square w/square pedestal foot, Sapulpa Clay, #23, 7" **10.00**

Wall pocket, boot form, Ada Clay, #133, 6" **18.00**

Wall pocket, Wagon Wheel, Prairie Green, #94Y, 9" **35.00**

Fruit Jars

Some of the earliest glass jars used for food preservation were blown, and corks were used for seals. During the 19th century, hundreds of manufacturers designed over 4,000 styles of fruit jars. Lids were held in place either by a wax seal, wire bail, or the later screw-on band. Jars were usually made in aqua or clear, though other colors were also used. Amber jars are popular with collectors, milk glass jars are rare, and cobalt and black glass jars often bring $3,000.00 and up if they can be found! Condition, age, scarcity, and unusual features are also to be considered when evaluating old fruit jars.

Amazon Swift Seal (in circle), blue, 1-qt **12.00**

Anchor Mason's Patent (roped anchor), clear, 1-qt **15.00**

Atlas E-Z Seal, aqua, bell shape, 1-pt **3.00**

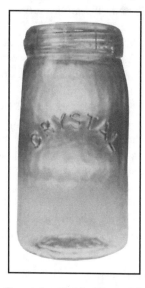

Crystal, Patd Nov 26-67/Pat Feb 4-73, aqua w/whittling marks, original glass screw cap, Hero Glassworks, quart, $75.00.

Atlas E-Z Seal, green, 1-pt ..**15.00**
Atlas Mason Patent, aqua, 1-qt .**4.00**
Ball Ideal, blue, sq, 1-pt **17.00**
Ball Improved, sq shoulder, sun-colored-amethyst, 1-pt ..**12.00**
Ball Mason Patent, clear, 1-qt .**5.00**
Ball Sanitary Sure Seal, blue, 1-qt **6.00**
Clark Peerless, aqua, 1-qt **4.50**
Clark's Peerless (in circle), clear, 1-qt **5.00**
Crown (crown) Imperial, aqua, 1-qt **4.00**
Decker's Iowana Mason City Iowa...Patd July 14 1908, clear, 1-qt **25.00**
Double Seal, clear, 1-qt **15.00**
Economy (base: Portland Ore), sun-colored amethyst, 1-pt **8.00**
Genuine Boyd's Mason, light green, ½-gal **21.00**

H&C (in circle), aqua, 1-qt ..**18.00**
Hazel Atlas E-Z Seal, aqua, 1-pt **15.00**
Improved Gem Made In Canada, clear, 1-qt **3.00**
Improved Mason Jar (in 2 lines), clear, 1-pt **10.00**
King (on banner below crown), clear, 1-qt **8.00**
Leotric, green, sm mouth, 1-qt .**12.00**
Lockport Mason, aqua, 1-qt **4.00**
Lustre RE Tongue & Bros Inc Phila (in circle), aqua, 1-pt **7.00**
Magic TM Mason Jar, clear, 1-qt **1.00**
Mason Ghost Whitney Etc, aqua, 1-qt **10.00**
Mason Improved Jar, clear, 1-qt **1.00**

Valve Jar Co., Philadelphia, Patent March 10th, 1868 (ca 1868-1875), aqua, glass lid and screw-down wire closure, quart, $160.00.

Mason's (cross) Improved, aqua, 1-pt **6.00**

Masons C.F.J. Co. (monogram) Improved, amber, glass insert and zinc screw band, amber, ½-gallon, $115.00.

Mason's IGCo Patent Nov 30th 1858, aqua, 1-qt **18.00**

Mason's II Patent Nov 30th 1858, aqua, 1-qt **33.00**

Mason's Improved, aqua, 1-pt .**8.00**

Mason's Patent Nov 20th 1858, aqua, solid star base, ½-gal **12.00**

Mason's Patent 1858, aqua, ½-gal **15.00**

Mason's X Patent Nov 30th 1858, aqua, 1-qt **30.00**

McDonald New Perfect Seal, blue, 1-pt **18.00**

Mom's (Mom) Mason Jar, clear, 1-qt **1.00**

Mrs Chapin's Mayonnaise Boston, Mass, clear, 1-pt **6.00**

Pacific Mason, clear, 1-qt **18.00**

Pine (P in square), clear, round, ½-gal **15.00**

Premium, clear, 1-qt **18.00**

Presto Supreme, clear, 1-pt ...**1.00**

Quick Seal in Circle, blue, 1-qt .**2.00**

Rath's Black Hawk Food Products...Waterloo Iowa, clear, 1-qt **10.00**

Safe Seal, blue, 1-pt **5.00**

Silicon (in circle), aqua, 1-qt .**18.00**

Smalley Self Sealer Wide Mouth, clear, 1-qt **4.00**

The Gem (1 line), aqua, 1-qt .**8.00**

TM Lighting, aqua, ½-gal ...**12.00**

Victory (in shield on lid), clear, 1-pt **5.00**

Victory (on lid), clear, 1-qt **6.00**

Wears (in oval), aqua, 1-qt ..**15.00**

Wears Jar (in circle), clear, 1-pt **9.00**

Gambling Collectibles

Prices for antique gambling chips and equipment have continued to escalate as evidenced by high prices realized at a May 1996 auction (Saratoga, New York) of gambling artifacts from several famous now-defunct casino clubs that operated in Saratoga from the 1930s through 1950s. Interest should spread and increase along with the rise of legal gambling in the US.

When evaluating these items, add a premium for: (1) equipment rigged for cheating; (2) items bearing the name of an old-time gambling saloon or manufacturer, particularly of the American West (e.g., Will & Finck, San Francisco; Mason, Denver; Mason, San Francisco), as signed and named pieces are worth at least 50% more than unsigned ones; (3) items typically found in American gambling halls of the middle and late 19th century (parlor game items of whist, bezique, cribbage, bridge, pinochle, etc., are not as valuable as those of faro, poker, craps, roulette, etc.); and (4) gambling supply catalogs which are dated and have many large, colorful pages and good graphics.

The most valuable chips, in descending order, are ivory poker chips (elaborately scrimshawed in more than a simple concentric design), mother-of-pearl chips and markers (engraved, at least 1/8" thick and preferably colored), casino chips (preferably from Nevada, the best from Las Vegas), illegal club chips, and clay composition poker chips.

Little or no value or collector interest is found in the following gambling items: (1) made after 1945, except for casino chips, gambling supply catalogs, and some early but post-1945 casino souvenirs; (2) plain (no design) paper, wood, and composition chips, regardless of age; chips with interlocking rims; hot-stamped casino-quality chips that cannot be identified (e.g., unknown monogram); and virtually all plastic (except Catalin), paper, and wood chips, unless there is some advertising connection; (3) homemade items (e.g., carnival wheels of fortune); (4) casino-type toys and combination game sets (e.g., plastic and brown Bakelite roulette wheels);

and (5) narrow, bridge-sized (2¼" wide) playing card decks. (Generally, only poker decks that are 2½" wide are collectible.) Finally, beware of the heavy, bulkier gambling antiques (e.g., professional crap tables) as storage and shipping problems limit the resale market.

Not listed here but of interest to many gambling collectors are a myriad of objects with gambling/playing card motifs: paintings and lithographs, ceramics, jewelry and charms, postcards, match safes, cigarette lighters, casino artifacts (ashtrays, swizzle sticks, etc.), souvenir spoons, tobacco tins, cigar box labels, song sheets, board games, etc. Values given here are for items in fine condition. Our advisor for this category is Robert Eisenstadt, who is listed in the Directory under New York. For further detailed information, refer to *Gambling Collectibles, A Sure Winner*, by Leonard Schneir.

Chip, scrimshawed ivory with a numeral design, 1½", $40.00. (Photo courtesy Robert Eisenstadt)

Book, Fools of Fortune by John Philip Quinn, 1890, EX .**160.00**

Book, Foster's Practical Poker by RF Foster, 1905, EX ...**105.00**

Book, Gambler's Tricks w/Cards Exposed & Explained, JH Green, 1858, EX **400.00**

Book, Official Rules of Card Games, Hoyle, US Playing Card Co, annual **10.00**

Book, Sucker's Progress... Gambling in America, H Asbury, 1938, EX **50.00**

Book, Thompson Street Poker Club, From Life, White & Allen, 1888, EX **150.00**

Book, Webster's Poker Book, HT Webster, 1925, EX **75.00**

Book, 40 Years Gambler on Mississippi, GH Devol, 1887, 1st edition, EX **250.00**

Card press, mahogany w/petit-point design, ca 1880 ..**325.00**

Card press, plain wooden box w/loose boards & threaded wooden dowel **85.00**

Card shuffler/dealer, auto-matic, 1940s, 5x5x5", common **20.00**

Catalog, Blue Book, KC Card Co, 50+ pages, 1930s-60s, any, from $20 to **50.00**

Cheat device, Jacob's ladder-type card holdout (up sleeve), mini-mum value **1,000.00**

Cheating device, card trimmer, brass & steel, attached blade **650.00**

Cheating device, corner rounder, brass & steel, unmarked .**600.00**

Chip, bone, plain, solid color, set of 100 ....**35.00**

Chip, bone w/design or color border, 1mm thick, set of 100 ....**75.00**

Chip, casino; Castaways...Las Vegas, $25, green w/black & yellow, 1963 ....**75.00**

Chip, Catalin or marbleized Bakelite, red, yellow & green, set of 100 ....**40.00**

Chip, clay, embossed, inlaid or engraved, ea, from $1 to .**7.00**

Chip, clay, plain, solid color, set of 100 ....**15.00**

Chip, clay or metal, w/casino name, minimum value ...**3.00**

Chip, clay w/molded design, set of 100, minimum value **20.00**

Chip, clay w/painted engrav-ing, set of 100, minimum value **30.00**

Chip, clay w/white plastic inlay, set of 100, minimum value **35.00**

Chip, dealer; clay w/goat head in relief, ea **50.00**

Chip, dealer; clay w/jackpot cup in relief, ea **50.00**

Chip, plastic, wood or rubber, no design, set of 100 ....**5.00**

Chip, scrimshawed ivory, marked 5 or 25, ea **40.00**

Chip, scrimshawed ivory w/con-centric circle design **10.00**

Chip, scrimshawed ivory w/quatro or floral design, ea **25.00**

Chip rack, marbleized Bakelite, ice-block type, 3x4x7", no chips **90.00**

Chip rack, marbleized Bakelite, ice-block type, 3x4x7", w/200 chips **170.00**

Chip rack, wood chest w/lid & pull-out rack, no chips, minimum value **70.00**

Chip rack, wood Lazy Susan (carousel) type, cover, no chips **10.00**

Faro (also Pharo) casekeeper, BC Wills & Co., Detroit, MI, celluloid strips and ivory beads, $450.00. (Photo courtesy Robert Eisenstadt)

Counter, mother-of-pearl, etched, elliptical, 1½", 1mm thick .**4.00**

Counter, mother-of-pearl, relief carving, 2½", 3mm thick .**35.00**

Dice, ivory,⅝", pr **80.00**

Dice, poker; celluloid; card symbols on sides, set of 5 ....**10.00**

Dice cage, felt-lined cardboard, thin wire & metal **25.00**

Dice cage, hide drums, heavy chrome, 9x14" **300.00**

Dice cup, ivory **100.00**

Dice cup, leather **15.00**

Faro dealing box, metal, open top, spring for cards, minimum value **300.00**

Faro layout, cloth attached to wood board, 40x16x1", minimum value **425.00**

Keno goose, polished walnut bowl between posts, 13x24" .**750.00**

Match safe, sterling w/engraved playing card etc, 1900s, from $100 to **300.00**

Needlepoint card table cover w/gambling & card images, minimum value **100.00**

Playing cards, faro; poker size w/sq edges, set of 52, minimum value **60.00**

Roulette pocketwatch, spinner hand, red & black numbers, 1900s, minimum value **100.00**

Roulette regulation table, w/wheel & 32" bowl, walnut, paw feet, Mason **5,000.00**

Roulette wheel, black Bakelite wheel & bowl, 9' **20.00**

Roulette wheel, 10" wood bowl w/wheel & simple design **150.00**

Roulette wheel, 24" wood bowl w/elaborate inlays & veneer, chrome trim **600.00**

Roulette wheel, 32" wood bowl w/elaborate inlays & veneer .**1,500.00**

Games

The ideal collectible game is one that combines playability (i.e., good strategy, interaction, surprise, etc.) with interesting graphics and unique components. Especially sought are the very old games from the 19th and early 20th centuries as well as those relating to early or popular TV shows and movies. As always, value depends on rarity and condition of the box and playing pieces.

Hand-held games, also called dexterity games or bead games, have been around for years, but it has only been recently that collectors have begun to take notice of them. These small, pocket-size toys involve moving a bead or another item around until you succeed in placing it in a certain position. They were made in many countries, Japan, Germany, and the US as well, and their values vary greatly depending on subject matter and age.

Dexterity game listings were provided by Phil Helley, see the Directory under Wisconsin.

$1,000,000 Chance of a Lifetime, Cardinal, 1986, EX **25.00**

Aggravation, CO-5, 1960s, EX (EX box) **30.00**

Annie, Parker Brothers, 1981, EX (EX box) **25.00**

Banana Tree, Marx, 1977, VG (EX box) **25.00**

Beverly Hills, Jax Ltd, 1982, EX (M box) **45.00**

Billionaire, Parker Brothers, 1973, EX (EX box) **33.00**

Bionic Woman, Parker Brothers, 1976, VG (VG box) **25.00**

Body Boggle, Parker Brothers, 1984, VG (EX box) **22.00**

Chase, TSR, 1987, EX (EX box) **27.00**

Circus Maximus, Avalon Hill, 1980, EX (EX box) **25.00**

Color Match, Ideal, 1982, EX (EX box) **31.00**

Commercial Crazies, Mattel, 1986, EX (EX box) **35.00**

Dexterity, Borden's Elsie the Cow, tin, glass & cardboard, 2½x3½" **135.00**

Dexterity, Boxers, aluminum, glass w/mirror, US Zone Germany, 2¼" **45.00**

Dexterity, Butterfly, aluminum, glass & cardboard, Germany, 1½" **20.00**

Dexterity, Cherry Blossoms, aluminum, glass, & cardboard, 1¼" dia **50.00**

Dexterity, Cocoa Marsh, tin & plastic, 1¼" dia **36.00**

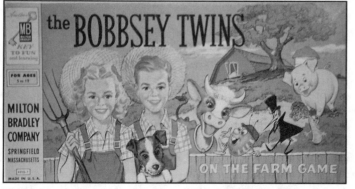

The Bobbsey Twins on the Farm Game, Milton Bradley, board game, 1957, MIB, $65.00.

Dexterity, General Electric, tin & plastic, 1½" dia **35.00**

Dexterity, Give It Wings, 5x3½" **30.00**

Dexterity, Hansel & Gretel, aluminum, glass & cardboard, W Germany, 2" **35.00**

Dexterity, Holsum Bread, tin & plastic, round, 2¼" **25.00**

Dexterity, Kelvinator Washer & Dryer, plastic, 2½x3" **25.00**

Dexterity, McDonald's, tin & plastic, 1¼" dia **75.00**

Dexterity, Monkey, Empire Buffet Restaurant, Milwaukee WI, 1¾" **45.00**

Dexterity, Old Stag Whiskey, key chain, round plastic, 1¾" .**8.00**

Dexterity, Pole Vaulter, w/mirror, US Zone Germany, 2¼" .**30.00**

Dexterity, Proud Fit Shoes, paper & plastic, round, 2" **18.00**

Dexterity, Red Goose Shoes, cardboard & plastic, round, 2¼" dia **30.00**

Dexterity, Subway Puzzle, wood & plastic, 4¼" tube **25.00**

Dexterity, Wisconsin Central Railway, picture of Chinaman, 1¾" **85.00**

Dexterity, Wisconsin Central Railway, picture of monkey, 1¾" **65.00**

Dinobones, Warren, 1986, VG (EX box) **30.00**

Double Trouble, Milton Bradley, 1987, EX (EX box) **24.00**

Dragonlance, TSR, 1988, EX (EX box) **47.00**

Duel, Lakeside, 1976, VG (EX box) **27.00**

Dungeon Dice, Parker Brothers, 1977, EX (EX box) **22.00**

Fortress America, Milton Bradley, 1986, VG (EX box) **85.00**

Girl Talk, Golden, 1988, EX (EX box) **25.00**

Go to Texas, Bright Ideas, 1979, VG (EX box) **37.00**

I Think You Think I Think, TSR, 1988, VG (EX box) **25.00**

Ink Blotz, Decipher, 1988, EX (M box) **35.00**

Jack & Jill Target Game, Cadeco-Ellis, 1948, VG (VG box) .**31.00**

Jetsons Game, Milton Bradley, 1985, EX (VG box) **25.00**

Jumpin', 3M, 1964, VG (VG box) **42.00**

Main Street, Aristoplay, 1982, EX (EX box) **39.00**

Mandinka, ES Lowe, 1978, VG (EX box) **37.00**

Manhunt, Milton Bradley, 1972, EX (VG box) **35.00**

Mary Hartman, Mary Hartman, Reiss, 1977, VG (EX box) .**43.00**

Mertwig's Maze, TSR, 1988, EX (EX box) **20.00**

Mid-Life Crisis, Game Works, 1982, EX (EX box) **27.00**

Mind Maze, Parker Brothers, 1970, VG (VG box) **25.00**

Operation, Milton Bradley, 1965, EX (EX box) **25.00**

Outwit, Parker Brothers, 1978, EX (EX box) **30.00**

Panzerforce, Lustron, 1979, VG (EX box) **50.00**

Password, 16th edition, Milton Bradley, 1970, EX (EX box) **24.00**

Paydirt, Sports Illustrated, 1985, VG (EX box) **25.00**

Rail Baron, Avalon Hill, 1977, G (G box) **22.00**

Real Ghostbusters Game, Milton Bradley, 1986, EX (EX box) **35.00**

Twiggy, Milton Bradley, 1967, from $45.00 to $60.00. (Photo courtesy Cindy Sabulis)

Relate, Whitman, 1972, VG (EX box) **25.00**

Richie Rich Game, Milton Bradley, 1982, VG (VG box) **30.00**

Ripley's Believe It or Not, 1984, EX (EX box) **29.00**

Risk, Parker Brothers, 1968, VG (EX box) **25.00**

Road Runner Game, Whitman, 1969, VG (EX box) **33.00**

Rook, Parker Brothers, 1963, VG (EX box) **25.00**

Snapshot, Cadaco, 1990, EX (EX box) **29.00**

Sod Buster, D Santee, 1980, EX (EX box) **30.00**

Space: 1999, Milton Bradley, 1976, VG (EX box) **30.00**

Spartan, SPI, 1975, EX (M box) **75.00**

Spill & Spell, Parker Brothers, 1972, VG (EX box) **22.00**

Stampin', Rainy Day Design, 1989, EX (EX box) **33.00**

Star Wars, Parker Brothers, 1982, EX (EX box) **35.00**

Starship Troopers, Avalon Hill, 1976, M (shrink wrapped) **35.00**

Take 5, Gabriel, 1977, VG (EX box) **15.00**

Telling Lies, Decipher, 1986, EX (EX box) **30.00**

Tiddle-Tac-Toe, Schaper, 1976, G (EX box) **25.00**

Tom & Jerry Game, Milton Bradley, 1977, VG (EX box) **26.00**

Topple, Kenner, 1979, VG (EX box) **29.00**

Tour of London, Waddington, 1984, VG (EX box) **30.00**

Trap Door, Milton Bradley, 1982, VG (EX box) **25.00**

Waterworks, Parker Brothers, 1975, VG (EX box) **30.00**

Web of Gold, TSR, 1989, M (shrink wrapped) **30.00**

Wheel of Fortune, Pressman, 1985, EX (EX box) **29.00**

Whirlwind, FASA, 1986, EX (EX box) **35.00**

Win by a Nose, Pressman, 1987, EX (EX box) **23.00**

WOW Pillow Fight Game, Milton Bradley, 1969, VG (VG box) **45.00**

Gas Station Collectibles

From the invention of the automobile came the need for gas service stations, who sought customers through a wide variety of advertising methods. While this is a specialized area of advertising collecting, there is a wide scope of items available as well as crossover attraction to both automobilia and advertising collectors. For further information we recommend *Huxford's Collectible Advertising* by Sharon and Bob Huxford and *Value Guide to Gas Station Memorabilia* by B.J. Summers and Wayne Priddy. Both are published by Collector Books.

Pump sign, Sky Chief, porcelain, marked Made in USA 3-7-46, 18x12", EX+, $130.00.

Banner, Texaco Fire-Chief, cloth, A Greater..., 30x17", VG+ **160.00**
Blotter, Esso Leaps Ahead, tiger, 3½x8", used **3.00**
Booklet, Esso Sports Stamps, 1950s premium, EX **5.00**
Booklet, Kendall Oil, 50 change tags, complete, M **25.00**
Checkers game, Standard Oil, EX (original box) **100.00**
Coin, Hyvis Oil, chart for mileage on back **10.00**
Display, Kendall, red silk banner w/gold fringe **35.00**
Gas globe, General Motor Fuel, knight at top, metal body, 15" dia, NM **500.00**
Gas globe, Mobilgas, green on white w/red, metal body, 15" dia, NM **440.00**
Guide, Texaco Lubrication, much text, 9½x4", NM **50.00**
Letter opener, Shell, red w/yellow base, older logo **15.00**
Mug, coffee; Gulf, 1920s station painted on glass, limited edition **5.00**
Pencil, mechanical; Esso, oil-can top, Standard Oil of New Jersey **15.00**
Pencil, mechanical; Southwestern Petroleum, cactus, oil-filled top **20.00**
Penknife, D-A Lubricant Co, Indianapolis, 1930s **35.00**
Pin-back button, Goodyear Tires, crescent moon & Earth w/in tire, EX **25.00**
Pin-back button, Mobiloil Arctic, celluloid over metal, 3½" dia, EX **160.00**
Pitcher, Esso, Put a Tiger in Your tank, glass, 2-qt **15.00**

Thermometer/ashtray, Texaco, metal with paper advertising thermometer, 3½", EX, $70.00.

Pocketknife, Esso, metal gas pump shape, 2½", EX **75.00**

Pump plate, Indian Gasoline, curved porcelain, multicolor, 18x12", NM **275.00**

Puzzle, Phillips 66, plastic slide tiles, 5x4", NM **5.00**

Radio, Sunoco, looks like gas pump, working, NM **45.00**

Screwdriver, Phillips 55, older logo **10.00**

Sign, Champion Spark Plug Service, tin flange, 12x18", NM **125.00**

Sign, Dunlop Tires, tin, black, yellow & red, 12x54", NM .**125.00**

Sign, Esso Credit Cards Honored, porcelain, 2-sided, 14x18", NM **200.00**

Sign, Pennzoil, porcelain, bell logo, 3-color, 2½x8", EX+ **300.00**

Sign, Shell Gasoline, tin flange, shell diecut, 17½x22", VG **230.00**

Thermometer, Quaker State Motor Oil, metal, 4-leaf clover, 39", EX **120.00**

Tie clasp, Mobil, metal Pegasus w/red enameling, EX in box **75.00**

Tin, Allstate Brake Fluid, green & gold, empty, 1-qt, EX **5.00**

Tin, American Motors Coolant, 1-qt, full, M **25.00**

Tin, Amoco Permalube, pierced top, 1-qt **12.00**

Tin, Cities Service Auto Polish & Cleaner, green & white ..**5.00**

Tin, Conoco All Season Super Motor Oil, 5-qt, 9½x7" dia, G+ **25.00**

Tin, Falcon Motor Oil, falcon logo, 1-qt, 5½x4", NM **35.00**

Tin, grease; Allstate, gold, green & white, 1960s, 1-lb **5.00**

Tin, grease; MacMillan Ring Free, blue & orange, 1-lb **15.00**

Tin, Quaker State Wheel Bearing; keywind, green & white, 1-lb **15.00**

Tin, Rainproof Wax Polish; 1920s car on lid, red, M **25.00**

Tin, Union 76 Year-Around Anti-Freeze & Coolant, empty .**5.00**

Tire pressure gauge, Schrader, balloon tires **15.00**

Tumblers, Esso, set of 6 in original box, 1955, EX **35.00**

Gaudy Italian

Here's a new category of collectible pottery you may want to start picking up while it's still very reasonable. Marked only 'Italy,' it has a rather primitive style that has all the charm of a countryside in an Italian village. It was made from about 1950 until the 1970s, handmade and hand painted, and though flowers seem to be most in evidence, you'll find items decorated with fruit and animals as well. Some of the designs are very reminiscent of Blue Ridge, and in fact, may have been copies.

Basket, 10" to 12", ea, from $20 to **22.00**
Basket, 4", from $6 to **8.00**
Basket, 6" to 8", ea, from $10 to **15.00**
Bowl, vegetable **10.00**
Bowl, vegetable; w/lid **15.00**
Box, ring; sm **5.00**
Cigarette box, sq **15.00**
Lamp, bedroom; sm, from $20 to **35.00**
Lamp, living room; lg, minimum value **45.00**
Plate, dinner **8.00**

Geisha Girl China

More than sixty-five different patterns of tea services were exported from Japan around the turn of the century, each depicting geishas going about the everyday activities of Japanese life. Mt. Fuji is often featured in the background. Geisha Girl Porcelain is a generic term collectors use to identify them all. Many of our lines contain reference to the color of the rim bands, which many collectors use to tentatively date the ware. For more about this lovely china, we recommend *Schroeder's Antiques Price Guide* (Collector Books).

Bowl, berry; Oni Dance A, 9-lobed, red-orange w/gold, sm ..**14.00**
Bowl, dessert; Garden Bench H, 3 reserves, cobalt **8.00**
Butter pat, Baskets of Mums B, red-orange w/gold, 3⅛" .**10.00**
Butter pat, Fan A, ladies on bridge, red border, 4¼" ...**8.00**
Cocoa pot, Basket A, ladies gathering shells, conical, 6½" .**50.00**
Leaf dish, Geisha Band, red-orange w/gold **18.00**
Match holder, Geisha in Sampan, pine green border **28.00**
Plate, Blue Hoo, cobalt bird, ladies, red-orange border, 7½" ..**12.50**

Snack set, Garden Bench D, $24.00. (Photo courtesy Elyce Litts)

Plate, Inside the Teahouse, apple green, scalloped, 8½" **40.00**

Plate, lemon; Art Show, ladies viewing screens, red w/gold, 5¾" **17.50**

Ring tree, Garden Bench Q, gold hand extends from decorated base **50.00**

Roll tray, Mother & Son B, melon ribs, red w/gold lacing ..**24.00**

Salt shaker, Child Reaching for Butterfly, red border, blue top **8.50**

Saucer, Flower Gathering A, blue w/gold lacing **7.50**

Teacup, Peacock, handleless, red-orange w/gold buds **18.00**

Teacup & saucer, Bamboo Trellis, red w/gold, patterned exterior **25.00**

Teacup & saucer, Bicycle Race, 2 ladies w/flags, gold tires & trim **32.50**

Teapot, Parasol E, red-orange w/gold buds **25.00**

Vase, Cloud A, ladies & clouds, cobalt w/gold, 5½" **35.00**

GI Joe

Toys are the big news of the '90s, as far as collectibles go, and GI Joe dolls vie for a spot near the top of many a collector's want list.

Introduced by Hasbro in 1964, 12" GI Joe dolls were offered in four basic packages: Action Soldier, Action Sailor, Action Marine, and Action Pilot. A Black figure was included in the line, and there were representatives of many nations as well. Talking dolls followed a few years later, and scores of accessory items such as vehicles, guns, uniforms, etc., were made to go with them all. Even though the line was discontinued in 1976, it was evident the market was still there, and kids were clamoring for more. So in 1982, Hasbro brought out the 'little' 3¾" GI Joe dolls, each with his own descriptive name. Sales were unprecedented. You'll find the small figures easy to find, but most of them are 'loose' and played with. Collectors prefer old store stock still in the original packaging; such examples are worth from two to four times more than those without the package.

12" Figures and Accessories

Action Sailor, MIB, $325.00. (Photo courtesy Cindy Sabulis)

Air Cadet Hat, EX **25.00**

Air Force Dress Doll, complete w/accessories, EX (EX+ box) **330.00**

Ampicat, 6-wheeled vehicle, MIB **75.00**

Army Poncho, green, EX **10.00**

Astronaut, complete w/accessories, silver space suit, NM ..**175.00**

Belt, black, cloth, EX **6.00**

Canteen, w/cover, EX **12.00**

Combat Soldier, Action Man, complete w/accessories, M (VG box) **95.00**

Crash Crew Pants, VG **20.00**

Deep Freeze, complete w/accessories, EX **180.00**

Detonator Gun, w/detonator, Action Man, MIP **5.00**

Diver's Weighted Belt, EX ..**24.00**

German Stormtrooper, complete w/accessories (replaced sling), VG **295.00**

Green Beret Hat, EX **45.00**

Iron Knight Tank, Action Man, M (NM box) **175.00**

Jacket, from the Mouth of Doom, EX **12.00**

Joseph Colton Arctic Explorer, w/all accessories, #783, M **190.00**

Marine Demolition, complete w/accessories, EX **150.00**

Marine Field Phone, camo, vinyl, EX **12.00**

Military Police Trousers, brown, MOC **70.00**

Navy Attack, complete w/accessories, EX **225.00**

Parachute, white cloth, w/strings, EX **25.00**

Raft, orange, EX **5.00**

Scramble Pilot Coveralls, G ..**40.00**

Shore Patrol, complete w/accessories, VG **265.00**

Ski Patrol Jacket, EX **18.00**

Talking Action Soldier, complete w/accessories, #7590, NM (VG box) **350.00**

Team Vehicle, yellow ATV, winch, hook, rope, VG+ (VG-box) **85.00**

Walkie-Talkie, EX **5.00**

3¾" Figures and Accessories

Toll Booth, with hammer, 1984, NM, $14.00.

Armadillo Mini Tank, 1984, EX .**8.00**

Astro Viper, 1988, MIP **12.00**

Blizzard, complete w/accessories, 1988 ....**8.00**

Captain Grid Iron, 1990, MIP .**11.00**

Cobra Claw, 1984, EX **10.00**

Countdown, 1989, MIP **18.00**

Deep Jay, 1989, MIP **13.00**

Falcon Glider, w/Grunt, complete w/ID Card, EX (glider G) .**60.00**

Flint, 1985, MIP **55.00**

Heavy Duty, 1991, MIP **8.00**

Lowlight, 1983-85, MIP **32.00**

Machine Gun, EX **5.00**

Mega Marine Mega-Viper, 1993, MIP **11.00**

Monkey Wrench, complete w/accessories, 1986 ....**7.00**

Mr Mindbender, 1983-85, MIP .**28.00**

Ninja Force, Bushido, 1993, MIP **5.00**

Pathfinder, 1990, MIP **11.00**

Recoil, 1989, MIP **20.00**

Ripper, 1985, MIP **26.00**

Sgt Slaughter, 1988, MIP **9.00**

Sky Patrol Drop Zone, w/parachute pack, brown, 1990, MIP **18.00**

Slip Stream, complete w/accessories, 1986 ....**10.00**

Strato Viper, mail-in, 1988, MIP .**12.00**

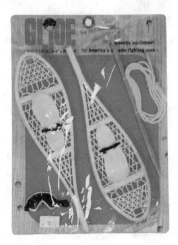

Snow Shoes set, with ice pick & rope, 1964, MIB, $55.00.

Tiger Force Roadblock, complete w/accessories, 1988 ....**8.00**

Whirlwind, twin battle gun, 1983, EX **15.00**

Glass Animals and Birds

Nearly every glasshouse of note has at some point over the years produced these beautiful models, some of which double for vases, bookends, and flower frogs. Many were made during the 1930s through the '50s and '60s, and these are the most collectible. But you'll also be seeing brand new examples, and you need to study to know the difference. A good reference to help you sort them all out is *Glass Animals of the Depression Era* by Lee Garmon and Dick Spencer (Collector Books). See also Boyd; Fenton.

Bird, medium dark blue, Viking Glass, 9½" **25.00**

Bird in flight, Amber Marigold, wings out, Westmoreland, 5" wide **25.00**

Blue jay, flower holder, crystal, Cambridge **125.00**

Bunny, cotton-ball dispenser, crystal frost, ears back, Paden City **60.00**

Cardinal, Green Mist, Westmoreland **20.00**

Cardinal head, Silver Mist, Fostoria, 6½" **125.00**

Colt, crystal, rearing, Heisey ..**200.00**

Deer, milk glass, sitting or standing, Fostoria, ea **55.00**

Donkey, Meadow Green Carnival, Imperial **95.00**

Donkey, Ultra Blue, Imperial ..**110.00**

Duck, cigarette box, red, Duncan & Miller, 6" **170.00**

Duck, dark teal, Viking's Epic Line, 9" **35.00**

Duck, flower block, crystal, Heisey **240.00**

Duck, mama, crystal, Fostoria .**25.00**

Duck, standing, crystal, New Martinsville/Viking's Epic Line, 9" **35.00**

Duck, Ultra Blue, standing, Imperial, 2⅝" 45.00

Duck, vaseline, Viking, 5" ...25.00

Duck w/3 ducklings, amber, Fostoria, set 50.00

Egrette, orange, Viking, 12" .45.00

Fish, canape plate, cobalt, Imperial 30.00

Fish, canape plate, teal, Imperial 25.00

Fish, match older, crystal, Heisey, 3x2¾" 150.00

Fish, paperweight, red carnival, Fenton limited edition ..65.00

Frog, crystal satin, Cambridge .25.00

German shepherd, crystal, New Martinsville, 5" 75.00

Goldfish, crystal, vertical, Fostoria 95.00

Goose, crystal, wings half, Heisey 95.00

Goose, light blue, Paden City, 5" 115.00

Goose, wings up, crystal, Heisey 100.00

Horse, aqua blue, Viking, 11½" 95.00

Horse, bookend, crystal, rearing, LE Smith, ea 25.00

Horse head, bookends, milk glass, Indiana, 6", pr 45.00

Irish setter, ashtray, Flamingo, Heisey 45.00

Mopey dog, crystal, Federal, 3½" 10.00

Pelican, amber, Fostoria, 1991 commemorative 55.00

Pony, crystal, Paden City, 12" .100.00

Pouter pigeon, any color, Westmoreland, 2½", ea .25.00

Ringneck pheasant, crystal, Heisey, 11¾" 140.00

Robin, crystal, Westmoreland, 5⅛" 20.00

Rooster, butterscotch slag, LE Smith, limited edition, #208 ......85.00

Rooster, Epic; red, Viking, 9½" (reproduced) 60.00

Scolding Bird, crystal, Imperial, $175.00.

Scottie, crystal frost, hollow, Cambridge 75.00

Scottie, crystal, Heisey 125.00

Seal, persimmon, Viking, 9¾" long 15.00

Sparrow, crystal, head up, LE Smith, 3½" 15.00

Sparrow, crystal, Heisey ...120.00

Squirrel, amber, running, Fostoria 35.00

Squirrel on curved log, crystal, Paden City, 5½" 65.00

Swan, Crown Tuscan, Cambridge, 8½" 125.00

Swan, crystal, open back, Duncan & Miller, 7" 45.00

Swan, crystal, solid, Duncan & Miller, 3" 20.00

Swan, crystal, solid, Duncan & Miller, 5" 30.00

Swan, milk glass, LE Smith, lg 45.00

Turtle, amber, LG WRight, 10" long 85.00

Turtle, ashtray, crystal, Westmoreland **10.00**
Whale, crystal, Fostoria **20.00**
Wolfhound, crystal, New Martinsville, 7" **95.00**
Wood duckling, Sunshine Yellow Satin, standing, Imperial .**15.00**
Wren, red, Westmoreland, 2½" .**22.50**
Wren on perch, light blue on white, Westmoreland, 2-pc **40.00**

Glass Knives

Glass fruit and cake knives, which are generally between 7½" and 9¼" long, were made in the United States from about 1920 to 1950. Distribution was at its greatest in the late 1930s and early 1940s. Glass butter knives, which are about 5" to 6½", were made in Czechoslovakia. Colors of the fruit and cake knives generally follow Depression glass dinnerware: crystal, light blue, light green, pink, and more rarely amber, forest green, and white (opal). The range of butter knife colors is even broader, including bicolors with crystal. Glass knives are frequently found with hand-painted decorations. Many were engraved with a name and occasionally with a greeting. Original boxes are frequently found along with a paper insert extolling the virtues of the knife and describing its care. As long as the original knife shape is maintained and the tip is not damaged, glass knives with nicked or reground blades are acceptable to collectors. Our advisor, Adrienne Escoe, is listed in the Directory under California. See also Clubs and Newsletters.

Aer-Flo (Grid), crystal **30.00**
Aer-Flo (Grid), forest green, 7½" **250.00**
Aer-Flo (Grid), pink, 7½" **75.00**
Block, crystal, MIB **20.00**
Block, green **30.00**
Block, pink, Atlantic City engraving, 8¼" **30.00**
Buffalo Knife (BK Co), clear w/hand-painted floral handle **25.00**
Butter, green/crystal, 6¼" ...**25.00**
Dagger, crystal, 9¼" **75.00**
Dur-X (3-Leaf), blue, 9½" **22.50**
Dur-X (3-Leaf), crystal, 8½" ..**12.00**
Dur-X (5-Leaf), blue, 9½", MIB .**25.00**
Dur-X (5-Leaf), blue, 9¼" **20.00**
Dur-X (5-Leaf), crystal, 8½" .**12.00**
Plain handle, green, 9" **30.00**
Plain handle, light pink, 9" .**35.00**
Rose Spray, green, 8½" **70.00**
Stonex, amber, 8¼" **135.00**
Stonex, crystal **45.00**
Stonex, green, 8¼", MIB **70.00**
Stonex, opal, 8½" **135.00**

Buffalo Knife (B.K. Co.), clear with hand-painted floral handle, $25.00. (Photo courtesy Adrienne Escoe)

Thumbguard, crystal, M in plain box **20.00**
Vitex (3-Star), blue, 9¼", MIB .**28.00**
Vitex (3-Star), crystal, 8½" ..**10.00**
Vitex (3-Star), pink, 9¼" **28.00**

Glass Shoes

While many glass shoes were made simply as whimseys, you'll also find thimble holders, perfumes, inkwells, salts, candy containers, and bottles made to resemble shoes of many types. Our advisor for this category is Libby Yalom, author of *Shoes of Glass*; see the Directory under Maryland for information on how to order her book. Numbers at the beginning of our descriptions refer to her book. See also Degenhart.

#130, Daisy and Button, amber, George Duncan and Sons, 4¼x4¾", $47.00.

#105, clear & stippled blue, 4 hobnails, hollow sole, 1¾x4¾" .**39.00**
#117, crystal, Sowerby peacock mark in heel, #RD87058, 2⅜x4⅞" **49.00**

#127, Daisy & Button boot, crystal, 4¼x4¾" **47.00**
#17, Daisy & Button, open front, blue, 3x5⅞" **40.00**
#172, frosted crystal hanging match holder w/side tab, 4x3⅜" **49.00**
#179, high-shoe roller skate, amber, 4x3½" **33.00**
#189, boot, milk glass, no initials on base, 5⅜x3¾" **44.00**
#192, stippled w/scalloped top & vertical scallops, blue, 5x5" **65.00**
#2, Duncan shoe w/mesh sole, crystal, lg **35.00**
#216, bootee, horizintal ribs, 2 sm flowers, green, 2¼x4⅛" .**38.00**
#227, baby shoe, milk glass w/pink bow, 2¼x4⅛" **36.00**
#236, attached pr of baby shoes, blue opaque, 2x3⅛x2⅝" .**55.00**
#245, boot jar, embossed snowflakes on lid, amber, 3x3" **70.00**
#258, heavy right shoe, 5-scallop back, green, 3⅝x6½" **65.00**
#266, man's bedroom slipper, amethyst, 1950s, 1½x5⅛" .**20.00**
#274, plain w/hollow sole, solid heel, crystal, ca 1915, 2⅝x4¾" **20.00**
#289, high-button shoe, amethyst, advertising on base, 5½x4⅜" **47.00**
#303, stirrup cup, vaseline opalescent, 2¾x4" **80.00**
#307, similar to Libbey shoes, frosted crystal, 3½x6⅜" **75.00**
#319, Dutch-style shoe, blue, 3x8¼" **85.00**
#320, milk glass w/colored flower on vamp, rigaree at top, 3¾x4⅞" **135.00**

#355, multicolor millefiori w/crystal heel & rolled edge, 2¼x5¼" **75.00**

#359, frosted burmese, ruffled edge, 2½x6⅜" **80.00**

#36, Daisy & Button, Bryce Bros, amber **37.00**

#371, boot, pink & white latticinio, 3¾x2⅝" **90.00**

#378, made as a candy dish, crystal, marked Baccarat, 1956-70s, 10" **135.00**

#385, Dutch shoe w/3 ridges on vamp, 3 buttons, crystal, 3⅛x7" **45.00**

#386, sm diamond pattern back, plain front, crystal, 3½x7½" **125.00**

#396, boot match older, green, 4½" long **40.00**

#408, Daisy & Button, apple green, 2½x11¾x4½" ...**130.00**

#414, shoe lamp, amber, Patd June 30, 1868, 3x6" .**1,000.00**

#430, Dutch-style shoe, crystal frosted, hollow in front, 2x4⅞" **40.00**

#442, stirrup cup, crystal, applied straps, 3¼" high **85.00**

#453, Victorian, blown, crystal w/blue threading, 1¾x3⅝" **190.00**

#462, shoe bottle, crystal, laced front, 2⅞x4" **35.00**

#471, man's shoe bottle, laces & stitching, crystal, 2⅞x4⅛" **52.00**

#476, man's shoe bottle, 10 buttons ea side, green, 1⅞x4" **65.00**

#479, boot, root beer frost, 2⅛x3¼" **30.00**

#495, thimble holder, blue, marked B&R, 2⅜x4" **80.00**

#77, shoe bottle w/metal top, crystal, Pat Apl'd For, 4¼x5¾" **100.00**

#92, English Sowerby (resembles Gillinder), crystal, 2½x5⅞" **65.00**

Graniteware

Graniteware is actually a base metal with a coating of enamel. It was first made in the 1870s, but graniteware of sorts was made well into the 1950s. In fact, some of what you'll find today is brand new. But new pieces are much lighter weight than the old ones. Look for seamed construction, metal handles, and graniteware lids on such things as tea- and coffeepots. All these are indicators of age. Colors are another, and swirled pieces — cobalt blue and white, green and white, brown and white, and red and white — are generally older, harder to find, and therefore more expensive. For a comprehensive look at this popular collectible, we recommend *The Collector's Encyclopedia of Graniteware, Colors, Shapes and Value*, Books I and II, by Helen Greguire (Collector Books).

Bread box, white with black trim and letters, vented lid, EX, $125.00.

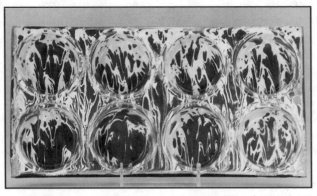

Muffin pan, cobalt large swirl, 7x14", VG+, $425.00.

Basin, gray mottle, 4x14", EX .**40.00**

Bowl, soup; Crysolite swirl, 9½", EX **85.00**

Bread riser, cobalt & white med mottle, w/lid, 17" dia, EX **425.00**

Coffee biggin, white w/black trim, 4-pc, M **125.00**

Coffee boiler, brown & white lg swirl, bail handle, NM .**495.00**

Coffee boiler, solid gray, EX .**85.00**

Coffeepot, gray swirl, 4-cup, NM **75.00**

Colander, solid gray, side handles, 12" dia, NM **25.00**

Cream can, gray mottle, 5", M .**195.00**

Creamer, blue & white lg mottle, blue strap handle, squatty shape, VG **395.00**

Custard cup, green & cream, 2¼x3⅝" top dia, M **55.00**

Dipper, Windsor, blue lg swirl, black hollow handle, EX **95.00**

Egg cup, white w/blue chicken wire, cobalt trim, 1½x1⅞", NM **135.00**

Grater, solid blue, rounded side, flat handle, M **125.00**

Ladle, cobalt blue & gray lg mottle, white interior, EX **95.00**

Mold, fish form, solid white, ring for hanging, lg, NM **175.00**

Muffin pan, gray lg mottle, 8 cups, NM **75.00**

Mug, gray, marked US on bottom **65.00**

Pail, milk; solid gray, tin lid w/strap handle, seamed, 2-qt, NM **75.00**

Pan, jelly roll; turquoise swirl, white interior, 1x9¼", NM **45.00**

Pan, tube; solid gray, EX **45.00**

Pitcher, milk; white w/black trim, 6", NM **36.00**

Pitcher, water; light green w/dark green trim, 8", NM **38.00**

Plate, red & white lg swirl w/black trim, lightweight, 1960s, M **35.00**

Roaster, solid blue, Savoy, w/lid **45.00**

Salt box, gray lg mottle, EX ..**525.00**

Skillet, gray lg mottle, 1¼x5¾" dia, EX **75.00**

Skimmer, gray med mottle, perforated, handled, NM **35.00**

Soap dish, white w/no trim, fluted, 2" deep, NM **45.00**

Spatula, cobalt blue w/white interior, perforated, EX **75.00**

Sugar bowl, dark green shading to lighter green, EX **275.00**

Syrup, gray & white lg mottle, NM **215.00**

Teapot, Blue Willow-type pattern on white, NM **185.00**

Teapot, gray swirl, gooseneck spout, domed, 4-cup, 8½", NM **60.00**

Thermos, white w/black trim, VG **130.00**

Tray, gray med mottle, oval, NM **165.00**

Tumbler, blue & white fine mottle, black trim, 2¾x2¾", NM .**115.00**

Water pail, blue & white lg swirl w/black trim, wooden bail handle, NM **200.00**

Griswold

Cast-iron cooking ware was used extensively in the 19th century, and even today, lots of folks think no other type of cookware can measure up. But whether they buy it to use or are strictly collec-tors, Griswold is the name they hold in highest regard. During the latter part of the 19th century, the Griswold company began to manu-facture the finest cast-iron kitchenware items available at that time. Soon after they became established, they introduced a line of lightweight, cast-aluminum ware that revolutionized the industry. The company enjoyed many prosperous years until its closing in in the late 1950s. You'll recognize most items by the marks, which generally will include the Griswold name; for instance, 'Seldon Griswold' and 'Griswold Mfg. Co.' But don't over-look the 'Erie' mark, which the company used as well. For lots of information and photographs, we recommend *Griswold Cast Collectibles* by Bill and Denise Harned (L-W Book Sales).

Ashtray, #570A **60.00**
Cornstick pan, #21, 7-stick .**100.00**
Dutch oven, #8 Tite Top, w/lid .**80.00**

Crispy cornstick pan, Griswold #262, miniature, 4x8½", $125.00.

Egg pan, #129, square **40.00**
Grease pot **75.00**
Lid, skillet; #468, self-basting .**55.00**
Long pan or iron heater, #8, Erie,
　deep oval **9.00**
Mold, Turk's head, #140 ....**200.00**
Muffin pan, #19 ....**185.00**
Patty irons, #1, boxed set **45.00**
Popover pan, #18, 6-cup **100.00**
Skillet, #3, Erie **50.00**
Skillet, #8, chicken fryer, smooth
　bottom, w/lid **65.00**
Skillet, Eagle Stove Works
　#12 ....**300.00**
Vienna roll pan, #6 ....**135.00**
Waffle iron, #11, square **150.00**

Hall

　Most famous for their extensive lines of teapots and colorful dinnerwares, the Hall China Company still operates in East Liverpool, Ohio, where they were established in 1903. Refer to *The Collector's Encyclopedia of Hall China* by Margaret and Kenn Whitmyer (Collector Books) for more information. See also Clubs and Newsletters. For listings of Hall's most popular dinnerware line, see Autumn Leaf.

Arizona, jug, Eva Zeisel, 3-qt, from
　$20 to **25.00**
Arizona, plate, Eva Zeisel, from $7
　to **9.00**
Blue Blossom, casserole, Thick
　Rim, from $50 to **60.00**
Blue Blossom, cookie jar, Five
　Band, from $150 to **175.00**
Blue Bouquet, bowl, fruit; 5½",
　from $5 to **7.50**
Blue Bouquet, cup, from $10 to .**12.00**
Blue Bouquet, plate, 9", from $12
　to **14.00**
Blue Garden, salt & pepper shak-
　ers, canister style, pr, from $70
　to **90.00**
Blue Willow, ashtray, from $7
　to **10.00**
Blue Willow, casserole, 7½", from
　$55 to **65.00**
Bouquet, bowl, coupe soup; Eva
　Zeisel, 9", from $10 to ...**12.00**

Blue Bouquet, jug, Radiance shape, from $75.00 to $80.00.

Red Poppy: Grease jar, $24.00; Salt and pepper shakers, Teardrop shape, $28.00 for the pair.

Bouquet, egg cup, from $25 to ..**28.00**

Bouquet, vase, Eva Zeisel, from $27 to **32.00**

Bricks & Ivy, drip-o-lator coffeepot, from $25 to **30.00**

Buckingham, ashtray, Eva Zeisel, from $7 to **8.00**

Buckingham, casserole, Eva Zeisel, 2-qt, from $32 to **37.00**

Cactus, bowl, Five Band, 8¾", from $22 to **27.00**

Cactus, creamer, Viking, from $18 to **22.00**

Cameo Rose, butter dish, ¼-lb, from $40 to **50.00**

Cameo Rose, salt & pepper shakers, pr, from $20 to **25.00**

Caprice, cup, AD; Eva Zeisel, from $5 to **7.50**

Caprice, platter, Eva Zeisel, 17", from $22 to **27.00**

Carrot, bowl, Thick Rim, 8½", from $22 to **27.00**

Carrot, custard, Radiance, from $14 to **16.00**

Crocus, bowl, oval, from $25 to ..**30.00**

Crocus, creamer, Art Deco, from $18 to **22.00**

Crocus, plate, 8¼", from $8 to .**9.00**

Crocus, tidbit, 3-tier, from $47 to .**52.00**

Eggshell Buffet Service, casserole, Dot, oval, 9¾", from $42 to .**47.00**

Eggshell Buffet Service, shirred egg dish, from $20 to **25.00**

Fantasy, egg cup, Eva Zeisel, from $18 to **22.00**

Fern, gravy boat, Eva Zeisel, from $12 to **14.00**

Fern, salt & pepper shaker, Eva Zeisel, pr, from $14 to ..**18.00**

Flamingo, batter bowl, Five Band, from $85 to **95.00**

Floral Lattice, canister, Radiance, from $90 to **110.00**

Floral Lattice, syrup, Five Band, from $35 to **45.00**

French Flower, sugar bowl, Boston, w/lid, from $25 to **30.00**

Frost Flowers, celery bowl, oval, Eva Zeisel, from $13 to .**15.00**

Game Bird, sugar bowl, w/lid, from $20 to **25.00**

Game Bird, teapot, New York, from $100 to **125.00**

Harlequin, ladle, Eva Zeisel, from $11 to **13.00**

Heather Rose, bowl, Flare shape, 8¾", from $12 to **15.00**

Heather Rose, mug, Irish coffee; from $14 to **16.00**

Homewood, bowl, flat soup; 8½", from $8 to **10.00**

Homewood, coffeepot, Terrace, from $45 to **55.00**

Meadow Flower, bean pot, New England, #4, from $95 to **110.00**

Meadow Flower, cookie jar, Five Band, from $140 to **160.00**

Medallion, bowl, Lettuce (green), #2, 5¼", from $8 to **10.00**

Medallion, drip-o-lator coffeepot, from $45 to **55.00**

Medallion, stack set, ivory, from $22 to **27.00**

Mulberry, casserole, Eva Zeisel, 2-qt, from $30 to **35.00**

Mulberry, cup, Eva Zeisel, from $5 to **6.00**

Mums, creamer, New York, from $14 to **16.00**

Mums, gravy boat, from $22 to **27.00**

Mums, teapot, New York, from $125 to **150.00**

No 488, bowl, 9¼" dia, from $30 to **40.00**

No 488, cup & saucer, from $13.50 to **16.50**

Orange Poppy, cake safe, from $25 to **30.00**

Orange Poppy, drip jar & lid, Radiance, from $18 to ..**20.00**

Orange Poppy, plate, 7¼" **8.00**

Orange Poppy, platter, oval, 13¼", from $25 to **30.00**

Orange Poppy, teapot, Streamline, from $240 to **260.00**

Pastel Morning Glory, casserole, Medallion, from $27 to .**32.00**

Pastel Morning Glory, pie baker, from $25 to **30.00**

Pastel Morning Glory, plate, 10", from $22 to **25.00**

Primrose, ashtray, from $8 to .**10.00**

Primrose, plate, 9¼", from $5 to **6.50**

Radiance, bowl, red or cobalt, #1, 3½", from $8 to **10.00**

Red Poppy, bowl, cereal; 6", from $10 to **12.00**

Red Poppy, custard, from $9 to **11.00**

Red Poppy, French baker, fluted, from $14 to **16.00**

Red Poppy, salt & pepper shakers, Teardrop, pr, from $24 to **28.00**

Ribbed, French casserole, stick handle, from $45.00 to $50.00.

Refrigerator Ware, butter dish, Hercules, Westinghouse, from $22 to **27.00**

Ribbed, baker, russet or red, diagonal ribs, 12-oz, from $4 to **6.00**

Sears' Arlington, creamer, from $7 to **9.00**

Sears' Arlington, gravy boat, w/under-plate, from $12 to **14.00**

Sears' Fairfax, bowl, fruit; 5¼", from $3.50 to **4.50**

Sears' Monticello, bowl, oval, 9¼", from $14 to **16.00**

Sears' Monticello, plate, 10", from $6 to **7.00**

Sears' Mount Vernon, casserole, w/lid, from $27 to **32.00**

Sears' Mount Vernon, plate, 8", from $3 to **4.00**

Sears' Richmond/Brown-Eyed Susan, pickle dish, 9", from $4 to **5.00**

Serenade, platter, 13¼", from $18 to **22.00**

Serenade, sugar bowl, w/lid, New York, from $12 to **14.00**

Silhouette, bowl, salad; 9", from $16 to **18.00**

Silhouette, cup & saucer, from $13.50 to **16.50**

Silhouette, jug, #4, Medallion, from $25 to **30.00**

Silhouette, mug, beverage; from $37 to **42.00**

Silhouette, salt & pepper shakers, metal, lg, pr, from $12 to .**14.00**

Springtime, ball jug, #3, from $45 to **55.00**

Springtime, bowl, oval, from $18 to **22.00**

Sundial, batter jug, color other than red or cobalt, from $65 to **75.00**

Sunglow, bowl, salad; Eva Zeisel, 11¾", from $11 to **13.00**

Teapot, Airflow, canary or turquoise, 5-cup, from $37 to **42.00**

Teapot, Aladdin, any solid color other than red or cobalt, from $35 to **45.00**

Teapot, Albany, gold label, from $50 to **60.00**

Teapot, Globe, red, from $120 to **140.00**

Teapot, Hollywood, yellow (or any common color), 6-cup, from $35 to **40.00**

Teapot, musical, working, from $175 to **225.00**

Teapot, New York, old gold decoration, 2-cup, from $55 to ..**65.00**

Tulip, bowl, flat soup; 8½", from $16 to **18.00**

Tulip, bowl, Radiance, 7½", from $12 to **14.00**

Tulip, creamer, modern, from $10 to **12.00**

Tulip, plate, 10", from $20 to .**25.00**

Viking, drip-o-lator coffeepot, from $28 to **35.00**

Wildfire, bowl, 9½" dia, from $22 to **27.00**

Wildfire, cake plate, from $18 to **22.00**

Hallmark

Since 1973 the Hallmark Company has made Christmas ornaments, some of which are today worth many times their original price. Our suggested values reflect the worth of those in mint condition and in their original boxes. Refer to *The Ornament Collector's Price Guide, Hallmark's*

Ornaments and Merry Miniatures, by our advisor, Rosie Wells, for more information. She is listed in the Directory under Illinois. See also Clubs and Newsletters.

Betsy Clark, children's choir and orchestra on white glass ball, QX 108-1, 1974 (2nd in series), 3¼" dia, MIB, from $75.00 to $85.00.

Across the Miles, QX 315-7, 1991 ....**14.00**
Baby-sitter, QX 275-6, 1986 .**10.00**
Batman, QX 585-3, 1994 .....**28.00**
Bellringer, QX 403-9, 1983 .**138.00**
Betsy Clark Home for Christmas, WX 271-4, #3, 1988 ....**24.00**
Charmers, WX109-1, 1974 ..**45.00**
Christmas Owl, QX 444-1, 1984 ....**35.00**
Christmas Teddy, QX 404-2, 1981 ....**20.00**
Country Goose, QX 518-5, 1985 .**14.00**
Currier & Ives, QX 209-1, 1976 .**50.00**
Disney, QX 207-6, 1978 ....**82.00**
Elvis, QX 562-4, 1992 ....**22.00**
Fred Flintstone & Barney Rubble, QX 500-3, 1994 ....**30.00**
Friends Are for Fun, QX 528-9, 1991 ....**22.00**

General Store, QLX 705-3, 1986 .**65.00**
Grandmother, QX 267-6, 1978 ...**48.00**
Holiday Highlights, Santa, QX 307-6, 1978 ....**80.00**
Kermit the Frog, QX 495-6, 1982-83 ....**100.00**
Lion King, Timon & Pumba, QX 536-6, 1994 ....**25.00**
Looney Tunes, Tasmanian Devil, 1994 ....**55.00**
Mom & Dad, QX 442-5, 1989 .**25.00**
Niece, QX 573-2, 1993 ....**12.00**
Norman Rockwell, QX 196-1, 1976 ....**75.00**
Nutcracker, QLX 726-1, 1992 ..**55.00**
Peppermint Mouse, QX 401-5, 1981 ....**30.00**
Rabbit, QX 139-5, 1977 .....**100.00**
Raggedy Ann, QX 165-1, 1975 .**50.00**
Santa's Workshop, QLX 737-5, 1993 ....**55.00**
Snowgoose, QX 107-1, 1974 ..**80.00**
Space Shuttle, QLX 739-6, 1995 ....**35.00**

Yesteryears: Train QX 181-1, 1976 MIB, from $170.00 to $175.00.

Tree Topper, Christmas Star, QX 702-3, 1978 ....**45.00**
Uncle Sam, QX 449-1, 1984 ..**45.00**

Winnie the Pooh, QX 206-7, 1979 ....**38.00**

Halloween

Halloween items are fast becoming the most popular holiday-related collectibles among today's collectors. Although originally linked to pagan rituals and super-stitions, Halloween has long since evolved into a fun-filled event; and the masks, noisemakers, and jack-o'-lanterns of earlier years are great fun to look for. Within the last ten years, the ranks of Halloween col-lectors have grown from only a few to thousands, with many overcom-pensating for lost time! Prices have risen rapidly and are only now lev-eling off and reaching a more rea-sonable level. As people become aware of their values, more items are appearing on the market for sale, and warehouse finds turn up more frequently. Our advisor for this category is Pamela E. Apkarian-Russell, the Halloween Queen; she is listed in the Directory under New Hampshire.

Basket/candy holder, paperboard, pumpkin face, Germany, 1916", 5" **150.00**
Basket/candy holder, paperboard, pumpkin face, Germany, 1916, 3½" **125.00**
Candy box, Clark's Black Jack Caramels, 1950x, 10x9", EX **40.00**
Centerpiece, black cat w/accordion body, crepe-paper & card-board, 10" **70.00**

Poster, Spook Show, dancing skele-tons and ghost, 72x30", $200.00. (Photo courtesy Pamela Apkarian-Russell)

Cookie cutter, Trick or Treat, metal, 6 in box w/Halloween scene **65.00**
Costume, Banana Splits, yellow & red bodysuit, Ben Cooper, 1969, M **30.00**
Costume, Doctor Doom, 1-pc bodysuit, Ben Cooper, 1967, MIP **100.00**
Costume, King Kong, Ben Cooper, 1976, MIB **20.00**
Costume, Tinkerbelle, Disney, Ben Cooper, in orig box **25.00**
Decoration, magpie, black & orange die-cut paper, Dennison, 9", M **22.00**
Diecut, cat dressed in Puss 'n Boots-type outfit, Germany, lg **125.00**
Doll, Jack Skellington, talk-ing **125.00**

Tambourines, tin: Jack-o'-lantern with dancing children, $40.00; black cat face, $50.00. (Photo courtesy Pamela Apkarian-Russell)

Doll, Sally, Nightmare Before Christmas, M (coffin box), from $300 to **350.00**

Doll, witch, composition, metal glasses, crepe-paper clothes, 1920s **500.00**

Doll, witch, wooden, Poppy Doll Co, in original box **65.00**

Figurine, cowboy w/rope & pistol, orange & black plastic, 3½" **100.00**

Figurine, girl holds cat, jack-o'-lantern at feet, Rockwell, bisque **400.00**

Figurine, jack-o'-lantern on green cart w/yellow wheels, plastic, 6x5" **100.00**

Game, Casper the Friendly Ghost, Milton Bradley **45.00**

Jack-o'-lantern, blow-up beachball type, Nightmare Before Christmas **75.00**

Jack-o'-lantern, papier-mache, fanged paper insert, American, 1940s, 7" **110.00**

Lamp shade, Casper the Ghost & friends on merry-go-round, 1960s, 8x8" **50.00**

Lantern, orange cat face, original paper insert, American, 5" **145.00**

Mask, gauze, 3-colored, 1960s .**3.00**

Mask, molded papier-mache, Black man, ca 1920 ......**85.00**

Mask, plastic, Nixon, Carter, Reagan, Oliver Hardy, Max Headroom, ea **12.00**

Mug, jack-o'-lantern w/vulture handle, Fitz & Floyd **65.00**

Nodder, cat w/bobbing head, glass eyes, Germany, 1920s .**350.00**

Noisemaker, frying pan shape w/jack-o'-lantern, tin, VG .**12.00**

Noisemaker, tin, Art-Deco sexy witch & skyline, round .**20.00**

Noisemaker, tin, black cat's face on orange background ..**12.00**

Noisemaker, tin, w/owl **14.00**

Party hat, smiling jack-o'-lantern w/fringe on checkered band, paper **65.00**

Poster, Halloween figures & Palmer Cox Brownie, Deco design, 3x18" **800.00**

Posters, Nightmare Before Christmas, German, sm, set of 4 ......**150.00**

238

Pull toy, clown in colored hat & ruff, Rosen USA **85.00**

Pull toy, plastic orange cat in colored shirt w/jack-o'-lantern, Rosen **85.00**

Skeleton, papier-mache, 72", in mirror-lined coffin, w/crown & beads **600.00**

Harker

One of the oldest potteries in the East Liverpool, Ohio, area, the Harker company produced many lines of dinnerware from the late 1920s until it closed around 1970. Refer to *A Collector's Guide to Harker Pottery* by Neva W. Colbert (Collector Books) for more information.

Amy, bean pot, metal rack ..**75.00**

Amy, hi-rise jug **22.00**

Amy, pie plate **8.00**

Amy, plate, dinner **5.00**

Black-Eyed Susan, saucer, 6" .**2.00**

Black-Eyed Susan, tidbit tray, 3-tier **12.50**

Calendar plate, Heritance shape, 1960 ....**3.00**

Calico Tulip, cake plate **17.50**

Calico Tulip, condiment jar, metal lid **5.00**

Cameo Rose, cup **5.00**

Cameo Rose, rolling pin, blue .**98.00**

Chesterton, cake set, pink floral, 8-pc **25.00**

Chesterton, snack set, gray & pink, 12-pc **60.00**

Colonial Lady, bowl, batter .**42.00**

Colonial Lady, cup & saucer .**7.50**

Colonial Lady, pie plate, 9" .**30.00**

Dainty Flower, cup & saucer, Swirl **10.00**

Deco Dahlia, cake lifter **22.00**

Deco Dahlia, cake tray, 10¾" .**27.50**

Deco Dahlia, pie plate, 10" .**30.00**

Deco Dahlia, plate, Virginia, 6" .**3.00**

Deco Dahlia, scoop **26.00**

Heritance, plate, dinner; 16-sided **3.00**

Ivy, creamer & sugar bowl ..**12.50**

Ivy, plate, dinner **6.00**

Modern Tulip, bowl, 6" **5.00**

Modern Tulip, custard **6.00**

Amy, spoon or cake lifter, $12.00 each; Dinner plate, $5.00.

Modern Tulip, teapot **18.00**
Pastel Tulip, gravy boat **14.00**
Pastel Tulip, plate, dinner **8.50**
Petit Point, fork & spoon **25.00**
Petit Point, rolling pin **75.00**
Poppy, bowl, utility; 11" **17.50**
Red Apple, drip jar, Skyscraper .**15.00**
Red Apple, plate, dinner **6.00**
Shadow Rose, cup & saucer ..**9.00**
Shadow Rose, platter **13.00**
White Rose, bowl, soup **12.00**
White Rose, cake/pie lifter ..**12.50**
White Rose, plate, dinner **12.00**
White Rose, plate, 10" **12.00**
Wood Song, plate, 7" **8.00**

Hartland

Hartland Plastics Inc. of Hartland, Wisconsin, produced a line of western and historic horsemen figures during the 1950s, which are now very collectible. Using a material called virgin acetate, they molded such well-known characters as Annie Oakley, Bret Maverick, Matt Dillon, and many others, which they painted with highest attention to detail. In addition to these, they made a line of sports greats as well as religious statues. See Clubs and Newsletters for ordering information regarding the book *Hartland Horses and Riders* by Gail Fitch.

Babe Ruth, EX, from $125 to .**175.00**
Brave Eagle, NM **200.00**
Bret Maverick, miniature series,
  NM **75.00**
Bullet, w/tag, NM **75.00**
Dale Evans, purple, NM **300.00**
Dick Groat, EX, from $800
  to **1,000.00**

Don Drysdale, NM/M, from $300
  to **400.00**
Ernie Banks, EX, from $200
  to **225.00**
Harmon Killebrew, EX, from $300
  to **325.00**
Henry Aaron, NM **200.00**
Jim Bowie, w/tag, NM **250.00**
Little Leaguer, 6", NM/M, from
  $200 to **250.00**
Lone Ranger, miniature series,
  NM **75.00**
Minor Leaguer, 4", EX, from $50
  to **75.00**
Paladin, NMIB **350.00**
Rifleman, miniature series, repro
  rifle, EX **75.00**

Rifleman, Lucas McCain, 8" figure on 8" horse, complete, NMIB, $350.00. (Photo courtesy Kerry & Judy's Toys)

Roger Maris, NM/M, from $350
  to **400.00**
Sgt Preston, repro flag, NM .**750.00**
Stan Musial, NM/M, from $200
  to **275.00**

Ted Williams, NM/M, from $225
to **300.00**
Wyatt Earp, w/tag, NMIB .**275.00**
Yogi Berra, w/mask, EX, from
$150 to **175.00**

Head Vases

Many of them being Japanese imports, head vases were made primarily for the florist trade. They were styled as children, teenagers, clowns, and famous people. There are heads of religious figures, Blacks, Orientals, and even some animals. One of the most common types are ladies wearing pearl earrings and necklaces. Refer to *Head Vases, Identification and Value Guide,* by Kathleen Cole (Collector Books) for more information.

Lady with hat and gold trim, Lefton, $90.00 to $110.00. (Photo courtesy Loretta DeLozier)

Blond girl in green hat & coat, Caffco (paper label), #E3283, 7½" **65.00**

Blond girl w/flip hairdo, white collar, Inarco, #2782, 6" **37.50**
Blond in black & white, bow at neck, pearls, Inarco, #E-1066, 4½" **32.50**
Blond in pale blue ruffled bonnet, bow tied at side, unmarked, 5½" **42.50**
Blond in white hat & dress, hand up, pearls, Inarco, #E241, 6½" **47.50**
Blond lady in flat hat, hands crossed, pearls, Rubens, #495, 5¾" **42.50**
Blond w/black hat & dress, pearls, hand to face, Inarco, #3190/L, 7" **42.50**
Brunette in black hat, hand to face, pearls, Napco, #C4891A, 8½" **125.00**
Girl in ponytails, eyes closed, white bodice, unmarked, 5½" **32.50**
Lady in bonnet w/heart-shaped brim, Rubens (label), #484, 5½" **37.50**
Lady in flat black hat, yellow dress, hand to face, unmarked, 4½" **22.50**
Lady in flat hat w/flower at band, Rubens #499B, 6" **42.50**
Lady in long white curls, hand to face, Japan, 5½" **42.50**
Lady in long white curls, ruffled bodice, Relpo, #K1335, 8" **125.00**
Lady in pink flowered hat, white gloves, Relpo, #A-1373S, 4½" **32.50**
Lady in pink hat & dress w/gold trim, unmarked, 4" **32.50**
Lady in pink turban w/flower, pearls, Napco, #C4899, 5½" **42.50**

Doris Day look-alike, fur collar, Enesco, 6", from $55.00 to $65.00.

Lady w/flower band in brown hair, dangle earrings, unmarked, 7½" **42.50**

Lady w/frosted blond hair, leaf pin, pearls, Napcoware, #C7474, 9" **150.00**

Lady w/rose in hair, hand to face, Inarco, #193/M, 1961, 6" **42.50**

Lady w/side-swept hair, blue ruffled bodice, pearls, unmarked, 6½" **47.50**

Victorian lady, high ruffled collar w/gold coleslaw, unmarked, 6½" **52.50**

White lady w/gold trim, marked Glamour Girl, 6½" **22.50**

Hippie Collectibles

The 'Hippies' perpetuated the 'Beatnik' genre of rebellious, free-thinking Bohemian nonconformity during the decade of the 1960s. Young people created a 'counterculture' with their own style of clothing, attitudes, music, politics, and behavior. They created new forms of art, theatre, and political activism. The epicenter of this movement was the Haight-Ashbury district of San Francisco. The youth culture culminated there in 1967 in the 'Summer of Love.' Woodstock, in August 1969, attracted at least 400,000 people. Political activism against the Viet Nam War was intense and widespread. Posters, books, records, handbills, and other items from that era are highly collectible because of their uniqueness to this time period. Our advisor for this category is Richard Synchef, who is listed in the Directory under California.

Key:

SF—San Francisco

FSM—Free Speech Movement

Magazines

Avant Garde, Ralph Ginsberg editor, NY, 1968-71, #1 - 12, ea, from $40 to **200.00**

Life, May 25, 1970, Tragedy at Kent State **25.00**

Ramparts, Mar '67, Social History of Hippies, re: Haight-Ashbury scene **65.00**

Saturday Evening Post, Nov 2, 1968, Bob Dylan cover story **25.00**

Paperback Books

Electric Tibet, N Hollywood: Dominion, 1969, study of SF music scene **50.00**

Killings at Kent State, IF Stone, NY Review Book, December 1970 ....**45.00**

Wavy Gravy, Hog Farm & Friends, forward: Kelsey, NY/Link, re: Woodstock **70.00**

Posters

Blushing Peony, Victor Moscoso art, Haight St store ad, '67, 14x20" **100.00**
Can You Pass Acid Test, Kensey & Pranksters, Ginsberg, etc, rare, 1965 ....**1,900.00**
Dick Gregory for President/Mark Lane for Vice, Peace & Freedom Party, 1968, 22x29" **400.00**
Dope Plus Capitalism Equals Genocide, Black Panthers, ca 1967, 14x17" **400.00**
HALO Benefit for Haight-Ashbury Legal Organization, May 30, 1966, Mouse, Kelley & Griffin art, 14x18" **80.00**
Human Be-In, Gathering of the Tribes, Jan 14, 1967, SF/Bindweed Press, Mouse & Kelley art, 14x20" **450.00**
Kendrick & Assoc, Eller art, hippies face riot police, 1970, 22x29" **125.00**
March & Rally Against War, April 24, 1971, National Peace Action Coalition, superimposed peace sign on yellow, 22x14" ..**80.00**
Out of Southeast Asia Now!, Demonstrate Nov 6, National Peace Action Coalition, 1971, 11x17" **80.00**
Stand for McCarthy Rally, Sacramento, Aug 10, white on blue, 18x23" **150.00**
The Trip, American International Pictures, classic '60s movie, 40x60" **100.00**

Would You Die To Save This Face?, stern-face photo of Lyndon Johnson, International Poster Corp, 1968, 21x29" **60.00**

Records

FSM's Sounds & Songs of the Demonstration, FSM, Berkeley, LP, +booklet **120.00**
Hoffman, Abbie; Wake Up America, NY/Big Toe, LP, 1969 .**100.00**
Kensey, K; & Merry Pranksters, Acid Test, Sound City Prod, SF, 1966 ....**350.00**
Leary, Timothy; LSD, NY/Pixie #1069, LP, 1966 ....**125.00**
Rod McKuen Takes a SF Hippie Trip, Tradition/Everest, LP, ca 1969 ....**25.00**

Miscellaneous

Admission ticket, Woodstock Music & Art Fair, Globe, 1969, from $100 to **120.00**
Book, Freewheeling Frank, Secretary of (Hell's) Angels, Frank Reynolds, as told to Michael McClure, NY/Grove, 1967 ...**65.00**
Book, High Priest, Timothy Leary, NY/World, 1968, a '60s classic **100.00**
Book, Journal of Psychedelic Drugs, Vol 2 #1, Marijuana, Dr Smith, SF **45.00**
Book, Psychedelic Review, #9, 1967, Leary, Metzner, Brand & others **80.00**
Book, Quotations From...Mao Tse-Tung (Little Red Book), 1st printing, 1966 ....**120.00**
Bumper sticker, McGovern/ Eagleton, blue & white, 1972, 12x4" .**40.00**

Bumper sticker, Nixon's My Man, Nixon as hippie, 3-color, 12x3" **50.00**

Comic, underground; Yellow Dog #5, Apex Novelties, SF, 1970 ....**55.00**

Comic, underground; Zap #5, Apex Novelties, SF, 1970, 1st printing **50.00**

Figurine, Hippie girl w/sign: Join Our Love-In, Napcoware, 1970s, 6" **75.00**

Figurine, Hippie man w/sign: Fight Hate, Napcoware, 1970s, 6" **75.00**

Handbill, Communications Co, advice/info re: Summer of Love, 300 produced during 1967, ea, from $35 to **300.00**

Handbill, McCarthy Is Happening, May 25, 1968, Santa Clara, 9x4" **200.00**

Handbill, publicizing 1st 'Be-In,' 5 different ones, any, from $300 to **500.00**

Handbill, Yippie! Chicago Aug 25-30, pre-'68 Democrat Convention Youth International Party, red, white & blue, 8½x11" ..**350.00**

Newspaper, Black Panther, 1967-74, per issue, from $40 to **250.00**

Newspaper, SF Oracle, 12 issues re: Summer of Love 1967, ea, $60 to **350.00**

Pillow, inflatable plastic, Peter Max, ca 1960-70, 16x16", any of 8, ea **80.00**

Pin-back button, Bomb Now, Pray Later, black on white, 1970s, 1½" **35.00**

Pin-back button, Free Speech, FSM, in white on blue, Berkeley, CA, 1964 ....**50.00**

Pin-back button, Dick Gregory for President, late 1960s, rare, 1½", from $50.00 to $60.00. (Photo courtesy of Paper Pile, San Anselmo, CA/PJ Gibbs, _Black Collectibles Sold in America_)

Pin-back button, Out Now, Nov 6th Demonstrate Against War, Nat'l Peace Action Coalition, 1971, 1¾" **35.00**

Pin-back button, Stop the Draft, white letters on red, ca 1969, 2" **25.00**

Program/magazine, for the Woodstock Music & Art Fair, 52-page, rare **400.00**

Protest button, March on WA-SF April 14 Out Now, 1971, NACP, 1⅝" **25.00**

Puzzle, Life, Peter Max, Schisgall 1970, box: 5⅜x7⅜", 500-pc **75.00**

Stickers, various peace signs, Atomic Energy Group, 1967, ea, from $5 to **10.00**

Holly Hobbie and Friends

About 1970 a young homemaker and mother, Holly Hobbie, approached the American Greeting

Plate, Start Each Day in a Happy Way, American Greetings Collectors Edition, 10½", from $8.00 to $10.00.

Company with some charming country-styled drawings of children. Since that time over four hundred items have been made with almost all being marked HH, H. Hobbie, or Holly Hobbie. For further information we recommend our advisor, Helen McCale, listed in the Directory under Missouri.

Dinnerware, porcelain, blue girl, adult, 45-pc **700.00**
Dinnerware, porcelain, girl w/rose, adult, 45-pc **600.00**
Dinnerware, porcelain, girl w/rose, adult luncheon, 20-pc .**250.00**
Dinnerware, porcelain, green girl, adult, 45-pc **600.00**
Dinnerware, porcelain, green girl, adult luncheon, 20-pc .**250.00**
Egg, porcelain, vertical, various sayings **8.00**
Figurine, The Recital **155.00**
Lamp, oil; colonial, various sayings, handle ea side, 10" **20.00**
Lamp, oil; hurricane, porcelain globe, 7¼" **15.00**

Planter, scroll or book shape, ea **10.00**
Plaque, oval, 4½x6" **10.00**
Plaque or trivet, 5x7" tile **8.00**
Plate, sterling silverplate, limited edition, 10" **300.00**
Plate, The Recital **6.00**
Platter, Happiness Is Having Someone To Love, gold border, 10½x14" **35.00**
Platter, To the House of a Friend, gold border, 10½x14" **35.00**
Sand bucket, metal, child's, lg, G **20.00**
Sand bucket, child's, sm, G ..**12.00**
Sand sifter, metal, child's, G .**20.00**
Sprinkling can, metal, child's, G .**15.00**
Wall planter **10.00**
Wall planter, tinted **12.00**
Wastebasket, metal **8.00**

Holt Howard

Ceramic novelty items marked Holt Howard are hot! From the late 1950s, collectors search for the pixie kitchenware items such as cruets, condiments, etc., all with flat, disk-like pixie heads for stoppers. In the '60s, the company designed and distributed a line of roosters — egg cups, napkin holders, salt and pepper shakers, etc. Items with a Christmas theme featuring Santa or angels, for instance, were sold from the '50s through the '70s, and you'll also find a line of white cats. Most pieces are not only marked but dated as well. Our advisor for this category is April Tvorak, listed in the Directory under Colorado.

Onion jar, pixie head finial, from $65.00 to $75.00.

Salt and pepper shakers, Santa, 1950s, from $35.00 to $40.00 for the pair.

Bank, Dandy Lion, bobbing head, from $140 to **160.00**

Bell, holly decoration **15.00**

Bud vase, white cat in plaid cap & neckerchief, from $65 to **75.00**

Butter dish, embossed rooster, ¼-lb **35.00**

Candle holder, boy on shoe .**22.00**

Candle holder, Mary holding Jesus, ea **45.00**

Cherries jar, Pixie head finial, from $65 to **80.00**

Coffeepot, embossed rooster, from $70 to **85.00**

Cookie jar, white cat's head form **45.00**

Egg cup, double; rooster figural **18.00**

Ketchup jar, embossed rooster **35.00**

Letter holder, white cat w/coiled-wire back **25.00**

Mayonnaise jar, Pixie winking head finial, from $45 to .**60.00**

Mug, Santa, from $10 to **12.00**

Planter, camel **15.00**

Platter, embossed rooster, oval **25.00**

Punch bowl, Santa, w/8 santa mugs, 9-pc set **95.00**

Salt & pepper shakers, Christmas angels, pr **45.00**

Salt & pepper shakers, mice in baskets, pr **35.00**

Salt & pepper shakers, Pixie, pr .**68.50**

Snack set, tomato, 1 cup & 1 plate, 1962 ....**14.00**

Spoon rest, figural rooster, from $30 to **35.00**

String holder, white cat's head only, from $35 to **45.00**

Homer Laughlin

Founded in 1871, the Homer Laughlin China Company continues today to be a leader in producing quality tablewares. Some of their earlier lines were made in large quantity and are well marked with the company name or HLC logo; collectors find them fun to use as well as to collect, since none are as yet very expensive. Refer to *The Collector's Encyclopedia of Homer Laughlin China* by Joanne Jasper and *The Collector's Encyclopedia of Fiesta* by Sharon and Bob Huxford (both published by Collector Books). Our advisor, Darlene Nossaman, is listed in the Directory under Texas. *The Laughlin Eagle* is listed in Clubs and Newsletters. See also Fiesta; Harlequin; Riviera.

Empress Shape, early 1900s (available in Flying Bluebirds, Pink Moss Rose, Rose and Lattice, Gold Garland)

Bowl, coupe soup; 8" **12.00**
Bowl, fruit/sauce; 5" **5.00**
Bowl, vegetable; oval, 9" **16.00**

Butter dish, w/lid, 7½" dia ..**35.00**
Casserole, oval, w/lid, 11" **35.00**
Creamer, 1-pt **12.00**
Egg cup, Boston **18.00**
Pitcher, 1½-qt **40.00**
Plate, 6" **6.00**
Plate, 8" **8.00**
Plate, 9" **10.00**
Plate, 9¾" **12.00**
Platter, 11" **18.00**
Platter, 13" **24.00**
Sauceboat, ¾-pt **18.00**
Saucer, 5" **4.00**
Sugar bowl, w/lid, 5½" **15.00**
Teacup **8.00**
Teapot, 2-qt **45.00**

Hudson Shape, early 1900s (available in Carnation Beauty, Pink Aster, Rose Border, Favorite)

Bowl, fruit/sauce; 5" **6.00**
Bowl, soup; 7" **10.00**
Bowl, vegetable; 9" dia **15.00**
Casserole, w/lid, 9" **40.00**
Creamer, 1-pt **15.00**
Pitcher, 1½-qt **35.00**
Plate, 6" **6.00**
Plate, 8" **8.00**
Plate, 9" **10.00**
Plate, 9¾" **12.00**
Platter, 11" **20.00**

Shapes: Empress creamer, $12.00; Kwaker creamer, $12.00; Hudson sugar bowl, with lid, $20.00; Nautilus regular sugar bowl, with lid, $12.00; The Angelus creamer, $16.00. (Photo courtesy Darlene Nossaman)

Platter, 13¾" **25.00**
Sauceboat, ¾-pt **18.00**
Saucer, 5½" **4.00**
Spooner, 4¼" **35.00**
Sugar bowl, w/lid, 5½" **20.00**
Teacup, 8-oz **7.00**
Teapot **50.00**

Kraft Blue and Kraft Pink Shape, 1930s (white handles and blue knobs)

Bowl, cereal; 6" **8.00**
Bowl, cream soup; 5" **10.00**
Bowl, fruit; 5½" **6.00**
Bowl, soup; 8½" **10.00**
Bowl, vegetable; 8¾" dia **12.00**
Creamer **8.00**
Creamer, novelty **12.00**
Egg cup, double **12.00**
Plate, 10" **10.00**
Plate, 6" **5.00**
Plate, 9" **8.00**
Platter, 10" **12.00**
Platter, 12" **15.00**
Saucer **3.00**
Sugar bowl, w/lid **10.00**
Teacup **7.00**
Teapot **25.00**

Kwaker Shape, 1920s (available in Dream Poppy, Vestal Rose, Vandemere, Presidental)

Bowl, coupe soup; 7¼" **8.00**
Bowl, fruit/sauce; 4" **5.00**
Bowl, vegetable; oval, 8¾" ...**15.00**
Butter dish, w/lid, 7¼" **40.00**
Casserole, w/lid, 10" **35.00**
Creamer, ⅔-pt **12.00**
Pitcher, 3¼-pt **40.00**
Plate, 10" **9.00**
Plate, 6" **5.00**
Plate, 9" **8.00**

Platter, 11½" **15.00**
Platter, 13½" **20.00**
Sauceboat, 7" **15.00**
Saucer, AD **4.00**
Saucer, 5" **4.00**
Sugar bowl, w/lid, 5" **14.00**
Teacup **6.00**
Teacup, AD **10.00**
Teapot, 2-qt **55.00**

Nautilus Regular Shape, 1930s (available in Cardinal, Colonial, Old Curiosity Shop, Magnolia)

Bowl, fruit/sauce; 5" **4.00**
Bowl, soup; 7" **8.00**
Bowl, vegetable; 9" dia **14.00**
Casserole, w/lid **35.00**
Creamer **8.00**
Onion soup **10.00**
Pickle dish, 6" **10.00**
Plate, 10" **8.00**
Plate, 7" **6.00**
Plate, 9" **8.00**
Platter, 11½" **16.00**
Platter, 13½" **18.00**
Sauceboat **12.00**
Saucer **2.00**
Sugar bowl, w/lid **12.00**
Teacup **6.00**

The Angelus Shape, early 1900s (available in Rosemere, Gold Wreath, Art Floral, Wild Rose)

Bowl, fruit/sauce; 5¼" **5.00**
Bowl, soup; 8" **10.00**
Bowl, vegetable; oval **18.00**
Casserole, w/lid, 9¼" **45.00**
Creamer **16.00**
Pitcher, 2-qt **40.00**
Plate, 10" **12.00**
Plate, 7½" **8.00**
Plate, 9½" **10.00**

Platter, 11½" **22.00**
Platter, 13½" **26.00**
Sauceboat, ¾-pt **18.00**
Saucer, 5" **4.00**
Sugar bowl, w/lid **20.00**
Teacup, 8-oz **8.00**
Teapot, 3-pt **65.00**

Horton Ceramics

Horton Ceramics, owned by Horace and Geri Horton, began operations in Eastland, Texas, in 1947. Mrs. Geri Horton was a multi-talented artist and designed all the ceramics, while Mr. Horton ran the business end. The company produced vases, planters, figurines, ashtrays, western dinnerware, and kitchen accessories. These items were sold to florist, variety, department, grocery, and gift shops all over the United States. Each item is usually marked with a mold number and 'horton ceramics' in lower case letters. The company was sold in 1961. Our advisor, Darlene Nossaman, is listed in the Directory under Texas.

Butter warmer, red apple design, Special Gift, 4" **4.00**
Figurine, clown, multicolor, Special Gift, 6" **4.00**
Figurine, cowboy boot, brown & yellow, Special Gift, 6" ...**7.50**
Figurine, sailboat, yellow, brown & turquoise, Special Gift, 10" **9.00**
Mug, Davy Crockett, Special Gift **25.00**
Planter, African violet, purple, #705, 4" **3.50**
Planter, baby bootie, pink or blue, #B4, 4" **4.50**
Planter, blue birds, #N880, oval, 6" **6.00**
Planter, cheerleader girl, pink skirt, #B9, 10" **10.00**
Planter, contemporary shape, greens, #37, 6" **3.50**
Planter, football boy, blue pants, #B8, 10" **10.00**
Planter, rooster, white w/black & red, #455, 8" **7.00**
Planter, speckled yellow & white, #809, 9" **4.50**
Planter, trotting horse, oval, #W44, 3" **6.50**

Planter, bluebirds on white, #N880, oval, 6", $6.00; Mug, Davy Crockett, Special Gift, $25.00. (Photo courtesy Darlene Nossaman)

Vase, brown cedar glaze, #V14, 10" **8.00**

Vase, flower motif, greens & yellow, #205, 5" **5.00**

Vase, fluted foot, 2-tone, #C8, 5" **6.50**

Vase, Madonna, blue, #M2, 7" .**12.00**

Vase, pitcher & bowl, pink, white or green, #AT7&8, 10" ..**15.00**

Wall pocket, flower, fish or fruit, #BS504, 4" **10.00**

Hull

Established in Zanesville, Ohio, in 1905, Hull manufactured stoneware, florist ware, art pottery, and tile until about 1935, when they began to produce the lines of pastel matt-glazed artware which are today very collectible. The pottery was destroyed by flood and fire in 1950. The factory was rebuilt and equipped with the most modern machinery which they soon discovered was not geared to duplicate the matt glazes. As a result, new lines — Parchment and Pine, and Ebb Tide, for example — were introduced in a glossy finish. During the '40s and into the '50s, their kitchenware and novelty lines were very successful. Refer to *Robert's Ultimate Encyclopedia of Hull Pottery* and *The Companion Guide*, both by Brenda Roberts (Walsworth Publishing), for more information. Brenda also has authored a third book, *The Collector's Encyclopedia of Hull Pottery* which is published by Collector Books.

Gingerbread Man, cookie jar, Mirror Brown, #323, from $295.00 to $325.00.

Avocado, salt shaker, w/cork, 3¾" **6.00**

Avocado, steak plate, oval, 11¾x9" **12.00**

Bank, Corky Pig, Mirror Brown, 1957 Patent trademark, 5", from $60 to **75.00**

Blossom, casserole, floral on white, open, #21, 7½" **45.00**

Blossom, creamer, floral on yellow to white, #28, 4½" **45.00**

Blossom Flite, bowl, console; flowers on basketweave, #T-10, 16½" **145.00**

Bouquet, pitcher, multicolor floral on yellow to ivory, #22, 64-oz **175.00**

Bow Knot, cup-&-saucer wall pocket, B-24, 6" **260.00**

Bow Knot, vase, bow & floral on blue to green, #B-3, 6½" **170.00**

Butterfly, ashtray, butterfly & flowers on ivory heart shape, #B-3, 7" **45.00**

Centennial, salt shaker, unmarked, 3" **30.00**

Country Belle, coffee cup, white w/blue flower & bell stencil .**7.00**

Country Belle, gravy boat w/tray, white w/blue flower & bell stencil **28.00**

Country Squire, cookie jar, green agate w/white trim, 94-oz **45.00**

Country Squire, water jug, green agate w/white trim, 80-oz .**32.00**

Crestone, gravy boat, turquoise, w/lid, 32-oz **25.00**

Dogwood, candle holder, cornucopia form, #512, 3¾" .**125.00**

Dogwood, vase, flared rim, handles, #510, 10½" **360.00**

Ebb Tide, creamer, shell form, #E-15, 4" **85.00**

Floral, bowl, salad; yellow on ivory w/brown band at top, #49, 10" **75.00**

Gingerbread Man, coaster, Mirror Brown, #399, 5x5", from $35 to **40.00**

Gingerbread Man, cookie jar, Mirror Brown, #323, from $295 to **325.00**

Gingerbread Man, server, Mirror Brown, #198, 10x10" **75.00**

Heartland, creamer, brown heart stencil on ivory w/yellow trim **15.00**

Heartland, salt & pepper shakers, brown heart stencil, handles, pr **32.00**

Magnolia, basket, floral on pink to blue, matt, #10, 10½" .**360.00**

Magnolia, candle holder, floral on ivory, glossy, #H-24, 4" .**45.00**

Magnolia, candle holder, floral on pink, low handles, matt, #27, 4" **50.00**

Magnolia, teapot, floral on ivory, glossy, #H-20, 6½" **175.00**

Magnolia, vase, floral on pink matt, low handles, #20, 15", from $375.00 to $500.00.

Magnolia, vase, floral on ivory, gold handles, glossy, #H-2, 5½" .**50.00**

Magnolia, vase, floral on pink matt, sm handles, #13, 4¾" **50.00**

Magnolia, vase, floral on pink to yellow matt, sm handles, #15, 6¼" **65.00**

Mardi Gras/Granada, vase, cream w/low handles, #49, 9" ..**55.00**

Mardi Gras/Granada, vase, pink to blue, handles, #48, 9" ...**60.00**

Mirror Almond, creamer, 8-oz .**14.00**

Mirror Almond, plate, luncheon; 9⅜" **9.00**

Mirror Brown, baker, rectangular, #534, 7-pt **40.00**

Mirror Brown, bowl, mixing; #538, 8" **12.00**

Mirror Brown, bowl, soup or salad; 3569, 6½", from $6 to **8.00**

Tuscany, basket, green and cream, twig handle, 8¼", from $60.00 to $85.00.

Mirror Brown, casserole, oval, #544, w/lid, 2-pt, from $18 to ..**20.00**

Mirror Brown, coffeepot, #522, 8-cup, from $30 to **35.00**

Mirror Brown, gravy boat, #511 ....**14.00**

Mirror Brown, ice jug, #514, 2-qt, from $22 to **26.00**

Mirror Brown, mug, #302, 1980s, 10-oz, from $3 to **5.00**

Mirror Brown, plate, dinner; #500, 10¼" **8.00**

Mirror Brown, platter, fish; #596, 11", from $40 to **50.00**

Mirror Brown, server, #873H, w/handle, from $70 to .**85.00**

Mirror Brown, sugar bowl, #519, 12-oz, w/lid, from $5 to **7.00**

Mirror Brown, tidbit tray, 2-tier, #592, from $60 to **70.00**

Novelty, Basket Girl, blue bonnet, glossy, #954, 8" **45.00**

Novelty, clown planter, #82, 6¼" **40.00**

Novelty, flowerpot, embossed rings on yellow flared form, #95, 4½" **20.00**

Novelty, leaf dish, burgundy & dark green, #85, 13" **40.00**

Novelty, planter, poodle stands upright beside leafy vase, #114, 8" **55.00**

Novelty, planter, twin geese, green & white, #95, 7¼" **60.00**

Open Rose, ewer, floral on pink, #105, 7" **270.00**

Open Rose, vase, floral decor on pink swan form, #135, 6¼" **175.00**

Parchment & Pine, candle holder, unmarked, 5" long **35.00**

Poppy, planter, floral on blue to pink, handles, #602, 6½" **255.00**

Poppy, wall pocket, floral on pink to blue, cornucopia form, #609, 9" **400.00**

Provincial, baking dish, brown w/white trim, 3-pt **22.00**

Provincial, plate, salad; 6½" .**11.00**

Ridge, creamer, gray or sand, 8-oz **10.00**

Ridge, tray, gray or sand, 7¼" ..**5.00**

Ring, bowl, salad/soup; brown, 12-oz **9.00**

Ring, creamer, brown **12.00**

Rosella, sugar bowl, white open roses on ivory, R-4, 5½" **65.00**

Rosella, vase, embossed open roses on ivory, #R-15, 8½" ...**135.00**

Serenade, vase, birds on white hat shape, #S-4, 5¼" .**70.00**

Sunglow, bowl, pink floral on yellow, #50, 9½" **45.00**

Sunglow, flowerpot, pink floral on yellow, #97, 5½" **40.00**

Tangerine, coffee mug, 9-oz ...**6.00**

Tangerine, sugar bowl, w/lid, 12-oz **12.00**

Tokay, cornucopia vase, pink grapes on pink to green, #10, 11" **75.00**

Tuscany, vase, green grapes on ivory, integral handles, #12, 12" **95.00**

Water Lily, creamer, floral on walnut to apricot, L-19, 5" ..**80.00**

Water Lily, ewer, floral on pink to yellow, #L-3, 5½" **80.00**

Water Lily, jardiniere, floral on pink to yellow, #L-23, 5½" **125.00**

Wildflower (numbered), candle holder, double; floral on pink, #69, 4" **150.00**

Wildflower (numbered), sugar bowl, floral on pink, #74, 4¾" **275.00**

Woodland, cornucopia vase, floral on ivory to pink, #W-2, 5½" **75.00**

Woodland, ewer, floral, on yellow to pink, sm handles, #W-3, 5½" **55.00**

Woodland, window box, floral on ivory to pink, rectangular, #W-14, 10" **170.00**

Imperial Glass

Organized in 1901 in Bellaire, Ohio, the Imperial Glass Company made carnival glass, stretch glass, a line called NuCut (made in imitation of cut glass), and a limited amount of art glass within the first decade of the century. In the mid-'30s, they designed one of their most famous patterns (and one of their most popular with today's collectors), Candlewick. Within a few years, milk glass had become their leading product.

During the '50s, they reintroduced their NuCut line in crystal as well as colors, marketing it as 'Collector's Crystal.' In the late '50s they bought molds from both Heisey and Cambridge. Most of the glassware they reissued from these old molds was marked 'IG,' one letter superimposed over the other. When Imperial was bought by Lenox in 1973, an 'L' was added to the mark. The company changed hands twice more before closing altogether in 1984.

In addition to tableware, they made a line of animal figures, some of which were made from Heisey's molds. *Glass Animals of the Depression Years* by Lee Garmon and Dick Spencer is a wonderful source of information and can help you determine the value and the manufacturer of your figures.

Numbers in the listings were assigned by the company and appeared on their catalog pages. They were used to indicate differences in shapes and stems, for instance. Collectors still use them.

For more information we recommend *Imperial Glass* by Margaret and Douglas Archer; *Elegant Glassware of the Depression Era* by Gene Florence; *Imperial Carnival Glass* by Carl O. Burns; and *Imperial Glass Encyclopedia, Vol. I A-Cane*, edited by James Measell. Our advisor, Joan Cimini, is listed in the Directory under Ohio. See also Clubs and Newsletters.

Ashtray, Heart, ruby red slag, satin or glossy **20.00**

Bell, Hobnail, amber carnival, #42340 ....45.00

Bell, Suzanne, white carnival, IG mark, 6" 40.00

Bowl, Grape, rubigold carnival, crimped edge, #47C, 9" .40.00

Bowl, jelly; Cape Cod, crystal, 3" 12.00

Box, Beaded Jewel, rubigold carnival, #975 ....30.00

Butter dish, ruby red slag, glossy 75.00

Cake plate, Cape Cod, low footed, square, 10" 95.00

Candlesticks, Rose, red slag, glossy, 3½", pr 30.00

Candy dish, Herringbone, red slag, glossy, w/lid 45.00

Champagne, Cape Cod, verde green, #1602 ....16.50

Cocktail, Crocheted Crystal, 4½", 3½-oz 12.50

Compote, Zodiac, peacock carnival, Heisey mold, w/lid .45.00

Cup, coffee; Cape Cod, crystal, #160/37 ....7.00

Decanter, wine; Grape, rubigold carnival, w/6 wines 150.00

Figurine, cygnet, caramel slag .55.00

Goblet, Cape Cod, red, wafer stem 22.00

Goblet, Grape, ruby 25.00

Goblet, Kite & Panel, Aurora Jewels (cobalt carnival), #29/9 ....40.00

Marmalade, Cape Cod, crystal, #160/89, 4-pc 45.00

Mug, Robin, red slag, glossy .45.00

Nappy, Pansy, rubigold carnival, handled, #478, 5½" 25.00

Pitcher, Mayflower or #678, peacock carnival, water size, w/6 tumblers 190.00

Pitcher, Williamsburg, cobalt blue, water size, 2-qt 55.00

Pitcher, Windmill, peacock carnival, water size, w/6 tumblers 190.00

Plate, Cape Cod, red, #160/5D, 8" .24.00

Plate, torte; Cape Cod, crystal, cupped, 13" 35.00

Punch bowl, Crocheted Crystal, 14" 65.00

Salt cellar, red slag, 4-toed, #61 .18.00

Toothpick holder, rubigold carnival, Collector's Crystal, #505 ....12.00

Toothpick holder, 3 in 1 Diamond, red slag, glossy, #1 ....15.00

Tumbler, Cape Cod, 16-oz, $30.00.

Tumbler, juice; Cape Cod, amber, footed, #1602, 5-oz 20.00

Tumbler, Tiger Lily, pink carnival 18.00

Vase, Beaded Block, cobalt opalescent, 6" 75.00

Vase, Lace Edge, rubigold carnival, 4-toed, 5" **25.00**
Vase, Rose, Labelle, rubigold carnival, #181, 6¼" **40.00**
Wine/cigarette holder, Eagle, red slag, glossy or satin **35.00**

Indiana Carnival Glass

Though this glass looks old, it really isn't. It's very reminiscent of old Northwood carnival glass with its grape clusters and detailed leaves and vines, but this line was actually introduced in 1972! Made by the Indiana Glass Company, Harvest (the pattern name assigned by the company) was produced in blue, lime green, and marigold. Although they made a few other carnival patterns in addition to this one, none are as collectible or as easy to recognize.

This glassware is a little difficult to evaluate as there seems to be a wide range of asking prices simply because some dealers are unsure of its age and therefore its value. If you like it, now is the time to buy it!

Harvest values given below are based on items in blue. Adjust them downward a price point or two for lime green and even a little more so for marigold. For further information we recommend *Garage Sale and Flea Market Annual* (Collector Books). Our advisor, Ruth Grizel, is listed under Iowa. See also King's Crown; Clubs and Newsletters.

Butter dish, stick type, ¼-lb, 8" **25.00**
Candlesticks, footed bowl shape, 4x4½" dia, pr **35.00**
Candy box, w/lid, 6½" **30.00**

Center bowl, Harvest, embossed grapes, leaves and vines, pedestal foot, 12x8½" dia, $35.00.

Candy dish, lace edge, footed, w/lid, 6½" **30.00**
Canister/candy jar, 7" **30.00**
Canister/cookie jar, 9" **45.00**
Creamer & sugar bowl on tray, 3-pc **30.00**
Goblet, 9-oz, set of 4, from $25 to **30.00**
Pitcher, 10½" **50.00**
Tumbler, 14-oz, set of 4, from $35 to **40.00**
Wedding bowl, footed, w/lid, 10x6¾" **35.00**

Japan Ceramics

Though Japanese ceramics marked Nippon, Noritake, and Occupied Japan have long been collected, some of the newest fun-type collectibles on today's market are the figural ashtrays, pincushions, wall pockets, toothbrush holders, etc., that are marked 'Made in Japan' or simply 'Japan.' In her books called *Collector's Guide to Made in Japan Ceramics* (there are two in the series), Carole Bess White explains the pitfalls you will encounter when you try to determine production dates. Collectors refer to anything produced before WWII as 'old,' and anything made after 1952 as 'new.' You'll find all you need to know to be a wise shopper in this book.

See also Black Cats; Blue Willow; Cat Collectibles; Egg Timers; Enesco; Fishbowl Ornaments; Flower Frogs; Geisha Girl; Head Vases; Holt Howard; Lefton; Moss Rose; Nippon; Noritake; Occupied Japan; Rooster and Roses; Sewing Collectibles; Toothbrush Holders; Wall Pockets.

Decanter, cowboy figural, matt green checkered shirt and red bandana, 7½", with 6 yellow and opalescent lustre shot glasses, all marked, $65.00 for the set. (Photo courtesy Carole Bess White)

Bank, smiling friar, comical look, glossy, black mark, 5¼" .**15.00**
Bell, Colonial lady figural, Seattle Washington souvenir, 4¾" .**20.00**
Bell, lady w/basket of flowers figural, semimatt, black mark, 4½" **15.00**
Biscuit barrel, black hunt scene on cream, glossy, 5¾" **50.00**
Biscuit barrel, multicolor floral reliefs on white w/cobalt, 7" **50.00**
Bookends, black poodle w/gold on brown clay body, gold mark, 6", pr **20.00**
Bookends, boy & girl, black & white, glossy, black mark, 6", pr **30.00**
Bookends, Scottie w/lg red bow at neck, lustre, red mark, 6½", pr **35.00**
Bowl, multicolor geometric lustre decor, 8-sided, reed handle, 8" **30.00**
Bowl, multicolored fruit along rim, Goldcastle mark, 8½" ...**45.00**

Bowl, striped leaf form w/floral decor & gold, gold mark, 6¼" **4.00**

Cache pot, elephant w/open howdah, multicolor, glossy, 3½" **15.00**

Candle holders, mottled lustre, flared base, red mark, 6¼", pr **35.00**

Candy dish, 3 Oriental ladies support bowl, blue mark, 4½" **75.00**

Chamberstick, floral on rustic crackle, shield back, red mark, 6" **35.00**

Cheese dish, green & black floral branch on white, Moriyama, 6¼" **35.00**

Cigarette box, dog figural w/ashtray back, Goldcastle, black mark **45.00**

Cigarette box, dogs on lid, opal lustre & multicolor, glossy, 3" sq **25.00**

Cigarette holder, figural elephant w/match holder howdah, lustre, 5½" **65.00**

Cigarette holder, floral w/yellow lustre, Goldcastle mark, 3¼" **25.00**

Condiment set, blue & orange lustre, 3-pc on cloverleaf tray, 3¾" **35.00**

Condiment set, 2 sm ducks rest on lg duck tray, multicolor lustre **50.00**

Creamer & sugar bowl, elephant figurals w/multicolor lustre, 4¼", pr **50.00**

Creamer & sugar bowl, hen figurals w/multicolor lustre, 3¼", pr **50.00**

Cup & saucer, green & black floral branch on white, Moriyama **30.00**

Incense burner, cottage form, multicolor, 4½" **17.50**

Incense burner, elephant w/pagoda on back, multicolor, glossy, 5¾" **20.00**

Incense burner, red flowers on blue 6-sided shape, footed, 2¾" **17.50**

Marmalade set, geometric lustre, 8-sided, attached underplate, w/ladle **70.00**

Plate, tomato form, black mark, 5¼" **10.00**

Powder box, Colonial lady, white w/shiny gold, Goldcastle mark 6¾" **25.00**

Powder box, Colonial lady in ornate blue gown, glossy, black mark, 7" **35.00**

Relish, divided heart shape w/green crackle, black mark, 7½" **20.00**

Salt & pepper shakers, floral on basketweave w/brown bands, 4¾", pr **15.00**

Salt & pepper shakers, Geisha stands amid flower shakers on tray **35.00**

Salt & pepper shakers, tomato form, green mark, 2", pr **15.00**

Tea set, child's; floral w/tan lustre, black mark, 1930s, serves 6 ....**200.00**

Teapot, Deco-style multicolor lustre, black mark, 6½", from $32 to **47.00**

Teapot, yellow shamrocks on red gloss, black mark, 6", from $32 to **47.00**

Vase, black cat figure before blue geometric-form vase, 4¼" **25.00**

Vase, calico hippo, mouth open wide, black mark, 3¼" ..**20.00**

Vase, floral on pink crackle, classic shape, black mark, 7¼" **38.00**

Vase, geometric multicolor w/white, blue handles, Goldcastle mark, 5½" ...**35.00**

Vase, orange & black w/gold lustre, Kinkozan, pre-WWII, 9¾" **100.00**

Jewelry

Today, anyone interested in buying gems will soon find out that antique gems are the best values. Not only are prices from one-third to one-half less than on comparable new jewelry, but the craftsmanship and styling of modern-day pieces are lacking in comparison. Costume jewelry from all periods is popular, especially Art Nouveau and Art Deco examples. Signed pieces are particularly good, such as those by Miriam Haskell, Eisenberg, Trifari, Hollycraft, and Weiss, among others.

There are several excellent reference books available if you'd like more information. Lillian Baker has written several: *Art Nouveau and Art Deco Jewelry; Twentienth Century Fashionable Plastic Jewelry; 50 Years of Collectible Fashion Jewelry;* and *100 Years of Collectible Jewelry.* Books by other authors include *Collectible Costume Jewelry* by Cherri Simonds, *Christmas Pins* by Jill Gallina; and *Collecting Antique Stickpins* by Jack and 'Pet' Kerins.

Bracelet, bangle, gold-filled w/chased decor **75.00**

Bracelet, charm; Sterling, silver w/18 charms **125.00**

Bracelet, Eisenberg, individual rhinestone links, flexible, 1960 ....**120.00**

Bracelet, Eisenberg Ice, ⅞" wide **140.00**

Bracelet, Lisner, faux opal, w/original tag **22.50**

Bracelet, Weiss, 19 7mm rhinestones in single row **20.00**

Cuff links, 18k yellow gold over sterling leaf w/8 mm cultured pearl **38.00**

Earrings, Carnegie, blue sapphires and rhinestones on gold, $90.00 for the pair.

Earrings, Coro, green rhinestones .**8.00**

Earrings, garnet set in 14k yellow gold, pr **85.00**

Earrings, Hollycraft, pastel faceted stones on gold-tone metal, 1960s **38.00**

Earrings, Kramer, Aurora Borealis, ¾" dia, pr **20.00**

Earrings, Marvella, lg gray baroque pearls on gold leaf, ⅞", pr **15.00**

Earrings, Robert, pearl & rhinestones on gold, pr **35.00**

Necklace, pearl drops on V-form bib, Victorian, $200.00.

Earrings, Sterling, pearl w/gold wash, clip type, pr **25.00**

Earrings, Weiss, flower-petal shape, marquise & round stones **20.00**

Earrings, 14k yellow gold filigree dangle type w/garnet, pr **85.00**

Locket, 10k yellow gold w/initials set in small jewels, 12k gold chain **125.00**

Necklace, cultured pearls, 5.5mm, 14k white gold clasp, 1 strand, 16" **100.00**

Necklace, gold-filled, garnet flower cluster in center, 3 sm garnets ea side, 18" **135.00**

Necklace, Miriam Haskell, pearl & 'gold' rope **75.00**

Necklace, Miriam Haskell, pearls w/lg puffed heart, 26" **180.00**

Necklace, Vendome, 3 strands of crystal beads & pearls ..**22.50**

Necklace, 14k gold-filled chain w/7 amethyst drops & 16 pearl spacers **90.00**

Pin, cameo, lady's head, black Bakelite **48.00**

Pin, cameo, white on black celluloid, 1⅞" **30.00**

Pin, Cini, star w/moonstone center **60.00**

Pin, Coro, enameled flower, 4" .**15.00**

Pin, Danecraft, sterling flower wreath, 1¼" dia **40.00**

Pin, gold-filled bar style w/carved design, 1930s, 2½" **35.00**

Pin, Jolle, green baguette & clear rhinestones on twisted leaf form **25.00**

Pin, Mexican silver, 3-D dragonfly, 1940s, 2½x2½" **75.00**

Pin, Monet, enameled daisy, 2¼" **8.00**

Pin, Sarah Coventry, gold leaf ..**7.50**

Pin, Sarah Coventry, rhinestones surround lg topaz, 5" dia .**25.00**

Pin, Sarah Coventry, Santa figural **40.00**

Pin, scarf; Boucher, gold-tone w/ white bamboo design **55.00**

Pin, scarf; Trifari, gold-tone feather design, 1960...............**25.00**

Pin, Schreiner NY, poodle, jet black stones...................**125.00**

Pin, sterling, fan-tailed goldfish, 2" **65.00**

Pin, Sterlingcraft by Coro, gold on sterling, birds on branch .**40.00**

Pin, Storet, clear, blue & pink stones on simple form ...**75.00**

Pin, sweater guard; horses, brass................................**28.00**

Pin, Trifari, gold bow **12.00**

Pin, Trifari, molded colored glass flowers on round rhodium shape **30.00**

Pin, Trifari, molded multicolor glass flowers, round shape, rhodium........................**30.00**

Pin, Trifari, poodle w/mother-of-pearl body...................**25.00**

Pin, Trifari, sterling pave feather **45.00**

Pin, unmarked, gold-tone crown w/multicolor stones & pearls **15.00**

Pins, swag; Corocraft Sterling, sword & sheath, hand paint & jewels.............................**145.00**

Ring, Cire Perdu, 14k yellow gold w/lg citron.......................**65.00**

Ring, Cire Perdu, 14k yellow gold w/lg pearl **75.00**

Ring, 10k yellow gold w/black enameling **50.00**

Ring, 14k yellow gold, .23ct marquise emerald solitaire **100.00**

Ring, 14k yellow gold, baby's, MIB **45.00**

Ring, 18k yellow gold w/7 cultured pearls **120.00**

Ring, Emmons, Aurora Borealis pave diamond shape, gold-tone, ca. 1970 ....**30.00**

Ring, Florenza, blue Aurora Borealis w/pink & purple rhinestones, glass novelty stone center, antiqued silver..........**45.00**

Ring, George Jensen, sterling, cut-out heart shape, Denmark **80.00**

Ring, Hollycraft, shades of blue rhinestones, adjustable, antiqued gold-tone, dated 1955 ....**55.00**

Ring, KJL, domed lg. blue cabachon encircled w/rhinestones, gold-tone, ca. 1970.......**145.00**

Ring, man's, 14k yellow gold, malachite & 6 sm diamonds.**235.00**

Tie pin, gold filled, pink shell cameo **50.00**

Johnson Brothers

Dinnerware marked Johnson Brothers, Staffordshire, has lately become the target of some aggressive collector activity, and for good reason. They made many lovely patterns, some scenic and some florals. Most are decorated with multicolor transfer designs, though you'll see blue or red transferware as well. Some, such as Friendly Village (one of their most popular lines), are still being produced, but the lines are much less extensive now, so the secondary market is being tapped to replace broken items that are no longer available anywhere else.

In addition to their company

Friendly Village, platter, 13½", from $25.00 to $30.00.

logo, the dinnerware is also stamped with the pattern name. Today they're a part of the Wedgwood group.

Coaching Scenes

Bowl, vegetable; 8", from $20 to **25.00**
Cup & saucer, from $10 to ..**15.00**
Plate, dinner; 10", from $10 to .**15.00**
Plate, 6", from $6 to **7.50**
Platter, oval, 14" **55.00**
Sugar bowl, w/lid **25.00**
Teapot, from $55 to **60.00**

Friendly Village

Bowl, cereal; 6" **6.00**
Bowl, fruit **4.00**
Bowl, vegetable; oval, from $18 to **22.00**
Bowl, vegetable; round, from $15 to **20.00**
Butter dish, from $25 to **35.00**
Coffeepot, from $45 to **55.00**
Creamer **18.00**

Cup & saucer, from $7 to **9.00**
Gravy boat w/stand, from $30 to **40.00**
Mug, from $9 to **12.00**
Plate, dinner **8.00**
Plate, salad **5.00**
Platter, turkey **125.00**
Platter, 11½", from $18 to ...**20.00**
Platter, 15", from $35 to **45.00**
Salt & pepper shakers, pr, from $15 to **20.00**
Sugar bowl, w/lid, from $18 to .**25.00**
Teapot, from $40 to **45.00**

Old Britain Castles

Bowl, cereal; 6", from $7 to .**10.00**
Bowl, vegetable; oval, from $20 to .**25.00**
Bowl, vegetable; round, from $16 to **20.00**
Coffeepot, from $50 to **65.00**
Creamer **18.00**
Cup & saucer, from $10 to ..**14.00**
Gravy boat, from $25 to **35.00**
Plate, dinner; 10", from $10 to .**14.00**
Plate, salad **6.00**
Plate, 6" **4.00**

Platter, 12", from $20 to **25.00**
Platter, 15", from $40 to **50.00**
Sugar bowl, w/lid **25.00**
Teapot **50.00**

Rose Chintz

Bowl, cereal; coupe, from $8 to .**12.00**
Bowl, vegetable; oval, from $20
    to **30.00**
Bowl, vegetable; round **25.00**
Chop plate, 12", from $55 to .**65.00**
Coffeepot, from $60 to **90.00**
Cup & saucer, demitasse **7.50**
Cup & saucer, from $8 to **12.00**
Egg cup, single **6.00**
Gravy boat, from $25 to **35.00**
Pitcher, 5½", from $35 to **45.00**
Plate, dinner; from $8 to **12.00**
Platter, 11½", from $20 to ...**25.00**
Sugar bowl, w/lid, from $25 to .**30.00**
Teapot, from $65 to **75.00**

Kentucky Derby Glasses

Kentucky Derby glasses are the official souvenir glasses sold filled with mint juleps on Derby Day. The first glass (1938), picturing a black horse within a black and white rose garland and the Churchill Downs stadium in the background, is said to have either been given away as a souvenir or used for drinks among the elite at the Downs. This glass, the 1939, and two glasses said to have been used in 1940 are worth thousands and are nearly impossible to find at any price. Our advisor, Betty Hornback, is listed in the Directory under Kentucky.

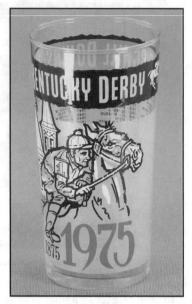

1975, 12.00.

1941, aluminum **800.00**
1941, plastic, Beetleware, from
    $3,000 to **4,000.00**
1945, regular **1,200.00**
1945, tall **425.00**
1946-47, ea **100.00**
1948 ....**180.00**
1948, frosted bottom **200.00**
1949 ....**180.00**
1950 ....**425.00**
1951 ....**550.00**
1952 ....**190.00**
1953 ....**135.00**
1954 ....**175.00**
1955 ....**135.00**
1956, 4 variations, from $150
    to **250.00**
1957 ....**110.00**
1958, Gold Bar **175.00**
1958, Iron Liege **185.00**
1959-1960, ea **80.00**
1961 ....**100.00**
1962 ....**65.00**
1963 ....**50.00**

1964	50.00
1965	60.00
1966	50.00
1967-1968, ea	47.00
1969	47.00
1970	55.00
1971	45.00
1972-1973, ea	38.00
1974, Federal	150.00
1974, mistake	18.00
1974, regular	16.00
1975	10.00
1976	14.00
1976, plastic	12.00
1977	10.00
1978-1979, ea	12.00
1980	18.00
1981-1982, ea	12.00
1983	9.00
1984	7.00
1984-1985, ea	9.00
1986	10.00
1986 ('85 copy)	18.00
1987-1989, ea	9.00
1990-1992, ea	7.00
1993-1995, ea	5.00
1996-1997, ea	3.00

King's Crown

This is a pattern that's been around since the late 1800s, but what you're most apt to see on today's market is the later issues. Though Tiffin made it early, our values are for the glassware they produced from the '40s through the '60s and the line made by Indiana Glass in the '70s. It was primarily made in crystal with ruby or cranberry flashing, but some pieces (from Indiana Glass) were made with gold and platinum flashing as well. Tiffin's tumblers are flared while Indiana's are not, and because Indiana's are much later and more easily found, they're worth only about half as much as Tiffin's. Refer to *Collectible Glassware from the '40s, '50s, and '60s* by Gene Florence (Collector Books) for more information.

Candy dish, footed, with lid, 10½", $70.00.

Ashtray, 5¼" sq	14.00
Bowl, cone, 11¼"	45.00
Bowl, flower floater, 12½"	40.00
Bowl, salad; 9¼"	56.00
Bowl, 5¾"	20.00
Cake salver, footed, 12½"	65.00
Candle holder, 2-light, 5½"	35.00
Compote, 7¼x9¾" dia	35.00
Creamer	22.50
Cup, punch	8.00
Pitcher	120.00
Plate, bread & butter	8.00
Plate, dinner; 10"	35.00
Plate, mayonnaise liner; 7¾"	12.50
Plate, party server; w/punch foot, 24"	115.00
Punch set, 15-pc w/plate	350.00

Stem, cocktail, 2¼" **12.50**
Stem, oyster cocktail, 4-oz ...**14.00**
Sugar bowl **22.50**
Tumbler, water; 8½-oz **13.00**
Vase, bud; 12¼" **60.00**

Kitchen Collectibles

From the early patented apple peelers, cherry pitters, and food choppers to the gadgets of the '20s through the '40s, many collectors find special appeal in kitchen tools. Refer to *Kitchen Antiques, 1790-1940,* by Kathyrn McNerney and *Kitchen Glassware of the Depression Years* by Gene Florence for more information. Both are published by Collector Books.

See also Aluminum; Appliances; Clothes Sprinkler Bottles; Cookie Cutters and Molds; Egg Timers; Enesco; Fire-King; Glass Knives; Graniteware; Griswold.

Glassware

Bowl, cobalt, Hazel Atlas, 6", from $17.50 to **20.00**
Bowl, Delphite Blue, square base, Pyrex, 12", from $20 to **25.00**
Bowl, drippings; white opaque w/red ships, McKee, 8-oz, from $35 to **40.00**
Bowl, green, slick handle, pouring lip, w/lid, US Glass **35.00**
Bowl, green dots on milk glass, 9", from $12.50 to **15.00**
Bowl, refrigerator, blue, Crisscross, w/lid, 4x4", from $25 to .**30.00**
Bowl, ultramarine, Jennyware, 10½", from $35 to **45.00**

Bowl set, fired-on colors, Pyrex, stacking set of 4, from $20 to **28.00**
Butter dish, crystal, deep bottom, Jennyware, from $50 to **60.00**
Butter dish, green, Butter embossed on lid, rectangular **40.00**
Butter dish, milk glass w/red ships, rectangular, McKee, from $22 to **25.00**
Butter dish, pink, bow finial, rectangular, from $50 to ...**60.00**
Canister, custard w/Coffee in black letters, square sides, tin lid **40.00**

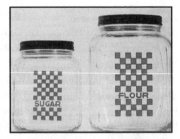

Canisters, checkerboard design on clear with tin lids: Sugar, from $18.00 to $20.00; Flour, from $20.00 to $22.50. (Photo courtesy Gene Florence)

Canister, Delphite Blue, Tea in black letters, tin lid, 20-oz **125.00**
Canister, Dutch decal on clear, square sides, tin lid, Hocking **20.00**
Canister, green clambroth, embossed ribs/paper label, glass lid, 47-oz **50.00**
Canister, multicolor Dutch boy on clear, red metal lid, from $15 to **20.00**
Casserole, white opalescent, w/lid, Fry, 7" square, in metal holder **50.00**

Coffee dripolator, clear, stacked cylinder style, sm, from $15 to **18.00**

Egg cup, Chalaine Blue, from $12 to **15.00**

Fish platter, white opalescent w/engraved decor, Fry, 17", from $50 to **60.00**

Grill plate, Azure Blue, Fry, 8½", from $30 to **40.00**

Ice bucket, pink elephants on clear, from $20 to **25.00**

Measure cup, Armour, Use Armour's Extract of Beef, 1-cup, from $20 to **25.00**

Measure cup, crystal, Pyrex, from $12.50 to **15.00**

Measure cup, green, slightly oval, 1-cup **50.00**

Measure cup, white opalescent, 3-spout, Fry, from $65 to .**75.00**

Measure pitcher, Delphite Blue, McKee, 2-cup, from $75 to **85.00**

Meat loaf pan, white opalescent, rectangular, w/lid, Fry, 9" **50.00**

Reamer, fired-on black, tab handle, Anchor Hocking, from $12.50 to **15.00**

Reamer, green, tab handle, Hazel Atlas, from $8 to **10.00**

Reamer, green transparent, ring handle, lg, from $20 to .**22.00**

Reamer, pink, ribbed, loop handle, Federal Glass, from $25 to **30.00**

Reamer, royal blue, straight sides, Fry, from $50 to **60.00**

Reamer, Sunkist, Chalaine Blue, from $175 to **195.00**

Reamer, Sunkist, yellow opaque, from $45 to **55.00**

Shakers, custard w/black script letters, square w/metal lids, pr **24.00**

Shakers, fired-on color, metal lid, ea, from $5 to **6.00**

Shakers, pink, flat, Jennyware, pr, from $55 to **60.00**

Sugar shaker, red dots on custard, McKee, from $22.50 to ..**25.00**

Teakettle, clear, globular, tin whistle top, Glasbake, from $25 to .**30.00**

Tumbler, green clambroth, horizontal ribs, plain rim, from $8 to **10.00**

Water bottle, green, vertical ribs, 32-oz, from $22 to **25.00**

Water bottle, red, plain or ribbed, Hocking, from $75 to **85.00**

Gadgets and Miscellaneous

Apple corer, tin, 5-shaped, handmade **22.00**

Apple peeler, cast iron, Hudson **65.00**

Tray, green well-in-tree design, 'Not Heat Resisting Glass,' Fry, from $70.00 to $80.00. (Photo courtesy Gene Florence)

Apple peeler, Goodell Improved Bay State, cast iron, EX **165.00**

Apple peeler, Sinclair, Scott & Co, Baltimore, cast iron, clamps on **110.00**

Apple peeler, tin, tubular handle, 6" **15.00**

Beater, Ladd, green glass bowl w/crank metal top, green handles ...**35.00**

Biscuit cutter, Kreamer, strap handle **8.00**

Bottle warmer, Sunbeam, Chicago Flexible Shaft, chromed metal, 1950s **265.00**

Cake mold, tin, center tube, fluted & scalloped sides, 2x8" ...**8.00**

Cake pans, tin, square w/crimped rim, set of 3: 8", 7", 6" ...**80.00**

Can opener, cast-iron bull form, tail forms handle, 6¾" ..**95.00**

Cheese slicer, tin blade w/long wood handle on pine board **45.00**

Cherry seeder, metal, hand-held, finger hole ea side, Perfection, 4" .**15.00**

Cherry seeder, The Electric, cast iron, stands on 4 legs ...**65.00**

Cherry seeder, tinned cast iron, Enterprise #2, Pat..., 1903, 12x9" **45.00**

Chopper, wrought iron w/rectangular blade, wood handle, 6¾x7" **50.00**

Churn, Dazey #40, 4-qt **110.00**

Churn, Lightning, 2-qt **95.00**

Colander, tin w/strap handle, footed, 4¾x11½" dia **30.00**

Cream whip, black tinned wire, spiral base, ca 1890s, 1-pc, 16" **30.00**

Cream whip, black wire w/tin plate, Horlick, 2" wide beaters, 9½" **32.00**

Egg & cream beater, Dunlap Sanitary **20.00**

Egg beater, hand-held, plastic handle **5.00**

Egg beater, Turbine, 1908 ...**35.00**

Egg separator, tin, JA Frost Grocer **12.50**

Egg separator, Town Talk Flour, tin **15.00**

Flour scoop, Jenny Wren Ready Mixed Flour, tin **10.00**

Food grinder, cast iron, Puritan #10, table-top type, EX **10.00**

Grater, punched tin, half-circle shape **35.00**

Grater, punched tin on oak board, 19" w/handle **80.00**

Ice crusher, chrome & black, Dazey, standing style ...**20.00**

Ice pick, heavy metal w/green painted wood handle **12.00**

Juicer, Handy Andy **35.00**

Lemon squeezer, cast iron, fluted bowl, 8" L **20.00**

Mayonnaise maker, Wesson Oil **75.00**

Milk bottle cap opener, iron, Jack Spratt **6.50**

Mixer, Lightning, 1-qt glass jar **265.00**

Mixer, New Keystone, 1-qt glass jar **155.00**

Mixer, Vidrio, electric, w/green base **100.00**

Mold, gray tin, fluted skirt, diamond or oval shape, marked A&J **12.50**

Noodle cutter, Titantonio's, cast iron, clamps to table **55.00**

Nutmeg grater, Gem, Caldwell, tin, mechanical, EX **125.00**

Nutmeg grater, tin, spring mechanism, crank handle, 4⅝" .**55.00**

Mixer/churn, Ladd #2, from $85.00 to $100.00. (Photo courtesy Gene Florence)

Nutmeg grater, tin & wood, 4½" **105.00**

Pie crimper, all wood w/well-shaped handle, 7" **175.00**

Potato masher, heavy twisted wire w/wooden handle, hotel size, 22½" **35.00**

Raisin seeder, cast iron, Enterprise, lg **50.00**

Rolling pin, curly maple, turned stationary handles, 18⅝" **60.00**

Sifter, tin, Lee's Favorite Flour, crank handle, 6x5", EX .**25.00**

Stove-blacking brush, iron handle, black bristles, Peoples ..**30.00**

Teakettle, tin, curved spout, arched handle, brass knob, 10½" **65.00**

Trivet, twisted wire, footed, some rust, 9" dia **55.00**

Vegetable slicer, tinned blade w/wire handle, hand operated, ca 1900 ....**12.00**

Vegetable washer, oval wire, 2-pc, EX **60.00**

Whip, Fries Cream Whip ..**100.00**

Wrench, fruit jar; wire w/rubber grips, Ho-Ho, Monticello IA **7.50**

Knife Rests

Several scholars feel that knife rests originated in Germany and France with usage spreading to England and later to America as travel between countries became more widespread. Knife rests have been documented from 1720 through 1839, and they're being made yet today by porcelain manufacturers and glasshouses to match their tableware patterns. Some of the present-day producers are located in France, Germany, and Poland.

Knife rests of pressed glass, cut crystal, porcelain, sterling silver, plated silver, wood, and bone have been collected for many years. Signed knife rests are especially desired. It was not until the Centennial Exhibition in Philadelphia in 1876 that the brilliant new cut glass rests, deeply faceted and shining like diamonds, appeared in shops by the hundreds. There were sets of twelve, eight, or six; some came boxed. Sizes of knife rests vary from 1¼" to 3¼" for individual knives and from 5" to 6" for carving knives. Glass knife rests were made in many colors such as purple, blue, green, vaseline, pink, and

Val St. Lambert Belquigue, amber glass, 1963, $100.00. (Photo courtesy Beverly Ales)

cranberry. It is important to note that prices may vary from one area of the country to another and from dealer to dealer. For further information we recommend our advisor, Beverly L. Ales, listed in the Directory under California. See also Clubs and Newsletters.

Art France, glass horse, pr .**100.00**
Cut crystal, squash form **75.00**
Cut crystal, w/star on end of ball, 3" **70.00**
Cut crystal, 8-sided bar w/diamond cut on ball end, 5½" **60.00**
Imperial, milk glass, marked IG **35.00**
Lalique France, marked, frosted ends **95.00**
Meissen, marked X w/sword logo on end, pr **165.00**
Pressed glass, green, 3½", pr .**60.00**
Quimper, #499, 1950s, from $40 to **65.00**
Quimper, blue, registered 1883, HB, #797 ....**75.00**
Sabino, blue glass w/duck end **50.00**

Silverplate, children hopping over stile **125.00**
Silverplate, squirrel w/lg bar on tail, Simpson, Hall & Miller **195.00**
Waterford, marked, lg **100.00**

Kreiss

One of the newest areas of collecting interests are items marked Kreiss which were imported from Japan during the 1950s. It's so new, in fact that we're not even sure if it's pronounced 'kriss' or 'kreese,' and dealers' asking prices also suggest an uncertainty. There are several lines. One is a totally off-the-wall group of caricatures called Psycho Ceramics. There's a Beatnick series, Bums, and Cave People (all of which are strange little creatures), as well as some that are very well done and tasteful. Others you find will be inset with colored 'jewels.' Many are marked either with an ink stamp or an in-mold trademark (some are dated).

Weird wood, felt, and fur figures, set of 3, all marked Kreiss Corp. Japan, $55.00. (Photo courtesy June Moon)

Ashtray, man w/tomahawk .**35.00**
Bank, Beatnik Santa **75.00**
Bank, poodle **65.00**
Bookends, good monk/bad monk, pr **75.00**
Egg cup, I'm an Egghead **65.00**
Figurine, Boxing Champ, from $40 to **45.00**
Figurine, Christmas Party ..**85.00**
Figurine, clown w/umbrella **50.00**
Figurine, convict w/ball & chain **85.00**
Figurine, drunk leans on pink elephant, sm elephant beside, 4½x5" **35.00**
Figurine, Hawaiian dancer, female, 6" **55.00**
Figurine, If You're So Smart Why Aren't You Rich, w/rhinestones **65.00**
Figurine, Psycho Ceramics, ea, from $85 to **225.00**
Mug, bum in garbage can **65.00**
Salt & pepper shakers, bear cubs, pr **35.00**
Salt & pepper shakers, monks w/hair, pr **35.00**

Shelf sitters, Oriental couple, pr **30.00**
Vanity set, Mermaid, 4-pc set, from $60 to **65.00**

Lefton China

Since 1940 the Lefton China Co. has been importing and producing ceramic giftware which may be found in shops throughout the world. Because of the quality of the workmanship and the beauty of these items, they are eagerly sought by collectors of today. Lefton pieces are usually marked with a fired-on trademark or a paper label found on the bottom of each piece. Our advisor is Loretta De Lozier, author of *Collector's Encyclopedia of Lefton China*; she is listed in the Directory under Iowa.

Animal, #3026, horse w/hat, detailed porcelain, 3½", pr **42.00**

Animal, #80521, English
Pointer **48.00**
Bank, #13384, Hubert the Lion .**53.00**
Bone dish, #4398, Poinsettia,
6" **20.00**
Box, #4714, French Rose, heart-
shaped perfume sachet w/rib-
bon **21.00**
Box, candy; #2089, Della
Robbia **18.00**

**Figurine, #07319, clown holds
balloon on wooden stick, 1989,
4¼", from $13.00 to $18.00.**

Compote, #2027, latticed, white
w/gold **25.00**
Cookie jar, #3236, Mr Toodles,
9" **250.00**
Creamer & sugar bowl, #2689,
Heavenly Rose **65.00**
Creamer & sugar bowl, #3292, Mr
Toodles, 5" **55.00**
Creamer & sugar bowl, #953,
Americana **30.00**
Dish, #1178, Fruits of Italy, 2-com-
partment, 9½" **30.00**

Figurine, #10268, Chinese
w/lantern, 8", pr **150.00**
Figurine, #1700, girl w/trellis, 3-pc
(complete) set **85.00**
Figurine, #326, Little Adorables,
set of 6 ....**125.00**
Figurine, #3455, Now I Lay Me
Down To Sleep, Christopher
Collection **15.00**
Figurine, #582, man, porcelain,
white w/gold, 8" **115.00**
Figurine, #6188, Paper Boy,
4½" **18.00**
Jam jar, #2697, Dutch Girl, 5" .**55.00**
Jam jar, #3290, Mr Toodles,
4¼" **38.00**
Pitcher, #2562, To a Wild Rose,
6½" **95.00**
Planter, #5260, Dutch shoe w/boy
& girl, pr **65.00**
Plate, #2048, Green Holly, 9" ..**35.00**
Plate, #976, Americana, 10½" .**30.00**
Swan, #721, 7" white china bowl,
w/sponged-on gold & pink
roses **65.00**
Syrup jar, #1333, Sweetie Pie,
4½" **38.00**
Tray, dresser; #982, Tiffany
Rose **75.00**
Vase, #70444, Mardi Gras ...**45.00**
Wall pocket, #6767, Dainty
Miss **95.00**
Wall pocket, #744, boy w/basket,
7½" **95.00**

Letter Openers

Here's a chance to get into a
hobby where there's more than
enough diversification to be both
interesting and challenging, yet
requires very little room for display. Whether you prefer the

advertising letter openers or the more imaginative models with handles sculpted as a dimensional figure or incorporating a penknife or a cigarette lighter, you should be able to locate enough for a nice assortment. Materials are varied as well, ranging from silverplate to wood. For more information, we recommend *Letter Openers, Advertising and Figural* (L&W Book Sales).

Advertising, bronze, Industrial Trust & Savings Bank, 7¼" **5.00**

Advertising, bronze, Milwaukee Lace Paper Co, 8" **15.00**

Advertising, bronze, National Shawmut Bank of Boston,7⅜" **20.00**

Advertising, bronze, Rotary International, 8¾" **5.00**

Advertising, lithographed tin, Uneeda Bread Co, 8¼" .**45.00**

Advertising, metal & celluloid, AE Haines, 8⅞" **35.00**

Advertising, plastic, Bank Americard, 1965, 7¼" **5.00**

Advertising, plastic, Fuller Brush Co, 7¼" **1.00**

Advertising, plastic, Miller High Life, 9" **10.00**

Advertising, stainless steel, Peter's Shoes, 8" **45.00**

Advertising, stainless steel, VFW Ladies Auxiliary, 7" **5.00**

Advertising, steel, Underwood Typewriter Co, 9" **20.00**

Advertising, sterling, 1861-Wright Kay-1961, 7⅝" **45.00**

Aluminum, fleur-de-lis handle, ornate openwork blade, Italy, 7" ..**20.00**

Brass, alligator as handle & blade, Made in China, 6" **10.00**

Brass, Celtic dragon as handle w/wide blade, 8½" **20.00**

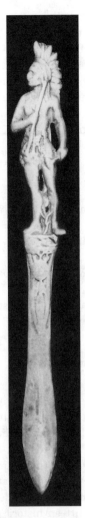

Brass, full-figured Indian chief handle, 8¾", $45.00.

Brass, owl w/sleepy eyes, Made in Israel, 7½" **10.00**

Brass, parrot w/long tail, flat w/engraved details, India, 7½" **10.00**

Bronze & tin, Egyptian death mask at handle, 5¼" **10.00**

Plastic, elephant at top, parade of elephants along edge, 6½" .**2.00**

Plastic, 2 colors w/wheat penny insert in handle, 8" **10.00**

Souvenir, brass, airplane, Washington DC, 8¼" **45.00**

Souvenir, plastic, Indianapolis Indians, 5½" **5.00**

Stainless steel, faux-jewelled leaf design, 7½" **15.00**

Steel, chicken foot as handle w/feather as blade, 9¼" **25.00**

Sterling, horse jockey as handle, Tiffany & Co, 1930s, 7" .**200.00**

Sterling, Old Master pattern handle, Towle Silversmiths, 7⅝" **30.00**

Sterling & mother-of-pearl, sickle form, 3½" **40.00**

Wood, hand-carved bust portrait w/painted details, 6¼" ..**10.00**

Liberty Blue

'Take home a piece of American history!,' stated an ad from the 1970s for this dinnerware made in Staffordshire, England. Blue and white depictions of George Washington at Valley Forge, Paul Revere, Independence Hall — fourteen historic scenes in all — were offered on different place-setting pieces. The ad goes on to describe this 'unique...truly unusual..museum-quality...future family heirloom.'

For every five dollars spent on groceries you could purchase a basic piece (dinner plate, bread and butter plate, cup, saucer, or dessert dish) for fifty-nine cents on alternate weeks of the promotion. During the promotion, completer pieces could also be purchased. The soup tureen was the most expensive item, originally selling for $24.99. Nineteen completer pieces in all were offered along with a five-year open stock guarantee.

For more information we recommend Jo Cunningham's book, *The Best of Collectible Dinnerware.*

Platter, 12", from $35.00 to $45.00.

Bowl, cereal; from $10 to **12.50**

Bowl, flat soup; 8¾", from $15 to **18.00**

Bowl, fruit; 5", from $4.50 to .**5.50**

Bowl, vegetable; oval **40.00**

Bowl, vegetable; round **35.00**

Butter dish, w/lid, ¼-lb, from $20 to **35.00**

Casserole, w/lid, from $65 to **75.00**

Creamer & sugar bowl, w/lid, original box **60.00**

Cup & saucer, from $7 to **9.00**

Gravy boat, from $30 to **35.00**

Gravy boat liner **15.00**

Mug, from $10 to **12.00**

Pitcher, water **95.00**

Plate, dinner; 10", from $7 to .**9.00**

Plate, luncheon, scarce, 8¾" .**12.00**

Plate, 6", from $3 to **4.50**

Platter, 14", from $55 to **65.00**

Salt & pepper shakers, pr ...**25.00**

Sugar bowl, w/lid **25.00**

Teapot, w/lid, from $95 to .**125.00**

License Plates

Early porcelain license plates are treasured by collectors and often sell for more than $500.00 per pair when found in excellent condition. The best examples are first-year plates from each state, but some of the more modern plates with special graphics are collectible too. Prices given below are for plates in good or better condition. Our advisor is Richard Diehl, who is listed in the Directory under Colorado.

Alabama, 1958 ....**14.50**
Alaska, 1967, totem pole **19.50**
Arkansas, 1926 ....**70.00**
California, 1975, blue **5.50**
Connecticut, 1956 ....**15.50**
Delaware, 1970 ....**8.50**
Florida, 1970-71 ....**5.50**
Georgia, 1951 ....**14.50**
Hawaii, 1973 ....**15.50**
Illinois, 1954 ....**5.50**
Iowa, 1959 ....**5.00**
Kentucky, 1976 ....**5.50**

Maryland, 1948 ....**20.00**
Michigan, 1976, Bicentennial, single **5.00**
Minnesota, 1949, Centennial ..**25.00**
Mississippi, 1932 ....**30.00**
Missouri, 1941 ....**11.50**
Montana, 1990 ....**4.50**
Nebraska, 1993, windmill **5.50**
New Hampshire, 1974 ....**4.50**
New Mexico, 1969 ....**8.50**
New York, 1937 ....**12.50**
North Dakota, 1973 ....**6.00**
Ohio, 1969 ....**4.00**
Oklahoma, 1976, Bicentennial .**15.50**
Pennsylvania, 1942 ....**9.50**
Rhode Island, 1951 ....**17.00**
South Carolina, 1953 ....**12.50**
South Dakota, 1962 ....**6.00**
Tennessee, 1965 ....**10.50**
Texas, 1973 ....**3.00**
Utah, 1947, This Is the Place .**18.50**
Vermont, 1920 ....**30.00**
Washington DC, 1992, A Capitol City **10.50**

Little Red Riding Hood

This line of novelties and kitchenwares has always commanded good prices on the col-

Pennsylvania, porcelain, 1913, 6x14", EX, $120.00 for the pair.

lectibles market, but recently dealer ads and show offerings have indicated that interest along with values are continuing to increase, no doubt following along with the same trend in figural cookie jars. Little Red Riding Hood was produced from 1943 to 1957. Some items were manufactured by the Hull Pottery of Crooksville, Ohio, who sent their whiteware to the Royal China and Novelty Company (a division of Regal China) of Chicago, Illinois, to be decorated, but a major part of the line was actually made by the Regal Company. For further information we recommend *The Collectors Encyclopedia of Cookie Jars Vol. I,* by Joyce and Fred Roerig.

Creamer, head pour, tab handle, $350.00.

Bank, standing **600.00**
Batter pitcher **425.00**
Cookie jar, closed basket, minimum value **350.00**
Cookie jar, open basket, red shoes **575.00**
Creamer, pours from head, tab handle **350.00**

Match holder, wall hanging .**800.00**
Salt & pepper shakers, lg, 5½", pr **175.00**
Salt & pepper shakers, standing, 3¼", pr **125.00**
Sugar bowl, crawling, unmarked **275.00**
Sugar bowl, side pour **175.00**
Teapot **365.00**
Vase, 2 handles, poppy decals .**95.00**
Wall pocket **550.00**

Lu-Ray Pastels

Introduced in 1938 by Taylor, Smith, and Taylor of East Liverpool, Ohio, Lu-Ray Pastels is today a very sought-after line of collectible American dinnerware. It was first made in these solid colors: Windsor Blue, Surf Green, Persian Cream, and Sharon Pink. Chatham Gray was introduced in 1948 and is today priced higher than the other colors. For more information, we recommend *Collector's Guide to Lu-Ray Pastels* by Kathy and Bill Meehan.

Bowl, baker; from $13 to **18.00**
Bowl, cream soup; w/saucer, from $68 to **85.00**
Bowl, fruit; from $4 to **6.00**
Bowl, lug soup; from $15 to ..**22.00**
Bowl, mixing; 7" **70.00**
Bowl, nappy; from $10 to **15.00**
Calendar plate, 9", from $35 to **50.00**
Chop plate, from $20 to **30.00**
Coaster, from $60 to **75.00**
Coffeepot, AD; Empire shape, introduced in 1940, from $125 to **150.00**

Juice jug, from $100.00 to $130.00.

Egg cup, double, from $12 to .**18.00**
Pickle tray, from $20 to **28.00**
Plate, 10", from $13 to **18.00**
Plate, 3-compartment, from $18
     to **25.00**
Plate, 6" **3.00**
Platter, 13", from $13 to **18.00**
Relish dish, center handle,
     4-compartment, from $65
     to **90.00**
Salt & pepper shakers, pr, from
     $10 to **16.00**
Teapot, flat spout, w/lid **68.00**
Tumbler, juice; from $30
     to **40.00**
Water jug, original footed design,
     from $65 to **75.00**

Lunch Boxes

In the early years of this century, tobacco companies often
packaged their products in tins
that could later be used for lunch
boxes. By the 1930s oval lunch
boxes designed to appeal to school
children were produced. The rectangular shape that is now popular
was preferred in the 1950s.
Character lunch boxes decorated
with the faces of TV personalities,
super heroes, Disney and cartoon
characters are especially sought
after by collectors today. Our values are for excellent condition
lunch boxes only (without the thermos unless one is mentioned in the
line). Refer to *Pictorial Price Guide
to Vinyl and Plastic Lunch Boxes
and Thermoses* and *Pictorial Price
Guide to Metal Lunch Boxes and
Thermoses* by Larry Aikens (L-W
Book Sales) for more information.
Our advisor is Terri Ivers; she is
listed in the Directory under
Oklahoma.

America on Parade, metal, 1976,
     EX **50.00**
Annie, metal, 1981, w/thermos,
     EX **23.00**
California Raisins, plastic, 1988,
     w/thermos, M **20.00**
Disney Express, metal, 1979,
     w/thermos, EX+ **22.00**

**Daniel Boone, yellow rim,
1965, EX, $150.00.**

Dragon's Lair, metal, 1983, VG .**14.00**
Dynomutt, metal, 1976, G ...**12.00**
Fall Guy, metal, 1981, w/thermos,
     EX- **30.00**

275

Floral, metal, 1970, EX **20.00**
Fox & the Hound, metal, 1982,
    EX+ **25.00**
Fruit Basket, metal, 1975, VG .**18.00**
Garfield, plastic, red, 1978,
    EX- **10.00**
Go-Bots, plastic, 1986, EX- ...**9.00**
Goober & the Ghost Chasers,
    metal, 1974, VG+ **28.00**
Home Alone, plastic, 1991, w/ther-
    mos, EX **12.00**
Indiana Jones, metal, 1984,
    VG **15.00**
Kermit the Frog, plastic,
    dome, 1988, w/thermos,
    EX **30.00**
Looney Tunes, plastic, red, 1978,
    EX- **12.00**
Mork & Mindy, metal, 1978,
    VG- **14.00**
Muppet School Bus, plastic, 1989,
    VG **11.00**
Muppet Show, metal, 1979,
    VG+ **15.00**
New Kids on the Block, plastic,
    1990, w/thermos, EX ...**9.00**
NFL, metal, 1978, VG+ **15.00**

Peanuts, metal, 1980, yellow,
    VG **10.00**
Return of the Jedi, metal, 1983,
    G **15.00**
Robin Hood, metal, 1974, VG .**25.00**
Rough Rider, metal, 1972,
    G **20.00**
Sport Goofy, metal, 1984, EX- ..**20.00**
Transformers, metal, 1986, EX+ .**20.00**
Weave Pattern, metal, 1972,
    EX **15.00**
Where's Waldo, plastic, 1990,
    w/thermos, EX- **8.00**

Thermos Bottles

Auto Race, King Seely Thermos,
    metal, 1967, NM **30.00**
Beverly Hillbillies, Aladdin, metal,
    1963, EX **60.00**
Boston Red Sox, Ardee, 1960s .**12.00**
Dick Tracy: The Movie, plastic,
    EX **2.00**
Dino-Riders, 1988 EX **4.00**
Disco Fever, Aladdin, 1980 .**30.00**
Food Fighters, Aladdin, plastic,
    1988 ....**10.00**

**Peanuts, King Seely Thermos, with thermos, 1966, NM,
$55.00. (Photo courtesy June Moon)**

GI Joe, King Seely Thermos, plastic, 1982 ....**10.00**

Gremlins, Aladdin, plastic, 1984 ....**8.00**

Gremlins, Aladdin, 1984 ....**8.00**

Hee Haw, 1970, NM **45.00**

Holly Hobbie, Aladdin, plastic, 1979 ....**5.00**

Hot Wheels, King Seely Thermos, metal, 1969 ....**25.00**

James Bond 007, metal, 1966, NM **60.00**

Kid Power, American Thermos, plastic, 1974 ....**20.00**

Knight Rider, King Seely Thermos, 1984 ....**12.00**

Land of the Lost, Aladdin, plastic, 1975 ....**35.00**

MAD Collectibles

MAD, a hotly controversial and satirical publication that was first published in 1952, spoofed everything from advertising and politics to the latest movies and TV shows. Content bordered on a unique mix of lofty creativity, liberalism, and the ridiculous. A cult-like following has developed over the years. Eagerly sought are items relating to characters that were developed by the comic magazine, such as Alfred E. Neuman or Spy Vs Spy. Our advisor, Jim McClane, is listed in the Directory under New Jersey.

Bust, bisque, sold through MAD Magazine, early 1960s, 3¾" **300.00**

Bust, sold through MAD Magazine, early 1960s, 5½" **400.00**

Calendar, any dated 1976 through 1981, ea **12.00**

Campaign kits, 1960, 1964 or 1968 issue, complete, ea, from $150 to **400.00**

Coffee mug, any of 6 styles, 1988, ea **15.00**

Computer game, MAD's Spy vs Spy **20.00**

Disquise kit, Imagineering Corp, 1987 ....**20.00**

Doll, Alfred E Newman, What Me Worry tie, 1961, 20" **350.00**

Game, Parker Brothers, board type, dated 1979 ....**10.00**

Game, Parker Brothers, card type, 1980 ....**15.00**

Halloween costume, tuxedo style, plastic mask, Collegeville, 1960, MIB **250.00**

Model kit, Alfred E Newman, Aurora, 1965, MIB **150.00**

Necktie, Watson Bros, 1992 .**35.00**

Magazine, Special Bring Back Arbor Day Issue, July, 1976, NM, $10.00.

277

Pen, Spy vs Spy, Applause, 1988, M **20.00**

Record, Fink Along With MAD, 33⅓ rpm, 1963, original sleeve, M **80.00**

Record, Musically MAD, 33⅓ rpm, 1959, original sleeve, M .**50.00**

Skateboard, 1988 ....**50.00**

Squirt toy, any of 8 variations, Imagineering Corp, 1987, ea **20.00**

Sunglasses, any of 4 variations, Imagineering Corp, 1989, ea **30.00**

Sweatshirt, 1993 ....**25.00**

T-shirt, various styles, 1980s, ea **15.00**

T-Shirt, What Me Worry?, I Read MAD!, late 1950s **400.00**

Tie bar, late 1950s **200.00**

Watch, various styles, limited edition, Applause, 1988, ea .**65.00**

Marbles

Because there are so many kinds of marbles that interest today's collectors, we suggest you study a book on that specific subject such as one by Everett Grist, published by Collector Books. In addition to his earlier work on antique marbles, he has written a book called *Machine-Made and Contemporary Marbles* as well. His latest title is *Everett Grist's Big Book of Marbles*, which includes both antique and modern varieties. Remember that condition is extremely important. Naturally, chips occurred; and though some may be ground down and polished, the values of badly chipped and repolished marbles are low.

In our listings, values are for marbles in the standard small size unless noted otherwise and in excellent to near-mint condition. Watch for reproductions of the comic character marbles. Repros have the design printed on a large area of plain white glass with color swirled through the back and sides. While common sulfides may run as low as $100.00, those with a more unusual subject or made of colored glass are considerably higher, sometimes running as much as $1,000.00 or more.

Agate, hand-cut dye, 1" **45.00**

Banded Lutz, opaque black base **32.00**

Banded Swirl, bright colors .**25.00**

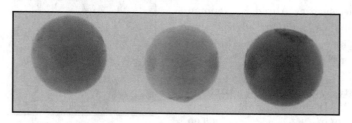

Solid opaque marbles: green, pink, and blue, ¾" dia, $75.00 each. (Photo courtesy Everett Grist)

Bennington, pink, 1" **75.00**
Cat's-eye, banana; Peltier Glass
    Company, 1" **2.00**
China, glazed, single color, inter-
    secting lines, 1" **4.00**
Clambroth, white base, single
    color **80.00**
Cleary, colored, ⅝" **20.00**
Comic, Skeezix **100.00**
Corkscrew, Akro Agate, 2-color,
    white base, 1" **15.00**
Crockery, unglazed, lined **4.50**
Divided Core Swirl, 4 bands .**8.00**
End of the Day, onionskin lutz,
    pink & white core, NM .**90.00**
Flinty, Akro Agate, red, ⅝" ...**7.00**
Helmet Patch, Akro Agate, 1" .**10.00**
Latticinio Core Swirl, red core ..**60.00**
Oxblood Slag, MF Christensen &
    Sons, ⅝" **75.00**
Peerless Patch, Peltier Glass
    Company, black aventurine,
    ¾" **12.00**
Peppermint Swirl, mica in blue
    bands **115.00**
Pinpoint Pontil Transitional, ⅝" .**30.00**
Popeye Corkscrew, Akro Agate,
    dark blue & yellow, ⅝" .**15.00**
Rainbow, Marble King, wasp,
    1" **30.00**
Regular Pointed Transitional,
    1" **30.00**
Ribbon Core Swirl, ¾"-1" **45.00**
Slag, MF Christensen & Sons,
    red **7.00**
Sparkler, Akro Agate, ⅝" **12.50**
Submarine, colored base, ⅝" .**90.00**
Sulfide, common unpainted ani-
    mals, clear glass, 1⅝", mini-
    mum value **100.00**
Sunbursts, Master Marble, tiger
    eye, ¾" **16.00**
Swirl, Christensen Agate, 2 opaque
    colors (no white) **15.00**

Marilyn Monroe

The famous nude calendar shot by Tom Kelley in 1953 catapulted her to stardom, and by January of 1954, Marilyn had become 20th-Century Fox's biggest box-office attraction and Hollywood's leading sex goddess. Her hairstyle and wardrobe were imitated by women, and she was admired by men the world over. Some of her best-remembered films include *How To Marry a Millionaire, The Seven Year Itch,* and *River of No Return.* But fame was short-lived and took its grim toll. In 1962 Marilyn was found dead in her apartment, an apparent suicide.

Magazine, Hit, 1949, EX, $65.00.

Book, Forever Marilyn, Marie
    Cahill, hardcover, M **10.00**
Calendar, Marilyn, Hallmark,
    1994, M **15.00**
Calendar, Marilyn, Landmark,
    1990, M **15.00**
Calendar, Unpublished Marilyn,
    Andre de Dienes, 1995, M .**20.00**

Calendar, nude with lace overlay, 1954, 15x9", minor soiling, $80.00.

Crossfire Comics, #12, all Marilyn Monroe inside, M **20.00**

Doll, 7 Year Itch, Tri-Star, 1982, 11½", MIB **90.00**

Magazine, Inside Story, July 1960, mostly Marilyn on cover, NM **25.00**

Magazine, Ladies' Home Journal, July 1973, mailing label, G **20.00**

Magazine, Liberty, Fall 1973 .**30.00**

Magazine, Life, August 17, 1962, Memories of Marilyn, NM .**30.00**

Magazine, Look, November 17, 1953, mailing label **25.00**

Magazine, Modern Screen, June 1955, NM **40.00**

Magazine, Modern Screen, September 1954, VG **40.00**

Magazine, Ms, August 1986, M ..**25.00**

Magazine, Photoplay, April 1954, NM **40.00**

Magazine, Photoplay, December 1953, spine damage, mailing label **40.00**

Magazine, Photoplay, September 1975, mailing label **35.00**

Magazine, Premier Telecard, February 1994, M **10.00**

Magazine, Redbook, July 1955, NM **45.00**

Magazine, Screen Stories, August 1956, NM **40.00**

Magazine, Screen Stories, February 1961, VG **40.00**

Magazine, Screen Stories, July 1957, NM **40.00**

Magazine, Screen Stories, November 1954, EX **35.00**

Plaque, green, color picture of Marilyn & nameplate, 7x5" **20.00**

Postcard, Marilyn's house in Beverly Hills, older **5.00**

Postcards, A Postcard Book, 30 different, 1989 ....**15.00**

Program, Bus Stop, Marilyn illustration, Roxy Theatre ...**65.00**

Sheet music, Ladies of Chorus, framed **200.00**

Sketch, by MacPherson, w/certificate, M **100.00**

Trade cards, complete set, #1-#20 & #21-#40 ....**50.00**

Window waver, Star Pool, M .**125.00**

Match Safes

The popularity of match safes began around 1850 and peaked in the early 1900s. These small containers were designed to safely carry matches on one's person. They were made from numerous materials including tin, brass, sterling, gold, tortoise shell, and aluminum. They became a popular advertising media at the turn of the century. Most safes can be distinguished from other smalls by their rough striking surface. Match safes have been and are still being reproduced; there are many sterling reproductions currently on the market. Our advisor is George Sparacio, who is listed in the Directory under New Jersey.

Advertising, El Wilto Cigar, plated metal, German, 1⅝x2⅝", VG **35.00**

Agate, moss green, round end, stone striker, brass trim, 2¾x1", EX **125.00**

Barrel form, striker ea end, plated brass, 1½x2½", EX **65.00**

Beaver on lid, maple leaves on body, sterling, 2½x2½", EX **200.00**

Boar figural, squatting, plated brass, 1¾x3", EX **185.00**

Book form, ivory w/sterling initial, 2x1¼" **68.00**

Boy Scout, cylinder w/stamped emblem on bottom, plated brass, 3", EX **18.00**

Coin motif, Gorham sterling, 2½x1⅝", EX **125.00**

Columbian Expo, Bryant & May decor, litho tin, 1½x¾", VG **60.00**

Cotton bale form, plated brass w/ties, 2⅞x1½", EX **60.00**

Crown lid w/Iron Cross, plated brass, 2¾x1⅜", EX **115.00**

Deer leg & hoof figural, fur covered, 3x1", EX **95.00**

Elephant on tooth figural, ring on side, brass, 3x1", EX ...**125.00**

English fob type, ring on side, sterling, 1⅝x2½", EX **55.00**

Firemen/Home Insurance, sterling, Kerr, 2½x1¾", EX **350.00**

Gladstone's bust figural, plated brass, 2½x1¼", EX **235.00**

Jackknife, textured sides, faux blades, plated brass, 2⅞x1⅛", EX **190.00**

Kate Greenaway decor, Springtime, copper, 3x1½", EX **65.00**

King Edward VII, commemorative, book form, vulcanite w/gold, 2x1½" **55.00**

Knapsack, Diamond Match, brassy metal, 1⅝x1⅜", EX **12.00**

Safe with cigar cutter, mother-of-pearl sides, ¾x2¼", EX, $125.00. (Photo courtesy George Sparacio)

Moss agate, rounded end, stone striker, brass trim, 2¾x1", EX **125.00**

Oriental decor w/compass on side, brass, 2¾x1¾", EX **180.00**

Oriental embossed decor ea side, brass, 1¾x2¾", EX **85.00**

Pocket watch form, plated brass, 2", EX **125.00**

Queen Victoria, commemorative, book form, vulcanite w/gold, 2x1½" .**95.00**

Queen Victoria 1887 Jubilee, hinged, plated brass, 1⅜x2⅝", EX **95.00**

Ruler form, brass w/aluminum, 2½x1¾", EX **225.00**

Shoe form (work type), brass w/studs on sole, 1⅜x2¼", EX **140.00**

St Louis World's Fair, insert type w/cutter, plated brass, 2¾", EX **65.00**

Trick, Magic Drawer, leather-wrapped, w/advertising, 1⅜x2⅝", EX **55.00**

Turtle figural w/real shell back, plated brass body, 1¾x2½", EX **275.00**

Matchcovers

Since their inception during the seven-year gap between the 1933 Chicago Century of Progress and the 1939 New York World's Fair, organized matchcover clubs have furnished tens of thousands of collectors with hours of fun and hobby. The 1933 Chicago extravaganza offered a limited number of matchcovers, while the 1939 New York World's Fair produced over 250 fair and related matchcovers for collectors.

Clubs grew and flourished for the next twenty years. Then during the 1940s, due to the publicity surrounding the New York Fair and a pioneering group of New York collectors, over one million people were known to maintain collections. Today matchcovers can still be picked up free at many restaurants, hotels, casinos, and businesses throughout America. For many the hobby is a fascinating and inexpensive way to learn about America, document vacations and trips, and just enjoy the satisfaction of collecting.

Information about matchcover collecting can be gained by joining America's foremost club, The American Matchcover Collecting Club (AMCC) (see Clubs and Newsletters). Dues are currently $23.00 yearly, for which members receive quarterly issues of *The Front Striker Bulletin* with mail auctions, a membership roster, a membership card, free matchcovers, and full membership privileges. Pricing information can be found in the book, *The Matchcover Collector's Price Guide, 2nd Edition,* by our advisor and the club's director, Bill Retskin (listed in the Directory under North Carolina).

For serious collectors, it should be noted that only about half of all the matchcovers ever produced are collectible. Of that 50%, less than 5% are worth more than a quarter. There are still thousands of valuable matchcovers in garages, attics, basements, and storerooms all over America. AMCC offers a complete matchcover appraisal service for estates and insurance purposes. Anyone writing for club or estate information will receive an immediate reply

Right to left: Fraternal Order of Eagles, $2.00 to 3.00; Moose Lodge, $2.00 to $3.00; V.F.W., $3.00 to $4.00; Native Sons of the Golden West, $3.00 to $4.00; B.P.O.E., $2.00 to $3.00. (Photo courtesy Bill Retskin)

and several collectible matchcovers. Please include an SASE with your request.

Listed here are typical prices realized within the last twelve months from the Quarterly *Front Striker Bulletin* mail matchcover auction.

Key:

20S — 20 stick size
30S — 30 stick size
B — on the back
BS — striker on back
B/W — black and white photo
C — covers
F — on the front
FL — full-length design
FS — front striker (understood if not indicated)
I — inside of matchcover
MM — manufacturer's mark (manumark)

MS — mixed sizes
S — saddle (between F & B)
SD — stock design

Banks from NC, ND, WV or VT, 45C, 30S, MS, from $7 to **10.00**

Bluebird System, Chicago & Joliet w/bus (F), routing (I), from $5 to **10.00**

Budweiser w/logo & King of Beers (F), Bud (S), FL copy, from $5 to **8.00**

CCC Camp, Company 1730 Camp Bunker, Project F-7, (F), from $10 to **14.00**

Central of Georgia Serving Great Southeast w/trains (F/B), from $10 to **12.00**

Chicago Maids Set #2: Hot Number, Plenty Doggie...; 1941, from $15 to **20.00**

Country Club of Virginia w/logo (F/B), blank (S), 30S, BS, from $3 to **5.00**

Decatur Cartage Co Inc w/logo, 17 offices & phones (I), FL, from $8 to **14.00**

Drink Coca-Cola w/bottle (B), Babe Ruth League logo (F), from $25 to **30.00**

Gas Stations from WI, 35C, from $12 to **18.00**

Golden Gate Int'l Expo, Tower of the Sun at Night (FL), from $4 to **10.00**

Gunther Field Exchange...Alabama (B), Keep 'em Flying! (S), from $8 to **14.00**

HMCS Fraser, Royal Canadian Navy w/Navy crest (B), from $6 to **10.00**

Holiday Inn, all w/cities in black, SD, 50C, MS, from $7 to **10.00**

Hyatt Hotels, 100C, 30S, MS, from $32 to **45.00**

Improved Order of Red Men...Indianapolis (B), RI 4103 (S), from $10 to **12.00**

Mickey Mantle's Holiday Inn, Joplin, w/photo (F), map (I), from $25 to **30.00**

Midway Diner, Hammonton, NJ, Midway Diner on sign (FL), from $7 to **17.00**

New York Times (F), person in occupation (F), set of 12, from $65 to **80.00**

Olds & Pontiac Auto Dealers, 1956, SD, 50C, 30S, from $12 to **18.00**

Outdoor set 1: Always Keep, Don't Try, Never Drive; 3-pc, from $3 to .**5.00**

Sophie Tucker, B/W photo (F), Opening...Chez Paree, from $15 to **18.00**

St Louis (S), University Club (F/B), dark blue & white, from $4 to **7.00**

Strike at Seat of Trouble, Buy War Bonds (F), Hitler (B), from $65 to **80.00**

Strop Taxi, Dial 5811, 24 Hour Service, Raleigh, NC (F/B), from $4 to **7.00**

Travelodge South Pacific Series, 1979, set of 13 boxes, from $3 to **6.00**

USO Club...Virginia (F), USO (S), USO logo (B), from $5 to .**7.00**

USS Arizona w/anchor (F), US Navy (S), ship & name (B), from $4 to **7.00**

Vote for Herbert Hoover, Charles Curtis w/photos (F), from $45 to **60.00**

Walker Cocktail, Type 4, Universal Match, 1934, set of 12, from $20 to **25.00**

McCoy

A popular collectible with flea market goers, McCoy pottery was made in Roseville, Ohio, from 1910 until the late 1980s. They are most famous for their extensive line of figural cookie jars, more than two hundred in all. They also made amusing figural planters, etc., as well as dinnerware, and vases and pots for the florist trade. Though some pieces are unmarked, most bear one of several McCoy trademarks. Beware of reproductions made by a company in Tennessee who is using a very close facsimile of the old McCoy mark. They are making several cookie jars once produced by McCoy as well as other now-defunct potteries. Some of these (but by no means all) have been dated with the number '93' below the mark.

For more information refer to *The Collector's Encylopedia of McCoy Pottery* by Sharon and Bob Huxford and *McCoy Pottery, Collector's Reference & Value Guide,* by Margaret Hanson, Craig Nissen, and Bob Hanson (both available from Collector Books). See also Cookie Jars; Clubs and Newsletters.

Basket, basketweave on blue, hanging, unmarked, 7½", from $35 to **40.00**

Beverage server, Sunburst Gold, McCoy mark, 11", from $60 to **80.00**

Bookends, birds, pastel, marked NM, 1940s, 6", pr, from $100 to **150.00**

Bookends, lily form w/decor, 1948, 5½x5", pr, from $85 to .**100.00**

Bookends, rearing horse, blue, USA mark, 1940s, 8", pr, from $80 to **100.00**

Cuspidor, embossed grapes on green, McCoy mark, 6", from $35 to **40.00**

Dog feeder, Man's Best Friend His Dog on side, 7½", from $50 to **60.00**

Ferner, embossed butterflies on green, rectangular, unmarked, 9" L **65.00**

Flower bowl ornament, fawn, white, unmarked, 3¾", from $40 to **60.00**

Flower bowl ornament, peacock, white, unmarked, 4¾", from $40 to **60.00**

Flower holder/planter, stretch goat, pastel, unmarked, 4¾x5¼" **70.00**

Flower holder/planter, stretch lion, pastel, unmarked, 5½x7½" **200.00**

Flowerpot, embossed butterflies on coral, NM mark, 3¾", from $35 to **45.00**

Frame, blue & white speckles, oval, unmarked, 13x7½", from $40 to **50.00**

Jardiniere, Basketweave, green or white, 7½", from $35 to **50.00**

Jardiniere, embossed butterflies on yellow, NM mark, 4½" **30.00**

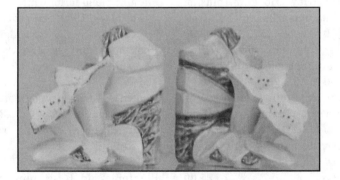

Bookends, lily among green leaves, 1948, 5½x5", from $85.00 to $125.00 for the pair.

Planter, quail, ivory and tan, 7x9", from $45.00 to $65.00.

Matchbox holder, painted flower on white, McCoy mark, 5¾" .**35.00**

Paperweight, football w/gold decor, unmarked, 1940s, from $85 to **100.00**

Pitcher, elephant figural, white, NM mark, 1940s, 75x", from $250 to **300.00**

Pitcher, embossed ribs, glossy, McCoy mark, 9½", from $25 to **50.00**

Pitcher, Hobnail, pastel matt, bulbous, unmarked, 48-oz, from $75 to **95.00**

Planter, baby crib form, pink or blue, unmarked, 6½" L, from $50 to **60.00**

Planter, banana form, yellow matt, NM mark, 8½" L, from $30 to **40.00**

Planter, dragonflies embossed on blue matt, unmarked, 5", from $30 to **35.00**

Planter, duck w/egg figural, yellow, decorated, McCoy mark, 3¼x7" **25.00**

Planter, grapes on leafy base form, McCoy mark, from $75 to .**100.00**

Planter, lamb figural, cold-paint details, McCoy mark, 4½x5" **65.00**

Planter, lion figural, any standard color, unmarked, 14½" L, ea **55.00**

Planter, Mammy stitting on yellow scoop, McCoy mark, 7½" L **165.00**

Planter, Mary Ann shoe, pastel, NM mark, 5" L, from $20 to **35.00**

Planter, pelican figural, glossy or matt, NM mark, 5¾x7¾" .**45.00**

Planter, piano form, white, yellow or black, 1959, 6x5", from $60 to **85.00**

Planter, rabbit w/carrot, cold-paint details, McCoy mark, 7¼" **85.00**

Planter, shell form in pastel matt, NM mark, 1940s, 5½x7½" **32.50**

Planter, swan form, white w/painted details, McCoy mark, 7½" **35.00**

Planter, Wild Rose, pink roses on yellow, McCoy mark, 3½x8" **45.00**

Reamer, yellow or white, 1949, 8" L, from $45 to **60.00**

Vase, angelfish figural white or green, unmarked, 6", from $100 to **150.00**

Vase, Blossomtime, applied flower, upturned handles, McCoy mark, 8" **40.00**

Vase, blue w/emb sailboats, footed, unmarked, 9", from $35 to **50.00**

Vase, bulbous, long angle handles, pastel, USA mark, 1940s from $35 to **45.00**

Vase, bulbous fish figural, yellow or rose, NM mark, 3¼x4¼" **70.00**

Vase, butterflies embossed on blue, handles, USA mark, 10" **135.00**

Vase, contrasting leaf, chartreuse overdrip at top, McCoy mark, 9" **85.00**

Vase, cornucopia; pastel matt, McCoy mark, 1940s, 7", from $30 to **40.00**

Vase, flared cylinder, low handles, pastel, unmarked, 1940s, 12", ... **90.00**

Vase, flared cylinder, low handles, yellow gloss, unmarked, 1940s, 8" **30.00**

Vase, hand form, white, unmarked, 1940s, 6½", from $60 to **75.00**

Vase, Hands of Friendship (aka Praying Hands), blue, NM mark, 3x4" **42.50**

Vase, heart form w/embossed flowers, pink, unmarked, 6", from $45 to **60.00**

Vase, Hobnail, pastel, square sides, flared rim, NM mark, 8", from $50 to **60.00**

Vase, leaves embossed on brown glossy, handles, McCoy mark, 8" **45.00**

Vase, orange on leafy base form, McCoy mark, from $40 to **60.00**

Vase, peacock on green, handles, McCoy mark, 1948, 8", from $35 to **45.00**

Vase, swan figural, open back, yellow, NM mark, 3½x4¾" .**70.00**

Vase, swan figural, pastel, unmarked, 6", from $20 to **25.00**

Vase, turtle figural, open back, yellow, NM mark, 2x4¼" ...**70.00**

Vase, yellow matt, inverted cylinder w/handles, USA mark, 10" **55.00**

Vase, 3-lily form, white or yellow, McCoy mark, 8½", from $40 to **60.00**

Wall pocket, bellows form w/embossed flowers, multicolor, 9½" **80.00**

Wall pocket, birdbath form, yellow, green & brown, McCoy mark, 6½" ....,....**90.00**

Wall pocket, butterfly figural, green, white or yellow, NM mark, 7x6" **225.00**

Wall pocket, cuckoo clock form, no gold, from $125 to **150.00**

Wall pocket, embossed berries & leaves on glossy, unmarked, 7" L **175.00**

Wall pocket, fan form, pastel, McCoy mark, from $60 to **75.00**

Wall pocket, iron on trivet form, McCoy mark, 8½x6", from $50 to **75.00**

Wall pocket, lily bud, pink, NM mark, 6", from $50 to ...**75.00**

Wall pocket, pear among green leaves form, from $50 to .**60.00**

Wall pocket, umbrella form, Sunburst Gold, from $70 to **85.00**

Wall pocket vase, flower form, turquoise or white, unmarked, 6" **40.00**

Metlox

Since the 1940s, the Metlox company of California has been producing dinnerware lines, cookie jars, and decorative items which today have become popular collectibles. Some of their most popular patterns are California Provincial (the dark green and burgundy rooster), Red Rooster (in red, orange, and brown), Homestead Provincial (dark green and burgundy farm scenes), and Colonial Homestead (farm scenes done in red, orange, and brown). See also Cookie Jars. For more information, refer to *Collector's Encyclopedia of Metlox Potteries* by Carl Gibbs, Jr.

Woodland Gold, salad bowl, 11", from $50.00 to $60.00; Salad fork and spoon set, from $50.00 to $55.00. (Photo courtesy Carl Gibbs, Jr.)

California Aztec, bowl, lug soup; from $30 to **35.00**

California Aztec, butter dish, from $95 to **100.00**

California Aztec, platter, sm, from $45 to **50.00**

California Ivy, cream soup, from $25 to **28.00**

California Ivy, cup & saucer, from $12 to **16.00**

California Ivy, egg cup, from $22 to **25.00**

California Ivy, gravy boat, 12-oz, from $28 to **30.00**

California Ivy, jam & jelly, from $30 to **35.00**

California Ivy, mug, 7-oz, from $18 to **20.00**

California Ivy, plate, dinner; 10¼", from $12 to **13.00**

California Provincial, bowl, cereal; 7¼", from $16 to **18.00**

California Provincial, mug, no lid, 1-pt, from $32 to **35.00**

California Provincial, platter, oval, 11", from $40 to **45.00**

California Rose, coffeepot, 8-cup, from $45 to **50.00**

California Rose, cup & saucer, from $8 to **10.00**

California Strawberry, bowl, vegetable; 8⅛", from $30 to .**35.00**

California Strawberry, pitcher, 1½-pt, from $30 to **35.00**

California Strawberry, sugar bowl, w/lid, 12-oz, from $22 to ..**25.00**

Geranium, cup & saucer, from $9 to **11.00**

Geranium, sugar bowl, w/lid, 11-oz, from $18 to **20.00**

Geranium, teapot, 4½-cup, from $50 to **55.00**

Homestead Provincial, cookie jar, from $90 to **95.00**

California Provincial, Platter, oval, 11", $45.00; Lug soup bowl, 5", from $22.00 to $25.00. (Photo courtesy Carl Gibbs, Jr.)

Homestead Provincial, gravy boat, 1-pt, from $40 to **45.00**

Homestead Provincial, salt & pepper shakers, pr, from $28 to **30.00**

Miniature, bird, wings up, 5", from $40 to **45.00**

Miniature, fawn, 4¼", from $35 to **40.00**

Miniature, sailboat, 2½", from $30 to **35.00**

Nostalgia Line, Cadillac, from $75 to **85.00**

Nostalgia Line, Clydesdale, 9x9", from $175 to **185.00**

Nostalgia Line, Mama or Papa, ea, from $40 to **45.00**

Nostalgia Line, pony cart, from $55 to **60.00**

Nostalgia Line, train set, 3-pc, from $150 to **160.00**

Poppet, Dutch girl, 5", from $25 to **35.00**

Poppet, Effie, cymbal lady, 7¾", from $35 to **45.00**

Poppet, Grover, w/4" bowl, from $55 to **65.00**

Poppet, Monica, nun, 8", from $35 to **45.00**

Poppet, Penelope, nursemaid, 7¾", from $25 to **35.00**

Provincial Blue, coffee canister & lid, from $60 to **65.00**

Provincial Blue, cup & saucer, from $16 to **18.00**

Provincial Blue, egg cup, from $28 to **30.00**

Provincial Fruit, coaster, 3¾", from $16 to **18.00**

Provincial Fruit, plate, salad; 7½", from $9 to **10.00**

Provincial Fruit, suar bowl, w/lid, 8-oz, from $22 to **25.00**

Provincial Fruit, tumbler, 11-oz, from $28 to **30.00**

Red Rooster Provincial, bowl, fruit; from $12 to **14.00**

Red Rooster Provincial, cup & saucer, from $14 to **16.00**

Red Rooster Provincial, plate, luncheon; 9", from $15 to ...**18.00**

Red Rooster Provincial, teapot, 42-oz, 6-cup, from $110 to **120.00**

Sculptured Daisy, butter dish, from $50 to **55.00**

Sculptured Daisy, mug, 8-oz, from $18 to **20.00**

Sculptured Daisy, oval baker, 11",
from $45 to **50.00**

Sculptured Daisy, salt & pepper
shakers, pr, from $22 to ..**24.00**

Sculptured Daisy, sugar bowl,
w/lid, 8-oz, from $28 to .**30.00**

Sculptured Zinnia, bowl, cereal;
7⅜", from $13 to **14.00**

Sculptured Zinnia, creamer, 10-oz,
from $20 to **22.00**

Sculptured Zinnia, plate, bread &
butter; 6⅜", from $7 to ...**8.00**

Sculptured Zinnia, platter, oval,
14¼", from $40 to **45.00**

Woodland Gold, bowl, soup; 6¾",
from $14 to **15.00**

Woodland Gold, mug, 8-oz, from
$18 to **20.00**

Woodland Gold, plate, dinner;
10¼", from $12 to **13.00**

Woodland Gold, salt & pepper shakers, pr, from $20 to **24.00**

Milk Glass

Milk glass has been used since
the 1700s to make tableware,
lamps, and novelty items such as
covered figural dishes and decorative
wall plaques. Early examples were
made with cryolite and ring with a
clear bell tone when tapped. For
more information, refer to *Collector's
Encyclopedia of Milk Glass* by Betty
and Bill Newbound. See also Animal
Dishes; Westmoreland.

Bowl, Daisy & Ray, upturned handles, 4¾x8", from $15 to .**20.00**

Bowl, Versailles, Dithridge, M
paint, 7¼" **30.00**

Box, handkerchief; 3 Kittens, EX
paint, 5x5¾", from $65 to .**70.00**

Butter dish, Lace & Dewdrop,
Kemple, 6x6½", from $35
to **40.00**

Cake stand, hole in center of plate,
footed, 6¾x10⅜" square .**10.00**

Candlesticks, embossed tassels,
rope handle, EX paint, pr,
from $30 to **35.00**

Candy dish, 3-compartment,
painted flowers on lid, 6" dia,
from $25 to **30.00**

Compote, Jenny Lind, smooth base
w/floral decor underneath, US
Glass **125.00**

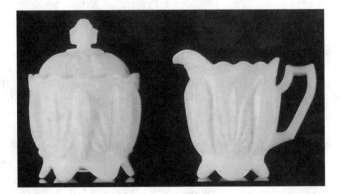

**Sugar bowl and creamer, Cactus, Fenton reproduction of
an original Greentown pattern, $45.00. (Photo courtesy
Betty and Bill Newbound)**

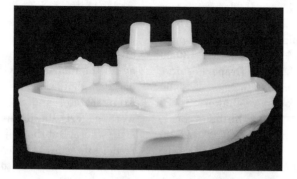

Covered dish, Battleship Maine, 7¾" long, $95.00.

Compote, open hand, Atturbury, 8¾x9" **75.00**

Covered dish, prairie schooner, 5⅞" L, from $175 to **195.00**

Creamer, Blackberry, Hobbs, Brockunier & Co **35.00**

Creamer, Paneled Wheat, 5¾", from $35 to **40.00**

Creamer, Primrose, 6-sided, 8 feet, Westmoreland Specialty Co **20.00**

Egg cup, chick base, 1½" **15.00**

Ginger jar, Regent line, hand-painted roses, Consolidated, 7½" **35.00**

Goblet, Dewberry, Kemple, 6", from $12 to **15.00**

Goblet, Diamond & Dart, 6", from $12 to **15.00**

Jar, no decor, screw-on glass lid, 4¾", from $25 to **35.00**

Jar, painted flowers, metal screw-on lid, 5", from $25 to ...**30.00**

Mug, Bird & Wheat, bar handle, Atterbury, 3½" **35.00**

Mug, Mephistopheles in high relief ea side, 3½" **95.00**

Novelty, coal scuttle, wire handle, Kemple, 3x4½" **15.00**

Novelty, Easter egg, New Arrival, embossed, paint traces, 4" .**45.00**

Novelty, slipper, Daisy & Button, cat emerging **15.00**

Paperweight, rabbit, Imperial (Heisey mold), 2¾" **35.00**

Pitcher, Iris, painted decor, Westmoreland, 8¾", from $95 to **100.00**

Planter, horse and cart figural, 4⅛x9⅜", from $30 to **35.00**

Plate, Columbus embossed in center, 1492-1892 on chest, 9¾" **40.00**

Plate, Eagle, Flag & Star border, silk-screened Niagara Falls, 7⅜" **25.00**

Plate, Fleur-de-Lis border, 7¼" .**12.50**

Plate, painted floral, beaded edge, Westmoreland, 7½", from $12 to **15.00**

Plate, painted fruit, lacy edge, Kemple, 7¼", from $10 to .**12.00**

Plate, Pinwheel border, 8" ...**25.00**

Plate, Scroll & Waffle, McKee, 7¼" **20.00**

Plate, 3 Kittens, paint traces, 8" **35.00**

Platter, nude lady reclining on open fan, fiery opalescence, N-339, 7" **60.00**

Reamer, rounded cone embossed McK, footed, sm **25.00**

Ring box, scroll design, paint traces, 1½x2" **15.00**

Rolling pin, blown, cork stopper, from $120 to **130.00**

Rose bowl, Heavy Drape, Fostoria, 4", from $25 to **30.00**

Salt & pepper shakers, panelled sides, bulbous base, 6½", pr **25.00**

Salt cellar, swan form, 3⅞" L, from $15 to **20.00**

Salt shaker, Feathered Scroll, bulbous, metal lid, 4¼", from $20 to **25.00**

Sugar bowl, ring handle, slit in lid for spoon, Atterbury **45.00**

Sugar bowl, swans on sides, ring handles, Atterbury **20.00**

Sugar shaker, Tulip, 4", from $60 to **65.00**

Syrup pitcher, Dot & Thumbprint, applied handle, 6½", from $50 to **55.00**

Toothpick holder, boy w/basket or marble shooter, Portieux, 3½" **110.00**

Toothpick holder, tramp's shoe, black & gold paint traces, 2" **35.00**

Toothpick holder, 3 swan handles, Westmoreland, 2⅜", from $25 to **30.00**

Top hat, Daisy & Button, 1½", from $8 to **12.00**

Vase, corncuopia, Westmoreland's 1933 line, 6", from $30 to **35.00**

Vase, hat shaped, birds embossed on sides, 3½x6x4" **25.00**

Model Kits

The best-known producer of model kits today is Aurora. Collectors often pay astronomical prices for some of the character kits from the 1960s. Made popular by all the monster movies of that decade, ghouls like Vampirella, Frankenstein, and the Wolfman were eagerly built up by kids everywhere. But the majority of all model kits were vehicles, ranging from as small as 3" up to 24" long. Some of the larger model vehicle makers were AMT, MPC, and IMC. Condition is very important in assessing the value of a kit, with built-ups priced at about 50% lower than one still in the box. Other things factor into pricing as well — who is selling, who is buying, and how badly they want it, locality, supply, and demand.

For information about Aurora models, we recommend *Aurora, History and Price Guide,* by Bill Bruegman (Cap'n Penny Productions, Inc); to learn more about models other than Aurora, refer to *Collectible Figure Kits of the '50s, '60s & '70s, Reference and Value Guide*, by Gordy Dutt (see Directory under Ohio for ordering information), and *Classic Plastic Model Kits* by Rick Polizzi (Collector Books). For additional listings we recommend *Schroeder's Collectible Toys, Antique to Modern* (Collector Books). See also Clubs and Newsletters.

Adams, Hawk Missile Batter, #154, 1/40 scale, 1958, MIB **75.00**

Airfix, Lunar Module, #3013, 1/72 scale, 1979, MIB **20.00**

AMT, Star Trek, USS Enterprise, #951, MIB (sealed) **55.00**

Aurora, Captain Action #480, 1966-67, MIB, $330.00. (Photo courtesy John and Sheri Pavone)

AMT/Ertl, Batman, Batmobile, #6877, 1/25 scale, 1989, MIB **20.00**

Aoshima, Delorian, #1800, 1/24 scale, 1990, MIB **25.00**

Aurora, Blue Knight of Milan, #B472, 1963, M (EX+ box) **16.00**

Aurora, Customized Corvette, 1963, MIB (sealed) **26.00**

Aurora, Dracula, Glow-in-the-Dark, assembled, 1972, NM **35.00**

Aurora, Gladiator, #V406, ⅛ scale, 1964, MIB (sealed) **245.00**

Aurora, Hulk, Comic Scenes, MIB **75.00**

Aurora, Mummy, #427, 1/8 scale, 1963, NMIB, minimum value **265.00**

Aurora, Pan-Am Boeing 747 Jumbo Jet, 1971, NMIB **40.00**

Aurora, Russian Stalin Tank, #323, 1972, M (G box) ..**35.00**

Aurora, Viking Ship, #320, 1/80 scale, 1962, MIB **60.00**

Bachmann, US WWII B-29 Super Fortress, 1960s, MIB **15.00**

Bandai, Ultraman, #0003523, 1/350 scale, 1990, MIB .**16.00**

Eldon, Invader Show Car, 1st issue, EX (EX box) **15.00**

Halcyon, Alien, Alien Face Hugger, #V02, 1/1 scale, 1991, vinyl, MIB **112.00**

Hawk, Lotus Race Car, green, #02, 1/32 scale, MIB **10.00**

Heller, Lunar Orbiter Apollo, #021, 1/100 scale, MIB ...**7.00**

Imai, Armoured Knights, Kaiser Maxmillian II, #1395, 1/12 scale, MIB **15.00**

Lifelike, Dutch Flintlock Pistol, #09230, 1/1 scale, MIB **35.00**

Aurora, Mummy #427, NMIB, $265.00 minimum value.

Revell, California Highway Patrol Bike, Harley-Davidson, 1976, M in VG box, $65.00.

Lindberg, Flintstones, Flintmobile, #72411, 1994, MIB **15.00**

Monogram, Garbage Truck, reissue, 1/24 scale, MIB (sealed) **20.00**

Monogram, Invaders, UFO #6012, 1/72 scale, 1979, MIB ...**70.00**

Monogram, 1963 Cobra Convertible, blue, #2764, 1/25 scale, MIB **10.00**

MPC, Dukes of Hazzard, Daisy's Jeep CJ, #0662, 1/25 scale, 1980, MIB **50.00**

MPC, Laser Warriors, Phantom Intruder, #2306, 1984, MIB **5.00**

MPC, Wacky Races, Penelope's Pussycat, #901, 1969, MIB (sealed) **140.00**

MPC, 1976 AMC Pacer Stock Car, #1-7601, white, 1/25 scale, MIB **22.00**

MRC, Stargate, Anubis #01, 1/9 scale, 1994, MIB **30.00**

Pyro, Moorish Miquelet Pistol, #227, 1/1 scale, 1960, MIB **35.00**

Realspace, Gemini/Titan, 1/144 scale, MIB **22.00**

Revell, Apollo 11-Hornet+3, #354, 1/490 scale, 1969, MIB .**45.00**

Revell, Deal's Wheels, Swine Hut #1356, 1970, MIB (sealed) .**75.00**

Revell, Dune, Ornithopter #1775, 1/50 scale, 1985, MIB ...**45.00**

Revell, Goodyear Blimp, #999, 1/169 scale, 1977, MIB (sealed) **16.00**

Revell, Hardy Boys Van, #1398, 1/25 scale, 1977, MIB ...**55.00**

Revell, Moon Ship, #1825, 1/96 scale, 1957, MIB **240.00**

Revell, Shuttle Challenger, #4526, 1/144 scale, 1982, MIB .**16.00**

Sevans, Dr Who, Dalek, #1, 1/5 scale, 1987, MIB **46.00**

Tamiya, Triceratops, #6901, 1/35 scale, 1982, MIB **10.00**

Union, Shuttle Challenger #15, 1/288 scale, 1980s, MIB .**20.00**

Moon and Star

A reissue of Palace, an early pattern glass line, Moon and Star was developed for the market in the 1960s by Joseph Weishar of Island Mould and Machine Company (Wheeling, West Virginia). It was made by several companies. One of the largest producers was L.E. Smith of Mt. Pleasant, Pennsylvania, and L.G. Wright (who had their glassware made by Fostoria, Fenton, and Westmoreland) carried a wide assortment in their catalogs for many years. It is still being made on a very limited basis, but the most collectible pieces are those in red, blue, amber, and green — colors that are no longer in production. The values listed here are for pieces in red or blue. Amber and green prices (and crystal) should be 30% lower.

Water pitcher, 1-qt, 7½", $65.00.

Ashtray, patterned moons at rim, star in base, 6-sided, 5½" .**18.00**
Banana boat, allover pattern, moons form scallop along rim, 12" **45.00**
Basket, allover pattern, scalloped rim, solid handle, 9", from $30 to **35.00**

Bell, patterned body, plain rim & handle, 6", from $25 to .**30.00**
Bud vase, patterned top, plain lower body & foot, 6", from $18 to **22.00**
Butter/cheese dish, patterned lid, plain base, 7" dia **40.00**
Cake plate, allover pattern, low collared base, 13" **50.00**
Cake stand, allover pattern, plate removes from standard, 11" **65.00**
Candle bowl, allover pattern, footed, 8" **28.00**
Candle holder, allover pattern, bowl style w/ring handle, 2x5½" **18.00**
Candle holders, allover pattern, flared base, 4½", pr **25.00**
Candle lamp, allover pattern, candlestick base, matching shade, 3-pc **50.00**
Candle lamp, patterned shade, clear base, 2-pc, 7½" **25.00**
Canister, allover pattern, 1-lb, from $12 to **15.00**
Canister, allover pattern, 2-lb, from $15 to **18.00**
Canister, allover pattern, 3½-lb, from $18 to **22.00**
Canister, allover pattern, 5-lb, from $22 to **25.00**
Compote, allover pattern, footed, flared crimped rim, 5" **22.00**
Compote, allover pattern, raised foot, patterned lid, 7½x6" **40.00**
Compote, allover pattern, scalloped foot on stem, patterned lid, 8x4" **35.00**
Compote, allover pattern, scalloped rim, footed, 5x6½", from $18 to **20.00**

Compote, allover pattern, scalloped rim, footed, 7x10" **45.00**

Creamer & sugar bowl (open), disk foot, sm, from $25 to **28.00**

Cruet, 6¾", from $40 to **45.00**

Goblet, water; plain rim & foot, 4½" **12.00**

Goblet, water; plain rim & foot, 5¾" **15.00**

Jardiniere, allover pattern, patterned lid & finial, 9¾" **85.00**

Lamp, oil; allover pattern, all original, 10", from $100 to **125.00**

Lighter, allover patterned body, metal fittings **35.00**

Nappy, allover pattern, crimped rim, 2¾x6" dia **18.00**

Plate, patterned body & center, smooth rim, 8" **25.00**

Relish dish, allover pattern, 1 plain handle, 2x8" dia **18.00**

Salt & pepper shakers, allover pattern, metal tops, 4x2" dia, pr **25.00**

Sherbet, patterned body & foot, plain rim & stem, 4¼x3¾" **15.00**

Spooner, allover pattern, scalloped w/straight sides, footed, 5¼x4" **30.00**

Sugar bowl, allover pattern, straight sides, patterned lid, 8x4½" **35.00**

Syrup, allover pattern, metal top, 4½x3½" **40.00**

Tumbler, iced tea; plain flat rim & disk foot, 11-oz, 5½" **20.00**

Tumbler, plain rim & disk foot, 7-oz, 4¼", from $12 to **15.00**

Mortens Studios

Animal models sold by Mortens Studios of Arizona during the 1940s are some of today's most interesting collectibles, especially among animal lovers. Hundreds of breeds of dogs, cats, and horses were produced from a plaster-type composition material constructed over a wire framework. They

Cocker Spaniel, 5¼", $55.00 to $65.00.

range in size from 2" up to about 7", and most are marked.

Airedale **95.00**
Boston Terrier, ivory marks on black, standing, 6x6" **75.00**
Boxer pup, playing **55.00**
Cocker Spaniel pup w/paw up, #841 ....**55.00**
Collie puppy **40.00**
Dachshund, recumbent **48.00**
Dalmatian, #112, sm **50.00**
Doberman, standing, 6x7" ...**70.00**
English Setter, #848 ....**65.00**
German Shepherd, standing, 7" .**85.00**
Great Dane, recumbent, black details on tan, 7½x6½" .**75.00**
Horse, mane erect **110.00**
Lion, recumbent, 4x6" **135.00**
Persian cat **48.00**
Springer Spaniel, 5" **65.00**
Wire-Hair Terrier, sitting, #829 ....**55.00**

Moss Rose

Though the Moss Rose pattern has been produced by Staffordshire and American pottery companies alike since the mid-1800s, the line we're dealing with here was primarily made from the late 1950s into the 1970s by Japanese manufacturers. Even today you'll occasionally see a tea set or a small candy dish for sale in some of the chain stores. (The collectors who're already picking this line up refer to it as Moss Rose, but we've seen it advertised just lately under the name Victorian Rose, and some companies called their lines Chintz Rose or French Rose.) The pattern consists of a briar rose with dark green mossy leaves on stark white glaze. Occasionally an item is trimmed in gold. In addition to dinnerware, many accessories and novelties were made as well. Our advisor for this category is April Tvorak; she is listed in the Directory under Colorado.

For further information on items made by Lefton, see *The Collector's Encyclopedia of Lefton China* by Loretta DeLozier (Collector Books). Refer to *Schroeder's Antiques Price Guide* for information on the early Moss Rose pattern.

Sugar bowl and creamer, French Rose, Lefton #4071, 2¾", from $8.00 to $10.00 for the pair. (Photo courtesy Loretta DeLozier)

Ashtray/cigarette box **15.00**
Bowl, sauce **4.00**
Bowl, soup **6.00**
Butter dish **15.00**
Cottage cheese dish **10.00**
Cup & saucer **6.00**
Cup & saucer, demitasse **8.00**
Egg cup, sm **6.00**
Plate, dinner **5.00**
Plate, salad **4.00**
Platter **12.00**
Teapot **20.00**
Teapot, demitasse **25.00**
Teapot, electric **22.00**

Movie Memorabilia

Vintage movies are meshed in our minds with fond memories of high school dates at drive-ins; of memorable performers like Vivian Leigh and Clarke Gable; of wonderful dancers like Rogers and Astaire; of terrifying monsters like Frankenstein and Dracula; of plush theatres, singing cowboys, and side-splitting comics. Posters, lobby cards, and souvenir booklets from those days before video stores, when Hollywood stars were epitomized as the ultimate in glamor and sophistication and movies were our number-one source of entertainment, are highly collectible today — so are movie magazines, autographs, and any of the vast assortment of retail merchandise items that promote a particular performer or movie. Especially valuable are items from the '20s and '30s that have to do with such popular stars as Jean Harlow, Bella Lugosi, Carol Lumbard, and Gary Cooper. See also Autographs; Beatles; Character Clocks and Watches; Dolls, Celebrity; Elvis Presley; Games; Marilyn Monroe; Paper Dolls; Pin-back Buttons; Rock 'n Roll; Shirley Temple; Western Heroes.

Poster, From Russia With Love, Sean Connery, 1963, 55x39", NM, $750.00.

Insert card, Chief Crazy Horse, Victor Mature, 1955, VG .**10.00**
Insert card, Old Yeller, 1974 reissue, EX **20.00**
Insert card, Silent World, Jacques Cousteau, 1956, EX **20.00**
Insert card, Your Cheatin' Heart, George Hamilton, 1965, EX **75.00**
Lobby card, Bad Seed, Nancy Kelly & Patty McCormack, 1956, EX **7.50**
Lobby card, Canyon River, George Montgomery, 1956, NM, 6 for **16.00**

Lobby card, The Hunchback of Notre Dame, Gina Lollobrigida and Anthony Quinn, NM, $25.00. (Photo courtesy John and Sheri Pavone)

Lobby card, East of Eden, James Dean fighting, 1955, NM **80.00**

Lobby card, Giant From the Unknown, Bob Steele, 1958, NM **15.00**

Lobby card, Hanging Tree, Gary Cooper, EX **15.00**

Lobby card, In the Heat of the Night, Portier & Steiger, 1967, VG **8.00**

Lobby card, Law of the Lawless, Robertson & DeCarlo, 1964, VG **6.00**

Lobby card, Where the Hot Wind Blows, Lollobrigida & Montand, 1960, EX **15.00**

Poster, Across the Great Divide, Robert Logan, 1977, 1-sheet, M **12.50**

Poster, Adromeda Strain, Arthur Hill & David Wayne, 1971, 1-sheet, G **5.00**

Poster, Against All Odds, Rachel Ward & Jeff Bridges, 1984, 27x24", EX **10.00**

Poster, Billion Dollar Brain, Michael Caine, 1967, 1-sheet, VG **8.00**

Poster, Cry Baby, Johnny Depp, 2-sided, 1990, 1-sheet, EX **15.00**

Poster, Dead Ringer, Bette Davis, 1964, 22x28", from $40 to **60.00**

Poster, Dog Day Afternoon, Al Pacino, 1974, 1-sheet, EX **32.00**

Poster, Fireball 500, Avalon & Funicello, 1966, half-sheet, VG **20.00**

Poster, Firm, The; Tom Cruise, 2-sided, 1993, 1-sheet, NM **35.00**

Poster, French Connection, Gene Hackman, 1971, 27x41", from $40 to **65.00**

Poster, Greatest, Mohammed Ali, 1977, 27x41", from $45 to .**75.00**

Poster, Herbie Goes Bananas, Leachman & Korman, 1980, 1-sheet, EX **20.00**

Poster, Julius Caesar, M Brando & J Mason, 1953, 27x41", from $125 to **175.00**

Poster, Lady in Cement, Frank Sinatra & Raquel Welch, 1968, 1-sheet, EX **40.00**

Poster, Gone With the Wind, 1954 reissue, framed, 28x22", NM, $300.00.

Poster, Look Who's Talking, Travolta & Alley, 1989, 1-sheet, EX **10.00**

Poster, Main Event, Barbra Streisand & Ryan O'Neal, 1979, 1-sheet, EX **15.00**

Poster, Mame, Lucille Ball, 1974, 27x41", from $30 to **40.00**

Poster, Predator, A Swarzenegger & Carl Weathers, 1987, 1-sheet, NM **25.00**

Poster, Raiders of Lost Ark, Harrison Ford, 1981, 27x41", from $55 to **80.00**

Poster, Revenge of the Jedi, Hamill, Ford & Fisher, 1983, 1-sheet, NM **90.00**

Poster, Some Kind of Wonderful, Stoltz & Thompson, 1987, 1-sheet, M **25.00**

Poster, Taking Care of Business, Charles Grodin, 1990, 1-sheet, NM **12.50**

Poster, Tea & Sympathy, Deborah Kerr, 1956, 27x41", from $55 to **85.00**

Poster, Two Mules for Sister Sara, MacLaine/Eastwood, 1970, 24x27", EX **40.00**

Poster, Where Eagles Dare, Clint Eastwood, 1968, 14x36", from $45 to **75.00**

Pressbook, Horror of Dracula, Peter Cushing, 1948, M **40.00**

Pressbook, No Deposit No Return, Niven, McGavin & Knotts, 1975, NM **12.00**

Pressbook, Rocky III, Sylvester Stallone, ca 1982, NM .**10.00**

Soundtrack, James Bond, From Russia w/Love, 1953, NM in sleeve **18.00**

Window card, Green Years, Charles Coburn, 1946, NM **45.00**

National Geographics

The National Geographic Magazine was first introduced in October 1888. There was only one issue that year, and it together with the three published in 1889 make up Volume I, the most valuable group on the market. Volume I, No. 1, alone is worth about $12,000.00 in very good condition. A complete set of magazines from

1888 to the present is worth approximately \$30,000.00 to \$60,000.00, depending on condition, as condition and price are closely related. As time goes by, values of individual issues increase. The most sought-after years are pre-World War I: 1888–1914. Still, some postwar recent issues command good prices. Prices are for single monthly issues, complete with all pages, covers and ads. Note that there are a few special out-of-print issues that are worth more. For further information our advisor, Don Smith (listed in the Directory under Kentucky), offers a listing including special issues and maps.

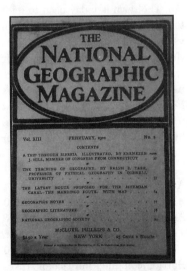

February 1902, Vol XIII #2, black and white, minor fading and soiling, \$50.00 at auction.

1915-1916, ea	**11.00**
1917-1924, ea	**9.00**
1925-1929, ea	**8.00**

1930-1945, ea	**7.00**
1946-1955, ea	**6.00**
1956-1967, ea	**5.50**
1968-1989, ea	**4.50**
1990-present, ea	**2.00**

Niloak

Produced in Arkansas by Charles Dean Hyten from the early 1900s until the mid-1940s, Niloak (the backward spelling of kaolin, a type of clay) takes many forms — figural planters, vases in both matt and glossy glazes, and novelty items of various types. The company's most famous product and the most collectible is their swirl or Mission Ware line. Clay in colors of brown, blue, cream, red, and buff are swirled within the mold, the finished product left unglazed on the outside to preserve the natural hues. Small vases are common; large pieces or unusual shapes and those with exceptional coloration are the most valuable. Refer to *The Collector's Encyclopedia of Niloak, A Reference and Value Guide,* by David Edwin Gifford (Collector Books) for more information.

Note: The terms '1st' and '2nd art mark' used in the listings refer to specific die-stamped trademarks. The earlier mark was used from 1910 to 1924, followed by the second, very similar mark used from then until the end of Mission Ware production. Letters with curving raised outlines were characteristic of both; the most obvious difference between the two was that on the first, the final upright line of the 'N' was thin with a solid club-like terminal.

Bowl, Mission/Swirl, inverted rim, 2nd art mark, 4½" **100.00**
Bowl/ashtray, Mission/Swirl, 2nd art mark, 1¼x4¾" **100.00**

Flower bowl, Mission/Swirl, second art mark, 4¾x4½", from $160.00 to $180.00. (Photo courtesy David Gifford)

Jardiniere, Mission/Swirl, 1st art mark, 8¼" **450.00**
Lamp base, Mission/Swirl, open bottom, unmarked, 7½", from $275 to **325.00**
Match stick holder, Mission/Swirl, marked Patent Pend'g, 2" .**120.00**
Vase, bud; Mission/Swirl, stick form, flared base, 8¼" .**175.00**
Vase, Mission/Swirl, bulbous, 1st art mark, 8⅛" **200.00**
Vase, Mission/Swirl, classic form w/flared rim, 1st art mark, 8¼" **175.00**
Vase, Mission/Swirl, classic form w/flared rim, 2nd art mark, 4¼" **70.00**

Vase, Mission/Swirl, cylindrical, marked Patent Pend'g, 7½" **210.00**
Vase, Mission/Swirl, flared cylinder w/sm neck, 1st art mark, 10¼" **250.00**
Vase, Mission/Swirl, inverted rim, 2nd art mark, 3" **80.00**
Vase, Mission/Swirl, shouldered form, 10¼" **250.00**
Vase, Mission/Swirl, 1st art mark, 3" **80.00**

Nippon

In complying with American importation regulations, from 1891 to 1921 Japanese manufacturers marked their wares 'Nippon,' meaning Japan, to indicate country of origin. The term is today used to refer to the highly-decorated porcelain vases, bowls, chocolate pots, etc., that bear this term within their trademark. Many variations were used. Refer to *The Collector's Encyclopedia of Nippon Porcelain* (there are four volumes in the series) by Joan Van Patten (Collector Books) for more information.

Ashtray, Egyptian portrait in center, 3 rests, triangular, 4¾" .**175.00**
Ashtray, moose in center, 3 rests, 6-sided, green mark, 6" high **140.00**
Bottle, cologne; multicolor roses w/gold on white, blue mark, 6" **225.00**
Bowl, acorns & branches in relief, handles, green mark, 7½" long **200.00**
Bowl, nut; nuts on branches, scalloped rim, green mark, 6" **75.00**

Plate, flowers and leaves, marked, 8½", from $50.00 to $80.00. (Photo courtesy Joan Van Patten)

Box, trinket; butterflies on white w/gold trim, green mark, 3¼" dia **90.00**

Cake plate, floral reserve on blue, floral rim, green mark, 11" **175.00**

Candlestick, farm scenic on pyramidal shape, green mark, 8" **185.00**

Candlestick, Gouda-style decor, 6-sided, green mark, 8", pr .**175.00**

Candy dish, palm scenic, lobed rim w/3 ring handles, green mark **75.00**

Coffeepot, palm scenic, brown stick handle, blue mark, 6¾" **165.00**

Compote, Deco motif on white w/gold, square M-in-wreath mark, 3½" **80.00**

Creamer, floral branches on cream w/gold, blue mark, 5½", 6½" **95.00**

Creamer & sugar bowl, river scene w/gold on white, hand-painted mark **110.00**

Cup, brown birds & florals on white w/gold trim, green mark **15.00**

Cup & saucer, bouillon; red & cream w/gold, w/lid, unmarked, 4" **110.00**

Cup & saucer, fruits on white w/ornate band & gold beadwork, blue mark **65.00**

Egg warmer, floral on white w/gold, holds 4, center handle, blue mark **165.00**

Ferner, Deco florals on footed box shape, green mark, 5½" **200.00**

Hair receiver, river scenic on round footed shape, green mark, 3" **55.00**

Mug, floral & beadwork on white w/colored bands at top & bottom, 5" **175.00**

Mustard pot, dainty flowers on white, round handles, green mark, 4" **50.00**

Nappy, Oriental figures on open fan, cobalt trim, ring handle, mark **50.00**

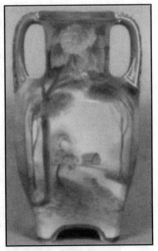

Vase, pastoral scene in earth tones, handles, marked, 7', from $150.00 to $200.00. (Photo courtesy Joan Van Patten)

Pitcher, wide gold floral bands on white, gold handle, blue mark, 7" **200.00**

Plate, brown leafy branch on shaded brown tones, green mark, 7½" **70.00**

Plate, Capitol building in center, gold trim, souvenir, blue mark, 9" **175.00**

Plate, lobster center, gold floral rim, green mark, 8¾" **185.00**

Plate, sampan scenic in natural tones, plain rim, green mark, 7½" **95.00**

Rolling pin, porcelain w/printed advertising, wood handles, mark, 10" **175.00**

Salt & pepper shakers, blue phoenix birds on white, marked, 3¼", pr **45.00**

Serving dish, butterflies on white, center handle, blue mark, 7" dia **95.00**

Soap dish, gold & floral band on white, blue mark, 7¼" dia **75.00**

Tea strainer, floral & gold on cream, side handle, green mark, 4½" **100.00**

Teapot, fox-hunt scene, Greek Key trim, blue mark, 2-cup, 5" **225.00**

Tile, Egyptian profile, geometric rim, 8-sided, green mark, 6¼" **175.00**

Toast rack, holds 2 slices, floral on cream, marked, 5" **145.00**

Toothpick holder, floral & gold on white, angle handles, green mark **50.00**

Vase, exotic birds on white, bulbous, Kenilworth Studios mark, 7" **125.00**

Vase, floral on white, gold integral handles, footed, blue mark, 5½" **175.00**

Vase, geometrics & Greek key trim on tan, handles, green mark, 8" **200.00**

Vase, landscape scenic in earth tones, brown handles, green mark, 5" **100.00**

Vase, pastel floral on white, sm handles, square sides, green mark, 6½" **125.00**

Vase, river scene, brown angle handles, blue mark, 5½" **155.00**

Noritake

Since the early 1900s the Noritake China Company has been producing fine dinnerware, occa-

Noritake, candlesticks, red mark, 1¾", $100.00 for the pair. (Photo courtesy Joan Van Patten)

Match holder, Deco-style girl and whippet, red mark, $115.00 to $130.00. (Photo courtesy Joan Van Patten)

sional pieces, and figural items decorated by hand in delicate florals, scenics and wildlife studies. Azalea and Tree in the Meadow are two very popular collectible lines you will find listed here. Refer to *The Collector's Encyclopedia of Noritake, First and Second Series* by Joan Van Patten; and *Early Noritake* by Aimee Neff Alden (all published by Collector Books) for more information.

Azalea

Bonbon, #184, 6¼" **50.00**
Cake plate, #10, 9¾" **40.00**
Creamer & sugar bowl, #7 ..**45.00**
Cup & saucer, #2 ....**20.00**
Egg cup, #120 ....**60.00**
Mustard jar, #191 ....**60.00**
Plate, dinner; #13, 9¾" **28.00**
Platter, #56, 12" **58.00**
Relish, oval, #18, 8½" **20.00**
Salt & pepper shakers, bell form, #11, pr **30.00**
Teapot, #15 ....**110.00**
Vase, fan form, footed, #187 ....**185.00**

Tree in the Meadow

Bowl, oatmeal **10.00**
Butter pat **15.00**
Cheese dish **45.00**
Cup & saucer **25.00**
Gravy boat **40.00**
Lemon dish **15.00**
Mustard jar, w/lid & spoon .**30.00**
Plate, dinner **25.00**
Platter, 10" **20.00**
Spoon holder **40.00**
Teapot, strap handle **50.00**

Miscellaneous

Ashtray, frog sits at side, black rim, 1 rest, green mark, 3½" dia .**200.00**
Bowl, butterflies & flowers on red to purple, handles, red mark, 7" ..**70.00**
Bowl, floral on gray w/green & white rim, flower applied at rim, 6½ **75.00**
Bowl, floral w/lg green leaves on orange lustre, red mark, 7½" **90.00**
Bowl, parrot on branch, blue lustre rim & handles, green mark, 8¾" **75.00**

Bowl, river scenic, 3 sm pierced handles, simple rim, green mark, 7" **60.00**

Bowl, silver floral overlay on white, closed handles, square, red mark, 7" **100.00**

Candy basket, pagoda & river scene, pink handle, red mark, 7½" dia **65.00**

Candy dish, Deco-style flowers on red, boat form, handles, red mark **75.00**

Candy dish, river scenic, butterfly shape w/center handle, red mark **95.00**

Condiment set, 3 bird forms on long oval tray, green mark, 7½" **110.00**

Cosmetic jar, bird finial, multicolor & lustre, red mark, 4" high **140.00**

Creamer & sugar bowl, blue & white w/rose finial, green mark, w/lid **60.00**

Flower frog, mermaid beside flower, multicolor, red mark, 3½" **300.00**

Flower frog, mushrooms on knoll, lustre, red mark, 3½" **150.00**

Sugar shaker, owl figural, multiple lustres, green mark **130.00**

Sugar shaker & creamer, floral on white w/gold, red mark, 6½", pr **70.00**

Vase, 3 lustre-glazed stumplike forms on base, red mark, 6" **185.00**

Novelty Telephones

Novelty phones representing a well-known advertising or cartoon character are proving to be the focus of a lot of collector activity — the more recognizable the character the better. Telephones modeled after a product container are collectible too, and with the intense interest currently being shown in anything advertising related, competition is sometimes stiff and values are rising. For further information we recommend *Schroeder's Collectible Toys, Antique to Modern* (Collector Books).

Kermit the Frog, push-button style, 1983, NM, $275.00. (Photo courtesy John Thurmond)

Bart Simpson, MIB **35.00**

Batmobile (First Movie), MIB .**60.00**

Bozo the Clown, Telemania, MIB **75.00**

Garfield, eyes open & close, 1980s, from $15 to.....................**35.00**

Inspector Gadget, figural, 1984, MIB **60.00**

Joe Cool, Seika, 1992, M **60.00**

Little Green Sprout, EX+ **75.00**

Little Orphan Annie, 1983, unused, M **85.00**

Mickey Mouse, Unisonic, NM .**65.00**

Pizza Man, 1980s, EX+ **37.50**

Raid Bug, EX+ **125.00**
Snoopy & Woodstock, American Telephone, touch-tone, 1970s, EX, from $75 to **100.00**
Star Trek Enterprise Spaceship, MIB **75.00**
Tyrannasaurus Rex, MIB **75.00**
Ziggy, 1989, MIB **75.00**
7-Up Can, EX+ **30.00**

Occupied Japan

Items with the 'Occupied Japan' mark were made during the period from the end of World War II until April 1952. Porcelains, novelties, paper items, lamps, silverplate, lacquer ware, and dolls are some of the areas of exported goods that may bear this stamp. Because the Japanese were naturally resentful of the occupation, it is felt that only a small percentage of their wares were thus marked. Although you may find identical items marked simply 'Japan,' only those with the 'Occupied Japan' stamp command values such as we've suggested below. For more information we recommend the series of five books on Occupied Japan collectibles written by Gene Florence for Collector Books. Items in our listings are ceramic unless another material is noted, and figurines are of average, small size. See also Clubs and Newsletters.

Bookends, penguins, black, blue, orange & white, 4", pr ..**35.00**
Box, piano form, metal, red velvet lined **20.00**
Butter dish, green basketweave, rectangular **20.00**
Creamer, collie's head form, Ucagco, 4½" **25.00**
Creamer, floral w/gold, 3" ...**15.00**
Cup & saucer, demitasse; floral, hexagonal **18.00**
Cup & saucer, demitasse; lacy flower on black **15.00**
Cup & saucer, fancy gold trim, Shofu China, 2⅝" **10.00**
Cup & saucer, pink & red flowers, Trimont Co **15.00**
Dinnerware, set for 4, w/creamer & sugar bowl, up to **250.00**
Doll, celluloid, Kewpie, 2¾" ..**22.00**
Easter basket, woven wicker, 7x7" **40.00**
Figurine, bellboy w/luggage, EX colors, 4" **22.00**
Figurine, Black fiddler in red & blue, 6" **40.00**

Creamer and sugar bowl on tray, floral pattern on white, $30.00 for the set. (Photo courtesy Gene Florence)

Toby jug, parson figural, $100.00. (Photo courtesy Gene Florence)

Figurine, Black horn player, 6¼" **42.00**

Figurine, boy on fence, Hummel type, 4" **20.00**

Figurine, boy w/guitar & dog, 4½" **20.00**

Figurine, bride & groom, bisque, 6" **45.00**

Figurine, cat playing sax, bisque, 4" **32.00**

Figurine, cherub on boot, bisque, Ucagco, 6x4" **68.00**

Figurine, collie, porcelain, 5" .**28.00**

Figurine, Colonial man in blue coat & tricorner hat, 10½" **70.00**

Figurine, Colonial man w/flowers, lady w/basket, 8", pr **60.00**

Figurine, cowboy & cowgirl, bisque, 6½", pr **42.50**

Figurine, Dutch boy & girl w/detachable buckets, blue, 4½", pr **30.00**

Figurine, girl in long apron, 8¼" **38.00**

Figurine, girl w/bird, Hummel type, bisque, 4" **22.00**

Figurine, girl w/doll, 4¼" **14.00**

Figurine, Indian chief w/tomahawk, 6" **40.00**

Figurine, Indian w/bow & arrow, 5⅞" **32.00**

Figurine, man seated, 3" **15.00**

Figurine, Oriental dancer w/green headdress holds fan, 6¼" ..**20.00**

Figurine, Oriental musical couple, 4", pr **22.00**

Figurine, peacock w/ lg plume tail, 5" **12.00**

Figurine, youthful gentleman, Florence look-alike, 9" ..**45.00**

Furniture, chest, tiny applied roses on white, 3" **14.00**

Furniture, china cabinet w/dishes, 2¼" **18.00**

Incense burner, elephant w/howdah lid, gold trim, Ucagco **37.50**

Lamp, Colonial couple, new silk shade, 15" **75.00**

Mint dish, fish figural, gold metal, 3-footed **12.50**

Mug, elephant figural, trunk forms handle, 4¾" **22.00**

Mug, face of winking man, 4" .**38.00**

Planter, farmer & cart **17.50**

Planter, frog in weeds, 3⅝x3" .**17.50**

Planter, Oriental boy w/rickshaw, hand painted **15.00**

Planter, shoe house, red roof, blue shoestring, 4¼x5" **15.00**

Planter, wheelbarrow, 2½" ..**10.00**

Plaque, cup & saucer form, 4" **15.00**

Plate, flamingos, Souvenir of Miami Florida, reticulated rim, 7¼" **35.00**

Plate, German Shepherd, 4" .**25.00**

Plate, old mill scene, 5¼" **25.00**

Reindeer, celluloid, 7x7½" ...**12.50**

Salt & pepper shakers, boots w/spurs, metal, marked in heel, pr **20.00**

Salt & pepper shakers, chef & stove, 5", pr **37.50**

Salt & pepper shakers, graduates, pr **22.00**

Salt & pepper shakers, red bird, 3¼", pr **20.00**

Teapot, aluminum, 9" **35.00**

Teapot, floral on brown, sm .**20.00**

Teapot, tomato form, Maruhon Ware, 4½" **37.00**

Vase, florals on green, maroon trim, 3" **20.00**

Vase, multicolor floral on blue, marked Meiko China, 3⅛" **18.00**

Vase, swan figural, multicolor details, 5" **20.00**

Wall plaque, flying duck figural, 6½", EX **28.00**

Wall pocket, iris form **16.00**

Old MacDonald's Farm

Made by the Regal China Co., items from this line of novelty ware designed around characters and animals from Old MacDonald's farm can often be found at flea markets and dinnerware shows. Values of some pieces are two to three times higher than a few years ago. The milk pitcher is especially hard to find. Our advisor for this category is Rick Spencer; he is listed in the Directory under Utah.

Butter dish, cow's head **220.00**

Canister, flour, cereal, coffee; med, ea **220.00**

Canister, pretzels, peanuts, popcorn, chips, tidbits; lg, ea **300.00**

Canister, salt, sugar or tea; med, ea **220.00**

Canister, soap or cookies; lg, ea **300.00**

Cookie jar, barn **275.00**

Creamer, rooster **110.00**

Grease jar, pig **175.00**

Pitcher, milk **400.00**

Salt & pepper shakers, churn, gold trim, pr **90.00**

Creamer, rooster, $110.00; Sugar bowl, hen on nest, $125.00.

Salt & pepper shakers, feed sacks w/sheep, pr **195.00**
Shakers, boy & girl, pr **75.00**
Spice jar, assorted lids, sm, ea .**100.00**
Sugar bowl, hen **125.00**
Teapot, duck's head **250.00**

Paper Dolls

Though the history of paper dolls can be traced even farther back, by the late 1700s they were being mass produced. A century later, paper dolls were being used as an advertising medium by retail companies wishing to promote sales. But today the type most often encountered are in book form — the dolls on the cardboard covers, their wardrobe on the inside pages. These have been published since the 1920s. Celebrity and character-related dolls are the most popular with collectors, and condition is very important. If they have been cut out, even when they are still in fine condition and have all their original accessories, they're worth only about half as much as an uncut doll. In our listings, if no condition is given, values are for mint, uncut paper dolls.

American Beauty Paper Dolls, #1548 Merrill, 1951, M in folder **45.00**
Annie Paper Doll Kit, #4330 Milton Bradley Magicrayon, 1983, MIB **12.00**
Barbie, Ken & Midge, #1976 Whitman, 1963, near complete **16.00**
Betty Grable, #1558 Merrill, 1951, uncut, in original folder .**100.00**
Beverly Hillbillies, #1955 Whitman, 1964, uncut, M **70.00**
Blondie (TV show), #4434, Saalfield, 1968, uncut, M **38.00**

National Velvet, #1958 Whitman, 1961, complete and uncut, M in folder, $45.00.

Bridal Paper Dolls, #1967 Whitman, 1971, uncut, in original folder **20.00**

Campus Queens, #2139 Whitman, 1947, partially cut, in original folder **15.00**

Chitty-Chitty Bang-Bang, #1982 Whitman, 1968, cut, in original folder, NM **18.00**

Debbie Reynolds, #1948 Whitman, 1962, cut, in original folder **20.00**

Debbie Reynolds Cut-Outs, #1956 Whitman, 1960, cut, NM in original folder **35.00**

Dodie, #6044 Saalfield, 1971, unused, MIB **32.00**

Donnie & Marie Osmond, #1991 Whitman, 1977, uncut, M .**22.00**

Elizabeth Taylor as Cleopatra, Blaise, 1963, MIB **40.00**

Esther Williams, #1563 Merrill, 1950, 3 dolls, EX in original folder **42.50**

Flintstones' Pebbles, #6685 Wonder, 1974, uncut, in original folder **12.50**

Grace Kelly Cut-Out Dolls, #2069 Whitman, 1956, 2 dolls, uncut, NM **110.00**

Green Acres Magic Stay-On..., #4773 Whitman, 1967, 2 dolls, EX in box **30.00**

Hayley Mills Summer Magic Cutouts, #1966 Whitman, 1963, uncut, M **35.00**

Heidi, #1954 Whitman, 1966, uncut, in original folder .**15.00**

Indian...Dolls w/Pictures To Color, #4406 Saalfield, 1956, NM in origianl folder **25.00**

Jaclyn Smith, Charlie's Angels Kelly, #112 Toy Factory, 1977, MIB **45.00**

Welcome Back Kotter Sweathogs, #108 Toy Factory, 1976, MIB, $30.00. (Photo courtesy June Moon)

Janet Leigh, #2733 Lowe, 1948, uncut, in original folder, from $55 to **70.00**

Julia, #6055 Saalfield, 1968, MIB **45.00**

Lennon Sisters, #1995 Whitman, 1963, cut, NM in original folder **15.00**

Little Ballerina, #1963 Whitman, 1961, EX in original folder **25.00**

Little Lulu, #1979 Whitman, 1973, uncut, in original folder **20.00**

Lois, #3967 Whitman, 1941, wooden, uncut **30.00**

Mary Poppins, #1982 Whitman, 1966, uncut, M **40.00**

Miss America, #1976 Whitman, 1979, uncut, M in original folder **12.00**

My Fair Lady, Columbia Broadcasting, 1965, uncut, M **35.00**

Nanny & the Professor, #4213 Saalfield, 1970, NM **35.00**

National Velvet, #1958 Whitman, 1961, cut, EX in folder .**25.00**

Neighborhood Kids, #1985 Whitman, 1980, uncut, in original folder **8.00**

Pat Boone Cutouts, #1968 Whitman, 1959, uncut, M **50.00**

Patience & Prudence, #2411 Lowe, 1957, VG **35.00**

Patti Doll Book: Alive-Like Face, #3921 Lowe, 1961, uncut, in original folder **20.00**

Playhouse Kiddles, #1954 Whitman, 1971, uncut, M **30.00**

Raggedy Ann & Andy, #1979 Whitman, 1966, uncut, M **26.00**

Rock Hudson, #2087 Whitman, 1957, uncut, NM **65.00**

Sandra & Sue Statuette Dolls, #1180 Whitman, 1948, uncut, in original folder **45.00**

Saturday Night Live, Gilda Radner, M **12.00**

Shirley Temple, #290 Saalfield, uncut, 6 pages of clothes .**135.00**

Storybook Kiddles Sweethearts, #1956 Whitman, 1969, uncut, M **30.00**

Sweetie Pie, #2482 Lowe, 1948, unpunched doll/cut clothes, in original folder **18.00**

That Girl, #4479 Saalfield, 1967, uncut, M **38.00**

Tiny Country Fair Press Out, #1935 Whitman, 1975, uncut, in original folder **6.00**

Tuesday Weld, #5112 Saalfield, 1960, cut, NMIB **25.00**

Uncle Sam's Little Helpers, #2450 Saalfield, 1943, uncut, in original folder **75.00**

Walt Disney's Annette, #1971 Whitman, 1960s, cut, in original folder, from $18 to **30.00**

Western Paper Dolls, #1541 Saalfield, 1950, uncut, in original folder **25.00**

White House w/Tricia, Julie & Pat Nixon, #4475 Saalfield, 1969, NM **35.00**

Paperback Books

Though published to some extent before then, most paperback book collectors prefer those printed from around 1940 until the late 1950s, and most organize their collections around a particular author, genre, publisher, or illustrator. Remember — (as is true with any type of ephemera) condition is extremely important. Unless noted otherwise, our values are given for books in near-fine condition. (Book dealers use the term 'fine' to indicate 'mint' condition.) For more information and hundreds of values, refer to *Huxford's Paperback Value Guide* by Sharon and Bob Huxford (Collector Books).

Abbott, AC; Wild Blood, Gold Medal 208, 1951, VG+ **7.00**

Ackworth, Robert C; Dr Kildare, Lancer 71-308, 1962, tie-in, VG **8.00**

Allingham, Margery; China Governess, Avon 70578, 1990, tie-in, VG **5.00**

Arthur, Burt & Budd; Action at Truxton, Avon F229, 1965, VG **2.25**

Avallone, Michael; Felony Squat, Popular 60-8036, 1967, tie-in, VG **7.00**

Avallone, Michael; Keith the Hero, Curtis 05005, 1970, tie-in, VG **8.00**

Barker, A; Rogue Planet, Pocket 80710, 1976, Space 1999 tie-in, EX **10.00**

Barrett, Monte; Tempered Blade, Popular Library 270, 1950, G+ **2.00**

Bernard, R; Army of Undead, Pyramid R-1711, 1967, Invaders tie-in, VG **10.00**

Blackburn, Thomas W; Short Grass, Bantam 207, 1948, VG+ **4.50**

Bowie, Sam; Chisum, Ace 10470, Wayne movie tie-in, 1970, VG+ **6.00**

Brand, Max; Silvertip's Chase, Pocket 634, 1949, VG **3.50**

Brand, Max; The Outlaw, Pocket 979, 1951, VG+ **6.00**

Burnett, WR; Asphalt Jungle, Pocket 5078, 1961, 3rd print, tie-in, VG **13.00**

Chadwick, Joseph; Gunsmoke Reckoning, Gold Medal 149, 1951, VG+ **7.00**

Charteris, L; Trust the Saint, Coronet 02287, 1978, tie-in, EX **8.00**

Chastain, T; Death Stalk, Award AN1428, 2nd printing, 1974, tie-in, VG **5.00**

Cheshire, Giff; Wenatchee Bend, Ace G759, 1968, VG **2.00**

Church, R; Mork & Mindy, Pocket 82729, 1979, tie-in, VG ...**5.00**

Clegg, B; Doctor Who-Enlightenment, Target 19537, 1984, tie-in, VG **5.00**

Corle, Edwin; Billy the Kid, Bantam A1246, 1954, VG **3.50**

Dean, M; Cry in Night, Pioneer 102, 1987, Dallas tie-in, VG **4.00**

Deming, R; The Hit, Pyramid X-2214, 1970, Mod Squad tie-in, VG **8.00**

Doctorow, EL; Welcome to Hard Times, Signet D1959, 1961, VG+ **6.00**

Fairman, Paul W; Lancer, Popular Library 50-2349, 1968, EX **3.50**

Fairman, PW; Bridget Loves Bernie, Lancer 74795, 1972, tie-in, EX **10.00**

Field, Peter; Maverick's Return, Pocket 1161, 1957, VG+ .**5.00**

Fisher, Clay; Big Pasture, Pocket 1137, 1956, VG **4.50**

Foreman, LL; Desperado's Gold, Pocket 702, 1950, VG+ ...**6.00**

Fox, Brian; Outlaw Trail, Award AS1006, 1972, TV tie-in, VG **5.00**

Franklin, Max; Charlie's Angels, Ballantine 25665, 1977, tie-in, VG **5.00**

Friend, E; Green Hornet in Internal Light, Dell 3231, 1966, tie-in, VG **15.00**

Gardner, Erle S; Cast of Lonely Heiress, Pocket 6027, 1960, VG **10.00**

Gaskell, Mrs; Cranford, Panther 03888, 1972, tie-in, VG ...**4.00**

Gill, Tom; Border Feud, Popular Library 397, 1952, VG **4.00**

Gill, Tom; Firebrand, Popular Library 119, 1946, VG 5.00

Grave, Stephen; Florida Burn, Avon 39930, 1985, Miami Vice tie-in, VG 5.00

Gruber, Frank; Man From Missouri, Popular Library 761, VG+ .5.00

Heath, Charles; A-Team, Dell 10009, 1984, tie-in, VG ...5.00

Hickok, Will; Restless Gun, Signet 1541, 1948, VG 4.00

Hine, Al; Bewitched, Dell 0551, 1965, tie-in, VG 7.00

Hopson, William; Gunfire at Salt Fork, Gold Medal 569, 1956, VG+ 7.00

Hunter, Evan; Chisholms, Bantam 10517, 1979, tie-in, VG .5.00

Jahn, Michael; Rockford Files, Starr 39819, 1975, tie-in, EX 13.00

Johnston, William; Ben Casey, Lancer, 70-006, 1962, tie-in, VG 9.00

Johnston, William; Fonzie Drops In, Tempo 7452, 1974, tie-in, VG 6.00

Kane, Bob; Batman Vs Penguin, Signet D2970, 1955, TV tie-in, VG 13.00

Keene, James; Texas Pistol, Dell 930, 1947, VG+ 4.00

Kerrigan, Kate L; Another World II, Ballantine 25860, 1978, tie-in, VG 5.00

Ketchum, Philip; Feud at Forked River, Gold Medal 772, 1958, VG+ 6.00

King, David; Desert Danger, Paperback Library 53-411, 1967, tie-in, VG 6.00

Knight, David; Dragnet: Case No 561, Pocket 1120, 1956, tie-in, VG 13.00

L'Amour, Louis; Broken Gun, Bantam J3098, 1966, VG+ .7.00

L'Amour, Louis; Conagher, Bantam 28101, 36th printing, tie-in, VG 4.00

L'Amour, Louis; Man From Broken Hills, Bantam Q2377, 1975, VG+ 6.00

Leighton, FS; Patty Goes to Washington, Ace F-278, 1964, tie-in, VG 9.00

LeMay, Alan; Cattle Kingdom, Signet 672, 1948, VG+ 7.00

Lomax, Bliss; Gunsmoke & Trail Dust, Dell 271, 1949, VG+ 6.00

Loomis, Noel; Have Gun Will Travel, Dell First Edition B156, 1960, EX 15.00

Matheson, Richard; Somewhere in Time, Ballantine #28900, 1980, 2nd issue, Christopher Reeve and Jane Seymour on cover, movie tie-in, VG, $15.00.

Mason, F Van Wyck; Wild Drums Beat, Pocket 977, 1953, VG **3.50**

Matheson, Richard; Gunfight, Berkley 13901, 1993, EX .**3.50**

McCulley, Johnston; Mark of Zorro, Dell 553, 1951, VG **10.00**

Mulford, Clarence E; Orphan Outlaw, Pyramid 25, 1950, G+ **3.00**

Nye, Nelson, Hired Hand, Pocket 1060, 1955, VG **3.50**

O'Connor, Richard; Pat Garret, Ace G502, biography, 1963, VG+ .**3.00**

Owen, D; Ponderosa Kill, Paperback Library 52-757, 1968, tie-in, VG **8.00**

Pearl, Jack; Garrison's Gorillas; Dell 2798, 1967, tie-in, VG **8.00**

Peeples, Samuel A; Outlaw Vengeance, Pocket 760, 1951, VG+ **6.00**

Queen, Ellery; Face to Face, Signet Y6872, 3rd printing, VG **4.00**

Racina, Thom; Quincy ME #2, Ace 69946, 1977, tie-in, VG **5.00**

Racina, Thom; Sweet Revenge, Berkley 03559, 1977, Beretta tie-in, VG **5.00**

Raine, Wm MacLeod; Colorado, Avon 500, 1952, G+ **3.50**

Raine, Wm MacLeod; Rustler's Gap, Popular Library 213, 1950, G+ **2.00**

Robbins, Harold; Pirate, Pocket 82529, 4th printing, no date, VG **4.00**

Ross, M; Barnabas Collins, Paperback Library 62-001, TV tie-in, VG **10.00**

Ross, M; Dark Shadows, Paperback Library 52-386, 1966, tie-in, VG **8.00**

Savage, Les Jr; Wild Horse, Gold Medal 111, 1950, VG **5.00**

Sackett, Susan; Letters to Star Trek, Ballantine #25522, 1977, TV tie-in, fine condition, $10.00.

Scott, Bradford; Curse of Texas Gold, Pyramid 264, 1957, G+ **2.75**

Shapiro, Herbert; High Pockets, Signet 688, 1948, VG+ **6.00**

Sharkey, Jack; Addams Family, Pyramid R-1229, 1965, tie-in, VG **13.00**

Shavelson, M; Ike, Warner 92-045, 1979, tie-in, VG **5.00**

St John, G; M*A*S*H Trivia...Quiz Book, Warner 32000, 1983, VG **4.00**

Steelman, Robert; Winter of Sioux; Ballantine 334k, 1959, VG+ **4.00**

Stevens, Serita D; Cagney & Lacy, Dell 11050, 1985, tie-in, VG **5.00**

Stratton, Chris; Gunsmoke, Popular 08146, 1970, tie-in, VG **8.00**

Thompson, Thomas; Trouble Rider, Ballantine 74, 1954, VG+ **5.00**

Tiger, John; Death Twist, Popular 50-2311, 1968, I Spy tie-in, VG **8.00**

Turner, Robert; Lonely Man, Avon 780, 1957, Palance movie tie-in, VG+ **8.00**

Ward, Brad; Man From Andersonville, Ace S148, 1956, VG **5.00**

Wells, Lee E; Tonto Riley, Pocket 865, 1952, VG+ **6.00**

Whittington, Harry; Man in Shadow, Avon T196, 1957, movie tie-in, G+ **3.50**

Wilcox, Collin; McCloud, Award AN1203, 1973, tie-in, VG **6.00**

Wilson, David; Corpse Maker, Award An1365, 1974, tie-in, VG **6.00**

Wohl, Burton; All in the Family, Bantam Q2566, 1976, VG **4.00**

Pennsbury

From the 1950s through the 1970s, dinnerware and novelty ware produced by the Pennsbury company was sold through tourist gift shops along the Pennsylvania turnpike. Much of their ware was decorated in an Amish theme. A group of barbershop singers was another popular design, and they made a line of bird figures that were very similar to Stangl's, though much harder to find.

Ashtray, Amish, 5" **25.00**
Ashtray, Such Schmootzers, 5" .**30.00**
Bowl, Dutch Talk, 9" **90.00**
Bowl, Green Rooster, 3" **35.00**
Butter dish, Folk Art, w/lid, 5x4" .**45.00**
Candle holder, Maypole Dance, 5½" **60.00**
Candy dish, Hex, 6-cup **75.00**
Casserole, Black Rooster, w/lid, 10¼x8¼" **100.00**
Chip & dip, Holly, 11" **100.00**
Coffeepot, Black Rooster, 6-cup, 8" **85.00**
Desk basket, National Exchange Club, 5" **40.00**

Barbershop Quartet: Coaster, 5" dia, $30.00; Pitcher, 7¼", $70.00; Mug, 5", $40.00.

Mug, Amish Couple **25.00**
Mug, beer; Amish Couple **30.00**
Mug, beer; Barbershop Quartet,
  marked, 4¾" **30.00**
Mug, coffee; Black Rooster ..**20.00**
Mug, Swallow the Insult **35.00**
Pie pan, Mother Serving Pie,
  9" **85.00**
Pie pan, Red Rooster, 9" **55.00**
Pitcher, Tulip, 4" **40.00**
Pitcher, Yellow Daisies, 4" ..**35.00**
Plaque, Baltimore & Ohio RR,
  5¾x7¾" **55.00**
Plaque, Don't Be So Doppich, 4"
  dia **25.00**
Plaque, Don't Stand Up While Room
  Is in Motion, 6" dia **50.00**
Plaque, Horse & Carriage, 6" .**50.00**
Plaque, Toleware, brown, 5x7" ..**40.00**
Plaque, US Frigate Constitution,
  11x8" **90.00**
Plate, Amish, Chatting, 8" ..**65.00**
Plate, Daily Bread **60.00**
Platter, Red Rooster, oval, 11" ..**45.00**
Pretzel bowl, Amish couple .**75.00**
Salt & pepper shakers, Red
  Rooster, 2½", pr **25.00**
Snack set, Red Rooster **25.00**
Tray, Crested Birds, octagonal,
  3x5" **30.00**
Tray, Horses, 5x3" **30.00**
Vase, Dartmouth insignia, 10" ..**30.00**
Wall pocket, clown & donkey,
  6½" **95.00**

Pez Dispensers

Originally a breath mint targeted for smokers, by the '50s Pez had been diverted toward the kid's candy market, and to make sure the kids found them appealing, the company designed dispensers they'd be sure to like — many of them characters the kids could easily recognize. On today's collectible market, some of those dispensers bring astonishing prices!

Though early on collectors preferred the dispensers with no feet, today they concentrate primarily on the character heads. Feet were added in 1987, so if you want your collection to be complete, you'll buy both styles. For further information and more listings, see *Schroeder's Collectible Toys, Antique to Modern* (Collector Books). Our values are for mint dispensers. Very few are worth collecting if they are damaged or have missing parts.

Policeman, no feet, $25.00; Stewardess, no feet, $95.00.

Baloo, w/feet **20.00**
Barney Bear, w/feet **20.00**
Bouncer Beagle, w/feet **6.00**
Bugs Bunny, w/feet, from $1 to .**3.00**
Casper, no feet **70.00**
Chick in Egg, no feet **12.00**
Cool Cat, w/feet **35.00**

Santa Claus, full body, $125.00.
(Photo courtesy June Moon)

Cow, no feet, blue **45.00**
Dino, w/feet, purple, from $1
    to **3.00**
Donald Duck, no feet **15.00**
Donald Duck's Nephew, no feet ..**20.00**
Dumbo, w/feet, blue head **20.00**
Fat-Ears Rabbit, no feet, yellow
    head **10.00**
Frog, w/feet, whistle head ...**30.00**
Garfield, w/feet, teeth, from $1
    to **10.00**
Gorilla, no feet, black head .**45.00**
Hulk, no feet, dark green **20.00**
Indian Chief, no feet, mar-
    bleized **65.00**
Indian Chief, no feet, yellow head-
    dress **45.00**
Lamb, no feet **10.00**
Lucy, w/feet, from $1 to **3.00**
Miss Piggy, w/feet, from $1 to .**3.00**

Monkey Sailor, no feet, w/white
    cap, M **25.00**
Papa Smurf, w/feet, red **5.00**
Pumpkin, no feet, from $10 to .**15.00**
Raven, no feet, yellow beak .**30.00**
Rhino, w/feet, whistle head ...**6.00**
Road Runner, no feet **6.00**
Rooster, w/feet, white or yellow
    head, ea **25.00**
Rudolph, no feet **25.00**
Scrooge McDuck, w/feet **6.00**
Sheik, no feet **30.00**
Smurfette, w/feet, blue **5.00**
Snoopy, w/feet, from $1 to **5.00**
Speedy Gonzales, w/feet **10.00**
Thumper, w/feet, no copyright .**30.00**
Tweety Bird, no feet **10.00**
Tyke, w/feet **6.00**
Winnie the Pooh, w/feet **25.00**
Wolfman, no feet **185.00**
Zorro, no feet, w/Zorro logo .**75.00**

Pfaltzgraff Pottery

Since early in the 17th century, pottery has been produced in
York County, Pennsylvania. The
Pfaltzgraff Company that operates
there today is the outgrowth of
several of these small potteries. A
changeover made in 1940 redirect-
ed their efforts toward making the
dinnerware lines for which they
are now best known. Their earliest
line, a glossy brown with a white
frothy drip glaze around the rim,
was called Gourmet Royale. Today
collectors find an abundance of
good examples, and many are
working toward reassembling sets
of their own. Village, another very
successful line, is tan with a sten-
cilled Pennsylvania Dutch-type

Gourmet Royale, casserole, stick handle, 1-qt, $18.00.

floral design in brown. Recently discontinued, we predict that this pattern will bear watching as more and more shoppers turn to secondary market sources to replace and replenish their services.

Giftware consisting of ashtrays, mugs, bottle stoppers, a cookie jar, etc., all with comic character faces were made in the 1940s. This line was called Muggsy, and it is also very collectible, with the mugs starting at about $50.00 each. For more information, refer to *The Collector's Encyclopedia of American Dinnerware* by Jo Cunningham (Collector Books) and *Pfaltzgraff, America's Potter,* by David A. Walsh and Polly Stetler, published in conjunction with the Historical Society of York County, York, Pennsylvania.

Our advisor for this category is Jo-Ann Bentz, who is listed in the Directory under Pennsylvania.

Gourmet Royale, baker, #323, oval, 9½", from $20 to **22.00**

Gourmet Royale, bean pot, #11-3, 3-qt, w/warmer, from $48 to **50.00**

Gourmet Royale, bowl, #241, oval, 7x10", from $15 to **17.00**

Gourmet Royale, bowl, mixing; 10", from $15 to **17.00**

Gourmet Royale, bowl, mixing; 8", from $12 to **14.00**

Gourmet Royale, bowl, soup; 2¼x7¼", from $6 to **8.00**

Gourmet Royale, bowl, vegetable; 9¾" **15.00**

Gourmet Royale, casserole, hen on nest, 2-qt, from $70 to ..**90.00**

Gourmet Royale, casserole, stick handle, 1-qt, from $18 to **20.00**

Gourmet Royale, chafing dish, w/handles, lid & stand, 8x9", from $30 to **32.00**

Gourmet Royale, coffee server, metal & wood stand, 10¾", from $100 to **125.00**

Gourmet Royale, flour scoop, sm, from $12 to **15.00**

Gourmet Royale, ladle, sm, from $12 to **15.00**

Gourmet Royale, marmalade, from $18 to **20.00**

Gourmet Royale, mug, #392, 16-oz, from $12 to **14.00**

Gourmet Royale, plate, dinner; #88R, 10", from $8 to **10.00**

Gourmet Royale, plate, salad; 6¾", from $3 to **4.00**

Village, cup and saucer, $3.00; Cereal bowl, 6", $2.50; Salad plate, 8", $2.00; Dinner plate, 10", $3.00. (Photo courtesy Jo Cunningham)

Gourmet Royale, platter, #320, 14", from $20 to **25.00**

Gourmet Royale, rarebit, #330, lug handles, oval, 11", from $15 to **18.00**

Gourmet Royale, roaster, #325, oval, 14", from $30 to ...**35.00**

Gourmet Royale, salt & pepper shakers, bell shape, pr, from $25 to **35.00**

Gourmet Royale, souffle dish, #398, ribbed, 8½", from $20 to **22.00**

Gourmet Royale, teapot, #0381, 6-cup, from $18 to **22.00**

Heritage, demitasse cup & saucer, #283 ....**4.50**

Heritage, teapot, #555, 24-oz, from $10 to **14.00**

Muggsy, ashtray **125.00**

Muggsy, cigarette server ...**125.00**

Muggsy, clothes sprinkler bottle, Myrtle, white, from $150 to **175.00**

Muggsy, mug, action figure (golfer, fisherman, etc), any, from $65 to **80.00**

Muggsy, tumbler **60.00**

Village, baker, #236, rectangular, 2-qt, from $10 to **12.00**

Village, beverage server, #490, lighthouse form, dome lid, from $15 to **20.00**

Village, bowl, fruit; #008, 5", from $2 to **3.00**

Village, bowl, serving; #010, 7", from $4 to **5.50**

Village, butter dish, #028, ¼-lb, from $6 to **8.00**

Village, casserole, #315, w/lid, 2-qt, from $15 to **18.00**

Village, cookie jar, #540, 3-qt, from $12 to **15.00**

Village, creamer & sugar bowl, #020, lighthouse form, from $10 to **12.00**

Village, napkin holder, #086, from $4 to **6.00**

Village, pepper mill, from $6 to .**8.00**

Village, picture frame, #352, from $7 to **9.00**

Village, plate, dinner; #004, 10¼", from $2 to **3.00**

Village, platter, #016, 14", from $8 to **11.00**

Village, salt & pepper shakers, #025, lighthouse form, pr, from $5 to **7.00**

Village, thermal carafe, 1-liter .**15.00**

Village, utencil crock, #500, 6½", from $5 to **7.00**

Pie Birds

What is a pie bird? It is a functional and decorative kitchen tool most commonly found in the shape of a bird, designed to vent steam through the top crust of a pie to prevent the juices from spilling over into the oven. Other popular designs were elephants and black-faced bakers. The original vents that were used in England and Wales in the 1800s were simply shaped like funnels.

From the 1980s to the present, many novelty pie vents have been added to the market for the baker and the collector. Some of these could be obtained from Far East Imports; others have been made in England and the US (by commercial and/or local enterprises). Examples can be found in the shapes of animals (dogs, frogs, elephants, cats, goats, and dragons), people (policemen, chefs with and without pies, pilgrims, and carolers), or whimsical figurals (clowns, leprechauns, and teddy bears). New for the 1990s is an array of holiday-related pie vents. Please note that incense burners, one-hole pepper shakers, dated brass toy bird whistles, and ring holders (for instance, the elephant with a clover on his tummy) should not be mistaken for pie vents.

Consequently a collector must be on guard and aware that these new pie vents are being sold by dealers (knowingly in many instances) as old or rare, often at double or triple the original cost (which is usually under $10.00). Though most of the new ones can't really be called reproductions since they never existed before, there's a black bird that is a remake, and you'll see them every-where. Here's how you can spot them: they'll have yellow beaks and protruding white-dotted eyes. If they're on a white base and have an orange beak, they are the older ones. Another basic tip that should help you distinguish old from new: older pie vents are air-brushed versus being hand painted. Our advisor for this category is Lillian M. Cole, who is listed in the Directory under New Jersey.

Rooster, multicolored details on white, ceramic, $45.00.

Benny the Baker, Cardinal China **85.00**
Bird, all black or all white, Imported, 4", ea **4.00**
Bird, cobalt, stoneware, New Hampshire pottery, new, 4¼" **10.00**
Black chef, half figure, England, new **39.00**

Black chef & cook, multicolor paint, Taiwan, pr **10.00**
Black clown, hat, striped shirt & pants w/suspenders, England, new **39.00**
Blackbird on log, marked Artone Pottery England **50.00**
Bluebirds on nest, 1950s, USA, copyright on back **100.00**
Canary, yellow w/pink lips, Josef Originals **22.00**
Chef, all white, 1995, repro, pinhole vent **5.00**
Crow dressed as chef, holds pie, marked SB, England, new **30.00**
Duck w/long neck, blue, pink or yellow, 1940s-50s, USA, ea .**25.00**
England, white, embossed logo 'Tala 1899,' 1996 ....**10.00**
Funnel, Pyrex glass **30.00**
Funnel, Royal Commemorative, England **35.00**
Green Willow, decaled, new .**15.00**
Mammy, airbrushed, brown skin tone, 1940s **110.00**
Rooster, multicolored details on white, ceramic **45.00**
Songbirds, gold beaks & feet, 1950s, USA, ea **65.00**

Pin-Back Buttons

Because most of the pin-backs prior to the 1920s were made of celluloid, collectors refer to them as 'cellos.' Many were issued in sets on related topics. Some advertising buttons had paper inserts on the back that identified the company or the product they were advertising. After the 1920s lithographed metal buttons were produced; they're now called 'lithos.' See also the Beatles; Elvis Presley; Marilyn Monroe; Political.

Alaska, polar bear, multicolor, M **4.00**
Alka-Seltzer, I Ate the Whole Thing, red & blue, 1960s, 1" **1.00**
All the Arms We Need, line-drawn boy & girl hugging, 1½" **3.50**
Archie Bunker, red, white & blue, 1972, M **4.00**
Atlanta '88 Delta, Official Airline...Democratic...Convention, 2½" **6.00**
Atlantis, 5 astronaut portraits w/names surrounding shuttle, 3½" **6.00**
Beverly Hills 90210, cast portrait, multicolor, 4" **2.00**
Bugs Bunny, Six Flags, multicolor, 1981 ....**5.00**
Bundles for Britain, red, white & blue, 1940s, NM **6.00**
California State Fair, blue & white, 1985 ....**5.00**
Cardinals, black, white & red, 2" **1.00**
Catwoman, DC Comics, multicolor **3.50**
Chrysler '73 When You're Hot, You're Hot, gulls & sun, 3" **4.00**
Culligan for Soft Water, red, white & blue,½" **1.00**
Earth Day, blue & white, 1990 .**2.50**
General Electric, If You Can Dream It..., blue & white, 2" **2.50**
Gould Electric, logo, red, white & blue, 2" **1.00**
Happy Birthday Donald Duck, 1934-1984, Donald's face & candle, 2½" **8.00**

Hard Rock Cafe, Save the Planet, Love All Serve All, 1½" ..2.00

Hawaii, waves spelling Hawaii, blue & white 2.50

Horseshoe Club, Reno casino, multicolor 4.00

I'm Fighting in the War Against Aids!, 1" 2.00

It All Happens in Las Vegas, rainbow, multicolor 2.50

Jack Carson, Quaker Puffed Wheat & Rice, multicolor, VG 4.00

Johnny's Back, Only on Video!, Carson portrait, 2¼" 5.00

K-Mart Loves (heart) Me!, red, white & blue, ½" 1.50

Mack Trucks, 3-D bulldog, yellow, 1" 2.50

Michael Jackson Victory Tour, multicolor 2.50

Mickey Mouse's 50th Birthday, multicolor, M 50.00

Milwaukee Zoo, gorilla portrait, multicolor 2.50

Moscow 1980 (Olympics), Misha mascot & rings, multicolor 5.00

People Free Libraries, Uncle Sam pointing, 2¼" 5.00

Pond's, Discover How Beautiful Your Skin Can Be, oval, multicolor, 2" 3.00

Remember...Only You Can Prevent Forest Fires!, Smokey portrait, 1½" 3.00

Riviera, Las Vegas, multicolor .3.00

Save With Franklin Gas, blue, white & yellow, 1" 8.00

Snoopy Cub Scout, multicolor .2.50

Universal Office Products, Satisfaction Guaranteed, 3-color 1.50

Western Airlines, logo, blue, white & red, 2" 2.00

Yogi Bear wearing DARE shirt, multicolor 3.50

Pep Pins

In the late '40s and into the '50s, some cereal companies packed a pin-back button in each box of their product. Quaker Puffed Oats offered a series of movie star pin-backs, but Kellogg's Pep Pins are probably the best known of all. There were eighty-six different Pep pins, so theoretically if you wanted the whole series, as Kellogg hoped you would, you'd have to buy at least that many boxes of their cereal. Pep pins came in five sets, the first in 1945, three more in 1946, and the last in 1947. They were printed with full-color lithographs of comic characters licensed by King Features and Famous Artists — Maggie and Jiggs, the Winkles, and Dogwood and Blondie, for instance. Superman, the only D.C. Comics character, was included in each set. Most Pep pins range in value from $10.00 to $15.00 in NM/M condition; any not mentioned in our listings fall into this range. The exceptions are evaluated below. Our advisor for Pep pins is Doug Dezso, listed under New Jersey in the Directory.

BO Plenty 30.00

Brenda Star 16.00

Corky 16.00

Dagwood 30.00

Dick Tracy 30.00

Felix the Cat 75.00

Flash Gordon 30.00

Flat Top 30.00

Jiggs 25.00

Kayo 20.00

Tess Trueheart and Vitamin Flintheart, $15.00 each.

Maggie **25.00**
Mama De Stross **30.00**
Mama Katzenjammer **25.00**
Olive Oyl **30.00**
Orphan Annie **25.00**
Phantom **75.00**
Popeye **30.00**
Superman **35.00**
Uncle Walt **20.00**
Winkles Twins **75.00**

Pinup Art

This is a relatively new area of collector interest, and nice examples such as calendars, magazines, playing cards, etc., by the more collectible artists are still easy to find and not terribly expensive. Collectors often center their attention on the work of one or more of their favorite artists. Some of the better known are Petty, Vargas, Ballantyne, Armstrong, DeVross, Elvgren, Moran, and Phillips. Pinup art was popular from the '30s into the '50s, inspired by Hollywood and its glamorous leading ladies. Our advisor, Denis Jackson, issues price guides on illustrations, old magazines, and pinups. Mr. Jackson is listed in the Directory under Washington.

Book, Stolen Sweets, FW Smith, 1970s **42.00**
Booklet, 11 pinups by Mozert, Brown & Bigelow, 1940s, 4¼x5¼" **50.00**
Calendar, blond in bikini, J Erbit, 1949, 33x16" **75.00**
Calendar, Women of History, Bill Randall, 1968 ....**28.00**
Calendar note pad, Aiming High, G Elvgren, 1961, 4½x8" **12.00**
Calendar note pad, Bet You Are, Earl Moran, 1936 ....**16.00**
Calendar note pad, blond & vacuum, G Elvgren **12.00**
Greeting card, Nursery Rhyme for Grownups, MacPherson, 1950s **25.00**

Calendar, 1959, Brown & Bigelow, Freeman Elliot, EX, $45.00. (Photo courtesy Dunbar Gallery)

Ink blotter, Jill Needs a Jack, Elvgren, 1949 ....**12.00**

Magazine, Paris Nights, Consolidated Magazines, 1930s, NM ...**15.00**

Magazine cover, Motion Picture, Garbo, Mozert, Jan 1937 .**60.00**

Magazine cover, Wink, harem girl, Peter Driben, Feb 1955 .**25.00**

Matchbook cover, various artists, 1940s-60s, unused, ea, from $2.50 to **3.50**

Playing cards, girl in hammock, J Erbit, US Playing Cards, 1950s, MIB **25.00**

Playing cards, nude & pelican, Elvgren, single deck, MIB **35.00**

Print, A Smile Worthwhile, Billy DeVross, 8x10" **18.00**

Print, Adorable, brunette, red & white gown, Armstrong, '50, 4x5½" **16.00**

Print, Beautiful Armfull, girl w/flowers, Art Frahm, 9x11" **13.00**

Print, Carmelita, Gene Pressler, 12x15" **40.00**

Print, Day Dreams, Billy DeVross, 3x5" **11.00**

Print, Diane, Earl Moran, 1950, 16x20" **65.00**

Print, Double Feature, girl walking boxer, W Otto, 8x10" **14.00**

Print, Enchanting, nude on rock, Elvgren, 1955, 10x17½" **75.00**

Print, girl in sailor hat on ship's rail, Elvgren, 7x9½" **13.00**

Print, Happy Landing, blond in pink ski suit, DeVross, 1944, 8x10" **12.00**

Print, Happy Moments, blond w/puppy, J Erbit, 16x30" .**30.00**

Print, Howdy, cowgirl on fence, Zoe Mozert, 12x14" **35.00**

Print, Irresistible, brunette, Armstrong, 1950, 11x23" **70.00**

Print, Miss Sylvania adjusting garter, G Elvgren, 1961, 16x34" **65.00**

Print, Red Shoes, Peter Driben, 1940s, 22x28" **65.00**

Print, signed DeVross, $30.00.

Print, Reflections, blond nude on couch w/mirror, J Erbit, 16x20" **45.00**

Print, Retirement Plan, redhead in teddy, G Elvgren, 5¾x17" **24.00**

Print, Say It Again, blond on phone, Earl Moran, 1952, 22x28" **175.00**

Print, Service w/Pleasure, tennis girl, Armstrong, 8½x11" .**30.00**

Print, Sharon, brunette in green gloves, DeVross, 1955, 7½x9½" **35.00**

Print, Susan, blond in jeans w/daisies, Earl Moran, 16x20" **45.00**

Print, That's a Deal, brunette in bikini, Armstrong, 4½x6" **17.50**

Political Collectibles

Pennants, posters, badges, pamphlets — in general, anything related to a presidential campaign or politicians — are being sought by collectors who have an interest in the political history of our country. Most valued are items from a particularly eventful period or those things having to do with an especially colorful personality. See also Matchcovers.

Apron, Jimmy Carter for President, green cloth, smock style, M **50.00**

Ashtray, ceramic, President & Mrs John F Kennedy, color transfer, 6" **12.00**

Badge, Honored Guest of GOP National Convention, Kansas City MO, EX **35.00**

Badge, Republican Citizen dinner, w/blue ribbon, 1952, EX .**55.00**

Badge, Roosevelt/Barner, red, white & blue cello in brass frame, EX **18.00**

Badge, Staff member of Connecticut Constitutional Convention, 1956, EX ...**35.00**

Badge, 1948 GOP Convention, Philadelphia PA, NM .**65.00**

Balloon, Vote Kennedy, white on blue, unused **10.00**

Balloon, Wallace for President, unused, 1972 ....**5.00**

Bank, Rockefeller for Governor, painted metal, ¾x2½", NM **12.50**

Bank, Uncle Sam, Roseville, ceramic with blue shading, 4½", from $125.00 to $150.00. (Photo courtesy Dunbar Gallery)

Banner, Franklin Roosevelt, red, white & blue cloth, 6x5", NM **15.00**

Banner, LBJ for the USA, red, white & blue plastic, 30x19", NM **20.00**

Book, Re-Elect Nixon...Club Fun Book, Nupaco, copyright 1972, M **12.50**

Book, Torch Is Passed...,
Associated Press, hardcover,
1963, NM 22.50
Booklet, A Dozen Reasons To
Elect Woodrow Wilson, 1944,
NM 10.00
Booklet, Public Officers of MA, full
page of Congressman JFK,
1951-52 ....75.00
Box, Spiro Agnew Mouthwash,
waxed cardboard, 1970, 5x2",
NM 7.50
Buckle, Carter on brass peanut
shape, 3¼x1¾", NM 10.00
Bumper sticker, Re-Elect Hillary's
Husband in 1996, M 1.50
Car window attachment, Reagan
for President, plastic ele-
phant 10.00
Doll, Teddy Kennedy, cloth carica-
ture, 1980, 5½" 15.00
Earrings, Goldwater on gold-colored
metal circle, 1" dia, pr 10.00
Flasher key chain, Kennedy/J Manford
Core, black & white 7.50
Flasher ring, John F Kennedy, 1917-
1963, child size, EX 10.00
Fob, Cox/Roosevelt, Our Choice,
nickel, EX 50.00
Guide, Nixon Inaugural, embossed
gold seal, 1973, 32-page,
NM 10.00
Key, 1960 Delegate at Republican
Convention, EX 27.50
Lapel badge, portait, Kennedy
Will Win, blue, white & black,
5" 60.00
Lapel pin, Jimmy Carter for
President in '76, 1" dia,
MOC 7.50
License plate, Al Smith the Happy
Warrior, EX 100.00
License plate, California, Perot,
yellow on black, 2x4", M .3.00

Figure, Barry M. Goldwater,
Remco, 1964, NMIB, $35.00.

Mask, Richard Nixon, rubber, nat-
ural colors, 1970s, NM .25.00
Medal, Nixon Inaugural, bronze,
Nixon-Agnew portraits, 1973,
2¾" 25.00
Pamphlet, Anti-Suffrage Association,
1968, EX 20.00
Paperweight, bust of Herbert
Hoover, copper paint on heavy
metal, EX 27.00
Pennant, Eisenhower Inauguration,
January 20, 1953, cloth, 17",
NM 22.50
Pennant, Nixon's the One, w/por-
trait, 4-color, 1968, 26" L .7.00
Photo card, Robert Kennedy por-
trait, information on back,
5½x8½" 4.00
Pillowcase cover, Franklin D
Roosevelt, 1933, EX 65.00
Postcard, George Wallace portrait,
multicolor photo, M 2.00
Postcard, President & Mrs Kennedy,
AAA Novelty, ca 1961,
M 5.00

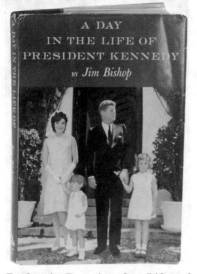

Book, A Day in the Life of President Kennedy, by Jim Bishop, Random House, 1964, 1st edition, with dust jacket, EX, $10.00.

Poster, Carter & Mondale, Challenging Leadership..., 1976, 20x16" **12.50**

Poster, Nixon/Agnew, w/25 celebrities (sketch), 1968, 27x20", M **27.50**

Poster, Robert F Kennedy portrait, ...For President, 1968, 18x12" **22.50**

Program, Eisenhower Inaugural, January 20, 1953, 48-page, NM **25.00**

Program, JF Kennedy Inaugural, January 20, 1961, 64-page, NM **27.50**

Ribbon, Shriver/McGovern, EX **10.00**

Scarf, silk-screened portrait on rayon, 1965, M **17.50**

Stove cover, Herbert Hoover for President, G **15.00**

Sunglasses, Barry Goldwater, black cardboard, NM **12.00**

Sunvisor, Carter/Mondale '80, green & white fabric w/elastic band, M **10.00**

Ticket, contribution; Landon/Knox, 1936, EX **25.00**

Ticket, Democratic National Convention, FD Roosevelt portrait, 1936 ....**20.00**

Ticket, Nixon Inauguration, 1973, 2¾x7" **5.00**

Tie bar, LBJ on gold-tone Texas shape, 1½" **7.50**

Tie clip, Let's Back Jack, white plastic on gold-tone, EX **10.00**

Token, Senator Birch Bayh ...**4.00**

Window decal, Kennedy for President, JFK photo, shield shape, 5½" **15.00**

Wristwatch, Ronald Reagan, digital, caricature in garbage can, MOC **30.00**

Pin-Back Buttons

Celluloid pin-back buttons ('cellos') were first widely used in the 1896 presidential campaign; before that time medals, ribbons, and badges of various kinds predominated. By the 1920s buttons with designs lithographed directly on metal ('lithos') became more common. The most attractive and interesting designs are found on 'classic' buttons made between 1900-15, and they (along with the plainer but very scarce buttons for presidential candidates of the 1920s) are also the most expensive.

Prices for political pin-back buttons have increased considerably in the last few years, more due to speculative buying and selling rather than inherent scarcity or unusual demand. It is still possible, however, to find quality collectible items at reasonable prices. In flea markets, recent buttons tend to be overpriced; the goal, as always, is to look for less familiar items that may be priced more reasonably.

Most collectors look for presidential items, but buttons for 'causes' (such as civil rights and peace) as well as 'locals' (governors, senators, etc.) are becoming increasingly popular as well. Picture buttons are the most desirable, especially the 'jugates' which show both presidential and vice-presidential candidates. Recently, 'coattail' items, featuring presidential and local candidates on the same button, have attracted a lot of interest. Most buttons issued since the 1964 campaign, with a few notable exceptions, should be in the range of $2.00 to $10.00. The listing here therefore concentrates on earlier items.

Condition is critical: cracks, scratches, spots, and brown stains ('foxing') seriously reduce the value of a button. Prices are for items in excellent condition. Reproductions are common; many are marked as such, but it takes some experience to tell the difference. The best reference book for political collectors is Edmund Sullivan's *Collecting Political Americana*, the second edition of which has been recently published.

Adlai Stevenson Our Next President, portrait, 4-color, w/ribbon, EX **12.50**

Better a Third Termer Than a Third Rater (Roosevelt), blue & black, EX **10.00**
Bury Barry, black & white cello, NM **4.00**
Clinton/Gore Volunteer, red, white & blue **1.25**
Eisenhower portrait, Peace & Prosperity w/Eisenhower, 3-color **3.50**
For President Lyndon B Johnson, w/portrait, 6", NM **10.00**
For the Love of Ike Vote Republican, red, white & blue cello **6.00**
Ford for President, portrait, black, red & white litho **1.00**
Franklin Roosevelt portrait, multi-color, EX **5.00**

Goldwater, The Best Man for the Job, 3½", $12.00.

Goldwater for '68, black letters on yellow **4.00**
Goldwater in '64, portrait flasher, black & white in gold-tone frame **8.00**
Hell No We Won't Go, red, white & blue, 3½" **4.00**
Humphrey for President, portrait, red, white & blue, flasher, 2½" **4.00**

I Like Ike Even Better, red, white & blue litho 1.50

Jimmy Carter Inauguration, January 20, 1977, multicolor cello, w/ribbon 8.00

Keep a Firm Grip on the Reins LBJ, red, white & blue, EX 6.00

Nixon for President, elephant hanging from ribbon below, EX 18.00

Nixon/Agnew, portraits, red, white & blue, 3½" 5.00

Nixon/Lodge, portraits, red, white & blue litho, M 5.00

Pat for First Lady, Pat Nixon portrait, black & white, 1960 .5.00

President Nixon, Now More Than Ever, red, white & blue, 1972 ....1.50

Roosevelt (Franklin D), red, white & blue litho, light scratches 3.50

Roosevelt/Garner Club, green & gold cello, 1936, VG 6.00

Socialist Party Workers of the World Unite for President Debs 110.00

Taft League of Massachusetts, portrait, sepia tone, EX .70.00

Truman Was Screwy To Build a Porch for Dewey, blue & white, EX 20.00

Viva LBJ, red, white & blue cello, black & white portrait, EX .8.00

Welcome Our Heroes Home, WWII, red, white & blue 2.00

Precious Moments

Little figurines with inspirational messages called Precious Moments were created by Samuel J. Butcher and are produced by Enesco Inc. in the Orient. They're sold through almost every gift store in the country, and some of the earlier, discontinued models are becoming very collectible. Refer to *Precious Collectibles*, a magazine published by Rosie Wells Enterprises Inc. for more information. See also Clubs and Newsletters.

Bell, Jesus Loves Me, #E-5209, Dove mark 48.00

Bell, The Purr-fect Grandma, #E-7183, Olive Branch mark .50.00

Candle climbers, Joy to the World, #E-2344, Cross mark, pr .95.00

Container, Forever Friends, #E-9283, Fish mark 60.00

Doll, Katie Lynne, #E-0539, Olive Branch mark 180.00

Doll, PD, #12475, Dove mark ..80.00

Doll, Trish, #12483, Dove mark .80.00

Figurine, Be Not Weary in Well Doing, #E-3111, Dove mark 75.00

Figurine, Brotherly Love, #100944, Bow & Arrow mark 75.00

Figurine, Dropping in for Christmas, #E-2350, Hourglass mark .75.00

Figurine, God Understands, #E-1379B, Hourglass mark .90.00

Figurine, Jesus Loves You, #E-9276, Cross mark 25.00

Figurine, Love Is Patient, #E-9251, Cross mark 75.00

Figurine, Our First Christmas Together, #E-2377, Fish mark 85.00

Figurine, The Lord Bless You & Keep You, #E-3114, Dove mark 55.00

Figurine, Winter's Song, #12092, Dove mark 120.00

Frame, Blessed Are the Pure of Heart, #E-0521, Cedar Tree mark 45.00

Figurine, He Careth For You, #E-1377B, no mark, $95.00.

Musical, Lord Keep My Life in Tune, #12580, Flower mark 160.00

Musical, Silent Night, #15814, Flame mark 65.00

Musical, The Purr-fect Grandma, #E-7184, Fish mark 80.00

Night light, God Bless You With Rainbows, #16020, Flower mark 100.00

Ornament, God Gave His Best, #15806, G Clef mark 25.00

Ornament, Joy to the World, #E-2343, Triangle mark 55.00

Ornament, Peace on Earth #E-5389, Olive Branch mark 35.00

Plate, Jesus Loves You, #E-9276, Cross mark 35.00

Plate, The Voice of Spring, #12106, Olive Branch mark 65.00

Plate, Winter's Song, #12130, Dove mark 65.00

Thimble, God Sent His Love, #15865, Dove mark 45.00

Thimble, Oh Holy Night, #522554, Bow & Arrow mark 22.00

Purinton

Popular among collectors due to its 'country' look, Purinton Pottery's dinnerware and kitchen items are easy to learn to recognize due to their bold yet simple designs, many of them of fruit and flowers, created with basic hand-applied colors on a creamy white gloss. For more information we recommend *Purinton Pottery, An Identification and Value Guide,* by Susan Morris (Collector Books).

Baker, Pennsylvania Dutch, 7" dia 45.00

Bean pot, Normandy Plaid, 3¾" .50.00

Bowl, Apple, scalloped border, 12" 40.00

Candle holder, Saraband, 2x6"
dia **20.00**
Candy dish, Normandy Plaid, center handle, 6¼" **35.00**
Canister, Fruit, oval, red trim,
9" **60.00**

**Vinegar cruet, Apple, 10", $45.00;
Oil cruet, Apple, 5", $35.00.**

Cookie jar, Pennsylvania Dutch,
slant top, wooden lid ..**125.00**
Cup & saucer, Heather Plaid, 2½",
5½" dia **13.00**
Honey jug, Ivy-Yellow Blossom,
6¼" **35.00**
Jardiniere, Windflower, 5" ..**30.00**
Jug, Dutch; Fruit, 1-pt **45.00**
Jug, Dutch; Mountain Rose, 2-
pt **85.00**
Jug, Kent; Apple, 1-pt **35.00**
Jug, Kent; Maywood, 1-pt ...**25.00**
Jug, Kent; Red Blossom, 1-pt .**30.00**
Plate, dinner; Apple, 9¾" **15.00**
Plate, dinner; Ming Tree,
9¾" **20.00**
Platter, meat; Provincial Fruit,
11" **40.00**

Relish tray, Starflower, 3-compartment, basket handle, 8" L .**45.00**
Sugar bowl, Intaglio, w/lid, 5" .**30.00**
Tea & toast set, Intaglio, 8½" plate
w/indent, 2½" cup **25.00**
Teapot, Fruit, 2-cup **45.00**
Teapot, Mountain Rose, 4-cup,
5" **75.00**
Wall pocket, Heather Plaid, 3½" .**35.00**

Puzzles

Of most interest to collectors of vintage puzzles are those made of wood or plywood, especially the early hand-cut examples. Character-related examples and those representing a well-known personality or show from the early days of television are coming on strong right now, and values are steadily climbing in these areas. See also Rock 'n Roll.

Atom Ant, jigsaw, Whitman,
14x18", NMIB **25.00**
Bat Masterson, jigsaw, Colorforms,
1960s, set of 2, NMIB ...**35.00**
Beverly Hillbillies, jigsaw, Lamar,
1963, family portrait, M in EX
box **27.00**
Bonanza, jigsaw, Milton Bradley,
1964, 100-pc, 10x19", EX .**25.00**
Broken Arrow, jigsaw, Built-Rite,
1958, NMIB **25.00**
Buffalo Bill, frame-tray, Built-
Rite, 1956, color, 11x13",
NM **30.00**
Capt Kangaroo, Mr Green Jeans &
Teddy, jigsaw, Fairchild,
1971, MIB **25.00**
Cisco Kid, frame-tray, Doubleday,
Cisco w/horse, 10x12",
VG+ **25.00**

Cisco Kid, set of 3, Saafield, 1950s, color, 10x11", EX in box .65.00

Daktari, jigsaw, Whitman, 1967, 100-pc, EX+ in repaired box **12.00**

Davy Crockett, frame-tray, Jaymar, defending fort, 11x14", EX+ in EX box **35.00**

Deputy Dawg, jigsaw, Fairchild, 1977, NM in NM box **12.00**

Dino, frame-tray, Hanna-Barbera, 8x10", VG in EX box **18.00**

Ducks & Geese, Springbok/Puzzles in Round, '66, 500-pc, 20", EX in box **5.00**

Farrah Faucett, 1977, MIB (sealed) **25.00**

Flintstones, frame-tray, Pebbles on Dino, Whitman, 1963, 11x14", EX+ **20.00**

Frankenstein, jigsaw, Golden, 1990, 200-pc, MIB **6.00**

Gabby Hayes, frame-tray, Milton Bradley, 1950s, 10x14", EX .**17.50**

Gunsmoke, jigsaw, Jr Jigsaw, NM **35.00**

Hopalong Cassidy, jigsaw, Milton Bradley, set of 3, NM in EX box **125.00**

James Bond, Thunderball, jigsaw, MIB, from $30 to **38.00**

Lariat Sam, jigsaw, Fairchild, 1977, EX+ in box **15.00**

Love Bug, frame-tray, M (sealed) **18.00**

Marlin Perkins Wild Kingdom, jigsaw, 1971, MIB (sealed) .**20.00**

Milton the Monster, jigsaw, Whitman, 1967, NMIB .**45.00**

Oliver, jigsaw, Jaymar, 1968, 100-pc, NM in EX+ box **25.00**

Raggedy Ann & Andy, frame-tray, Milton Bradley, 1955, EX+ **18.00**

Howdy Doody Puzzles, Milton Bradley, 1950s, copyright by Kagran Corporation, boxed set of 3, each 9x12", NM, from $50.00 to $75.00. (Photo courtesy June Moon)

Range Rider, frame-tray, Gabriel, 1955, set of 4, 10x12", VG+ **30.00**

Roger Ramjet, frame-tray, 1966, 18", EX, from $20 to **30.00**

Roy Rogers, frame-tray, Whitman, 1950s, Roy w/Dale & Bullet, NM **40.00**

Roy Rogers, frame-tray, 1950s, Roy at saddle, VG **15.00**

Santa Claus, frame-tray, Whitman, 1966, 11x14", EX+ **10.00**

Sky Hawks, frame-tray, Whitman, 1970, EX+ **8.00**

Smokey Bear, frame-tray, Whitman, 1969, EX+ **15.00**

Superman, jigsaw, Whitman, 1965, 150-pc, EX+ **25.00**

Welcome Back Kotter, frame-tray, Whitman, 1977, MIP, sealed **12.50**

Zorro, jigsaw, Garcia & Diego, MIB **55.00**

Racing Collectibles

The Indianapolis 500 race has been a popular event since 1911, and the Daytona 500 along with other NASCAR events draw ever increasing crowds — as well as the many vendors that follow them hawking souvenirs. Many fans become ardent about following their favorite driver and want items such as clothing, dolls, books, postcards, programs, yearbooks, etc. Some drivers own their own copyright and manufacturing rights which limits the number and type of items that might otherwise be found. Our advisors, Jim and Nancy Schaut, are listed in the Directory under Arizona.

Ashtray, Indianapolis 500 Speedway, white china w/gold ..**20.00**
Belt buckle, Car Craft Street Machine Nationals, 1981 .**30.00**
Bobbin' head doll, in red & white car, Indianapolis 500 on car, M **500.00**
Bobbin' head doll, Indianapolis 500 in gold on front of blue shirt, M **300.00**
Book, American Automobile Racing, Bochrock, soft back **25.00**
Book, Andretti, Bill Libby, Tempo paperback, 1970 ....**15.00**
Book, King Richard, The Richard Petty Story, Libby & Petty, w/jacket **20.00**
Decanter, Al Unser, Johnny Lightning, blue racer w/gold, #2, M **75.00**
Decanter, Mario Andretti, red racer, Old Mr Boston #9, M **50.00**
Flyer, NASCAR Orange Show Speedway Racing News, CA, 1-sheet, 1967 ....**5.00**
Folder, Indianapolis 500, 1965 Qualifying, GC Murphy Special #67 ....**15.00**
Glass, Altamonte (CA) Raceway, checkered flags **5.00**
Handout, Grumpy's Toy X, Vega, color, 1973 ....**10.00**
Hatpin, Garlits/Kendal Rear Engine Dragster **25.00**

Coin bank, Dale Earnhardt, NASCAR limited edition, 1:24 scale, diecast metal, 8", MIB, $25.00.

Hatpin, Quartermidgets of America, red, white & blue 8.00

Magazine, Drag Racing, February, 1964 ....10.00

Magazine, Hot Rod, any single edition from 1950-1970 in EX condition 5.00

Magazine, Popular Hot Rodding, January, 1963-67, ea 3.00

Magazine, Sports Illustrated, Indianapolis 500/Bob Sweikert cover, NM 30.00

Mug, Indianapolis 500, frosted glass, wooden handle, Bill Vukovich 40.00

Newsletter, IMCA, Off the Cuff, National Speedways Racing Notes, 1958 ....10.00

Newsletter, Quartermilestones, current issue 3.50

Newspaper, Motorsport News, 1967 ....5.00

Patch, Hang Ten Funny Car, OCR 500, Orange County, CA .3.00

Penknife, brass, embossed open racing car #7, 1920s 65.00

Pennant, Indianapolis Motor Speedway, white letters on blue, 1940s, M 250.00

Pennant, Indianapolis 500, colorful, dated 1984, M 10.00

Pillow sham, Souvenir of Indianapolis Speedway, race scene on silk 30.00

Pin, NHRA membership; red, white & blue, 1990 ....8.00

Pin, Top Eliminator, US Nationals, no date 5.00

Pin-back button, Lake Mead Gold Cup, 1960 ....5.00

Pit pass, Altoona Speedway, May 27, 1939 ....20.00

Pit pass, SCCA, Road Atlanta, 1970 ....10.00

Pit pass, USAC, 7th Annual CA 500, w/pin-back button, 1976 .10.00

Postcard, Glidden Tour, Halladay Press car, Streator Motor Cars, 1910 ....10.00

Postcard, Indianapolis 500, Dallenback (signed) & #6 car, 5x7" 15.00

Postcard, NASCAR, #21 Purolator 1973 (?) Mercury driven by D Pearson 10.00

Postcard foldout, Iowa State Fair souvenir, shows cycles racing, 1929 ....5.00

Press pass, Altoona Speedway, dated June 11, 1938 .....20.00

Press release, Don Garlits, 1980, supplement 5.00

Program, Atlanta Drag Strip Association, 1964 National Fuel & Gas Drag Race .25.00

Program, Clear Lake Spectacular, hydroplanes, 1983, VG ...5.00

Program, Indianapolis 500, 1932, EX 150.00

Program, Indianapolis 500, 1980s, ea 10.00

Program, Internationale ADAC-Flugplazrennen Munchen-Neubiberg, 1974 ....20.00

Program, Lake Tahoe World Championship Regatta, hydroplanes, 1965, M ...10.00

Program, Midwinter Open Sprint Car Midget Championships, 1983 ....5.00

Program, NASCAR Spring Sizzler, Stafford Motor Speedway, 1976 ....10.00

Program, NASCAR Winston Racing Series, Motordrome Speedway, PA, 1992 ......3.00

Program, NASCAR Winston Western 500, Riverside, 1981 ....6.00

Soda bottle, Richard Petty, a Carolina Legend, 33 Years of Stock Car Racing, Pepsi, 12-oz, common, M, $12.00.

Program, SCCA, Long Beach Grand Prix, 1978 ....**10.00**

Program, SCCA, Watkins Glen, shows drivers, 1972 ......**15.00**

Program, Thompson Speedways, NESMRA Challenge Cup Classic, 1971 ....**10.00**

Program, 3rd Annual LA Times 500, Grand National Stock Car Race, 1976 ....**10.00**

Program, 5th Annual National Championship Drag Races, Detroit, 1959 ....**50.00**

Publication, SCCA Haybale, Jim Clark article, 1963 edition **15.00**

Rulebook, AHRA, 1970, Cobra Torino on back cover **10.00**

Rulebook, NASCAR, Super Stocks & Figure Eights, Englewood CO, 1970 ....**10.00**

Seat cushion, Indianapolis 500 Speedway, 1970s car, black & white check **25.00**

Ticket, Indianapolis 500, AJ Foyt & car, 1965 ....**25.00**

Tie bar, AMA Gypsy Tour, brass, AMA logo, dated 1963 ..**25.00**

Trophy, Beeline Dragway, early 1960s class winner trophy **25.00**

Tumbler, Indianapolis 500, Indy logo, winners through 1967, M **20.00**

Yearbook, 1981 Indy Car World Series, 144-page **10.00**

Radios

Novelty radios are those that carry an advertising message or are shaped like a product bottle, can, or carton; others may be modeled after the likeness of a well-known cartoon character. It's sometimes hard to recognize the fact that they're actually radios. To learn more, we recommend *Collector's Guide to Novelty Radios* by Marty Bunis and Robert F. Breed (Collector Books).

Transistor radios are also popular. First introduced in 1954, many feature space-age names and futuristic designs. Prices here are for complete, undamaged examples in at least very good condition. All are battery operated and AM unless noted otherwise. For further information, we recommend *Collector's Guide to Transistor*

Raid Bug, digital clock and AM/FM radio, S.C. Johnson & Sons Inc., rare, 7x7", M, $225.00. (Photo courtesy Marty and Sue Bunis)

Radios by Marty and Sue Bunis (Collector Books). If you have vintage radios you need to evaluate, see *Collector's Guide to Antique Radios* (Bunis, Collector Books).

Novelty

AMF Bowling Pin, NM **85.00**

Big Bird, 2-dimensional figure, NM **15.00**

Bugs Bunny w/Carrot, working, EX **25.00**

Campbell's Tomato Soup Can, NM, from $35 to **50.00**

Coca-Cola Bottle, MIB (sealed) .**45.00**

F-1 Racer, MIB **25.00**

Fudgie Wudgie, 1970s, chocolate ice cream bar, MIB **75.00**

Gumby, Lewco, 1970s, NM .**150.00**

Hamburger Helper, hand figural, MIB **50.00**

Heinz Ketchup Bottle, NM ..**50.00**

Hockey Puck, Flyer, MIB **40.00**

Joe Cool Wet Tunes, China, 1992, MIB **30.00**

Lil' Sprout, M **50.00**

Male Chauvinist Pig, M **60.00**

McDonald's French Fries, 1977, no battery cover, working, EX **50.00**

Mork From Ork Eggship, 1978, working, EX+ **50.00**

Oscar the Grouch, portable AM, Oscar in trash can, M (EX box) **42.00**

Planters Cocktail Nuts Can, MIB **55.00**

Pound Puppy, unused, MIB .**15.00**

Raggedy Ann & Andy, EX+..**22.50**

Shell Super X-Motor Oil Can, NM **45.00**

Skittles, circular, M **75.00**

Snoopy, Determined #351, sitting on strap, black & white, EX **20.00**

Snoopy on Doghouse, Determined #354, 1970s, 7", EX **40.00**
Spice Rack, EX **40.00**
Starsky & Hutch Car, CB radio, w/booklet, MIB **50.00**
Sunoco Gas Pump, yellow & blue, 4", EX **25.00**
Turtle, gold-tone metal, working, EX **65.00**
Vending machine form, Westinghouse Cold Drinks, EX in box ..**145.00**

Transistor

Admiral, 228, horizontal, turquoise, 6 transistors, AM, battery ...**35.00**
Admiral, 4P24, horizontal, tan, 4 transistors, AM, 1957 ...**35.00**
Airline, GEN-1214A, vertical, 8 transistors, AM, 1961, battery **30.00**

Bulova, #250, plastic, AM, battery operated, 5x3x1¼", EX/NM, $350.00. (Photo courtesy Marty and Sue Bunis)

Ambassador, A-880, horizontal, plastic, 8 transistors, AM, battery **25.00**
Arvin, 60R58, tan cowhide, 7 transistors, leather handle, AM, battery **20.00**
Channel Master, 6474, horizontal, 6 transistors, AM, 1965, battery **10.00**
Columbia, C-605, horizontal, leather, 5 transistors, AM, 1962, battery **15.00**
Continental, TR-751, vertical, 7 transistors, AM/SW, 1961, battery **30.00**
Crown, TR-820, horizontal, 4 transistors, AM, 1959, battery **40.00**
Eico, RA-6, horizontal, leather, 6 transistors, AM, 1961, battery **15.00**
Elgin, R-1800, vertical/clock radio, 10 transistors, AM, 1964, AC **10.00**
Emerson, 842, horizontal, leather, 6 transistors, AM, 1956, battery **35.00**
Emerson, 880, vertical, 8 transistors, AM, 1962, battery .**40.00**
GE, P-9001A, horizontal, 7 transistors, AM, 1962, battery **25.00**
GE, P725B, horizontal, plastic, 6 transistors, AM, 1958, battery **25.00**
Global, GR-823, horizontal, plastic, 8 transistor, AM/SW, battery **25.00**
Hitachi, TH-812R, horizontal, leather, 8 transistors, AM, 1964 ....**15.00**
JC Penney, 628, horizontal, 7 transistors, AM, 1962, battery **25.00**
Lafayette, FS-235, vertical, 6 transistors, AM, 1963, battery ...**35.00**

Linmark, T-80, vertical, 8 transistors, AM, 1960, battery .35.00

Lloyd's, TR-10L, horizontal, leather, 10 transistors, AM, 1964 ....10.00

Magnavox, AM-61, vertical, plastic, 6 transistors, AM, 1965, battery 20.00

Midland, 10-410, horizontal, leather, 10 transistors, AM, 1964 ....10.00

MMA, 8TP-416, vertical, 6 transistors, AM, 1963, battery .15.00

Motorola, 6X31N, horizontal, metal case, AM, 1957, battery 50.00

Norelco, L3X19T/97, horizontal, 7 transistors, AM/2 SW, 1964, battery 25.00

Olympic, 766, vertical, leather, 6 transistors, AM, 1959, battery 30.00

Panasonic, R-102, vertical, 6 transistors, AM, 1964, battery ...15.00

Philco, NT-601BK, horizontal, 6 transistors, AM, 1965, battery 15.00

RCA, 1-RG-41, horizontal, 6 transistors, AM, 1963, battery ..20.00

RCA, 3RG14, vertical, 6 transistors, AM, 1962, battery .20.00

Realtone, TR-806B, horizontal, 6 transistors, AM, 1963, battery 40.00

Regency, TR-22, horizontal, leather, 4 transistors, AM, 1959, battery 35.00

Sharp, BP-460, horizontal, 6 transistors, AM, 1963, battery ...15.00

Silvertone, 1217-700, horizontal, leather, 7 transistors, AM, 1961 ....20.00

Sony, 2R-30m vertical, plastic, 7 transistors, AM, battery .25.00

Star-Lite, FM-900, horizontal, 9 transistors, AM/FM, 1965, battery 15.00

Toshiba, 6P-10, horizontal, 6 transistors, AM, 1963, battery 25.00

Truetone, DC3084A, horizontal, leather, 6 transistors, AM, 1960 ....20.00

Vesper, G1110, horizontal, 9 transistors, AM/FM, 1963, battery 15.00

Ramp Walkers

Ramp walkers date back to at least 1873 when Ives produced a cast-iron elephant walker. Wood and composite ramp walkers were made in Czechoslovakia and the USA from the 1920s through the 1940s. The most common were made by John Wilson of Watsontown, Pennsylvania. These sold worldwide and became known as 'Wilson Walkies.' Most are two-legged and stand approximately 4½" tall.

Plastic ramp walkers were manufactured primarily by the Louis Marx Co. from the 1950s through the early 1960s. The majority were produced in Hong Kong, but some were made in the USA and sold under the Marx logo or by the Charmore Co., a subsidiary of Marx.

The three common sizes are: 1) small premiums about 1½" x 2"; 2) the more common medium size, 2¾" x 3"; and 3) large, approximately 4" x 5". Most of the smaller walkers were unpainted, while the medium and large sizes were hand or spray painted. Several of the walking types were sold with wooden or colorful tin lithographed ramps.

For more extensive listings and further information, see *Schroeder's Collectible Toys, Antique to Modern* (Collector Books.) Randy Welch is our advisor for ramp walkers; he is listed in the Directory under Maryland.

Hap and Hop soldiers, Marx, light wear, 2¾", $20.00.

Astro, Hanna-Barbera, Marx .**150.00**
Cow, plastic, w/metal legs, sm .**15.00**
Dog, Czechoslovakian **20.00**
Donald Duck, pulling nephews in wagon, Marx **35.00**
Eskimo, Wilson **75.00**
Goofy Grape, Funny Face Kool-Aid, w/plastic coin weight **60.00**
Horse, plastic, lg **30.00**
Jiminy Crickett, w/cello, Marx .**30.00**
Lion w/Clown, Marx **25.00**
Mickey Mouse, pushing lawn roller, Marx **35.00**
Penguin, Wilson **25.00**
Pluto, all plastic, Marx **20.00**
Popeye & Wimpy, plastic, heads on springs, lg **65.00**

Sailor, Wilson **30.00**
Santa, w/open gold sack, Marx .**45.00**
Wimpy, Wilson **175.00**

Records

Records that made it to the 'Top Ten' in their day are not always the records that are prized the highest by today's collectors, though they treasure those which best represent specific types of music: jazz, rhythm and blues, country and western, rock 'n roll, etc. Many search for those cut very early in the career of artists who later became superstars, records cut on rare or interesting labels, or those aimed at ethnic groups. A fast-growing area of related interest is picture sleeves for 45s. These are often worth more than the record itself, especially if they feature superstars from the '50s or early '60s.

Condition is very important. Record collectors tend to be very critical, so learn to watch for loss of gloss; holes, labels, or writing on the label; warping; and scratches. Unless otherwise noted, values are for records in like-new condition — showing little sign of wear, with a playing surface that retains much of its original shine, and having only a minimal amount of surface noise. To be collectible, a sleeve should have no tape, stickers, tears, or obvious damage.

Refer to *The American Premium Record Guide* by Les Docks for more information on extended play and 78 rpm records.

Extended Play

Baker, Chet; The Wind/Trickleydidlier, Columbia 1909, VG+ **15.00**

Boone, Pat; Ain't That a Shame, Dot 1049, G **8.00**

Christy, June; Interlude/Give Me the Simple Life, Capitol 902, VG+ **15.00**

Cole, Nat King; Cachito/Maria Elena, Capitol #1031, NM **20.00**

Davis, Jackie; Irresistable You/Where in the..., Capitol 815, VG ..**10.00**

Day, Doris; Ten Cents a Dance/At Sundown, Columbia 2090, VG **10.00**

Ellington, Duke & Orchestra; Jazz Lips/Merry-Go-Round, Columbia 1, VG **10.00**

Everly Brothers, So Sad/You Thrill Me, Warner Brothers 1381, VG **10.00**

Garland, Judy; Chicago/Swanee, Capitol 1569, NM **20.00**

Griffin, Ken; Pretend/When You Wore a Tulip, Columbia 1778, VG **10.00**

Lewis, John; Cabin in the Sky/In Other Words, Columbia 8871, VG **10.00**

Mathis, Johnny; Johnny's Mood Vol III, Columbia 15263, NM .**20.00**

Pied Pipers, Dream/Cuddle Up..., Capitol 586, NM **20.00**

Sinatra, Frank; Lonesome Road/You'd Be So Nice..., Capitol 803, NM ..**20.00**

Smith, Keely; Sweet & Lovely/East of the Sun, Capitol 1073, VG .**10.00**

Starr, Kay; Goin' to Chicago Blues/Indiana, Capitol 1254, VG **10.00**

Young, Faron; If You Ain't Lovin'/Sweet Dreams, Capitol 1096, NM **20.00**

Children's Records

Alice in Wonderland/Pinocchio, storyteller, VG **3.00**

Baa-Baa Black Sheep, 1976, 45 rpm, EX **8.00**

Ballad of Davy Crockett, 1950s, 45 rpm, EX **20.00**

Bozo at the Circus, 1970, 78 rpm, EX **25.00**

Brady Bunch Phonographic Album, LP **55.00**

Captain Kangaroo, CBS, 1956, 78 rpm, photo sleeve, NM ..**20.00**

Casper the Friendly Ghost, Wonderland, 1965, 33⅓ rpm, EX **10.00**

Curious George Takes a Job, Scholastic, '69, 33⅓ rpm, +booklet, EX+ **10.00**

Daniel Boone, Til Records, 1977, 33⅓ rpm, +black & white poster, NM **15.00**

Dick Tracy, Mercury, 1947, 2 records, unused, EX+ ...**80.00**

Disney Presents Great Composers #1919, 1962, 33⅓ rpm, stereo, M **15.00**

Disney's Little Toot, 1952, 33⅓ rpm, picture sleeve, EX .**10.00**

Donald Duck & His Friends, 45 rpm, 1-sided, in Disneyland mailer **25.00**

Emmet Kelly, Clown & Kids, 1968, soundtrack, M, sealed sleeve **20.00**

Flintstones & Jose Jimenez, 1965, EX **30.00**

Frosty the Snowman, 1951, 45 rpm, EX **12.00**

Green Hornet, 1966, 45 rpm, EX in sleeve **30.00**

Heidi, 1972, 4 songs, 33⅓ rpm, EX in sleeve **4.00**

Hopalong Cassidy, Story of Topper, 45 rpm, G- in G sleeve ..**55.00**

Howdy Doody & You, RCA Little Nipper, 45 rpm, G **5.00**

Jetsons First Family on the Moon, 1977, EX **15.00**

Lone Ranger He Helps the Colonel's Son, Decca, 1951, 4th in series, EX **20.00**

Mickey Mouse Club March, 1955, 45 rpm, EX **25.00**

Mickey Mouse Pledge, G **10.00**

Peter & the Wolf, 1949, 78 rpm, 2 records, EX in EX sleeve .**35.00**

Popeye the Sailor Man, Diplomat Records, 1960, 33⅓ rpm, EX **18.00**

Puff the Magic Dragon, 1983, M in sealed sleeve **8.00**

Quick Draw McGraw & Treasure of Sarah's Mattress, 1951, VG in sleeve **14.00**

Robin Hood Starring Top Cat, 1965, EX **25.00**

Roy Rogers' Thank You God, 45 rpm **22.00**

Ruff & Reddy Friends, 1959, 45 rpm, EX **25.00**

Snow White & 7 Dwarf's Whistle While You..., 1948, picture sleeve, EX **12.00**

Sword in the Stone, 1963, 45 rpm, EX **20.00**

Three Little Kittens, 1960, 45 rpm, EX **8.00**

Three Little Pigs, Peter Pan, 1960s, VG in sleeve **15.00**

Treasure Island Starring Sinbad Jr, EX in sealed sleeve ..**35.00**

Twinkles & His Pals, Little Golden Records, 1961, 78 rpm, NM **39.00**

Woody Woodpecker's Talent Shoe, 1975, EX **8.00**

Zorro, 1958, w/dialogue, soundtrack, VG **15.00**

LP Albums

Acuff, Roy; Teasure of Country Hits, Hickory 147, NM .**40.00**

Berry, Chuck; 20 Greatest Hits, Black Tulip 28005, NM .**12.00**

Brooks, David; Brigadoon, RCA Victor, LSO/1001, stereo, G **8.00**

Cash, Johnny; Folsom Prison Blues, Share 5001, VG+ **10.00**

Channing, Dolly; Hello Dolly, RCA, LS0D1087, stereo, M **10.00**

Chitty-Chitty Bang-Bang, w/picture book, United Artists, SLP108, M **9.00**

Clark, Petula; My Love, Warner Bros 1630, NM **25.00**

Clark, Roy; Heart to Heart, ABC Paramount 123731, NM .**12.00**

Como, Perry; Sentimental Date, Philips 1177, NM **60.00**

Egyptian, Jean Simmons & Victor Mature, Decca, DL9014, G **12.00**

Everly Brothers, A Date With..., Warner Bros 1395, G- **5.00**

Grimes, Tammy; Unsinkable Molly Brown, Cap SW2152, stereo, NM **10.00**

Ink Spots, Ink Spots, Decca 5071, NM **50.00**

Jan & Dean, Golden Hits, Liberty 3248, VG- **20.00**

Jones, Jack; Call Me Irresponsible, Kapp 3328, VG+ **30.00**

Kerr, Deborah/Brenner, Yul; King & I, Capitol, W740, 1956, G **7.00**

Lee, Brenda; That's All, Decca 4326, VG- **10.00**

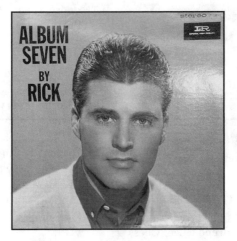

Nelson, Ricky; Album Seven, Imperial IR, Stereo 12082, VG, $25.00.

Lettermen, Lettermen, Capitol 1761, NM **40.00**

Lone Ranger, Tonto & Silver; Don Reid, Decca, DL75125, stereo, M **12.00**

MacLaine, Shirley/Davis Jr, Samson; Sweet Charity, Decca 74502, M **6.00**

Midnight Cowboy, Vaccaro & McGiver, United Artists, UAS3918, VG **9.00**

Miller, Roger; Golden Hits, Smash 67073, NM **40.00**

Orlando, Tony & Dawn; Greatest Hits, Arista 4045, NM ..**12.00**

Porgy & Bess, Tod Duncan & Anne Brown, Decca, DL79024, stereo, M **10.00**

Queen, Nems of the World, Elektra 112, VG **6.00**

Reeves, Del; Struttin' My Stuff, United Artists 6571, NM .**30.00**

Sinatra, Nancy; Boots, Reprise 6202, NM **40.00**

Smothers Brothers, Think Ethnic, Mercury 30777, NM **50.00**

Taylor, D/Laughlin, .T; Trial of Billy Jack, ABC, D853, mono, M **9.00**

Tillotson, Johnny; Tillotson Touch, MGM 4224, NM **40.00**

Williams, Hank; Greatest Hits, MGM 3918, NM **15.00**

Young, Burt/McKeon, Day; Uncle Joe Shannon, United, LA935, stereo, M **7.00**

45 rpms

Ad Libs, Giving Up, Share 104, VG **3.00**

Alpert, Herb; Tiajuana Taxi/Zorba the Greek, A&M 8407, M **3.00**

Anka, Paul; Hello Jim, RCA 47-8195, NM **4.00**

Bachelors, Diane/I Believe, London 59210, M **5.00**

Beach Boys, Do It Again, Capitol 2239, VG **3.00**

Belafonte, Harry; Hold 'Em Joe, RCA 47-0322, VG **3.00**

Anka, Paul; Love Me Warm and Tender/I'd Like To Know, 47-7977, EX, $4.00.

Berry, Chuck; Brenda Lee, Chess 1906, VG- 1.50

Boone, Pat; April Love, Dot 15660, VG 3.00

Bostic, Earl; April in Portugal, King 5564, VG+ 4.00

Bowie, David; Fame/Golden Years, RCA 10938, M 12.50

Brown, James; Don't Be a Drop-Out, King 6056, M 5.70

Campbell, Glen; Gentle on My Mind, Capitol 5939, VG 3.00

Captain & Tennille, Muskrat Love/Can't Stop Dancin', A&M 8603, M 4.50

Castaways, Liar Liar, Lana 151, VG 4.00

Charles, Ray; America the Beautiful/Sunshine, Crossover 985, M 20.00

Charles, Ray; Without Love There Is Nothing, ABC-Paramount 10453, VG 3.00

Chiffons, One Fine Day, Lauri 3179, VG 3.50

Cole, Nat King; Ramblin' Rose, Capitol 4804, VG+ 5.00

Cooke, Sam; Cupid, RCA 47-7883, VG 3.50

Creedence Clearwater Revival, I Put a Spell on You, Fantasy 617, NM 4.00

Crosby, Bing; Teddy Bear's Picnic/ Rudolph..., MCA 27159, M 6.50

Day, Doris; Everybody Loves a Lover, Columbia 4-41195, NM 3.50

Def Leppard, Animal/I Wanna Be..., Mercury 888832, picture sleeve, M 4.50

DeShannon, Jackie; Love Will Find a Way, Imperial 66419, VG 3.00

Domino, Fats; Blueberry Hill, Imperial 1082, VG 3.00

Donovan, Hurdy Gurdy Man, Epic 5-10345, VG 3.00

Dowell, Jim; Wooden Heart, Smash 1708, VG 3.00

Easy Riders, East Virginia/John Henry, Columbia 4-41347, VG+ 3.50

Edwards, Tommy; Love Is All We Need, MGM 12722, VG 3.00

Equals, Baby Come Back, RCA 47-9583, VG- 1.50

Everly Brothers, Brand New Heartache/Like Strangers, Barnaby 508, M 3.50

Francis, Connie; Follow the Boys, MGM K13127, VG+ 3.50

Francis, Connie; Where the Boys Are, MGM K19271, VG 4.50

Gaylord, Ronnie; Don't You Forget About Me, Mercury 70425, VG+ 4.00

Gaylords, Molly-O, Mercury 70778, VG 3.50

Gentrys, Keep On Dancing, MGM K13379, VG 3.50

Haley, Bill; Candy Kisses, Warner Bros 5145, VG **5.00**

Herman's Hermits, Can't You Hear My Heartbeat, MGM K 13310, VG- **1.50**

Jackson, Stonewall; Waterloo, Columbia 4-41393, VG+ ..**4.00**

James, Tommy; Hanky Panky, Roule 4686, VG+ **3.50**

King, Ben E; So Much Love, ATCO 6413, NM **4.00**

Lennon, John; Happy Xmas/Listen the Snow..., Capitol 1842, M **12.50**

Lettermen, Never My Love, Capitol 2132, NM **4.00**

Lewis, Jerry Lee; Break-Up, Sun 303, VG **6.00**

Martin, Dean; Who's Sorry Now, Capitol F1458, NM **4.50**

Mathis, Johnny; Chances Are, Columbia 4-40993, NM ..**4.00**

Miller, Roger; Dang Me, Smash 1881, VG+ **3.00**

Nelson, Ricky; Hello Mary Lou, Imperial X5741, VG **4.00**

Nelson, Sandy; Lion in Winter, Imperial 66350, NM **4.00**

Ocean, Billy; Love Zone, Arista 9510, picture sleeve, M ...**2.50**

Page, Patti; Say Wonderful Things, Columbia 4-42791, VG+ **4.00**

Paul & Paula, First Quarrel, Phillips 40114, VG+ **4.00**

Peter, Paul & Mary; Leaving on a Jet Plane, Warner Bros 1340, VG **3.00**

Prado, Perez; Patricia/Twist, RCA 47-8006, VG **3.50**

Reese, Della; Everyday, RCA 47-7750, NM **3.75**

Rivieras, California Sun, Lana 136, VG+ **5.00**

Ronettes, You Came You Saw..., A&M 1040, NM **4.00**

Royaltones, Seesaw, Jubilee 5362, VG **3.50**

Sherman, Bobby; Julie Do Ya Love Me, Metro 194, VG **2.50**

Sherman, Bobby; Waiting at the Bus Stop, Metro 222, VG **3.00**

South, Joe; Walk a Mile in My Shoes, Capitol 2704, NM .**4.00**

Stevens, Dodie; No, Dot 16103, VG **3.00**

Sting, We'll Be Together, A&M 2983, picture sleeve, M ...**3.50**

Street People, Jennifer Tomkins, Music 1365, VG **3.00**

Supremes, I Hear a Symphony, Motown 1083, NM **4.00**

Supremes, The Happening, Motown 1107, VG **3.00**

Thomas, BJ; I Can't Help It, Sceptor 12194, NM **3.50**

Thomas, Cliff; Leave It to Me, Sun 63 RI, NM **3.00**

Twitty, Conway; I'm Used To Losing You, MCA 40857, NM **3.00**

Vinton, Bobby; Roses Are Red, Epic 5-9509, NM **3.75**

Warwick, Dee Dee; I Want To Be w/You, Mercury 72584, VG .**3.00**

Wilder Brothers, Old Chimney, Wing 90039, VG+ **3.50**

Williams, Dick; Hillbilly Rock, RCA 47-6599, VG+ **3.50**

Wilson, J Frank; Last Kiss, Virgo 6001, NM **3.00**

78 rpms

Autry, Gene; Back in the Saddle Again, Okeh 05080, G+ .**15.00**

Autry, Gene; South of the Border, Columbia 30242, VG **30.00**

Autry, Gene; Take Me Back to My Boots & Saddle, Vocalion 4172, VG- 25.00

Bill Haley & Comets, Rock Around the Clock, Decca 29124, M 10.00

Brooks, Hadda; Swingin the Boogie, Modern Music 101, G+ 5.00

Como, Perry; Juke Box Baby, RCA 6427, VG- 5.00

Crothers, Scat Man; Hound Dog, Tops 290, G 5.00

Danny & the Jrs, At the Hop, ABC Paramount 9871, M 10.00

Hill, David; Jellybean, Aladdin 3354, VG+ 15.00

Ink Spots, The Gypsy, Decca 18817, VG- 10.00

James, Etta; W-O-M-A-N, Modern 972, NM 25.00

Jones, Grandpa; It's Raining Here This Morning, King 502, VG+ 25.00

Lovett Sisters, Until I Lost You, Imperial 8233, VG+ 10.00

Magic Stars, Stand by Me, Phoenix 009, VG 15.00

Moody, James; Over the Rainbow, Prestige 896, NM 10.00

Moore, Martha; Yo Yo Yo, Deluxe 6038, NM 30.00

Murray, Billy; That's Why I Never Married, Victor 16851, VG- 10.00

Page, Patti; I Went to Your Wedding; Mercury 5800, G- 3.00

Ramblers, She Had It Taken, Top Hat 1014, VG- 10.00

Reed, Lula; Watch Dog, King 4688, VG- 10.00

Ritter, Tex; Jealous Heart, Capitol 179, G- 5.00

Rogers, Roy; I'll Be Honest w/You, Decca 6016, G+ 10.00

Shore, Dinah; Lavender Blue, Columbia 38299, G+ 6.00

Travis, Merle; Information Please, Capitol 40072, VG- 5.00

Wilson, Jackie; Lonely Teardrops, Brunswick 55105, M 10.00

Red Wing

Taking their name from the location in Minnesota where they located in the late 1870s, the Red Wing Company produced a variety of wares, all of which are today considered noteworthy by pottery and dinnerware collectors. Their early stoneware lines, Cherry Band and Sponge Band (Gray Line), are especially valuable and often fetch prices of several hundred dollars on today's market. Production of dinnerware began in the '30s and continued until the pottery closed in 1967. Some of their more popular lines — all of which were hand painted — were Bob White, Lexington, Tampico, Normandie, Capistrano, and Random Harvest. Commercial artware was also produced. Perhaps the ware most easily associated with Red Wing is their Brushware line, unique in its appearance and decoration. Cattails, rushes, florals, and similar nature subjects are 'carved' in relief on a stoneware-type body with a matt green wash its only finish.

We have listed only their very collectible dinnerware lines here; for more information, we recommend *Red Wing Art Pottery, 1920s – 1960s*, by B.L. Dollen. To learn about their stoneware production, refer to *Red Wing Stoneware, An Identification and Value Guide,* and *Red Wing Collectibles,* both by Dan and Gail de Pasquale and Larry Peterson. All are published by Collector Books. See also Clubs and Newsletters.

Dinnerware

Bob White, butter dish, ¼-lb .**75.00**
Bob White, plate, 10½" **12.50**
Bob White, sugar bowl, w/lid .**28.00**
Bob White, teapot **100.00**
Capistrano, bowl, berry; 5½" .**8.00**
Capistrano, plate, 6½" **5.00**
Capistrano, platter, 15" **15.00**
Country Garden, gravy boat .**22.00**
Country Garden, plate, 10½" .**15.00**
Country Garden, plate, 8" ...**10.00**
Frontenac, butter dish **16.50**
Frontenac, trivet **50.00**
Lexington Rose, pitcher, water .**65.00**
Lotus, cup & saucer **10.00**
Lotus, plate, 7½" **7.00**

Lute Song, casserole **35.00**
Lute Song, platter, 13" **20.00**
Lute Song, teapot **65.00**
Magnolia, bowl, fruit; 5¼" **5.00**
Magnolia, rim soup **15.00**
Random Harvest, coffeepot, tall .**45.00**
Random Harvest, plate, 10" .**12.50**
Round-Up, bowl, divided veg-
    etable **95.00**
Round-Up, creamer **50.00**
Round-Up, cruets, pr **275.00**
Round-Up, plate, 10½" **35.00**
Round-Up, plate, 7½" **20.00**
Smart Set, bread tray **100.00**
Smart Set, cup & saucer **38.00**
Smart Set, pitcher, water; 14" .**125.00**
Smart Set, plate, 10" **35.00**
Tampico, cup & saucer **14.00**
Tampico, gravy boat, w/attached
    underplate **50.00**
Tampico, platter, 13¼" **20.00**
Town & Country, bowl, 5" ...**15.00**
Town & Country, cup & saucer,
    forest green w/white interi-
    or **27.50**
Town & Country, shaker, lg .**25.00**

Lotus, plate with metal handle, $15.00.

Town & Country, sugar bowl, bronze, w/lid 65.00
Village Green, butter dish, w/lid 25.00
Village Green, salt and pepper shakers, pr 20.00
Village Green, warmer 18.00

Rock 'n Roll

Concert posters, tour books, magazines, sheet music, and other items featuring rock 'n roll stars from the '50s up to the present are today being sought out by collectors who appreciate this type of music and like having these mementos of their favorite preformers around to enjoy. Our advisor for this category is Bojo (Bob Guttuso); he is listed in the Directory under Pennsylvania. See also Beatles; Elvis Presley; Paperback Books; Records.

Bill Haley and the Comets, souvenir glass from concert at Monroe College, 1948, 4½', from $20.00 to $25.00.

Aerosmith, pen, promo for Pump, X-rated, 1990-91 World Tour 15.00
Alice Cooper, cup, clear plastic, promo for Trash, red, 4" ..9.00
Andy Gibb, flip book, promo for Shadow Dancin', 3x3¾" .24.00
Andy Gibb, jigsaw puzzle, 200-pc, sealed, 11x17" 12.00
Bee Gees, jigsaw puzzle, 1979, 11x17", M (sealed) 25.00
Bee Gees, puffy stickers, 4 styles, 6 ea, 1979, per set 5.00
Black Sabbath, frisbee, promo for the Tour of the Black Mass, 1979 ....20.00
Bob Seger, backstage pass, unused, w/Thunderbirds, 1986 ....4.00
Cheap Trick, bowtie, promo, printed white on black 28.00
Fleetwood Mac, backstage pass, 'Tusk' in 1980 ....5.00
Freddy & the Dreamers, button, 'I Love...,' black, red & white, 3½" 18.00
Gregg Allman, slingshot, heavy duty, promo for I'm No Angel 35.00
Humble Pie, flip book, promo for Roach Card, 1x4" 24.00
KISS, backstage pass, laminated, Japan Tour 15.00
KISS, comb, many colors to choose from, Australian, ea 9.00
KISS, guitar Pick, Gene Simmons, white w/black autograph & logo 15.00
KISS, jacket, colorful flame design, w/photos & logo, child size 90.00
KISS, necklace, Peter Criss, autographed style in gold, original package, 78" 32.00

KISS, necklace, 3-D logo in silver or gold finish, ea **10.00**
KISS, Poster Put-ons, sealed stickons, tour pictures, lg **7.00**
KISS, puzzle, Destroyer, complete, w/box **30.00**
Lita Ford, wristband, black leather, studded w/metal 'Lita,' promo **15.00**
Michael Jackson, slipper socks, size 8, 1984 ....**19.00**
Monkees, backstage pass, 20th Anniversary Tour **7.00**
Monkees, button, 'I'm an Official...Fan,' blue & white (bootleg) **4.00**
Monkees, flip books, ea **14.00**
Monkees, Mickey, finger puppet, brown Sears box **36.00**
Monkees, Monkee Mobile, Corgi, diecast, w/all figures, 5" .**190.00**
Monkees, Monkee Mobile, Husky, diecast w/all figures, 3" .**50.00**
Monkees, sunglasses, w/original hang tag **44.00**
Partridge Family, paperback #5, Terror by Night, w/cover, 1971 ....**5.00**
Poison, first aid kit, pill form, w/band-aids, Unskinny Bop promo **24.00**
Police, puffy stickers, 1 style, 5 stickers **5.00**
Queen, calling card, foreign, credit card size **20.00**
Rolling Stones, key chain 3-D viewer, Voodoo Lounge, 5 different, ea **10.00**
Rolling Stones, 3-D LP flasher, Satanic Majesty's Request, 8" square **18.00**
Van Halen, puffy stickers, w/David Lee Roth, 3 styles, 5-7 per sheet **5.00**

New Kids on the Block, doll (Donnie), Hasbro, 1991, 12", MIB, $40.00.

Warrant, mug, promo for Cherry Pie, ceramic **14.00**

Rooster and Roses

Since our last edition, this line of dinnerware seemed to appear out of the blue — suddenly there it was, by the tablesfull at the flea markets, by the *boothfull* at the antique malls. It's Rooster and Roses, a quaint and provincial line of dinnerware made in Japan from the '40s and '50s. The rooster has a yellow breast with black crosshatching, a brown head, and a red crest and waddle. There are full-blown roses, and the borders are yellow with groups of brown diagonals.

Several companies seem to have made the line, which is very extensive. In the short time we've been recording shapes, we've found more than seventy-five.

Our advisor for this category is Jacki Elliott; she is listed in the Directory under California.

Wall Pocket, marked UCAGCO, 7", $45.00.

Ashtray, round or square, from $15 to **20.00**
Biscuit jar, wicker handle, from $50 to **65.00**
Bowl, 8" **25.00**
Butter dish, ¼-lb, from $20 to .**25.00**
Candy dish, leaf handle, from $15 to **20.00**
Chamberstick, saucer base, ring handle, from $20 to **25.00**
Creamer & sugar bowl, w/lid, lg **25.00**
Cruets, cojoined w/twisted necks, sm **20.00**

Cup & saucer, from $15 to ..**25.00**
Flowerpot, buttress handles, 5", from $35 to **45.00**
Jam jar, attached underplate, from $25 to **35.00**
Measuring cup set, 4 pcs w/matching ceramic rack, from $35 to **45.00**
Mug, from $25 to **30.00**
Napkin holder, from $30 to .**40.00**
Pitcher, bulbous, 5", from $18 to **22.00**
Plate, dinner; from $25 to ...**35.00**
Recipe box, from $20 to **25.00**
Salt & pepper shakers, applied rose, square, pr **23.00**
Salt box, wooden lid, from $45 to **55.00**
Stacking tea set, teapot, creamer & sugar bowl, from $70 to ..**80.00**
Teapot, from $55 to **65.00**
Wall pocket **45.00**

Roselane Sparklers

A line of small figures with a soft shaded finish and luminous jewel eyes was produced during the late 1950s by the Roselane Pottery Company who operated in Pasadena, California, from the late 1930s until possibly the 1970s. The line was a huge success. Twenty-nine different models were made, including elephants, burrows, raccoons, fawns, dogs, cats, and fish. Not all pieces are marked, but some carry an incised 'Roselane Pasadena, Calif.,' or 'Calif. U.S.A'; others may have a paper label. Our advisor for this category, Lee Garmon, is listed in the Directory under Illinois.

Owl, modern, black w/gold trim, lg plastic eyes, 1960-70s, 5¼" .**18.00**
Siamese cat, 7½" **15.00**
Whippet dog, sitting, 7½" **14.00**

Rosemeade

Novelty items made by the Wapheton Pottery Company of North Dakota from 1941 to 1960 are beginning to attract collectors of American pottery. Though smaller items (salt and pepper shakers, figurines, trays, etc.) are readily found, the larger examples are scarce and can be very expensive. The name of the novelty ware, 'Rosemeade,' is indicated on the paper labels (many of which are still intact) or by the ink stamp.

For more information refer to *Collector's Encyclopedia of the Dakota Potteries* by Darlene Hurst Dommel (Collector Books). Our advisor for this category, Bryce L. Farnsworth, is listed in the Directory under North Dakota.

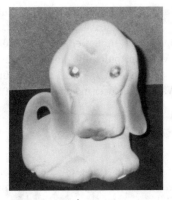

Hound dog, 4", $12.00. (Photo courtesy Lee Garmon)

Angelfish, 4½" **14.00**
Basset hound, 3¼x1¼" **12.00**
Boy w/dog, 5½" **30.00**
Deer, standing, unmarked, 5½", from $10 to **14.00**
Dog, 2", from $6 to **8.00**
Elephant, sparkler eyes & headpiece, 6", from $15 to **20.00**
Girl w/bouquet, in-mold mark, 5" **30.00**
Kitten, sitting, 1¾" **7.00**
Owl, baby; 2¼" **12.00**

Rosemeade, Hors d'oeuvre tray, with pheasant, $140.00.

Ashtray, state shape, Vermont .**75.00**
Ashtray/figurine, turkey **110.00**
Bank, Jamestown buffalo ..**320.00**
Bell, elephant **200.00**
Bookends, wolfhounds, pr .**235.00**
Creamer & sugar bowl, duck figu-
    rals, white **90.00**
Creamer & sugar bowl, turkey fig-
    urals **180.00**
Figurine, mountain goat, lg .**320.00**
Figurine, pheasant rooster, tail
    up, on base, 3¾" **95.00**
Figurine, seal, black, set of 3 ..**45.00**
Pin, Prairie Rose **500.00**
Pitcher, ball shape, sm **25.00**
Salt & pepper shakers, bull & cow,
    tan, pr **240.00**
Salt & pepper shakers, Northern
    Pike, pr **270.00**
Salt & pepper shakers, oxen, red,
    pr **130.00**
Salt & pepper shakers, pheasant
    roosters, striding, pr ...**100.00**
Salt & pepper shakers, quail, pr .**80.00**
Salt & pepper shakers, Scottie dog
    heads, pr **50.00**
Salt & pepper shakers, skunks,
    pr **50.00**

Salt & pepper shakers, tulips, pink
    w/green leaves, 2¼", pr .**45.00**
Spoon rest, sunflower shape .**180.00**
TV lamp, palomino horse against
    foliage **500.00**
Wall pocket, deer in foliage, 5" .**60.00**

Royal China

Several lines of the dinnerware made by Royal China
(Sebring, Ohio) are very collectible, especially their Currier
and Ives pattern, decorated with
scenes of early American life in
blue on a white background, and
Blue Willow. Since the same
blanks were used for all lines, they
will all be the same size. Currier
and Ives as well as the Willow pattern was made in both blue and
pink. (Pink Willow is not as easy to
find as the blue nor as collectible.)
For further information we recommend our advisor, BA Wellman,
listed in the Directory under
Massachusetts.

**Royal China, Blue Willow, teapot, $65.00. (Photo courtesy
Mary Frank Gaston)**

Blue Willow

Ashtray, 5½" **12.00**
Bowl, cereal; 6¼" **12.00**
Butter dish, ¼-lb **35.00**
Casserole **30.00**
Creamer **6.00**
Plate, cake; w/handles, 10½" ..**20.00**
Platter, 13" **28.00**
Teapot **65.00**

Colonial Homestead

Bowl, fruit nappy; 5½" **3.00**
Bowl, soup; 8½" **7.50**
Cup & saucer **5.00**
Gravy boat **12.00**
Plate, salad; rare, 7¼" **6.00**
Platter, oval, 13" **18.00**

Currier and Ives

Ashtray, 5½" **13.00**
Bowl, cereal; 6¼" **10.00**
Bowl, vegetable; 10" **25.00**
Bowl, vegetable; 9" **20.00**
Butter dish, Fashionable **35.00**

Currier and Ives, calendar plate, 1973, 10", $15.00.

Casserole, tab handles **150.00**

Creamer, angle handle **6.00**
Creamer & sugar bowl, handled .**20.00**
Cup & saucer **5.00**
Gravy boat **15.00**
Lamp, candle; w/globe **75.00**
Pie plate, 10" **25.00**
Plate, bread & butter; 6¼" **3.50**
Plate, chop; marked, 11" & 12¼",
    ea **25.00**
Plate, dinner; 10" **6.00**
Plate, luncheon; 9" **13.00**
Platter, oval, 13" **30.00**
Teapot **125.00**
Tray, for gravy boat, 7¼" **15.00**
Tumbler, water; glass, 4¾" .**15.00**

Memory Lane

Ashtray **10.00**
Bowl, cereal; 6½" **10.00**
Bowl, dessert; 5½" **3.50**
Bowl, vegetable; 9" **20.00**
Bowl, vegetable; deep, 10" ...**25.00**
Butter dish, ¼-lb **30.00**
Creamer **6.00**
Cup & saucer **5.00**
Plate, chop; 12¼" **25.00**
Plate, dinner; 10" **6.00**
Plate, luncheon; 9" **13.00**
Plate, salad; rare, 7¼" **10.00**
Platter, oval, 13" **30.00**
Sugar bowl, handled, w/lid ..**15.00**
Tumbler, iced tea; glass **15.00**

Old Curiosity Shop

Bowl, cereal; 6¼" **5.00**
Bowl, vegetable; 9" **18.00**
Cake plate, 10" **15.00**
Creamer **6.00**
Cup & saucer..........................**5.00**
Plate, dinner; 10" **4.00**
Salt & pepper shakers, pr ...**15.00**
Sugar bowl, handled w/lid **9.00**

Royal Copley

Produced by the Spaulding China Company of Sebring, Ohio, Royal Copley is a line of novelty planters, vases, ashtrays, and wall pockets modeled after appealing puppy dogs, lovely birds, innocent-eyed children, etc. The decoration is airbrushed and underglazed; the line is of good quality and is well received by today's pottery collectors. We recommend *Royal Copley, Books I and II,* by Leslie Wolfe, edited by our advisor, Joe Devine, who is listed in the Directory under Iowa.

Figurine, Blackamoor, 8½", from $22.00 to $25.00.

Bank, pig, paper label, lg, 7½" .**55.00**
Bank, teddy bear, sitting upright, paper label, 7½" **85.00**
Coaster, pheasants flying, paper label, 4⅝" **17.00**

Figurine, kingfisher, paper label, 5" **30.00**
Figurine, Oriental boy holding jar, paper label, 7½" **15.00**
Figurine, rooster, white, paper label, lg, 8" **75.00**
Figurine, spaniel, brown tones, collar at neck, paper label, 6" **18.00**
Lamp, dancing girl, complete w/ original shade **90.00**
Pitcher, Pome Fruit, green stamp, 8" **48.00**
Planter, cockatiel on kidney-shaped planter, w/label, 8½" **40.00**
Planter, dog at mailbox, black & white, paper label, 8½" ..**60.00**
Planter, dog beside suitcase, rare **45.00**
Planter, dog w/string bass, paper label, 7" **90.00**
Planter, kitten in cradle, bow at neck, paper label, 7½" **70.00**
Planter, Peter Rabbit, paper label, 6½" **40.00**
Planter, poodle resting, paper label, 6½" **36.00**
Planter, salmon, jumping, gray only, paper label, 6½x11½" **60.00**
Planter, Siamese cats before basketweave planter, 9" **95.00**
Planter, teddy bear, paper label, 7½" **70.00**
Plaque/planter, mill scene, signed in script, 8" **50.00**
Vase, mare & foal, embossed mark, 8½" **38.00**
Vase, star & angel, depression for candle, paper label, 6¾" **28.00**
Vase/planter, kitten on stump, paper label, 6½" **32.00**

Royal Haeger, Haeger

Manufactured in Dundee, Illinois, Haeger pottery has recently become the focus of much collector interest, especially the artware line and animal figures designed by Royal Hickman. These were produced from 1938 through the 1950s and are recognized by their strong lines and distinctive glazes.

Ashtray, #1273, free-form, 8" .**6.00**
Bowl, #3002, octagon shape, w/pedestal, 8½" **12.00**
Bowl, console; R-467, beaded, 15" **8.00**
Candle holder, R-485, upright, flower & candle combo, 7½", pr **18.00**
Candle holder, R-622, Chinese figure, yellow, 5" **12.00**
Cigarette box, R-684, turtle figural, w/lid, 9½" L **30.00**
Cookie jar, pig, standing, Bartlow Bros Inc, Korn Top **80.00**

Figurine, R-130, cock pheasant, 12" **25.00**
Figurine, R-683, panther, black, 18" **35.00**
Figurine, R-165, nude torso, 14" **50.00**
Figurine, R-408, racing horse, double, 10" **65.00**
Figurine, R-618, Thought ..**150.00**
Figurine, R-992, stag, standing, 7" **30.00**
Pitcher, Earth Graphic Wraps, #8188, squat, 8" **35.00**
Planter, #617, fawn figural, 6½" **8.00**
Planter, R-766, Rudolf the Red-Nosed Reindeer, 9½" **65.00**
Planter/bookend, #1240, moon fish, 10" **30.00**
Vase, console; R-248, plume feather, 10" **20.00**
Vase, pillow; R-651, 8" **20.00**
Vase, R-501, beehive w/flowers, 7" **15.00**
Wall mask, R-1198/R-1199, Comedy & Tragedy, 11", ea **25.00**

Toe Tappers, ca 1970s, seven in the series, from 8½" to 12" tall, each, $35.00.

Wall pocket, R-724, rocking
horse **15.00**

Russel Wright Dinnerware

Dinnerware designed by
Wright, at one time one of
America's top industrial engi-
neers, is today attracting the
interest of many. Some of his more
popular lines are American
Modern, manufactured by the
Steubenville Pottery Company
(1939-'59), and Casual by Iroquois,
introduced in 1944. He also introduced several patterns of melmac
dinnerware and an interesting
assortment of spun aluminum
serving and decorative items such
as candleholders, ice buckets,
vases, and bowls.

To calculate values for items
in American Modern, add 100% to
the suggested prices in the following listings for examples in these
colors: White, Bean Brown,
Cantaloupe, and Glacier Blue. In
Casual, Brick Red, and Aqua
items go for about 200% more than
any other color, while those in
Avocado Yellow are priced lower
than our suggested values. Unless
otherwise described, values are
given for glassware in Coral and
Seafoam; other colors run about
10% to 15% less. For more information refer to *The Collector's
Encyclopedia of Russel Wright
Designs* by Ann Kerr (Collector
Books). Mrs. Kerr is listed in the
Directory under Ohio.

Dinnerware

Bowl, bouillon; Sterling, 7-oz .**12.00**
Bowl, cereal/soup; Harker White
Clover, clover decor **14.00**
Bowl, lug soup; Residential,
Melmac **12.00**

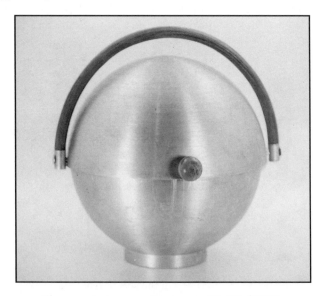

Bun warmer, spun aluminum, 10", EX, $75.00.

Bowl, oval vegetable; Highlight, Citron or Nutmeg, ea ...**55.00**
Bowl, oval vegetable; Home Decorator, Melmac, shallow **12.00**
Bowl, vegetable; American Modern **22.00**
Butter dish, Highlight, White, Pepper or Blueberry, ea .**175.00**
Casserole, Harker White Clover, clover decor, w/lid, 2-qt **50.00**
Casserole, spun aluminum ..**85.00**
Celery dish, American Modern .**25.00**
Coffeepot, Casual, w/lid **85.00**
Creamer, Home Decorator, Melmac **10.00**
Creamer, individual; Sterling, 1-oz **10.00**
Cup, Meladur, Melmac, 7-oz .**8.00**
Cup & saucer, American Modern .**15.00**
Cup & saucer, Knowles **14.00**
Gravy, American Modern **20.00**
Knife or soup spoon, stainless, ea **70.00**
Mug, Casual, 13-oz **65.00**
Mug, Highlight, Citron or Nutmeg, ea **55.00**
Pitcher, water; restyled Casual, 2-qt **150.00**
Plate, chop; American Modern .**30.00**
Plate, dinner; American Modern, 10" **10.00**
Plate, dinner; Harker White Clover, clover decor, 9" .**14.00**
Plate, dinner; Highlight, White, Pepper or Blueberry, ea .**30.00**
Plate, dinner; Meladur, Melmac, 9" **8.00**
Plate, salad; Snow Glass **65.00**
Platter, American Modern, 13" .**25.00**
Platter, Casual, Aqua or Brick Red, oval, 12¾", ea **50.00**
Platter, Knowles, Antique White or Grass, 13", ea **18.00**
Platter, Sterling, oval, 10½" ..**17.00**

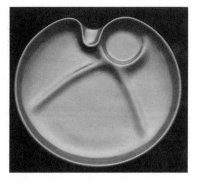

Plate, hostess/party; Casual, in charcoal: $60.00. (Photo courtesy Ann Kerr)

Relish server, Highlight, Citron or Nutmeg, ea **55.00**
Salt & pepper shakers, American Modern, pr **14.00**
Serving accessory, spun aluminum, sm **115.00**
Sherbet, American Modern glassware, 2½" **25.00**
Sugar bowl, Casual, stacking, 4" **12.00**
Sugar bowl, Highlight **30.00**
Tumbler, iced tea; Flair, 14-oz .**65.00**
Tumbler, juice; Pinch, 6-oz ..**35.00**
Tumbler, water; American Modern glassware, 11-oz **30.00**
Tumbler, water; Pinch, 11-oz .**35.00**

Salt Shakers

You'll probably see more salt and pepper shakers during your flea market forays than T-shirts and tube socks! Since the 1920s they've been popular souvenir items, and a considerable number have been issued by companies to advertise their products. These advertising shakers are always good, and along with miniature shakers (1½" or under) are some of the more valuable. Of course, those that have a crossover interest with other categories of collecting — Black Americana, Disney, Rosemeade, Shawnee, Ceramic Arts Studios, etc. — are often expensive as well. There are many good books on the market; among them are *Salt & Pepper Shakers, Identification & Values, Books I, II, III, and IV*, by Helene Guarnaccia; and *The Collector's Encyclopedia of Salt & Pepper Shakers* (there are two in the series) by Melva Davern (all published by Collector Books). See also Clubs and Newsletters; Advertising; Ceramic Arts Studio; Character Collectibles; Disney; Gas Station Collectibles; Shawnee; Rosemeade.

Cardinals, $12.00

African natives (heads & shoulders), carved wood, pr, from $8 to **10.00**

Amish woman seated in chair (2-pc), painted ceramic, from $12 to **14.00**

Anthropomorphic cacti, Grand Canyon on bases, painted ceramic, pr **22.50**

Babies in diapers w/boxing gloves, painted ceramic w/gold, pr ..**12.00**

Baby boy & girl in cabbage heads, painted ceramic, pr, from $14 to **16.00**

Barbeque pit & picnic table, painted ceramic, mini, pr, from $22 to **24.00**

Barred Plymouth Rock chickens, painted ceramic, pr, from $18 to **22.00**

Bellhop boys, painted ceramic, Germany, pr, from $35 to .**45.00**

Black couple's heads & shoulders, chalkware, USA, 2", pr, from $70 to **75.00**

Boot & saddle, green painted ceramic, pr, from $12 to **15.00**

Bowling ball & pin, painted wood, pr, from $6 to **8.00**

Boxers, painted ceramic, pr, from $16 to **18.00**

Boy & girl, red & blue plastic, on puzzle base that fits together, pr **20.00**

Bread man & woman, ceramic, Goebel #73034/#73035, pr, from $20 to **25.00**

Bride & groom, young 1 side/old on back, painted ceramic, pr, $18 to **22.00**

Cat w/fiddle & cow jumping over moon, painted ceramic, pr, from $15 to **18.00**

Clowns, painted ceramic, Napco, 1947, pr, from $22 to **24.00**

Couple's faces fit together, We're a...Match, painted ceramic, pr **15.00**

Cowboy Santa & cowgirl wife, painted ceramic, pr, from $22 to ...**25.00**

Diary & love letters, painted ceramic, mini, pr, from $20 to **22.00**

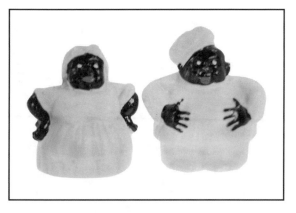

Mammy and Chef, 2½", $35.00.

Dog & doghouse, painted ceramic, cork bottoms, pr, from $10 to **15.00**

Drunk & lamppost, painted ceramic, from $12 to **14.00**

Dustpan & whisk broom, painted ceramic, mini, pr, from $20 to **24.00**

Easter bunny & egg, painted ceramic, pr, from $10 to **12.00**

Easy chair & ottoman, painted ceramic, pr, from $12 to .**14.00**

Eskimo boy & girl, painted ceramic, sticker: 1959 Alaska, pr, $12 to **15.00**

Ferdinand the Bull, painted ceramic, unmarked, pr, from $35 to **45.00**

Football players, comic, painted ceramic, Napco, 1958, pr, from $14 to **16.00**

Fox & goose, painted ceramic, pr, from $40 to **50.00**

Girl saying prayers & bed, painted ceramic, pr, from $14 to **18.00**

Hawaiian hula girl & male musician, painted ceramic, pr, from $14 to **18.00**

Hippos, pink-painted ceramic, comic style, pr, from $8 to **10.00**

Horse heads, silver-colored metal, pr, from $15 to **18.00**

Humpty Dumpty (head seperates from body), painted ceramic, $65 to **70.00**

Indian on rearing horse (2-pc), painted ceramic, pr, from $16 to ...**18.00**

Jack-o'-lanterns w/pilgrim hats, painted ceramic, ca 1980, pr, $10 to **12.00**

Kissing pr in native costume, All Nations Series, Napco, 3½", pr **24.00**

Kitchen graters, painted ceramic, heavy & realistic, pr, from $15 to **20.00**

Mary & her lamb, painted bone china, Parkcraft, mini, pr **24.00**

Mexican couple, bright colors w/black, painted ceramic, Josef, pr **22.00**

Mickey Mouse, plastic, Wilton, Walt Disney, Hong Kong, 1972, pr **40.00**

Mormon Temple & Tabernacle, painted ceramic, lightweight, pr **12.00**

Tappan Chefs, 1960s, 4", $25.00.

Mouse couple dressed as people, painted ceramic, pr, from $10 to **12.00**

Oranges w/green stems, painted ceramic, glossy, pr, from $8 to **12.00**

Pilgrim's Progress, Thanksgiving couple, Fitz & Floyd, pr, from $25 to **30.00**

Policeman & risque lady, painted wood, pr, from $35 to **40.00**

Pool balls, painted plastic, shiny, France, pr, from $22 to .**28.00**

Porpoises on waves, silver-colored metal, pr, from $18 to ...**22.00**

Rainbow trout, painted ceramic, realistic, pr, from $8 to .**10.00**

Roly poly boy & girl, painted plastic, pr, from $15 to **20.00**

Santa w/horn & howling Dalmatian, painted ceramic, Otagiri, pr .**20.00**

Santas, painted ceramic, full bee in V mark (Goebel), pr, from $45 to **55.00**

Skunk & flower, Ponsettia Studio, painted ceramic, pr, from $18 to **25.00**

Squirrels, silver-colored metal, pr, from $12 to **15.00**

Strawberries on leafy screw-on bases, painted ceramic, pr, from $8 to **10.00**

Suitcase & valise, painted ceramic, mini, pr, from $6 to **8.00**

Telephone (2-pc), green & yellow painted ceramic, 1950s, from $14 to **18.00**

Train engine & car, painted ceramic, mini, pr, from $14 to ..**16.00**

Valentine heart split in 2 forms shakers, painted ceramic, from $8 to **10.00**

Vegetable people in sports attire, painted ceramic, pr, from $20 to **24.00**

Watering cans w/garden poem, painted ceramic, pr, from $8 to **10.00**

Watermelon wedges, painted ceramic, realistic, pr, from $8 to **12.00**

Woody Woodpecker & girlfriend, Walter Lantz, cold paint, 1990, pr **55.00**

Scottie Dogs

An amazing array of Scottie dog collectibles can be found in a wide range of prices. Collectors might choose to specialize in a particular area, or they may enjoy looking for everything from bridge tallies to original portraits or paintings. Most of the items are from the 1930s and 1940s, although you'll find Scottie items that were made both before and after those dates. Many were used for advertising purposes; others are simply novelties. Scottie collectors are among the most avid; many like to communicate with one another and gather to display their collections. There have been instances in which individuals and/or groups have shopped an area, leaving very little that was unique behind, causing first a shortage of merchandise and then an escalation of prices. For further information we recommend contacting Donna Palmer, who is listed in the Directory under Washington. She has been collecting, buying, and selling Scottie items for many years. See also Clubs and Newsletters.

Bank, black & white w/oversized head, sits upright, glossy ceramic, 5" 20.00
Bookends, ceramic, w/glasses & book, white w/blue & black, 4", pr 25.00
Bookends, ceramic, white lustre w/black trim, red bow tie, 6½", pr 35.00
Coaster, aluminum, embossed Scottie, 3⅛" dia, 6 for ...35.00
Figurine, black w/white, glossy, ears up, rectangular base, Japan, 4" 10.00
Figurine, white w/black details & airbrushed trim, sitting, Japan, 10" 45.00
Lighter, standing Scottie w/pull-out mechanism, wood base, 2½x3" 35.00
Magazine, Youth's Companion, Scottie on plaid cover, November 1936 ....10.00
Pipe rest, Duk-It, McDonald's Products, metal dog at side, 3½x4" 20.00

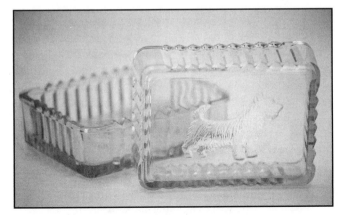

Powder jar, transparent pink with embossed Scottie on lid, $40.00.

Print, Check & Double Check, Drayton, 2 Scotties eye each other 40.00

Tray, glass, metal & wood, red, black & white, 12x18" .135.00

Tumbler, clear glass w/painted black Scottie, 4¾" 22.50

Wall pocket, ceramic, white w/brown spots by blue fence, Japan, 5½" 20.00

Scouting Collectibles

Founded in England in 1907 by Major General Lord Baden-Powell, scouting remains an important institution in the life of young boys and girls everywhere. Recently scouting-related memorabilia has attracted a following, and values of many items have escalated dramatically in the last few years. Early first edition handbooks often bring prices of $100.00 and more. Vintage uniforms are scarce and highly valued, and one of the rarer medals, the Life Saving Honor Medal, is worth several hundred dollars to collectors. Refer to *A Complete Guide to Scouting Collectibles* by Rolland J. Sayers for more information. Mr. Sayers is listed in the Directory under North Carolina.

Backpack, woven oak basket, 1930s-40s, EX 40.00

Badge, Girl Scout, Thanks medal, 10k gold w/blue ribbon, 1930 ..50.00

Button, 1973 National Jamboree, celluloid, pin-back, 1¼" dia ..20.00

Calendar, Girl Scouts, color photos, 1956, 16x10", EX ...20.00

Calendar, Girl Scouts 50th Anniversary, 1962, 16x10", NM 20.00

Calendar, Norman Rockwell, Men of Tomorrow, 1948, 14x8", EX+ 20.00

Camera, Official Girl Scout, Univex, 1937, EX 50.00

Camera, Seneca Boy Scout, in litho box 40.00

Diary, 1926, linen cover, some entries, 240 pages, $25.00; Diary, 1938, paperback, unused, 256 pages, $25.00.

Canteen, Official, aluminum w/cloth cover & strap, 1950s, MIB 20.00

Cap, Den Mother's, Garrison type, blue, w/pin, 1960s 5.00

Diary, pocket; Official, paperback, 1934, some entries, 192-page, EX 25.00

Doll, Girl Scout, Terri Lee, hard plastic, 1949-53, 16" 20.00

First aid kit, Johnson & Johnson, green, square, 1940 ......15.00

Handbook, Lion Cub Scout, dated 1948, 155-page, EX 20.00

Insignia, Explorer Scout, bronze on blue twill, 1950s, M 20.00

Jumper, Boy Scout Sea Explorers, blue wool, w/patch, 1950s, NM 75.00

Neckerchief, US Grant Pilgrimage, 1968, EX 20.00

Neckerchief, 1947 National Jamboree, any variation 8.00

Neckerchief slide, Abraham Lincoln Council, bronzed metal, EX .20.00

Necktie, Air Explorer Scoutmaster, blue clip-on, 1960s, NMIB .40.00

Patch, Eagle Scout, oval embroidered design on khaki square, 1950s, EX 50.00

Patch, 1966 Yahara Invitational Canoe Race, embroidery on white twill 20.00

Photo book, 1964 National Jamboree souvenir, lg format, paperback, EX 20.00

Pin, lapel; 1957 National Jamboree, octagonal, gold-tone, ¾", EX .22.00

Pocketknife, Boy Scout, Shrade #1066, 2-blade, bone handle, 1978-80 ....5.00

Pocketknife, Girl Scout, bronze collar monogram, 1920s, 1¼", EX 20.00

Sash, 1950-60s, w/23 merit badges, EX 70.00

Scarf, Girl Scouts 1960 National Jamboree, silk, w/logo 7.00

Sewing kit, green cover, w/contents, 1930-40 ....15.00

Shoes, Official Boy Scout, leather, Weinbrenner Shoe Co, 1970s, M 35.00

Signal set, twin; Boy Scout Official, 1950s, EX in box 25.00

Sleeve patch, Cubmaster, embroidery on green twill, 1950s, EX 20.00

Sleeve patch, National Jamboree Southeast Region, 1981, M .20.00

Uniform, Girl Scout, dark green, complete, 1940 ....30.00

Uniform, Girl Scout, dress, hat w/emblem, belt & purse, 1950s, EX 75.00

Vest, Boy Scout, red felt, w/40 patches, 1970s, EX 40.00

Sewing Items

Sewing notions from the 1800s and early 20th century, such as whimsical figural tape measures, beaded satin pincushions, blown glass darning eggs, and silver and gold thimbles are pleasant reminders of a bygone era — ladies' sewing circles, quilting bees, and beautifully hand-stitched finery. For further information we recommend *Antique and Collectible Thimbles and Accessories* by Averil Mathis; and *Toy and Miniature Sewing Machines, An Identification and Value Guide*, by Glenda Thomas. *Collector's Guide to Made in Japan*

Ceramics, Identification and Values, by Carole Bess White is a good source for photos of figural ceramic pincushions. All are published by Collector Books.

Figural Ceramic Pincushions

Girl with basket, multicolored shiny glazes, inscribed From Frank Pattee Christmas 1931, black mark, 5", from $20.00 to $32.00.

Bird on perch beside lg flower (cushion), multicolored, 3½" ..**17.50**
Boy w/mandolin beside shell, multicolored, Occupied Japan, 2¾" **10.00**
Calico disc horse, multicolor on white, red mark, 3" **30.00**
Calico elephant sits beside lg red hat, 3¼" **20.00**
Camel, white lustre w/basket cushion on back, red mark, 3¼" **20.00**
Cat & mouse, Art Deco style, multicolored w/yellow lustre, 2¾" **17.50**

Dog w/ball, multicolored, black mark, 2¾", from $12 to .**18.00**
Dog w/boy at neck stands beside top hat, red & black lustre, 4" **30.00**
Dog w/cushion on back, tan lustre, unmarked, 1¾", from $12 to **18.00**
Elephant, opening in back, glossy white, post-1960, unmarked, 2½" **5.00**
Girl w/big basket, multicolored, red mark, 3¾", from $18 to .**28.00**
Lion, Art Deco angular style, tan lustre, red mark, 2½", $12 to **20.00**
Penguin, blue & white lustre, black mark, 3", from $12 to ...**28.00**

Toy Sewing Machines

Artcraft Little Lady, pink w/flowers, ca 1955, from $75 to **95.00**
Casige, gold scrolls & green buds, pre-WWII, 5x2x5", from $100 to **135.00**
Casige, sunflowers & scrolls, chain stitch, 7x4¼x8", from $85 to **100.00**
Elan Junior, plays Blue Danube Waltz, 1956, 7x4x9¼", from $100 to **150.00**
Electric Little Modiste, battery or manual, Japan, 1950s, from $40 to **60.00**
Gateway Junior Model NP-1, 1940s-50s, 7x4½x8½", EX, from $35 to **50.00**
KAYanEE Sew Master, sheet metal, floral decor, hand operated, from $75 to **100.00**
Kittie Model #606, plastic, battery or manual, China, 6½", MIB **25.00**

Lockstitch #8130, plastic, 1980-90s, 7½x4¾x10", MIB, from $15 to **25.00**

National American Girl, steel w/black enamel, 1930s, 6¾x9x4" **100.00**

Playskool, plastic & wood, JC Penney, Hasbro, 1960s, 8", from $25 to **40.00**

Raggedy Ann, plastic, Bobbs-Merrill, 1977, 6x3½x7", M, from $30 to **35.00**

Singer Model 20, cast metal, oval base, 1914, 6¼x3x7", from $150 to **175.00**

Thimbles

Advertising, aluminum, from $2 to **6.00**

China, painted roses w/gold trim, modern **10.00**

Gabler, sterling, wide Delft enamel border, marked **37.50**

Goldsmith-Stern, sterling, tiny cherub faces around band **125.00**

Ketcham & McDougal, sterling, spread-wing eagle, KMD mark **115.00**

Noritake, bone china, white w/gold rim **15.00**

Simons, sterling, floral design .**65.00**

Simons, sterling, plain band, scrolled rim **25.00**

Simons, sterling, plain band, vermicelli top, marked **75.00**

Simons, sterling, repousse medallion, marked **60.00**

Simons, sterling, snail border, reeded rim **55.00**

Simons, sterling, 10-panel w/diamond indentations **34.00**

Stern Bros, sterling, gold band, anchor in cap **65.00**

Stern Bros, sterling, paneled, SBC mark **40.00**

Unmarked, sterling, chased roses & leaves **50.00**

Unmarked, sterling, Domestic Sewing Machines advertising, EX **55.00**

Unmarked, sterling, Louis XV rim, engraved initials **38.00**

Unmarked, sterling, palmate border **55.00**

Unmarked brass, simple decor .**10.00**

Waite-Thresher, sterling, chased wave scroll, marked **28.00**

Waite-Thresher, sterling, fleur-de-lis, scrolled rim, marked **55.00**

Webster, sterling, overlapping flowers, marked **50.00**

Wedgwood, jasper ware **25.00**

Miscellaneous

Clamp, quilting frame; cast iron, pr **27.50**

Crochet hook, covered metal, resembles fountain pen .**12.00**

Darner, black glass egg, sterling repousse handle, P&B mark, EX **55.00**

Darner, mold-blown blue glass foot form **27.50**

Emery, red strawberry w/sterling leaf top **60.00**

Knitting gauges, celluloid, black hoof shapes w/fur trim, 1¾", pr **55.00**

Knitting needles, unmarked sterling, 14", pr, EX **78.00**

Measure, celluloid, ad for Lydia Pinkham, spring type, lg .**70.00**

Measure, celluloid, dog w/big eyes, pink & white, 2" **60.00**

Measure, celluloid, flower basket form, Germany **90.00**

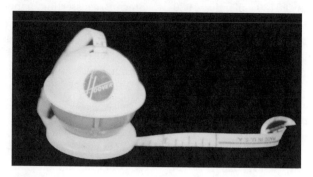

**Measure, plastic, Hoover canister vacuum cleaner, 2",
EX, $32.00.**

Measure, celluloid, ship form, red,
Japan **85.00**

Measure, plastic, apple form, M .**30.00**

Measure, plastic, Hoover advertising on gray, 1½" dia **32.00**

Measure, plush, bear figural,
Japan **30.00**

Needle book, Tunbridge,
mosaic, flannel pages,
2¼x2½" **85.00**

Needle case, celluloid, umbrella
form, 3¾" **125.00**

Needle case, sterling, engraved
decor, flat & narrow, 2¼",
EX **75.00**

Needle case, vegetable ivory, egg
shape w/pierced decor ..**65.00**

Scissors, cut steel, engraved
shanks, 4" **50.00**

Scissors, gilt over metal, French
style, 4", M **160.00**

Scissors, sterling, floral daisy at
base of shanks, EX **90.00**

Sewing kit, red leather shoe,
holds 5 sm spools, aluminum
needle **32.50**

Tatting shuttle, cloisonne, design
ea side, EX **125.00**

Tatting shuttle, heavy brass,
3¼x¾" **60.00**

Thimble case, brass w/embossed
flowers, snap closure, 2 loops
to hang **85.00**

Thimble case, sterling, walnut
figure w/chatelain loop, 1",
NM **185.00**

Thimble case, Tartan Ware, egg
shape, Stuart **245.00**

Thimble stand, base metal, cat on
2½" dia base **80.00**

Thread winder, ivory, rectangular,
flat, 2" **45.00**

Tatting shuttle, sterling with daisies in relief, 3", $95.00.

Planter set, cab and trailer, #681, $55.00.

Shawnee

The novelty planters, vases, cookie jars, salt and pepper shakers, and 'Corn' dinnerware made by the Shawnee Pottery of Ohio are attractive, fun to collect, and still available at reasonable prices. The company operated from 1937 until 1961, marking their wares with 'Shawnee, U.S.A.,' and a number series, or 'Kenwood.' Refer to *The Collector's Guide to Shawnee Pottery* by Janice and Duane Vanderbilt, and *Shawnee Pottery, An Identification and Value Guide,* by Jim and Bev Mangus (both by Collector Books) for more information. Note: Large shakers with decals and gold trim are very hard to find and have a minimum value of $225.00 for the pair. Our advisor for this category is Richard Spencer, listed in the Directory under Utah. See also Cookie Jars.

Bank, tumbling bear **125.00**

Bookends, flying geese, gold trim, marked Shawnee 4000, pr **75.00**
Bowl, mixing; Corn Line, marked #5, 5" **25.00**
Butter dish, Corn Line, marked #72 ....**50.00**
Butter dish, Lobster Ware, marked USA 927 ....**65.00**
Carafe, Valencia, w/lid, no mark **30.00**
Coffee cup, AD; Valencia **37.00**
Coffeepot, Pennsylvania Dutch, marked USA 52 ....**150.00**
Creamer, Corn Line, marked #70 ....**25.00**
Creamer, Dutch style, red feather decor, marked USA 12 .**40.00**
Creamer, Snowflake, marked USA **17.00**
Creamer, White Corn, marked USA, 12-oz **30.00**
Egg cup, Valencia **15.00**
Figurine, gazelle, black & white w/gold trim, marked USA 614, 5" **85.00**
Figurine, raccoon, decals w/gold .**110.00**
Figurine, tumbling bear **60.00**

Flower frog, swan, high base, no mark, 4¼" 30.00
Lamp, flamenco dancers, multicolored, no mark 45.00
Lamp, Victorian man, no mark .35.00
Pitcher, fruit, marked Shawnee 80 ....70.00
Planter, baby buggy, pink, marked USA, miniature 10.00
Planter, dog & jug, marked USA 610 ....10.00
Planter, mouse & cheese, gold trim, marked USA 705 .32.00
Planter, poodle on bicycle, marked USA 712 ....32.00
Planter, spaniel & doghouse, marked Shawnee USA .22.00
Planter, wheelbarrow, wood-grain, marked USA 775 ....8.00
Salt & pepper shakers, chef, sm, pr 15.00
Salt & pepper shakers, flowerpots, all white, sm, pr 55.00
Salt & pepper shakers, fruit, gold trim, marked USA 8, pr .55.00
Salt & pepper shakers, Muggsy, gold trim, lg, pr 150.00
Salt & pepper shakers, Muggsy, sm, pr 65.00
Salt & pepper shakers, wheelbarrow, gold trim, sm, pr ...55.00
Salt box, Fernware, yellow, marked USA 80.00
Snack jar, Lobster Ware, marked #925 ....175.00
Sugar bowl, Sunflower, marked USA 40.00
Sugar bowl, White Corn, marked USA 40.00
Teapot, cottage shape, multicolored, USA 7, 5-cup, minimum value 350.00
Teapot, embossed clover buds, yellow, marked USA, 7-cup 100.00

Teapot, embossed rose, solid gold, marked USA 200.00
Teapot, Rosette, marked USA, 5-cup 30.00
Utility jar, green basketweave, marked USA 80.00

Sheet Music

The most valuable examples of sheet music are those related to early transportation, ethnic themes, Disney characters, a particularly popular actor, singer, or composer, or with a cover illustration done by a well-known artist. Production of sheet music peaked during the 'Tin Pan Alley Days,' from the 1880s until the 1930s. Covers were made as attractive as possible to lure potential buyers, and today's collectors sometimes frame and hang them as they would a print. Flea markets are a good source for sheet music, and prices are usually very reasonable. Most are available for under $5.00. Some of the better examples are listed here. Refer to *The Sheet Music Reference and Price Guide* (Collector Books) by Anna Marie Guiheen and Marie-Reine A. Pafik and *Collector's Guide to Sheet Music* by Debbie Dillon (L-W Book Sales) for more information.

Bury Me Out on the Prairie, Manoloff, 1935 ....5.00
Cattle Call, Tex Owens, 1943 .3.00
Come Away Little Girl, Pfeiffer cover, 1910 ....15.00
Cutey Boy, Williams & Greenberg, Pfeiffer cover, 1913 ....10.00

Darling Lily, Mercer & Mancini, from Darling Lili, Andrews cover, 1970 ....3.00

Don't Let It Happen Again, Al J Neiburg & Robert Levenson, 1934 .....5.00

Drifting in a Lover's Dream, Herbert Leslie, 1933 ....3.00

Ev'ry Time We Say Goodbye, Cole Porter, 1944 ....5.00

Fascination, Manning & Marchetti, Dick Jacobs photo cover, 1945 ....5.00

Frosty the Snow Man, Steve Nelson & Jack Rollins, 1950 ....3.00

Georgia on My Mind, Correll & Carmichael, Carmichael photo cover, 1941 ....10.00

Girl in the Bonnet of Blue, Ross Parker, Merman artwork, 1938 ....3.00

Gone With the Wind, Magidson & Wrubel, movie cover, 1937 .10.00

Goodnight Irene, Ledbetter & Lomax, photo cover, 1950 .3.00

Happy in Love, Jack Yellen & Sammy Fain, 1941 ....5.00

He's Got the Whole World in...Hands, G Love, Laurie London cover, 1957 ....2.00

Hello Dolly (from musical), Jerry Herman, 1963 ....5.00

Honey Bun (from South Pacific), Rogers & Hammerstein, 1949 ....3.00

How Deep Is the Ocean, Irving Berlin, 1932 ....5.00

I Couldn't Sleep a Wink..., Adamson & McHugh, photo cover, 1943 .5.00

I Learned a Lesson I'll Never Forget, Janette Davis photo cover, 1944 ....3.00

I'll Share It All w/You (from Annie Get Your Gun), Irving Berlin, 1946 ....5.00

I'm Henry the Eighth I Am, Murray & Weston, Herman Hermits cover, 1965 ....3.00

If You Were the Only Girl, Clifford Grey and Nat Ayer, Perry Como photo cover, $5.00. (Photo courtesy Guiheen/Pafik)

I Need You Now, Jimmy Crane & Al Jacobs, Eddie Fisher cover, 1953 ....3.00

I Sent My Wife to the 1,000 Isles, Al Jolson, Jolson cover, 1916 ....10.00

I've Got a Lovely Bunch..., Heatherton, Nick artwork, 1949 ....5.00

I Wish I Were Back in Your Arms Tonight, Conrad, Lewis & Sherman, 1930 ....3.00

If I Were a Carpenter, T Hardin, Cash & Carter photo cover, 1966 ....3.00

Island in the Sun (from movie), Belafonte & Burgess, Belafonte cover, 1956 ....3.00

Just a Prayer Away, Tobias & Kapp, Crosby photo cover, 1944 .3.00

Kid w/the Rip in His Pants, Jack Owens, 1944 ....**5.00**

Let It Rain! Let It Pour!, Friend & Donaldson, 1925 ....**5.00**

On the Atchison, Topeka and the Santa Fe, Mercer and Warren, 1934, Judy Garland photo cover, $15.00. (Photo courtesy Guiheen/Pafik)

Little Home I Am Building for You, Billy Day, Pfeiffer artwork, 1917 ....**10.00**

Little White Church in Niche, RE Oliver, Tito Guizar photo cover, 1934 ....**5.00**

Love & Marriage (from Our Town), Cahn & Van Heusen, Sinatra cover, 1955 ....**5.00**

Making Memories, L Kusick & E Snyder, Frankie Lane cover, 1967 ....**3.00**

Melody of Love, T Glazer & H Englemann, Four Aces cover, 1954 ....**5.00**

Mimi (from Love Me Tonight), Hart & Rogers, Chevalier photo cover, 1932..........**10.00**

My Cup Runneth Over (from I Do! I Do!), T Jones & H Schmidt, 1966 ....**5.00**

My Mother's Waltz, Dave Franklin, Bing Crosby photo cover, 1945 ....**5.00**

No Other Love, Russell & Weston, Jo Stafford photo cover, 1950 ....**3.00**

Oh You Beautiful Doll, Brown & Ayer, Starner artwork, 1911 ....**10.00**

Once in a While, Green & Edwards, Tommy Dorsey photo cover, 1937 ....**5.00**

Over the Rainbow (Wizard of Oz), Harburg & Arlen, Garland cover, 1939 ....**35.00**

Petite Waltz, Ellington, Claire & Heyne, Lombardo photo cover, 1950 ....**10.00**

Please Please Me, Beatles ...**20.00**

Put on a Happy Face (Bye Bye Birdie), Adams & Strouse, 1960 ....**5.00**

Ramblin' Rose, Sherman & Sherman, Nat King Cole photo cover, 1948 ....**3.00**

Rocked in the Cradle of the Deep, Knight, Baker photo cover, 1935 ....**10.00**

Say a...Prayer for Me, Gilbert & Nichols, R Etting photo cover, 1930 ....**10.00**

She's Drivin' Me Wild, Gerald Marks & Buddy Fields, 1925 ....**5.00**

So Near & Yet So Far (You'll Never Get Rich), Cole Porter, 1941 ......**5.00**

Somewhere Over There, Pulver & O'Keefe, Pfeiffer artwork, 1918 ....**10.00**

Steam Heat (Pajama Game), Adler & Ross, 1954 ....**3.00**

Sweet Marie, Warman & Moore, Powell & Dunne photo cover, 1946 ....5.00

Tennessee Waltz, Stewart & King, Patti Page photo cover, 1948 ....5.00

There's a Cabin in the Pines, Billy Hill & M Fisher, 1933 ....5.00

There's a Song in the Air, F Flaxington Harker, 1934 .3.00

This Ole House, Stuart Hamblen, 1954 ....3.00

Til There Was You (from Music Man), Meredith Wilson, 1950 ....5.00

Try Little Tenderness, Woods, Campbell & Connelly, Sinatra cover, 1932 ....3.00

Underneath the Harlem Moon, Gorden & Revel, Black face cover, 1932 ....10.00

Volarie, Parish & Modugno, McGuire Sisters cover, 1958 ....3.00

Watermelon Weather, Francis & Carmichael, Como & Fisher cover, 1952 ....5.00

We're in the Army Now, Taylor, Olsen & Jones, 1917 .....15.00

What a Wonderful World, Weiss & Thiele, L Armstrong cover, 1967 ....3.00

When I Grow Up (Curly Top), Heyman & Henderson, S Temple cover, 1935 ....10.00

When the Sun Comes Out, Ted Koeler & Harold Arlen, 1941 ....3.00

White Sport Coat & Pink Carnation, Marty Robbins, Robbins cover, 1957 ....5.00

Woodstock, Joni Mitchell, Crosby, Stills, Nash & Young cover, 1969 ....3.00

Yesterday, John Lennon & Paul McCartney, 1965 ....5.00

You Made Me Love You, McCarthy & Monaco, Jolson cover, 1913 ....10.00

You're a Natural (College Swing), Loesser & Sherwin, 1938 .5.00

You're the Only Star in My...Heaven, G Autry, Autry & Light cover, 1938 ....5.00

You've Come Home (from Wildcat), C Leigh & C Coleman, 1960 ....3.00

Shell Pink Glassware

Made by the Jeannette Glass Company from 1957 until 1959, this line is made up of a variety of their best-selling shapes and patterns. The glassware has a satiny finish, and the color is the palest of peachbloom. Refer to *Collectible Glassware of the '40s, '50s, and '60s* by Gene Florence (Collector Books).

Candy jar, raised grapes and leaves, footed, $25.00.

Ashtray, butterfly shape.....17.50

Bowl, fruit; footed, 9" high ..**35.00**

Bowl, fruit; gondola shape, 17½" **27.50**

Bowl, Lombardi, 4-toe, plain center, 11" **28.00**

Candlesticks, 2-light, pr **65.00**

Compote, Windsor, common, 6" **12.00**

Cookie jar, w/lid, 6½x5¾" ..**125.00**

Creamer, Baltimore Pear **55.00**

Honey jar, beehive shape, notched cover **38.00**

Pitcher, Thumbprint, footed, 24-oz **27.50**

Relish, vineyard design, 4-part, octagonal, 12" **40.00**

Snack set, plate w/indent & cup, feather design **15.00**

Tumbler, juice; Thumbprint, footed, 5-oz **8.00**

Vase, heavy beaded bottom, 9" .**85.00**

Shot Glasses

Shot glasses, old and new, represent a fresh area of interest to today's collectors and are relatively easy to find. Basic values are given for various categories of shot glasses in mint condition. These are general prices only. Glasses that are in less-than-mint condition will obviously be worth less than the price given here. Very rare and unique items will be worth more. Sample glasses and other individual one-of-a-kind oddities are a bit harder to classify and really need to be evaluated on an individual basis. For more information we recommend *Shot Glasses: An American Tradition* by our advisor for this category, Mark Pickvet. He is listed in the Directory under Michigan, and information about a newsletter is given in our Clubs and Newsletters section.

Glass, Old Valley Whiskey, 3 men holding bottle, rare, $120.00. (Photo courtesy Shot Glass Exchange)

Aluminum **3.00**

Black porcelain replica **4.00**

Glass, barrel shape **7.50**

Glass, Carnival colors, plain or fluted **45.00**

Glass, Carnival colors w/patterns **60.00**

Glass, coated inside & out w/black enamel to look like porcelain **4.00**

Glass, Culver, 22k gold **8.00**

Glass, cut, whiskey tumbler .**100.00**

Glass, Depression, clear, tall .**6.00**

Glass, Depression, general designs, tall **8.00**

Glass, Depression colors, patterns or etching **25.00**

Glass, Depression colors, plain .**10.00**

Glass, European, gold trim, round, sm **3.00**

Glass, general, enameled design .**3.00**

Glass, general, etched designs .**7.50**

Glass, general, frosted, w/gold trim **6.00**

Glass, general, frosted designs .**4.00**

Glass, general, gold designs ..**8.00**

Glass, general, square **7.50**

Glass, general advertising **4.00**

Glass, general tourist **3.00**

Glass, inside eyes **7.50**

Glass, Mary Gregory/Anchor Hocking Ships **150.00**

Glass, nude **25.00**

Glass, pop or soda advertising .**15.00**

Glass, pressed design, whiskey tumbler **75.00**

Glass, ruby flashed **40.00**

Glass, square, w/etching **10.00**

Glass, square, w/pewter **15.00**

Glass, square, 2-tone bronze/ pewter **17.50**

Glass, Taiwan Tourist **2.00**

Glass, Tiffany, Galle or fancy art **750.00**

Glass, tourist, Taiwan **3.00**

Glass, tourist, turquoise & gold **7.50**

Glass, whiskey or beer advertising, modern **5.00**

Glass, 19th-Century cut patterns **35.00**

Porcelain, general **7.50**

Porcelain, tourist **4.00**

Silhouette Pictures

Silhouette pictures with the subject matter reverse painted on the glass (which is sometimes curved) were popular dime-store items from the '20s until the '50s, and you'll often see them at flea markets and antique malls. Subjects range from animals and trees to children and courting couples, and some may incorporate an advertising or perhaps a thermometer. Refer to *The Encyclopedia of Silhouette Collectibles on Glass* (Shadow Enterprises), by Shirley Mace for more information. She is listed in the Directory under New Mexico.

Benton, man pushing woman in swing, full-color background, $35.00.

Benton, couple in opera booth, convex glass, #BG 45-19, 4x5" **32.00**

Benton, couple out for a stroll, convex glass, #BG 68-11, 6x8" **38.00**

Benton, man gives flowers to woman, convex glass, #BG 68-5R, 6x8" **60.00**

Benton, man proposes to woman, convex glass, #BG 68-26, 6x8" **40.00**

Benton, man smoking pipe while reading paper, convex glass, #BG 45-15 ....**25.00**

Benton, woman picking flowers, convex glass, #BG 45-21, 4x5" **30.00**

C&A Richards, Per Aspera Ad Astra, 3x7", $45.00. (Photo courtesy Shirley Mace)

Benton, woman playing piano, convex glass, #BG 45-14, 4x5" **25.00**

Bilderback's, lady w/parasol, convex glass, #BI 9D-1, 9" dia **35.00**

Buckbee-Brehm, Gay Nineties, flat glass, #BB 68-12, 6x8" ...**15.00**

Buckbee-Brehm, Love Letter, flat glass, #BB 46-3, 4x6" **23.00**

C&A Richards, Elfin Music, flat glass, #RI 57-760, 5x7" ..**45.00**

C&A Richards, John Alden, flat glass, #RI 44-592, 4x4" ..**22.00**

Deltex, Blossoms, flat glass, #DE 45-27, 4x5" **20.00**

Fisher & Flowercraft, boy & dog fishing, flat glass, #FI 44-2, 4x4" **18.00**

Newton, Land of the Free, flat glass, #NE 57-14, 5x7" .**22.00**

Newton, Out Where the West Begins, flat glass, #NE 810-4, 8x10" **28.00**

Peter Watson, sailboat at sea, convex glass, #PW 5D-5, 5" dia ...**15.00**

Reliance, A Fickle Wind, flat glass, #RE 34-63, 3x4" **20.00**

Reliance, Anticipation, flat glass, #RE 57-121, 5x7" **25.00**

Reliance, Baltimore Oriole, flat glass, #RE 710-23, 7x10" **22.00**

Reliance, Beau Brummel, flat glass, #RE 57-125, 5x7" **18.00**

Reliance, Blossom Time, flat glass, #RE 711-36, 7x11" **30.00**

Reliance, Cardinal, flat glass, #RE 710-21, 7x10" **22.00**

Reliance, Courtship, flat glass, #RE 44-83, 4x4" **15.00**

Reliance, Double Dutch, flat glass, #RE 711-33, 7x11" **30.00**

Reliance, Gift Bearer, flat glass, #RE 55-151, 5x5" **14.00**

Reliance, Lucky April Showers, flat glass, #RE 34-64, 3x4" .**20.00**

Reliance, Spring in the Park, flat glass, #RE 44-87, 4x4" .**18.00**

Reliance, Tulip Time, flat glass, #RE 711-34, 7x11" **22.00**

Tinsel Art, baby & butterfly, flat glass, #TA 710-16, 7x10" .**18.00**

Skookum Dolls

The Skookums Apple Packers Association of Wenatchee, Washington, had a doll made from their trademark.

Skookum figures were designed and registered by a Montana woman, Mary McAboy, in 1917. Although she always made note of the Skookum's name, she also used the 'Bully Good' trademark along with other information to inform the buyer that 'Bully Good' translated is 'Skookums.' McAboy had an article published in the March 1920 issue of *Playthings* magazine explaining the history of Skookum dolls. Anyone interested can obtain this information on microfilm from any large library.

In 1920 the Arrow Novelty Company was making the dolls, but by 1929 the H.H. Tammen Company had taken over their production. Skookums were designed with life-like facial characteristics. The dried apple heads of the earliest dolls did not last, and they were soon replaced with heads made of a a composition material. Wool blankets formed the bodies that were then stuffed with dried twigs, leaves, and grass. For the remainder of the body, they used cloth and felt.

Skookum dolls with wooden legs and felt-covered wooden feet were made between 1917 and 1949. After 1949 the legs and feet were made of plastic. The newest dolls have plastic heads. A 'Skookums Bully Good Indians' paper label was placed on one foot of each early doll. Exact dating of a Skookum is very difficult. McAboy designed many different tribes of dolls simply by using different blanket styles, beading, and backboards (a device used for carrying the papoose).

Our advisor for this category is Jo Ann Palmieri; she is listed in the Directory under New Jersey.

Female with baby, 14" to 16" tall, from $175.00 to $225.00. (Photo courtesy Pat Smith)

Child, wooden legs & feet, 6", from $40 to **50.00**
Child, wooden legs & feet, 8", from $60 to **70.00**
Female, plastic legs & feet, 10", from $35 to **45.00**
Female, plastic legs & feet, 12", from $50 to **60.00**
Female, plastic legs & feet, 4", from $20 to **25.00**
Female, plastic legs & feet, 6", from $25 to **35.00**
Female, wooden legs & feet, 10" to 12", from $125 to **150.00**

Female w/baby, wooden legs & feet, 14" to 16", from $175 to 225.00

Male, plastic legs & feet, 10", from $35 to 45.00

Male, plastic legs & feet, 12", from $50 to 60.00

Male, plastic legs & feet, 4", from $20 to 25.00

Male, plastic legs & feet, 6", from $25 to 35.00

Male, wooden legs & feet, 10" to 12", from $150 to 175.00

Male, wooden legs & feet, 14" to 16", from $200 to 350.00

Snowdomes

The term snowdome refers broadly to any water-filled paperweight, but there are several distinctly different styles. Round glass globes which sit on a separate base have been made in a variety of shapes and materials and were first designed in the middle of the 19th century. Flea markets offer this type (which were made in America and Italy in the '30s and '40s) as well as newer ones which are produced today in Austria and the Orient.

Small plastic half-moons with blue backs often serve as souvenirs or Christmas toys. This style originated in West Germany in the 1950s. Dozens of other shapes followed, including round and square bottles, short and tall rectangles, cubes, and other simple shapes.

Figurals made of plastic were especially popular in the 1970s. Either the entire object was an unusual shape or a figure of an animal, mermaid, etc., was draped over a large plastic dome. Today snowdomes of this type are made of glass, ceramic, or artplas (very heavy plastic) in elaborate shapes. Some collectors buy all three styles while others specialize in only one type.

For further information we recommend contacting Nancy McMichael, author of *Snowdomes*, the first illustrated book on this subject, and editor of *Snow Biz*, the first newsletter and collector club. She is listed in the Directory under the District of Columbia. See also Clubs and Newsletters.

Souvenir, Australia and I Love Jerusalem, $18.00 each. (Photo courtesy Nancy McMichael)

Advertising, Co name on base, oily liquid, 1950s, 2¾" glass globe 50.00

Ashtray, Bakelite, glass globe w/scene, decaled base, 1930s 55.00

Award, oily liquid, black or brown base, ca 1950s, 2¾" glass globe 60.00

Bank, all plastic, souvenir scene, square base, slit in back .8.00

Black subjects in glass globe, ceramic base 100.00

Calendar, perpetual; all plastic, 2 knobs either side of square base 8.00

Cartoon character, plastic, sm .10.00

Christmas theme, plastic half-moon, sm 5.00

Commemorative (moon landing, etc), plastic bottle form .25.00

Disney character, plastic dome, marked Monogram, 1960s 30.00

Disney character, styles other than above listing 12.00

Figure, animal draped across lg plastic dome 10.00

Figure, animal w/water ball 'tummy,' 1970s 12.00

Figure, cartoon character, plastic, 1970s 50.00

Figure, clown w/water ball 'tummy,' 1970s 30.00

Figure, Indian w/water ball 'tummy,' 1970s 40.00

Fraternal, oily liquid, glass globe on black base, flat sides, 1950s 60.00

Marx, copyrighted plastic half-moon, 1960s, set of 6, MIB 50.00

Religious theme, saint in glass globe, decal on plastic base, 1930s 40.00

Roly-poly, Santa or snowman on top half of water compartment, 1970s 20.00

Saint or souvenir scene in glass atop shell base, Italy, 1940s 12.00

Shakers, souvenir scene or place plaque inside, plastic, 1950s, ea 12.00

Snowman, glass globe on plastic or ceramic base, 1940s 30.00

Souvenir, glass w/bisque figure, ceramic base, decal, ca 1940s 40.00

Souvenir, plastic, city, any shape 7.00

Souvenir, plastic, sm tourist attraction, any shape 8.00

Souvenir, plastic, state, any shape 6.00

Souvenir, plastic, television shape 7.00

Souvenir, plastic, treasure chest shape 8.00

World's Fair, glass w/bisque Trylon & Perisphere, 1939 ....75.00

World's Fair, plastic half ball on red calendar base 20.00

World's Fair, plastic half-moon shape 15.00

World War II general or serviceman, glass globe on ceramic base 50.00

Soda Pop

A specialty area of the advertising field, soft drink memorabilia is a favorite of many collectors. Now that vintage Coca-Cola items have become rather expensive, interest is expanding to include some of the less widely known flavors — Dr. Pepper, Nehi, and Orange Crush, for instance.

If you want more pricing information, we recommend *Huxford's Collectible Advertising* by Sharon and Bob Huxford. Our advisors for this category are Donna and Craig Stifter; they are listed in the directory under Illinois.

Coca-Cola

Since it was established in 1891, the Coca-Cola Company has issued a wide and varied scope of advertising memorabilia, creating what may well be the most popular field of specific product-related collectibles on today's market. Probably their best-known item is the rectangular Coke tray, issued since 1910. Many sell for several hundred dollars each. Before 1910 trays were round or oval. The 1903 tray featuring Hilda Clark is valued at $5,000.00 in excellent condition. Most Coca-Cola buffs prefer to limit their collections to items made before 1970.

For more information we recommend *B.J. Summers' Guide to Coca-Cola. Collectible Coca-Cola Toy Trucks* by Gael de Courtivron, and *Goldstein's Coca-Cola Collectibles* by Sheldon Golden. All are published by Collector Books.

Ashtray, Coca-Cola & baseball, Partners, 1950s, from $65 to **100.00**
Ashtray, glass, Drink...in Bottles...JJ Flinn Co in red, 1950s, M **75.00**
Banner, Atlanta...Super Bowl XXVIII, 102x34", NM, from $50 to **60.00**

Window display, 3-D cardboard diecut, fountain scene with soda jerk, 1950s, 24x36", $400.00. (Photo courtesy Donna and Craig Stifter)

Book, 100 Best Posters, hardcover, 1941, EX+ **40.00**
Bottle carrier, aluminum, lift handle, holds 12 bottles, 1950s, NM **110.00**
Bottle opener, metal, Shirts for the Coke Set on solid handle, EX+ **25.00**
Buckle, chrome plate w/applied gold truck, Year 5 Record No Accident **130.00**
Calendar, complete pad, 1944 .**275.00**
Calendar, complete pad, 1958 .**200.00**
Calendar holder, tin, Things Go Better w/Coke, 1960, from $50 to **85.00**
Clock, metal, maroon w/red logo, Drink Coca-Cola, 1951, 17½" dia **110.00**
Clock, plastic & metal, Things Go Better..., disk logo, 16" square, VG **60.00**

Clock, plastic light-up, Things Go Better..., 1960s, 15" square **145.00**

Cooler, picnic, red vinyl box-type, fishtail logo, NM **40.00**

Decal, Things Go Better... (receding words), 1960s, NM .**25.00**

Doll, Santa, holds bottle & white book, white boots, 1950s-60s, VG **45.00**

Fountain glasses, 1960s, box of 12 ....**65.00**

Festoon, cardboard, girls faces, 1951, 5 pcs w/envelope **1,000.00**

Game, Shanghai, MIB **20.00**

Ice pick/bottle opener, metal w/wood handle, Compliments..., 1940s-50s **40.00**

Menu board, light-up, 1960s, EX **115.00**

Menu holder, plastic, Things Go Better w/Coke, 1960s **25.00**

Paper cup, Things Go Better... in red on white square, 1960s, 3½" **3.00**

Pencil holder, ceramic, 75th Anniversary, shaped like 1896 dispenser **185.00**

Pin, 5-Year Service, 1950s ..**45.00**

Playing cards, cowgirl, 1951, complete, NMIB **75.00**

Playing cards, It's the Real Thing, party scene, 1972, NMIB ..**25.00**

Playing cards, nurse, spotter deck, 1943, NMIB, from $65 to .**100.00**

Postcard, bottling plant photo, black & white, NM **30.00**

Radio, upright vending machine, red & white, 1966, MIB **200.00**

Record, Buy the World a Coke, New Seekers, M **15.00**

Sign, button, Drink...Sign of Good Taste, red, 1950s, 16" dia, EX **225.00**

Sign, cardboard, Here's Something Good, circus scene, 1952, 20x36" **275.00**

Sign, cardboard, You Taste Its..., lady w/bottle, 1942, 20x36", EX **485.00**

Sign, cardboard, Zing, girl in pool, 1963, 20x36" **200.00**

Sign, cardboard diecut, hand-held bottle, 1950s, 9", M **85.00**

Sign, cardboard stand-up diecut of Eddie Fisher, 1954, 19", EX **250.00**

Sign, light-up, glass & metal, w/clock, Lunch w/Us, 1950s **400.00**

Sign, light-up, Sign of Good..., flowers around edge, 1957, 12" dia **200.00**

Sign, neon, Official Soft Drink of Summer above palm tree, NM **1,100.00**

Sign, paper, Plastic Cooler for Picnics..., 1950s, 27x16", NM **40.00**

Sign, plastic, Big King Size, shows bottle, 1950s **45.00**

Sign, porcelain, Delicious & Refreshing, bottle, 1950s, 24" square, EX **250.00**

Sign, porcelain, die-cut bottle, 1950s, 16" **150.00**

Sign, tin, Take Home a Case Today, 1950s, 19x28" ..**200.00**

Sign, tin, tire rack display, 1960s **375.00**

Sign, tin bottle, Wherever You Go..., skier, 1960s, 18", NM **200.00**

Sign, tin button, Drink Coca-Cola, 1950s, 16" dia **185.00**

Sign, tin button, Drink Coca-Cola in Bottles, 1950s, 12" dia ...**115.00**

Thermometer, glass front, Things Go Better..., 1964, 12" dia ...**165.00**

Thermometer, tin, emb button on top, 1950s, 9" **125.00**
Toy truck set, Buddy L, Brute Coca-Cola Set, 1981, 5-pc, NMIB **50.00**
Tray, girl w/bottle, screened ground, 1950, 13x10½", NM **125.00**

Dr. Pepper

A young pharmacist, Charles C. Alderton, was hired by W.B. Morrison, owner of Morrison's Old Corner Drug Store in Waco, Texas, around 1884. Alderton, an observant sort, noticed that the drugstore's patrons could never quite make up their minds as to which flavor of extract to order. He concocted a formula that combined many flavors, and Dr. Pepper was born. The name was chosen by Morrison in honor of a beautiful young girl with whom he had once been in love. The girl's father, a Virginia doctor by the name of Pepper, had discouraged the relationship due to their youth, but Morrison had never forgotten her. On December 1, 1885, a US patent was issued to the creators of Dr. Pepper.

Bottle opener, wall mount, embossed lettering, NM **20.00**
Calendar, complete pad, 1954 .**150.00**
Calendar, complete pad, 1968 ...**50.00**
Clock, metal & glass, light-up, 1960s, 20" sq **200.00**
Clock, metal frame, glass front, 1950s, 15" dia **200.00**
Drinking glass, ...Good for Life!, label & clock, M **220.00**

Calendar, 1945, woman in party dress in front of mirror, complete, 22x13½", EX, $250.00.

Menu board, tin, Drink Dr. Pepper in oval logo, 1960s, 20x28" **75.00**
Sign, cardboard, Lift for Life, cheerleader, 1950s, 19x32", EX, from $325 to **400.00**
Sign, celluloid, 1940s, 8½x11", from $350 to **600.00**
Sign, paper, Frosty Man Frosty!, chef, 1950s, 15x25", NM .**30.00**
Sign, tin, bottle on white background, 1960s, 14x48" .**150.00**
Sign, tin, Drink Dr. Pepper in red oval on silver, 1960s, 11x28" **65.00**
Sign, tin, Drink...Distinctively, red & white, 12x29", NM **135.00**
Thermometer, plastic, bottle cap shape, 1960s **50.00**

Hires

Did you know that Hires Root Beer was first served to fairgoers at the Philadelphia Centennial in 1876? It was developed by Charles E. Hires, a druggist who experimented with roots and herbs to come up with the final recipe. The company originally chose the Hires boy as their logo, and if you'll study his attire, you can sometimes approximate a guess as to when an item he appears on was manufactured. Very early on he appeared in a dress, and from 1906 until 1914 it was a bathrobe. He sported a dinner jacket from 1915 until 1926.

Ashtray, glass, bottle shape, EX+ **12.00**
Booklet, How To Make Hires Root Beer at Home, EX **10.00**
Bookmark, pictures ducks, rare, EX **28.00**
Calendar, man w/frothy mug & 8-pack carton, full pad, 1957, M **25.00**
Cutout, cardboard, bottle w/menu, 1950s, 18x32" **125.00**
Cutout, tin, bottle shape, 1950s, 48", from $275 to **375.00**
Decal, Drink Hires Root Beer on bottle cap, EX **15.00**
Door push, tin, It's High Time..., chrome frame, 4x30", G+ **35.00**
Ice cream scoop, plastic, Only One Taste Says Hires to You, EX **10.00**
Menu board, tin, Hires Root Beer, red on white, 27x19", EX+ **85.00**
Menu board, tin, 1950s, 15x28" **150.00**
Mug, ceramic, Drink Hires It Is Pure on red diamond, 5½x4", EX **35.00**

Mug, glass, applied label in script on slanted band, M **35.00**
Pencil clip, celluloid, round head, blue, gold & black, rare, EX **75.00**
Sign, cardboard diecut, bottles, glass & sandwich tray, 10x9½", VG+ **25.00**
Sign, tin, bottle & Drink Hires, 1950s, 10x28" **100.00**
Sign, tin, Hires R-J Root Beer, red, white & blue, 12" dia, NM **100.00**
Sticker, pointing Hires boy, NM **50.00**
Thermometer, glass front, 1960s, 15" dia **200.00**
Thermometer, tin, bottle shape, 1950s, 18", from $125 to .**175.00**
Thermometer, tin, bottle shape, 27x8", NM **150.00**
Tray, lady in white oval on woodgrain background, vertical, 13", VG+ **250.00**

Nehi

Coupon, Drink...For Health..., bottle at right, NM **65.00**
Fountain glass, applied color label, white band w/logo, 1940s .**85.00**
Menu board, Gas Today, round chalkboard area, 1940s, 42x15" **500.00**
Pocketknife, Remington, metal engraved boot-shaped handle, EX **110.00**
Sign, cardboard, ping-pong game scene, 1950s, 11x28" **65.00**
Sign, tin, Drink Nehi Beverages, bottle on white oval, 1940s, 17x45" **150.00**
Sign, tin flange, Drink Nehi, Ice Cold, bottle on white, 1940s, 13x18" **325.00**

Sign, tin flange, Drink Nehi Beverages & bottle, 1940s, 13x18" **225.00**

Tray, bathing beauty in ocean wave, vertical, 13", VG+ **145.00**

Nesbitt's

Thermometer, 1950s, 24", $125.00. (Photo courtesy Donna and Craig Stifter)

Bottle carrier, cardboard, 6-pack, 1940s **25.00**

Calendar, complete pad, 1953 .**65.00**

Dispenser, glass, no jug, 1950s, from $100 to **175.00**

Menu board, tin, 1950s, 20x28", from $50 to **75.00**

Picnic cooler, 1950s **45.00**

Push bar, tin plate on wire frame, 1950s **80.00**

Sign, cardboard, child dressed as boxer, 1950s, 22x35" ...**100.00**

Sign, cardboard, clown w/children, 1950s, 20x36" **325.00**

Sign, cardboard, twins sitting at table, 1950s, 20x36" **275.00**

Sign, cardboard diecut, lady in hat & gloves w/bottle, 1950s, 23x21" **85.00**

Sign, tin, Drink & 5¢ above bottle, 1950s, 49x16" **275.00**

Thermometer, logo over bottle & thermometer, 1950s, 24" **125.00**

Orange-Crush

Bottle opener, metal Crushy figure, NM **16.00**

Bottle opener/spoon, metal, EX .**40.00**

Calendar, Competition for American Artists, 1945, complete, EX+ **40.00**

Calendar, complete pad, 1957 .**50.00**

Clock, glass & metal, bottle cap on face, 1950s, 15" dia **225.00**

Decal, lg amber bottle, 30x9", EX+ **35.00**

Door plate, porcelain, Revenez Merci, 9x3½", NM **175.00**

Sign, cardboard, New! & bottle, Crushy figure, Served Here, 14x11", EX **80.00**

Sign, celluloid, ...Carbonated Beverages, Crushy singing, 9" dia, EX .**500.00**

Sign, celluloid, 1950s, 9" dia, from $75 to **125.00**

Sign, tin, bottle cap shape, Enjoy..., 18" dia, EX **195.00**

Sign, tin, bottle cap shape, 1950s, 36" dia, $175 to **275.00**

Sign, tin, Enjoy a Fresh New Taste, 1960s, 12x28" **85.00**

Sign, tin, Feel Fresh!..., Crushy figure, diamond shape, 16x16", EX **220.00**

Sign, tin diecut, New Flavor Guarding Bottle..., 1930s, NM **650.00**

Sign, tin flange, Enjoy w/bottle cap, 1950s, 14x18" **175.00**

Thermometer, glass front, 1950s, 12" dia, from $125 to ..**175.00**

Thermometer, tin, bottle shape, 1950s, 30" **125.00**

Thermometer, tin, image of bottle, 1950s, 16" **175.00**

Tray, bottles & diamonds for kaleidoscopic design, 12" dia, VG **110.00**

Tray, serving; tin, bottle cap, 1950s, 12" dia **65.00**

Yo-Yo, wooden, Crushy Ski Top Drink Orange-Crush, EX+ **50.00**

Pepsi-Cola

Pepsi-Cola has been around about as long as Coca-Cola, but since collectors are just now beginning to discover how fascinating this line of advertising memorabilia can be, it's generally much less expensive. You'll be able to determine the approximate date your items were made by the style of logo they carry. The familiar oval was used in the early 1940s, about the time the two 'dots' (represented in our descriptions by an equal sign) between the words were changed to one. But the double dots are used nowadays as well, especially on items designed to be reminiscent of the old ones — beware! The bottle cap logo was used from about 1943 until the early to mid-'60s with variations. For more information refer to *Pepsi-Cola Collectibles* by Bill Vehling and Michael Hunt and *Introduction to Pepsi Collecting* by Bob Stoddard.

Sign, cardboard easel-back, 1930s-40s, 15x19", NM, $650.00. (Photo courtesy Gary Metz)

Blotter, Drink...Delicious Healthful, black on brown, G 70.00

Bottle carrier, tin, oval Pepsi-Cola logo, rounded handle, VG+ 40.00

Bottle crate, wood w/stamped Pepsi-Cola logo, EX 70.00

Bottle opener, wall mount, embossed Pepsi-Cola, G .20.00

Calendar, lady walking dog, complete pad, 1951, 16x33" .650.00

Calendar, Light Refreshment, bottle cap, glass & bottle, 1956, EX+ 325.00

Calendar, Paintings of the Year, 1947, complete, EX+ 40.00

Calendar, paper tear-off on cardboard frame w/easel back, 1954 ....125.00

Calendar, 6 pages, 1950, 13x22" 375.00

Can, cone-top w/cap, 1940s-50s, 12-oz, EX 240.00

Can, flat-top, slanted bottle cap on diagonal stripes, 1960s, VG+ ...40.00

Clock, glass & metal, bottle cap on face, 1950s, 15" dia 275.00

Clock, light-up, logo at 12, lines between 3, 6 & 9, square, 1969, VG+ 55.00

Clock, light-up, stylized bottle cap, metal frame, round, 1950s, NM 375.00

Display, cardboard diecut w/3-D bottle, New Single..., 10x14", M .215.00

Display rack, tin, Drink...Ice Cold on bottle cap, NM 255.00

Game, Big League Baseball, 1950s-60s, EX 95.00

Paper cup, Pepsi's Best, Pepsi-Cola bottle cap, red, white & blue, NM 18.00

Pocketknife, Pepsi-Cola 5¢ in blue on bone-colored handle, 3", EX 60.00

Score sheet, Pepsi-Cola flanked by the Pepsi cops above, 8x4¼", NM 5.00

Sign, cardboard, Be Sociable...Have a..., 1960, 37x25" 150.00

Sign, cardboard, Big Shot, 2 children, W Darrow Jr art, 1943, 11x28" 200.00

Sign, cardboard, More Bounce to the Ounce, 1950, 11x28" 250.00

Sign, cardboard, Santa scene, Your Good Old Friend, 1951, 11x28" 285.00

Sign, cardboard, self-framed, Certified Quality, 1950, 21x27" 275.00

Sign, cardboard cutout, lady w/glass, easel-back, 1951, 20x48" 450.00

Sign, cardboard cutout, lady w/6-pack, easel-back, 1960 ..125.00

Sign, counter-top light-up, Drink..., contour logo, 1950s, 14" dia, EX 175.00

Sign, plastic light-up, w/cardboard back, embossed Santa, 1956, 26" 175.00

Sign, tin, die-cut bottle cap, 1951, 18" dia 175.00

Sign, tin, Say Pepsi Please, image of bottle, 1965, 18x48" .125.00

Stadium cushion, Pepsi logo on blue, M 30.00

Thermometer, Have a Pepsi, slanted bottle cap, 1956, 27" .75.00

Tip tray, Compliments of Pepsi-Cola, banded rim, rectangular, NM 35.00

Toy truck, Marx, plastic flatbed w/wood wheels, no cases, EX+ 75.00

Tray, deep-dish, lg Pepsi-Cola bottle cap in center, 12" dia, EX 150.00

Royal Crown Cola

Bottle, applied color label, 1940s 7.00
Bottle, embossed, 1940s **10.00**
Bottle carrier, cardboard, 6-pack, 1940s **25.00**
Calendar, Anne Blyth, complete pad, 1950, from $100 to **145.00**
Calendar, Arlene Dahl, complete pad, 1953 ....**200.00**
Calendar, complete pad, 1956 .**85.00**
Calendar, complete pad, 1959 .**75.00**
Calendar, complete pad, 1963, from $45 to **65.00**
Calendar, complete pad, 1964 .**65.00**
Calendar, Loretta Young, complete pad, 1952 ....**175.00**
Calendar, Wanda Hendrix, complete pad, 1950 ....**100.00**
Clock, glass & metal, logo in center, 1940s, 15" dia **250.00**
Clock, glass & metal, 1950s, 16" square **100.00**
Clock, reverse-painted glass light-up, 15x15", NM **175.00**
Cutout, cardboard, 3-D, Enjoy Today's Modern RC, 1950s, 15x21" **225.00**
Cutout, cardboard carton display, little boy, 1950s **100.00**
Lighter, aluminum flip-top, crown above name, VG **25.00**
Playing cards, oval image of bottle, scalloped border, NMIB **30.00**
Sign, cardboard, Claudette Colbert or Mary Martin, 1940s, 11x28", each **75.00**
Sign, cardboard, First Choice, Anytime, original frame, 1940s, 11x28" **115.00**
Sign, cardboard, June Haver, 1940s, 26x40" **185.00**

Sign, cardboard, Mary Martin, 1950s, 26x40", from $100 to **150.00**
Sign, cardboard, My Mom Knows Best, 1940s, 11x28" **50.00**
Sign, cardboard, RC Tastes Best, Bing Crosby, 26x31", NM **250.00**
Sign, cardboard, Veronica Lake, 1940s, 26x40" **175.00**
Sign, cardboard stand-up diecut, Hedy Lamarr, 1940s-50s, 9", EX **100.00**
Sign, tin, Enjoy Royal Crown Cola, 1960s, 12x28" **75.00**
Thermometer, tin, embossed RC logo on top, bottle at right, 1940s **150.00**
Thermometer, tin, RC on top, logo below, better Taste Calls..., 1940s **175.00**

7-Up

Though it was originally touted to have medicinal qualities, by 1930 7-Up had been reformulated and was simply sold as a refreshing drink. The company that first made it was the Howdy Company, who by 1940, had changed its name to 7-Up, to correspond with the name of the soft drink. Collectors search for the signs, thermometers, point-of-sale items, etc., that carry the 7-Up slogans.

Bank, can shape, NM **25.00**
Bottle, plastic display, 1960s, 28" **65.00**
Bottle carrier, cardboard, 6-pack, Fresh Up 7-Up, 1950s ..**10.00**
Bottle opener, heavy brass, M series, VG **20.00**

Bottle topper, Top O' the Mornin', leprechaun & shamrocks, NM **12.00**

Box of straws, Get Real Action...Your Thirst Away!, 1960s **145.00**

Calendar, complete, pad, 1955, 9½x20" **300.00**

Calendar, complete pad, lady w/bouquet of roses, 1950, 9½x20" **375.00**

Calendar, complete pad, 1960, from $15 to **25.00**

Clock, Get Real Action...7-Up Your Thirst Away!, 1960s, 17¾" sq **150.00**

Clock, glass & metal, 1950s, 14" dia, from $175 to **275.00**

Dispenser, counter; Bakelite, 3 spigots, 1950s, 7½x11" **250.00**

Display, iceberg shape holds glass bottle at slant, 1940s ..**425.00**

Drinking glass, Don't Drink Water..., boy in stream, 5", NM **20.00**

Fountain glass, emerald green w/applied color label, 1950s **20.00**

Matchbook, Nothing Does It..., square logo, 20-stick, front strike, NM **2.00**

Menu board, tin, hand-held bottle above chalkboard, 27x19", EX+ ...**70.00**

Sign, tin, Your 'Fresh Up' above hand holding bottle, raised border, 1947, 20x28", EX, $225.00.

Sign, cardboard, So Good w/..., bottles & popcorn, 1950s, 21x34" **65.00**

Sign, cardboard hanger, hand w/bottle, 1947, 5x9½" ...**40.00**

Sign, cardboard stand-up, Fresh Up, grocery man, 1948, 12x9", NM **65.00**

Sign, flange, Real...Sold Here & bubbles on round disk, G **95.00**

Sign, foil on cardboard, bottles in bucket, embossed, 1960s, 12x16" **85.00**

Sign, plastic light-up, Fresh Up...Nothing Does..., 1950s, 11" sq **200.00**

Sign, porcelain, Fresh Up, bottle, green band, 1951, 16x40", VG+ **210.00**

Sign, tin, Fresh Up, black, red & white, 12x19", EX+ **90.00**

Sign, tin, Fresh Up, bottle at top, 1954, 18½x27", from $75 to **125.00**

Sign, tin, Fresh Up! It Likes You, for corner, 1950s, 8x10½", pr **145.00**

Sign, tin, Nothing Does It Like Seven-Up, 1950s, 13x44".**150.00**

Sign, tin, 7-Up Your Thirst Away, multicolored, 1963, 12x30", VG+ **10.00**

Sign, tin flange, bottle, 1954, 18x20", from $350 to ..**475.00**

Sign, tin flange, circular shape, 7-Up Sold here, 1940s, 14x18" **350.00**

Syrup jug, green glass w/paper label, 1950s **20.00**

Thermometer, glass & metal, Fresh Clean Taste, 1950s, 10" dia **100.00**

Thermometer, glass & metal, 7-Up the Uncola, 1960s, 12" dia **50.00**

Thermometer, tin, bottle, The All-Family Drink, 1950s, from $30 to **50.00**
Tie bar, oval celluloid emblem w/7-Up logo, M **18.00**
Tray, serving; tin, Fresh Up w/...Family Drink, 1950s, 12½" dia **110.00**

Sports Collectibles

Memorabilia related to sports of any kind is attracting a following of collectors, many of which specialize in the particular sport that best holds their interests.

Album, Official 1970 Pro Football Stars Photostamp Album, 30-page, M **25.00**
Almanac, 1955 Baseball **20.00**
Bank, Philadelphia Flyers, porcelain, Imco, Japan, 1970s, M **20.00**
Baseball, Angels, Official American League, signed Ryan ...**125.00**
Baseball, McPhail, vintage Mickey Mantle signature (yellowed) **225.00**
Baseball, Official American League, signed Joe DiMaggio **150.00**
Baseball, Official NL Giles, 1950s Brooklyn Dodgers team autograph, NM **495.00**
Baseball, Tigers, Official Detroit Ball, 19 signatures, NM **75.00**
Baseball bat, signed Frank White, classic Worth bat, M **35.00**
Baseball glove, Rawlings, Mickey Mantle signature model, EX **57.00**

Baseball, signed Pete Rose, 9-11-85, 4,192 (hits), $45.00.

Basketball, NBA Spalding, signed Larry Bird **225.00**
Book, Babe Ruth, Tom Meany, hardcover, 1970, EX+ ...**20.00**
Book, Baseball in the '30s, D Honig, Crown, 1989, w/dust jacket, M **30.00**
Book, Cooperstown, Alvin Hall, Meckler, 1991, w/dust jacket, M **10.00**
Book, Hank Aaron, B Gutman, Thistle, 1973, black & white photos, EX **10.00**
Book, How To Box/How To Train, J Romano, softcover, 1944, 96-page, EX **8.00**
Book, One for the Record, G Plimpton, Harper & Row, 1974, EX **65.00**
Book, Playing the Field, C Euchner, Johns Hopkins, 1993, w/jacket, M **17.50**
Book, Primitive Baseball, H Frommer, Antheneum, 1988, w/jacket, EX **20.00**
Booklet, Quick, Yogi Berra cover, 1952, EX+ **25.00**
Boxing gloves, Everlast, signed Sugar Ray Leonard, pr **110.00**

**Shoes, Joe DiMaggio, $400.00.
(Photo courtesy Dunbar Gallery)**

Broadside, Joe Louis fight, photo of Joe in fighting pose, NM .**40.00**

Cap, Cincinnati Reds, signed Ray Washburn, game-used ..**50.00**

Folder, 1964 Tokyo Olympics, set of 6 color photo cards, M in mailer **8.00**

Football, signed Jerry Rice .**150.00**

Football, signed Joe Montana .**140.00**

Football helmet, signed Joe Namath **275.00**

Golf ball, signed Lee Trevino .**30.00**

Gum card pack, Wrestling (66/11), Topps, 1st series, 1985, M (sealed) **2.00**

Hat, Chicago Bulls, signed Michael Jordan **50.00**

Helmet, NY Jets, signed Joe Namath **275.00**

Jersey, Official Champion NY Jets Throwback, signed Joe Namath **175.00**

Jersey, Official NFL Proline, Jo Montana autograph, w/certificate, NM **165.00**

Magazine, Basketball's Best, NBA Pictorial Review, 1955-56, EX **17.50**

Magazine, Wrestling, Vol 1 #2, February 1951, 52-page, 8½x11" **15.00**

Newspaper, Boston Globe, The Bird Legend, February 4, 1993, complete, NM **35.00**

Patch, Brooklyn Dodgers Ebbets Field on blue & white cloth ball shape **50.00**

Pencil, wooden baseball bat form, Baseball's 100th Anniversary, mini **28.00**

Pennant, Mets National League Champions 1986, logo & members, 30", M **7.50**

Pennant, NY Yankees American... Champions, purple & white, 1940s, NM **150.00**

Pennant, Philadelphia Eagles, green w/white lettering, early, NM **40.00**

Pennant, Philadelphia Eagles NFC Champions Super Bowl XV, 1981, M **12.50**

Pennant, Philadelphia The Sixers, 1982-83 World Champions, 30", M **7.50**

Pennant, Ted Williams portrait & signature on felt, NM ...**90.00**

Photo, Dream Team III, 8x10" .**250.00**

Photo, Ebbetts Field, color, 1948, scarce, NM **100.00**

Photo, Sport Magazine premium, Joe DiMaggio, dated 1947, NM **50.00**

Pin-back button, Harlem Globetrotters team picture, M **20.00**

Pin-back button, LIU (Long Island University), 1940s-50s, 1¼" **1.00**

Pin-back button, NY Giants, red, white & blue, vintage, 1¾", NM **10.00**

Pin-back button, Oscar Robertson portrait w/ball, Specs International **20.00**

Pocketknife, 1939 Baseball Centennial, striped Bakelite handle, 3¾" **220.00**

Postcard, signed Jackie Robinson in blue ink, 3x5", NM .**250.00**

Poster, Billy Conn vs Joe Louis, boxing scene, 1946 Title, EX+ **275.00**

Program, football; Illinois vs Notre Dame, 1945, EX- **45.00**

Scorecard, Detroit Tigers vs Cleveland, unused, 1951, EX **20.00**

Scorecard, Dodgers vs Giants, unused, 1951, M **45.00**

Ticket, boxing; Baer vs Louis, full ticket, May 23, 1941, NM **150.00**

Ticket, football; Army vs Notre Dame, 1947, EX **40.00**

Ticket, 1948 Baseball World Series, EX+ **75.00**

Ticket, 1976 Baseball All Star, EX+ **30.00**

Ticket, 1980 Super Bowl, full ticket, NM **150.00**

Wristwatch, Michael Jordan, Wilson, black leather band, NM ..**50.00**

Yearbook, Chicago White Sox, 1961, EX+ **40.00**

Yearbook, Cincinnati Royals, 1969, NM **100.00**

Yearbook, Philadelphia Eagles, w/lg fold-out poster, 1976, 64-page **18.00**

Yearbook, Philadelphia Phillies 1976 Bicentennial edition, 72-page **22.50**

Yearbook, Pirates, 1955, spine wear, missing back cover **18.00**

Yearbook, San Diego Padres, Dave Winfield on cover, 1980, 48-page **12.50**

Stangl

The Stangl Company of Trenton, New Jersey, produced many striking lines of dinnerware from the 1920s until they closed in the late 1970s. Though white clay was used earlier, the red-clay patterns made from 1942 on are most often encountered and are preferred by collectors. Decorated with both hand painting and sgraffito work (hand carving), Stangl's lines are very distinctive and easily recognized. Virtually all is marked, and most pieces carry the pattern name as well.

Fruits and Flowers: Cup and saucer, $15.00; Plate, 8", $15.00.

Bowl, cereal; Fruit, 5½" **15.00**
Bowl, cereal; Thistle **15.00**
Bowl, Concord, 4¼x12¾" **50.00**
Bowl, coupe soup; Starflower, 7½" **16.00**
Bowl, divided vegetable; Thistle **40.00**
Bowl, fruit; Festival **10.00**
Bowl, fruit; Provincial **10.00**
Bowl, lug soup; Thistle **15.00**
Bowl, lug soup; White Dogwood .**15.00**
Bowl, salad; Thistle, 10" **40.00**
Bowl, vegetable; Thistle, round .**35.00**

Creamer & sugar bowl, Magnolia, w/lid **20.00**
Cup, Concord **11.00**
Cup, Kiddieware, clown **65.00**
Cup & saucer, Golden Harvest .**18.00**
Gravy boat, Orchard Song, from $12 to **15.00**
Gravy boat, Thistle, w/stand .**35.00**
Pitcher, Garden Flower, 2-qt .**48.00**
Pitcher, Provincial, 1-qt **35.00**
Plate, chop; Country Garden, 1-qt **50.00**
Plate, chop; Golden Harvest, 12" **20.00**
Plate, chop; Magnolia, 14¼" .**40.00**
Plate, Concord, 8⅛" **12.00**
Plate, Country Life, w/rooster, 6" **45.00**
Plate, dinner; Golden Harvest, 10" **14.00**
Plate, Festival, 6" **5.00**
Plate, Fruit, 8", from $15 to .**20.00**
Plate, grill; Golden Blossom, 11", from $18 to **20.00**
Plate, Kiddieware, Little Bo Peep, 9" **100.00**
Plate, Magnolia, 10" **20.00**
Plate, Magnolia, 8", from $6 to ..**8.00**
Plate, Thistle, 10⅛" **18.00**
Plate, Thistle, 6" **6.00**
Plate, Town & Country, blue, 10" **45.00**
Platter, Country Garden, oval, 14¾" **50.00**
Relish, Thistle **22.00**
Relish, Yellow Tulip, from $20 to **22.50**
Salt & pepper shakers, Florette, pr **12.00**
Salt & pepper shakers, Roxanne, pr **15.00**
Shakers, Thistle, pr **20.00**
Sugar bowl, Mountain Laurel, w/lid **15.00**

Tidbit, First Love, 2-tier, from $15 to **20.00**
Tile, Golden Blossom **15.00**
Vase, Antique Gold, 4" **10.00**

Star Trek Collectibles

Star Trek has influenced American culture like no other show in the history of television. Gene Roddenberry introduced the Star Trek concept in 1964, and it has been gaining fans ever since. The longevity of the television show in syndication, the release of six major motion pictures, and the success of Star Trek the Next Generation television show have literally bridged two generations of loyal fans. This success has spawned thousands of clothing, ceramic, household, jewelry, and promotional items; calendars; plates; comics; coins; costumes; films; games; greeting and gum cards; party goods; magazines; models; posters; props; puzzles; records and tapes; school supplies; and a wide assortment of toys. Most of these still turn up at flea markets around the country, and all are very collectible. Double the value for an excellent condition item when the original box or packaging is present. For further information and more listings, see *Schroeder's Collectible Toys, Antique to Modern* (Collector Books).

Bookmark, Captain Kirk, Antioch, EX **1.00**
Bowl, cereal; plastic, 1975, EX, from $10 to **15.00**

Inter-Space Communicator, Lone Star, 1974, MIB, $55.00. (Photo courtesy June Moon)

Calendar, Star Date 1977, EX .**25.00**

Coloring book, Rescue at Raylo, Whitman, Kirk on cover, 1978, EX+, from $8 to **10.00**

Comic Book, Gold Key #8, photo cover, G **14.00**

Costume, Captain Kirk, 1976, NM (Star Trek box) **40.00**

Display piece, Spaceshuttle Galileo, lights ups/talks, 1992, M, from $125 to **175.00**

Eraser, Mr Spock, 1983, EX, from $8 to **10.00**

Figure, Captain Kirk, Motion Picture, Mego, 3¾", MOC, from $28 to **35.00**

Figure, Commander Riker, Next Generation, Galoob, 3¾", MOC, from $12 to **15.00**

Figure, Dr McCoy, Motion Picture, Mego, 3¾", MOC, minimum value **35.00**

Figure, Ilia, Mego, 12½", MIB, from $65 to **85.00**

Figure, Lt Commander Data, Galoob, 1st series, 3¾", MOC **125.00**

Figure, Scotty, Star Trek III, Ertl, 3¾", MOC **25.00**

Figure, Spock, Mego, 12", NMIB .**75.00**

Game, Star Trek the Motion Picture, Milton Bradley, 1979, NMIB, from $25 to **40.00**

Lunch box, Star Trek the Next Generation, purple plastic, 1988, EX **10.00**

Model kit, USS Enterprise Bridge, built up, EX+ **20.00**

Ornament, USS Enterprise, Hallmark, M **285.00**

Photo mug, Mr Spock, MIB ..**17.50**

Pin-back button, black & white photos of Kirk & Spock, 1976, 2¼", M, from $5 to **10.00**

Playset, Command Communication Console, Mego, 1976, M in EX box, from $70 to **80.00**

Postcard book, set of 48 cards, M **35.00**

Puzzle, frame-tray, Whitman, 1978, MIP (sealed), from $10 to **12.00**

Space Launching gun, AHI, 1976, MOC **65.00**

T-shirt, gold, 1990, adult size, EX, from $15 to **25.00**

Utility belt, w/phaser, tricorder & communicator, Remco, 1975, M in VG box **150.00**

Vehicle, Klingon Warship, Dinky, MIB, from $75 to **85.00**

Vehicle, USS Enterprise, Star Trek II, Corgi, 1982, MOC, from $18 to **25.00**

Wristwatch, Bradley/20th Century - Paramout, Swiss movement, 1980, M, from $65 to **85.00**

Star Wars Collectibles

Capitalizing on the ever-popular space travel theme, the movie 'Star Wars' with its fantastic special effects was a mega box office hit of the late 1970s. A sequel called 'Empire Strikes Back' (1980) and a third adventure called 'Return of the Jedi' (1983) did just as well, and as a result, licensed merchandise flooded the market, much of it produced by the Kenner Company. Refer to *Modern Toys, American Toys 1930 to 1980,* by Linda Baker and *Schroeder's Collectible Toys, Antique to Modern* (both by Collector Books) for more information.

Bank, Darth Vader, plastic, EX+ .**18.00**

Book, Empire Strikes Back, pop-up, EX **10.00**

Cookie jar, R2-D2, ceramic, MIB **175.00**

Figure, A-Wing pilot, Power of the Force, 3¾", MOC **115.00**

Figure, Admiral Ackbar, Return of the Jedi, w/accessories, 3¾", M **6.00**

Figure, B-Wing Pilot, Return of the Jedi, 3¾", MOC, from $15 to **10.00**

Figure, Ben Obi-Wan Kenobi, 12", from $95 to **115.00**

Figure, Bossk, Return of the Jedi, 3¾", MOC **60.00**

Figure, C-3PO, Empire Strikes Back, removable limbs, 3¾", MOC **45.00**

Figure, Chewbacca, 12", EX .**65.00**

Figure, Darth Vader, Power of the Force, 3¾", MOC, from $65 to **80.00**

Figure, Greedo, Empire Strikes Back, 3¾", MOC, from $85 to .**100.00**

Figure, Sy Snootles and the Rebo Band, Return of the Jedi, 1983, MIB, $125.00. (Photo courtesy June Moon)

Figure, Han Solo, Empire Strikes Back, Hoth gear, 3¾", M .**14.00**

Figure, Jawa, Power of the Force, 3¾", MOC, from $65 to .**75.00**

Figure, Lando Calrissian, Skiff Guard outfit, 3¾", M **10.00**

Figure, Luke Skywalker, Empire Strikes Back, Hoth gear, 3¾", M **15.00**

Figure, Princess Leia, Empire Strikes Back, Hoth outfit, 3¾", MOC **70.00**

Figure, Rebel Soldier, Empire Strikes Back, w/accessories, 3¾", M **8.00**

Figure, Snaggletooth, Empire Strikes Back, 3¾", MOC .**80.00**

Lobby card set, Empire Strikes Back, 11x14", set of 8, EX **75.00**

Mask, Stormtrooper, Don Post, full head, M **75.00**

Pendant, figural w/movable parts, 1978, M, ea **15.00**

Playset, Bespin Control Room, Micro Collection, MIB (sealed) **55.00**

Playset, Hoth Ice Planet, EX .**30.00**

Plush toy, Ewok, 15", NM ...**24.00**

Speaker phone, Darth Vader, MIB **125.00**

Sticker, Empire Strikes Back, puffy, 1980, MIP **10.00**

Toothbrush, Oral B, MIB (sealed), ea **8.00**

Vehicle, Ewok Combat Glider, MIB **22.00**

Vehicle, Imperial Troop Transport, EX in EX box **65.00**

Vehicle, Landspeeder, diecast, NM **35.00**

Vehicle, Millennium Falcon, diecast, EX **50.00**

Vehicle, Scout Walker, w/instructions, no insert, otherwise NMIB **50.00**

Vehicle, TIE Bomber, diecast, EX **250.00**

Vehicle, X-Wing Fighter, Micro Collection, w/1 figure, NM **55.00**

Wristwatch, Fantasm, Darth Vador or Millennium Falcon, MIP, ea **40.00**

Strawberry Shortcake Collectibles

Strawberry Shortcake came onto the market around 1980 with a bang. The line included everything to attract small girls such as swimsuits, bed linens, blankets, anklets, underclothing, coats, shoes, sleeping bags, dolls and accessories, games, toys, and delightful items to decorate their rooms. It was short lived, though, lasting only until near the middle of the decade. Our advisor is Geneva Addy; she is listed in the Directory under Iowa.

Doll, Raspberry Tart, MIB, $26.00.

Bake Shoppe, lg strawberry opens to reveal shop, complete, MIB .**40.00**

Berry Bake Shoppe, stove, stand & accessories in lg strawberry, M **40.00**

Butterfly, Flitter-Bit, roll-along toy that carries dolls, MIB .**30.00**

Carousel, sunflower merry-go-round for 4 dolls, M **30.00**

Carrying case, lg red plastic strawberry to hold 4 dolls **15.00**

Christmas lights, Strawberry Shortcake figurals, electric, 1 strand **25.00**

Dog, Pupcake, belongs to Huckleberry Pie, scented name tag **30.00**

Doll, Apple Dumplin' w/Tea Time Turtle, rag doll w/yarn hair, 13" **35.00**

Doll, Cupcake or Custard (puppy or kitten), machine washable, M, ea **30.00**

Doll, Huckleberry Pie, w/removable hat, clothes, & comb **26.00**

Doll, Purple Pieman w/Berry Bird, MIB **30.00**

Doll, Raspberry Tart, rag doll w/yarn hair, 15" **35.00**

Doll, Strawberry Shortcake, rag doll w/yarn hair, 15" **35.00**

Doll, Strawberry Shortcake, scented, poseable, removable clothes, MIB **26.00**

Doll, Strawberryland Miniature, ea **6.00**

Garden House gazebo w/table & chairs, barbeque, etc, complete **35.00**

Necklace, enameled Strawberry Shortcake pendant on gold-tone chain **10.00**

Necklace, ring & bracelet, w/Strawberry Shortcake figure, ea **10.00**

Outfit, Berry Wear, made for 5½" & 3⅝" dolls, from $20 to **25.00**

Outfits, sold in pairs, for 5½" doll, MIP, from $20 to **25.00**

Play Doh Play Set, complete w/molds, vehicle & playmat, M **10.00**

Roller skates **35.00**

Snail cart, snail pulls basket that converts to table, complete **30.00**

Strawberryland Miniature, Blueberry Garden Shoppe, w/accessories **25.00**

Strawberryland Miniature, Raspberry Soda Shoppe **25.00**

Strawberryland Miniature, Shortcake House, w/accessories **25.00**

Strawberryland Miniature, Strawberry Shortcake or friend, ea **25.00**

Tumbler, glass, 6" **6.50**

Vehicle, Big Berry Trolley, 1982 ....**20.00**

Wristwatch, digital, MIB **65.00**

Swanky Swigs

Swanky swigs are little decorated glass tumblers that once contained Kraft Cheese Spread. The company has used them since the Depression years of the 1930s up to the present time, and all along, because of their small size, they've been happily recycled as drinking glasses for the kids and juice glasses for adults. Their designs range from bright-colored flowers to animals, sailboats, bands, dots, stars, checkers, etc. There is a combination of 223 verified colors and patterns. In 1933 the original swanky swigs came in the Band pattern; at the present time they can still be found on the grocery shelf, now a clear plain glass with an indented waffle design around the bottom.

They vary in size and fall into one of three groups: the small size sold in Canada, ranging from 3¹⁄₁₆" to 3¼"; the regular size sold in the United States, ranging from 3⅜" to 3⅞"; and the large size also sold in Canada, ranging from 4³⁄₁₆" to 5⅝".

A few of the rare patterns to look for in the three different groups are: small group, Band No. 5 (two red and two black bands with the red first); Galleon (two ships on each glass in black, blue, green, red or yellow); Checkers (in black and red, black and yellow, black and orange, or black and white, with black checkers on the top row); and Fleur-de-lis (black with a bright red filigree design).

In the regular group: Dots Forming Diamonds; Lattice and Vine (white lattice with colored flowers); Texas Centennial (cowboy and horse); Special Issues with dates (1936, 1938, and 1942); and Tulip No. 2 (black, blue, green, or red).

Rare glasses in the larger group are Circles and Dots (black, blue, green, or red); Star No. 1 (small stars scattered over the glass in black, blue, green, or red); Cornflower No. 2 (dark blue, light blue, red, or yellow); Provincial Cress (red and burgundy with maple leaves); and Antique No. 2 (assorted antiques on each glass in lime green, deep red, orange, blue, and black).

A word of warning! Once you start looking for swanky swigs, it becomes very addictive. Our advisor for this category is Joyce Jackson, she is listed in the Directory under Texas.

Note: The letter C immediately following the size in our descriptions indicates that those examples were made for the Canadian market; 'US' has been used to identify those sold in this country.

Antique No 1, any color, 1954, 3¼", C **10.00**

Bustlin' Betty, 3³⁄₄", US $2.50; Texas Centennial, 3³⁄₄", US $30.00.

Antique No 1, any color, 1954, 3¾", US **2.50**

Antique No 1, any color, 1954, 4¾", C **20.00**

Antique No 2, any color, 1974, 4⅝", C **25.00**

Bachelor Button, red, white & green, 1955, 3¼", C.........6.00

Bachelor Button, any color, 1955, 3¾",US **3.00**

Bachelor Button, red, white & green, 1955, 4¾",C **15.00**

Band No 1, red & blk, 1933, 3⅜",US...........................**3.00**

Band No 2, black & red, 1933, 3⅜", US **3.00**

Band No 2, black & red, 1933, 4¾", C **20.00**

Band No 3, white & blue, 1933, 3⅜", US..............................**3.00**

Band No 4, blue, 1933, 3⅜", US **3.00**

Bicentennial Tulip, any color, 1975, 3³⁄₄₈", US **15.00**

Bustlin' Betty, any color, 1953, 3¼, C **10.00**

Bustlin' Betty, any color, 1953, 4¾", C..............................**20.00**

Carnival, any color, 1939, 3½", US .**6.00**

Checkerboard, any color, 1936, 3½", US **20.00**

Checkerboard, any color, 1936, 4¾", C **20.00**

Circles & Dot, any color, 1934, 3½", US **4.00**

Circles & Dot, any color, 1934, 4¾", C **20.00**

Colonial, clear w/waffle design, 1976, 4⅜", C **10.00**

Coin Design, clear w/indented design around bottom, 3⅛" or 3½", ea, C......................**2.00**

Cornflower No 1, any color, 1941, 3³⁄₁₆", C **10.00**

Cornflower No 2, any color, 1947, 3½", US **3.00**

Cornflower No 2, any color, 1947, 3³⁄₁₆", C **10.00**

Cornflower No 2, any color, 1947, 4³⁄₁₆", C **20.00**

Crystal Petal, clear, 1951, 3½" .**2.00**

Ethnic Series, any color, 1974, 4⅝", C **20.00**

Forget-Me-Not, any color, 1948, 3½", US **3.00**

Forget-Me-Not, any color, 1948, 3³⁄₁₆", C **10.00**

Galleon, any color, 1937, 3⅛", C .**12.00**

Hostess Design, clear, 1960, 3⅛" or 3¼", ea, C **2.00**

Hostess Design, clear, 1960, 3¾", US **1.00**

Hostess Design, clear, 1960, 4⅝", C...........................**5.00**

Kiddie Kup, any color, 1956, 3¼", C **10.00**

Kiddie Kup, any color, 1956, 4¾", C **20.00**

Petal Star, clear w/indented star pattern, 3¼", C.......**2.00**

Posy Pattern, jonquil, violet or tulip, 1941, 3½", ea, US .**3.00**

Posy Pattern, jonquil, violet or tulip, 1941, 3³⁄₁₆", ea, C .**10.00**

Posy Pattern, jonquil, violet or tulip, 1941, 4⅝", ea, C ..**20.00**

Provencial Crest, red & burgundy, 1974, 4⅝", C **25.00**

Sailboat No 1, blue, 1936, 3½", US.**12.00**

Sailboat No 2, any color, 1936, 3½", US **12.00**

Special Issue, blue, 1936, 3½", US .**50.00**

Special Issue, red, 1938, 3½", US **50.00**

Sportsmen Series, any, 1976, 4⅝", C...................................**25.00**

Stars No 1, any color, 1935, 4¾", C **20.00**

Stars No 1, any color other than yellow, 1935, 3½", US **4.00**

Stars No 1, yellow, 1935, 3½", US **15.00**

Stars No. 2, clear w/orange stars, 1971, 4⅝", C **5.00**

Tulip No 1, any color, 1937, 3½", US **3.00**

Tulip No 1, any color, 1937, 3¼", C **10.00**

Tulip No 1, any color, 1937, 4⅝", C **20.00**

Tulip No 2, any color, 1938, 3½", US **20.00**

Tulip No 3, any color, 1950, 3¼", C **10.00**

Tulip No 3, any color, 1950, 3⅞", US **3.00**

Tulip No 3, any color, 1950, 4¾", C **20.00**

Wildlife Series, goose, moose, bear or fox, 1975, 4⅝", ea, C .**20.00**

Swizzle Sticks

Swizzle sticks, stirrers used for mixed drinks, first became popular in 1934 with the end of prohibition. They may be made of Bakelite, metal, wood, plastic, or glass. Collectors fall into two categories: those who prefer figural glass examples and those who like the advertising sticks. Advertising sticks in glass and plastic are the most popular today. Eagerly sought by collectors are Bakelite bats, railroad sticks, airline sticks, and Worlds' Fairs-related sticks. Our advisor for this category is Tom Maimone who can be found listed in the Directory under New York. Mr. Maimone has written several articles on swizzle sticks and is a member of the International Swizzle Stick Collectors Association.

Advertising, plastic figural ballerina, Tropicana, Havana, Cuba, $2.00. (Photo courtesy Tom Maimone)

Advertising

Airline, American Airlines logo **25**

Airline, TWA, plastic giraffe **25**

Bakelite, bat, Essex House, NY .**5.00**

Bakelite, bat, Jack Dempsey's .**10.00**

Glass rod, amber, Gilbey's Liquor **2.00**

Glass rod, cobalt blue, Lincoln Hotel **2.00**

Glass tube w/rolled paper inside, cobalt blue spoon end **4.00**

Glass tube w/rolled paper inside, Green River Whiskey **2.00**

Bakelite bat, Jack Dempsey's, $10.00; Wooden knocker, Lou Walter's, Latin Quarter, $2.00. (Photo courtesy Tom Maimone)

Las Vegas clubs, plastic, 1970s-80s, ea **25**

Metal, golf club shape, Old Taylor Whiskey **2.00**

Plastic, common varieties (Seagrams, etc), ea, from 10¢ to **25**

Plastic, figural skull, Ivanhoe, Chicago **1.00**

Railroad, plastic, NY Central straight stick **25**

Railroad, plastic figural domeliner train **5.00**

Wooden knocker, Concord Hotel, NY **2.00**

Wooden knocker, Lou Walter's, Latin Quarter **2.00**

World's Fair, cobalt blue glass, Souvenir NY 1939 ....**8.00**

Figurals

Angel, clear glass, 1970s **2.00**

Bird, multicolored glass, Czechoslovakian, 1930s **8.00**

Christmas tree, green glass, 1970s **2.00**

Tiara Exclusives

Collectors are just beginning to take notice of the glassware sold through Tiara in-home parties, their Sandwich line in particular. Several companies were involved in producing the lovely items they've marketed over the years, among them Indiana Glass, Fenton, Dalzell Viking, and L.E. Smith. In the late 1960s, Tiara contracted with Indiana to produce their famous line of Sandwich dinnerware (a staple at Indiana Glass since the late 1920s). Their catalogs continue to carry this pattern, and over the years, it has been offered in many colors: ruby, teal, crystal, amber, green, pink, blue, and others in limited amounts. We've listed a few pieces of Tiara's Sandwich below, and though the market is unstable, our values will serve to offer an indication of current values. Unless you're sure of what you're buying, though, don't make the mistake of paying 'old' Sandwich prices for Tiara. To learn more about the two lines, we recommend *Collectible Glassware from the '40s, '50s, and '60s,* by Gene Florence (Collector Books).

Ashtray, 4 rests, 7⅜", from $5 to **7.00**

Basket, Sandwich, amber, footed, 10", from $25.00 to $32.50.

Bowl, salad; 5", from $2 to **3.50**
Candle holder, 8½", pr, from $15 to **18.00**
Canister, 7½", from $8 to **10.00**
Creamer, 5", from $4 to **5.00**
Cup, 9-oz, from $2.50 to **3.50**
Egg tray, 12", from $10 to ...**14.00**
Pitcher, 68-oz, from $20 to ..**25.00**
Plate, dinner; 10", from $6 to ..**8.00**
Platter, footed, from $12 to .**15.00**
Saucer, 6", from $1 to **2.00**
Sugar bowl, footed, 2-handled, open, 5", from $4 to **5.00**
Tray, serving; high rim edge, 10", from $9 to **12.00**
Vase, footed, 3¾", from $6 to ..**8.00**

Toothbrush Holders

Children's ceramic tooth-brush holders represent one of today's popular collecting fields, with some of the character-related examples bringing $150.00 and up. Many were made in Japan before WWII. For a comprehensive look at toothbrush holders and current market values, we recommend *A Pictorial Guide to Toothbrush Holders* by our advisor, Marilyn Cooper (see the Directory under Texas).

Annie Oakley, hanging, 2 holes, Japan, 5¾", from $90 to .**100.00**
Aviator, standing, celluloid, 1 hole, 6⅛", from $110 to **120.00**
Bear, hanging, chalkware, brown, black & red, 1 hole, 6", from $45 to **55.00**
Bellhop w/Flowers, w/tray, 1 hole, Japan, 5¼" **75.00**
Bonzo, w/side tray, mouth holds brush, Germany, 3⅝" .**135.00**
Boy in Knickers, standing, no tray, 2 holes, Japan, 4¾", from $65 to **75.00**
Boy on Elephant, hanging, w/tray, 3 holes, Japan, 6¼" **85.00**
Boy w/Cap & Tie, dog at side, hanging, 3 holes, Japan, 6¼" **75.00**
Bulldog, sitting, no tray, 1 hole, Japan, 3½", from $50 to .**60.00**
Cat w/Bass Fiddle, hanging, w/tray, 2 holes, Japan, 6" **120.00**
Children in Auto, hanging, w/tray, 2 holes, Japan, 5" **80.00**
Circus Elephant, hanging, bright colors, 1 hole, Japan, 5⅜", from $75 to **85.00**
Clown, hangs, painted cast iron, arms hold brush, 3¾", M, from $200 to **225.00**
Clown, juggling, hanging, w/tray, 3 holes, Japan, 5" **85.00**
Cow, hanging, w/tray, 3 holes, Japan, 6" **90.00**
Duck, hanging, chalkware, yellow, red & black, 2 holes, 4¾", from $35 to **45.00**

Cat w/Bass Fiddle, 2 holes, Japan, 6", from $110.00 to $120.00. (Photo courtesy Marilyn Cooper)

Ducky Dandy, hanging, 2 holes, Japan, 4¼", from $150 to **175.00**

Elephant, toothbrush through mouth, tan lustre, Japan, 3", from $85 to **95.00**

Flapper Girl, standing, no tray, 2 holes, 4¼", from $110 to **120.00**

Little Red Riding Hood, hanging, 2 holes, Japan, 5¼", from $95 to **110.00**

Man w/Derby Hat, hanging, no tray, 2 holes, Japan, 5½", from $75 to **85.00**

Mandolin Player, standing, 1 hole, 4⅛" **100.00**

Mexican Boy, hanging, w/tray, 2 holes, Japan, 5½" **90.00**

Old King Cole, hanging, 1 hole, Japan, 5¼", from $85 to .**100.00**

Old Mother Hubbard, shaker top, Germany, 6¼" **375.00**

Old Woman in Shoe, hanging, w/tray, 3 holes, Japan, 4½" **80.00**

Penguin, hanging, black & white, 3 holes, Japan, 5½", from $85 to **95.00**

Pinocchio & Figaro, standing, 1 hole, Shafford, 5¼" **475.00**

Pirate w/Sash, hanging, w/tray, 2 holes, Japan, 6" **90.00**

Popeye, bisque, standing, no tray, 1 hole, Japan, 5", from $475 to **500.00**

Popeye, standing, 1 hole, Japan, 5" **500.00**

Rabbit, hanging, green, red & black, 1 hole, Germany, T696, 5½" **90.00**

Soldier w/Sash, hanging, 2 holes, Japan, 6", from $70 to ..**80.00**

Uncle Willie, hanging, red & yellow attire, FAS-Japan, 5", from $80 to **85.00**

Toys

Toy collecting is a very popular hobby, and if purchases are wisely made, there is good potential for investment. Most of the battery-operated toys made from the '40s through the '60s were made in Japan, even though some were distributed by American companies such as Linemar and Cragstan, who often sold them under their own names. Because of their complex mechanisms, few survive. Condition is very important in evaluating a battery-op, and the more complex their movements, the more they're worth.

Japanese wind-up toys are another fun and exciting field of toy collecting. The fascination with Japanese toys stems from their simplistic but exciting actions and bright and attractive colors. Many of the boxes that these toys came in are almost as attractive as the toys themselves!

Toys from the 1800s are rarely if ever found in mint condition but should at least be working and have all their original parts. Toys manufactured in the 20th century are evaluated more critically. Compared to one in mint condition, original box intact, even a slightly worn toy with no box may be worth only about half price. Character-related toys, space toys, toy trains, and toys from the '60s are among the most desirable. Several good books are available, if you want more information: *Modern Toys, American Toys 1930 to 1980,* by Linda Baker (Collector Books); *Collectible Male Action Figures,* by Paris and Susan Manos (Collector Books); *Collector's Guide to Tootsietoys,* by David E. Richter (Collector Books); *Toys, Antique and Collectible,* and *Character Toys and Collectibles,* by David Longest (Collector Books); *Collecting Toys Soldiers, Collecting Toy Trains,* and *Collecting Toys,* by Richard O'Brien. For more information and additional listings, see *Schroeder's Collectible Toys, Antique to Modern* (Collector Books). See also Character Collectibles; Star Trek; Star Wars.

Battery-Operated

Allis-Chalmers HD 5 Crawler, 1955, 8", EX **175.00**
B-Z Porter, Modern Toys, 1950s, 7½", MIB **375.00**
Blacksmith Bear, AI, 1950s, 9½", MIB **400.00**
Blushing Cowboy, Y, 1960s, NM **125.00**
Blushing Willie, Y, 1960, 10", NMIB **100.00**
Chippy the Chipmunk, Alps, 12", MIB **250.00**
Cock-A-Doodle-Doo Rooster, Mukuni, 8", VG **50.00**

Josie the Walking Cow, Rosco, 12½", EX with original box, $200.00.

Ford Mustang Stunt Car, Japan, 1969, litho tin, MIB, $125.00. (Photo courtesy Dunbar Gallery)

Concrete Mixer, Linemar, 9", NMIB **240.00**

Cragston One-Armed Bandit, Y, 1960s, NMIB **275.00**

Dennis the Menace Playing Xylophone, Rosko, 1950s, MIB **300.00**

Drinking Dog, Y, 1950s, M .**125.00**

Dune Buggy, TPS, 11", EX+ .**100.00**

Farmland Cup Ride, MIB .**325.00**

Fido the Xylophone Player, Alps, 9", EX (VG box) **250.00**

Fred & Barney Car, AHI, 1974, rare, NM **175.00**

Gino Neapolitan Balloon Blower, Tomiyama, 10", MIB ..**225.00**

Happy Naughty Chimp, Daishin, 1960, MIB **100.00**

Hippo Chef Cutey Cook, Y, 10", MIB **1,275.00**

Hooty the Happy Owl, Alps, 9", NM (EX box) **150.00**

Jocko the Drinking Monkey, Linemar, 11", VG+ **100.00**

Linus Loveable Lion, Illco/Hong Kong, 1970, MIB **40.00**

Lucky Seven Dice Throwing Monkey, Alps, 1960, MIB **165.00**

Major Tooty, plays drums, Alps, 14", MIB **275.00**

Mickey Mouse Loop the Loop, MIB **175.00**

Mother Goose, Cragston, 1950, EX **100.00**

Musical Jolly Chimp, CK, 10½", MIB **100.00**

Peppermint Twist Doll, Haji, 12", MIB **375.00**

Pinky the Clown, Alps, 10½", NM **225.00**

Playful Puppy, MT, 7½", MIB .**300.00**

Puffy Morris, Y, 10", MIB .**375.00**

Reading Bear, Alps, 1950s, 9", M **525.00**

Santa Bank, Trim-A-Tree, H&C, 11", NMIB **300.00**

Santa Copter, MT, 1960, 8½", MIB **150.00**

Santa on Rotating Globe, HTC, 15", MIB **675.00**

Skipping Monkey, TN, 1960s, NMIB **100.00**

Smarty Bird, Ideal, 1964, working, EX **60.00**

Southern Pacific Model Train, Japan, unused, MIB ...**200.00**

Surfing Snoopy, Mattel #3477, M 60.00

Swan the Queen on the Water, MIB 500.00

Tinkling Trolley, MT, 10½", MIB 200.00

Turn-O-Matic Gun Jeep, TN, 10", NMIB 175.00

Wild West Rodeo Bubbling Bull, Linemar, 6½", MIB 375.00

Windy the Juggling Elephant, TN, 10½", EX 85.00

Yo-Yo Clown, Alps, 9", NM .400.00

Friction

Action Clown Mobile, plastic, Mattel #463, 1952, 7", NMIB 85.00

Army Jeep Set, tin, Sanshin/Japan, 5", NM (EX box) 200.00

Batman Car, tin w/vinyl figure, ASC, 1959, 8½", NM (EX box) 1,600.00

Broderick Crawford Highway Patrol Car, English, 11", NM (NM box) 350.00

Champion Racer #98, Indy-style racer w/driver, ETC, 19", G- 500.00

Circus Boat, litho tin & vinyl, German, 7", NM (EX box) 200.00

Citroen Wagon, painted & litho tin, French, 1950s, 8", VG (orig box) 120.00

Clown Jalopy Cycle, litho tin, TPS, 9", NMIB 700.00

Comet Racer #37, litho tin, rubber tires, Y/Japan, 9", NM (EX box) 95.00

Continental Super Special, convertible, Cragston, 13¾", NMIB 650.00

Disney Express Bus, litho tin, MT/Japan, 10", NM (NM box) 600.00

Duckmobile, litho tin, celluloid figure, Japan, 6½", M (VG box) 390.00

Dump Truck, red & white w/black tires, Yonezawa, 14", NM (VG box) 225.00

Fire Car, litho tin, SSS, mk Josteele FD, 6", NMIB 225.00

Fire Pumper, tin body w/wood seats/boiler, DP Clark, 10", G- 385.00

Fire Truck, plastic w/rubber tires, 1950s, 11", NM 250.00

Flappy Duck, litho tin, TT, 5½", NMIB 45.00

Flying Car, futuristic car w/spinning blade, Masuya, 8", NMIB 275.00

Friendly Cycle, litho tin, German, 8", EX 425.00

Golden Racer #3, litho tin, SN/Japan, 11", NM (EX box) 210.00

Highway Patrol Cycle, litho tin, ATC, 10", MIB 360.00

Dick Tracy Sparkling Riot Car, Marx, 6½", EX in original box, $245.00.

Honeymooners, Jackie Gleason's
bus, Wolverine, 1950s, 9",
NM **300.00**
Honk-Along Children Bus, litho
tin, Kanto Toys, 8½", EX+ (EX
box) **130.00**
Hot Rod, trunk mk Century, TN,
7", EX (VG box) **150.00**
Huckleberry Hound, litho
tin, Linemar, 1961, 10",
NMIB **675.00**
Jalopy Stock Car #10, litho tin,
NGS/Cragstan, 6", NM (EX+
box) **120.00**
Louie & His Dream Car, litho tin,
celluloid figure, Linemar, 5",
NMIB **575.00**
Merry-Go-Round Truck, litho tin,
TN, 8", EX **175.00**
Mickey Mouse Motorcyclist,
litho tin, Linemar/WDP,
3½", EX **325.00**
Monkee Mobile, tin w/plastic figures,
ASC, 12", M (VG box) ..**455.00**
Police Car, black & white litho tin,
German, 10", EX **440.00**
Sparking Choo Choo, litho tin,
Kraemer/German, 1950s, 17",
M (VG box) **160.00**

Wind-Ups

Atom Motorcycle, litho tin, TN,
11½", VG **250.00**
Bagpipe Player, hand-painted,
Gunthermann, 10½", EX .**465.00**
Bear, fur-covered tin, brown,
Occupied Japan, 5", NM ..**45.00**
Betty, litho tin, Lindstrom, 1930s,
8", NM **300.00**
Charlie Chaplin, tin w/cloth outfit,
Schuco, 6½", G **900.00**
Dancing Lassie, litho tin,
Lindstrom, 8", EX+ **155.00**

**Donald Duck the Drummer,
Linemar, litho tin, 6", NM, from
$650.00 to $675.00. (Photo courtesy Antique Treasures & Toys)**

Donald Duck Waddler, celluloid,
K, 3", EX+ (EX box) **650.00**
Doodle-Bug, plastic, full-figure
driver, Nosco, 1950, 10",
MIB **230.00**
Flamenco Dancer, hand-painted tin,
Gunthermann, 8", G **415.00**
Flying Fish Boat, litho tin, Asahi,
11", VG **50.00**
Ford Saloon, blue, Minic, 3½", NM
(EX+ box) **150.00**
Girl w/Baby, cloth clothing & hair,
Schuco, NM **165.00**
Go-Kart, advances w/sound, Schuco
#1055, 6", NMIB **385.00**
Happy Skaters, rabbit skates,
TPS/Cragstan, 6", NM (EX+
box) **650.00**
Hott & Trott, Black banjo &
piano players, Unique Art,
5½", EX **1,000.00**

Jack Sprout, painted tin, Gunthermann, 1900s, repainted, 6½", EX 460.00

Jolly Pig, celluloid, advances w/clown pulling his tail, 7", MIB 135.00

Krazy Kat on Scooter, tin, 1920s, EX 1,200.00

Li'l Abner & his Dogpatch Band, litho tin, Unique Art, 1945, 7", NMIB 875.00

Military Motorcycle w/Sidecar, litho tin, SFA, 4", VG ..250.00

Military Motorcycle w/Sidecar, litho tin, TN, 8", EX ...300.00

Minstrel, painted tin, plays banjo, 8", G 500.00

Motorcycle w/Driver, red, Technofix/ US Zone, 7", VG 280.00

Musical Merry-Go-Round, litho tin, Ohio Art, 1954, 9", NM (EX+ box) 525.00

Nautilus Submarine, 20,000 Leagues Under the Sea, Sutcliffe, MIB 475.00

Oreo Tailspin Pup, Orianna Metal Products, 1940s, 5", MIB 100.00

Peacock, Eberl, 10", EX 250.00

Pigmyphone, green litho tin, Bing, 3x6x6", EX 390.00

Racer #3, red, Schuco, 5½", EX 175.00

Roadster, litho tin, Kingsbury, repainted, 11", G 200.00

Rubber Neck Willie, celluloid, vibrates around/spins cane, 6½", NM 200.00

Scottie Dog, tin & plush, Schuco, 4½", NM 175.00

See-Saw Circus, Lewco Products, 1940s, VG 200.00

Smitty Scooter, Nifty, 1920s, 8", G 675.00

Solisto Monkey Violinist, Schuco, 4½", EX 275.00

Spark Plug (Wa-Gee Walker), gold cloth & felt over tin, 9", VG 440.00

Sweeping Mammy, Lindstrom, 1930s, 8", NM (EX+ box) 400.00

Tractor, litho tin, Mettoy, 7½", NM (EX box) 100.00

Tractor, tin, Distler, 7", EX .325.00

Water-Driven Mill, painted tin, German, early 1900s, 11", EX 400.00

Trolls

The first trolls to come to the United States were molded after a 1952 design by Marti and Helena Kuuskoski of Tampere, Finland. The first to be mass produced in America were molded from wood carvings made by Thomas Dam of Denmark. As the demand for these trolls increased, several US manufacturers became licensed to produce them. The most noteworthy of these were Uneeda doll company's Wishnik line and Inga Dykin's Scandia House True Trolls. Thomas Dam continued to import his Dam Things line.

The troll craze from the '60s spawned many items other than dolls such as wall plaques, salt and pepper shakers, pins, squirt guns, rings, clay trolls, lamps, Halloween costumes, animals, lawn ornaments, coat racks, notebooks, folders, and even a car.

In the '70s, '80s, and '90s more new trolls were produced. While these trolls are collectible to some, the avid troll collector still prefers those produced in the '60s. Remember, trolls that receive top dollar must be in mint condition.

For more information we recommend *Collector's Guide to Trolls* by Pat Peterson (Collector Books). Our advisor is Roger Inouye, who is listed in the Directory under California.

Santa, marked Chuck-O-Luck, green suit and eyes, pink hair and white beard, 3½", $65.00. (Photo courtesy Roger Inouye)

Bamboozle Bear, white mohair, yellow felt bow at neck, rare **28.00**
Caveman, green eyes, yellow hair, leopard-skin outfit, Dam, 12" **150.00**
Christmas Stocking, Norfin, lg vinyl head, M, pr **6.00**
Clown, Dam, painted-on clothes, yellow eyes, '65, 5½", from $175 to **250.00**
Doll face, petal-shaped red & white costume, Wishnik, 7" ...**20.00**

Elephant, blue hollow plastic, fuzzy hair, Japan, 1960s, 3", EX+ **25.00**
Elephant w/drum, Dam, 1964, 3", NM **50.00**
Giraffe, amber eyes, gray hair, Dam, 12", G **125.00**
Hawaiian Troll, vinyl, 1964, 3", M **18.00**
Hobbit, yellow mohair, nude, gloved hands, 2½" **8.00**
Indian, dark skin, headband, outfit & shoes, 1960s, 3½", EX+ ...**15.00**
Leprechaun, w/jacket, 1969, EX **25.00**
Lion, Dam, lg, M **125.00**
Love Bug, original clothes, Regal, 4½", EX **115.00**
Moontik, mohair body w/rubber feet, shake eyes, Uneeda Wishnik, 18" **100.00**
Neanderthal man, painted eyes, Bijou Toy, 1963, 7½", EX .**32.00**
Nude, any eye or hair color, Dam, 3", G **8.00**
Pixie face, nude, molded yellow hair, painted eyes, Wishnik, 7" .**20.00**
Santa, bank, 7" **68.00**
Sappy Claws, Dam, M **28.00**
She-nik, white mohair to floor, yellow eyes, S on front of dress, 5" **14.00**
Thumbsucker, long white mohair, purple felt dress, Norfin, 18" **85.00**
Vampire, jointed, Hong Kong, 1966, 3", M **20.00**
Viking, wood body, black rabbit fur, w/spiked mace, tin shield, 2½" **5.00**
Voodoo doll, black plastic, white hair, red eyes, white clothes, 3", M **15.00**
Weird Creature, real animal hair, 1960s, 3", MIB **30.00**

TV Guides

For most people, their *TV Guide* spends a week on top of their TV set or by the remote and then is discarded. But to collectors this weekly chronicle of TV history is highly revered. For many people, vintage *TV Guides* evoke happy feelings of the simpler days of their youth. They also search for information on television shows not to be found in reference books. As with any type of ephemera, condition is very important. Some collectors prefer issues without address labels on the cover. Values are given for guides in fine to mint condition. Our advisor is Jeffrey M. Kadet, *TV Guide* Specialist, who is listed in the Directory under Illinois.

1953, November 13-19, Jimmy Durante cover, Pride of Family article **30.00**

1954, August 21-27, Steve Allen & Jayne Meadows cover, J Paar article **28.00**

1955, May 7-13, Peggy Wood of Mama cover, Capt Midnight article **15.00**

1956, August 4-10, Jackie Cooper & Cleo cover, Milton Berle article **10.00**

1957, April 13-19, Nanette Fabray cover, Ronald Reagan article **9.00**

1957, December 28-January 3, Ricky Nelson cover, E Arden Show article **50.00**

1958, July 12-18, Lucille Ball cover, John Russell article **35.00**

1958, November 29-December 5, Victor Borge cover, Tuesday Weld article **10.00**

1959, May 9-15, Edd Byrnes of 77 Sunset Strip cover **25.00**

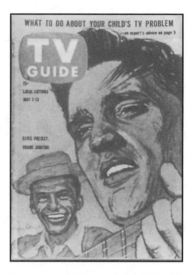

1960, May 7-13, Elvis and Frank Sinatra on cover, articles on TV westerns and Steve Allen, $45.00.

1960, October 1-7, Dinah Shore cover, Andy Griffith Show article **12.00**

1961, April 15-21, Mitch Miller cover, Surfside 6 article **8.00**

1961, August 19-25, Troy Donahoe cover, Elizabeth Montgomery article **7.00**

1962, June 9-15, Efram Zimbalist Jr cover, Bob Newhart article **10.00**

1963, December 14-20, Sinatra, Crosby & Martin cover, Lewis article **35.00**

1963, May 4-10, Cast of The Virginian cover, John F Kennedy article **17.00**

1964, March 7-13, Richard Chamberlain cover, SJ Perelman article ..10.00

1964, September 26-October 2, Dan Blocker cover, Sophia Loren article 21.00

1965, July 24-30, Raymond Burr cover, Munsters article ...8.00

1965, October 16-22, Red Skelton cover, Roaring Chicken article 7.00

1966, April 16-22, Petticoat Junction girls cover, Bob Hope article 17.00

1966, December 3-9, Cast of Rat Patrol cover, Dark Shadows article 45.00

1967, June 10-16, Smothers Brothers cover, Time Tunnel article 27.00

1967, October 21-27, Mia Farrow cover, High Chaparral article 15.00

1968, July 6-12, Barbara Eden cover, Alejandro Ray article 22.00

1968, March 9-15, Jackie Gleason cover, Jack Benny article .8.00

1969, May 31-June 6, Cast of Family Affair cover, W Brennan article 6.00

1970, January 31-February 6, Debbie Reynolds cover, Room 222 article 5.00

1970, September 12-18, Special Fall Preview cover, 1970-71 shows 20.00

1971, February 6-12, Cast of the Odd Couple cover 16.00

1971, October 9-15, Dick Van Dyke & Hope Lange cover, Bonanza article 15.00

1972, March 18-24, Sonny & Cher cover, James Garner article 7.00

1972, November 18-24, Bea Arthur as Maude cover, Waltons article .8.00

1973, February 3-9, Bill Cosby cover, Hawaii Five-O article 4.00

1973, June 9-15, Richard Widmark cover, Bob Newhart article 4.00

1973, October 6-12, Diana Rigg of Diana cover, Wolfman Jack article 15.00

1974, January 19-25, Bob Hope cover, Larry Hagman article 5.00

1974, July 61-2, Lucille Ball cover, Wimbledon article 12.00

1975, June 21-27, Cast of the Jeffersons cover, Olympics article 8.00

1975, November 15-21, Soul & Glaser of Starsky & Hutch cover 20.00

1976, January 10-16, Ron Howard & Henry Winkler of Happy Days cover 20.00

1976, May 8-14, Lindsay Wagner, Bionic Woman cover, T Snyder article 14.00

1976, November 13-19, Dorothy Hamill cover, Charlie's Angels article 5.00

1977, April 16-22, Frank Sinatra by Hirschfeld cover 7.00

1977, June 25-July 1, Cast of the Waltons cover, F Fawcett article 15.00

1977, October 22-28, Welcome Back Kotter Cast cover, Rafferty article 12.00

1978, June 17-23, Valerie Harper cover, Battlestar Galactica article 7.00

1979, June 30-July 6, Dukes of Hazzard cover, Quinn Cummings article 12.00

1979, March 24-30, Ricardo Montalban cover, Animal House article 5.00

1980, October 25-31, Barney Miller by Hirschfeld cover 5.00

1981, May 16-22, Cast of Hart to Hart cover, Inga Swenson article 7.00

1982, November 20-26, Cast of Three's Company cover ..5.00

1982, September 18-24, Victoria Principal cover, Alex Karras article 7.00

1983, March 26-April 1, Chamberlain & Ward of Thorn Birds cover 20.00

1983, October 15-21, Larry Hagman & Joan Collins cover 4.00

1984, September 15-21, George Burns & Catherine Bach cover 5.00

1985, September 21-27, Michael J Fox cover, Moonlighting article 7.00

1986, October 18-24, Box Bonsall of Family Ties cover, P Duffy article 6.00

1987, June 13-19, Waxman & Gless of Cagney & Lacy cover 6.00

1988, July 2-8, Cast of Designing Women cover, Dana Carvey article 5.00

1989, May 20-26, Rosanne Barr of Rosanne cover, BL Stryker article 6.00

1990, November 3-9, November to Remember cover, Cheer's 200th article 8.00

1991, August 3-9, Madonna: MTV's 10th Anniversary cover 12.00

1992, April 18-24, Cast of Home Improvement cover 5.00

1993, July 31-August 6, Patrick Stewart of Star Trek cover 10.00

1994, July 2-8, Reba McIntire cover, X-Files article 10.00

Universal

Located in Cambridge, Ohio, Universal Potteries Incorporated produced various lines of dinnerware from 1934 to the late 1950s, several of which are very attractive, readily available, and therefore quite collectible. Refer to *The Collector's Encyclopedia of American Dinnerware* by Jo Cunningham (Collector Books) for more information. See also Cattail Dinnerware.

Calico Fruit, refrigerator jug, with lid, $35.00.

Ballerina, chop plate 15.00
Ballerina, creamer & sugar bowl 20.00
Ballerina, egg cup 12.00
Ballerina, gravy boat 15.00
Bittersweet, cup & saucer ...14.00
Bittersweet, platter, oval, 13½" 28.00

Bittersweet, salt & pepper shakers, pr **12.50**
Calico Fruit, bowl, mixing; w/lid, 8¾" **40.00**
Calico Fruit, bowl, 9" **18.00**
Calico Fruit, pepper shaker .**20.00**
Calico Fruit, platter **12.00**
Calico Fruit, utility shaker .**12.00**
Mount Vernon, bowl, soup; 8" ..**12.50**
Mount Vernon, sugar bowl, from $10 to **12.50**
Poppy, butter dish, from $22.50 to **25.00**
Poppy, gravy boat **15.00**
Woodvine, bowl, mixing; 4" .**20.00**
Woodvine, sugar bowl, w/lid .**18.00**

Valentines

In terms of collectibility, today's interest in good examples from the 1940s through the 1960s, including mechanicals, penny valentines, and boxed cards, makes that time frame the fastest-growing period in the history of valentines. Within the general spectrum, there are many subdivisions with diversified appeal that can cross over into other collections, such as Black memorabilia, advertising, transportation, cartoon characters, folk art, and so on.

Please keep these factors in mind when assessing the value of your valentines: age, condition, size, category, and whether or not an artist's signature is present. All of these factors were taken into consideration when the following valentines were priced. Also, it is important to remember that they tend to be priced higher on the East Coast than the West, primarily due to higher demand there. Our advisor for this category is Katherine Kreider, who is listed in the Directory under Pennsylvania.

In the listings that follow, HCPP stands for honeycomb paper puff, and MIG indicates valentines marked Made in Germany.

Betty Rubble of the Flintstones, flat, 1962, 4¾", EX, $5.00. (Photo courtesy Katherine Kreider)

Booklet, Little Bo Peep, 1940s, USA, 6½x3¾", EX............**5.00**
Dimensional, flower basket, HCPP, USA, 1926, 8½x8", EX ..**10.00**
Easel-back, big-eared golfer, Made in Germany, 1930s, 8½x4¾", NM **10.00**
Easel-back, button boy, hand painted, 3½x3½", EX **3.00**
Flat, druggist, comic, 1930s, 8x7½", EX **5.00**
Flat, Gone with the Wind, USA, 3¼x2¾", EX **3.00**

Flat, Little Burglar, 4¼x3¼" .**2.00**
Flat, penny valentine, no marker, USA, 5¼x5½", EX **3.00**
Flat, teddy bear, Hallmark, 1948, 8½x6¾", EX **3.00**
Flat, Whitney, 4x3", EX **1.00**
Flat, 3 Little Pigs, USA, 4½x5", EX **5.00**
Gift-Giving, w/original fingernail file, USA, NM **5.00**
Mechanical, flat, bear cub, Steiner Litho Co, 8x3½", EX **5.00**
Mechanical, flat, monkey grinder, Carrington Co, 7x9", EX .**5.00**
Mechanical, flat, paper-doll sailor, 9x3½", EX **5.00**
Mechanical, Pekingese dog, 6¼x5", VG **5.00**
Oh Boy Gum, original gum wrapper, USA, 4x5", EX **10.00**
Punchout, 3½x2¾x½", EX **1.00**
Wishing well, Hallmark, 1960s, 9½x7x4½", NM **3.00**

Vernon Kilns

From 1931 until 1958, Vernon Kilns produced hundreds of patterns of fine dinnerware that today's collectors enjoy reassembling. They retained the services of famous artists and designers such as Rockwell Kent and Walt Disney, who designed both dinnerware lines and novelty items. Examples of their work are at a premium.

Barkwood, bowl, fruit; 5½" **7.00**
Barkwood, mug, 9-oz **20.00**
Barkwood, salt & pepper shakers, lg, pr **22.00**
Brown-Eyed Susan, bowl, mixing; 8", from $25 to **35.00**
Brown-Eyed Susan, casserole, round, from $35 to **45.00**
Brown-Eyed Susan, cup, AD .**22.00**
Brown-Eyed Susan, plate, salad .**12.00**
Brown-Eyed Susan, salt & pepper shakers, regular, pr, from $10 to **15.00**
Chintz, bowl, rim soup **18.00**
Chintz, plate, luncheon **15.00**
Chintz, teapot **60.00**
Coral Reef, egg cup **48.00**
Coral Reef, tumbler **42.50**
Delores, plate, dinner; 10½" .**15.00**

Harvest, teapot, 6-cup, $65.00.

411

Gingham, bowl, oval, 10".......**20.00**
Gingham, coffeepot, AD; 2-cup .**20.00**
Gingham, plate, dinner; from $12
   to **14.00**
Gingham, sugar bowl, w/lid ..**15.00**
Hawaiian Flowers, cup &
   saucer **25.00**
Hawaiian Flowers, plate, salad;
   7½" **20.00**
Hawaiian Flowers, sauce boat .**40.00**
Homespun, bowl, mixing; 6", from
   $20 to **25.00**
Homespun, creamer, individual,
   from $14 to **18.00**
Homespun, plate, grill; 11", from
   $18 to **22.00**
Lei Lani, bowl, coupe soup; 7½" .**18.00**
Lei Lani, cup & saucer **45.00**
Lei Lani, plate, bread & butter;
   from $7 to **10.00**
May Flower, bowl, serving; 9" .**25.00**
May Flower, pitcher, 2-qt **40.00**
Moby Dick, bowl, fruit; brown .**15.00**
Moby Dick, plate, blue, 9" ...**65.00**
Native California, creamer ..**15.00**
Native California, plate, dinner;
   from $15 to **18.00**
Native California, plate, luncheon;
   square **15.00**
Organdie, bowl, mixing; 8" ..**35.00**
Organdie, bowl, 1-pt **20.00**
Organdie, cup, custard; 3" ...**25.00**
Organdie, pitcher, ½-pt **25.00**
Organdie, sauce boat **25.00**
Sherwood, bowl, coupe soup ..**7.00**
Sherwood, bowl, 7½" **8.00**
Sherwood, plate, dinner **8.00**
Sherwood, tumbler **11.00**
Ultra California, coffepot, AD; 2-
   cup **70.00**
Ultra California, plate, dinner .**24.00**
Wheat, bowl, salad; footed base,
   12" **60.00**
Wheat, platter, 16" **45.00**

View-Master Reels & Packets

View-Master, the invention of William Gruber, was first introduced to the public at the 1939-1940 New York World's Fair and at the same time at the Golden Gate Exposition in California. Since then, thousands of reels and packets have been produced on subjects as diverse as life itself. Sawyers' View-Master even made two different stereo cameras for the general public, enabling people to make their own personal reels, and then offered a stereo projector to project the pictures they took on a silver screen in full-color 3-D.

View-Master has been owned by five different companies: the original Sawyers Company, G.A.F. (in October 1966), View-Master International (in 1981), Ideal Toy Company, and Tyco Toy Company (the present owners).

Unfortunately, after G.A.F. sold View-Master in 1981, neither View-Master International, Ideal, nor Tyco Toy Company have had any intention of making the products anything but toy items, selling mostly cartoons. This, of course, has made the early non-cartoon single reels and the three-reel packets desirable items.

The earliest single reels from 1939-1945 were not white in color but were originally dark blue with a gold sticker in the center. They came in attractive gold-colored envelopes. Then they were made in a blue and tan combination. These early reels are more desirable, as the print runs were low.

Most white single reels are very common, as they were produced from 1946 through 1957 by the millions. There are exceptions, however, such as commercial reels promoting a product and reels of obscure scenic attractions, as these would have had smaller print runs. In 1952 a European division of View-Master was established in Belgium. Most reels and items made there are more valuable to a collector, since they are hard to find in this country.

In 1955 View-Master came up with the novel idea of selling packets of three reels in one colorful envelope with a picture or photo on the front. Many times a story booklet was included. These became very popular, and sales of single reels were slowly discontinued. Most three-reel packets are desirable, whether Sawyers or G.A.F., as long as they are in nice condition. Nearly all viewers are common and have little value except the very early ones, such as the Model A and Model B. These viewers had to be opened to insert the reels. The blue and brown versions of the Model B are rare. Another desirable viewer is the Model D, which is the only focusing viewer that View-Master made. Condition is very important to the value of all View-Master items, as it is with most collectibles. Our advisor is Mr. Walter Sigg, who is listed in the Directory under New Jersey.

Camera, Mark II, w/case ...**100.00**
Camera, Personal Stereo, w/ case **100.00**
Close-up lens, for Personal Camera **100.00**
Film cutter, for cameras **100.00**
Packet, Addams Family or Munsters, 3-reel set **50.00**
Packet, Belgium made, 3-reel set, from $4 to **35.00**
Packet, miscellaneous subject, 3-reel set, from $3 to **50.00**
Packet, scenic, 3-reel set, from $1 to **25.00**
Packet, TV or movie, 3-reel set, from $2 to **50.00**
Projector, Stereo-Matic 500 .**200.00**
Reel, Belgium made, from $1 to .**10.00**
Reel, blue, from $2.50 to **10.00**
Reel, commercial, brand-name product (Coca-Cola, etc), from $5 to **50.00**
Reel, gold center, gold-colored package **10.00**
Reel, Sawyers, white, early from 25¢ to **5.00**
Reel, 3-D movie preview (House of Wax, Kiss Me Kate, etc) .**50.00**
Viewer, Model B, blue or brown, ea **100.00**
Viewer, Model D, focusing type **30.00**

Tru-View

Tru-Vue, a subsidiary of the Rock Island Bridge and Iron Works in Rock Island, Illinois, first introduced their product to the public at the 1933 Century of Progress Exposition in Chicago. With their popular black and white 3-D filmstrips and viewers, Tru-Vue quickly became the successor to the stereoscope and stereocards of the 1800s and early 1900s. They made many stereo views of cities, national parks, scenic attractions, and even some foreign countries. They produced children's stories, some that featured personalities and nightclubs, and many commercial and instructional filmstrips.

By the late 1940s, Sawyers' View-Master had become a very strong competitor. Their full-color 7-scene stereo reels were very popular with the public and had cut into Tru-Vue's sales considerably. So it was a tempting offer when Sawyers made a bid to buy out the company in 1951. Sawyers needed Tru-Vue, not only to eliminate competition but because Tru-Vue owned the rights to photograph Disney characters and the Disneyland theme park in California.

After the take-over, Sawyers' View-Master continued to carry Tru-Vue products but stopped production of the 3-D filmstrips and viewers. Instead they adopted a new format with 7-scene 3-D cards and a new 3-D viewer. These were sold mainly in toy stores and today have little value. All of the pictures were on a cheaper 'Eastmancolor' slide film, and most of them have today faded into a magenta color. Many cards came apart, as the glue that was used tends to separate quite easily. The value of these, therefore, is low. (Many cards were later remade as View-Master reels using the superior 'Kodachrome' film.) On the other hand, advertising literature, dealer displays, and items that were not meant to be sold to the public often have considerable collector value.

When G.A.F. bought View-Master in 1966, they gradually phased out the Tru-Vue format.

Card, from $1 to **3.00**
Filmstrip, children's story, from $1 to **3.00**
Filmstrip, commercial (promoting products), from $20 to ..**50.00**
Filmstrip, instructional, from $5 to **15.00**
Filmstrip, ocean liner **15.00**
Filmstrip, personality (Sally Rand, Gypsy Rose Lee, etc), from $15 to **20.00**
Filmstrip, scenic, from $1 to ..**5.00**
Filmstrip, World's Fair **7.50**

Wall Pockets

If you've been interested enough to notice, wall pockets are everywhere — easily found, relatively inexpensive, and very diversified. They were made in Japan, Czechoslovakia, and by many, many companies in the United States. Those made by companies best known for their art pottery (Weller, Roseville, etc.) are in a class of their own, but the novelty, just-for-fun wall pockets stand on their own merits. Examples with large, colorful birds or those with unusual modeling are usually the more desirable. There are three books we recommend for more information: *Collectors Guide to Wall Pockets, Affordable and Others,* by Marvin and Joy Gibson (L-W Books); *Collector's Encyclopedia of Wall Pockets* by Betty and Bill Newbound; *Wall Pockets of the Past* by Fredda Perkins; and *Collector's*

Guide to Made in Japan Ceramics by Carole Bess White. (The last three are all published by Collector Books.) See also Cleminson; McCoy; Shawnee; other specific manufacturers.

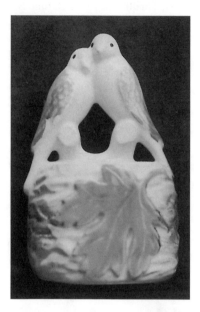

Lovebirds on a nest, with flat back and bottom, Morton Pottery, 6½", $20.00. (Photo courtesy Fredda Perkins)

Baby w/swan, marked Bradley Exclusives, Japan, from $15 to **20.00**

Bananas, yellow bunch on brown stem, Gilner, 5" **10.00**

Bird on basket w/floral branch, multicolored, Japan, 8¼" **25.00**

Bluebird w/Oriental scene, impressed Japan mark, 2½x3½" **15.00**

Cornucopia w/cattails & applied duck, airbrushed, Pat 149244, 7" **20.00**

Cupid holding up lg red heart, light brown hair, Japan, 5" ...**15.00**

Elephant w/trunk up, white lustre w/multicolored accents, Japan, 7" **45.00**

Fruit cornucopia, no mark, 5⅝" **15.00**

Girl w/rag doll, multicolored details on white, marked USA 810, 6½" **25.00**

Japanese lady w/basket on back, multicolored costume, Japan, 8½" **75.00**

Kitten, brown head & paws emerging from green bag, unmarked, 5½" **20.00**

Lustre pocket w/painted scene, Japan, 6¼", from $25 to .**35.00**

Madonna holy water font, Italy, 8" **25.00**

Peacock, blue, green, pink or white, marked USA, 6½" **15.00**

Scoop, cylindrical w/handle, embossed flowers, light blue, 9" **12.00**

Serenity Prayer, Norcrest Japan label, 7" **15.00**

Telephone, crank style w/flower & leaf design, L&F Ceramics, 7" **20.00**

Violin w/purple & yellow pansies, green & gold details, 6½" .**12.00**

Woodpecker on log, beak at hole, Japan, 7¼", from $25 to .**35.00**

Western Collectibles

Items such as chaps, spurs, saddles, and bits represent possibly the most colorful genre in the history of our country, and collectors, especially from the western states, find them fascinating. The romance of the Old West lives on through relics related to those bygone days of cowboys, Wild West shows, frontier sheriffs, and boomtown saloons. Our advisor, Dan Hutchins, is listed in the Directory under Iowa.

Bit, bridle; US Military, 1909, #3 ....**115.00**

Bit, Crocket, silver mounted, rare pattern, ca 1930s-40s ..**200.00**

Bit, half breed; Buermann, silver-inlaid Santa Barbara style, 1920s-30s **450.00**

Bit, Humane; Visalia, silver mounted **325.00**

Bit, JR McChesney, Pauls Valley, OK, pattern #30 ....**225.00**

Bit, prison made, lady-leg style, German silver mounted, 1920s **660.00**

Bit, ring; Mexican, unmarked .**25.00**

Bit, shoemaker; Buermann, Newark, NJ **200.00**

Bit, spade; Buermann, silver-inlaid Arizona pattern, 1920s **350.00**

Book, California Bit & Spur, author signed, limited edition of 1,000 ....**300.00**

Book, Thrilling Lives of Buffalo Bill & Pawnee Bill, c 1911 ....**40.00**

Bootjack, Naughty Nellie, ca 1920 ....**145.00**

Boots, cowgirl; custom made for rodeo, ca 1940s, VG paint **385.00**

Cartridge belt, Anson Mills, Patent 1881, dog face buckle **150.00**

Catalog, Colt Fire Arms, the Arm of Law & Order, 1935 ...**35.00**

Catalog, Porter, Phoenix, AZ, #38 ....**45.00**

Catalog, Racine Blanket, 1912 .**220.00**

Catalog, Visalia Stock Saddle Co, San Francisco, ca 1931, 40 pages **175.00**

Chaps, Vanco, Sacramento, California, fancy, bat-wing style with suite card decorations, heart-shaped and floral studs, and 6 sterling silver 2" string conchos, sold for $3,700.00 at auction. (Photo courtesy Dan Hutchins)

Chaps, cowgirl; unmarked, woolly white, EX **1,600.00**

Chaps, HH Heiser, plain, bat-wing style **400.00**

Chaps, RT Frazier, Pueblo, CO, plain w/ border spots & tooled belt **.450.00**

Coat & hat rack, horn construction, ca 1910 .... **360.00**

Cuffs, unmarked, brass spotted, 1920s-30s **75.00**

Cuffs, unmarked, star-studded pattern **200.00**

Poster, Monster Beery Exhibitions, Dayton, OH, 1913, shows gear **350.00**

Program, Forepaugh Wild West Show, ca 1910 .... **225.00**

Program, Tom Mix Circus & Wild West, 1937 .... **160.00**

Rifle scabbard, William Wellman, White Sulphur Springs, MT, ca 1910 .... **175.00**

Saddle, child's; unmarked, ca 1910-20 .... **475.00**

Saddle, T Quinn, rounded skirts, high cantle & horn, 1910s, EX carving **1,125.00**

Saddle, Wise & Rose Makers, Colorado Springs, CO, ca 1910 .... **400.00**

Saddle pockets, CP Shipley, Kansas City, MO, ca 1910 to 1920 .... **400.00**

Saddlebags, courier's; US Military, Quarter Master's mark **.145.00**

Saddlebags, Otto Ernst, Sheridan, WY, large border stamping, ca 1910 .... **475.00**

Spurs, Buermann, marked pattern #1284, w/conchos, original leathers **400.00**

Spurs, JB Mull, chased iron, dated February 1913, w/2" 16-point rowels **450.00**

Spurs, Mexican, 2" heel bands, ½" rowels, tooled leather, 10" **550.00**

Spurs, parade; Crockett, overlaid sterling silver, 1950s ..**675.00**

Spurs, Spanish/Moorish reproduction, ornate brass, 1930s **165.00**

Western Heroes

Interest is very strong right now in western memorabilia — not only that, but the kids that listened so intently to those after-school radio episodes featuring one of the many cowboy stars that sparked the airwaves in the '50s are now some of today's more affluent collectors, able and wanting to search out and buy toys they had in their youth. Put those two factors together, and it's easy to see why these items are so popular. *Character Toys and Collectibles* by David Longest and *Schroeder's Collectible Toys, Antique to Modern* (both by Collector Books). have lots of good information on Western heroes. See also Character Watches; Movie Memorabilia.

Davy Crockett

Davy Crockett had long been a favorite in fact and folklore. Then, with the opening of Disney's Frontierland and his continuing adventures on 1950s television, came a surge of interest in all sorts of items featuring the likeness of Fess Parker in a coonskin cap. Millions were drawn to the mystic and excitement surrounding the settlement of our great country. Due to demand, there were many types of items produced for eager fans ready to role play their favorite adventures.

Davy Crockett Guitare, marked EC France/WDP, 24", EX in original box, $350.00.

Belt, metal arrow-shaped buckle, NM **25.00**
Bolo tie, 1955 ....**35.00**
Comic book, Dell #664, Great Keelboat Race, Disney, EX .**25.00**
Gun, multicolor litho tin clicker revolver, Wyandotte, 1950s, 8", VG **25.00**
Lamp, covered wagon w/western scenes, Cactus Craft, 1950s, 8" **120.00**
Mug, Davy Crockett...1786-1836, black on white, EX **9.50**
Neckerchief, dark blue, EX .**25.00**
Patch, 4½x6" **12.00**
Pin, long rifle form **20.00**
Shoe holder, hanging; vinyl .**70.00**
Toy watch, EX (on card) **12.00**
Wallet, red vinyl w/hat made of real fur, 1950s, EX **30.00**

Wastebasket, litho tin, 1955, 11" **95.00**

Gene Autry

First breaking into show business as a recording star with Columbia Records, Gene went on to become one of Hollywood's most famous singing cowboys. From the late 1930s until the mid-'50s, he rode his wonder horse 'Champion' through almost ninety feature films. He did radio and TV as well, and naturally his fame spawned a wealth of memorabilia originally aimed at his young audiences, now grabbed up just as quickly by collectors.

Coloring book, Whitman, 1950, 48 pages, unused, NM **20.00**
Comic book, Dell #54, EX+ ..**25.00**
Guitar, plastic, w/instruction booklet, Emenee, 1955 ....**100.00**
Paint book, 1940, EX **40.00**
Postcard, black & white portrait w/horse, 1940s **10.00**
Poster, Valley of Fire, 1951, 27x41" **75.00**
Ring, w/flag **50.00**
Song book, Cowboy Songs & Mountain Ballads, picture cover, 1950s, EX **15.00**

Hopalong Cassidy

One of the most popular western heroes of all time, Hoppy was the epitome of the highly moral, role-model cowboys of radio and the silver screen that many of us grew up with in the '40s and '50s. He was portrayed by Bill Boyd who personally endorsed more than 2,200 items targeting Hoppy's loyal followers. If you just happen to be a modern-day Hoppy aficionado, you'll want to read *Collector's Guide to Hopalong Cassidy Memorabilia* by Joseph Caro (L-W Book Sales). See also Clubs and Newsletters.

Hopalong Cassidy Ear Muffs, Bailey, 1950, EX in original box, $225.00.

Autograph book, stylized photos & raised designs, 1950s, 5x5", unused **165.00**

Badge, older pin-back w/clasp, original, EX **50.00**

Bank, bronze-colored plastic bust **75.00**

Board game, Milton Bradley, complete, EX, w/EX original box **90.00**

Coaster, black on yellow, advertising Spun Honey, 4", EX **7.50**

Coloring book, Funtime, 1954, NM **45.00**

Ice cream cup lid, Dixie, 1930s .**25.00**

Mirror, black frame w/black out-line of Hopalong & signature, 5x7" **50.00**

Money clip, silver w/photo insert, EX **50.00**

Pencil, gold letters on green, unused **15.00**

Pennant, white on black felt, 1950s, 27" **65.00**

Picture, black & white glossy, reproduction publicity shot **5.00**

Pin-back button, Hopalong Cassidy Savings Club, 1950, 3", EX **45.00**

Ring, Bar-20, 1950s, VG **50.00**

Token, face of Hopalong, size of 50¢ pc, EX **10.00**

Wristwatch, Good Luck From Hoppy on back, US Time/William Boyd, VG **80.00**

The Lone Ranger

Recalling 'those thrilling days of yesteryear,' we can't help but remember the adventures of our hero, The Lone Ranger. He's been admired since that first radio show in 1933, and today's collectors seek a wide variety of his memorabilia; premiums, cereal boxes, and even carnival chalkware prizes are a few examples. See Clubs and Newsletters for more information.

Ballpoint pen, silver metal, Everlast Pen, 1950s, EX, on original card **165.00**

Blotter, Bond Bread, 1940s, NM **20.00**

Coloring book, Whitman, 1950s, NM **25.00**

Doll, Gabriel Industries Inc, 1973, 10", VG **12.00**

Pencil box, cardboard w/sliding tray, American Pencil Co, 1949, EX **80.00**

Pin-back button, Lone Ranger Bond Bread Safety Club Star, VG **30.00**

Tattoo transfers, Swell (bubble gum), 1960s, set of 4, NM **25.00**

Roy Rogers

Growing up during the Great Depression, Leonard Frank Sly was determined to make his mark in the entertainment industry. In 1938 after landing small roles in films featuring Gene Autry and others, Republic Studios (recognizing his talents) renamed their singing cowboy Roy Rogers and placed him in his first leading role in *Under Western Stars.* By 1943 he had become America's 'King of the Cowboys.' And his beloved horse, Trigger, was at the top with him. For further information about Roy and other singing cowboys, we recommend *Silver Screen Cowboys, Hollywood Cowboy Heroes, Roy Rogers, Singing Cowboy Stars,* and the forthcoming *Western Comics* — all written by our advisor, Robert W. Phillips, listed in the Directory under Oklahoma.

Roy Rogers Camera and Binocular Set, Herbert George Co., complete, EX in original box, $680.00 at auction.

Alarm clock, desert scene, galloping motion, Ingraham, 1950s, 4x4", EX **175.00**
Bandana, 1950s **100.00**
Box, Bunkhouse Boots, head shot photo w/logo, 10x4", EX .**135.00**
Give-A-Show Slide Strip, Kenner, 1962, set of 7, NM **15.00**
Guns & double holster set, Classy Products, 1955 ....**400.00**
Horseshoe set, lithograph tin bases, Ohio Art, NM, w/original box **265.00**
Paint set, 1950s, unused, NM, w/original box **125.00**

Pencil set, illustrated cardboard box w/generic materials, EX **55.00**
Pin-back button, black & white photo on gray, 1940s, 1¼", VG+ **25.00**
Playset, Rodeo Ranch, Marx #3922, complete, NM, w/original box **265.00**
Wristwatch, Dale Evans, Ingraham-Bradley, 1957, replaced band o/w VG **85.00**

Miscellaneous

Annie Oakley, bread label, black & white photo on yellow, Wonder Bread **35.00**
Annie Oakley, game, Milton Bradley, 1955, NM, w/original box **100.00**
Annie Oakley, gun & holster set, Daisy, 1955, w/original box **225.00**

Bat Masterson, coloring book, Saalfield, 1959, EX+ **25.00**

Bat Masterson, holster set w/cane & vest, Carnell, 1958, MIP .**150.00**

Bonanza, cup, litho tin, photo of Cartwrights w/out Adam, 1960s **15.00**

Bonanza, cup, litho tin, photo of Cartwrights w/Adam, 1960s, 3" **30.00**

Brave Eagle, outfit, complete w/headdress, NM, w/original box **125.00**

Bronco Billy, pocketknife, 2-blade, picture on green background, EX **35.00**

Buck Jones, sheet music, Hidden Valley, 1936, 9x12" **40.00**

Buffalo Bill, playset, Atlantic, 18-pc, MIB **15.00**

Cheyenne, guns & double holster set, Daisy, 1959 ....**125.00**

Daniel Boone, card game, Ed-U-Cards, EX, w/EX plastic box **15.00**

Daniel Boone, game, Fess Parker Trail Blazer, Milton Bradley, EX **25.00**

Deputy, board game, Milton Bradley, 1960, 9½x19x2" **50.00**

Durango Kid, photo, Dixie Ice Cream, 1937, 8x10" **45.00**

Gabby Hayes, charm **25.00**

Ken Maynard, exhibit card, 1930s, 3½x5½" **15.00**

Kit Carson, cap gun, Kilgore, NM **60.00**

Lash Larue, knife, plastic case, Smoky Mountain Knife Works, 1990s **10.00**

Matt Dillon, writing tablet, 1950s, unused **10.00**

Maverick, comic book, Dell #9, EX **25.00**

Patsy Montana, song folio, 1941, 100 pages, VG **25.00**

Pawnee Bill, show token, Wild West Co, bronze, ca 1905 ......**300.00**

Restless Gun, coloring book, unused, M **50.00**

Rifleman, hat, felt, Tex-Felt Co, 1958 ....**70.00**

Rin-Tin-Tin & Rusty, belt buckle, EX **65.00**

Sugarfoot, coloring book, 1959, unused, M **65.00**

Restless Gun hat, felt, EX, $42.00. (Photo courtesy June Moon)

Tex Ritter, record, Capitol Records, 78 rpm, w/original 10x12" sleeve **40.00**

Tom Mix, blotter, Tom Mix Circus, 1930s, 3x6", NM **65.00**

Tom Mix, photograph, Dixie Ice Cream, 1930s **125.00**

Wild Bill Hickok & Jingles, box (for outfit), Leslie-Henry, 14x11", EX **85.00**

Wyatt Earp, badge, Wyatt Earp Ent, 1957, 2", VG **20.00**

Zorro, board game, Parker Bros, 1966, M, w/original box **65.00**

Zorro, coloring book, Whitman, 1960s, EX **20.00**

Zorro, costume, B Cooper, MIB .**150.00**

Zorro, pin-back button, copyright Disney, 3" **35.00**

Zorro, pinwheel, marked WDP, 1950s-60s, 18", EX **30.00**

Zorro, travel bag, vinyl, 1960, 12x7x4" **75.00**

Westmoreland

Originally an Ohio company, Westmoreland relocated in Grapesville, Pennsylvania, where by the 1920s they had became known as one of the country's largest manufacturers of carnival glass. They are best known today for the high quality milk glass which accounted for 90% of their production. For further information we recommend contacting the Westmoreland Glass Society, Inc., listed in Clubs and Newsletters. See also Glass Animals and Birds.

Ashtray, Beaded Grape, #1884, milk glass, 4" **12.00**

Bell, crystal w/holly, #1902, fluted rim **25.00**

Bell, ruby w/floral, #1902, ruffled rim, 5" **45.00**

Bottle, cologne; Panelled Grape, #1881, milk glass w/gold trim **55.00**

Bowl, fruit; Old Quilt, #500, milk glass, footed, 9" **45.00**

Bowl, Lotus, #1921, milk glass, oval, lg **50.00**

Bowl, Rose Trellis, #1967, milk glass (plain), crimped rim **25.00**

Candle holders, Dolphin, milk glass, 3½", pr **25.00**

Candle holders, Lattice Edge, #1890, milk glass, pr **25.00**

Candle lamp, #1972, blue mist shade w/decal, milk glass base, mini **35.00**

Celery vase, Old Quilt, #500, milk glass **20.00**

Compote, Seashell & Dolphin, #1048, milk glass, 8" **35.00**

Cordial, Thousand Eye, #1000, crystal, 2-oz **10.00**

Creamer & sugar bowl, Maple Leaf, #1928, milk glass **35.00**

Egg cup, double; American Hobnail, #77, milk glass **18.00**

Goblet, water; Della Robbia, #1058, milk glass **14.00**

Ivy ball, Panelled Grape, #1881, milk glass **45.00**

Mayonnaise bowl, Lotus, #1921, pink, 4" w/7" underplate .**25.00**

Pansy basket, green marble, #757 ....**35.00**

Plate, Beaded Edge, #22, milk glass, Christmas decor, 7" **25.00**

Plate, Contrary Mule, #17, milk glass **35.00**

Plate, Della Robbia, #1058, crystal w/lustre stain, 14" **95.00**

Princess Feather, plate, #201, Golden Sunset, 8", $30.00. (Photo courtesy Ruth and Frank Grizel)

Plate, Forget-Me-Not, #2, milk glass **10.00**

Plate, Heart, #32, green mist .**20.00**

Plate, One Hundred & One, #101, crystal w/ruby & ruby flowers **55.00**

Plate, Wicket, #30, green mist .**20.00**

Plate, Woof-Woof, milk glass, Westmoreland Specialty Co **50.00**

Plate, 3 Owls, purple carnival, 1974 limited edition **50.00**

Puff box, #1902, green w/daisies .**30.00**

Punch cup, Multi-Fruit, #81, milk glass **10.00**

Punch ladle, Panelled Grape, #1881, milk glass, from $55 to **60.00**

Salt & pepper shakers, High Hob, #550, milk glass, pr **20.00**

Salt & pepper shakers, Pansy, #757, milk glass, pr **50.00**

Sherbet, Old Quilt, #500, milk glass **20.00**

Straw jar, #1813, crystal mist w/blue china rose **45.00**

Toothpick holder, Panelled Grape, #1881, milk glass **35.00**

Tumbler, water; American Hobnail, low foot, 11-oz, from $12 to **15.00**

Vase, Lily of the Valley, #241, blue opalescent **55.00**

Vase, Old Quilt, #500, milk glass, fan form **15.00**

Vase, Swan, #115, electric blue carnival opalescent, 6½" **55.00**

Vase, Tear Drop, #231, milk glass **75.00**

Votive candle holder, #1976, crystal mist w/flower decor, flat, 2½" **18.00**

World's Fairs & Expositions

Souvenir items have been distributed from every fair and exposition since the mid-1850s. Examples from before the turn of the century are challenging to collect, but even those issued for much later events are desirable as well. For information on earlier fairs see *Schroeder's Antiques Price Guide* (Collector Books).

1939 Golden Gate International Exposition

New York World's Fair, 1939, ashtray, gold-tone metal with 12 white rests, $40.00. (Photo courtesy Lee Garmon)

Book, Illustrated Catalogue Art Exhibition by CA Artists, 44 pages **12.50**
Book, Magic in the Night, softcover, Crocker Co, 16 pages, 12x9", NM **22.50**
Dollar, gilt bronze, Pledge of Allegiance over flag, M **17.50**
Matchbook, Towers of the East at Night, unused, NM **6.00**
Medal, aluminum, 2 Union Pacific trains, Aluminum Co of America, M **2.50**
Paperweight, miniature brass horseshoe w/embossed scenes, 2x2⅜" **35.00**

Pin-back button, blue enamel on brass, scene w/setting sun, NM **15.00**
Pin-back button, celluloid, bridge in sun, blue & orange, EX **24.00**
Thermometer, gold-plated metal key shape w/celluloid view, 8½x3" **40.00**
Towel, Expo scenes on terry cloth, 22x42", M **55.00**

1939 New York

Ashtray, square w/Trylon & Perisphere in center, 4 rests, Syroco **25.00**
Book, Dominican Republic at NY World's Fair, 30 pages, 8½x11", EX **7.50**
Change purse, embossed & painted leather, 3½", EX **7.50**
Pamphlet, Rip Van Winkle Discovers Radio, EX **8.00**
Postcard, Bridge of Tomorrow, Grinnel Litho, NM **3.00**
Tray, Trylon & Perisphere painted on metal, 17½x11½", EX .**35.00**
Vase, NY World's Fair 1940, Trylon & Perisphere, ruby stain, 3¾" **25.00**

1962 Seattle

Medal, gilt brass, 30 Tons of Silver Dollars..., Space Needle, M **3.50**
Plate, ceramic, color transfer, reticulated rim, hangs, 5" **8.00**
Token, gilt brass, Good for One Dollar..., M **3.50**
Tumbler, clear w/blue scene, Seattle World's Fair 1962, 4¾" **9.00**

Seattle World's Fair, 1962, tumblers, single color with black and white matt finish on frosted glass, gold trim, 16-oz, from $7.00 to $9.00 each.

1964 New York

Board game, Milton Bradley, 1964, complete, EX, in original box **35.00**

Bookend, ceramic, 3-D Unisphere on base, brown & gold, 5" .**6.50**

Flashlight, gilt tin & plastic, Unisphere decal, 3¼", EX .**9.00**

Lapel clip, tin, I Have Seen...General Motors Futurama, M **3.50**

Locket, gold-tone blue & orange enamel, Unisphere on front, EX **45.00**

Map, Official Souvenir, foldout, lists every attraction, NM (in cover) **7.50**

Pin, enamel on brass, Peace Through... on Unisphere form, 1½", MIB .**7.50**

Plaque, ceramic, Unisphere, skyline, Statue of Liberty, etc, 9x8" **7.00**

Plate, ceramic w/5 color views, skyline in center, 7¼", M **15.00**

Postcards, 14 views, Unisphere & Pool of Reflections on cover, M **5.00**

Ring, multicolored flasher on gold-tone band, M **15.00**

Shopping bag, Miles Shoes World of Fashion for the Fair, 16x17" **45.00**

T-shirt, Unisphere in full color on front, EX **45.00**

Token, brass, One Fare, Long Island Railroad **2.50**

Tumbler, frosted glass w/scene & dates, 7" **10.00**

DIRECTORY

The editors and staff take this opportunity to express our sincere gratitude and appreciation to each person who has in any way contributed to the preparation of this guide. We believe the credibility of our book is greatly enhanced through their efforts. Check these listings for information concerning their specific areas of expertise.

You will notice that at the conclusion of some of the narratives, the advisor's name is given. This is optional and up to the discretion of each individual. We hope to add more advisors with each new edition to provide further resources to you, our readers. If you care to correspond with anyone listed here in our Directory, you must send a SASE with your letter.

Alabama
Cataldo, Gene
Gene's Cameras
2603 Artie St., SW Ste. 16
Huntsville, 35804
205-536-6893

Arizona
Schaut, Jim and Nancy
P.O. Box 10781
Glendale, 85318-0781
602-878-4293
e-mail: nschaut@aztec.asu.edu
Specializing in automobilia and racing memorabilia

California
Ales, Beverly L.
4046 Graham St.
Pleasanton, 94566-5619
510-846-5297
Specializing in knife rests and editor of *Knife Rests of Yesterday and Today*

Cox, Susan
Main Street Antique Mall
237 E Main St.
El Cajon, 92020
619-447-0800 or fax 619-447-0185
Author of *Frankoma Pottery, Value Guide and More;* also specializing in American pottery (California pottery in particular),

Horlick's advertising, matchbooks, and advertising pencils

Elliott, Jackie
9790 Twin Cities Rd.
Galt, 95632
209-745-3860
Specializing in Rooster and Roses

Escoe, Adrienne
4448 Ironwood Ave.
Seal Beach, 90740
Specializing in glass knives; Editor of *Cutting Edge,* newsletter

Harrison, Gwynne
P.O. Box 1
Mira Loma, 91752-0001
909-685-5434
Buys and appraises; Autumn Leaf edits newsletter

Inouye, Roger
765 E Franklin Ave.
Pomona, 91766
909-623-1368
Specializing in trolls

Lewis, Kathy and Don
187 N Marcello Ave.
Thousand Oaks, 91360
Authors of *Chatty Cathy Dolls, an Identification and Value Guide*

426

Mallette, Leo A.
2309 S Santa Anita Ave.
Arcadia, 91006-5154
Specializing in Betty Boop

Synchef, Richard M.
16 Midway Ave.
Mill Valley, 94941
fax 415-381-4145
Specializing in Beatnik and Hippie
collectibles

Utley, Bill; Editor
Flashlight Collectors of America
Newsletter
P.O. Box 4095
Tustin, 92781
714-730-1252 or fax 714-505-4067
Specializing in flashlights

Van Ausdall, Marci
P.O. Box 946
Quincy, 95971
916-283-2770 or fax 916-283-4449
Specializing in Betsy McCall dolls;
edits newsletter

Connecticut
Sabulis, Cindy
P.O. Box 642
Shelton, 06484
203-926-0176
Specializing in dolls from the '60s-
'70s (Liddle Kiddles, Barbie,
Tammy, Tressy, etc.); co-author of
*The Collector's Guide to Tammy,
the Ideal Teen*

Colorado
Diehl, Richard
5965 W Colgate Pl.
Denver, 80227
303-985-7481
Specializing in license plates

Tvorak, April
P.O. Box 126
Canon City, 81215-0126
719-269-7230

Specializing in Kitchen Independence,
Kitchen Prayer Ladies, Pyrex, Fire-
King (guides available), and Holt
Howard

District of Columbia
McMichael, Nancy
P.O. Box 53262
Washington, 20009
Author of *Snowdomes,* (Abbeville
Press); editor of *Snow Biz*
newsletter
Information requires SASE

Florida
Poe, Bill and Pat
220 Dominica Cir.
E Niceville, 32578-4068
904-897-4163 or fax 904-897-2606
Buy-sell-trade fast-food collectibles,
cartoon character glasses, PEZ,
Smurfs, and California Raisins; for
a 70-page catalog (published twice a
year in January and July) send $3
US delivery

Idaho
McVey, Jeff
1810 W State St. #427
Boise, 83702
Author of *Tire Ashtray Collector's
Guide* available for $12.95 post-
paid; SASE for my 300+ sale item
catalog

Illinois
Garmon, Lee
Glass Animals
1529 Whittier St.
Springfield, 62704
217-789-9574
Co-author of *Glass Animals and
Figural Flower Frogs of the
Depression Era;* specializing in
glass animals, Royal Haeger,
Royal Hickman, Roselane
Sparklers, Borden's Elsie, Reddy
Kilowatt, Elvis Presley, and
Marilyn Monroe

Klompus, Eugene R.
The National Cuff Link Society
P.O. Box 346
Prospect Hts., 60070
847-816-0035
Specializing in cuff links and
men's accessories; edits newsletter

Rodrick, Tammy
1509 N 300 St.
Sumner, 62466
618-947-2240
Specializing in Avon

Stifter, Craig and Donna
P.O. Box 6514
Naperville, 60540
630-717-7949
Specializing in soda memorabilia
such as Coca-Cola, Hires, Pepsi, 7-
Up, etc.

TV Guide Specialists, Jeff Kadet
P.O. Box 20
Macomb, 61455
309-833-1809
Buying and selling of *TV Guide*
from 1948-1990s

Wallin, Richard
Box 1784
Springfield, 62705
217-498-9279
Specializing in airline memorabilia

Indiana
Hoover, Dave
1023 Skyview Dr.
New Albany, 47150
Specializing in fishing collectibles

Iowa
Addy, Geneva D.
P.O. Box 124
Winterset, 50273
515-462-3027
Specializing in Imperial Porcelain,
Pink Pigs, and Strawberry
Shortcake collectibles

De Lozier, Loretta
1101 Polk St.
Bedford, 50833
712-523-2289
Author of *Collector's Encyclopedia
of Lefton China, Identification and
Values* (Collector Books); specializing in Lefton China and research

Devine, Joe
D&D Antique Mall
1411 3rd St.
Council Bluffs, 51503
712-232-5233 or 712-328-7305
Specializing in Royal Copley

Grizel, Ruth
P.O. Box 205
Oakdale, 52319-0205
fax 391-626-3216
Specializing in Indiana Glass,
Westmoreland, L.E. Smith, and
L.G. Wright, among others; author
of *The Collector's Guide to Modern
American Slag Glass;* editor of *The
Glass Post*

Kansas
Anthony, Dorothy Malone
World of Bells Publications
802 S Eddy
Ft. Scott, 66701
Specializing in bell research and
publication; author of *World of
Bells,* #5 ($8.95); *Bell Tidings*
($9.95); *Lure of Bells* ($9.95);
Collectible Bells ($10.95); and
More Bell Lore ($11.95); auto-
graphed copies available from the
author; please enclose $2.00 for
postage

Kentucky
Hornback, Betty
707 Sunrise Ln.
Elizabethtown, 42701
502-765-2441
Specializing in Kentucky Derby
and horse racing memorabilia

Don Smith's National Geographic
Magazine
3930 Rankin St.
Louisville, 40214
502-366-7504
Specializing in *National Geographic*
magazines and related material;
guide available

Maryland
Gordon, Steve
P.O. Box 632
Olney, 20830-0632
301-439-4116 or fax 301-439-7296
Specializing in beer cans and
breweriana

Losonsky, Joyce and Terry
7506 Summer Leave Ln.
Columbia, 21046-2455
Authors of: *The Illustrated Collector's
Guide to McDonald's® Happy Meal®
Boxes, Premiums, and Promotions*©
($9 plus $2 postage); *McDonald's®
Happy Meal® Toys in the USA,* in full
color ($24.95 plus $3); *McDonald's®
Happy Meal® Toys Around the
World,* in full color, ($24.95 plus $3);
and *Illustrated Collector's Guide to
McDonald's® McCAPS®,* ($4 plus $2).
Autographed copies available from
the authors

The Shoe Lady
Yalon, Libby
P.O. Box 7146
Adelphi, 20783
301-422-2026
Specializing in glass and china
shoes and boots. Author of *Shoes of
Glass* (with updated values) avail-
able from the author by sending
$15.95 plus $2 to above address
Welch, Randy
27965 Peach Orchard Rd.
Easton, 21601-8203
410-822-5441
Specializing in ramp-walking fig-
ures and tin wind-up toys

Massachusetts
Bruce, Scott
P.O. Box 481
Cambridge, 02140
617-492-5004
Publisher of *Flake* magazine; author
of *Complete Cereal Boxography,
Cerealizing America* (Faber and
Faber), and *Cereal Box Bonanza —
the 1950s* (Collector Books).
Specializing in buying, selling, trad-
ing cereal boxes, cereal displays, and
cereal premiums; free appraisals
given

Schmuhl, Marian H.
7 Revolutionary Ridge Rd.
Bedford, 01730-2057
617-275-2156
Specializing in dollhouse furnishings

Wellman, BA
P.O. Box 673
Westminster, 01473-1435
Specializing in all areas of
American ceramics; identification
and price guides available on
Ceramic Arts Studio; researcher
on Royal China

Michigan
Pickvet, Mark
P.O. Box 90404
Flint, 48509
Specializing in shot glasses; Author
of *Shot Glasses: An American
Tradition,* (167 pages of information,
over 1,000 illustrations, current val-
ues) available for $12.95 plus $2.50
postage from Antique Publications,
P.O. Box 553, Marietta, OH 45750

Missouri
Allen, Col. Bob
P.O. Box 85
St. James, 65559
Author of *A Guide to Collecting
Cookbooks;* specializing in cook-
books, leaflets, and Jell-o memorabilia

McCale, Helen L.
P.O. Box 397
Butler, 64730-0397
816-679-3690
Specializing in Holly Hobbie

Van Hoozer, Gary, Publisher/ Editor
Rural Heritage Magazine
812 N Third St.
Tarkio, 64491
816-736-4528
Specializing in old farm items, tractors to smaller collectibles

Nevada
Hunter, Tim
1668 Golddust
Sparks, 89436
702-626-5029
Author of *The Bobbing Head Collector and Price Guide*

New Hampshire
Chris Russell
   and The Halloween Queen
Pamela Apkarian-Russell
4 Lawrence St. & Rt. 10
Winchester, 03470
Specializing in Halloween collectibles
and postcards of all kinds

Holt, Jane
P.O. Box 115
Derry, 03038
Specializing in Annalee dolls

New Jersey
Cole, Lillian M.
14 Harmony School Rd.
Flemington, 08822
908-782-3198
Specializing in collecting pie birds,
pie vents, and pie funnels; also pie
bird research

Dezso, Doug
864 Paterson Ave.
Maywood, 07607
Co-Author of *Candy Containers* (Collector

Books); Specializing in candy containers,
nodders, Kellogg's Pep pin-back buttons,
Shafford cats, and Tonka toys

McClane, Jim
232 Butternut Dr.
Wayne, 07470
201-616-1538
Specializing in MAD collectibles

Palmieri, Jo Ann
27 Pepper Rd.
Towaco, 07082
201-334-5829
Specializing in Skookum Indian dolls

Sigg, Walter
3-D Entertainment
P.O. Box 208
Swartswood, 07877
Specializing in View-Master and
Tru-View reels and packets

Sparacio, George
P.O. Box 791
Malaga, 08328
609-694-4167
Specializing in match safes

Visakay, Stephen
P.O. Box 1517
W Caldwell, 07007-1517
Specializing in vintage cocktail shakers; by mail and appointment only.
Author of *Vintage Bar Ware*

Warren, Adrienne
1032 Feather Bed Ln.
Edison, 08820
908-381-7083 (EST)
Specializing in Smurfs, Garfield, Warner
Brothers, and other character collectibles

Yunes, Henri
971 Main St., Apt. 2
Hackensack, 07601
201-488-2236
Specializing in celebrity and character dolls

New Mexico

Hutchins, Dan
Hutchins Publications
P.O. Box 1283
Las Vegas, 87701
Author of *Old Cowboy Saddles and Spurs, Identifying the Craftsmen Who Made Them* and *Old West Cowboy Collectibles Auction Update and Price Guide;* available from the author; specializing in Western Americana research and collectibles

Mace, Shirley
Shadow Enterprises
P.O. Box 1602
Mesilla Park, 88047
505-524-6717 or 505-523-0940
e-mail: Shmace@nmsu.edu
Author of *Encyclopedia of Silhouette Collectibles on Glass* (available from the author)

New York

Dinner, Craig
Box 4399
Sunnyside, 11104
718-729-3850
Specializing in figural cast-iron items (door knockers, lawn sprinklers, doorstops, windmill weights, etc.)

Doucet, Larry
Dick Tracy Collectibles
2351 Sultana Dr.
Yorktown Hts., 10598
Specializing in Dick Tracy memorabilia; for free appprasials, send photos, detailed descriptions, and SASE; also an active buyer

Eisenstadt, Robert
P.O. Box 020767
Brooklyn, 11202-0017
718-625-3553 or fax 718-522-1087
Specializing in gambling chips and other gambling-related items

Gerson, Roselyn
P.O. Box 40
Lynbrook, 11563
516-593-8746
Collector specializing in unusual, gadgetry, figural compacts and vanity bags and purses; author of *Ladies' Compacts of the 19th and 20th Centuries*, available from the author for $34.95 plus $2 postage, and *Vintage Vanity Bags and Purses* (Collector Books)

Lederman, Arlene
Arlene Lederman Antiques
150 Main
St. Nyack, 10960
914-358-8616
Specializing in vintage cocktail shakers, 18th through 20th-century antiques, furniture, glass, decorative accessories, and collectibles

Luchsinger, Paul P.
1126 Wishart St.
Hermitage, 16148
412-346-2331
Specializing in antique and unusual corkscrews

Maimone, Tom
53 W Court St.
Warsaw, 14569
716-786-5674
Specializing in advertising and figural swizzle sticks

Weitman, Stan and Arlene
101 Cypress St.
Massapequa Park, 11758
516-799-2619 or fax 516-797-3039
Authors of *Crackle Glass, Identification and Value Guide*; specializing in crackle glass

North Carolina

Brooks, Ken and Barbara
4121 Gladstone Ln.
Charlotte, 28205
704-568-5716
Specializing in Cattail Dinnerware

Retskin, Bill
P.O. Box 18481
Asheville, 28814
704-254-4487 or fax 704-254-1066
e-mail: matchclub@circle.net
Author of *The Matchcover Collector's Price Guide;* editor of *The Front Striker Bulletin,* the official publication of the American Matchcover Collecting Club (AMCC)

Sayers, Rolland J.
Southwestern Antiques and Appraisals
P.O. Box 629
Brevard, 28712
Specializing in Boy Scout Collectibles. Author of *Guide to Scouting Collectibles,* available from the author for $19.95 plus $3.50 postage

North Dakota
Farnsworth, Bryce L.
1334 14½ St.
S Fargo, 58103
Specializing in Rosemeade

Ohio
Bruegman, Bill
137 Casterton Ave.
Akron, 44303
216-836-0668 or fax 216-869-8668
Author of *Toys of the Sixties; Aurora History and Price Guide;* and *Cartoon Friends of the Baby Boom Era.* Write for information about his magazine and mail order catalog.

Cassidy, Brad
1350 Stanwix
Toledo, 43614
419-385-9910
Specializing in Fisher-Price pull toys and playsets up to 1986

Cimini, Joan
63680 Centerville-Warnock Rd.
Belmont, 43718

Specializing in Imperial; also has Candlewick matching service
Dutt, Gordy
Gordy's/KitBuilders Magazine
Box 201
Sharon Center, 44274-0201
216-239-1657 or fax 216-239-2991
Author of *Collectible Figure Kits of the '50s, '60s, and '70s* ($24 US postpaid), containing over 400 photographs with information and values; specializing in models other than Aurora, Weirdos, and Rat Finks

Grubaugh, Joan
GB Publications
2342 Hoaglin Rd.
Van Wert, 45891
419-622-4411 or fax 419-622-3026
Author of *Gerber Baby Dolls and Advertising Collectibles* ($39.95 plus $4 postage), 224 pages with colored photos of Gerber Baby dolls and collectibles as well as pricing information

Kerr, Ann
P.O. Box 437
Sidney, 45365
513-492-6369
Author of *Collector's Encyclopedia of Russel Wright Designs* (Collector Books); specializing in work of Russel Wright with interests in 20th-century decorative arts

Knauss, Nada Sue
12111 Potter Rd.
Weston, 43569
419-669-4735
Specializing in figural flower frogs

Marsh, Thomas
914 Franklin Ave.
Youngstown, 44502
216-743-8600 or 800-845-7930
Publisher and author of *The Official Guide to Collecting Applied Color Label Soda Bottles* Volumes I

and II ($28.95 each postpaid); specializing in applied colored label soda bottles and related items

Oklahoma

Phillips, Robert W.
Phillips Archives of Western
  Memorabilia
1703 N Aster Pl.
Broken Arrow, 74012
918-254-8205 or fax 918-252-9363
Author of *Roy Rogers, Singing Cowboy Stars, Silver Screen Cowboys,* and *Western Comics;* authority on Classic Western comics, TV westerns, character collectibles, country-western music; ardent western researcher and guest columnist

Terri's Toys and Nostalgia
Terri Mardis-Ivers
419 S First St.
Ponca City, 74601
405-762-8697 or 405-762-5174
fax 405-765-2657
e-mail: tivers@pcok.com
Specializing in character collectibles, advertising items, Breyer and Hartland figures, etc.

Oregon

Morris, Tom
Prize Publishers
P.O. Box 8307
Medford, 97504
503-779-3164
Author of *The Carnival Chalk Prize;* specializing in carnival chalkware figures

Pennsylvania

Bentz, Jo-Ann
Dealer at Shep's Grove, D15 & D16
P.O. Box 146AA Beaver Rd., R.R. #3
Birdsboro 19508-9107
610-582-0311
Specializing in Hull Mirror Brown, Pfaltzgraff Gourmet Royale and other lines

BOJO/Bob Gottuso
P.O. Box 1403
Cranberry Twp., 16066-0403
phone or fax 412-776-0621
Specializing in the Beatles and rock 'n roll memorabilia

Greenfield, Jeannie
310 Parker Rd.
Stoneboro, 16153
Specializing in egg timers, cake toppers, and Jasco bells

Homestead Collectibles
Art and Judy Turner
P.O. Box 173
Mill Hall, 17751
717-726-3597
Specializing in Jim Beam decanters and Ertl die-cast metal banks

Huegel, Joan L.
1002 W 25th St.
Erie, 16502
Specializing in bookmarks

Kingsbury Productions and Antiques
Katherine Kreider
P.O. Box 7957
Lancaster, 17604-7957
717-892-3001
or
4555 N Pershing Ave., Ste. 33-138
Stockton, CA 95207
209-467-8438
Specializing in valentines

Posner, Judy
May-October:
R.D. 1, Box 273
Effort, 18330
717-629-6583
or
November-April:
4195 S Tamiami Trail, #183
Venice, FL 34293
941-497-7149

e-mail: Judyandjef@aol.com
Specializing in figural pottery, cookie jars, salt and pepper shakers, Black memorabilia, and Disneyana; sale lists available

Texas
Cooper, Marilyn M.
P.O. Box 55174
Houston, 77255
Author of *The Pictorial Guide to Toothbrush Holders* ($22.95 postpaid)

Jackson, Joyce
900 Jenkins Rd.
Aledo, 76008
817-441-8864
Specializing in Swanky Swigs

Nossaman, Darlene
5419 Lake Charles
Waco, 76710
817-772-3969
Specializing in Homer Laughlin china information and Horton Ceramics

Pringle, Joyce
Chip and Dale Collectibles
3500 S Cooper
Arlington, 76015
817-467-7030
Specializing in Boyd art glass, Summit, and Moser

Woodard, Dannie
P.O. Box 1346
Weatherford, 76086
817-594-4680
Author of *Hammered Aluminum, Hand Wrought Collectibles,* and publisher of *The Aluminist* newsletter ($12 for 6 issues)

Utah
Spencer, Rick
3953 S Renault Cir.
West Valley, 84119
801-973-0805

Specializing in Shawnee, Roseville, Weller, Van Telligan, Regal, Bendel, Coors, Rookwood, Watt; also salt and pepper shakers, cookie jars, etc., cut glass, radios, and silver flatware

Virginia
Cranor, Rosalind
P.O. Box 859
Blacksburg, 24063
Author of *Elvis Collectibles* and *Best of Elvis Collectibles* (each at $19.95 with $2.50 postage), available from the author

De Angelo, Larry
516 King Arthur Dr.
Virginia Beach, 23464
804-424-1691
Specializing in California Raisin collectibles

Giese, David
1410 Aquia Dr.
Stafford, 22554
703-569-5984
Specializing in character shaving mugs and razor blade banks

Henry, Rosemary
9610 Greenview Ln.
Manassas, 22100
Specializing in cookie cutters, stamps, and molds

Reynolds, Charlie
Reynolds Toys
2836 Monroe St.
Falls Church, 22042
703-533-1322
Specializing in banks, figural bottle openers, toys, etc.

Washington
Jackson, Denis C.
Illustrator Collector's News
P.O. Box 1958
Sequim, 98382
360-683-2559 or fax 360-683-9708

e-mail: ticn@daka.com
Specializing in pinup art, illustrations, and old magazines; issues prices guides

Palmer, Donna
Our Favorite Things
3020 Issaquah Pine Lake Rd. #557
Issaquah, 98027
206-392-7636
General line but specializing in Scottie dog collectibles

Thompson, Walt
Box 2541
Yakima, 98907-2451
Specializing in charge cards and credit-related items

Wisconsin
Helley, Phil
Old Kilbourn Antiques
629 Indiana Ave.
Wisconsin Dells, 53965
608-254-8659
Specializing in Cracker Jack items, radio premiums, dexterity games, toys (especially Japanese wind-up toys), banks, and old Dells souvenir items marked Kilbourn

Clubs and Newsletters

Akro Agate Collectors Club and *Clarksburg Crow*
Roger Hardy
10 Bailey St.
Clarksburg, WV 26301-2524
304-624-4523
Annual membership fee: $20

The Aluminist
Dannie Woodard
P.O. Box 1347
Weatherford, TX 76086
817-594-4680
Subscription: $12 per year

American Game Collectors Assn.
49 Brooks Ave.
Lewiston, MA 04240

The American Matchcover Collecting Club (AMCC)
P.O. Box 18481
Asheville, NC 28814
704-254-4487 or fax 704-254-1066
e-mail: matchclub@circle.net
Dues: $23 per year and includes quarterly issues of *The Front Striker Bulletin,* a membership roster and card, free matchcovers, and full membership privileges

Antique and Collector Reproduction News
Mark Cherenka, Circulation Dept.
P.O. Box 71174
Des Moines, IA 50325
800-227-5531
Monthly newsletter showing differences between old originals and new reproductions; subscription: $32 per year

The Antique Trader Weekly
P.O. Box 1050
Dubuque, IA 52004

Subscription: $32 (52 issues) per year; Sample: $1

Association of Map Memorabilia Collectors
8 Amherst Rd.
Pelham, MA 01002
413-253-3155
Autographs of Times
Tim Anderson
P.O. Box 461
Provo, UT 84603
801-226-1787 (afternoons, please)
Free sample catalog of hundreds of autographs for sale

Avon Times
c/o Dwight or Vera Young
P.O. Box 9868, Dept. P.
Kansas City, MO 64134
Send SASE for information

Beatlefan
P.O. Box 33515
Decatur, GA 30033
Subscription: $15 (US) for 6 issues

The Bell Tower
P.O. Box 19443
Indianapolis, IN 46219

Betsy McCall's Fan Club
Marci Van Ausdell, Editor
P.O. Box 946
Quincy, CA 95971
e-mail: DREAMS707@aol.com
Subscription: $12.50 per year or send $3 for sample copy

The Bobbing Head Collector
Tim Hunter
1668 Golddust
Sparks, NV 89436
702-626-5029

Bookmark Collector
Joan L. Huegel
1002 W 25th St.
Erie, PA 16502
Quarterly newsletter, $5.50 per year ($6.50 in Canada). Send $1 plus SASE for sample copy

Boyd's Crystal Art Glass
Jody & Darrell's Glass Collectibles Newsletter
P.O. Box 180833
Arlington, TX 76096-0833
Publishes 6 times a year; subscription includes an exclusive glass collectible produced by Boyd's Crystal Art Glass. LSASE for current subscription rates or send $3 for sample copy

Candy Container Collectors of America
P.O. Box 352
Chelmsord, MA 10824-0352

The Carnival Pump
International Carnival Glass Assoc., Inc.
Lee Markley
Box 306
Mentone, IN 46539
Dues: $15 per family per year payable each July 1st

CAS Collectors Association (Ceramic Arts Studio)
P.O. Box 46
Madison, WI 53701
608-241-9138

Cat Collectors Club
Cat Talk Newsletter
Marilyn Dipboye
33161 Wendy Dr.
Sterling Heights, MI 48310
Subscription: $18 per year

Compact Collector Chronicles
Powder Puff Newsletter
P.O. Box 40
Lynbrook, NY 11563
516-593-8746
Contains information covering all aspects of compact collecting, restoration, vintage ads, patents, history, and articles by members and prominent guest writers. A 'Seekers and Sellers' column and dealer listing is offered free to members

The Cookie Jar Collectors Express
Paradise Publications
Box 221
Mayview, MO 64071
816-584-6309

Cookie Jarrin' With Joyce: The Cookie Jar Newsletter
R.R. 2, Box 504
Walterboro, SC 29488

Cookies Newsletter
Rosemary Henry
9610 Greenview Ln.
Manassas, VA 22110
Published 6 times a year, subscription $10.

The Copley Courier
1639 N Catalina St.
Burbank, CA 91505

Cowboy Collector Newsletter
Joseph J. Caro, Publisher
P.O. Box 7485
Long Beach, CA 90807
310-428-6972

Cracker Jack® Collector's Assoc.
The Prize Insider Newsletter
Larry White
108 Central St.
Rowley, MA 01969
508-948-8187

Subscription: $18 per year or $24 per year for family membership

Currier & Ives China by Royal
c/o Jack and Treva Hamlin, Editor
R.R. 4, Box 150 Kaiser St.
Proctorville, OH 45669
614-886-7644

The Daze
Teri Steel, Editor/ Publisher
Box 57
Otisville, MI 48463
810-631-4593
The nation's marketplace for glass, china, and pottery

Doll Castle News Magazine
P.O. Box 247
Washington, NJ 07882
908-689-7042 or fax 908-689-6320

Doorstop Collectors of America
Jeanie Bertoia
2413 Madison Ave.
Vineland, NJ 08630
609-692-4092
Membership: $20 per year, includes 2 newsletters and convention; send 2-stamp SASE for sample

Farm Antique News
Gary Van Hoozer, Publisher/Editor
812 N Third St.
Tarkio, MO 64491
816-736-4528
A bimonthy magazine available by sending $14 per year which includes one free classified ad; actively sells, trades, and welcomes inquires

FBOC (Figural Bottle Opener Collectors)
Donna Kitzmiller
117 Basin Hill Rd.
Duncannon, PA 17020
717-834-4867
Please send SASE for information

Fiesta Club of America
P.O. Box 15383
Loves Park, IL 61132-5383
Send $20 for 1 year's subscription and newsletter

Fiesta Collector's Quarterly
China Specialties Inc.
19238 Dorchester Cir.
Strongville, OH 44136
$12 (four issues) per year

Fisher-Price Collector's Club
Jeanne Kennedy
1442 N Ogden
Mesa, AZ 85205
Monthly newsletter with information and ads; send SASE for more information

FLAKE, The Breakfast Nostalgia Magazine
P.O. Box 481
Cambridge, MA 02140
617-492-5004
Bimonthly illustrated issue devoted to one hot collecting area such as Disney, etc.; plus letters, discoveries, new releases, and ads; single issue: $4 ($6 foreign), annual: $20 ($28 foreign); free 25-word ad with new subscription

Flashlight Collectors of America Newsletter
Bill Utley
P.O. Box 4095
Tustin, CA 92681
714-730-1252 or fax 714-505-4067
$12 for four issues per year; single copies and back issues are $3 each

Frankoma Family Collectors Association
c/o Nancy Littrell
P.O. Box 32571
Oklahoma City, OK 73123-0771
Membership dues: $20 (includes quarterly newsletter and annual convention); send SASE for more info.

The Front Striker Bulletin
Bill Retskin
P.O. Box 18481
Asheville, NC 28814
704-254-4487 or fax 704-254-1066
Quarterly newsletter for matchcover collectors $17.50 per year for
1st class mailing + $2 for new
member registration

GAB! (Glass Animal Bulletin!)
P.O. Box 143
North Liberty, IA 52317
Monthly publication for all animal
collectors including animal dishes;
free monthly ads with $16 yearly
subscription

Glass Knife Collectors Club
Adrienne Esco
4448 Ironwood Ave.
Seal Beach, CA 90740
562-430-6479

The Glass Post
P.O. Box 205
Oakdale, IA 52319-0205
phone or fax 319-626-3216
Monthly publication for buying,
selling, and trading all kinds of
glassware; free monthly ads with
$25 yearly subscription

Grandma's Trunk
The Millards
P.O. Box 404
Northport, MI 49670
616-386-5351
Auction and set price lists in newspaper format for all types of paper
ephemera; subscription: $5 yearly
bulk rate or $8 for 1st class

Hall China Collectors' Club Newsletter
P.O. Box 360488
Cleveland, OH 44136

Hartland Newsletter
Gail Fitch
1733 N Cambridge Ave. #109
Milwaukee, WI 53202
Send $8 for 6 issues or $4.50 for 3
issues of monthly newsletter.
Classified ads are $2 for 50 words.
Please send SASE for information
and order form for book, *Hartland
Horses and Riders,* which covers
horses and western heroes made
from 1947 to present day

Head Hunters Newsletter
c/o Maddy Gordon
P.O. Box 83 H
Scarsdale, NY 10583
Subscription: $20 yearly for 4
quarterly issues. Ads free to sub-
scribers

International Figure Kit Club
Gordy's
P.O. Box 201
Sharon Center, OH 44274-0201
216-239-1657 or fax 216-239-2991

International Nippon Collectors Club
(INCC) and Newsletter
c/o Phil Fernkes
112 Oak Ave N
Owatonna, MN 55060
Publishes newsletter 6 times per year

Just for Openers
John Stanley
3712 Sunningdale Way
Durham, NC 27707-5684
919-419-1546

*Kitchen Antiques & Collectibles
News* Newsletter
Kana & Darlene DeMore, Editors
4645 Laurel Ridge Dr.
Harrisburg, PA 17110
717-545-7320

Knife Rests of Yesterday and Today
Beverly L. Ales
4046 Graham St.
Pleasanton, CA 94566-5619
Subscription: $20 per year for 6
issues

The Laughlin Eagle
c/o Joan Jasper, Publisher
1270 63rd Terrace South St.
Petersburg, FL 33705

License Plate Collectors Hobby Magazine
Drew Steitz, Editor
P.O. Box 222
E Texas, PA 18046
phone or fax 610-791-7979
Bimonthly publication with pho-
tographs, classifieds, etc.; $18 per year

Marble Collectors' Society of America
P.O. Box 222
Trumbull, CT 06611
Send SASE for information

McDonald's® Collecting Tips Newsletter
Meredith Williams
Box 633
Joplin, MO 64802
Send SASE for information

McDonald's® Collector Club
c/o Joyce and Terry Losonsky
7506 Summer Leave Ln.
Columbia, MD 21046-2455
301-381-3358

SUNSHINE Chapter, McDonald's®
 Collector's Club
c/o Bill and Pat Poe
220 Dominica Cir. E.
Niceville, FL 32578-4068
904-897-4163 or fax 904-897-2606
Annual membership is $10 per
individual ($15 per family) and
includes 6 newsletters and 2
McDonald's® Only shows per year

Model & Toy Collector Magazine
Toy Scouts, Inc.
Bill Bruegman
137 Casterton Ave.
Akron, OH 44303-1552
216-836-0668 or fax 216-869-8668

National Association of Avon
 Collectors
c/o Connie Clark
6100 Walnut, Dept. P
Kansas City, MO 64113
Send large SASE for information

The National Association of Paper
 and Advertising Collectors
P.O. Box 500
Mount Joy, PA 17552

National Autumn Leaf Collectors'
 Club
c/o Gwynne Harrison
P.O. Box 1
Mira Loma, CA 91752-0001
909-685-5434

National Blue Ridge Newsletter
Norma Lilly
144 Highland Dr.
Bloutville, TN 37617
Subscription: $15 per year

The National Cuff Link Society
Eugene R. Klompus, President
P.O. Box 346
Prospect Hts., IL 60070
847-816-0035
Information clearinghouse offers
networking, history, researching,
price guidance and appraisal information. $25 membership includes
subscription to *The Link,* the
Society's giant quarterly publication as well as free appraisals, shop
discounts and free locator services
for lost 'singles' or wanted pairs.
The Society's annual convention

includes workshops, competitions and networking opportunities.

National Graniteware Society
P.O. Box 10013
Cedar Rapids, IA 52410

National Imperial Glass Collectors' Society, Inc.
P.O. Box 534
Bellaire, OH 43906
Dues: $15 per year (+$1 for each additional member of household), quarterly newsletter: *Glasszette*

National Society of Lefton Collectors and *The Lefton Collector*
Loretta DeLozier
11101 Polk St.
Bedford, IA 50833
712-523-2289

National Milk Glass Collectors' Society and *Opaque News*
c/o Helen D. Storey
46 Almond Dr., Cocoa Townes
Hershey, PA 17033
Please send SASE for information

National Reamer Association
c/o Larry Branstad
R.R. 3, Box 67
Frederic, WI 54837

National Toothpick Holder Collectors' Society
Joyce Ender, Treasurer
Box 246
Sawyer, MI 49125
Dues: $15 (single) or $20 (couple) per year; includes monthly *Toothpick Bulletin* newsletter

National Valentine Collectors Association
Evalene Pulati
P.O. Box 1404
Santa Ana, CA 92702
714-547-1355

The Nelson-McCoy Express
Carol Seman, Editor
7670 Chippewa Rd., Ste. 406
Brecksville, OH 44141-2310
e-mail: McCjs@aol.com

Nutcracker Collectors' Club and Newsletter
Susan Otto, Editor
12204 Fox Run Dr.
Chesterland, OH 44026
216-729-2686
$10 annual dues for quarterly newsletter and free classified ads

The Occupied Japan Club
c/o Florence Archambault
29 Freeborn St.
Newport, RI 02840-1821
Publishes *The Upside Down World of an O.J. Collector,* a bimonthly newsletter. Information requires SASE

On the Lighter Side
International Lighter Collectors
Judith Sanders, Editor
136 Circle Dr.
Quitman, TX 75783
903-763-2795 or fax 703-763-4953 Annual convention held in different cities in the US; send SASE when requesting information

Paper Collectors' Marketplace
Doug Watson, Publisher/Editor
470 Main St.
Scandinavia, WI 54977-0128
715-467-2379 or fax 715-467-2243 (8 am to 8 pm, Monday-Saturday) Subscription: $19.95 per year

Paper Doll News
Emma Terry
P.O. Box 807
Vivian, LA 71082

Paper Pile Quarterly
Ada Fitzsimmons, Publisher/Editor
P.O. Box 337
San Anselmo, CA 94979-0337
Subscription: $17 per year

Pez Collector News
Richard & Marianne Belyski
P.O. Box 124
Sea Cliff, NY 11579
516-676-1183

Pie Birds Unlimited Newsletter
Lillian M. Cole
14 Harmony School Rd.
Flemington, NJ 08822
908-782-3198

Pottery Collectors Express
P.O. Box 221
Mayview, MO 64071-0221

Quint News
Dionne Quint Collectors
P.O. Box 2527
Woburn, MA 01888
617-933-2219

Red Wing Collectors Newsletter
Red Wing Collectors Society, Inc.
Doug Podpeskar
624 Jones
St. Eveleth, MN 55734-1631
218-744-4845
Please include SASE when requesting information

Rosevilles of the Past Newsletter
Jack Bomm, Editor
P.O. Box 656
Clarcona, FL 32710-0656
407-294-3980
Subscription $19.95 per year

Roy Rogers - Dale Evans Collectors Association
Nancy Horsley, Exec. Secretary
P.O. Box 1166
Portsmouth, OH 45662-1166

Salt & Pepper Novelty Shakers Club
Irene Thornburg
581 Joy Rd.
Battlecreek, MI 49017
616-963-7953

Shawnee Pottery Collectors' Club
c/o Pamela Curran
P.O. Box 713
New Smyrna Beach, FL 32170-0713

The Shot Glass Club of America
Mark Pickvet, Editor
P.O. Box 90404
Flint, MI 48509
$6.00 yearly membership includes newsletter

The Silver Bullet
Terry and Kay Klepey
P.O. Box 553
Forks, WA 98331
Yearly subscription for Lone Ranger enthusiasts and collectors is $12 ($20 Canadian); sample copy available for $4. Please allow 2 to 4 weeks to process a new subscription

Smurf Collectors' Club
24 Cabot Road West, Dept. P
Massapequa, NY 11758
Specializing in Smurf memorabilia, 1957-1990

Snow Biz
c/o Nancy McMichael
P.O. Box 53262
Washington, D.C. 20009
Quarterly newsletter (subscription: $10 per year) and collector's club, annual meeting/swap meet

The Trick or Treat Trader
C.J. Russell & the Halloween Queen Antiques
P.O. Box 499
4 Lawrence St. & Rt. 10
Winchester, NH 03470

Subscription: $15 per year for 4 issues or $4 for sample

Troll Monthly
5858 Washington St.
Whitman, MA 02382
800-858-7655 or 800-858-Troll

Vernon Views
Newsletter for Vernon Kilns collectors
P.O. Box 945
Scottsdale, AZ 85252
Quarterly issue available by sending $10 for a year's subscription

View-Master Reel Collector
Roger Nazeley
4921 Castor Ave.
Phil., PA 19124
215-743-8999

Vintage Fashion & Costume Jewelry
  Newsletter/Club
P.O. Box 265
Glen Oaks, NY 11004
718-969-2320   or   718-939-3095

Yearly subscription: $15 (US) for 4 issues; sample copy available by sending $5

Westmoreland Glass Society
Steve Jensen, President
4809 420 St. SE
Iowa City, IA 52240
319-337-9647
Publishes 6 newsletters per year; meets in March and August

The Willow Word
P.O. Box 13382
Arlington, TX 76094
Subscription: $23 (US) for 6 20-page issues per year; includes free ads to readers and lots of photos

World's Fair Collectors' Society, Inc.
Michael R. Pender, Editor
P.O. Box 20806
Sarasota, FL 34238
813-923-2590
Dues: $17 per year

INDEX